Please
return
materials
on time

CHINA

A NEW HISTORY

CHINA
A NEW HISTORY

Second Enlarged Edition

John King Fairbank
and
Merle Goldman

THE BELKNAP PRESS OF
HARVARD UNIVERSITY PRESS
Cambridge, Massachusetts
London, England · 2006

Designed by Marianne Perlak

Library of Congress Cataloging-in-Publication Data

Fairbank, John King, 1907–1991
China : a new history / John King Fairbank and Merle Goldman.—2nd. enl. ed.
p. cm.
Includes bibliographical references and index.
ISBN 0-674-01828-1 (pbk.: alk. paper)
1. China—History. I. Goldman, Merle. II. Title.
DS 735.F27 2005
951—dc22   2005053695

For Wilma, Laura,
and Holly Fairbank

Contents

Preface to the Enlarged Edition   xv

Preface to the Original Edition   xvii

Introduction: Approaches to Understanding China's History   I
  The Variety of Historical Perspectives   *I*
  Geography: The Contrast of North and South   *4*
  Humankind in Nature   *14*
  The Village: Family and Lineage   *17*
  Inner Asia and China: The Steppe and the Sown   *23*

PART ONE
Rise and Decline of the Imperial Autocracy   27

1. Origins: The Discoveries of Archaeology   29
  Paleolithic China   *29*
  Neolithic China   *31*
  Excavation of Shang and Xia   *33*
  The Rise of Central Authority   *37*
  Western Zhou   *39*
  Implications of the New Archaeological Record   *40*

2. The First Unification: Imperial Confucianism   46
    The Utility of Dynasties 46
    Princes and Philosophers 49
    The Confucian Code 51
    Daoism 53
    Unification by Qin 54
    Consolidation and Expansion under the Han 57
    Imperial Confucianism 62
    Correlative Cosmology 64
    Emperor and Scholars 66

3. Reunification in the Buddhist Age   72
    Disunion 72
    The Buddhist Teaching 73
    Sui–Tang Reunification 76
    Buddhism and the State 79
    Decline of the Tang Dynasty 81
    Social Change: The Tang–Song Transition 83

4. China's Greatest Age: Northern and Southern Song   88
    Efflorescence of Material Growth 88
    Education and the Examination System 93
    The Creation of Neo-Confucianism 96
    Formation of Gentry Society 101

5. The Paradox of Song China and Inner Asia   108
    The Symbiosis of Wen and Wu 108
    The Rise of Non-Chinese Rule over China 112
    China in the Mongol Empire 119
    Interpreting the Song Era 126

6. Government in the Ming Dynasty   128
    Legacies of the Hongwu Emperor 128
    Fiscal Problems 132
    China Turns Inward 137
    Factional Politics 140

7. The Qing Success Story   143
    The Manchu Conquest 143
    Institutional Adaptation 146

The Jesuit Interlude 151
Growth of Qing Control in Inner Asia 152
The Attempted Integration of Polity and Culture 154

PART TWO
Late Imperial China, 1600–1911

163

8. The Paradox of Growth without Development

167

The Rise in Population 167
Diminishing Returns of Farm Labor 170
The Subjection of Women 173
Domestic Trade and Commercial Organization 176
Merchant–Official Symbiosis 179
Limitations of the Law 183

9. Frontier Unrest and the Opening of China

187

The Weakness of State Leadership 187
The White Lotus Rebellion, 1796–1804 189
Maritime China: Origins of the Overseas Chinese 191
European Trading Companies and the Canton Trade 195
Rebellion on the Turkestan Frontier, 1826–1835 197
Opium and the Struggle for a New Order at Guangzhou,
1834–1842 198
Inauguration of the Treaty Century after 1842 201

10. Rebellion and Restoration

206

The Great Taiping Rebellion, 1851–1864 206
Civil War 209
The Qing Restoration of the 1860s 212
Suppression of Other Rebellions 214

11. Early Modernization and the Decline of Qing Power

217

Self-Strengthening and Its Failure 217
The Christian–Confucian Struggle 221
The Reform Movement 224
The Boxer Rising, 1898–1901 230
Demoralization 232

12. The Republican Revolution, 1901–1916   235

A New Domestic Balance of Power   235
Suppressing Rebellion by Militarization   236
Elite Activism in the Public Sphere   238
The Japanese Influence   240
The Qing Reform Effort   241
Constitutionalism and Self-Government   244
Insoluble Systemic Problems   247
The Revolution of 1911 and Yuan Shikai's Dictatorship   250

PART THREE
The Republic of China, 1912–1949   255

13. The Quest for a Chinese Civil Society   257

The Limits of Chinese Liberalism   257
The Limits of Christian Reformism   260
The Tardy Rise of a Political Press   262
Academic Development   263
The New Culture Movement   266
The May Fourth Movement   267
Rise of the Chinese Bourgeoisie   269
Origins of the Chinese Communist Party   275

14. The Nationalist Revolution and the Nanjing Government   279

Sun Yatsen and the United Front   279
The Accession to Power of Jiang Jieshi (Chiang Kaishek)   283
The Nature of the Nanjing Government   286
Systemic Weaknesses   289

15. The Second Coming of the Chinese Communist Party   294

Problems of Life on the Land   294
Rural Reconstruction   299
The Rise of Mao Zedong   301
The Long March, 1934–1935   305
The Role of Zhou Enlai   307
The Second United Front   310

16. China's War of Resistance, 1937–1945   312
   Nationalist Difficulties   312
   Mao's Sinification of Marxism   316
   Mao Zedong Thought   321
   The Rectification Campaign of 1942–1944   323
   American Support of Coalition Government   326

17. The Civil War and the Nationalists on Taiwan   331
   Why the Nationalists Failed   331
   Nationalist Attack and Communist Counterattack   334
   Taiwan as a Japanese Colony   337
   Taiwan as the Republic of China   339

PART FOUR
The People's Republic of China   343

18. Establishing Control of State and Countryside   345
   Creating the New State, 1949–1953   345
   Collectivizing Agriculture   352
   Collective Agriculture in Practice   354
   Beginning Industrialization   357
   Education and the Intellectuals   359
   The Anti-Rightist Campaign, 1957–1958   365

19. The Great Leap Forward, 1958–1960   368
   Background Factors   368
   The Disaster of 1959–1960   372
   Revival: Seizing Control of Industrial Labor   374
   Party Rectification and Education   376
   The Sino–Soviet Split   378
   The Great Leap Forward as a Social Movement   380

20. The Cultural Revolution, 1966–1976   383
   Underpinnings   383
   Mao's Aims and Resources   385
   Role of the People's Liberation Army   387
   How the Cultural Revolution Unfolded   389

The Red Guards   392
The Seizure of Power   393
Foreign Affairs   395
Decentralization and the Third Front   397
The Succession Struggle   400
The Cultural Revolution in Retrospect   401
Aftermath   404

21. The Post-Mao Reform Era   406
    by Merle Goldman

    Epilogue: China at the Start of the Twenty-first Century   457
    by Merle Goldman

    Note on Romanization and Citation   472
    Suggested Reading   473
    Publisher's Note   429
    Illustration Credits   531
    Author Index   535
    General Index   545

    Illustrations follow pages 104, 200, and 328

Maps

1. Land Forms of China 6–7
2. Population Distribution in 1980 8–9
3. Geographical Features 10
4. Provinces 12
5. Macroregions 13
6. The Three Dynasties: Xia, Shang, and Zhou 36
7. The Qin and Other Warring States 50
8. Commanderies and Kingdoms of the Han Empire, 206 BC 58
9. Tang Empire at Its Greatest Extent (Eighth Century) 80
10. Population Distribution in the Han Dynasty, AD 2 90
11. Population Distribution in the Tang Dynasty, AD 742 90
12. Population Distribution in the Song Dynasty, ca. 1100 91
13. The Northern Song and Liao (Qidan) Empires, ca. 1000 114
14. The Southern Song and Jin (Ruzhen) Empires in 1142 116
15. Mongol Conquests and the Yuan Empire in 1279 120
16. The Grand Canal System of the Sui, Song, and Yuan Dynasties 125
17. The Ming Empire at Its Greatest Extent 131
18. The Voyages of Zheng He 136
19. Rise of the Manchus 144
20. Foreign Encroachments 202
21. Nineteenth-Century Rebellions 215
22. The Long March 306
23. The Japanese Invasion of China 315
24. The People's Republic of China 346–347

Tables

1. Major periods in Imperial China   24
2. China's prehistory   31
3. Divisions of the Mongol empire under Chinggis Khan's successors   119
4. Events in China, 1796–1901   188
5. Major turning points, 1901–1916   242
6. Rural administrative units and average characteristics,
    1974 and 1986   355

Preface to the Enlarged Edition

John King Fairbank devoted his life to writing and teaching on China, a country whose history and society absorbed him throughout his adult years. This book is a fitting conclusion to his career.

Fairbank, who was affectionately referred to as JKF by his colleagues and students, began as a scholar of British history. But he was drawn to the study of China by the publication of its diplomatic archives in 1932, when he was in China doing research for his dissertation. That dissertation emerged as the pioneering monograph *Trade and Diplomacy on the China Coast*, which launched the study of Qing dynasty documents and China's interaction with the West. In 1936 Fairbank joined the Harvard University History Department, where he introduced the history of modern China to its curriculum. His lectures, given with wry wit and humorous slides, presented history as a story. For the next five decades he continued to teach at Harvard, to work for the United States government in Washington, D.C., and in China during World War II, and to write, co-author, and edit over three dozen books plus hundreds of articles, reviews, commentaries, and congressional testimonies. Fairbank was the dean of modern Chinese studies not only in the United States but in most of the world—a teacher, mentor, administrator, public educator, and historian.

I first met JKF in 1953 when I entered Harvard's East Asian Regional Studies master's program. He subsequently became my Ph.D. thesis advisor and invited me to become a Research Associate of Harvard's East Asian Research Center (later renamed the Fairbank Center for East Asian Research), where I have been ever since. He was an inspiring and demanding graduate advisor. As with the scores of other future historians of China whom he trained, he relentlessly guided, cajoled, and pushed me through the Ph.D. process and then the publication of my first book. Even after I began teaching at Boston University and had my own students, he remained a constant, dominating presence. Sometimes he would call before 7:00 in the morning, usually on weekends, to tell me how much he liked a piece I had written and to suggest ways it could have been "even better."

At the time Fairbank completed this book, the post-Mao reform period had been under way for little more than a decade and could not yet be analyzed in historical context. My contribution, Chapter 21 and the Epilogue, deals with the reform period in more detail, providing greater perspective than the first edition could. My views also diverge somewhat from those of Fairbank. Another of JKF's notable qualities was his willingness to take on and encourage students who were interested in topics and approaches different from his own.

Whereas Fairbank emphasized demographic and institutional factors and stressed China's uniqueness, I tend to be more interested in intellectual and political history and to see more overlap between Confucian and Western views. Whereas he saw the post-Mao era as a continuation of China's repressive, backward recent history, I view it as more open to change. His darker view was due in part to the fact that this book was completed in the aftermath of the violent crackdown in Tiananmen Square on June 4, 1989. In his preface, he notes that while in most aspects Chinese civilization before the nineteenth century was far more advanced than that in the West, in modern times, China had fallen far behind. Even its revolution, he asserted elsewhere, has been the longest, most difficult, and bloodiest in modern history. He often despaired whether China would ever be able to catch up with the developed world.

This question remains unanswered today. Fairbank often pointed out that China has the extraordinary problem of having to feed, house, and provide a livelihood for the largest population in the world, 1.2 billion and growing. But as my epilogue points out, despite many difficulties, China in the post-Mao era appears to be finding its way to deal with its problems and has acquired the potential to revive its greatness of old. Whether or not China succeeds in becoming a great power, it will have a major impact on the rest of the world in the years to come.

Merle Goldman
December 1997

Preface to the Original Edition

Since the 1970s, as part of the modernization defining the current phase of the great Chinese revolution, China has been emerging as a more diverse and dynamic place. "One China, One Culture" may still be the patriotic slogan of 1,250,000,000 people in China, echoing the old Confucian governing elite's persistent ideal of political unity. But the Chinese experience of invasion, rebellion, civil war, and reform since the 1930s has shattered the ancient sanction for central autocracy and local acquiescence. Education and economic modernization among the great mass of the Chinese people are creating new opportunities, new careers and lifestyles. Fresh ideas and political institutions cannot lag far behind.

Along with this transformation in Chinese life has come a dynamic growth in China studies the world over. During the last twenty years an outpouring of skilled monographs has begun to modernize our view of China's history and institutions. This new view has rendered obsolete the old sinologue's all-about-China approach to the country as a single entity inhabited by "the Chinese." Archaeologists excavating thousands of sites, historians researching in the great new archives, social scientists investigating localities have all begun to break up the unitary One-China monolith.

China: A New History takes account of much of this recent work. Yet the perpetual seesaw between fresh evidence and interpretation gives any new history a fuzzy outline, bounded by many unresolved questions. The path of historical wisdom is to find out what issues are still in dispute, to identify major current questions, rather than to try to resolve them all here and now. Our libraries are littered with the pronouncements of writers who knew all about China but could not see how much they did not know. The expansion of our knowledge has expanded the circumference of our ignorance.

The plan of this book is as follows: After noting several lines of approach to the Chinese scene, we look first at the newest chapter in the story, China's prehistory. Since 1920 archaeology has broken through the ancient crust of Chinese myth and legend, confirming much of it. Scientific excavation has found Peking Man, traced the growth of Neolithic China, and exhumed the Bronze Age capitals of the once-legendary Shang and Xia dynasties. We start with a firm picture of the extraordinary continuity of a largely self-contained civilization.

Next, we trace the growth of the imperial autocracy, of the elite, and of the state and society they governed. New studies of the major periods—Han, Tang, Song, Ming, and Qing—allow us to appreciate the sophistication of China's achievements. Never have so few ruled for so long over so many. Yet this success in autocracy and elitism left a problem. The imperial mixture—the ruler's ritual leadership, the elite's self-indoctrination in moral principles, the bureaucracy's clever self-regulating mechanisms among the people, and the violent punishments held in reserve—all created a self-sufficient and self-perpetuating civilization. But it did not form a nation-state with a government motivated to lead the way in modernization.

China's history when surveyed over the last two thousand years contains a great paradox that bothers all Chinese patriots today. In comparison with Europe, the China of the eleventh and twelfth centuries was a forerunner, far ahead in most aspects of civilization, whereas in the nineteenth and twentieth centuries China lagged far behind. When Francis Bacon remarked around 1620 that the world was being made over by printing, gunpowder, and the magnet, he did not refer to the fact that they all three had appeared first in China. Nowadays, however, it is generally conceded that the China of AD 1200 was on the whole more advanced than Europe. So why and how did China fall behind? Among the world's major peoples, why have the Chinese become latecomers on the way to modernity? If living conditions and the amenities of life in China and Europe were generally comparable as recently as the eighteenth century, how did China so spectacularly fail to follow the European lead in industrialization? To so large a question there is no single, monocausal answer. In Part Two we pursue this intriguing question from several angles.

In Part Three, we look at the rise to power of the Chinese Communist Party under Mao Zedong and, in Part Four, at its amazing vicissitudes since 1949. Once the modern revolution in Chinese thought got under way in the 1890s, it became evident that no foreign model could fit the Chinese situation, that many models would be used but none would be adequate, and that the creative Chinese people would have to work out their salvation in their own way. Having had a unique past, they would have their own unique future.

This conclusion, unsettling to many, has now coincided with a further worldwide realization that the species *Homo sapiens sapiens* (as it has reassuringly designated itself) is itself endangered. The twentieth century has already seen more man-made suffering, death, and assault on the environment than all previous centuries combined. Perhaps the Chinese have finally joined the great outside world just in time to participate in its collapse. A few observers, less pessimistic, believe that in the end only a survival capacity like that exhibited by the Chinese for three millennia can save us.

By taking a fresh, newly informed look at China's long history, at its multichanneled reforms, rebellions, and revolutions and its record of admirable successes and grievous failures in the modern century, we may find the long-term trends and contemporary conditions that will shape China's future and affect our own.

JKF
September 12, 1991

Introduction: Approaches to
Understanding China's History

The Variety of Historical Perspectives

The fact that Chinese history is best known in China, just as Western history is best known in America and Europe, creates discordant perspectives between China and the outside world. For example, Chinese know that Manchu tribal leaders christened their new state Qing ("Pure") in 1636, the year that Americans (at least those around Boston) remember as the founding of Harvard, the New World's first college. After 2 million or so Manchus took power over 120 million or so Chinese, the Qing dynasty governed the Chinese people for 267 years while their numbers rose to about 400 million. At its midpoint in the 1770s, the Qing dynasty, governing the Chinese empire from Beijing, completed its conquest of Mongolia, Central Asia, and Tibet, while a few million American rebels in their thirteen colonies declared their independence of Britain.

Now that the United States is top nation in succession to eighteenth-century France and nineteenth-century Britain, historical perspective is more necessary than ever. In China the United States' democratic market economy faces the last communist dictatorship, yet behind Chinese communism lies the world's longest tradition of successful autocracy. It is now trying to achieve economic modernization without the representative political democracy that Americans view as their special gift to the world's salvation. U.S. citizens who feel inclined to bash China's dictatorship may usefully recall their nation's own difficulties in the exercise of freedom and power, which call into question the appropriateness of the American model for China's modern transformation. The United

States has, for example, had trouble recently with its national leadership. One president was assassinated for reasons not yet known which we prefer not to ask about. Another president resigned to avoid impeachment for lying. A more recent president from Hollywood lived a fantasy life, lying to himself and the public to make us feel good, while creating an underclass beneath our democracy and ending the Cold War with the Soviet Union. Meanwhile, in far-off China, Chairman Mao Zedong killed millions and millions of Chinese while calling it a class struggle for revolution. His successor in 1989 was so stuck in China's autocratic tradition that, when confronted with unarmed petitioners for democracy, he made the mistake of sending in tanks to shoot down hundreds of them on primetime television.

Today the old men in Beijing do not want China flooded with the commercial world's pop culture. Academic Americans welcome 40,000 bright students from China and want them free to think about modern problems. In America these include the drug and gun industries and shooting in the streets. The Chinese have to reduce their birthrate to avoid drowning in a population of more than a billion. Female infanticide is one way, birth control and abortion are others. Many Americans meanwhile want to save every fetus as a sacred human being, never mind its mother or its future.

Among all these bizarre and poignant ironies, one unanswered question haunts all Chinese patriots today. The Chinese Han empire had been contemporary with and bigger than the Roman Empire. Indeed, China was once the superior civilization of the world, not only the equal of Rome but far ahead of medieval Europe. Albert Feuerwerker, an economic historian disciplined against hyperbole, tells us that from 1000 to 1500 AD "no comparison of agricultural productivity, industrial skill, commercial complexity, urban wealth, or standard of living (not to mention bureaucratic sophistication and cultural achievement) would place Europe on a par with the Chinese empire" (in Ropp 1990). So why did China fall behind in modern times? How could it be ignominiously contemned by Western and even Japanese imperialists in the late nineteenth century?

The answer lies partly in China and partly in the West. From the time of the Industrial Revolution that began about 1750 in England, science and technology have been radically transforming the modern world. Since 1978 "modernization" has been China's national goal. The high drama of a great people making a modern comeback is particularly moving in this case because of the Chinese people's residual conviction of their innate superiority. The twentieth century has generally acknowledged the superlative quality of Shang bronzes, Song paintings, and other aspects of China's heritage. And since 1950 Joseph Needham and his collaborators in the fourteen and more volumes of *Science and Civilisation in China* have described the impressive array of early Chinese discoveries and inventions, far more than the well-known paper, printing, gunpowder, and compass. Nathan Sivin suggests that premodern science in China and Europe superficially resembled each other more than either one resembled modern science. Although Europe had inherited ways of thought that made it more ready for scientific thinking when the time came, in neither case was there much linkage between science and technology, between the theoretical scholar and the practical artisan. The dynamic combination of S&T is a modern creation.

Sivin also points out how, for example, the remarkable efficiency of the Chinese abacus as a calculator was limited to a dozen or so digits in a linear array and so was useless for advanced algebra. He suggests that the relative lack of Chinese mathematical innovations from the mid-1300s to the 1600s may have been the price paid for the convenience of the abacus. Here we have an example of how China's early precocity in invention could later hold her back. Indeed, I shall argue that the very superiority achieved by Song China would become by 1800 a source of her backwardness, as though all great achievements carry the seeds of their ossification.

China's precocity, it is now recognized, was not limited to the arts and technology. By almost any definition, an autocratic state appeared in ancient China, with institutions of bureaucratic administration, record-keeping, selection of officials by merit on the basis of examinations, and central control over the economy, society, literature, and thought. This Chinese autocracy presaged the rise of the modern absolutist state in seventeenth-century Europe. Our repertoire of social science concepts derived from the pluralistic Western experience seems still inadequate to encompass this early Chinese achievement.

If we wish to understand the social and human factors in China's falling behind the West in the modern period, we must look more closely at her prehistory, her rice economy, family system, Inner Asian invaders, classical thought, and many other features of her high civilization to see how they all may have played a part. Let us therefore identify certain major approaches to understanding China.

Geography: The Contrast of North and South

One's approach to China's diversity is first of all visual. To the traveler who flies through the vast gray cloud banks, mists, and sunshine of continental China, two pictures will stand out as typical, one of North China and one of the South (see Map 1). On the dry North China plain to the south of Beijing, where Chinese civilization had its first flowering, one sees in summer an endless expanse of green fields over which are scattered clusters of darker green, the trees of earth-walled villages. It is very like the view of the Middle West in the United States a few decades ago, where farmsteads and their clumps of trees were dispersed at roughly half-mile intervals. But where the American corn belt had a farm, on the North China plain there is an entire village. Where one American farmer's family lived with its barns and sheds among its fields in Iowa or Illinois at a half-mile distance from its neighbors roundabout, in China an entire community of several hundred persons lives in its tree-studded village, at a half-mile distance from neighbor villages. The American people, in spite of their farming background, have no appreciation of the population density that subtly conditions every act and thought of a Chinese farmer.

In South China the typical picture is quite different, and like nothing to which Americans are accustomed. There during much of the year the rice fields are flooded and present a water surface to the airborne observer. The green terrain is hilly, and the flat crescent-shaped rice terraces march up each hill almost to the top and on the other side descend again from near the crest, terrace upon terrace in endless succession, each embankment conforming to the lay of the land like the contour lines of a geographer's chart. Indeed, the curving pattern of the rice terraces seen from above is a visual index to the slope of the valleys in which they are built—narrow concave strips of paddy field touch the hilltops, the lower terraces grow broader and longer and bulge out as they descend to the valley floor. Gray stone footpaths are built on many of the embankments, forming intricate patterns. When the sun is out, one sees it from the air reflected brilliantly in the water of the rice fields. The sun seems to be shining up through the fields from below, so that the whole ornate network of the embankments and paths and hilltops appears to rush beneath one as though on a great rolling screen, a black lacework moving across the bright silver of shining water.

No one can fly over the rugged green hills of the South without wondering where the billion and more people of China live and what they eat—such vast reaches of mountain and valley seem largely uncultivable and sparsely settled. One's picture of a big empty landscape is mirrored statistically in the estimate that six sevenths of the population have to live on the one third of the land that is cultivable (see Map 2). The inhabited part of China is roughly half as large as the inhabited part of the United States, yet it supports five times as many people. This is made possible only by crowding some 2,000 human beings onto each square mile of cultivated earth in the valleys and floodplains. The United States has some 570,000 square miles under cultivation and could greatly increase this area; China has perhaps 450,000 square miles of cultivated land (less than one half acre of food-producing soil per person), with little prospect of increasing this area by more than a small fraction, even if it is used more intensively. In short, China must feed about 23 percent of the world's population from about 7 percent of the world's arable land.

The dry wheat-millet area of North China and the moist rice-growing areas of the South divide along a line roughly halfway between the Yellow (Huang) River and the Yangzi River on the thirty-third parallel (see Map 3). Rainfall, soil, temperature, and human usage create striking contrasts between these two economic regions.

China's rainfall patterns are created by the terrain. The Asian land mass changes temperature more readily than does the Western Pacific Ocean and its currents, and the cold dry air that is chilled over the continent in the wintertime tends to flow southeastward to the sea, with minimum precipitation. Conversely, the summer monsoon of moisture-laden air from the South China Sea is drawn inward and northward over the land mass by the rising of the heated air above it, and precipitation occurs mainly during the summer. The southerly wind of summer crosses the hills of South China first, and they receive a heavy, relatively dependable rainfall. North China, being farther from the South China Sea, receives less rainfall overall, and the amount of precipitation over the decades has varied as much as 30 percent from one year to the next. The average annual rainfall of the North China plain is about 20 to 25 inches, like that of the great American dustbowl, barely sufficient to maintain cultivation at the best of times. This high variability of rainfall from year to year constantly threatens to produce drought and famine.

North China's severe continental winters, not unlike those of the American Middle West, limit the growing season to about half the year. In southernmost China, crops are grown the year around, and rice is double-cropped and even triple-cropped. This explains why most of the

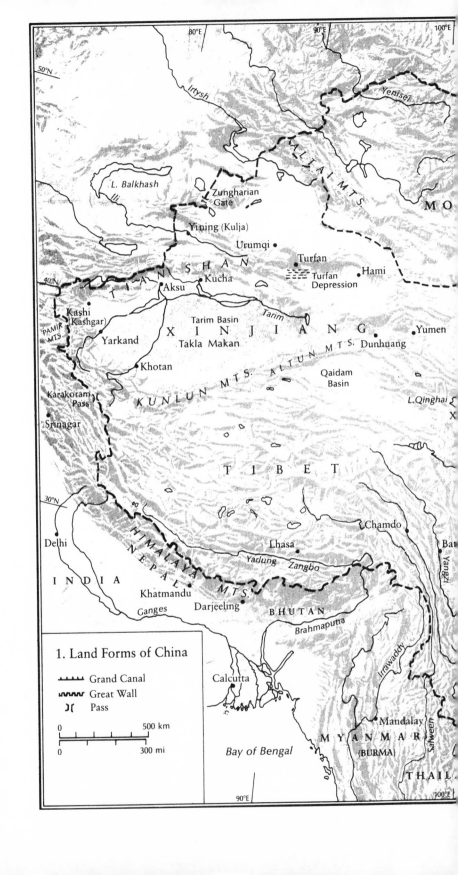

1. Land Forms of China

‒‒‒ Grand Canal
∿∿∿ Great Wall
)(Pass

0 ———————— 500 km
0 ———————— 300 mi

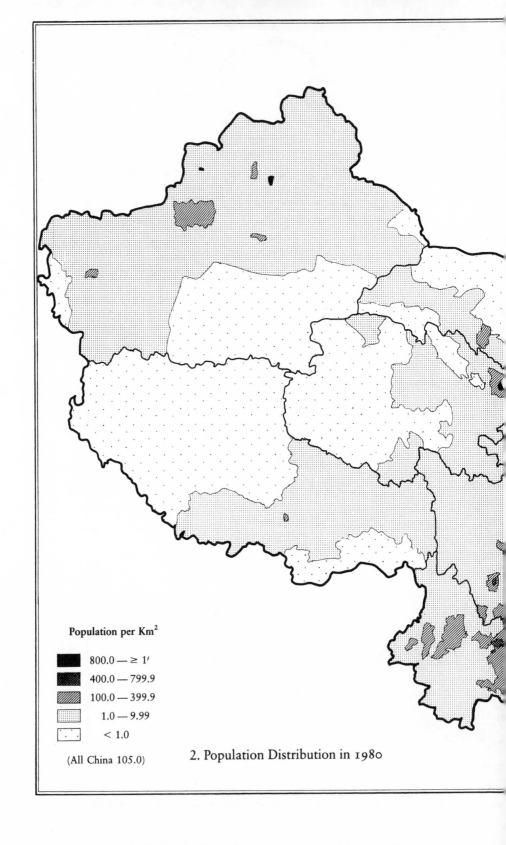

Population per Km²

- ■ 800.0 — ≥ 1′
- ■ 400.0 — 799.9
- ▨ 100.0 — 399.9
- ▨ 1.0 — 9.99
- ▫ < 1.0

(All China 105.0)

2. Population Distribution in 1980

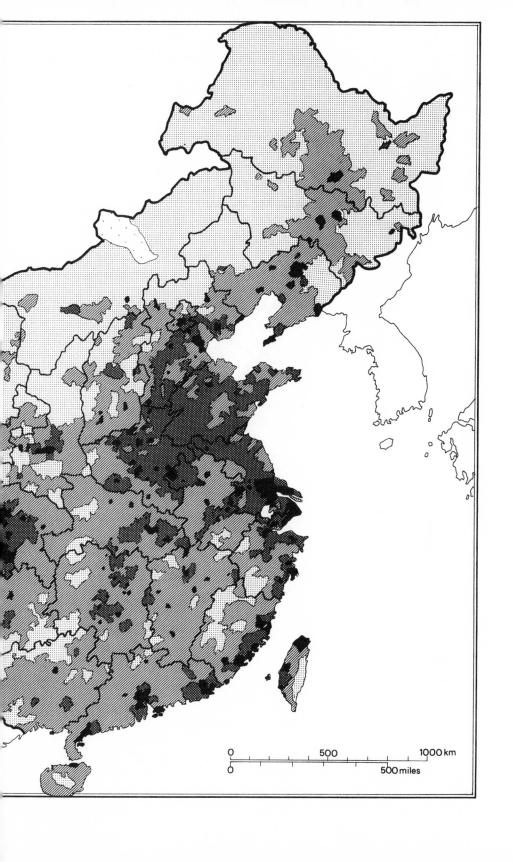

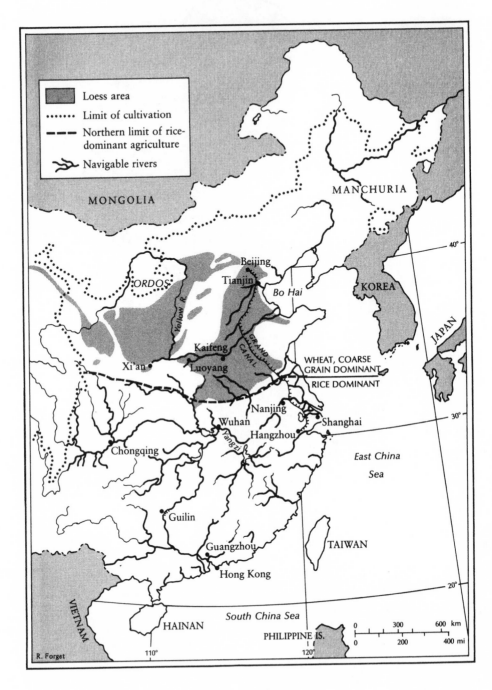

3. Geographical Features

Chinese people live in the more fecund rice country of the South. Rice culture, with its greater inputs of water and labor, until recent times yielded more than twice as much food as wheat-growing.

In both the North and South, natural resources are supplemented by unremitting human endeavor, of which the night-soil (human-excrement) industry is but one of the more spectacular forms. Without returning human waste to the land, or using equivalent chemical fertilizers, no region of China could produce enough food crops to sustain its present population. Each urban center sustains its surrounding truck gardens in this way; from the air Chinese cities can be seen surrounded by a belt of dense green crops that fade at the periphery.

Early travelers compared China with Europe in the variety of its languages and the size of its different provinces (see Map 4). For example, three regions along the course of the Yangzi River—Sichuan province to the west, the twin provinces of Hubei to the north and Hunan to the south, and the lower Yangzi delta—are each of them comparable to Germany in area and each bigger in population. Major provinces of China have distinctive dialects, cuisines, and sociocultural traditions that can trigger endless dinner conversations. But provinces are essentially political subdivisions of government. One new approach has been to divide China for analytic purposes by regions of economic geography.

In the last quarter-century, G. William Skinner's work on marketing and urbanization has led him to divide China into macroregions, each centering around a river drainage basin (see Map 5). Each region has a populous and productive core area on a waterway and a less populous and less productive periphery area in mountainous or arid terrain. A core area is naturally more powerful in human affairs, while a periphery becomes adjusted to its subordinate or marginal role. For example, deforestation, cultivation, and soil erosion in a periphery will tend to send useful alluvium down into a core, heightening their difference in fertility.

The precise limits and interrelationships of these analytically defined macroregions will be refined and improved upon. They are useful to historians because they reflect economic reality more accurately than the political provinces. In fact, provincial boundaries may be set not to enhance the power of economic factors but rather to counter them. Thus, the fecund Yangzi delta is divided among the provinces of Zhejiang, Jiangsu, and Anhui so that the preeminent economic strength of the region will not be under a single provincial government that might take over the state.

Macroregions center on waterways as transport routes for trade. In

4. Provinces

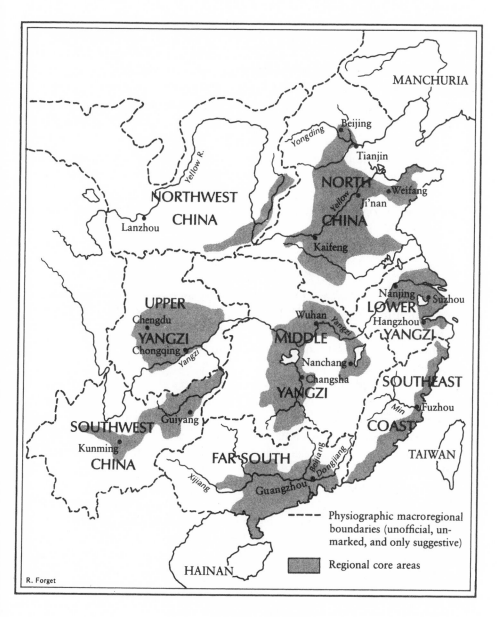

5. Macroregions

modern times the great cities—Guangzhou, Shanghai, Wuhan, even Tianjin—have grown up where sea trade met the waterborne commerce of the interior. Yet until recently China's foreign trade seldom lived up to the great expectations of the foreign merchants. Stretching so far from north to south, from the latitude of Canada to that of Cuba, China remains a subcontinent largely sufficient unto herself. Too easily we forget that Shanghai, at the mouth of the Yangzi River, is in the temperate latitude of New Orleans and Suez, while Guangzhou, on the West River, is in the latitude of Havana and Calcutta, well into the tropics.

In spite of the immensity and variety of the Chinese scene, this subcontinent has remained a single political unit, where Europe has not, for it is held together by a way of life and a system of government much more deeply rooted than our own, and stretching further back uninterruptedly into the past.

Humankind in Nature

No matter what elements of civilization—peoples or cultural traits—accumulated in China, they all became integrated in a distinctly Chinese way of life, nourished, conditioned, and limited by the good earth and the use of it. To cite but one example, from Neolithic times (12,000 years ago) to the present the people of North China have made pit dwellings or cave homes in the fine, yellow, windborne loess soil that covers about 100,000 square miles of Northwest China to a depth of 150 feet or more (see Map 3). Loess has a quality of vertical cleavage useful for this purpose. Many hundreds of thousands of people still live in caves cut into the sides of loess cliffs; these homes are cool in summer, warm in winter, and dangerous only in earthquakes.

Where forest land occurred, the Chinese, like other early peoples and recent American pioneers, achieved its deforestation. The consequent erosion through the centuries changed the face of the country, and erosion today is still a major problem. The waterborne loess deposits of the Yellow River have built up a broad floodplain between Shanxi province and the sea, and the process still goes on. Nothing so vividly conveys a sense of man's impotence in the face of nature as to watch the swirling coffee-colored flood of the Yellow River flowing majestically within its great earthen dikes across, and 20 feet above, the crowded plain 200 miles from the sea; and to realize that this vast yellow torrent is steadily depositing its silt and in this way building its bed higher above the surrounding countryside until the time when human negligence or act of God will allow it again to burst from the dikes and inundate the plain.

Deforestation, erosion, and floods have constantly been met by human efforts at water control. The planting of trees and damming of tributaries in the watershed of the Yellow River is a recent effort of the People's Republic. In previous periods China's rulers confronted in every flood season the debouching of the river upon the North China plain in full force. In prehistoric times, however, flooding of the plain was less of a problem than the reclamation of it from its primitive swamp and fen conditions; water-control techniques were developed for drainage purposes as well as for flood prevention and irrigation. Thus many generations of labor have been spent upon the land to make it what it is today, protected by dikes, crossed by canals and roads worn into the earth, irrigated by streams and wells, divided by paths and occasional remnants of grave land in their groves of trees, and all of it handed down from generation to generation.

This land that modern China has inherited is used almost entirely to produce food for human consumption. China proper (as distinct from Inner Asia; see below) cannot afford to raise cattle for food. Of the land that can be used at all, nine tenths is cultivated for crops, and only about 2 percent is pasture for animals. By comparison, in the United States only four tenths of the used land is put into crops, and almost half of it is put into pasture.

The social implications of intensive agriculture can be seen most strikingly in the rice economy, which is the backbone of Chinese life everywhere in the Yangzi valley and the South. Rice plants are ordinarily grown for their first month in seedbeds, while subsidiary crops are raised and harvested in the dry fields. The fields are then irrigated, fertilized, and plowed (here the water buffalo may supplement man's hoeing) in preparation for the transplanting of the rice seedlings. This transplanting is still done in large part by human hands, the rows of planters bending from the waist as they move backward step by step through the ankle-high muddy water of each terrace. This goes on in the paddy fields of a whole subcontinent—certainly the greatest expenditure of muscular energy in the world. When the rice has been weeded and is mature, the field is drained and the crop is harvested, again often by hand. Given an unlimited supply of water and of human hands, there is probably no way by which a greater yield could be gained from a given plot of land. In this situation land is economically more valuable than labor, or to put it another way, good muscles are more plentiful than good earth. Lacking both land and capital for large-scale agricultural methods, the Chinese farmer has focused on intensive, high-yield hand-gardening rather than extensive mechanized agriculture.

The heavy application of manpower and fertilizer to small plots of land has also had its social repercussions, for it sets up a vicious interdependence between dense population and intensive use of the soil whereby each makes the other possible. A dense population provides both the incentive for intensive land use and the means. Once established, this economy acquired inertial momentum—it kept on going. The back-breaking labor of many hands became the accepted norm, and inventive efforts at labor saving remained the exception. Early modernizers of China, in their attempts to introduce the machine, constantly ran up against the vested interest of Chinese manpower, since in the short run the machine appeared to be in competition with human hands and backs. Thus railways were attacked as depriving carters and porters of their jobs, and there was no premium upon labor-saving invention.

This unfavorable population-land balance had other implications as well. Pressure from rising population drove many Chinese farmers in the Late Imperial era to switch from grain production to the growing of commercial crops (such as cotton in the Yangzi delta). This offered a greater return per unit of land but not per individual workday. It was a survival strategy—Philip Huang (1990, 1991) calls it "involution"—in which substantial commercialization could take place without leading either to modern capitalist development or to the freeing of the Chinese farmer from a life of bare subsistence.

The ecology of the Chinese—their adaptation to the physical environment—has influenced their culture in many ways. Life on the great river floodplains has always been a hard life. "Heaven nourishes and destroys" is an ancient saying. On the broad stretches of the plain the patient Chinese farmers were at the mercy of the weather, dependent upon Heaven's gift of sun and rain. They were forced to accept natural calamity in the form of drought, flood, pestilence, and famine. This is in striking contrast to the lot of Europeans, who lived in a land of variegated topography. People in the West, either on the Mediterranean or on the European continent, were never far from a water supply and could usually supplement agriculture by hunting or fishing, provided they exercised initiative. From ancient times, seaborne commerce has played an immediate part in Western economies. Exploration and invention in the service of commerce became part of a Western struggle to overcome nature.

This different relation of human beings to nature in the West and East has been one of the salient contrasts between the two civilizations. Man has been at the center of the Western stage. The rest of nature has served as either neutral background or as an adversary. Thus Western religion is anthropomorphic, and early Western painting anthropocentric. To see how great this gulf is, we have only to compare Christianity with the relative impersonality of Buddhism, or compare a Song landscape, its tiny human figures dwarfed by crags and rivers, with an Italian primitive, in which nature is an afterthought.

Living so closely involved with family members and neighbors has accustomed the Chinese people to a collective life in which the group normally dominates the individual. In this respect the Chinese experience until recently hardly differed from that of other farming peoples long settled on the land. It is the modern individualist, be he seafarer, pioneer, or city entrepreneur, who is the exception. A room of one's own, more readily available in the New World than in the crowded East, has symbolized a higher standard of living. Thus, one generalization in the lore about China is the absorption of the individual not only in the world of nature but also in the social collectivity.

Today the balance between the collectivity of Chinese society and its beautiful natural surroundings is being destroyed by modernization. Chemicals and industrial effluents pollute the water, while use of unwashed soft coal for energy pollutes the air. Growth of a predominantly young population with an increasing life expectancy cannot be throttled down for decades to come. Meanwhile, deforestation and erosion coupled with the building of roads, housing, and installations are destroying the arable land. The world's biggest and most populous country is heading for an ecological nightmare that will require a great collective effort to overcome.

The Village: Family and Lineage

To understand China today, one basic approach is that of anthropology, which looks at the village and family environment from which modern China has just begun to emerge. Even now the Chinese people are still mostly farmers tilling the soil, living mainly in villages, in houses of brown sun-dried brick, bamboo, or whitewashed wattle, or sometimes stone, with earth or stone floors, and often paper, not glass, in the windows. Frequently half their meager material income goes for food. The Chinese still lack the luxury of space. Farmers' dwellings have usually about four small room sections for every three persons. Sometimes family members of both sexes and two or three generations all sleep on the same brick bed, which in North China may be heated by flues from the nearby stove. There is little meat in the diet. Manpower still takes the place of the machine for most purposes.

To Americans and Europeans with their higher material standard of living, the amazing thing about the Chinese farming people has been their ability to maintain a highly civilized life under these poor conditions. The answer lies in their social institutions, which have carried the individuals of each family through the phases and vicissitudes of human existence according to deeply ingrained patterns of behavior. These institutions and behavior patterns are among the oldest and most persistent social phenomena in the world. China has been a stronghold of the family system and has derived both strength and inertia from it.

Until very recently the Chinese family has been a microcosm, the state in miniature. The family, not the individual, was the social unit and the responsible element in the political life of its locality. The filial piety and obedience inculcated in family life were the training ground for loyalty to the ruler and obedience to the constituted authority in the state.

This function of the family to raise filial sons who would become loyal subjects can be seen by a glance at the pattern of authority within the traditional family group. The father was a supreme autocrat, with control over the use of all family property and income and a decisive voice in arranging the marriages of the children. The mixed love, fear, and awe of children for their father was strengthened by the great respect paid to age. An old man's loss of vigor was more than offset by his growth in wisdom. As long as he lived in possession of his faculties, the patriarch had every sanction to enable him to dominate the family scene. According to the law, he could sell his children into slavery or even execute them for improper conduct. In fact, Chinese parents were by custom as well as by nature particularly loving toward small children, and they were also bound by a reciprocal code of responsibility for their children as family members. But law and custom provided little check on paternal tyranny if a father chose to exercise it.

The domination of age over youth within the old-style family was matched by the domination of male over female. Even today, Chinese baby girls seem more likely than baby boys to suffer infanticide. A girl's marriage was arranged and not for love. The trembling bride left her own family behind and became at once a daughter-in-law under the control of her husband's mother. She might see secondary wives or concubines brought into the household, particularly if she did not bear a male heir. She could be repudiated by her husband for various reasons. If he died, she could not easily remarry. All this reflected the fact that a woman had no economic independence. Her labor was absorbed in household tasks and brought her no income. Farm women were almost universally illiterate. They had few or no property rights.

The inferior social status of women was merely one manifestation of the hierarchic nature of China's entire social code and cosmology. Ancient China had viewed the world as the product of two interacting complementary elements, *yin* and *yang*. *Yin* was the attribute of all things female, dark, weak, and passive. *Yang* was the attribute of all things male, bright, strong, and active. While male and female were both necessary and complementary, one was by nature passive toward the other. Building on such ideological foundations, an endless succession of Chinese male moralists worked out the behavior pattern of obedience and passivity that was expected of women. These patterns subordinated girls to boys from infancy and kept the wife subordinate to her husband and the mother to her grown son. Forceful women, whom China has never lacked, usually controlled their families by indirection, not by fiat.

Status within the family was codified in the famous "three bonds" emphasized by the Confucian philosophers: the bond of loyalty on the part of subject to ruler (minister to prince), of filial obedience on the part of son to father (children to parents), and of chastity on the part of wives but not of husbands. To an egalitarian Westerner the most striking thing about this doctrine is that two of the three relationships were within the family, and all were between superior and subordinate. The relationship of mother and son, which in Western life often allows matriarchal domination, was not stressed in theory, though it was naturally important in fact.

When a father saw the beginning of individuality and independence in his son, he might fear that selfish personal indulgence would disrupt the family. Strong bonds of intimacy between mother and son or son and wife threatened the vertical lines of loyalty and respect that maintained the family and the father's authority. In Jonathan Ocko's summary (in Kwang-Ching Liu, 1990), wives were "ineluctably destabilizing elements," promising descendants, yet always threatening the bond of obedience between parents and sons.

In addition to this common bond of loyalty to family, the old China was knit together by the common experience of a highly educated local elite, who were committed from childhood to studying and following the classical texts and teachings. Motherly nurture and fatherly discipline combined to concentrate the young scholar's effort on self-control and on the suppression of sexual and frivolous impulses. Instead, as Jon Saari's (1990) study of upper-class childhood in the late nineteenth century reiterates, the training of youth was in obedience above all. Once a boy entered his adolescent years, open affection from parents gave way to intensive training aimed at proper character formation.

The traditional family system was highly successful at preparing the Chinese to accept similar patterns of status in other institutions, including the official hierarchy of the government. The German sociologist Max Weber characterized China as a "familistic state." One advantage of a system of status is that a man knows automatically where he stands in his family or society. He can have security in the knowledge that if he does his prescribed part, he may expect reciprocal action from others in the system.

Within the extended family, every child from birth was involved in a highly ordered system of kinship relations with elder brothers, sisters, maternal elder brothers' wives, and other kinds of aunts, uncles, cousins, grandparents, and in-laws too numerous for a Westerner to keep track of. These relationships were not only more clearly named and differentiated than in the West but also carried with them more compelling rights and duties dependent upon status. Family members expected to be called by the correct term indicating their relationship to the person addressing them.

In South China the pioneer anthropologist Maurice Freedman (1971) found family lineages to be the major social institutions—each one a community of families claiming descent from a founding ancestor, holding ancestral estates, and joining in periodic rituals at graves and in ancestral halls. Buttressed by genealogies, lineage members might share common interests both economic and political in the local society. In North China, however, anthropologists have found lineages organized on different bases. Chinese kinship organization varies by region. Family practices of property-holding, marriage dowries, burial or cremation, and the like also have had a complex history that is just beginning to be mapped out.

The Chinese kinship system in both the North and South is patrilineal, the family headship passing in the male line from father to eldest son. Thus the men stay in the family, while the women marry into other family households, in neither case following the life pattern that Western individuals take as a matter of course. Until recently a Chinese boy and girl did not choose each other as life mates, nor are they likely even today to set up an independent household together after marriage. Instead, they usually enter the husband's father's household and assume responsibilities for its maintenance, subordinating married life to family life in a way that many Westerners would consider insupportable.

While the family headship passes intact from father to eldest son, the family property does not. Early in their history the Chinese abandoned primogeniture, by which the eldest son inherits all the father's property while the younger sons seek their fortunes elsewhere. The enormous significance of this institutional change can be seen by comparing China with a country like England or Japan, where younger sons who have not shared their father's estate have provided the personnel for government, business, and overseas empire and where a local nobility might grow up to challenge the central power. In China, the equal division of land among the sons of the family allowed the eldest son to retain only certain ceremonial duties, to acknowledge his position, and sometimes an extra share of property. The consequent parcelization of the land tended to weaken the continuity of family land-holding, forestall the growth of landed power among officials, and keep peasant families on the margin of subsistence. The prime duty of each married couple was to produce a son to maintain the family line, yet the birth of more than one son might mean impoverishment.

Contrary to a common myth, a large family with several children has not been the norm among Chinese peasants. The scarcity of land, as well as disease and famine, set a limit to the number of people likely to survive in each family unit. The large joint family of several married sons with many children all within one compound, which has often been regarded as typical of China, appears to have been the ideal exception, a luxury that only the well-to-do could afford. The average peasant family was limited to four, five, or six persons in total. Division of the land among the sons constantly checked the accumulation of property and savings, and the typical family had little opportunity to rise on the social scale. Peasants were bound to the soil not by law and custom so much as by their own numbers.

The farming village, which even today forms the bedrock of Chinese society, is still built out of family units that are permanently settled from one generation to the next and depend upon the use of certain land-holdings. Each family household is both a social and an economic unit. Its members derive their sustenance from working its fields and their social status from membership in it. The life cycle of the individual in a farming village is still inextricably interwoven with the seasonal cycle of intensive agriculture upon the land. The life and death of villagers follow a rhythm that interpenetrates the growing and harvesting of the crops.

Yet Chinese peasant life has not normally been confined to a single village but rather to a whole group of villages that form a market area. This pattern can be seen from the air—the cellular structure of market communities, each centered on a market town surrounded by its ring of satellite villages. The prerevolutionary Chinese countryside was a honeycomb of these relatively self-sufficient areas. From the market town, footpaths (or sometimes waterways) radiated out to a first ring of about six villages and continued on to a second ring of, say, twelve villages. Each of these eighteen or so villages had perhaps 75 households, and each family household averaged five persons—parents, perhaps two children, and a grandparent. No village was more than about two and a half miles from the market town, within an easy day's round trip with a carrying-pole, barrow, or donkey (or a sampan on a waterway). Together, the village farmers and the market-town shopkeepers, artisans, landowners, temple priests, and others formed a community of roughly 1,500 households or 7,500 people. The town market functioned periodically—say, every first, fourth, and seventh day in a ten-day cycle—so that itinerant merchants could visit it regularly while visiting a central market and the adjoining town markets five miles away in similar cycles—say, every second, fifth, and eighth day or every third, sixth, and ninth day. In this pulsation of the market cycle, one person from every household might go to the market town on every third day, perhaps to sell a bit of local produce or buy a product from elsewhere, but in any case to meet friends in the tea shop, at the temple, or on the way. In ten years a farmer would have gone to market a thousand times.

Thus while the villages were not self-sufficient, the large market community was both an economic unit and a social universe. Marriages were commonly arranged through matchmakers at the market town. There, festivals were celebrated, a secret society might have its lodge meetings, and the peasant community would meet representatives of the ruling class—tax gatherers and rent collectors. Yet here again recent research has already modified the stereotype. Prasenjit Duara (1988) has noted how villagers participated in several networks—of kinship relations, secret societies, religious cults, militia groups, or the security system of mutual responsibility—that were not necessarily coextensive with the market network.

Inner Asia and China: The Steppe and the Sown

The contrasts between North and South China are superficial compared with those between the pastoral nomadism of the plateaus of Inner Asia and the settled villages based on the intensive agriculture of China. Inner Asia denotes the originally non-Chinese regions abutting China in a wide arc running from Manchuria through Mongolia and Turkestan to Tibet. At various times of strength and conquest the Chinese empire has included Inner Asia, as indeed the People's Republic does today. Such Inner Asians as Mongols, Tibetans, and Manchus are counted among the 55 ethnic minorities that help to make up the People's Republic of China.*

The contrast between Inner Asia and China proper is a striking one in nearly every respect. On the steppe, population is thinly scattered; today there are only a few million Mongols and hardly more than that number of Tibetans in the arid plateau regions that more than equal the area occupied by over a billion Chinese who trace their ancestry to the Han dynasty (see Table 1). The thinness of population in Inner Asia in itself makes the life of the steppe nomads vastly different from the crowded life of the Han Chinese.

"Nomadism" of course does not mean aimless wandering over the grasslands but the seasonal migration of camps and flocks from one known place to another, perhaps to the hills in winter and the lowlands in summer, as climate and rainfall dictate, in search of pasture. Full nomads of this sort, dependent upon their horses and sheep, may have emerged from seminomadic societies on the edge of the grasslands that originally combined settled agriculture with hunting and warfare. Both acquired metallurgy in bronze and then iron.

Just as intensive agriculture molded the Chinese, so the sheep and horse economy of Inner Asia conditioned the nomad. The sophisticated technology of rice culture in South China's paddy fields had its counterpart in the care with which sheep, goats, camels, horses, and cattle must each be properly adjusted to the ground cover, terrain, and climate in

---

*Early Western explorers spoke of the deserts and mountains west of China and north of India as "Central Asia." Thus Inner Asia—inner from China—includes Central Asia.

Table 1. Major periods in Imperial China

Eastern Zhou	771–256 BC
Warring States	403–221 BC
Qin	221–206 BC
Earlier Han	206 BC–AD 8
Later Han	25–220
Period of North-South disunion	220–589
Northern Wei	386–535
Sui	589–618
Tang	618–907
Northern Song with Liao empire (Qidan) on north border	960–1125
Southern Song with Jin empire (Ruzhen) in North China	1127–1279
Yuan (Mongols)	1279–1368
Ming	1368–1644
Qing (Manchus)	1644–1912

the grasslands. From his flocks, the nomad secured food, sheepskins for clothing, shelter in the form of felt for his yurt, and fuel in the form of sheep dung. Cultivation of the soil being unreliable, he depended upon the management of his animals for a livelihood and upon his horses for mobility, which could save him from the aridity of the steppe. He therefore had to be constantly resourceful and ready for new ventures. Custom did not tie him to the land, but he remained dependent upon a certain minimum of trade with settled regions. He was often freer than the Chinese farmer and at the same time poorer than the Chinese landlord, since he could not accumulate immobile wealth from generation to generation. He was also a trained hunter and horseman, and so a potential warrior.

Succession to tribal leadership had to be settled not by simple inheritance as in a dynasty but more flexibly by tanistry—the election of an heir apparent for his (presumed) preeminent ability to carry on the leadership. Such a man might be found patrilineally among the chieftain's sons or laterally among the chieftain's brothers. Such an ambiguous system could justify any choice that the tribal leaders might make. They would accept an able leader, and so a charismatic chieftain like Chinggis (Genghis) Khan in the thirteenth century might quickly organize a tribal confederation of great military strength based on the firepower of mounted archers. Until recently the nomadic and seminomadic peoples to the north and west of China were a continuing factor in Chinese military and political life.

Here lies one source of China's "culturalism"—that is, the devotion of the Chinese people to their way of life, an across-the-board sentiment as strong as the political nationalism of recent centuries in Europe. Where European nationalism arose through the example of and contact with other nation-states, Chinese culturalism arose from the difference in culture between China and the Inner Asian "barbarians." Because the Inner Asian invaders became more powerful as warriors, the Chinese found their refuge in social institutions and feelings of cultural and aesthetic superiority—something that alien conquest could not take away.

We must therefore realize that Chinese history has embraced both the Chinese people and the Inner Asian non-Chinese who have repeatedly invaded the Chinese state and society and become integral components of them. In short, we must broaden our sights: the Inner Asian peoples have been a critical part of the history of the Chinese people. Even today the Chinese state assigns to the "autonomous regions" of the minority nationalities more land area than to the Han Chinese majority.

Rise and Decline of the Imperial Autocracy

SINCE HISTORIANS, like journalists, have constantly to generalize about complex situations, they easily accede to the need of ruling figures to stand forth as principal actors in the record. Short referents help—witness TR, FDR, IKE, JFK, and even Bush among American presidents. Such preeminence may be institutionalized, as when all communications from an embassy have to go out over the ambassador's name. How infinitely more prominent, then, was an emperor of China, whose individual reign title dated all records—as though our calendar read not 1991 and 1992 but Bush 3 and Bush 4. Is it even worth mentioning that an emperor was an autocrat? What else could he have been?

But autocracy is a matter of degree and takes various forms. It may be defined at one extreme as the capacity of a ruler to impose his will upon his state and society. This borders on despotism or tyranny. At a minimum autocracy is above the law, a law unto itself, making specific laws but not controlled by them.

In operational terms, however, an autocrat like the emperor of China had to contend with procedural rules as well as moral admonitions and his own interests and reputation. He needed staff cooperation and competent information and advice. For example, procedural rules might require that he could act only when a matter was formally presented to him, or only when others had prepared his choices to decide upon. His staff outnumbered him and slept in shifts. Personal freedom for such an autocrat might be hard to find, especially in an age that exalted imperial rites and ceremonies. He was burdened by many duties and manipulated by the system—by his courtiers during the day and by his harem at night. What a crowded life!

However, the aspects of Chinese autocracy that will be described in the following chapters are not those of the palace treadmill but rather certain other features that seem to have stood out in the Chinese case. First, one notes the *pervasiveness* of the imperial authority. The Chinese emperor seems to have had the final word in every aspect of life. Second, we see the resulting *politicization* of all these aspects, from dress to manners, books to paintings. One's every act might have political significance. Third is the emperor's careful refusal to allow any rival authority to arise, nor any untaxable income, that might challenge the imperial *monopoly of power*. In short, China's imperial institution at times was capable of strong leadership, and this fact seems to have contributed to China's early achievements. We cannot say the emperor did it all—far from it!— yet we may see the vigor of the imperial institution as a rough index to the strength of China's social cohesion and unity. But as time went on, how long could this quality of strong leadership survive the growth of the body politic?

1

Origins: The Discoveries
of Archaeology

Paleolithic China

One of the early forms of Western cultural imperialism toward China was the belief of some pundits and archaeologists that Chinese civilization had no prehistory of its own, that it arose suddenly from the diffusion of West Asian cultural traits like wheat, pottery, writing, or the horse-drawn chariot as a "civilization by osmosis," bit by bit coming across Central Asia from the West. Such assumptions out of ignorance have long since been overturned. The early stress on diffusion of cultural traits has given way to a realization that there were probably substantial contacts among primitive men over the eons.

In China, the study of prehistory through excavation is one of the newest developments. Part of China's modernization today lies in the steady advance of archaeology since the 1920s. Modernization efforts under both the Nationalist and the Communist governments, as the latest phase of China's modern revolution, have been matched by scientific discovery of China's prehistory. The story continues to unfold. Its importance lies in the cultural continuity that it discloses. Distinctive features of Chinese life today, such as autocratic government, come down directly from prehistoric times.

China has two north-south chains of mountains: one along the coast, running discontinuously from the northeast (formerly called Manchuria) through Shandong province and the southeast coast to Hong Kong and Hainan Island. The other chain is inland on the eastern edge of the Central Asian plateau, running from Shanxi province south through Sichuan to the southwest China upland. East of it in the north stretches the North China plain. Among the limestone hills on the edge of the plain twenty-seven miles southwest of Beijing near today's village of Zhoukoudian there are a number of caves. One particularly large cavern was originally the size of a football field (500 by 150 feet and in one area 120 feet from floor to ceiling). Beginning about 400,000 BP (before the present) this cave, which had a small entrance on the northeast, was inhabited by primitive people continuously for about 200,000 years until the interior was completely filled up with layers of their debris.

What a find for archaeologists! In 1921 a single tooth from the site was identified as belonging to a primitive species of human. The first skull was found in 1929. Careful excavation from 1921 to 1937 and since 1959 has exhumed about 100,000 stone tools, over 100 teeth, 14 skulls, and many other bones representing more than 40 individuals of *Homo erectus,* the same species of early humans as the ones found in Java (1891), Europe, the Middle East, and Africa.

They were little people. Peking Man stood about 5 feet, 2 inches tall, Peking Woman about 4 feet 9. They had very thick skull bones and receding chins, but their cranial capacity of 850–1300 cc may be compared with Java Man's 775–900 cc and the 1350 cc of early *Homo sapiens.* They were hunter-fisher-gatherers and used fire to illuminate their cave and to cook their meat, 70 percent of which consisted of deer, although bones of the leopard, bear, saber-toothed tiger, hyena, elephant, rhinoceros, camel, water buffalo, boar, and horse were also found. There were no burials or complete skeletons in the cave, but some skulls were bashed in, which suggests that Peking Man was a small-time cannibal or at least a head-hunter who savored brains. All in all, says K. C. Chang (1986), the Peking Man fossils were "paleoanthropology's greatest catch."

Other discoveries followed. After 1949 the widespread construction of roads, railways, dams, and foundations unearthed hundreds of new archaeological sites. Another skull of *Homo erectus* was found in 1964 in Shaanxi province, though it seemed more primitive than Peking Man. Chipped stone tools and human fossils from between 400,000 and 200,000 years BP (during the Lower or Early Paleolithic period; see Table 2) at a dozen or more sites show *Homo erectus* to have been widely dispersed in China, mainly in the provinces of the western mountain chain. A cranium was found in 1980–81 in Anhui province, and a partial skeleton was found in 1984 in Liaoning. Other finds are continuing.

At several sites excavated in the 1970s remains were found of early

Table 2. China's prehistory

1,000,000–200,000 BP	Lower (Early) Paleolithic
400,000–200,000	*Homo erectus* (Peking Man)
200,000–50,000 BP	Middle Paleolithic
	Early *Homo sapiens*
50,000–12,000 BP	Upper (Late) Paleolithic
	Homo sapiens sapiens
12,000–2000 BC	Neolithic
8000–5000	Beginning of agriculture
5000–3000	Yangshao Painted Pottery
3000–2200	Longshan Black Pottery
2200–500 BC	Bronze Age
2200–1750 BC	Xia
1750–1040 BC	Shang
1100–256 BC	Zhou
600–500 BC	Beginning of Iron Age

All dates are approximate except 256 BC. BP = before the present

Homo sapiens, dating between roughly 200,000 and 50,000 years BP (the Middle Paleolithic period). By roughly 50,000 to 12,000 years BP (the Upper or Late Paleolithic period), *Homo sapiens sapiens* (the later model) was widely dispersed in half a dozen or more local cultures throughout China. They were usually situated at points where mountains descended into plains and hunting could be combined with fishing and gathering. Judging by the stone tools left behind, these cultural regions had common features but also distinctive local characteristics even at this early time. Sites included the middle Yellow River valley, the Ordos region, the loess plateau of Shaanxi province, and the western edge of the North China plain—for example, the Upper Cave at Zhoukoudian seems to have served at this late time as a burial place. Seven skulls were found there, all battered. Archaeologists like K. C. Chang have concluded that Old Stone Age man in China was not a mere chipper of rocks; basic ideas of kinship, authority, religion, and art that can still be found in China today were already developing in these early cultures.

Neolithic China

The Neolithic Age that began in China about 12,000 years ago was marked by the spread of settled agricultural communities. At that time the Yellow and Yangzi Rivers had not yet deposited all the alluvial soil that today forms the plains between the western and eastern mountain chains. Today's North China plain between Shanxi* and Shandong was mainly lakes and marshes—Shandong was almost an island off the coast. Today's provinces of Hebei and Henan were still fens not easily habitable. Meanwhile, the central China section of the Yangzi was an enormous lake. Today's provinces of Hubei and Hunan were not yet cultivable, even for rice. The mountains were well forested, and animals were plentiful. Domestication of animals like the dog and pig was a minor problem compared with the domestication of crops. The hardy perennial plants that hunter-fisher-gatherer communities might have gradually begun to use for food had to be substituted by annual seed crops that could be regularly planted and harvested—in short, cultivated. At this time the fairly warm and moist climate of Paleolithic China had not yet shifted to the more arid and colder climate of the present day. Neolithic agriculture could start most easily in marginal areas where upland forest gave way to cultivable grassland and where an abundance of plants and animals could sustain human life with or without successful farming.

Discoveries at thousands of Neolithic sites show a beginning of settled agriculture below the southern bend of the Yellow River, on a border between wooded highlands and swampy lowlands. For example, the villagers of Banpo (now in the city of Xi'an) about 4000 BC lived on millet supplemented by hunting and fishing. They used hemp for fabrics. Dwellings were grouped in clusters that suggest kinship units. Arrowheads indicate hunting with bows. The villagers raised pigs and dogs as their principal domesticated animals and stored their grain in pottery jars decorated with fish, animal, and plant designs as well as symbols that were evidently clan or lineage markers. But this "Painted Pottery" (called Yangshao) culture of North China was paralleled by contemporary cultures found at sites on the southeast coast and Taiwan and in the lower Yangzi valley, where rice culture had already begun.

Overlying the Painted Pottery has been found a thinner, lustrous Black Pottery (called Longshan) more widely distributed throughout North China, the Yangzi valley, and even the southeast coast, indicating

*Names of provinces commonly use *shan* mountains, *xi* west, *dong* east, *he* river, *bei* north, *nan* south, and *hu* lake. Shanxi is "west of the mountains." Hunan is "south of the lake."

a great expansion of Neolithic agriculture with many regional subcultures. Thus, it seems that Neolithic China developed in several centers from Paleolithic origins.

Another achievement of Neolithic China was silk production. The exacting procedures of sericulture have been practiced in the Chinese farm economy throughout history. How to nourish silkworms on vast quantities of mulberry leaves, how to help them go through periods of quiescent moulting and then spin their cocoons, and finally how to unwind the cocoons to produce raw silk thread are all parts of a painstaking craft. The worms eat about 100 pounds of mulberry leaves to produce about 15 pounds of cocoons from which comes one pound of raw silk. This household industry began in North China in Neolithic times and remained a Chinese monopoly until silkworms were smuggled to the West in the sixth century AD.

Excavation of Shang and Xia

As of 1920 among the legendary Three Dynasties of ancient China—Xia, Shang, and Zhou—only the Zhou (Chou) was known directly from its own written records. The Shang dynasty's 30 kings and seven successive capitals were listed in chronicles compiled during the Zhou or shortly after. Many centuries later antiquarians of the Song era became interested in the bronze ritual vessels inherited from the Shang, some with inscriptions. But not until 1899 did scholars note that Chinese pharmacists were selling "dragon bones" inscribed with archaic characters. By the late 1920s private buyers had traced these "oracle bones" to a site near Anyang north of the Yellow River in Henan province. In 1928 archaeologists of the National Government's Academia Sinica began scientific excavations of the last Shang capital at Anyang that continued until Japan attacked China in 1937. After 1950 an earlier Shang capital was found near present-day Zhengzhou.

In these Shang capital cities were royal palaces and upper-class residences of post-and-beam construction on stamped-earth platforms, built in the basic architectural style we admire today in Beijing's Forbidden City. At Anyang were found the stamped-earth foundations, as hard as cement, of 53 buildings, with many stone-pillar bases. Subterranean pit houses nearby evidently were used as storage and service quarters. The aristocracy had the services of artisans who specialized in a highly developed bronze metallurgy, pottery, and many other crafts. The Shang bronzes, never surpassed in craftsmanship, are still one of humankind's great artistic achievements. The Shang king was served by diviners who handled the writing system and took the auspices by scapulimancy (applying a hot point to create cracks in animal shoulder blades, interpreting these cracks as the advice of the ancestors, and inscribing the results on the bones). This produced the famous "oracle bones" that first led to excavation at Anyang. Some 100,000 such bones have been collected. Questions and answers inscribed on the bones reveal that the Shang aristocracy lived a superior life, fighting in horse chariots, hunting for sport, performing rites and ceremonies, while served by scribes and artisans and supported by the agriculture of the surrounding village peasants, who lived in semisubterranean dwelling pits. Shang society was already highly stratified.

In the warmer and moister climate of the time, water buffalo were the principal domestic animals, and large herds of cattle must have been maintained to supply the bones for scapulimancy and the animals used by the hundreds in ritual sacrifices. Reverence for ancestors was expressed by rulers in the form of a fully ritualized religious observance. Royal tomb chambers deep in the earth were supplied with precious objects and many animal and human sacrifices. K. C. Chang concludes that these burials indicate most vividly a stratified society in which members of a lower class were sometimes the victims of ritual sacrifice. The Anyang excavations seem to have revealed only the royal core of a much larger capital area. Many Shang sites have also been found elsewhere in North China and Sichuan.

The power of the Shang king was also attested in the use of vast bodies of manpower for public works. The Shang capital at Zhengzhou had a roughly rectangular wall 4 miles around and as high as 27 feet, built of stamped earth. Pounding thin layers of earth within a movable wooden frame made a product as hard as cement. This building technique, which was found first in Longshan sites, has been used throughout China's history. Three thousand years later the walls of the capitals of the Ming dynasty (AD 1368–1644) at Nanjing and Beijing were also built of stamped earth. They were some 40 feet high and respectively 23 and 21 miles around, bigger and faced with brick but still built by massed labor. In other parts of the ancient world massed manpower was used to build many wonders, such as the Egyptian pyramids, but in China this custom has persisted to the present day.

In 1959 excavations at Erlitou (in the city of Yanshi not far from Luoyang and just south of the Yellow River) uncovered another site with large palaces that seems likely to have been a capital of the Xia dynasty. The Erlitou culture was widespread in the region of northwest Henan and southern Shanxi. It was a direct successor to the Longshan Black Pottery culture and preceded the early Shang, with radiocarbon dates of ca. 2100 to 1800 BC. With this all-but-final identification, the Xia and Shang components of the legendary Three Dynasties have taken tangible form. What do they tell us about China's origins?

First, there seems to have been a rather smooth transition from the innumerable Neolithic villages of the Longshan culture to the Bronze Age capital cities of the Three Dynasties, all of which we can view as successive phases of a single cultural development. Looking at the tools and weapons, the pots and bronze vessels, the domestication of crops and animals, the architectural layout of settlements and burials, and the evident practices of religion and government, we can see a high degree of cultural homogeneity and continuity. One dynasty succeeded another through warfare, but there is no evidence of violent intrusion by an outside culture. Moreover, Xia, Shang, and Zhou centered in three different areas and seem to have co-existed (see Map 6). The Shang and Zhou "succession" consisted of becoming the dominant center of ancient North China.

Second, these ancient capitals testify to the power of a kingship based on sedentary, land-locked agriculture, not on mobile, waterborne trade with other areas. To be sure, cowry shells found at Anyang must have come from the seacoast; and the Neolithic East Asians were seafarers when opportunity arose. We know this from the fact that a Neolithic site in northern Taiwan dated 4000–2500 BC (and a later Neolithic South Taiwan site dated 2500 to 400 BC) were uncovered on an island that today is 100 miles off the coast of Fujian province. As there was no land bridge from the mainland, and as the sea, though more shallow, did not vary sufficiently in depth to make crossing much easier than it would be today, we have to conclude that the Neolithic peoples living on the sea developed a nautical technology parallel with the Neolithic capacity for agriculture. So why did a robust sea trade not grow up in China comparable to that in the Middle East and Mediterranean? The difference lay in an accident of geography: few other early communities in East Asia could be reached from China by coasting or by sea trade. Chinese shipping developed on the Yangzi, between Shandong and South Manchuria and along the coast, but no great sea trade could grow up in the absence of accessible foreign countries.

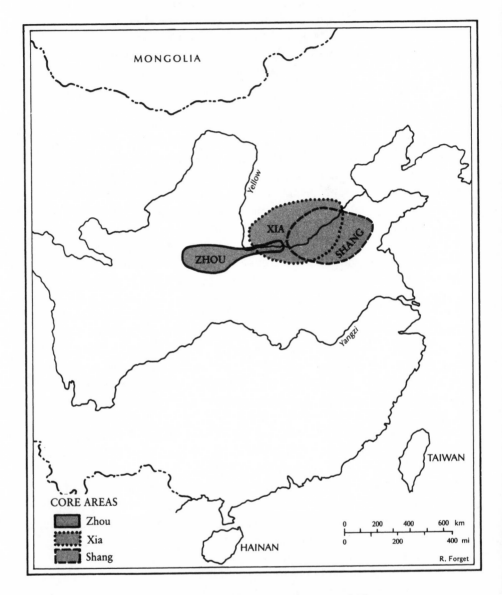

6. The Three Dynasties: Xia, Shang, and Zhou

The Rise of Central Authority

The deposits of Yangshao and then Longshan types of pottery in half a dozen or more areas on the North China plain and along the Yellow River and Lower Yangzi show the differentiation of local cultures. As contact grew among these Neolithic farming villages, networks of kinship and allied relationships created an opportunity for broader government from a central capital. Judging by what came later, it seems that family lineages, derived from large tribal clans, each set up their separate walled towns. The Shang oracle bones name about a thousand towns altogether. One lineage headed by a patriarch would establish relations by marriage with other lineages in other walled towns. Branch lineages could also be set up by migration to new town sites; and complex relations of subordination and superordination would ensue.

Toward the end of the third millennium BC the making of bronze from copper and tin deposits widely mined in North China coincided with the rise during the Xia and Shang dynasties of the first central government over a broad area. Bronze metallurgy was probably a natural further step in a technology that had developed techniques for shaping and firing Yangshao and Longshan pottery and then producing small copper objects such as knives. Whether the techniques of bronze metallurgy were indigenous or imported (or both), the central fact of bronze production was that only a strong authority could ensure the mining of ore. Judging by nineteenth-century examples, premodern mining required laborers, on hands and knees, to drag their heavy ore-sleds out through cramped and unventilated tunnels—work fit for slaves or prisoners. When it came to bronze casting by the piece-mold process, hundreds of skilled artisans would be needed to prepare and handle the molten metal. Making ritual vessels of bronze thus had several implications—first, that a royal authority was vitally concerned with rituals as an aspect of its power; and, second, that it was able to assign manpower to the onerous tasks of mining ores and refining metals.

We know that in both Xia and Shang the ruling family made use of elaborate and dramatic rituals to confirm their power to govern, especially the rituals of shamanism by which a priest (or shaman), often the ruler himself, would communicate with the spirits of the ancestors to secure their help and guidance. In this function the shaman would be helped by certain animals considered to have a totemic relation to the ancestors. On the Shang bronze ritual vessels these were represented by animal designs, especially by the bilateral animal masks (*taotie,* echoed much later, for example, in Amerindian totem poles). By practicing a religious cult of the ancestors, local rulers legitimized their authority. Some became lords over groups of towns, and group vied with group as well as region with region, until a single ruling dynasty could emerge in a distinct area.

Once under way, the expanding authority of the state would encompass settlements still at a Neolithic stage of pre–Bronze Age culture. Bronze weapons would help, and in their conquests we know that the late Shang after about 1200 BC used the two-horse war chariot that had empowered conquerors in West Asia from about 1500 BC. No doubt its concept had come across Central Asia. The spears and arrows of foot soldiers accompanied the chariot. Three men manned it—a driver in the center, flanked by a swordsman (or halberdier) and a bowman. Bronze fittings made the chariot motile. Men from each cluster of families in a lineage seem to have formed a military unit. Thousands of soldiers are mentioned as having taken thousands of prisoners, hundreds of whom might be sacrificed. The king claimed that his primacy rested on his personal merit, but there is no doubt that military power helped him.

In addition to warfare, the Xia and Shang expanded their domain by building new towns. Towns were not unplanned growths caused by trade or by migration of individual families but were planned and created by local rulers. Typically a king might decree the building of a town in a new region where farmland was to be opened up, and a town populace would be selected and dispatched to do the job. In the *Classic of Poetry (Shijing)* is a description of a town-founding in terms not inappropriate for a barn-raising by American pioneers:

> . . . left and right
> He drew the boundaries of big plots and little
> He opened up the ground, he counted the acres
> From west to east . . .
> Then he summoned his Master of Work
> Then he summoned his Master of Lands
> And made them build houses.
> Dead straight was the plumb line
> The planks were lashed to hold the earth;
> They made the Hall of Ancestors very venerable
> They tilted in the earth with a rattling
> They pounded it with a dull thud . . .
> They raised the outer gate
> The outer gate soared high.

They raised the inner gate
The inner gate was very strong.
They raised the great earth-mound
Whence excursions of war might start . . .

On balance, warfare and trade seem to have been no more important as factors in expansion than the overall superiority of the king's ritual and liturgical functions in his intercession with the ancestors and other forces of nature. Perhaps like the early Carolingian kings of France, the king's extensive travels suggest, as David Keightley observes, that he was head of a patrimonial state that was not yet fully bureaucratic, a state that was still more theocratic than secular in its institutional activity.

Western Zhou

With the conquest of the Shang dynasty by the Zhou, the Chinese state finally emerges. Here again, the new archaeological evidence such as inscriptions on bronzes and newly excavated Zhou oracle bones fit together with the literary record of ancient places, people, and events long known from the classics and earliest histories.

In its origins, the small Zhou tribe interacted with nomads on the north and with proto-Tibetan Qiang people on the west. They early learned how to tolerate and work with peoples of different cultures. After they finally settled in the Wei River valley, the Zhou rulers became vassals of the Shang until they became strong enough to conquer Shang in warfare in about 1040 BC. Each side mobilized from seven to eight hundred villages or petty "states." The victorious Zhou built a new capital at Xi'an (Chang'an). They transported many Shang elite families to manage the work of building and made use of Shang skills in ritual and government. Other Shang families were transported to populate and develop the west. Cho-yun Hsu and Katheryn Linduff (1988) conclude that the former Shang elite and the Zhou ruling class coalesced.

After conquering the eastern plain, the Zhou's power expanded by defeating nomads on the northwest and by campaigns southward into the Han and Yangzi River areas and southeast along the Huai River. Zhou rule was established by setting up what has been called a "feudal" network, enfeoffing *(fengjian)* sons of the Zhou rulers to preside over fifty or more vassal states. The Zhou investiture ceremony was an elaborate delegation of authority of a contractual nature. Along with symbolic ritual gifts the Zhou king bestowed upon a vassal lord the people of a certain area. The people, so bestowed, however, were more important than the land, and whole communities composed of descendants of a lineage might be moved to another area and be superimposed upon the local people to create another vassal state.

While the Zhou thus continued, like the Shang, to use kinship as a main element of political organization, they created a new basis of legitimacy by espousing the theory of Heaven's mandate. Where Shang rulers had venerated and sought the guidance of their own ancestors, the Zhou claimed their sanction to rule came from a broader, impersonal deity, Heaven *(tian)*, whose mandate *(tianming)* might be conferred on any family that was morally worthy of the responsibility. This doctrine asserted the ruler's accountability to a supreme moral force that guides the human community. Unlike a Western ruler's accession through the doctrine of the divine right of kings, which rested on birth alone, the Chinese theory of Heaven's mandate set up moral criteria for holding power.

Expansion of the Zhou central power involved a degree of acculturation of those who submitted, not least in the spread of the Chinese writing system and the rituals and administration that it served. The mainstream culture was that of the Central Plain *(zhongyuan)*, the core region of Shang–Zhou predominance. In peripheral areas were many non-Chinese whose different cultural status was marked by the fact that their names were not Chinese but were recorded in transliteration. They included both seminomads of the north, northeast, and northwest and tribal peoples of South China. By degrees, intermarriage, acculturation, and a beginning of bureaucratic government created the successor states that followed the Shang–Zhou dominance. These states inherited various cultural mixes and emerged as distinct political entities during the Warring States period, which began about 400 BC.

Implications of the New Archaeological Record

The cultural homogeneity of ancient China as revealed by the archaeological record contrasts remarkably with the multiplicity and diversity of peoples, states, and cultures in the ancient Middle East. Beginning about 3000 BC, Egyptians, Sumerians, Semites, Akkadians, Amorites (ruled by Hammurabi of Babylon), Assyrians, Phoenicians, Hittites, Medes, Persians, and others jostled one another in a bewildering flux of Middle Eastern warfare and politics. The record is one of pluralism with a vengeance. Irrigation helped agriculture in several centers—the Nile, the Tigris–Euphrates, and the Indus valleys. Trade flourished along with seafaring. Languages, writing systems, and religions proliferated. The contrast with ancient China could not have been greater.

Second, Middle Eastern technology predates Chinese in several respects. Painted pottery, the use of bronze, and the horse chariot appear earlier in the Middle East than in China, as does the subsequent use of iron, and this priority naturally suggests that these cultural elements were transmitted to China. But the precise connections between ancient China and the Middle East are still obscure and in dispute. We do know that some things failed to be transmitted from the Middle East. For example, despite precedents in Egypt, Mesopotamia, and India, the Yellow River did not at first lend itself to irrigation networks on the North China plain. The Chinese of Xia and Shang did not use metal agricultural tools nor draft animals and plows. The horse chariot functioned in the late Shang as an aristocratic vehicle as well as the main war machine, but its use in the Shang is not thus far accompanied by evidence of a barbarian horse-chariot invasion from the northwest and the steppe, as Western historians posited until recently from the example of early horse-chariot invasions in the Middle East.

Obscurity also clouds the influences coming into China from the south. For example, bronze metallurgy seems to have begun in Thailand before 3000 BC. Its relation to bronze in China is uncertain. On the whole, the Middle Eastern evidence of early and extensive communication between separate prehistoric cultures has made "diffusion" or the lack of it a dying issue. Each major culture was a local achievement, but cultures were hardly isolated. We can conclude that important influences from West Asia reached China as though "by osmosis," to be sure, but never in proportions so cataclysmic as to shatter China's cultural homogeneity.

This conclusion counters the early suggestion of pioneer archaeologists, mainly Western, that ancient China was given an absolutely essential impetus toward civilization by Middle Eastern contact filtered across Central Asia. The new evidence also militates against a more recent concept that ancient Chinese civilization grew from a single nuclear area in North China and that the Xia-Shang development was unique—"the cradle of the East," in P. T. Ho's phrase. To be sure, the combination of Zhou era chronicles about Xia, Shang, and Zhou and post-1920 excavations gives the Three Dynasties center stage in China's ancient history.

But excavation in East Asia as a whole, though just beginning, has already revealed separate though related pottery cultures south of the Yangzi, on China's southeast coast, and in northern Vietnam.

One source of Xia–Shang strength was the social order imposed by kinship and the ranking of lineages through their hierarchical segmentation, that is, branch lineages remaining subordinate to their parent lineages. Every individual had a status in his family group, and lineages had relationships of superiority and inferiority among themselves, all the way up to the dynastic power-holders. The ruler's top position rested also on his final authority both in the shamanistic religion of ancestor reverence that used bronze ritual vessels and in the warfare that featured chariots and bronze weapons. Royal burials involved human sacrifice in a society already highly stratified.

On the other hand, in the absence of significant seafaring, trade and technological innovation seem to have been quite secondary in the growth of central political authority. This finding of the archaeologists is not easy for Western historians to grasp, so deeply engrained in Western, especially Mediterranean, history is the evidence that early cities emerged on trade routes and empires grew by their command of commerce, especially on the sea. Ancient China's lack of sea trade left the merchants less important and disesteemed ideologically, and this made it easier for the Qin and Han rulers when they came to power to assert control over the merchants who had arisen in their societies.

Finally, the ruler's primacy rested on his monopoly of leadership not only in ritual and warfare but also in oracle-bone writing and the historical learning it recorded. The Shang writing system already evinced subject-verb-object syntax and methods of character formation by simple pictographs, abstract descriptive pictographs, and phono-pictographs that would remain basic in Chinese thereafter. Chinese characters began as pictures or symbols. The ancient character 木 meant a tree, two trees 林 meant a forest, and three 森, a dense growth. The symbols 一 二 三 are certainly easier than "one, two, three." 囗 indicates an enclosure or "to surround," while a smaller square 口 is the sign for the mouth and by extension means a hole, a pass, a harbor, and the like.

In its early growth the Chinese written language could not expand on a purely pictographic basis (like the joining of two trees to make a forest, noted above). A phonetic aspect had to be adopted. As a result, most Chinese characters are combinations of other simple characters.

One part of the combination usually indicates the root meaning, while the other part indicates something about the sound.

For example, take the character for east 東, which in the Beijing dialect has the sound "dong" (pronounced "doong," as in Mao Zedong's name). Since a Chinese character is read aloud as a single syllable and since spoken Chinese is also rather short of sounds (there are only about four hundred different syllables in the whole language), it has been plagued with homophones, words that sound like other words, like "soul" and "sole" or "all" and "awl" in English. It happened that the spoken word meaning "freeze" had the sound "dong." So did a spoken word meaning a roof beam. When the Chinese went to write down the character for freeze, they took the character for east and put beside it the symbol of ice 冫, which makes the character 凍 ("dong," to freeze). To write down the word sounding "dong" which meant roof beam, they wrote the character east and put before it the symbol for wood 木 making 棟 ("dong," a roof beam).

These are simple examples. Indeed, any part of the Chinese language is simple in itself. It becomes difficult because there is so much of it to be remembered, so many meanings and allusions. When the lexicographers of later times wanted to arrange thousands of Chinese characters in a dictionary, for instance, the best they could do in the absence of an alphabet was to work out a list of 214 classifiers or "radicals," one of which was sure to be in each character in the language. These 214 classifiers, for dictionary purposes, correspond to the 26 letters of our alphabet, but are more ambiguous and less efficient. Shang writing was already using "radicals" like wood, mouth, heart, hand, that indicated categories of meaning. From the start the governmental power of the Chinese writing system was at the ruler's disposal. Writing seems to have emerged more in the service of lineage organization and government than in the service of trade.

When we group together the shaman-priests, warriors, scribes, heads of lineages, and superintendents over artisans, we can see the rudiments of the ruling elite that developed. The emerging art of government made use of ritual and art, warfare, writing, and family connections, all of which contributed to the concept of culture. A next step was the assertion of central cultural superiority over the surrounding peoples by designating as "barbarians" (in the Greek cultural sense of βαρβαροι) those peoples who did not yet acknowledge the central government's supremacy. Such peoples were given generic names in the classics and histories: *Yi,* barbarians on the east, *Man* on the south, *Rong* on the west, and *Di* on the north. (When Westerners arrived by sea, they were officially designated until the late nineteenth century as *Yi.*) This custom of sharply distinguishing "inside" *(net)* and "outside" *(wai)* went along with calling China the "Central Country" *(zhongguo),* which began by ruling the "Central Plain" *(zhongyuan)* in North China. So strong is this nomenclature in the classics that were composed under the Zhou Dynasty that historians East and West have generally depicted ancient China of the Three Dynasties as a "culture island" surrounded by a sea of "barbarians" lacking in the civilized qualities of Chinese culture.

The new archaeological record suggests that things were not so simple. The Western Zhou, having intermingled with non-Chinese-speaking peoples on China's north and west peripheries, were adept at tolerating cultural differences while asserting the civilizing superiority of the culture of the Central Plain. Rather than outright military conquest, the process was often one of steady assimilation based on the efficacy of the Chinese way of life and government. The political unit was defined culturally more than territorially.

When we read that "barbarians" have been ever-present on the fringes of China's long history, we can realize that they were a basic category in the political system from the very beginning. We must not overlook the ancient Chinese assumption of a symbiosis between culture *(wenhua)* and temporal power. Subservience to the dynastic state required acceptance of its rituals and cosmology that gave it Heaven's mandate to rule over mankind. Nonacceptance of this politicized culture left one outside of Zhongguo. Yet if one's language was Chinese, acceptance was already partway assured by the very terms imbedded in the classics and in the spoken tongue itself. An identifiably similar way of life was widespread throughout late Neolithic China. The task of statebuilding during the Three Dynasties of the Bronze Age was to gain ever wider submission to or acceptance of the central dynastic ruling house. It functioned as the capstone of the social structure, the high priesthood of the ancestor cult, the arbiter of punishments, and the leader in public works, war, and literature. Among these omnicompetent functions K. C. Chang stresses the ruler's "exclusive access to heaven and heavenly spirits." The result was that the ruler engineered a unity of culture that was the basis for political unity in a single universal state. China of course was not alone in idealizing this kind of unity, which was sought in many of the ancient empires. But China's geographic isolation made the ideal originally more feasible, and as time went on it became more readily supportable in the state and society.

Overstated though these considerations may be, they represent a great fact emerging from Chinese archaeology—that by the beginning of the era of written history, the Chinese people had already achieved a degree of cultural homogeneity and isolated continuity hard to match elsewhere in the world. They had begun to create a society dominated by state power. To it all other activities—agricultural, technological, commercial, military, literary, religious, artistic—would make their contributions as subordinate parts of the whole. Yet it would be an error for us today, so long accustomed to the modern sentiment of nationalism, to imagine ancient China as an embryonic nation-state. We would do better to apply the idea of culturalism and see ancient China as a complete civilization comparable to Western Christendom, within which nation-states like France and England became political subunits that shared their common European culture. Again, because we are so aware of the all-encompassing power of the totalitarian states of the twentieth century, we would do well to avoid an anachronistic leap to judgment that the Shang and Zhou kings' prerogatives led inevitably to a sort of totalitarianism. We might better follow Etienne Balazs (1964), who called it a government by "officialism." As summarized by Stuart Schram (1987), "The state was the central power in Chinese society from the start, and exemplary behavior, rites, morality and indoctrinations have always been considered in China as means of government." We need only add that in addition to these liturgical functions the ruler monopolized the use of military violence.

2

The First Unification:
Imperial Confucianism

The Utility of Dynasties

Until this century dynastic families have provided most of the rulers over the human race. Kinship formed an in-group network to support the power-holder (or a rival) as well as a principle by which to settle (or dispute) the explosive question of the succession to power. Yet among European dynasties such as the Capetian kings of France (987–1328), the Norman and Plantagenet kings of England (1066–1485), the Hapsburgs (1273–1919), or the Romanovs (1613–1917), none ruled as large a state as China or maintained such a monopoly of central power. As institutions of government, the major Chinese dynasties are in a class by themselves. Neither Japan, India, nor Persia produced regimes comparable in scope and power. The Liu clan of Earlier Han provided 13 emperors and in Later Han 14 emperors, the Li clan of the Tang dynasty 23 emperors, the Zhu clan of the Ming dynasty 17 emperors, and the Aisin Gioro lineage of the Manchus 9 emperors (see Table 1).

By comparison, European dynasties were provincial potentates within the oikoumene of Christendom, ruling regional kingdoms. As Jacques Gernet points out, at the end of the seventeenth century the first modern state, the Kingdom of France, was just getting organized while China had long been a "great centralized empire governed by a uniform administrative system." Again, emperors have been quite different entities, East and West. Modern Europe, for example, at one time had emperors of France, Russia, Austria-Hungary, Germany, and the British Empire plus the Pope at Rome all making history *simultaneously*. China ideally, and most of the time in fact, had only one emperor on earth, like one sun in the sky.

Our first requirement, then, if we are to understand China, is to try to avoid imposing a European scale of judgment. For instance, European music and fine arts, technology, philosophy, and religion might come in all or part from outside the country one lived in. No European rulers governed self-sufficient lands or held the final word on law and justice, moral thought, religion, art, the military, and public works that was claimed by and for China's Sons of Heaven.

Periodizing Chinese history by dynasties makes more sense than the Western periodizing by centuries. China's dynasties, after all, were political ventures like American presidential administrations, full of human struggle, idealism, and knavery—a lot more concrete and intelligible than European centuries, few of which fit neatly over the movements and trends grouped under them. The sequence of dynasties was due to the inveterate Chinese impulse during a dynastic interregnum toward political reunification. Unity was so strong an ideal because it promised stability, peace, and prosperity. Yet unity seemed precariously dependent on historical rhythms. The waxing and waning of regimes, like that of people and families, called for constant attention.

Students have been impressed by the parallel sequences in ancient China and in the Graeco–Roman world: an age of philosophers and warring states, an age of unification and empire, and an age of disintegration and collapse of central power. Thus Confucius and his disciples were roughly contemporary with Plato and Aristotle; Alexander the Great preceded the First Emperor of the Qin (221 BC) by only a century; and the imperial systems of Rome and Han flourished contemporaneously. Similarly, the barbarians on the northern frontier grew more dangerous as each of these empires declined, and the economic and political disintegration within the "universal state," in Toynbee's phrase, was marked by the spread of foreign religions to which the distressed people turned for solace. The entrance of the northern nomads into China and the spread of Buddhism in the period from the third to the sixth centuries AD were actually contemporary with the inroads of the Goths and Vandals and the spread of Christianity in the West, the triumph, as Gibbon put it, of "barbarism and religion."

Within Chinese history, the most interesting parallel sequence of phases centers about the Han (206 BC–AD 220) and the Tang (618–907). Preceding each of these imperial eras was a time of intellectual ferment marked, respectively, by the philosophers of the late Zhou and by the flourishing of Daoism and Buddhism prior to the Tang. Each phase of imperial greatness was inaugurated by a short-lived powerful dynasty which unified the state, the Qin (221–206 BC) and the Sui (AD 589–618). Both the Han and the Tang, once established as a new unity, achieved an expansion of Chinese political power in neighboring regions, especially Central Asia, and a corresponding growth of foreign contact.

In the phenomena recorded so assiduously in the dynastic histories there is naturally a certain recurrence of data, since the chroniclers in each case were recording the life history of a ruling family that came to power, had its heyday, and shuffled from the scene. Toward the close of each regime, for example, natural calamities, earthquakes, floods, comets, eclipses, and other heavenly portents become more numerous in the record, evidence that the improper conduct of the ruler was losing him the Mandate of Heaven.

Autosuggestion, indeed, on the plane of public morale and social psychology, played its part in the dynastic cycle. For so great was the dynasty's dependence on its moral prestige that its loss of "face" in certain instances might set in motion a process whereby the ideology, as it were, turned against the regime and hastened its downfall. Once the literati who set the tone of ruling-class opinion became convinced that a dynasty had lost its moral claim to the throne, little could save it. This is a factor in Chinese politics today.

Time after time dynastic decline went hand in hand with the increasing inefficiency of the ruling house. The family in power accumulated over the generations a heavy load of dead wood, fastened upon it by the family system. This was most flagrantly visible in the peculations and profligacy of the emperor's maternal relatives, who became entrenched in the imperial household.

An economic interpretation has been used even more extensively to explain the dynastic cycle. This approach concentrates particularly upon the land tax. In each dynasty the progressive withdrawal of land from taxation to benefit the ruling class led to a dangerous reduction of imperial revenues. At the beginning of a dynasty the land and the population were usually estimated and recorded in a rough sort of census. New tax registers were used as a basis for revenue collection. As time went on there ensued a struggle between the interests of the imperial government and of the great families who lived under it. Gradually the ruling class were able to increase their land-holdings and to remove them from taxation by expedients such as the destruction of tax registers, official connivance, or legal falsification. The big lineages could then take under their wing small farmers as clients who paid less to the big household than they would have to the state. This created a vicious spiral in which a greater burden was placed upon the still-taxable land of the peasantry, at a time when the demands of the government for revenue were probably increasing. In this way a progressively smaller proportion of the land was expected to pay a progressively larger amount of revenue. Peasant disorders would eventually result.

In some cases the final collapse of a dynasty came through peasant rebellion under fervent religious leadership. Since no dynasty tolerated an organized opposition, its opponents had recourse to secret cults or societies.

Princes and Philosophers

The imperial institution that came to dominate Chinese society gained its sophistication and durability through long experience. In 771 BC the Zhou house moved its capital from the Wei valley near Xi'an eastward to Luoyang, thus inaugurating the Eastern Zhou. Already Zhou power was being gradually diminished by the growth of many aristocratic family-states out of its central control. By the so-called Spring-and-Autumn period (722–481 BC) there were about 170 such states, each centered in its walled capital. These states formed alliances and leagues and engaged in a diplomatic—military free-for-all, some absorbing others. By the era of Warring States (403–221 BC) only seven major states remained in the competition, most of them on the populous North China plain (see Map 7).

Already visible were two components of the eventual Chinese imperial government—military rulers and scholar-teachers. Both were concerned with the performance of ritual and ceremonies to keep human society in proper accord with the cosmic order of which it was a part. Our understanding of the ruler's role has been recently advanced by Mark Edward Lewis' (1990) study of sanctioned violence as a key to ancient China's state power and social order. He finds that the ruler's authority in each state was based on "ritually directed violence in the form of sacrifices, warfare and hunting." Since hunting as violence against animals was practice for war against men, the two major state services were actually sacrifices and warfare. Both involved the ritualized taking of life, and this defined the realm of political power. In the Zhou period as in the Shang, veneration of the ancestors through sacrifices, both animal and human, made use of the highest achievements of art—the bronze ritual vessels—and maintained the ruler's legitimacy by

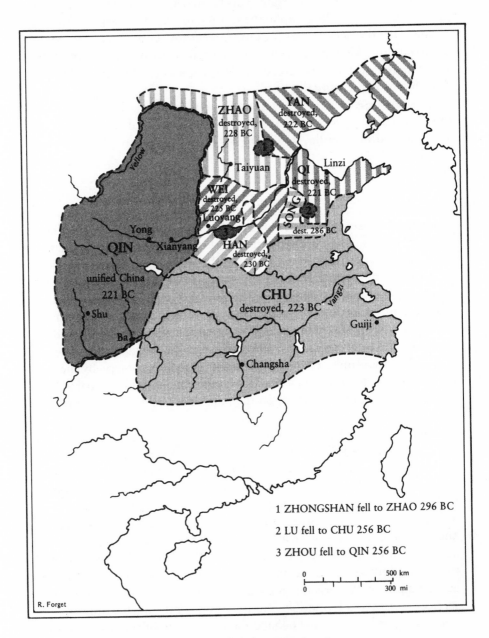

7. The Qin and Other Warring States

his liturgical activities. Hunting provided sacrificial animals, warfare sacrificial prisoners. Warfare was itself a religious service, replete with rituals of divination, prayers, and oaths preceding combat and ending in presentation of formal reports, booty, and prisoners at the ancestral altars. Participation in service to the ancestors and other deities through hunting, warfare, and sacrifices defined one's membership in the ruling class, who shared a common ancestry. Its hallmark was the privilege of eating meat.

Along with this military—liturgical basis for state power and social order, the Warring States also fostered, rather paradoxically, an age of philosophers who sought theoretical bases for those same things. During this time of rivalry and warfare, there was a widespread yearning for peace and order. Many people idealized a golden age of earlier times when according to legend all China had lived peacefully under one ruler. Violence inspired the late Zhou philosophers, who acted as what we now call consultants, advising rulers on how to get back to the golden age.

Confucius (551–479 BC) and his major disciple, Mencius (372–289 BC), were members of a considerable group of seminal thinkers in this era. Among the so-called "hundred schools" (meaning a great many), there were half a dozen major schools of thought whose writings survived. They were contemporaries of the great teachers in India (the Buddha, ca. 500 BC) and Greece (Plato, 429–347 BC, Aristotle, 384–321 BC, et al.) in what some have called the "axial age," when basic ways of thought were established in these early civilizations. The philosophers of the various schools of thought in China did not quell the disorder, and Confucianism would become an important philosophy only later, under the Han. Yet the Warring States context of sanctioned violence, with its killings and its ceremonies, helps us understand how the Confucian teaching arose and why it was eventually embraced.

The Confucian Code

Confucianism's rationale for organizing society began with the cosmic order and its hierarchy of superior-inferior relationships. Parents were superior to children, men to women, rulers to subjects. Each person therefore had a role to perform, "a conventionally fixed set of social expectations to which individual behavior should conform," as Thomas Metzger (in Cohen and Goldman, 1990) puts it. These expectations defined by authority guided the individual's conduct along lines of proper ceremonial behavior. Confucius had said (rather succinctly), "jun jun chen chen fu fu zi zi," which in its context meant "Let the ruler rule as he should and the minister be a minister as he should. Let the father act as a father should and the son act as a son should." If everyone performed his role, the social order would be sustained. Being thus known to others by their observable conduct, the elite were dependent upon the opinion and moral judgment of the collectivity around them. To be disesteemed by the group meant a disastrous loss of face and self-esteem, for which one remedy was suicide.

A major Confucian principle was that man was perfectible. In the era of Warring States, Chinese thinkers of the major schools had turned against the principle of hereditary privilege, invoked by the rulers of many family-states, and stressed the natural equality of men at birth. Mencius' claim that men are by nature good and have an innate moral sense won general acceptance. They can be led in the right path through education, especially through their own efforts at self-cultivation, but also through the emulation of models. The individual, in his own effort to do the right thing, can be influenced by the example of the sages and superior men who have succeeded in putting right conduct ahead of all other considerations. This ancient Chinese stress on the moral educability of man has persisted down to the present and still inspires the government to do the moral educating.

The Confucian code also stressed the idea of "proper behavior according to status" (li). The Confucian gentleman ("the superior man," "the noble man") was guided by li, the precepts of which were written in the ancient records that became the classics. Although this code did not originally apply to the common people, whose conduct was to be regulated by rewards and punishments (stressed by the Legalist school), rather than by moral principles, it was absolutely essential for government among the elite. This was the rationale of Confucius' emphasis on right conduct on the part of the ruler—an emphasis so different from anything in the West. The main point of this theory of government by good example was the idea of the virtue that was attached to right conduct. To conduct oneself according to the rules of propriety or li in itself gave one a moral status or prestige. This moral prestige in turn gave one influence over the people. "The people are like grass, the ruler like the wind"; as the wind blew, so the grass was inclined. Right conduct gave the ruler power. Confucius said: "When a prince's personal conduct is correct, his government is effective without the issuing of orders. If his personal conduct is not correct, he may issue orders but they will not be followed."

As a code of personal conduct, Confucianism tried to make each individual a moral being, ready to act on ideal grounds, to uphold virtue against human error, even including evil rulers. There were many Confucian scholars of moral grandeur, uncompromising foes of tyranny. But their reforming zeal—the dynamics of their creed—aimed to reaffirm and conserve the traditional polity, not to change its fundamental premises.

Western observers, looking only at the texts of the Confucian classics, were early impressed with their agnostic this-worldliness. As a philosophy of life, we have generally associated with Confucianism the quiet virtues of patience, pacifism, and compromise; the golden mean; reverence for the ancestors, the aged, and the learned; and, above all, a mellow humanism—taking man, not God, as the center of the universe.

All this need not be denied. But if we take this Confucian view of life in its social and political context, we will see that its esteem for age over youth, for the past over the present, for established authority over innovation has in fact provided one of the great historic answers to the problem of social stability. It has been the most successful of all systems of conservatism.

Daoism

It is aptly said that the Chinese scholar was a Confucian when in office and a Daoist when out of office. Daoism, which flourished among the common people, was the school most opposite to the elitist prescriptions of Confucianism. *Dao* means "the path," "the way." It expressed the common people's naturalistic cosmology and belief in the unseen spirits of nature, much of which was shared by the scholar-elite. Daoism was an enormous reservoir of popular lore. It also provided an escape from Confucianism, profiting by each revulsion of scholars against the overnice ritualism of the classics. It was a refuge from the world of affairs.

Traditionally Daoism stemmed from Laozi (lit., "The Old Master"), who was claimed by his followers to have been an elder contemporary of Confucius. The school of thought ascribed to him became a repository for a variety of beliefs and practices that Confucianism had refused, including early popular animism, alchemy, ancient magic, the search for the elixir of immortality and the Isles of the Blest, early Chinese medicine, and mysticism generally, both native and imported from India.

In general the Daoist philosophical writers who followed the brilliant literary example of Zhuangzi (369–286 BC?) raised their doubting questions from what we might now call a relativistic point of view. It was Zhuangzi who delighted succeeding generations by writing that he had dreamed that he was a butterfly playing in the sunshine and after he awoke he could not be sure whether he was still Zhuangzi who had dreamed that he was a butterfly, or actually a butterfly dreaming that it was the philosopher Zhuangzi. Applying the idea of the unity of opposites, the early Daoists argued that human moral ideas are the reflection of human depravity, that the idea of filial piety springs from the fact of impiety, that the Confucian statement of the rules of propriety is really a reflection of the world's moral disorder. Following this line of thought, the typical Daoist took refuge in a philosophy of passivity expressed in the term *wuwei*, meaning "action by inaction" or "effortlessness." This took the form of laissez-faire, of following one's unrationalized inner nature and accepting without struggle the experience of life. This was plainly the philosophy of those who condemned government meddling and moral crusading and who sought to be resigned to the burdens of life, since they could not be avoided.

Unification by Qin

As interstate rivalries intensified, the ingredients of a new order began to emerge that would contribute to the unification of the Warring States. Among these ingredients was the use of infantry armies in hilly terrain on the northern and southern frontiers, areas which were difficult for chariots to maneuver in. Another ingredient was the use of iron for tools as well as weapons, leading to greater agricultural production, more trade, and larger armies. Finally, non-Chinese tribes of Inner Asia began to use the horse in cavalry warfare, obliging the Chinese to do the same.

Much growth occurred in all the seven most persistent Warring States—for example, the state of Qi on the eastern edge of the North China plain in what is now Shandong province (Map 7). Able rulers had begun to build there a centralized administration with uniform taxes, law codes, a salt monopoly, and central army. Other states were comparable.

However, the most powerful growth occurred in the state of Qin. Though less renowned for culture, it was strategically well situated on the west where the Zhou had earlier risen to power. The Qin king *(wang)*, who was to create for himself the title of First Emperor *(Shi huangdi)*, had the advantage of reforms that for a whole generation had already been instituted by the ruler's Legalist adviser, Shang Yang (Lord Shang, d. 338 BC). The Legalist school, so called for its reliance on hard and fast rules *(fa,* not "law" in the modern sense), advocated rewards and punishments as the "two handles" by which to keep the people in order. Lord Shang was quite cynical (or realistic?) about it: "To club together and keep your mouth shut is to be good; to be alienated from and spy on each other is to be a scoundrel. If you glorify the good, errors will be hidden; if you put scoundrels in charge, crime will be punished." The ruler's aim was to preserve his power, never mind benefiting the people. There was no harmony of interests assumed between ruler and people.

Lord Shang's reforms had strengthened Qin power. The ruler's problem was the common one of how the center could dominate local lineages. For this purpose the Qin fostered bureaucracy. The state was divided into 31 counties, each administered by a centrally appointed magistrate who reported to the capital in writing. Next, a score of honorary ranks with exemption from labor service or taxes and (at certain levels) conferment of income from certain lands and people were used to create a new elite separate from the old aristocracy and dependent upon the ruler.

Meanwhile, the common people were permitted to buy and sell land, which stimulated farm enterprise, and criminal laws were promulgated so that severe punishments as well as rewards would be known to everyone and equally applicable to all persons. Legalist doctrines of government aimed at enforcing laws to support agriculture and strengthen the state over the family. For example, group responsibility was decreed not only within each family but among units of five or ten families, so that all within each unit were collectively to answer for any individual's wrongdoing. Under this system one's best protection was to inform on all malefactors without delay. Group ties and loyalties were thus undermined in favor of obedience to the state.

State control of the people enhanced Qin's military power. The state exalted its administrators and its farmers (who were potential soldiers) and downgraded merchants and artisans. Against other states Qin's defensible position on the west in the area of today's Shanxi and Shaanxi provinces and also in Sichuan, its first conquest, was strengthened economically by building canals and irrigation networks. In warfare, the horse chariots of antiquity had now been supplanted by cavalry and massed infantry armed with bronze or iron weapons and especially the crossbow.

Once Qin's armies had defeated the other states in 221 BC, the First Emperor divided his new empire into 36 commanderies *(jun)*, each subdivided into a number of counties *(xian)*. *(Junxian* has been shorthand for centralized bureaucratic rule ever since, as opposed to *fengjian* meaning decentralized or "feudal.") Each commandery was headed by a civil governor and a military commander, with an imperial inspector to watch the governor. County magistrates were centrally appointed, salaried, and subject to recall. Local aristocratic families were moved en masse to the capital, nongovernment arms were melted down, and some city walls were destroyed.

Writing was standardized and unified under two forms, the so-called small seal (actually rather complex-looking) script, used for inscriptions on stone and formal engravings, and a more cursive and simple clerical script used for everyday business. The latter won out when it was written by a brush on bamboo slips or strips of silk and then on paper (which was developed gradually during the first century AD). Weights, measures, and currency were also standardized. Imperial highways were built totaling over 4,000 miles, as many as in the Roman Empire. One was a "straight road" through the arid Ordos region to reach the frontier facing the nomads of the steppe. To the south, waterways and canals were cut to allow water transport for 1,200 miles from the Yangzi to Guangzhou (Canton).

If all this sounds overstated, and it does, our doubts must confront facts such as the 7,500 life-sized ceramic soldiers found in 1974 and still being excavated at the First Emperor's tomb near Xi'an. Here again archaeology is revealing more about ancient China than we had ever imagined. As late as the 1930s art historians were still saying that China had no sculpture in the round before the advent of Buddhism in the first century. How little we knew!

Recent scholarship casts doubt on the question of whether the First Emperor, who disliked hearing the complaints of scholars, actually had 460 of them buried alive. Derk Bodde (in *CHOC* 1) suggests the idea comes from a mistranslation; the scholars were merely murdered. Qin's Legalist-minded control of history by the burning of books was also far from complete, although the archives of conquered states were destroyed and the records of Qin alone were preserved.

Walls were built by Qin and other Warring States and later by some dynasties, but the hoary legend that Qin built the Great Wall of China has long since been exploded. The vast wall system visible today was mainly built by the Chinese Ming dynasty in the sixteenth century. In a fresh interpretation, Arthur Waldron (1990) has recently demonstrated how the Ming wall building, though of little military value for keeping out the non-Chinese nomads to the north, resulted from the officials' inability to decide on any better course, either to attack or to trade. Earlier rulers going back to the Qin had dealt with the nomads through trade, diplomacy, or warfare, not by fortifications alone.

Under the Qin, the First Emperor's ruthless exactions of men and taxes year after year exhausted the people and the state's other resources. After 37 years as ruler of the Qin state, he suddenly died at age 49 in 210 BC. His empire quickly disintegrated. Aside from unity of the known world, the First Emperor had sought mainly an elixir of immortality for himself. His five royal journeys to sacred mountains had been part of his search. His regime's ideology was quite inadequate to rule by. His successors, the emperors of the Earlier and Later Han dynasties (206 BC–AD 220) continued to extend Qin's methods of bureaucratic control, but did it more gradually and combined it with a comprehensive moral cosmology that focused on the emperor.

Consolidation and Expansion under the Han

The Han dynasty began its administration of the Chinese empire in 206 BC by setting up 14 commanderies to govern the western half of the empire, while permitting 10 aristocratic kingdoms to rule the more populous eastern half (see Map 8). The Han emperors put their sons to rule the kingdoms and gradually reduced their territories and the size of their courts. By 108 BC there were 84 commanderies and 18 kingdoms, smaller and more easily controlled. Meanwhile, the Han emperors conferred hundreds of marquisates, consisting of certain taxes from the land and the populace of a designated area, on relatives and men of merit who would (it was hoped) collect the taxes and be local aristocratic supporters of the throne.

The bureaucracy created by the Qin and Han buttressed the power of the state in many ways. One was the government post, which sent communications on the highways. Another was the institution of regional inspectors, who traveled through their designated areas and re-

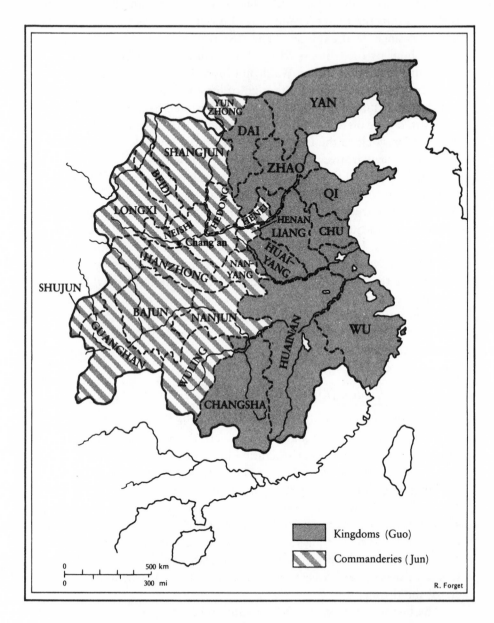

8. Commanderies and Kingdoms of the Han Empire, 206 BC

ported on local administration annually to the imperial secretariat at the capital city of Chang'an. The main problem was how to check the reemergence of aristocratic local families with their own resources of food and fighting men.

At the capital arose a similar problem for the Han ruler: how to avoid domination of the court by the family of an empress. When a Han emperor died, power resided in his widow, the empress dowager, to appoint her husband's successor from the Liu clan (the clan of the Han emperors). She might appoint a minor of the Liu clan as emperor, and a strong-man regent of her own clan to rule for him. Half a dozen families of empresses played this game. An emperor, however, could rely within the palace on the staff of eunuchs, whose castration fitted them to look after the women selected for the emperor's harem. There, by having several sons, the emperor hoped to find one worth selecting as his successor. Eunuchs, being entirely dependent on a young emperor as his servants and companions, might be his only reliable supporters against an empress's family. The palace was a center of intrigue.

Outside the palace, in order to control residents of the Earlier Han capital (Chang'an), the emperor divided the city into 160 wards, each within its own walls and gate and superintended by a select group of residents not unlike a street committee of today. The Han state also tried to dominate economic life. All urban trading was in the government markets, where officials set commodity prices and collected commercial taxes that went directly into the court treasury. The registered shop merchants in the cities were actively discriminated against: they were not allowed to own land, become officials, or enjoy a fine lifestyle (no silk clothing or riding on horseback!). By contrast, the unregistered merchants, who patronized the private inns on the post roads while trading to other cities and foreign countries, grew rich. They developed connections with officials, became big landowners, hoarded goods, speculated, and made great profits exporting gold and silks across the oases of the Silk Road to West Asia and Rome. In short, the evil of commerce tended to suborn the officials. A "merchant–official complex" might have acquired some power in the government had not Confucian values so strongly disesteemed the profit motive. In deference to the Confucian ideology, official pronouncements for the next 2,000 years would generally denigrate merchants, while officials in practice would profit from licensing, taxing, and sharing private deals with them. The merchants' dependence on official approval or cooperation would seldom stimulate risk-taking entrepreneurship.

The government also operated monopolies of manufactured goods whenever feasible, beginning with salt (a daily necessity for a grain diet) and iron (in demand for farming tools as well as weapons). In 117 BC the state set up 48 foundries with thousands of workers. The general idea of the salt monopoly was that licensed saltmakers would sell their product to the government or to licensed salt merchants, and government revenue would accumulate at each stage of production, transport, and sale. After much experimenting with minting copper coins by merchants and local authorities, the minting of "cash"—a copper coin with a square hole in its center—also became a central government monopoly. In the first century BC, for a population that was approaching 60 million, the Han minted in the average year about 220,000 strings of cash (each of 1,000 coins). This does not signify a highly developed money economy.

During the four centuries of Han rule, vast changes occurred in China—not only an increase of population but a growth of the landed estates of local magnates, who gained control of the lands of impoverished peasants when they could not pay their debts and then let them use the land as tenants. The government land tax was light, about one tenth to one thirtieth of the crop, whereas rent from sharecroppers to their landlords might be half to two thirds of the crop. Peasant labor service, or corvée, due the state for one month a year was increasingly commuted into cash payments. Peasants continued to pay a poll (or capitation) tax. As the Han government by degrees lost vigor, it gave up some of its monopolies and control of markets, while local aristocratic landed and merchant families grew stronger.

During these four centuries an upper class emerged as the dominant social group, tied by kinship to officialdom but locally independent and represented by men educated to be gentlemen. Its literate, artistic, and sumptuous lifestyle is dramatically evident in three tombs, dating from 186 BC to ca. 168, discovered at Mawangdui near Changsha in 1974. The well-preserved body of the Princess Dai in the innermost of a nest of four waterproof coffins was accompanied by 1,000 objects, including paintings, texts written on bamboo and silk, and variegated silks that the princess's Roman counterpart could hardly have matched for beauty and craftsmanship. Other Chinese luxury items included lacquerware, pottery, bronzes, and steel for weapons, produced by forging together two types of iron with different contents of carbon. Iron metallurgy may have begun later in China than in the Middle East but, once introduced, it developed rapidly.

Han economic growth in North China stimulated foreign trade and military expansion. Under the most energetic of the Han rulers, the Martial Emperor (Han Wudi, reg. 140–87 BC), Chinese armies penetrated into southern Manchuria and Korea to the northeast and into south and southwest China and northern Vietnam. In these areas commanderies could be established over farming peoples. Only on the north and northwest was there an unstable frontier.

Han foreign policy began with the need for stable relations with the far-flung tribal confederation of the Xiongnu—Turkish nomads whose mounted archers habitually raided North China for loot and supplies. During times when the Han were strong, they developed their own horse pastures and mounted archers, while usually enlisting the aid of nomad allies or mercenaries as well. One device was to subsidize the Southern Xiongnu as a client state to help fend off the warlike Northern Xiongnu. The alternative—punitive expeditions into the steppe—was costly and perilous; within a few weeks, lack of food supplies would oblige retreat, leaving the Xiongnu horde still intact and at large. When militarily weak, which was much of the time, Han emperors used a policy of "peace and kinship" *(heqin)*—entertaining the nomad chieftain, giving him Han princesses in marriage, and making lavish gifts, especially of silks. Nomad warriors learned that if they performed a ritual at Chang'-an in which they accepted Han suzerainty, they could profit substantially while having a good time. Ying-shih Yü notes that this appeasement policy was a forerunner of the unequal treaties of Song and late Qing times, which acknowledged China's military weakness.

Besides fighting or buying off the barbarians, Han rulers also learned how to use diplomacy to enlist some barbarians in fighting others. In the search for allies against the Xiongnu, the Han sent envoys across the Silk Road through the oases of Central Asia on the southern flank of the steppe nomads. Other tribal peoples like the Qiang (proto-Tibetans) menaced the trade route to the west; and in periods of strength, as under Wudi, the Han set up a Protectorate General of the Western Regions. At their high point, Chinese armies crossed the Pamirs into the center of Asia, where Alexander's Greek forces had penetrated more than two centuries earlier.

The Chinese techniques of barbarian-taming, we must realize, were not successful in the end. Thomas J. Barfield (1989), looking at the Inner Asian side, reminds us how Chinese rulers had to pay the powerful nomads either with gifts in response to their presenting tribute or with outright subsidies or involuntary loot when nomads raided. The fact was that goods from China were essential to nomad life. When China was unified, Barfield suggests, the steppe tribes were more likely to accept the overlordship of the nomad rulers who handled the China connection. China's strength made them more powerful.

Imperial Confucianism

The Han rulers' daily regimen of ceremonies and rites required the guidance of learned men at court. Han Wudi in particular fostered learning as one channel (in addition to recommendation) for recruitment of officials. He saw education as a way to strengthen his new upper class against the older aristocratic families, and he accepted Confucianism as the ideology in which the state's officials should be trained. To the despotic statecraft of Qin Legalism the Han added a monumental structure of ideas of largely Confucian origin that provided an all-encompassing state philosophy. This Legalist-Confucian amalgam we call Imperial Confucianism, to distinguish it both from the original teaching of Confucius, Mencius, et al. and from the secular and personal Confucian philosophy that arose during Song times and has since then guided so many lives in the East Asian countries of the old Chinese culture area—China, Korea, Vietnam, and Japan.

The essential point about the Legalist-Confucian amalgam was that Legalism was liked by rulers and Confucianism by bureaucrats. A ruler could use the material inducements of rewards and punishments (which were so material you could feel them) to keep the common people in order. But his administrators needed something more than benefits or intimidation to inspire their best efforts. The Confucians believed that the ruler's ceremonial observances and exemplary conduct gave him a certain virtue *(de)*—or, as A. C. Graham (1989) says, potency—that drew others to accept, support, or even venerate his rule. If his exercise of moral and cultured civility *(wen)* became ineffective, the ruler could always fall back on punishment and even military force *(wu)*. The ruler's use of violence remained his prerogative toward both his people and his officials. But he could not rule by force alone and so needed the Confucianists' help in showing his constant moral concern for benevolent and proper conduct. Under Confucian guidance the emperor day by day performed rituals and ceremonies that were his special function as Son of Heaven. (Today's White House foto-ops and sound-bites would have seemed quite natural to him.)

The limitations of the Confucians' status had been plain from the start. Confucius had aimed to train an elite who would become superior men, able both to secure the people's respect and guide the ruler's conduct. Confucius was neither out to become a ruler himself nor to educate the masses directly. His priorities put proper ritual first, humaneness second, and learning only third. By his example he showed the way for his own kind, who would later be the scholar-officials of the imperial era. China's social structure, in short, was already in place and the philosopher's task in his Chinese form of prophecy was not to arouse the masses but only to guide the rulers. As W. T. de Bary (1991) points out, the Confucians did not try to establish "any power base of their own . . . they faced the state, and whoever controlled it in the imperial court, as individual scholars . . . this institutional weakness, highly dependent condition, and extreme insecurity . . . marked the Confucians as *ju* [*ru*] ('softies') in the politics of imperial China." They had to find patrons who could protect them. It was not easy to have an independent voice separate from the imperial establishment.

The Han retained the Mandate of Heaven by an imperial cult of ritual observances, beginning with the Liu family ancestors but especially devoted to Heaven. Its attendant cosmology tied together all the phenomena of human experience and set the stage on which Confucianism by degrees came to play a central political role as an official teaching.

Early China's cosmology (her theory of the universe as an ordered whole) shows striking points of difference with Western thought. For example, the early Chinese had no creation myth and no creator-lawgiver out of this world, no first cause, not even a Big Bang. As Joseph Needham says, they assumed "a philosophy of organism, an ordered harmony of wills without an ordainer." This view contrasts with the inveterate tendency elsewhere in the world to assume a supernatural deity. Westerners looking at China have continually imposed their own preconceptions on the Chinese scene, not least because the Chinese, though they generally regarded Heaven as the supreme cosmic power, saw it as immanent in nature, not as transcendent. Without wading further into this deep water, let us note simply that Han thought as recorded in classical writings built upon the concept of mankind as part of nature and upon the special relationship between the ruler and his ancestors, concepts that were already important in Shang thought over a millennium earlier.

Correlative Cosmology

Han Chinese saw correspondences or mutual influences between Heaven, earth, and man—that is, between celestial phenomena, the world of nature on earth, and human society—from which they derived notions of their proper place in the universe. This "correlative cosmology," or what John B. Henderson (1984) calls "correspondences between microcosmic man and macrocosmic nature," can be seen, for example, in a Han work dated about 139 BC, the *Huainanzi*. This work explained that "the head's roundness resembles heaven and the feet's squareness resembles earth. Heaven has four seasons, five phases, nine sections, and 366 days. Man likewise has four limbs, five viscera, nine orifices, and 366 joints. Heaven has wind and rain, cold and heat. Man likewise has taking and giving, joy and anger . . . Thus the eyes and ears are the sun and moon; and the blood and pneuma are the wind and rain."

Once one begins to see close correspondences—numerological, anatomical, psychological, and moral—between *Homo sapiens* and the rest of nature, this is a game any number of philosophers can play. Even today the Chinese have a custom of assigning numbers to important events, like the May Fourth Movement of 1919—(in Chinese, 5–4). This strong numerological habit of thought found its fullest expression in the doctrine of the five phases. Numerologies using three, four, nine, and other numbers were all surpassed by the five phases or processes. Also known as the five elements, these were water, fire, wood, metal, and earth. Once started on this approach, Han cosmologists noted the five planets (all that were then visible), five seasons, five directions, five colors, five musical tones, five sage emperors, five viscera, five orifices, five animals, five grains, five mountains, five punishments, and the like. This system of fives could be used to explain change, since each phase is followed by a succeeding phase—wood producing fire, fire producing earth, earth producing metal, metal producing water, and water producing wood. Alternatively, the phases could be put in different sequences, such as wood conquered by metal, metal reduced by fire, fire extinguished by water, water blocked by earth, and earth manipulated by wood.

Application of this structure of correspondences was not automatic but arguable and gave great substance for philosophical discussion. There was a considerable problem, for example, in trying to mesh the five phases with the four seasons and other fours, like the quarters of the compass. Correlative thinkers in medieval Europe faced a similar problem when they had to relate, for instance, the nine muses to the eight celestial spheres. It was about like squaring the circle.

Chinese thinkers were ingenious in developing the vocabulary for correlative thinking through such devices as *yin* and *yang* or the ten celestial stems and twelve earthly branches (*gan* and *zhi*) which produced the sexagenary or 60-unit cycle for counting time. (Each of the 60 units could be represented by two characters respectively drawn from the set of 10 and the set of 12.) A considerable lore grew up about cycles of 60, but the broadest Chinese device was that of the 64 hexagrams in the *Classic of Changes* or *Yijing*. These were sets of six parallel lines either broken or unbroken. Each of the 64 resulting figures was given its specific connotations, which could be used in fortunetelling.

Correlative thought is not news to social anthropologists studying any early society. It was by no means unique to China. But it gained unusual currency in China and dominated thinking for an unusually long time, no doubt because of the centripetally organized Chinese state and society. The emperor was so much at the center of everything that the ideas of correlative thinking and particularly of the phenomenalism of his close interaction with nature could become an established doctrine.

Natural phenomena do not become less mysterious simply because we get used to them. Today we accept the idea of gravity by which we find all bodies influence other bodies at a distance. The early Han postulated the existence of a pervasive pneuma or ether *(qi)* through which human and natural processes interacted. Correlative cosmology can be called wrong only because it was not scientifically provable. The idea of resonance *(ganying)*, as when one pitch-pipe or one lute string induces a response from another, also inhered in the virtue of reciprocity (one good act must be balanced by a response). Another resonance was when the good example set by the conduct of the ruler moved the beholder to do likewise.

This early Han reasoning by correspondence helped Chinese observers of natural activities to move in the direction of scientific thought, as Nathan Sivin (1987) has pointed out, particularly in the realm of Chinese medicine. For example, certain puncture points in the human body were found to control nervous sensitivity in other parts of the body, although acupuncture anesthesia has developed only in this century.

Alchemists, who were the principal pioneers in Chinese science, made great use of correlative thinking. Indeed, its influence may be seen in almost every field of Chinese mental activity.

In the Western world correlative cosmology played a considerable role in Hellenistic thought contemporary with the early Han. Its influence among syncretic thinkers of the Renaissance would be even greater. Yet the arbitrary nature of some correspondences and the all-inclusiveness of some systems in the course of time produced skepticism. Leading Song scholars doubted the resonance between natural events and imperial conduct. Since correlative thinking made so much use of imagination and speculation, it could not stand up as a comprehensive explanatory device, especially in astronomy, where theories of correspondence could not handle the complex and extremely various phenomena of the heavenly bodies.

All this cosmological lore could be focused particularly on the correspondence between the ritual observances of the ruler and the cycle of the seasons or other celestial phenomena. As a proliferation from the early activity of the shamans who inscribed the oracle bones in the Shang period, the prescriptions for the emperor's ritual observances became very detailed. First of all, one kept careful note of heavenly events. Chinese celestial observations were remarkably precise, for example in tables showing the times and locations of the rising and setting of the major planets between 246 and 177 BC. Equally careful attention was paid to the ritual observances of the emperor, for reciprocal relations were seen between his conduct and natural events. Basic here was the concept of resonance noted above. This idea of mutual influence was particularly applicable to the relationship between the ruler and the heavens. Because mankind played a part in the cosmic process, human error could throw it out of order. Misgovernment on the part of the ruler might produce natural catastrophe; and so a meteor, an eclipse, an earthquake, or a flood could all be regarded as nature's commentary on the ruler's performance.

Emperor and Scholars

Here plainly was a tool which the Confucian adviser could use to affect the emperor's behavior. By means of correlative cosmology, portents could be interpreted for the ruler, as had been done by the magical shamans at Anyang. Because the classics were felt to offer insights into the art of government and hidden meanings that only erudite scholars could bring out, the scholars at court like Dong Zhongshu (c. 175–105 BC) found a great opportunity to become savants on how the ruler should fit into the cosmos and in turn was affected by it. Benjamin Schwartz (1985) remarks how Dong's "cosmological Confucianism confirms the cosmic status of the universal king" but then adds "in the case of Han Wu-ti [Wudi], Tung [Dong] also seems to have conceived of it as a weapon of inhibition and constraint." In other words, as Derk Bodde (1991) notes, portents could sometimes be falsely alleged to have occurred, faked for political purposes.

The Confucianists won out over the other schools of Warring States philosophy because they claimed to be, and became, indispensable advisers to the emperor. In its broad historical context this meant, as Arthur F. Wright phrased it, that "the literate elite . . . had entered into an alliance with monarchy. The monarch provided the symbols and the sinews of power: throne, police, army, the organs of social control. The literati provided the knowledge of precedent and statecraft that could legitimize power and make the state work. Both the monarch and the literati were committed to a two-class society based on agriculture."

The Han emperors stressed the worship of Heaven as their major rite and also maintained hundreds of shrines to deceased emperors, but their high officials at court became most concerned with the precedents set by former rulers as recorded in the classics. Han Confucianism came into its own when the imperial academy was founded in 124 BC. There were specialists on the five classics: the *Yijing* or *Classic of Changes* (for divination), the *Shujing* or *Classic of Documents* (or *History*), the *Shi-jing* or *Classic of Songs* (*Odes,* ancient folk poems), the *Chunqiu* or *Spring and Autumn Annals* (chronicles of Confucius' own state of Lu in Shandong, with their commentaries), and the *Liji* or *Record of Ceremonies and Proper Conduct.* The Han emperors, who had already asked for talented men to be recommended for examination and appointment, now added classical training to the criteria for official selection, plus written examinations in the Confucian classics. By the mid-second century AD, 30,000 students were reported at the academy, presumably listed as scholars, not resident all at once.

The Confucian code of personal conduct also came from examples in the classics as elucidated by scholars. Though this personal code would be most fully developed in Song Neo-Confucianism, certain basic themes emerged among pre-Han philosophers of various schools. Most fundamental was the stress on hierarchy so evident in prehistoric times, which assumed that order can be achieved only when people are organized in gradations of inferiority and superiority. This hierarchic principle in turn was the basis for a stress on duties rather than rights, on the evident assumption that if everyone did his duty everyone would get what he deserved. Thus, the filial son obedient to his parent would bask in the parent's approval. With all duties performed, society would be in order to everyone's benefit.

The most important of all duties was loyalty. In the form of filial piety it ensured parental control within the family. Within the state loyalty ensured the support of officials for the emperor and his dynasty. So deeply was this idea ingrained in official thinking that at times of dynastic overthrow servitors of the old dynasty might choose death rather than serve the new one.

The strength of this loyalty may account for a curious anomaly that haunts the imperial annals. Only one thing unaccounted for keeps cropping up in the biographies of eminent Confucian officials—some are beheaded. The fact that officials in the later dynasties are publicly beaten may be an unfortunate incidence of greater despotism. But beheading? Surely this is an important event not only for the victim but as a symbol of the values of the state. How can the emperor behead his ministers with a minimum of legal procedure, as an imperial right exercised since time immemorial?

Eventually the ritual would be less bloody: as recently as 1858 the emperor sent a silken bowstring to the grandee who had negotiated the first treaties with Britain, France, and the United States because he lost face in front of the foreigners. The grandee was permitted to kill himself, with the help of his servants.

Here certainly is a Legalist aspect of imperial Confucianism. Benjamin Schwartz (1985) reminds us that in Legalist texts the ruler is "admonished to use the full severity of the law against the unfilial and the unfraternal so that penal sanctions are introduced into the very heart of the family network where the bonds of family morality should reign supreme ... The virtue of the rulers was manifested as much in their righteous punishments as in the power of their moral influence."

Several assumptions seem implicit here. First is the emperor's role as a source of spontaneous, irrational, or unpredictable acts, as opposed to the routinized, predictable action (or inaction) of bureaucrats. The officials sought order. The emperor could shake them up with disorder. Second, the emperor was considered to have an arbitrary and unbridled power of life and death. The victim had no rights, partly because a doctrine of rights was not part of Chinese political theory. Third and most striking is the almost universal acceptance of the emperor's decision to execute an official. There is no court of appeal. Others may be outraged, but they have no recourse except various forms of protest or even group rebellion. This situation no doubt was an inheritance from the ritually sanctioned violence that Mark Lewis has documented from the era of Warring States, when killing of beasts in hunting and men in warfare was the ruler's professional specialty, even after human sacrifice was given up.

This leads one to wonder whether Western and modern Chinese scholars have not underestimated the transcendental role of the emperor in the Chinese belief system. Truly the Son of Heaven is the equivalent of what we would call God on earth, the one person who in Western parlance might be termed a god incarnate. The imperial temples were places of emperor worship. Perhaps we can understand the emperor's capacity to kill his officials only by appreciating his role as the central divinity of the Chinese state and society. The Confucianist had no fear of retribution in an afterlife because he lived in a day-to-day environment in which the imperial power might reward and also extinguish him. Where the West Asian or European, focused upon a faith in an afterlife, might fear going to Hell, the Confucianist, concerned with the here and now, could live in fear of the imperial wrath. God was on his throne within the palace at the capital. The aspiring official made his every move with this in mind. If an official was beheaded, it was simply to be accepted as what today our insurance agents would call an "act of God."

This line of thought raises a major question, the relationship between *wen* and *wu*. *Wen* means basically the written word and so by extension its influence in thought, morality, persuasion, and culture. Let us call it in the most general terms "the civil order." *Wu* connotes the use of violence and so stands for the military order in general. The Confucian-trained scholar class went to great lengths to exalt *wen* and disparage *wu*. Yet I wonder if *wu* (including the founding of dynasties, extermination of rebels and evildoers, and punishing of officials) should not be considered the stronger and *wen* the weaker element in the *wen—wu* combination. For example, was the virtue of loyalty (an aspect of *wen*) as powerful as the practice of intimidation (an aspect of *wu*)? Often it seemed that when he wanted to control a situation, the emperor's principal tactic was intimidation. Take for example the case of China's greatest historian Sima Qian. As Edwin Reischauer (Reischauer and Fairbank, 1960) says, he had "inherited a post as court astrologer and had access to the resources of the imperial library . . . he claimed to be simply completing the historical work which his father, Sima Tan, had commenced, but this may have been partly a pious excuse for what was in reality a most presumptuous undertaking—the continuation and amplification of what was supposed to be Confucius' greatest accomplishment, that is, the arrangement of the record of the past in proper form. Sima Qian was obviously a man of great daring as well as prodigious learning. In 99 BC he came to the defense of a prominent Chinese general who had been forced to surrender to the Xiongnu and Wu Di repaid him for his audacity by having him castrated."

As a punishment, losing one's testicles was the next thing to losing one's head because it potentially cut off the male offspring who in the secular religion of the Chinese elite would conduct the family rituals of veneration of ancestors that would comfort their spirits. In the period from 99 BC to his death about 85 BC Sima Qian was presumably completing his great work of organizing Chinese history. Should we believe that he was not intimidated by his castration?

Whether this intimidation had any effect on the *Records of the Historian (Shiji)* we can only imagine. Sima Qian's basic annals of Wudi's reign stop short after the introductory paragraph. Sima did not pursue the origins of imperial legitimacy—what sanctioned the emperor's capacity to execute or castrate his subjects. Perhaps there is something here that deserves critical reexamination.

As Thomas Metzger (1973) has pointed out, the emperor naturally "played on the whole range of available sanctions—coercive, remunerative and normative"—combining them to suit circumstances. "His use of terroristic violence was usually accompanied by outbursts of moral indignation aimed at achieving normative justification in the minds of the elite."

Along with the emperor's power over the scholar-official's life went his power over his books and education—the system of learning and its transmission. Nearly every dynasty sponsored the collecting of books; the Qin First Emperor's destructive concern for books and scholars had been only more vehement than that of other rulers. R. Kent Guy (1987) has concluded that if "the arts of ruling and writing developed together in ancient China, then a sense of the basic unity of the two acts may well have underlain both the Confucian and the Legalist views of scholarship and government."

A similar conclusion may be reached concerning education. Perhaps it is an overtranslation to call the imperial academy or *Taixue* (inaugurated in 124 BC and continued into the Southern Song) the "National University," or to call the *Guozijian* (from Song to Qing) the "Directorate of Education." Focused on the classics, these institutions might equally well be called indoctrination centers. The fact remains that imperial power, books, and scholars were all seen as integrally related aspects of government.

3

Reunification in the Buddhist Age

Disunion

As China's unity under the Han disintegrated, the Buddhist faith, which had been imported from India in the middle of the first century AD, gained adherents while state Confucianism went into a decline. Barbarism and religion accompanied the breakup of the Han empire as it did the Roman. But different results ensued in China than in Europe.

The basic mechanism of the Han dynasty's decline was the usual one: the rise of local or regional power to eclipse that of the central dynasty. Weakness at the center came from many causes: the succession of ineffectual Han emperors, their domination by the empress's family, usurpation of power by eunuchs, and many other factional rivalries at the court. Favoritism and corruption resulted in the appointment of inadequate personnel, rapacious exploitation of the people, disregard of the interests of merchants' and magnates' families, and a weakening of the dynasty's military capacity. Such weaknesses at the center interacted with the growth of local and regional power in the hands of aristocratic families possessing landed estates and walled cities as well as industries within them. The final disaster came in 220 from a revolt of formerly nomad aristocratic families in North China and their retainers, who had settled inside the Wall yet kept their skills and propensities for warfare.

At the time of this rebellion, two processes were at work that would lead to over three centuries of disunion between North and South China—first, the continual incursion of nomadic peoples into North China and, second (partly as a result of this), migration of Han Chinese to the warmer and more fertile areas of the Yangzi valley further south. This laid the basis for a dual development of small regional dynasties north and south. After the era known as the Three Kingdoms, from 220 to 265 AD, and a temporary reunification of the country between 280 and 304, there ensued in the centuries from 317 to 589 a succession known as the Six Dynasties in South China along and below the Yangzi and in North China a welter of competition among a total of Sixteen Kingdoms first and last.

The principal invaders in the north were no longer the Turkic Xiongnu, whose confederation had broken up, but a nomadic proto-Mongol people known as the Xianbei, who set up states in Gansu on the west and Hebei and Shandong on the east. Instead of a barbarization of the local Chinese culture, these less-civilized invaders quickly took on the trappings of Chinese aristocratic families, intermarried with the local Han people, and set up courts in the Chinese style. The most outstanding were the Toba Turks, who set up their Northern Wei dynasty (386–535) first at Datong in northern Shanxi and later (after they had conquered and reunified North China) at their second capital, Luoyang, just south of the Yellow River, which had been the capital of Later Han. Not least of the achievements of Northern Wei was their devotion to Buddhism and the great stone carvings they produced near their two capitals.

Buddhism spread rapidly not only in the north but also among the Six Dynasties of the south. In the great age of Buddhism in China from the fifth to the ninth centuries, Confucianism was largely left in eclipse and the Buddhist teachings as well as Buddhist art had a profound effect upon Chinese culture, both north and south.

The Buddhist Teaching

The Buddha, who lived probably during the sixth century BC in Nepal, began life as an aristocrat. After renouncing his palace and its harem and luxuries, he achieved through meditation an illumination in which he realized the great principle of the wheel of the law or the wheel of the Buddha. This may be defined as a theory of the "dependent origination" of life: that everything is conditioned by something else in a closed sequence, so that in effect the misery of life is dependent upon certain conditions, and by eliminating these conditions it is possible to eliminate the misery itself. Thus desire—which ultimately leads to misery—originates in dependence upon sensation, which in turn originates in dependence upon contact and the six senses, and so on. The Buddhist objective therefore becomes to cut the chain of conditions that bind one into this sequence of passions, desires, and attachments. From this premise that misery is conditioned and that the conditions can be destroyed, the early Buddhists developed many theories.

One central idea of peculiar interest today is that of the dharmas. This is actually a theory of elements or atoms, according to which an entity does not exist in itself but is made up of all its parts. The old Buddhist monks believed that man himself is composed merely of these many parts or dharmas; he has no personality, soul, or self. The dharmas are of several types. Some relate to form and substance, others to sensation, and others to mental activity. Taken together, they make a neat explanation of experience and form a basis for the denial of the existence of self. This is just what the Buddhist sought, as a way of escaping life's misery. Since all the elements of experience could be analyzed to be disparate, unconnected, and atomic, both in space and in time, it was held that a proper realization of this truth could lead to elimination of the illusion of the self and a release from the wheel of the law. This sort of escape or enlightenment, as you prefer, has been sought by mystics the world over and was eagerly pursued in medieval China.

Early Buddhism was institutionalized in a monastic order that may be compared and contrasted with the monasticism of Christianity at a later date. By these early Buddhist monks the sutras (traditional sermons and teachings of the Buddha) were finally written down.

By the time of its expansion from North India to the Far East the Buddhist school of the Mahayana (the "greater vehicle") had wrought profound changes in the ancient doctrines and made them more likely to appeal to the masses of the population. One of these developments was the idea of salvation, which became possible through the intercession of the bodhisattvas (or "enlightened ones") who had attained the enlightenment of the Buddha but continued their existence in this world in order to rescue others. The most famous of these deities has been the Chinese Goddess of Mercy or Guanyin, an abstraction of the principle of compassion. Another is the Buddha of Endless Light, Amitabha (in Chinese, Emituofo or O-mi-to-fo). Salvation of others through the efforts of these enlightened ones was made possible on the theory that merit could be transferred. Along with this notion went the concept of charity, which supplemented the original Buddhist faith and has made it in China and Japan a more positive social force.

The Mahayana school also developed a positive doctrine of nirvana, the state which it was the object of Buddhist effort to attain but which the Buddha himself had regarded as so completely indescribable that he had said nothing about it.

The Buddhist teachings were set forth in the great Buddhist canon or tripitaka. Translation of sutras from this canon became the chief work of the first Buddhist monks in China. They and their followers faced enormously complex linguistic as well as intellectual problems—how to translate from Sanskrit, which was polysyllabic, highly inflected, and alphabetic like English and other Indo-European languages, into the monosyllabic, uninflected, ideographic script of China; how to convey, in that rather terse and concrete medium, the highly imaginative and metaphysical abstractions of Indian mysticism.

In attempting to transfer or "translate" their new and alien ideas into terms meaningful for their Chinese audience, the early Buddhist missionaries ran into the problem that has faced all purveyors of foreign ideas in China ever since: how to select certain Chinese terms, written characters already invested with established meanings, and invest them with new significance without letting the foreign ideas be subtly modified, in fact sinified, in the process. For example, the Chinese character *dao* ("the way"), already so much used in Daoism and Confucianism, might be used variously for the Indian dharma or for yoga or for the idea of enlightenment, while *wuwei*, the "nonaction" of Daoism, was used for nirvana. The result was at least ambiguity, if not some watering down of the original idea.

Abstract ideas from abroad when expressed in Chinese characters could hardly avoid a degree of sinification. In addition, exotic and socially disruptive values were resisted. As Arthur Wright (1959) remarks, "The relatively high position which Buddhism gave to women and mothers was changed in these early translations. For example 'Husband supports wife' became 'The husband controls his wife,' and 'The wife comforts the husband' became 'The wife reveres her husband.' "

Non-Chinese invaders of North China, in the fourth century and after, accepted Buddhism partly because, like themselves, it came from outside the old order that they were taking over. Buddhist priests could be allies in fostering docility among the masses. For the Chinese upper class who had fled to the south, Buddhism also offered an explanation and solace, intellectually sophisticated and aesthetically satisfying, for the collapse of their old society. Emperors and commoners alike sought religious salvation in an age of social disruption. Great works of art, statues, and rock-cut temples have come down from this period. Fruitful comparisons and contrasts can be made between the roles of clergy and monasticism, the growth of sects, and relations of church and state, during this age of Buddhist faith in China and its later Christian counterpart in medieval Europe. Buddhist monasteries, for example, served as hostels for travelers, havens of refuge, and sources of charity. They also became great landowners and assumed quasi-official positions in the administration.

The early period of borrowing and domestication was followed by one of acceptance and independent growth. Chinese native Buddhism was influenced by Daoism, and influenced it in return, to an extent still being debated. New sects arose in China, catering to Chinese needs. Best known to us today through its influence on Oriental art was the school which sought enlightenment through practices of meditation (called in Chinese Chan, or in the Japanese pronunciation, Zen). Perhaps enough has been said to indicate the very complex interaction among such elements as Indian Buddhism, the barbarian invaders, native Daoism, and the eventual growth, flowering, and decay of Chinese Buddhism.

Sui-Tang Reunification

During the period of disunion the lack of central orthodoxy allowed the southern Six Dynasties, most of which set their capital at Nanjing, and the northern Sixteen Kingdoms to differentiate and innovate. Buddhism and Daoism inspired artists, philosophers, and writers. Many of the dynastic histories concern the transient small dynasties of this era.

The three centuries of the Sui-Tang dynasties (589–907) finally reestablished the Chinese ideal of unity that had developed under the Han. North China had been devastated by the nomad invasions, whereas South China along the Yangzi had prospered in relative peace. The 60 million people estimated for the Han dynasty in the year AD 2 (mainly in North China; see Map 10) had been reduced in number, but the migration of Han families to the south had begun to shift China's center of gravity (see Maps 11 and 12.). In modern times South China would have two thirds of the Chinese population. Yet in the sixth to tenth centuries the great bulk of China's people lived still on the easily unified North China plain, where a score of prefectures, each with 100,000 households (say, 500,000 people) were found. As Mark Elvin (Blunden and Elvin, 1983) has pointed out, the Roman Empire had "conspicuously lacked a comparable consolidated dominant region." North China's centrality and heavy population was a factor for unity. Whoever got control over it could rather easily subjugate the other areas, including South China.

The Sui and Tang dynastic founders had intermarried with nomadic tribal families who became sinicized. They were now the aristocratic families of Northwest China, located particularly in present-day Shanxi province and the ancient capital region running from the Wei valley along the south of the Yellow River to the North China plain. As under the Zhou and Qin, this northwest area derived military vigor from the nomadic peoples. From the herdsmen of the grasslands the Chinese acquired horses for cavalry warfare, trousers for riding astride, saddles and later stirrups, plus the breast harness and eventually the horse collar, which would be imitated in the West. The relations of these clans with Central Asia in trade and diplomacy were close and influential long before the Sui-Tang reunification within China.

The Sui founder was of a part-nomad Yang family with estates situated midway between the two ancient capitals of the Zhou and Han, Chang'an and Luoyang. The Tang dynastic founder was likewise a scion of a Li family of Turkic military origins and aristocratic status. These military aristocrats had intermarried both with Chinese and with each other's families so that they formed a large and homogeneous group of leaders, equal to the onerous tasks of conquest and administration. The nomad rulers of North China adopted Chinese ways, including language, dress, and methods of government so sedulously that their hybrid states seemed in the historical record to be properly Chinese.

The last of the Sixteen Kingdoms had already unified North China when the Sui founder took power in 581. He quickly produced a new legal code in 500 articles, brought order into local government, and continued several institutions begun by earlier kingdoms. These included the "equal field" system that was supposed annually to allot several acres of cultivable land to each adult male. He also continued the system of collective responsibility among groups of households, the territorially administered militia, and the military agricultural colonies on the frontier. The unified bureaucracy brought in tax revenues; price-regulating granaries bought grain in times of glut and sold it cheaply in times of shortage. Meanwhile, Buddhist monasteries became great landowners of increasing influence. The emperor's devout patronage created (in Arthur Wright's phrase), an "imperial Buddhism."

The Sui conquest of the south along the Yangzi was not very destructive, and the second emperor, Sui Yangdi, was able to mobilize the empire's resources for great projects. One was the extension of the Grand

Canal from Hangzhou north across the Yangzi to Yangzhou and then northwest to the region of Luoyang (see Map 16). By 609 it was extended from this far inland point in a northeasterly direction to the region of Tianjin and Beijing. By making use of local streams and lakes, barge transport could bring the food and commodities of the lower Yangzi up through North China to strengthen the northern frontier as well as feed the capital area. Large granaries were built (one could hold 33 million bushels).

This outburst of inordinate energy under an emperor with visions of grandeur has inspired comparisons between the short-lived reigns of Sui Yangdi and Qin Shihuang, each of whom overreached himself. Yangdi's attempt to conquer Korea exhausted his resources, and defeat there contributed to widespread rebellion and his loss of the Mandate.

The Tang founders were more prudent. They inherited the Sui achievements, including the enormous 5-by-6-mile capital Chang'an and the secondary capital Luoyang. Where the Han administrative departments had handled palace and dynastic family affairs cheek by jowl with countrywide matters, the Sui and Tang set up six ministries—personnel administration, finance, rites, army, justice, and public works—which would form the main echelons of China's government down to 1900. Other agencies included the censorate that scrutinized and reported on official and even imperial conduct and an early version of the examination system.

Under the second emperor the Tang armies spread outward in all directions, defeating the Koreans, expanding south into northern Vietnam, and most of all pushing their control into Central Asia until Chinese prefectures were actually functioning west of the Pamirs (see Map 9). This Tang expansion through the oasis trading cities of the Silk Road opened the way for increased contact with West Asia. The Tang capital at Chang'an became a great international metropolis, a focal point of the Eurasian world. Between 600 and 900 no Western capital could compete in size and grandeur.

Tang military prowess was matched by achievements in the fine arts and literature. Tang poetry became the model for later periods. The creative vigor of the Tang let it be a more open society, welcoming foreigners in its urban life from Japan, Korea, and Vietnam, as well as from Persia and West Asia. Buddhism had added an extra dimension to the Tang heritage from the Han. Younger states arising in East Asia modeled their institutions on the Tang.

Buddhism and the State

A comparison of Buddhism's role in China with that of Christianity in Europe shows one striking difference on the political plane. After the revival of central power by the Tang, under Buddhist influence Confucianism was gradually reinvigorated to support strong government. Eventually the imperial bureaucracy would bring the Buddhist church under firm control.

Buddhism's adaptation to Chinese ways is evident, for example, in education. As Eric Zürcher (1959) points out, the Buddhist Way was similar to Confucianism in emphasizing moral behavior. The Buddhist novice had to learn countless rules of conduct and maintain a constant struggle against sin, desire, and attachment. He had to observe the five rules, abstaining from killing, stealing, illicit sex, lying, and intoxication. The *sangha*—or community of monks and nuns, novices, and lay believers—had to observe a great number of vows. Along with this went the performance of good works and charity (a development that lies in the background of the Confucian "community compacts," *xiangyue,* of the Song and later, as we shall see).

During the Buddhist age in China from ca. 500 to 850 Buddhism did not diminish the power of the state as the sole source of political and social order. High culture was still dominated by the secular elite of the literati. This meant that the Buddhist community of believers was kept strictly within limits. Not until the sixth century did the *sangha* become what Zürcher calls a "secondary elite." Monks were recruited from families of high official status. This was anomalous because the members of the *sangha* as a corporate entity had severed their ties with the outside society. Toward the government it claimed to be autonomous, free of government control and taxes, and it even included women. Sooner or later this autonomy would make Buddhism a threat to the state.

Under the Tang the tendency was to bureaucratize Buddhism through administrative control, bestowal of titles, sale of ordination certificates, compilation of a Buddhist canon, and a system of clerical examinations to select talent. Monks had to undergo an arduous program of training and study before ordination. The clerical examinations for the Buddhist as for the Confucian classical scholar were under the Ministry of Rites. Education in Buddhist monasteries included study of the Confucian classics. Indeed, the Buddhist monasteries that prepared monks for the Confucian examination system seem like forerunners

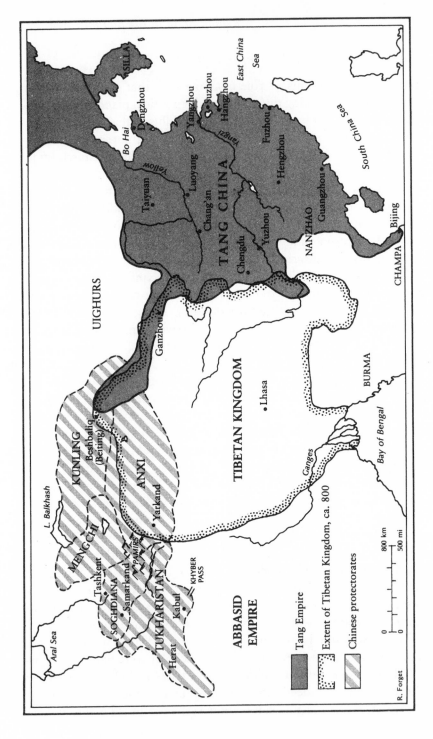

9. Tang Empire at Its Greatest Extent (Eighth Century)

of the academies of the Song period. Thus Buddhism, until the crackdown of 845, was consistently circumscribed in its educational efforts by the prior domination of Confucian teaching. However, Buddhism would have its indirect influence later in the amalgam known as Neo-Confucianism.

So little had Buddhism disrupted political tradition that the Tang government had relatively little difficulty in reducing the economic power of the Buddhist monasteries. The several persecutions of Buddhists, especially in the ninth century, were in part a struggle to keep land out of the hands of the church and more easily amenable to taxation. But no struggle between church and state developed in medieval China comparable to that in the West. The church—whether Buddhist or Daoist—was quite unable to achieve independence from the state. Its priesthoods and temples remained loosely decentralized, dependent on modest local support but without organized lay congregations or any nationwide administration, and passive in matters of politics.

Led by the example of Buddhism, the Daoist church, as distinct from the philosophers or alchemists, reached the masses with an imposing pantheon and many sects but failed to build up a worldly organization. Daoist monasteries and temples remained disconnected units, catering to popular beliefs. By its nature Daoism could not become a vigorous organized force in Chinese politics: it expressed an alternative to Confucianism in the realm of personal belief but left the field of practical action to the Confucians.

On the other hand, Daoists contributed to China's technology through the long-developed practices of alchemy, both in pursuit of the physiological goal of immortality and the more immediate bonanza of making gold. In their physiological and chemical experiments, they concocted elixirs and also searched for herbs, building up the great Chinese pharmacopoeia on which the world is still drawing. The alchemists contributed to the technology of porcelain, dyes, alloys, and eventually to other Chinese inventions like the compass and gunpowder. Many of their achievements, as Joseph Needham remarks, were "proto-science rather than pseudo-science."

Decline of the Tang Dynasty

The third Tang emperor was unfortunately a weakling, though his Empress Wu made up for it by wielding autocratic power for half a century (ca. 654–705), first through him, second through his young successors, and finally for a time as empress of a newly declared dynasty. China's only woman ruler, the Empress Wu was a remarkably skilled and able politician, but her murderous and illicit methods of maintaining power gave her a bad repute among male bureaucrats. It also fostered overstaffing and many kinds of corruption. In 657 the Tang government was using only 13,500 officials to rule a population of probably 50 million. By drawing a local militia (fubing) from self-sufficient farms and requiring them to perform labor service in each locality, the government reduced expenses. The administration still aimed to see independent, free-holding farmers, and so under the equal-field (juntian) system it reallocated land periodically according to population registers. But whereas the second emperor had ruled in a hands-on fashion with his councilors day by day, the manipulations of the Empress Wu made the imperial power more remote, conspiratorial, and despotic. She broke the power of the aristocratic clans of the northwest and gave more opportunity for the North China plain to be represented in the government. Examination graduates began to be a small elite within officialdom. Her record is still being debated.

Under the Emperor Xuanzong (who reigned from 713 to 755) the Tang reached its height of prosperity and grandeur, but weaknesses accumulated. First came military overexpansion, ruinously expensive. Tang forces were engaged on the frontiers in southwest China and also became overextended west of the Pamirs. There they were defeated by Arab forces in 751 near Samarkand. Meanwhile, the fubing militia had been made gradually into a professional fighting force grouped in nine commands, mainly on the frontiers under generals with wide powers to repel attack. Powerful generals got into court politics. As the Outer Court under the Six Ministries became more routinized and cumbersome, the high officials who led it as chancellors—actual surrogates for the emperor, ruling in his name—became increasingly involved in bitter factionalism, while the emperor used eunuchs to support his control from the Inner Court. Then in his old age Xuanzong fell for a beautiful concubine, Yang Guifei, and let the central power deteriorate. She adopted as her son her favorite general, An Lushan, who rebelled and seized the capitals in 755. From 755 to 763 a frightfully destructive rebellion raged across the land. When the emperor fled his capital and his troops demanded Yang's execution, his imperial love story came to a tragic (and often recounted) end. Tang rule was nominally restored after eight years, but over the next century and a half Tang power never fully revived.

The defeat of the An Lushan rebellion had the effect of setting up regional military commands that later became the basis for a new provincial layer of administration. While control of outer regions evaporated, the Tang regime within China had to cede power to the military. No longer was it able to govern from the center with uniform laws and institutions. The elite bureaucracy was unable to maintain countrywide procedures. Localism and particularism supervened, and the nominal unity of the Chinese state became a hollow facade.

Social Change: The Tang–Song Transition

Of the several movements for change during the late Tang dynasty, the most long-term was the decline of the aristocratic families that had dominated government. Later Han had seen a clear-cut though not statutory social distinction between elite families *(shi)* and commoners *(shu]* plus mean people *(jianmin)*. In its original meaning the term *shi* had designated "servitors," meaning the literate elite who served the state. From the Han to the end of the Tang, the "aristocratic" status of the great clans coincided with clan members' holding high office in government. The families of the elite were listed in official social registers. Marriage between them and commoners was frowned upon. During the post-Han period of disunion this elite provided roughly three quarters of government officials. During early Tang the proportion was more than half and later three fifths. Although the aristocratic clans of the northwest were mainly non-Chinese in origin, they were a major source of officials for the central government. As David Johnson (1977) says, "Unlike England or France, where a man could rise to a position of high social status through a career in law, medicine, commerce, the church or the military, in China there was only one significant occupational hierarchy: the civil service."

The lack of primogeniture in China meant that equal division of property among males was the common practice when the head of a family died. The imperial code of laws required partible inheritance and so prevented the rise of a landed nobility such as occurred in Europe. If a member of the family did not become an official for two or three generations, the family would sooner or later disintegrate. Each generation was potentially insecure and had to prove itself in official life. Family status was hereditary, but if a family that joined the elite through having members in high office was unable to produce additional members, its status would decline. However, a cushion was provided in that the Tang maintained various status groups outside the ranked bureaucracy from which one could re-enter official service.

Appointments to office were made by recommendation, first by the prefect, who was expected to rank all members of the elite within his jurisdiction according to a scale that eventually would consist of nine ranks, each one divided into upper and lower. Official appraisals of each prospective candidate for appointment were accumulated in dossiers. Through this system the elite perpetuated itself. Although the examination system got started in Sui–Tang times, it did not dominate the process whereby officials were recruited. Recruitment was a social rather than a legal process because in the social scene personal connections (guanxi) formed the fluid matrix in which candidates for office were advanced and family status was maintained. For example, the Northern Wei established its own list of major clans and made them equivalent to the Chinese list, so that families of nomad background could now move into Chinese life at the top level. Officially sponsored lists of the great clans' genealogies were produced between AD 385 and 713, evidently based on the recommendation lists submitted by the prefects. These established genealogies formed the basis for arranging marriages.

The Tang founders had felt this system obstructed the mobility of talent and turned against it. In this way the newly arisen Sino-barbarian families of the northwest, who now were taking power, struck a blow at the great Chinese families on the northeast of the North China plain. The Tang founders also denounced the large gifts that were being demanded by the old established families when their daughters were married. In 659 a revision of the national genealogy was 200 chapters long and contained 2,287 families from 235 clans. One aim of the revision was evidently to put the northeastern families in their place.

By the eighth century it appears that the holding of office had become the main criterion of family status, and the pedigrees of the great clans were less important. Everything now depended upon the official rank of the person listed, not on his family origins. Legally, officials were no longer regarded as a special elite. Though sons of officials were given a minor rank in the Tang legal code, there was no longer an upper-class status recognized in the code that gave special claims for appointment to office. The imperial institution had won out over the social interests of the great clans.

As Denis Twitchett (in *CHOC* 3) suggests, the Tang thus began the transition from rule by aristocratic families, in which the imperial house was merely *primus inter pares,* to rule of China by a trained bureaucracy selected by merit partly through the examinations. Decline of the aristocratic families left the central power more able to dominate local regions. The emperor would become a sacrosanct ruler set apart in his palace, remote from companions of the battlefield and dependent upon counselors who emerged from the new bureaucracy.

The aristocratic clans' loss of their dominance in government during the late Tang was accompanied by another great change—the government's retreat from its hands-on domination of China's economic life. The collapse of the equal-field system of land allotment in the countryside, and of official markets and price-setting in the cities, showed that the economy was outgrowing state control. Property began to accumulate in the hands of local magnates. In order to shore up the state's power, the tax system was rationalized by setting annual quotas to be collected on land, not persons, in summer and autumn. It was known from 780 as the two-tax system, that is, the combination of land tax and household tax. Tax quotas were set by consultation and provided the central government with some prospective security, although the new system acknowledged the government's inability any longer to control private wealth and free trade in land.

After the 755–763 rebellion, the government superintendence of trade also began to break down. Tang policy had been to keep trade regulated so that officially supervised markets with stable prices would assist peasant production but not permit the ignoble human propensity for profit-seeking. Tax revenues from trade were not considered important except when fiscal crises arose, although they always did in times of military need or dynastic decline. China's network of market communities (as described in the Introduction) would soon emerge under the Song and be too prolific for state control.

Finally, China had been militarized by the An Lushan rebellion, even while the Tang outposts in Central Asia had been overrun and much of the northwest was occupied by a Tibetan people, the Tanguts. Within China, the new provinces at first totaled some 30 units, mostly under military governors whose garrisons gave them power over local government. In contrast, the central government had almost no forces of its own and was several times in danger of takeover by Tangut invaders. The emperor's power after 763 rested precariously on four regions—the metropolitan province, the northwest frontier zone, the lower Yangzi, and the zone along the Grand Canal, which was the capital's lifeline. Several North China provinces remained out of central control and so took perhaps a quarter of the empire's population out of the revenue system, leaving the lower Yangzi and Huai valley region to be the dynasty's chief source of revenue.

A few Tang emperors after the rebellion succeeded in retrenchment and centralization of power, but the great age of the Tang had passed. The Inner Court was now plagued by the emperor's reliance on eunuch power while the Outer Court was wracked by intense factionalism.

In general, the rise of the Tang civil service contributed to a renewal of Confucianism, another aspect of the Tang–Song transition, researched most recently by David McMullen (1988). A continued development of classical scholarship had been fostered under the Tang by a school system, the examinations, the cult of Confucius, and state ritual as well as by historiography and secular literature. This growth of the scholar-elite during the Tang prepared the ground for the intellectual flowering of the Northern Song.

In 845 the Tang emperor decreed a broad, systematic repression of Buddhist monasteries, with their enormous tax-exempt land-holdings and resplendent city temples housing thousands of inmates. As many as a quarter of a million priests and nuns were forced back into lay life. Thereafter the government controlled Buddhist growth by its issuance of all ordination certificates to monks. The splendor of the Tang and of Chinese Buddhism declined together.

The power relations in North China at this time suggest that the actual interregnum in central power lasted all the way from the rebellion of 755 to 979. The military governors surviving from the Tang and their successors set up centralized, personally led military regimes that became the model for government during the interregnum and early Northern Song.

In its final half century the Tang was an object-lesson in anarchy. Officials, both civil and military, became so cynically corrupt and village peasants so ruthlessly oppressed that the abominable became commonplace. Loyalty disappeared. Banditry took over. Gangs swelled into armed mobs, plundering all in their path as they roamed from province to province. Emperors, their eunuchs, and officials lost control and were despised. For six years (878–884) the major bandit Huang Chao led his horde up and down the face of China, from Shandong to Fuzhou and Guangzhou, then to Luoyang and Chang'an, which was destroyed. By 907, the official end of the Tang dynasty, Turkic and other non-Chinese peoples occupied much of North China and warlordism flourished else-where.

Out of the debris emerged regional states known in North China as the Five Dynasties and in Central and South China as the Ten Kingdoms. The situation of general warlordism would be resolved only by the eventual domination of an imperial army at the new capital of the incoming Song dynasty in 960.

4

China's Greatest Age:
Northern and Southern Song

Efflorescence of Material Growth

A curious anomaly haunts the three centuries of the Song in China. On the one hand it was a great creative age that put China ahead of the rest of the world in technological invention, material production, political philosophy, government, and elite culture. Printed books, paintings, and the civil service examination system, for example, all attest to China's preeminence. On the other hand, during just this time of Chinese efflorescence, tribal invaders from Inner Asia gradually got military and administrative control over the Chinese state and people. Were Song China's cultural achievements related to the eventual non-Chinese domination? It is a vital question, though not a simple one.

In 960 the commander of the palace guard under the last of the Five Dynasties in North China was acclaimed by his troops as a new emperor. Thus catapulted into power, Zhao Kuangyin founded the Song dynasty. He and his successor, prudent and capable, pensioned off the generals, replaced the military governors with civil officials, concentrated the best troops in their palace army, built up the bureaucracy from examination graduates, and centralized the revenues. It was an exemplary job of controlling the military and establishing a new civil power. The century and a half of the Northern Song (960–1126) would be one of China's most creative periods, in some ways like the Renaissance that would begin in Europe two centuries later.

To appraise the strategic place of the Song in Chinese history, we must take several major approaches. The first is on the plane of material growth—in population and urbanization and in production, technology, and trade, both domestic and foreign.

China's population had reached about 60 million in mid-Han (around AD 2) and, after a probable decline in the era of disunion, seems to have approached 50 to 60 million again at the height of the Tang in the early 700s. It grew to perhaps 100 million in early Song and stood at about 120 million at the end of the twelfth century: say 45 million in the area north of the Huai River and 75 million along the Yangzi and southward (see Maps 10, 11, and 12.).

Population growth brought the rise of city life, which became most spectacular in the capital. As the political and administrative center of Northern Song, Kaifeng held a great concentration of officials as well as the service personnel, troops, and hangers-on attracted by the court. It was only four fifths the size of the Tang capital, Chang'an, but thrice that of ancient Rome. In 1021 the population was about 500,000 within the walls. Including the nine suburbs, it totaled roughly a million. By 1100 the registered households totaled 1,050,000 persons. Adding the army made about 1.4 million.

Such an urban concentration could be fed because Kaifeng was near the junction of the early Grand Canal and the Yellow River, at the head of barge transport from the Lower Yangzi grain basket. China's domestic and interregional trade was facilitated by cheap transportation on the Grand Canal, the Yangzi, its tributaries and lakes, and other river and canal systems. These waterways stretched for something like 30,000 miles and created the world's most populous trading area (see Map 16). Foreign trade would be at all times an offshoot of this great commerce within China.

Industry grew up at Kaifeng first of all to meet the needs of government. For example, North China then had large deposits of coal and iron, which water transport made cheaply accessible to the capital. The exhaustion of forest cover by about AD 1000 obliged iron smelters to use coal instead of charcoal in coke-burning blast furnaces. Moreover, using the cast iron thus produced, Song ironworkers developed a decarbonization method for steelmaking. By 1078 North China was producing annually more than 114,000 tons of pig iron (700 years later England would produce only half that amount).

From this the art of war gained coats of mail and steel weapons. Meanwhile a proto-artillery in the form of the catapult (trebuchet) was used in siege warfare, and gunpowder was used first in fire-lances, grenades, and bombards. Ancient sieges had been chancy because a besieged city, with its stored supplies, often could outlast the besiegers foraging in the barren countryside. The new Song weapons now could

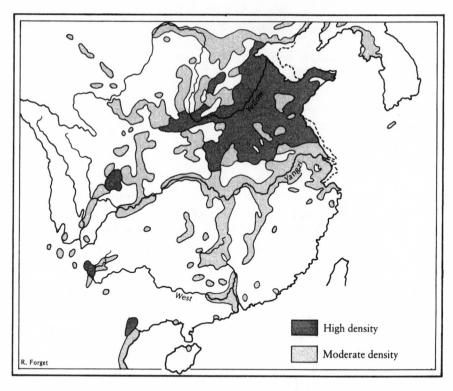

10. Population Distribution in the Han Dynasty, AD 2

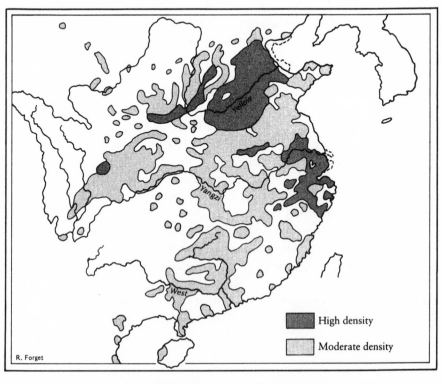

11. Population Distribution in the Tang Dynasty, AD 742

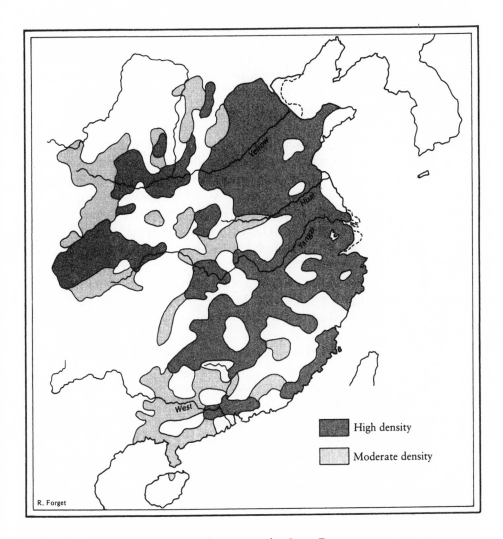

12. Population Distribution in the Song Dynasty, ca. 1100

batter walls and gates, explode gunpowder mines, and light fires within the walls.

Unfortunately for the Northern Song dynasty, this war technology was soon taken over by the Ruzhen invaders, who set up their Jin dynasty in North China after seizing Kaifeng in 1126. A new Song capital was established in the south at Hangzhou.

At its height in the early 1200s this great capital of the Southern Song stretched alongside the Qiantang River estuary for more than twenty miles, from the southern suburb of about 400,000 people through the imperial walled city of half a million and the northern suburb of say 200,000. Hangzhou had some Venetian features, as Marco Polo noted. Clear water from the large West Lake flowed through the city in a score or more of canals, which carried refuse on out east to the tidewater in the river estuary. The city embraced some seven square miles within its walls, bisected by the broad Imperial Way that ran from south to north. Before the Mongol conquest of 1279, Hangzhou had a population of more than a million (some estimates reach 2.5 million), making it the world's biggest city. Marco Polo's Venice had perhaps 50,000; we can understand why he was impressed by urban life in China.

During the Southern Song, foreign trade bulked large in Chinese government revenues for almost the only time before the nineteenth century. The demand for luxuries at Hangzhou and especially for spices imported via the Spice Route that ran from the East Indies to China, as well as to Europe, figured in the rapid growth of Song foreign trade. The demand was so high that the famous Chinese exports of silks and porcelains and also copper cash were not enough to balance the imports. The Islamic diaspora that had reached Spain and profoundly influenced Europe had similarly, by Song times, prompted a great increase of sea trade at the Chinese ports of Guangzhou (Canton), Quanzhou (Zayton), Xiamen (Amoy), Fuzhou, and Hangzhou. Chinese shipping went down the coast of East Asia to the Indies and across to India and even to east Africa, but the Southern Song foreign trade was still largely in Arab hands. Its taxation enabled the Southern Song to rely more on salt and trade taxes than on the traditional staff of imperial life, the land tax. One effect of this increase of commerce was to revive the use, inaugurated in the Tang, of paper money, beginning with government remittance notes to transfer funds, promissory notes, and other paper of limited negotiability, and finally arriving at a countrywide issuance of paper currency by the government. Like coal, this use of paper money was another thing that amazed Marco Polo.

Chinese nautical technology led the world during this period. China's big compartmented ships (with as many as four decks, four or six masts, and a dozen sails), which were guided by a stern post rudder and the use of charts and the compass, could carry 500 men. This technology was far ahead of West Asia and Europe, where Mediterranean galleys were still using muscle power and an inefficient steering oar.

These facets of the spectacular achievements of the Song are only examples. Any modern-minded expansionist looking back on all this growth and creativity can imagine how Song China, left to itself, could have taken over the maritime world and reversed history by invading and colonizing Europe from Asia. Seemingly the only thing lacking was motivation and incentives. This of course is a far-out fantasy, but it poses again the question of what impeded the further development of China's "medieval economic revolution," as Mark Elvin (1973) calls it. It is easy to point to barbarian invaders and blame the Mongol conquest for torpedoing the Song ship of state as it sailed so promisingly toward modern times. This has the attractiveness of any monocausal devil theory, but, as we shall see presently, the causes were various.

In the sections that follow we will see how the examination system became a major source of civil service bureaucrats, how the decreasing likelihood of actually getting a position in the civil service encouraged the scholar class *(shi)* to turn toward primary involvement in local affairs as leaders of the gentry, and how Neo-Confucian philosophy aided this shift in focus.

Education and the Examination System

The technological key to the growth of education under the Song was the printed book. As Tsien Tsuen-hsuin has recounted in his magistral volume on paper and printing, the first component of China's success in inventing the printed book was paper. Its development dated from the second or first centuries BC, but it was used in block printing only in late Tang. Northern Song was the first society with printed books. Europe lagged behind. Paper was cheaper when made of plant fibers in China than when made of rags in Europe, just as wood-block printing was simpler, cheaper, and better suited for Chinese characters than movable type. Printed matter was the life-blood of the expanding Song educated elite.

Printed books gave a great impetus to the education carried on in Buddhist monasteries as well as within families. The government had at first tried to control all printing, which was widespread. But by the 1020s it was encouraging the establishment of schools by awarding land endowments as well as books. The aim was to have a government school in every prefecture. The schools enrolled candidates, conducted Confucian rituals, and offered lectures. John W. Chaffee (1985) tells us that by the early 1100s the state school system had 1.5 million acres of land that could provide a living for some 200,000 students.

The examination system became an enormous and intricate institution central to upper-class life. During a thousand years from the Tang to 1905 it played many roles connected with thought, society, administration, and politics.

The first two Song emperors built up the examination system as a means for staffing their bureaucracy. The *yin* privilege by which higher officials could nominate their offspring as candidates for appointment still operated to make the official class partly self-perpetuating. But where the mid-Tang had got about 15 percent of its officials from examinations, the Song now got about 30 percent. Song examiners tried to select men ready to uphold the new civil order, who would be "loyal to the idea of civil government," says Peter Bol (1992). The examiners had to take precautions against cheating and so used devices such as searching candidates on entrance, putting numbers instead of names on their papers, and recopying papers to prevent readers from recognizing the writers' calligraphy. In 989 quotas of how many could pass were set up for each examination, so that certain geographical regions productive of high scholarship could not get too many winners in the competition.

Pioneer researchers some decades ago concluded that the Song examinations offered a career open to talent, letting in new men on their merits, but closer scrutiny now suggests that big families nevertheless continued to get their candidates into officialdom in disproportionate numbers, partly by virtue of superior home training, partly by influence through recommendations and connections. Chaffee found that during the three centuries of the Song the examinations became less and less important for gaining office and yet, paradoxically, more and more men became examination candidates. This reflected the fact that "the establishment" of official families increasingly found special ways to get degrees for their sons—for instance, by the *yin* privilege of recommendation, by passing various special or restricted examinations outside the regular competition, and, most amazingly, by simply taking the examinations and *failing* them time after time! (One is reminded of the report card that gives a backward child at least a grade of "A for Effort.") As a result, holders of regular degrees constituted in 1046 about 57 percent of the civil service; in 1119, 45 percent; in 1191, 31 percent; and in 1213, 27 percent. This declining rate of success was shown in the legislated (that is, decreed) pass-fail ratios as the number of candidates grew: 5 out of 10 were allowed to pass in 1023, 2 out of 10 in 1045, 1 out of 10 in 1093, 1 out of 100 in 1156, and 1 out of 200 in 1275. As more competed, fewer passed.

Thus, becoming classically educated and taking the examinations had become a certification of social status, whether or not one passed and whether or not one became an official. An exemplary community study by Robert Hymes (1986) traces how growth of the scholar class far outstripped the growth of state posts, leaving most examination degree-holders unable to enter the professional elite of the civil service. Among the 200,000 registered students, about half were candidates for examination in competition for about 500 degrees that would let them enter the civil service of, say, 20,000 officials. Thus, the road to office was blocked for most students. In this situation the growth of rural market communities with their need for local leadership attracted scholars to their home localities. An elite family's status in Southern Song began to depend less on office-holding by a family member and more on the family's wealth, power, and prestige in the local scene.

Hymes finds that the 73 families in his community's elite on the average maintained their elite status for about 140 years. He also finds "dense networks of connections"—familial, scholarly, and personal—joining official and commoner. Holding office in the civil service had become only one factor—and not a necessary one—in establishing elite status. In other words, the elite had broadened out to include local magnates, family heads, and informal public servants as well as ex-officials. The prerequisite for all was a classical education that qualified one culturally as a member of the class of *shi*—literati or "gentlemen." Such men, by their Confucian training, felt a sense of responsibility to keep the world materially and morally in order. They were guided by the creed of Neo-Confucianism, a philosophy of life that grew out of the debates of scholar-officials in the Northern Song.

The Creation of Neo-Confucianism

Confucianism asserted standards of perfect, unselfish conduct, and since backsliders were as common in China as elsewhere, Confucianists periodically called for reform. Indeed, most dynastic founders came into power to remedy evils. Once the examination system had taken hold and the Song bureaucrats shared a training in the classics, reformers naturally arose among them. As we look at this recurrent aspect of Confucianism, two features may be noted: reform-advocating officials normally hoped that the emperor would grant them power to make their reforms. They assumed that the imperial autocracy was the origin of all political power. They might strengthen it or use it but never sought to go behind it and consider any other forms of authority in state and society. Second, would-be reformers regarded the great mass of the common people as passive recipients of the benevolent despotism they sought to guide. They assumed merchants were perniciously addicted to greed and military men to violence. The reformer's job was to keep them in their place and secure a wise application of the unified central power represented by the emperor. Viewed this way, reform was a high calling, a means of preserving the imperial order and benefiting (while controlling) the mass of the people.

One early exemplar of the Confucianist reformer was Fan Zhong-yan, whose dedication was indicated in his maxim, "Before the rest of the world starts worrying, the scholar worries; after the rest of the world rejoices, he rejoices." As summarized by James T. C. Liu (in Fairbank 1957), Fan when prime minister of Northern Song pushed reforms in the bureaucracy against favoritism, in the examinations for practicality of subject matter, in land-holding to give local officials a chance to rely on income instead of squeeze, in defense to strengthen local militia, and the like. His call for a broader school system got some result, and Fan is also known as the founder of an exemplary "charitable estate" of land devoted to supporting the education of his own lineage members.

The most famous and controversial Song reformer was Wang Anshi. Though his reforms have been variously regarded, the most recent analysis sees him as a totalitarian-minded man ahead of his time. As a classicist, he regarded China's ancient sages down to Confucius as models of perfection whose intentions at least could still be followed. Wang's New Policies aimed to establish a "perfect, self-contained, and self-perpetuating system," as Peter Bol (1992) phrases it. Backed by the emperor from 1068, Wang bypassed the bureaucracy by getting his own people in office to pursue reforms to attack corruption and inequalities of wealth through vigorous state intervention in the economy. In effect, he tried to knock out the private sector, as we would now call it, by strictly limiting land-holding and private wealth, and by organizing the populace into mutual-responsibility groups for the purpose of controlling it. He would not tolerate opposition, which he considered immoral; in a properly unified state and society all men would have the same values, all people would function at their level in the hierarchy, and none would have independent means to support others and so possibly support dissent. There would be no loans from landlords to tenants; all people would depend entirely on the government. Meanwhile, the mutual-responsibility system would create community ties and would weaken the power of the family.

Since Wang's radical program attacked the basis of local family wealth that in turn produced examination candidates as well as local managers and merchants, Wang's reforms after some years of experiment and turmoil were shot down. The alternative approach that gained the day was typified by Wang's contemporary, the historian Sima Guang. Sima thought that imperial policy should not be guided by the perfect theoretical models of antiquity but by the study of history. He therefore compiled a most influential summary called *A Comprehensive Mirror for Aid in Government*, which chronicled dynastic rule from 403 BC to AD 959. Sima tried to choose events that showed how the policies of various kinds had worked out. This pragmatic approach urged the emperor to study his predecessors and not rock the boat by seeking perfection. The established order should be repaired, to be sure, but not transformed by a blueprint. Landlords and tenants were a natural result of the difference in human abilities. The key function of the ruler was the selection of talent, which was to be found among the Confucian-trained literati.

This conservative approach of keeping the imperial Confucian system going by always trying to remedy its defects and avoid its evils had a long-term effect on Chinese government. Wang had aimed to transform the state into an integrated social–political order led by political authority. It would make no distinction between government and society or between the political and the moral. Sima, on the other hand, saw the state as needing to be run by the literati as a separate social elite who came mainly from families with a tradition of official service and acquired their learning for that purpose.

Neo-Confucianism, as the Jesuits later named it, took shape in the

interests and as mediating between state and family. More than 700 years later the content would differ but the methods of criticism and self-criticism would resurface under the People's Republic. Both were exercises in applied morality.

For the scholar-elite, Zhu Xi promoted academies. He had contact with about 24 such unofficial institutions and taught 20 students in his own. The object of this teaching was the individual, who must learn how to achieve his own grasp of morality and bear responsibility for his moral self-cultivation in his effort to become a sage. Zhu hoped that proper government, finally, would rest upon "universal self-discipline beginning with the ruler's self-rectification." This could be aided by scholars' lectures to him (as part of court ritual) as well as by the subsequent judgments of the court historians. In discussing moral questions, minister and emperor should talk as equals.

Zhu Xi was a great editor of texts and writer of commentaries, but his main contribution was to raise the flag of Confucian moral righteousness and nail it to the mast. As Denis Twitchett (in *CHOC* 3) remarks, the Song era saw "the gradual change of China into an ideological society with a strong sense of orthodoxy." James T. C. Liu (1988) calls the Neo-Confucians "moral transcendentalists," although in time, he says, "neotraditionalism permeated the culture so completely that it lost the power to transform." The historical role of Zhu Xi and Neo-Confucianism is still in dispute: seven centuries of writings facilitate argument. One way in which Neo-Confucianism may have retarded China's modern growth was by its disesteem of trade. The attitude was that merchants did not produce things but only moved them around in search of profit, which was an ignoble motive.

We can better understand why there is continuing controversy over the meaning of translated Chinese texts if we look at the classical scholars' way of writing. As Joseph Needham has pointed out, they saw the world as a flux of concrete phenomena worth careful observation and chronological listing, but they did not make much use of analytic categories. Logical system building was not their forte. "Even in the case of such a giant as Chu Hsi [Zhu Xi]" says Derk Bodde (1991), "we have to derive his system from a bewildering assortment of recorded sayings, commentaries on the classics, letters to friends and other scattered documents. There is no single *summa* written by the master himself" (unlike his European contemporary Thomas Aquinas).

Writers of classical Chinese were by training compilers more than composers. Having memorized vast sequences of the classics and histories, they constructed their own works by extensive cut-and-paste replication of phrases and passages from those sources. This unacknowledged quotation today would be called plagiarism, but the Chinese writers from early times saw themselves as preservers of the record more than its creators.

Translation problems arose from the absence in Chinese grammar of particularities such as: singular and plural numbers; past, present, or future tenses; gender and case inflections showing relationships; as well as a means of showing the derivation of some words from others (except as might be indicated by radical and phonetic parts of characters). On the other hand, a reader can be guided to meaning by the rhythm, cadence, and balance of successive groups of characters, as I found during twenty-five years of teaching the translation of Qing official documents.

Another problem with classical Chinese was that there was little way to generalize or express abstractions—for example, to express the idea of being or existence as a nontemporal and nonactive abstraction. There was little use of theoretical hypotheses or conditions contrary to fact, nor of inductive and deductive logical reasoning. All this made it difficult to take novel foreign ideas into the writing system. In the end, this may have made it hard to develop the theoretical aspects of science. The best-known term problem in English translation was the phrase *gewu (ke-wu)*. Used by Zhu Xi and translated as "the investigation of things," it seemed to some modern scholars to call for scientific study of nature, but the term meant in fact, as Kwang-Ching Liu explains (1990), "acquisition of moral knowledge through the careful study of the classics and the scrutiny of the principles behind history and daily life."

The sources of imprecision just noted plus the constant growth of the modern philosophers' conceptual repertoire make Neo-Confucianism still a fertile field for new insights and interests.

Formation of Gentry Society

As China grew larger during the Song, a social structure became established that lasted in its general outline until the twentieth century. Upper-class families dominated Chinese life so much that sociologists have called China a gentry state, and even ordinary people may speak of the "scholar-gentry" as a class. But do not let yourself be reminded of the landed gentry, roast beef, and fox hunts of merry England, for "gentry" in the case of China is a technical term with two principal meanings and an inner ambiguity. It requires special handling. The characterization that follows is derived mainly from the Qing era (1644–1912), which has been the most fully studied. In its institutional arrangements, China's gentry society underwent a long and varied evolution, and its immense diversity is now being brought out by studies of local elites. But in order to appreciate diversity one must first acquire a general image, a China-wide model, as pioneer researchers tried to do.

Non-Marxists generally agree, first of all, that the gentry were not a mere feudal landlord class, because Chinese society was not organized in any system that can be called feudalism, except possibly before 221 BC. While "feudal" may still be a useful swear word, it has little value as a Western term applied to China. For instance, an essential characteristic of feudalism, as the word has been used with reference to medieval Europe and Japan, has been the inalienability of the land. The medieval serf was bound to the land and could not himself either leave it or dispose of it, whereas the Chinese peasant, both in law and in fact, has been free, if he had the means, to purchase land. In fact, it was the buying and selling of land in small and so not-too-costly plots that probably contributed to the extreme parcelization of cultivable land, with its many small strips of fields. At any rate, not calling the Chinese farmer's situation in life "feudal" by no means signifies that it was less miserable. But if the word is to retain a valid meaning for European and other institutions to which it was originally applied, it cannot be very meaningful in a general Chinese context.

The Chinese gentry, as their institutions developed from the Song period down to the Qing, can be understood only in a dual economic and political sense as connected both with land-holding and with degree-holding. A narrower definition would assign gentry status to those *individuals* who held degrees gained normally by passing examinations, or sometimes by recommendation or purchase. This narrow definition has the merit of being concrete and even quantifiable—the gentry in this sense were scholarly degree-holders, as officially listed, and not dependent for their status on economic resources, particularly land-owning, which is so hard to quantify from the historical record. Moreover, the million or so men who held the first-level degree under the Qing must be seen, as P. T. Ho suggests, as "lower gentry," barely removed from commoner status, whereas the small elite who after further years of effort went on up through the three rigorous week-long examination rounds at the provincial capital and at Beijing formed an "upper gentry" of great influence.

Gentry society was based on familism, which was dominated by the men within it. Women were inferior creatures, relatively expendable, who were usually married into other families. The gentry's aim was to preserve the family's elite status by training sons to become scholars and degree-holders. Under Neo-Confucianism the training of a young scholar from childhood was strong on discipline and perhaps shorter on affection. Self-control and unselfish hard mental work tended to crowd out frivolity, sexuality, muscular development, and even spontaneity. Testimony collected by Jon Saari from late Qing scholars paints a rather grim picture of education in gentry families.

The gentry as individuals served as public functionaries, playing political and administrative roles. Yet they were also enmeshed in family relations, on which they could rely for material sustenance. This political–economic dualism has led many writers to define the term gentry more broadly, as a group of *families* rather than of individual degree-holders only. Both the narrow and the broad definitions must be kept in mind.

The gentry families came to live chiefly in the walled towns, not in the smaller villages. They constituted a stratum of landowning families that intervened between the earth-bound masses of the peasantry, on the one hand, and the officials and merchants who formed a fluid matrix of overall administrative and commercial activity, on the other. They were the local elite, who carried on certain functions connected with the farming populace below and certain others connected with the officials above. In the agricultural community, the gentry included the big land-owners, whose high-walled compounds enclosing many courtyards, replete with servants and hoarded supplies and proof against bandits, dominated the old market towns. This was the type of "big house" celebrated in both Chinese and Western novels of China. As a local ruling class, the gentry managed the system of customary and legal rights to the use of land. These ordinarily were so diverse and complicated that decided managerial ability was required to keep them straight. The different ownerships of subsoil and topsoil, the varied tenant relationships, loans, mortgages, customary payments, and obligations on both sides formed such a complex within the community that many farmers could hardly say whether they were themselves mainly small landowners or mainly tenants.

For the officials of the old China the gentry families were one medium through whom tax collections were effected. By this same token, they were, for the peasantry, intermediaries who could palliate official oppression while carrying it out. The local official dealt with flood and famine, incipient rebellion, a multitude of minor criminal cases, and projects for public works all through the help of the gentry community. It was the buffer between populace and officialdom.

If a poor man could pass the examinations, he could become a member of the gentry in the narrow sense used above, even though he was not connected with a land-owning family. Nevertheless, the degree-holding individuals were in most cases connected with land-owning families, and land-owning families had degree-holding members. In general, the gentry families were the out-of-office reservoir of the degree-holders and the bureaucracy. The big families were the seedbed in which office-holders were nurtured and the haven to which dismissed or worn-out bureaucrats could return.

In each community the gentry had many important functions of a public nature (*gong* as opposed to official *guan* or private *si*). To generalize about such activities by millions of people over several centuries, we would do well to set up two views at either end of a continuum between idealistic and realistic. In the idealistic view that comes down to us through the gazetteers and other writings, the gentry-elite were moved by a sense of dutiful commitment to community leadership. So inspired, they raised funds for and supervised public works—the building and upkeep of irrigation and communication facilities such as canals, dikes, dams, roads, bridges, ferries. They participated in the Community Compact assemblies and they supported Confucian institutions and morals—establishing and maintaining academies, schools, shrines, and local temples of Confucius, publishing books, especially local histories or gazetteers, and issuing moral homilies and exhortations to the populace. In time of peace, they set the tone of public life. In time of disorder, they organized and commanded militia defense forces. From day to day they arbitrated disputes informally, in place of the continual litigation that goes on in any American town. The gentry also set up charities for their clan members and handled trust funds to help the community. Obviously, no one person could do all of these things. They are listed here to show the wide range of opportunities for gentry action.

Another function was to make contributions at official request to help the state, especially in time of war, flood, or famine. So useful were these contributions that most dynasties got revenue by selling the lowest literary degrees, thus admitting many persons to degree-holding status without examination. While this abused the system, it also let men of wealth rise for a price into the upper class and share the gentry privileges, such as contact with officials and immunity from corporal punishment.

The realistic view of the gentry's public functions begins with evidence from Song times that they might supervise the local periodic markets and play a role in the allocation and collection of taxes—in other words, undertake duties that officials had performed down to the early Tang. By Prasenjit Duara (1988) and others this has been seen as part of the gentry's "brokerage" function in local administration. It began with trade but was extended also into land tax collection, where it became tax-farming (promising to remit revenue quotas while keeping above-quota collections as personal fees).

In trade, the wholesale brokers *(yahang)* were middlemen who performed facilitative services for a fee. For example, an itinerant merchant would need reliable local assistance in dealing with dialects, customs, currency, porters, inns, markets, and the like. A local broker of this sort, probably a man of means, might be licensed by the state and might secure fees for his services, such as warehousing of goods, lodging, and transportation, as well as record-keeping for the state. He might be a well-to-do merchant himself. The wealthy salt merchants of Yangzhou, and the Cohong merchants in foreign staple trade at Guangzhou, were only the most famous among the innumerable brokers all over China who were licensed by and acted for the government. Since the gentry-elite were "licensed" by receiving their examination degrees, they can be seen as a specific subclass of "brokers" in the broad sense. Thus, when the gentry as private persons were used to oversee public activities in the field of taxation as well as public works, they might also receive fees or commissions as part of their income. As one might expect, their community leadership was not pure philanthropy but paid its way. This it continued to do as the Late Imperial gentry, having outgrown the available resources of land that could generate income, became more active in the public sphere as gentry managers, handlers of welfare institutions, and gentry merchants.

The local leadership and management functions of the gentry families explain why officialdom did not penetrate lower down into Chinese society. Or to put it the other way in terms of origin, the gentry had emerged to fill a vacuum between the early bureaucratic state and the Chinese peasant society that in the Song was outgrowing its control.

City studies inspired by G. W. Skinner (1977) have noted how in the two millennia from early Han to mid-Qing the territorial administrative structure of successive dynasties failed to grow, while the Chinese population increased sixfold. The basic-level counties or sub-prefectures *(xian)* totaled in the heyday of those regimes 1,180 in Han, 1,255 in Sui, 1,235 in Tang, 1,230 in Song, 1,115 in Yuan, 1,385 in Ming, and 1,360 in Qing, while the empire's population may have totaled 60 million in AD 80, 80 million in 875, 110 million in 1190, 200 million in 1585, and 425 million in 1850. Thus a county magistrate was responsible for 50,000 people in late Han but for 300,000 in late Qing. Skinner submits that the Qing administration simply could not have functioned with as many as 8,500 counties managed from Beijing. Instead of building up mechanically to such an unmanageable level, the Chinese state as it was expanding consolidated the counties in populous core areas while it created new counties on the peripheries. Meanwhile, it reduced its local administrative functions. For example, after the Tang the officially administered city marketing system was given up, the government stopped its "minute regulation of commercial affairs" generally, and it steadily withdrew from official involvement in local affairs. In its place came the rise of the gentry and their local functions.

In this way the imperial government from Song times on remained a superstructure of about the same nominal size. For example, there were about 18,000 official posts listed in the Tang, 20,000 in the Song, and 20,000 in the Qing. (Tables of organization were inherited.) The government did not directly enter the villages because it rested upon the gentry as its foundation. The many public functions of the local degree-holders made a platform under the imperial bureaucracy and let the officials move about with remarkable fluidity and seeming independence of local roots. Actually, the emperor's appointee to any magistracy could administer it only with the cooperation of the gentry in that area. All in all, in a country of over 400 million people, a century ago, there were fewer than 20,000 regular imperial officials but roughly 1.25 million scholarly degree-holders.

Continued superiority of the gentry families over the peasant mass was assured not only by landowning but also by the fact that the gentry mainly produced the "scholar-gentlemen" *(shi)* who carried on the great traditions of calligraphy, painting, literature, philosophy, and official life. If we stand back and look at China's gentry society in comparison with Europe until recent times, we cannot avoid being impressed. In the greatly changed circumstances of today, the belief system of the Neo-

1. Qin, third century BC. A soldier of the famous terracotta army buried at the tomb of the First Emperor of Qin near Xi'an, Shaanxi. The army totaled some 7,500 life-sized ceramic figures, individually sculpted and aligned in martial array underground to guard the emperor in the afterlife. This soldier probably held in his hands a bow or halberd.

2. Han, ca. AD 164. The First Emperor of Qin (219 BC) is trying to recover a sacred bronze tripod of earlier dynasties which has reappeared on the river bottom. It has the power of bestowing the Mandate of Heaven upon a ruler. The emperor's officials watch from the upper register. Below, boats and fish indicate the river. Men have been arranged on both banks to pull on the rope that has been attached to the tripod. But just as it reaches the surface, a dragon's jaws cut the rope. The three men on the right fall over backward. The four on the left are pulled forward by the weight of the heavy tripod as it sinks again to the bottom, indicating that the Qin empire will shortly come to an end.

3. Han, second century AD. A bronze representation of a familiar Han scene: an official seated in a two-wheeled chariot under a circular umbrella while his spirited horse between the curved shafts champs at the bit. Compare this three-dimensional version to the horse and chariot in the picture opposite.

4. *Above:* Northern Wei, ca. AD 525. This detail of a stone engraving celebrates Cai Shun, a paragon of filial piety. Under his care, his mother enjoyed a long life but finally died at the age of ninety. As she lay in her coffin before burial, a sudden fire broke out in the village. On the left, villagers work with frenzy to put out the flames. The son, dressed in his mourning clothes, has thrown himself across his mother's coffin to protect it and cries out to Heaven for aid. Though the rest of the village burned to the ground, Cai Shun's house and his mother's coffin were spared.

5. *Opposite:* Liao, AD 984. Because Guanyin has power to alleviate sufferings and is responsive to the prayers of the people, the popularity of this Buddhist deity of compassion among Chinese worshippers outstrips all others. A colossal clay statue of Guanyin standing fifty-two feet high is sheltered within this temple hall in Jixian, some sixty miles east of Beijing. The structure of the temple is entirely of wood, yet it has survived storms and earthquakes for a thousand years. The cross-section drawing is by Liang Sicheng, China's famous architectural historian.

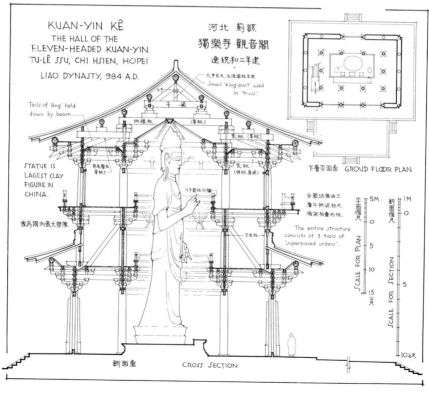

KUAN-YIN KÊ
THE HALL OF THE
ELEVEN-HEADED KUAN-YIN
TU-LÊ SSU, CHI HSIEN, HOPEI

LIAO DYNASTY, 984 A.D.

河北 薊縣
獨樂寺 觀音閣
遼統和二年建

父手巨大,与陳梁柱並用
Small 'king-post' used
in 'truss'.

Tails of 'Ang' held
down by beam.

平梁

四橡栿 (草栿)

乳栿 (草栿)

STATUE IS
LAGEST CLAY
FIGURE IN
CHINA.

郑尾壓在
乳栿下

乳栿 (明栿童柱)

斗予蜀柱以增

下層平面圖 GROUND FLOOR PLAN

全閣結構由三
層斗拱梁柱之
墙架相叠而成

像為國內最大塑像

平坐柱

The entire structure
consists of 3 tiers of
'superposed orders'.

5M.

1M

平面縮尺

斷面縮尺

SCALE FOR PLAN

SCALE FOR SECTION

5

10

10

15

斷面圖   CROSS SECTION

10尺

6. *Above:* Song, eleventh century. This painting is entitled "Scholars of the Northern Qi Dynasty Collating the Classical Texts," but the four scholars shown in this detail are at play as well as at work. Although the two seated on the far side of the large wooden platform have their brushes and papers in hand, the foreground pair appear to be smiling and teasing each other with pushing and pulling, while a small boy removes shoes on the right. Two maidservants have set out cups and heaping dishes of food, but one dish has been knocked over by the playful pair. On the left edge of the platform are still more diversions—a musical instrument, the *qin* (zither), and equipment for competing at throwing arrows into a vase.

7. *Opposite:* Song, eleventh century. Li Tang's painting of a traveling village doctor applying red-hot moxibustion conveys vividly the patient's terror. In this detail, his mate grasps his arms to hold him in place. At the right, huddled beside the doctor's insignia, is his young assistant. He has ready a soothing ointment, but meanwhile he giggles at the scene before him.

8. Song, twelfth century. "The Qingming Festival on the River" by Zhang
Zeduan is a famous handscroll, now seventeen feet long but originally even
longer. It follows the celebrants along the banks of the Bian River to the tower-
ing Water Gate of Bianliang (modern Kaifeng), the capital of the Northern Song
dynasty. In this detail, the heavily laden camels seen entering and exiting the
gate and the busy throngs passing by typify in brief the myriad details of daily
life in Zhang's home city, which the gifted artist has preserved for us through
eight centuries.

9. Song, twelfth century. A Tang general receives the submission of Inner Asian nomads. In this detail, General Guo Ziyi (697–781), facing an invasion by a more powerful force of Uighurs whose leaders had once served under him, goes unarmed to their camp. They recognize him, dismount, and pay homage. This line drawing is attributed to the famous artist Li Guanglin.

10. Song, twelfth–thirteenth century. In this album leaf bearing the title "Palace Ladies Bathing Children," the three palace ladies have their hands full. The child in the tub is having his nose wiped; behind him a lively one awaits his turn in the tub. On the far right, the child being dressed longs to escape, while the one on the far left runs for comfort to the lady's lap. The practice of painting informal, everyday activities of ladies in the court began in the Tang dynasty and was perpetuated in the Song imperial painting academies.

11. Song, 1210. The knickknack peddler's shoulder-pole is heavily weighted with toys. His wares captivate four mischievous small boys. In their midst stands a nursing mother whose baby also reaches out for a toy. A masterpiece of fine-line draftsmanship with brush and ink.

12. *Opposite:* Ming, fourteenth century. The Ming founder Hongwu, who reigned from 1368 to 1398, was reputed to be fierce and ugly. In this portrait of him wearing his imperial crown and royal robe, he has been described as "phoenix-eyed, dragon-jawed, and bespeckled all over the face."

13. *Above:* Ming, fifteenth century. A detail from a handscroll depicting six "Tartars on Horseback" who are delivering a riderless horse (not shown here) to be presented as tribute to the Chinese emperor. A Chinese rider leads the procession, but just behind him a bearded Tartar hurries to keep up. The picture is believed to be copied from a work by a tenth-century Qidan Tartar of Liao who excelled at painting the horses and nomadic peoples of his native steppe.

14. Ming, fifteenth century. A detail of a narrative handscroll representing a
well-known historical incident in the fourth century AD which involved a meri-
torious minister, Chen Yuanda, and his Turkic sovereign, described as "the At-
tila of Chinese history." Chen, compelled by his duties as a censor to admonish
the brutal ruler for his extravagant plans to enlarge the palace, chained himself
to a tree to make sure his reprimand would be heard in full. This detail shows
Chen clutching the tree as guards try to remove his chains. Two officials have
prostrated themselves and are pleading with the outraged Turkic ruler (not
shown here) that Chen be spared. In a later section, the ruler's Chinese wife
explains the Confucian tradition to her husband to exonerate Chen.

15. Ming, 1516. This picture of two blind beggars is a detail of a long hand-scroll. Zhou Chen, the artist, describes its inception in an inscription at the end: "I was idling under a window, and suddenly there came to my mind all the appearances and manners of the beggars and other street characters whom I often saw in the streets and markets. With brush and ink ready at hand, I put them into pictures in an impromptu way." Social commentary as seen here was an unorthodox subject for a Chinese painter, which explains why Zhou's painting bears no seals of famous connoisseurs or collectors.

消夏圖

江邨先生五十二玉照 廣陵禹之鼎

16. Qing, 1696. The subject of this hanging scroll is a lofty gentleman, Gao Shiqi (1645–1703), who was a close associate of the Kangxi Emperor and a leading collector of paintings. He is shown whiling away the summer by fishing from his skiff as a serving maid proffers him a drink.

Confucianists can again, in adjusted form, command respect and even allegiance. Its central message of the overriding need for self-discipline in the service of social order rings a welcome bell for many listeners.

The special Chinese need for order (and therefore authority) is explicated by social anthropologists like Patricia Ebrey (1984), whose study of a Song official's *Precepts for Social Life* forms a salubrious obligato to the philosopher's teaching. Under 200 topics the author advises how to get along with relatives, how to improve personal conduct, and how to manage a big family's affairs. Certain realities are at once thrust upon us: first of all, the extraordinary complexity of interpersonal relations when rules govern the roles assigned by status in kinship, age, sex, and law. We are reminded of the integral importance of servants, as well as concubines, maids, and others, in the "ministate" of the big household. How to beat a servant (don't do it yourself), how to buy a slave girl, how to discipline a son—the reader is offered practical and sensible guidance worthy of a Chesterfield or an Ann Landers. "The general rule with maids and concubines is to be careful of what is begun and take precautions concerning how things may end."

Most striking overall is the high degree of control to which everyone, including the master, is subjected. This is exerted not least by the ethical opinion of the group. Unlike the philosopher's ideal of absolute adherence to principle, the master of a gentry household is advised to think ahead, consider all sides, and be ever ready to compromise.

5

The Paradox of Song China
and Inner Asia

The Symbiosis of Wen and Wu

While Chinese creations in technology, government, art, thought, social organization, and the like all reached a high point in the Song, so did the invasion and takeover of power within China by the non-Chinese tribal peoples of Inner Asia. It seems a startling paradox that at its acme of civilization, China should be conquered by outsiders. The mystery deepens if we note that this conquest did not happen all at once but in fact began in 907 before the Song dynasty was set up and continued in fits and starts over three and a half centuries until 1279. So long-drawn-out a development can hardly be called accidental. What long-term trends were behind it?

One element of Song weakness was the buildup of a bureaucratism burdened with the costs of defense. Paul J. Smith (1991) even declares that "by the Southern Song the state had become parasitic." Behind this lay the Confucian disdain for the military, which classed them even lower than merchants. So deep-laid was this dislike that the military were excluded from the standard Confucian list of the four occupational groups or classes—scholar *(shi)*, farmer *(nong)*, artisan *(gong)*, and merchant *(shang)*. Derk Bodde (1991) tells us that this four-part division of society was never put forward by Confucius or Mencius but first appeared probably among Legalist writers of late Zhou and early Han. For twenty-one centuries since that time, however, the four classes have been standard fare in the lore about China.

Since military power founded dynasties and maintained them, built empires and defended them, there was usually a big military establishment. It is easy to argue that warriors—the military—were also an occupational group or class in China. Some have suggested that the *shi* recorded on Shang oracle bones were at that time "warriors" or later "servitors." Plainly the military were not listed as a fifth occupational class because the Confucian *wenren* (literati) who did the listing regarded practitioners of *wu* (violence) as their mortal enemies, incarnating the very evil of brute force that it was the Confucians' moral duty to extirpate in the cause of civilized behavior. To list them as a fifth profession would seem to condone them, legitimize their existence, give them moral stature.

A Confucianist might say further that the use of military force was always one of the measures available to the scholar-official ruling elite. One entered that class by becoming a scholar, then an official; an official might command troops. Scholar-generals often wielded military power. The troops were at first merely recruited or conscripted farmers. The only discrete military "class," a scholar might tell us, consisted of surrendered bandits, mercenary cavalry, drill sergeants, bowmen, or the like, a miscellaneous group, far down in the official system. The military examinations, rankings, and posts, though parallel to the civil ones, were explicitly disesteemed by the literati. As practitioners of violence, soldiers were part of the emperor's inner court, beyond control by the *wen*-complex of the bureaucracy. Eunuchs sometimes commanded troops.

Why have China scholars for 2,000 years gone along with this Confucian refusal to accept the military establishment as an occupational class? Professional military forces turn up all the time in Chinese history. Our refusal to look at them as a military class suggests that China scholars are still under the sway of the great Confucian myth of the state, government by virtue. Looked at from another angle, we see here one of the glories of old China, a reasoned pacifism, and one of its deepest weaknesses, an inability to avoid alien conquest from the grasslands.

Judging by the examination questions, says Peter Bol (1992), the Southern Song were quite conscious of their military problems, but they nevertheless relied upon mercenary troops from the dregs of society, who were poorly disciplined and could not be entrusted with decision-making powers even at the command level. Civilian domination of the military was part of the ruling elite's control of the state, but it left the state militarily weak. In size and military resources the Song more than equaled the Jin (and later the Mongols), but the Song civilian officialdom had little taste for violence. Charles Hucker (1975) and others conclude that the Chinese portion of the China–Inner Asia empire had become so civilized they lacked the martial values and sense of ethnicity (as opposed to culturalism) with which to fight off the invaders, who ordinarily promised to rule in the Chinese fashion. In effect, the Confucianists were specially fitted for administration, not for holding ultimate imperial power. After all, they had been trained to be civil servants in a literal sense, and they could foresee that resort to violence would breed more violence. Yet when all this has been said, the fact remains that the Southern Song held the all-conquering Mongols at bay for 45 years, almost two generations.

Perspective on Chinese rulers' Inner Asian relations is provided by Thomas J. Barfield's chronological account of the succession of tribal peoples in the grasslands. He concludes that in times of strength the Chinese connection with a tribal power fostered its hegemony in Inner Asia. Thus the Han, when strong, saw the long-continued Inner Asian dominance of the Xiongnu, and the Tang of the Uighur Turks. A balanced view of such relations is hampered by the evidence coming mainly from the Chinese side.

Lack of contact with Inner Asia handicapped the Song by making it harder to secure horses for warfare. The Qin-Han and Sui-Tang dynasties had all been in touch, through traders and envoys, with the power configurations of Inner Asia. They were adept at finding allies and using some peoples against others. The ineptitude of Song diplomacy—as in their initially helping the Ruzhen against the Qidan, only to be defeated later by the Ruzhen, and then helping the Mongols against the Ruzhen, only to be overrun later by the Mongols—was presumably due to their lack of direct contact with and only marginal participation in the life of Inner Asia. Song China after all coexisted with several peripheral states—Vietnam on the south, Nan Zhao on the southwest, Tibet, the Tangut Western Xia (Xixia) state on the northwest, and the Qidan Liao on the north—so that China was in fact, as Morris Rossabi (1983) puts it, diplomatically "among equals." The Ming claims of universal superiority would be asserted only after the Mongol empire of the thirteenth century had set an example.

From the Song period on, one sees within the imperial Confucian polity a civil administrative complex and a military power-holding complex ruling in tandem. Both were necessary to govern the state. The civil complex includes the examination degree-holders and scholar-official civil servants trained in Neo-Confucianism, together with the local elite or gentry class that produced them. The second and less studied component, the military complex, consists of the emperor, his family, and their nobility, army striking forces and garrison troops, plus the palace eunuchs and security apparatus (as we would now call it) that were all especially attached to the emperor.

Perhaps we can discern a certain division of functions between these two complexes. As suggested above, imperial autocracy was a necessary counterpart to bureaucratic administration. It could be a nonroutinized, autonomous source of innovation or sudden intervention. It was naturally unpredictable, often ruthless, potentially disastrous. In the well-organized Confucian order the emperor functioned both at the apex of the structure and yet at the same time represented in its highest form the principle of violent disorder. He was, for one thing, the great executioner.

Almost from the beginning the government of China had been a co-dominion of these two functions. Inner Asian tribal warriors had contributed to the imperial power-holding function through a continuing pattern of pastoral nomadic militarism. The other function was performed by Chinese Confucian civil administrators. Dynasties were militarist in origin, but once established, their bureaucracies were civilian. The ideology of each was suited to its needs. The men of violence who founded dynasties believed in the Mandate of Heaven, which was confirmed as theirs when resistance ceased. The scholar-administrators who staffed their bureaucracies looked down upon men of violence, who by their recourse to force *(wu)* showed themselves lacking in cultivation *(wen)*. The central myth of the Confucian state was that the ruler's exemplary and benevolent conduct manifesting his personal virtue *(de)* drew the people to him and gave him the Mandate. This could be said as long as rebels could be suppressed, preferably by decapitation.

The great weakness in this Confucian myth of the state was that the ruler, if he wanted to keep on ruling, could never dispense with his militaristic prerogative of decapitating whom he pleased *pour raison d'etat,* to preserve the dynasty. Thus, government under imperial Confucianism was conducted by bureaucrats who served under an autocrat, and they depended upon one another. In practice, a balance was often reached between *wen* and *wu* when Confucian-trained territorial administrators were allowed to command troops to destroy rebels. Many scholars specialized in military matters; some became able generals. Yet all held power only at the whim of the emperor.

While the Chinese under the Song perfected the classical examination system as the device for training obedient bureaucrats, the contemporary non-Chinese invaders of China—the Qidan (Liao dynasty), Ruzhen (Jin dynasty), and Mongols (Yuan dynasty)—proved the utility of militarism as the source of imperial power. The ancient adage that China could be ruled only in the Confucian civil fashion is only half true. Imperial Confucianism could function only as long as the ruling dynasty commanded enough violence to destroy rebels, and this type of power was the specialty of the non-Chinese tribesmen of Inner Asia. Thus one may discern a specialization of functions historically between Chinese administrators and Inner Asian power-holders such that Inner Asian non-Chinese participated increasingly in the imperial government and sometimes took it over.

The Rise of Non-Chinese Rule over China

Let us look back a moment at the rise of this Inner Asian component of China's polity. The Zhou and the Qin dynasties in Northwest China had derived some of their military vigor from contacts with the northern tribes and intermarriage, as had the Sui and Tang in their turn. It was only a further step for northern tribal invaders to take over part of China directly and rule it with Chinese help but through a non-Chinese dynastic house. This pattern of dual Sino-nomadic government was visible from the fourth century AD in southern Manchuria. It would reach its peak in the complete control that followed the Mongol and Manchu conquests.

Rule by cultural aliens posed an acute problem in Chinese political theory. From earliest times under the kings of Shang, the culture (including the Chinese writing system, use of ritual bronzes, shamanist consultation with the ancestors, and the ruler's ritual observances toward the powers of nature) had been part and parcel of the polity. The early tenet of sinocentrism was that the superiority of *Zhongguo*, the Central State, in *wen* (culture and civilization) would inevitably dominate the mere military violence *(wu)* of the Inner Asian tribes. This could be done by requiring that the non-Chinese tribal chieftains acknowledge China's superiority by bowing down before the emperor, who held Heaven's Mandate to govern China and whose magnificent benevolence and compassion naturally attracted outsiders to come and also be transformed by civilization.

In the absence of contact with any other state of equal cultural achievement, Han and Tang foreign policy thus became based on the tribute system, a reciprocal foreign relationship between superior and inferior comparable to the Three Bonds that kept China's domestic society in order. Since presentation of tribute offerings was normally reciprocated by lavish gifts from the emperor, accepting China's supremacy was materially worthwhile. In addition, the tribute system early became the institutional setting and indeed cover for foreign trade.

With the demise of the Tang central power, the ten or so successor states of tenth-century China were in a multistate polity a bit like that of the Warring States era before the Qin unification. In their relations with one another, the rulers fell back on some practices of those times, such as negotiating through envoys, although their multistate relations were now focused on the question of who would revive the central imperial power. But in this competition, non-Chinese rulers on the periphery of China now took part. When non-Chinese for the first time began to govern a Chinese populace in North China, the old amalgam of polity and culture had split apart. The Chinese world order set up by the Han and revived by the Tang as a system of thought and institutions to handle foreign relations had now collapsed.

Alien rule began with the rise of the Qidan (a Mongolian people from whom North China got the medieval European name Cathay), who maintained an empire for more than two centuries (916–1125) over parts of North China, Manchuria, and Mongolia. In origin the Qidan had been only seminomadic, relying on agricultural crops, especially millet, as well as on sheep, horses, and pigs. They rose to power by straddling the frontier between steppe and sown, where they could combine the military force of nomad cavalry with the economic sustenance of peasant tillage. The federation of tribes that founded the empire was led by the imperial Yelü clan, who prolonged their rule by adopting the Chinese institution of hereditary monarchy and many of the forms of Confucian government. As studied by K. A. Wittfogel (Wittfogel and Feng, 1949) and others, the Liao empire, as it called itself, was a dual state: its southern section encompassed 16 prefectures of North China (out of some 300 in the Song empire; see Map 13), and these were governed in the Chinese style through institutions of civil bureaucracy inherited from the Tang. The much larger northern part of the Qidan domain was governed by men on horseback as before. Thus, while the Qidan emperor's officials for the southern area were being recruited through a classical examination system, the mounted archers of the north were being mobilized and trained to serve in his elite guard, the *ordo* (from which derives our term "horde"). Eventually a dozen *ordos* were set up in separate areas, totaling perhaps 600,000 horsemen, a mobile shock force held in reserve.

This dual state rested on a population of perhaps 4 million, which made it somewhere about 1/15th the size of the Song empire to the south. Yet the Liao cavalry had such striking power that the Song finally paid them annual subsidies to keep peace on the border. The Northern Song emperors at Kaifeng bought off the Qidan by concluding treaties in 1005 and 1042 under which the Song accepted inferior status and paid an annual tribute. In 1044 similar terms were accepted in a treaty with the Tangut rulers of the Western Xia (Xixia) state in northwest China. For all its wealth and progress, the larger Song empire lacked the determination more perhaps than the means to conquer these barbarians.

13. The Northern Song and Liao (Qidan) Empires, ca. 1000

It is a striking fact, as Needham tells us, that gunpowder had been created by Chinese alchemists in the ninth century. Against the nomad invaders the Chinese used both simple bombs and fire-lances. This great breakthrough in military technology evidently had little significance for the classically trained Song statesmen. Here we find Confucianism slow to mount on the back of technology.

In 1125 the Liao state was taken over by the Tungusic Ruzhen (Jurchen) tribes from northern Manchuria, who took the dynastic name of Jin or "Golden." At first the pattern of dual government was continued. Like the Liao, the Sino-nomadic Jin empire could combine the horses of the grasslands and the grain of North China to mount military assaults and force the Song southward. From their founding in 960 the Song had had their capital at Kaifeng on the Yellow River at the head of the Grand Canal, but by 1126 the Jin attacks forced them to abandon North China. Song resistance to the Ruzhen Jin attacks was hamstrung by controversy over whether to fight or to appease the invaders. The issue came to a head in 1141 when the chief councilor and negotiator (Qin Gui) arranged the murder of a leading fighter, General Yue Fei, who was thereby immortalized as a model for later Chinese patriots. In 1142 the Southern Song by treaty ceded North China down to the Huai River and agreed to be a vassal of and pay annual tribute to the Jin. The North China plain combined with the lower Yangzi region had been the heartland of Chinese life, so that now for the first time a considerable segment of the Chinese people came under non-Chinese rule (see Map 14).

Once they had conquered North China, the Ruzhen of the Jin dynasty (1115–1234) totaled about 6 million in a North China population of about 45 million. The Qidan remaining from the Liao dynasty of 916–1125 may have made up about 4 million out of this total, so that the Ruzhen had to govern some 35 million Chinese subjects. For this task they relied at first on sinicized Qidan and on Han Chinese who had served the Qidan. They also recruited officials from the pool of Chinese government clerks. But the Ruzhen emperors soon found they had to sustain their central power in competition with their own Ruzhen tribal leaders, military aristocrats from the north who expected to control lands and peoples they had conquered. In self-defense the Jin emperor built up an imperial bureaucracy patterned on Confucian ways of government. Finding they needed classically trained examination candidates to staff this bureaucracy, in the last quarter of the twelfth century the Jin rulers at Kaifeng set up Ruzhen-language schools, translated the Con-

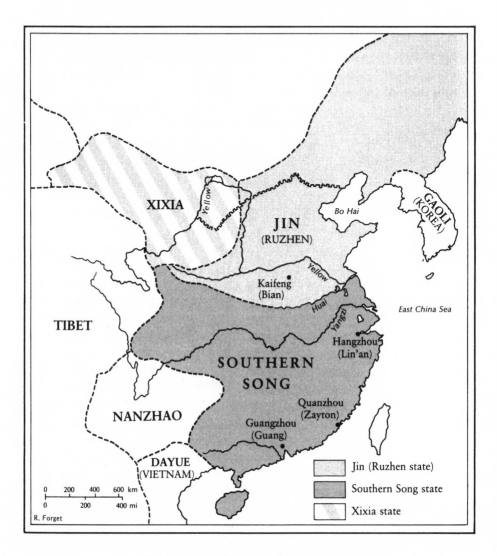

14. Southern Song and Jin (Ruzhen) Empires in 1142

fucian classics into Ruzhen, and set examinations for Ruzhen candidates. The major flow of recruits, however, came from the Han Chinese: in the quarter century after 1185 the expanded Chinese examinations produced at least 5,000 metropolitan *(jinshi)* degree-holders. Also important, as Peter Bol points out, was the spread of Confucian culture: "Tens of thousands acquired an examination education."

"Sinicization," however, is an inadequate description of what the Ruzhen rulers were seeking. Instead of "becoming Chinese," they were, on the contrary, developing their role as supporters of civil order *(wen zhi,* "civilization"). Their role had a supra-ethnic value as the means by which Chinese subjects and nomadic invaders could live together in peace and prosperity under a universal empire. In other words, China's original "culturalism" (the "Confucian" way of thought and action) could be promoted by non-Chinese rulers, who maintained their ethnic identity while functioning as rulers over China and Inner Asia. The Ruzhen thus developed the theoretical foundation for the multiethnic empire that would be brought to its highest point under their eventual descendants, the Manchus.

In claiming their dynasty's "legitimate succession" to its predecessors *(zhengtong),* the Jin rulers were aided by their adoption of traditional centralizing institutions and also by their performance of the appropriate imperial rituals. As outlined by Hok-lam Chan (1984), these rituals began with the reverence for the forces of nature and especially for the ancestors as practiced by the Shang; they maintained the belief in the Mandate of Heaven asserted by the Zhou along with the doctrine of benevolent rule by sage kings as propounded by Mencius and interpreted by the Confucian scholar-elite. The correlative cosmology of Earlier Han, centered around the cyclical theory of the Five Phases, was also continued. This theory, postulating correspondence between the order of nature and human events, had stressed the importance of the phase, color, and so forth to be associated with, and so legitimate, each dynasty. Han Wudi, for example, chose the Earth phase for Han plus the color yellow, the number 5, and so on. Later dynasties, small and big, continued to assert their legitimacy according to the Five Phases cycle— for example, Tang claimed its affinity to Earth in succession to Han, while the Song claimed Fire and the color red as its symbols of legitimacy. The Jin rulers therefore claimed the Earth power in succession to the Song.

The Ruzhen had moved their capital from Ha'erbin to Beijing in

1153 and then to the Northern Song site at Kaifeng in 1161. Some emperors achieved new heights of brutality by beginning a regular practice of having top officials flogged in open court in front of the emperor, quite contrary to the classic Chinese exemption of literati and especially officials from corporal punishment. Some executed hundreds of kinsmen, officials, and military leaders, trying to forestall opposition.

One of the last Jin emperors, on the other hand, has come down in history as a model Confucian ruler. In his era occurred a cultural revival led by Chinese Confucianist subjects of the Jin state morally committed to supporting the inherited culture of civil order. Between them, the Confucianist-minded Ruzhen rulers and their Chinese literati officials asserted that a non-Chinese dynasty could indeed support a "Chinese" (that is, Chinese and Inner·Asian) cultural tradition. In any case, the Jin dynasty's legitimacy was formally established when its official history was written under the Mongol Yuan dynasty.

The advent of Neo-Confucianism in Southern Song set up broader criteria for dynastic legitimacy. Such factors as victory in warfare, government procedures like the promotion of an imperial cult of ancestors, plus rituals and symbols, scholastic theories, control by intimidation, and mutual surveillance and popular (or elitist) acceptance all figured in legitimation in China much as they did in West Asia and Europe. But thanks mainly to Confucian scholarship, the Chinese criteria were far more unified and homogeneous. To some degree the Song philosophers' stress on the universality of their cosmology and values accommodated the non-Chinese invaders. On the level of political theory China was thereafter prepared, whenever the need arose, to accept government by tribal peoples of Inner Asia.

In the final analysis, the legitimation of non-Chinese rule in China consisted of the fact that it could not be avoided and so had to be rationalized. As Korean observers would later find, in China under the Manchus Chinese scholars might hate Qing rule but would leave no record of the fact. This inner hatred and outer acceptance was like that of most victims of despotism then and now. It required that one practice self-control and a sort of hypocrisy, a "feigned compliance," outwardly accepting while inwardly denying the validity of the ruling power. For most people this could lead to a seeming indifference to politics as none of their business, just as the rulers claimed.

Looking ahead, we may posit that the dynasties of conquest—Liao, Jin, and Yuan—form a connected sequence of incursions of Inner Asian military power into China and must be viewed as a single, if sporadic process. Liao lasted longest but occupied only a strip on the northern edge of North China. Yuan occupied all China but was the briefest. This puts the Jin dynasty in the strategic position of having learned how alien invaders could govern China's heartland, the North China plain, by co-opting Chinese personnel inherited from the defeated Northern Song. Jin rule in China seems comparatively neglected, overshadowed by the Mongol conquest.

China in the Mongol Empire

The Mongol conquest was a forerunner to the Western imperialism of nineteenth-century China, when Chinese society was again laid open to the culture shock of discordant foreign influences. The Yuan dynasty (1279–1368), in other words, must be examined as the seedbed of important phenomena that we see in the Ming and Qing (1368–1644–1912).

As a first step we must note the dramatic achievements of the Mongolian people in the creation of their great empire. The Mongol war machine was the culmination of a millennium of the mounted archer's military prowess all across Eurasia. After Chinggis Khan united the tribes in 1206 and his Mongol hordes erupted in all directions, his sons and grandsons ruled four khanates respectively in Persia, South Russia, Central Asia, and China (see Table 3). As conquerors, the Mongols' ferocious destructiveness gave them a bad reputation, especially among

Table 3. Divisions of the Mongol empire under
Chinggis Khan's successors

Great Khan (East Asia): Ogodei (third son of Chinggis), 1229–1241; Mongke (Mangu),* 1251–1259; Khubilai,* 1260–1294 (ruled over all China after 1279); Mongols expelled from China by Ming, 1368

Khanate of Chaghadai (Djaghatai, in Turkestan): Chaghadai (second son of Chinggis), 1227–1242; western part incorporated after 1370 in empire of Timur or Tamerlane, 1336–1405

Khanate of Persia (Il-khans): built up by Hulegu*; capture of Baghdad, 1258; dissolution after 1335

Khanate of Kipchak (Golden Horde) on lower Volga: built up by Batu,* 1227–1255; dominated Russia; conquered by Tamerlane and broken up in fifteenth century

---

*Grandsons of Chinggis Khan.

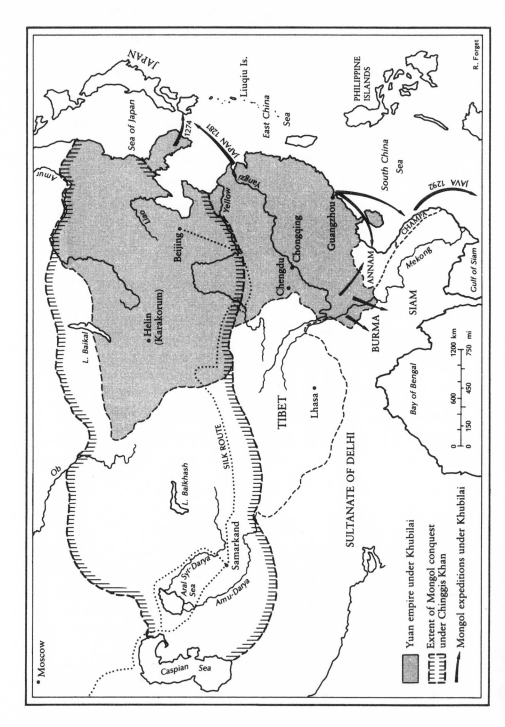

15. Mongol Conquests and the Yuan Empire in 1279

moral-minded Confucians. For example, their first invasion of the Jin empire in North China had left more than 90 towns burned to rubble.

The Mongols extinguished the Jin in 1234, and finally conquered the Southern Song only 45 years later, in 1279. Between those two dates they ruled the North China heartland, which had already experienced a century of alien domination, and learned that the empire could be conquered on horseback but not ruled on horseback, much as nineteenth-century European imperialists would learn that bayonets were no use for sitting on.

Eventually Chinggis's ablest grandson, Khubilai Khan, who reigned as chief of the Mongol world from 1260 to 1294, built his capital at Beijing (see Map 15). He became emperor of China in 1271, calling his dynasty Yuan ("origin") and ruling in Chinese style. Yet he was distracted by imperial politics and rivals for power. He also had to cater to his Muslim constituency as defender of the faith; and for the Mongol followers of Tibetan Lamaism he had to be a Buddhist universal ruler. This diversity of faiths reflected the cosmopolitanism of the multiethnic Mongol world, where even Nestorian Christianity from Central Asia had its devotees within the ruling family.

Although it is obvious that the humiliation of inferior status in their own country inflamed Chinese anti-Mongol feeling both at the time and in retrospect, the actual conditions of Chinese life in the Yuan era, as John Langlois (1981) suggests, present a mixed picture that calls for more reappraisal than it has yet been given. On the score of militarism, first of all, there is little doubt of the Mongol influence. The Chinese classical ideal had been that every farmer should also be potentially a self-sustaining soldier. Under the dynasties from Qin to Tang the army had been conscripted. The Qin-Han required all able-bodied males to serve for two years as a corvee obligation. Sui and early Tang used the *fubing* militia system, by which certain families, in return for tax exemptions, supplied soldiers to be available for service and provide their own equipment and rations. The early Tang had some 633 militia units, each of about 1,000 men, located mainly in the northwest and around the capital. The *fubing* were abolished in 749, and late Tang and Song raised hired-service mercenary armies whose personal qualities generally put them in bad repute.

In contrast, the Inner Asian tribesmen were by nurture and custom potential cavalrymen who easily became after their conquests a professional and also hereditary armed force. Each-farmer-a-soldier had been only an ideal, but each-hunter-a-soldier easily became a fact. The Ruzhen's basic unit of 300 families had supported 100 soldiers. Chinggis Khan by 1206 had under him 95 units, each of 1,000 with their supporting families and assigned pastures. Just as the Mongols were the first Inner Asians to conquer and rule all of China, so their greatest contribution to the empire was in military matters. As Ch'i-ch'ing Hsiao (1978) says, the Mongol conquerors "remained chiefly concerned with power. They tended to think in military terms" and gave China a new army organization that "contained most of the members of the conquering nation."

Once China was taken over, the Mongol garrison troops had to get their livelihood from their own agriculture and that of their slaves on the depopulated lands allotted to them in North China. The fighting capacity of their hereditary military households soon deteriorated. Mongol officers formed a segregated and self-perpetuating salaried aristocracy—the superior military wing of the imperial bureaucracy—but in general the Mongol soldiery in China became impoverished. They married Chinese women, but many lost their lands, even had to sell their families, sometimes absconded and became vagrants. To be hereditary soldiers in peacetime turned out to be a disaster.

One question debated by historians has been the degree to which Mongol rule made the Confucian government of China more despotic. The answer seems to be affirmative, but the reasons do not lie wholly with the Mongols. Perhaps the founder of the Ming would later be the most positive witness. The Mongols were despised—Chinese liked to say that they stank so that you could smell them downwind—and Mongol rule lasted less than a century, more brief than Ruzhen rule had been in North China. Except along the Great Wall the Mongols could not take root. But this does not mean some of their ways were not imitated.

In ruling China the Mongols' first problem was cultural. As full nomads from Outer Mongolia without much earlier contact with China, the Mongols were too different in speech, dress, customs, and background to bridge the cultural gap between themselves and the Southern Song Chinese. Being generally illiterate and comparatively few in number, in government they used West Asians (Uighur Turks, Arabs, even some Europeans like Marco Polo) and Sino-Ruzhen personnel of the conquered Jin empire. Southerners were slighted as of dubious loyalty, and they responded by avoiding government service. Yan-shuan Lao (in Langlois, 1981) has illustrated how southerners with top degrees were willing to be masters of private academies but refused to teach in government schools, which would make them officials even though at the lowest rank.

On the whole the cultural gap made for light government. Yuan punishments were apparently less severe than the Song; there were fewer irregular exactions added to the taxes. While Khubilai to be sure patronized Lamaism and Daoism as well as orthodox Confucianism, he pursued no literary inquisition. Mongol princes could enjoy their *appanages* and squabble among themselves. The Mongols could garrison key points, but they could not administer the government, police local communities, censor Chinese literature and drama, or provide China's intellectual and cultural leadership.

Comparing the Liao, Jin, and Yuan dynasties, Herbert Franke (in Schram, 1987) suggests that all three had a looseness of administration almost like colonial governments because of the oil-and-water mixture of Chinese and tribal ways. Thus, in their multiethnic, multilingual regimes each nationality used its own script—Qidan, Ruzhen, or Mongol. The Chinese continued to expect hereditary succession in a hierarchy of authority, whereas the invaders determined successors by election in a somewhat democratic or at least collective assembly of chieftains. For the Chinese the laws were uniform and pervasive, whereas the nomads applied to each person his customary tribal law. This diversity made for less centralization and not for monolithic despotism.

Since the examination system was not restored until 1315, the lack of administrators was made up by the increased use of yamen clerks. Many Chinese entered government by this route, but the clerks' weakness in Confucian indoctrination as well as the lack of Mongol surveillance fostered widespread corruption. To sustain Mongol power in the local scene, the Mongols used an extra layer of territorial officials. To critical places the court sent omnicompetent Mongol and sometimes Chinese officials who could act in both military and civil capacities, trouble shooters called *darugaci (daluhuachi),* who held their commissions directly from the emperor. In the last decades of Yuan rule, Confucian ways were being studied and used by Mongol governors to good effect, but they were undone by civil war among their unsinicized and diehard countrymen.

One trait of the Mongols was their nomadic yen to keep on the move, seeking more loot and slaves. Having expanded over the known world and finally overrun China, they used the captured Song fleet with its experienced captains and crews to send expeditions overseas. Yuan fleets of thousands of ships attempted to conquer Japan in 1274 and

1281, invaded Vietnam and Champa (in southern Indo-China), the Liu-qiu Islands, and in 1292 Java, all without success. Burma and Siam were also invaded. While the Mongol warriors had an urge to expand, they did little to get China's sea trade into the early maritime world system that was beginning to take shape on the sea routes around Asia. Mongol rule brought China several decades of domestic peace and caravan trade across Asia. A number of Europeans reached China by this route. It is a plausible theory that bubonic plague, which drastically reduced China's population in the years roughly from 1331 to 1354, was also transmitted through Mongol channels to Europe, where it became the Black Death of 1348–1349.

Khubilai's great public works such as the second Grand Canal system contributed to some degree of economic prosperity (see Map 16). The sea trade from West Asia and India was still largely in Arab hands because, as noted above, the Islamic diaspora had brought Muslim merchants to China not only over the Silk Road but also by the Spice Route that carried spices from the East Indies to China as well as to the eastern Mediterranean for Europe. Muslim merchant groups active in caravan trade across Central Asia as well as in maritime commerce were regulated and given loans by the Mongol rulers to invest in trade. As tax farmers they also helped the Mongols collect the agrarian surplus and channel some of it into trade. Commercial growth was signaled by the extensive issue of paper money, superintended by Muslim financiers at court.

By not using the southern Chinese in government but leaving their local communities intact, Mongol rule stimulated private Chinese scholarship. Many thousands of Chinese scholar-gentlemen found themselves unemployed by the state and free to pursue private ends, to become leaders in their communities and preservers of the Confucian Way. Thus the Yuan era saw the rise of Chinese drama, and painting flourished. Among these private scholars Zhu Xi's stress on the moral self-cultivation of the individual as the foundation of social order and good government was vigorously promoted. While the Zhu Xi school urged study of the practical world, the followers of another Neo-Confucian philosopher, Lu Xiangshan, advocated a more inward-looking contemplation. Along with these more philosophical trends developed the school of statecraft, a pragmatic how-to-govern approach to political institutions. Both these schools of thought, the moral and the utilitarian, stressed the virtue of loyalty, not so much to a given dynasty as to the

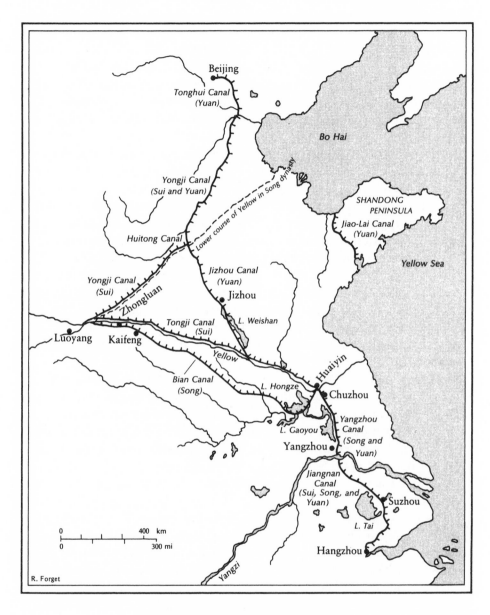

16. The Grand Canal System of the Sui,
Song, and Yuan Dynasties

Neo-Confucian Way. The Yuan era also saw a new attention to law as an antidote to arbitrary government.

Interpreting the Song Era

No high period of civilization can be characterized in simple terms. Yet scholarly interpretations of a great period have often become part of its historical record. So comprehensive and spectacular were the changes of the Song era that a Japanese historian (Naitō Konan) saw in them the birth of "modern" China, by which he meant the China that persisted until the late Qing in his own day, early in the twentieth century. Naitō saw two levels of power in this modern era: the despotic emperor with his "entourage and underlings," and "local Chinese society beneath the centrally appointed bureaucrats." This new modern age was characterized by the "decreasing importance of government for the vast majority of the Chinese people, accompanied by the increasing importance of culture" (Fogel, 1984). As part of this process Naitō saw the shift that we have noted from government by an oligarchy of aristocratic clans to government by a stronger imperial-dynastic clan through a trained and examined bureaucracy and local gentry-elite. Removed from daily informal contact with his old oligarchic colleagues, the emperor became more autocratic. "The result," as Denis Twitchett (in *CHOC* 3) puts it, "was a growing gulf both between the emperor and society and between the emperor and the officials through whom he ruled." Naitō's thesis, he adds, "has stood up remarkably well to the progress of modern research." Yet it does not deal in particular with the enormous drama of the Song efflorescence and the nomadic conquests that helped check it. An updated appreciation of China's spectacular growth under the Song and Yuan dynasties and of factors that eventually stunted it seems overdue.

A theory seems to me to emerge from the works of many scholars when surveyed and connected by a single observer. Others have expressed much the same thing in somewhat different terms. The hypothesis may be stated as follows: (1) that early China created a *politicized* state organized for purposes of central control both by bureaucratic methods of philosophic persuasion and by the imperial autocrat's use of violence; (2) that non-Chinese invaders from Inner Asia became integral *participants* in the Chinese polity by their military prowess and administrative skill; and (3) that the resulting Sino-nomadic imperial power continued to maintain the primacy of central *political control* over the subordinated processes of economic growth and cultural diversification.

In short, from the very beginning, the non-Chinese invaders helped maintain the political domination over economic and cultural life that had been inherited from ancient China. Politics was still (or especially) in command. The propensity for control above all was reinforced by the Neo-Confucian ideology that stressed loyalty to authority in a hierarchic social order and esteemed agricultural self-sufficiency over the less controllable growth of trade and foreign contact. Yet along with this persistent and increasing autocracy in government went the attendant trend mentioned above, "the increasing importance of culture" for the Chinese people. In other words, we are discussing here two levels: the state and the society lying beneath it.

Thus Naitō's second point about the diminished role of government and increased role of culture in local society is borne out by the formation of gentry society outlined above. This growth at the local level, however, left the emperor and court at his higher level still autocratic.

The influence on China of the great fact of alien conquest under the Liao–Jin–Yuan dynasties is just beginning to be explored. Its economic impact seems still uncertain. Certainly it was traumatic and probably, over all, a tremendous psychological disaster. Its effect on Ming China soon became quite obvious.

6

Government in the Ming Dynasty

Legacies of the Hongwu Emperor

During the 276 years of the Ming from 1368 to 1644 China's population doubled, from about 80 million to about 160 million. Destructive domestic warfare was largely avoided, and great achievements in education and philosophy, literature and art, reflected the high cultural level of the elite gentry society. But the Yuan-to-Ming transition was not very promising. The Ming regime was first militarized to drive out and hold off the Mongols and subsequently tried to maintain domestic stability and avoid influence from outside China. The Chinese resurgence that threw out the Mongol conquerors did not attempt a continuation of the Song but tried in theory to go back to the models of Han and Tang, all the while in fact continuing certain features of the Yuan.

The character of the Ming dynasty began with the mentality of the dynastic founder, Zhu Yuanzhang, who reigned as the Hongwu ("Vast Military") Emperor from 1368 to 1398. He was a peasant who had starved and begged as a boy, got his literacy from Buddhist priests, and joined an anti-Mongol religious sect. Rising as a rebel warlord, he bested his competitors in violence in the lower Yangzi region, got Confucian scholars' help in issuing pronouncements and performing rituals to claim the Mandate, drove out the fissiparous Mongol princes in 1368, and built a great capital at Nanjing (see Map 17).

The personality of this new autocrat, though extolled like that of any dynastic founder, on balance seems to have been a disaster for China. Ugly to look at, Hongwu was fiercely energetic, had violent fits of temper, and became paranoidally suspicious of conspiracies against himself. Frederick Mote (in *CHOC* 7) observes that many peculiarities of Ming rule stemmed "from the personal characteristics of this strange and powerful man."

Hongwu's aim was to maintain centralized control over the world's largest and most diversified state. To this end he issued a flood of admonitions and regulations to guide his subjects' conduct—law codes, commandments, ancestral instructions, a series of grand pronouncements, village and government statutes, and ceremonial regulations. As Edward Farmer says, these codes constituted a blueprint of the ideal social order and included sanctions to back it up. Hongwu was less a militarist than an ideologue, full of ideas.

When it came to practical action, Hongwu from his own experience understood the plight of the farming villages and used the repertoire of statecraft devices to hold down the land tax, to plant trees against erosion, to maintain the dikes on the Yellow and Yangzi Rivers, to keep the granaries stocked against famine, to support mutual-responsibility systems to suppress banditry and encourage the gentry to succor the needy. But his economic vision was limited to the conventional Confucian view of agriculture as the source of the country's wealth, trade as ignoble and parasitic, and frugality as the prime imperial virtue. His government tried to foster self-sufficient communities and so to have the populace police themselves, the army to feed itself, and the rural populace to provide the corvée labor for local roads and yamen services. His frugality extended to paying officials purely nominal salaries so that they had to maintain their establishments by nonstatutory fees. Thus Hongwu's version of no-new-taxes led inevitably to corruption.

Hongwu's main concern, however, was military. Because China had to prevent a Mongol resurgence, he copied the Yuan military system, establishing Chinese garrisons at strategic points and creating a hereditary military caste of soldiers who would sustain themselves by farming but be ever ready for war. Where the Mongol princes had formed a scattered nobility with big estates, Hongwu now made his commanders into a Chinese military nobility with ranks and emoluments superior to those of the top civil officials—at least until he suspected them of treason and killed a great number.

When required to choose between *wen* and *wu*—the civil and military complexes in imperial government—Hongwu was on the side of violence despite all the laws and moral homilies that he put out. Finding his prime minister plotting against him in 1380, he had him beheaded, along with everyone in his family or remotely connected, which totaled over the years about 40,000 persons. *(Guanxi* networks have their dangers!) Continued beheading of officials and several later purges may have swelled this total to 100,000 victims. The resulting loss of talent and reign of terror hardly allowed Confucian government to prosper. Beating (flogging with large or small bamboo staves) for punishment and humiliation in open court became a regular feature of Ming terrorism. The victim was held prone by men at his hands and feet and his bare buttocks were bastinaded while the prescribed blows were counted one by one. No ritual could have been more demeaning or life-threatening, for the skin was soon broken and infection of bloody tissue was hard to avoid. In 1519, for recommending that the emperor not continue to stay in the south away from his duties, 146 men were beaten, 11 of whom died. In 1524 officials objected to imperial honors for the emperor's mother and father because he had inherited the throne from his cousin: 134 were beaten and 16 died. One gets the impression that the emperor and his bureaucrats were often locked in an institutional struggle that imperial violence could not resolve.

Hongwu's mistakes of judgment can be traced in general to his all-consuming determination to assert and maintain his personal control. Thus Hongwu's obsession to hold central power (an imperative inherited from history) led him in 1380 to abolish the central secretariat and prime ministership so that he as emperor would be the civil and military CEO of the realm. This gave him control but also an extraordinary burden. One top specialist on Ming administration, Charles Hucker, notes that in one eight-day period Hongwu received 1,600 dispatches (called memorials) in which 3,391 issues were presented. At the rate of 200 documents in a 10-hour day, each document could get on average three minutes' consideration. In previous regimes day-to-day administration had been handled by a prime minister (or chancellor) with a staff. In the Ming and Qing governments this burden now fell upon the emperors. Since not all of them were supermen, the imperial office often became a bottleneck, and the government more easily sank into inefficient routine.

In abolishing the prime minister's office and secretariat, Hongwu had decapitated the civil bureaucracy. Its echelons of personnel and paper work had been headed by the prime minister as the top official of the Outer Court (the six ministries, censorate, and other offices at the capital). This meant that the Ming emperors had to govern through their personal entourages (the Inner Court), which led to reliance on eunuchs in administration as well as in military and other special matters. Eventually the court would have 70,000 eunuchs.

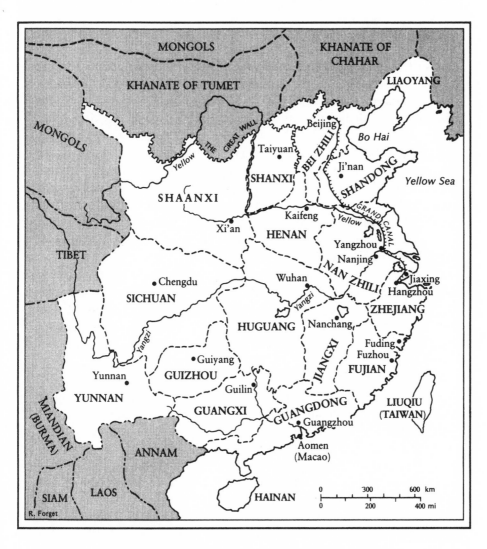

17. The Ming Empire at Its Greatest Extent

Fiscal Problems

The most glaring inadequacies in Hongwu's legacy, from the viewpoint of a fiscal historian like Ray Huang (1974), were in finance. To begin with, there was no separation between the government's funds and the emperor's. The third emperor Yongle (1402–1424) usurped the throne in a civil war and moved the capital to Beijing because that was his area of personal strength and also the strategic point for keeping the Mongols in check. In the Imperial City that surrounded the Forbidden City (palace complex) in Beijing was a three-square-mile area where more than 50 service offices or supply shops employed about 100,000 artisans and others to meet the needs of the imperial household, without any distinction between public and private functions. This accorded with the fact that the emperor's personal life and ceremonial conduct were a key part of the state's activity and subject to the scrutiny and comment of Confucian scholar-moralists in many ways.

Under eunuch management, palace expenditures went up without reason. So did the cost of the emperor's personal troops, the Embroidered-uniform Guard, who acted not only as bodyguards but also as special police and ran a fearsome prison for political offenders' "special treatment." The Guard began in 1382 with about 16,000 men but eventually grew to 75,000.

Hongwu himself, whatever his court and heirs may have done, aimed at extreme frugality. He set the land tax at about 10 percent of the agricultural product, not an onerous rate. By this seemingly benevolent lightness of taxation, he starved his government of revenue. From a modern point of view this prevented its performing service functions that could have helped the economic life of the people. In place of the government he expected local communities to make all sorts of private outlays in connection with tax payments. For control and tax purposes, the peasantry were organized from 1381 in registered groups of 110 households in a system known as *lijia*. Each year ten households headed by one leading household took responsibility for superintending tax payments and labor services (corvée) of the whole group. They also updated the official Yellow Registers of all lands and families. These duties rotated year by year for ten years and then began again in a self-perpetuating cycle.

This ingenious arrangement shared with similar inventions, like the *baojia* mutual surveillance and security system, a major drawback. It was a blueprint to show the masses how to perform the many kinds of duties devised for them by scholar-administrators; but its details left little room for alterations. When the system had to be adjusted to the realities of terrain and personal relations in village life, abuses kept creeping in so that in no long time it was riddled with corruption. As examples of this disastrous syndrome, let us look at taxation, army maintenance, and the provision of currency, all of which became sooner or later inadequate. Underlying all these problems was the freezing of government structure and institutions in the rigid mold decreed by the founder, so that the Ming administration was eventually unable to adjust them to China's changing needs.

In taxation, first of all, to obviate the burden of conveying to Beijing the revenues from localities all over the empire, transfers were arranged to move income directly from a specific revenue source to an authorized expenditure. The result was a complex criss-crossing network of automatic or at least statutory income and outgo, that hardened into inflexible precedent yet could not be policed against corruption because it was not kept in view by any one official. Ray Huang concludes that the major concern in the Ming fiscal system "was always governmental stability." Because every fiscal office had to get its revenue from innumerable different sources, the local officials could not assert their independence or improve the quality of their administration. No financial base was ever developed adequate to sustain a rebellion. "The empire's fiscal operations were so fragmented as to make them virtually safe from capture."

This fragmentation of revenue and expenditure left the central government impotent. A vast panoply of yamen runners, clerks, and other subofficial persons was almost constantly engaged in collecting the many kinds of taxes at the various times they were alleged to be due during the year. Since the land tax in its total amount was not inordinately burdensome to the economy, the real burden was the inefficiency of collection and the overstaffing of collecting agencies. In other words, millions of middlemen lived off the revenue system by participating in its cumbersome processes.

For example, there was no budget item to finance the maintenance of the Grand Canal. It was maintained by local corvée labor without any financing from the central government. By the mid-fifteenth century there were 11,775 grain boats handled by 121,500 officers and troops, who were supposed to receive their pay from their army rations. Since these transportation troops were seldom paid, they had to rely on carrying private cargo in their grain barges. In general, since every item of revenue had been listed before received as an expected payment, and the standing orders for delivery led to nominal disbursal before funds were collected, there was no flexibility possible. Any calamity like a flood required crisis management to raise special funds.

Second, the Ming records praising the self-sufficiency of the military in farming for their own food supply are unreliable. Ray Huang says that the army nowhere near paid for itself. The record stated the ideal, not the facts: Military officials kept no records, and Ming historians wanted to make the dynasty look good. The whole military farming program was a blueprint put out with no preparation, research, or experimentation to guide it. No control agency was set up, and administration was very lax. Households were pressed into military service but frequently deserted. Soldiers did not receive regular pay but only occasional unscheduled awards. The system merely turned soldiers back into farmers. The military establishment declined because its rations were cut. Soldiers therefore sold or mortgaged their land. The army went more and more unpaid, and its ranks were thinned by desertion. Military units shrank in size down to about 10 percent except on the frontiers, where the army had to be supplied. But since the unrealistic legend of a self-sufficient army still persisted, its financing methods could not be abolished or reorganized.

Third, the currency system was a failure, quite unable to keep up with the growth of trade. At first the government relied on paper currency, but Hongwu was unaware that unlimited paper money produces inflation, so he kept on handing out paper currency as awards. By 1425 the paper notes had only 1/40 to 1/70 of their original value. In the end, paper currency went out of use. Meanwhile, the government forbade the use of silver.

China's copper coins were made by casting, not stamping, and all had to be trimmed by hand. The Ming produced far fewer coins than the Song, although the demand was much greater. Often the government minted no new coins at all, and private counterfeiters filled the vacuum. The job of minting was then given to the provinces. But when producers used some lead in the mixture they lowered the coins' value. There continued to be a great coin shortage. Government failure to do a proper minting job led to most coins' being counterfeit, and their value declined to 6,000 to 1 tael of silver as opposed to the old standard of 1,000 to 1 tael. In short, the Ming government signally failed to provide a copper coinage for the use of the people, just at the time when growth of trade was increasing the need for money.

During the sixteenth century, the growth of foreign trade led to a sporadic but massive importation of silver especially from Japan and by various routes from the New World. As a result, China's original commodity economy became monetized. Payments to government in goods and services under the reform trend known as the Single Whip were gradually combined and commuted into money payments. The *lijia* tax payments demanded from local residents were gradually absorbed into the land tax even when preserved in the accounts. In doing their *lijia* labor service, instead of working on the roads or other public works, those who could would hire substitutes. Finally, they simply made money payments instead of performing services.

Unfortunately, the inflow of Japanese and New World silver did not give China a silver currency. Both copper cash and silver bullion were used in what amounted to a sort of bimetallic system. Local day-to-day transactions among the people used copper cash, though the government could seldom refrain from debasing it. But it was not possible to maintain a minted currency of fixed value in silver because the Ming never tried to mint silver dollars. Tax payment in raw bullion was not planned but merely resorted to out of necessity in the failure of all other currencies. In the clumsy circulation of pure lump silver, the unit of account (the ounce or tael) varied from place to place and also as between trades and between agencies of government. Twenty different silver tael units of account might be in common use in one city at one time, requiring a different "currency" for each major commodity, like salt or cotton cloth, and for payments going to certain other places. Each ingot had to be weighed and also assayed for its purity. The resulting multiplicity of silver tael units, and exchange arrangements among them, represented the domination of the money manipulator, who profited by this complexity, over any investor who wanted to put his money into planned productive enterprises.

The fiscal establishment seems to have followed the founder's strong sense of frugality because of his conviction that profit was in itself evil. Mercantile interests were felt to be inherently in conflict with those of society and the state and had to be curbed as far as possible. At the same time the state had to refrain from "enriching itself" because any gain to the government, in this naive view, automatically meant a loss to the people. The government failed to develop its potential economic power and resorted instead to political control as its basis of governing. It thus persistently neglected to build up the minimum financial strength required to operate its fiscal machinery. It neglected to invest even in trans-

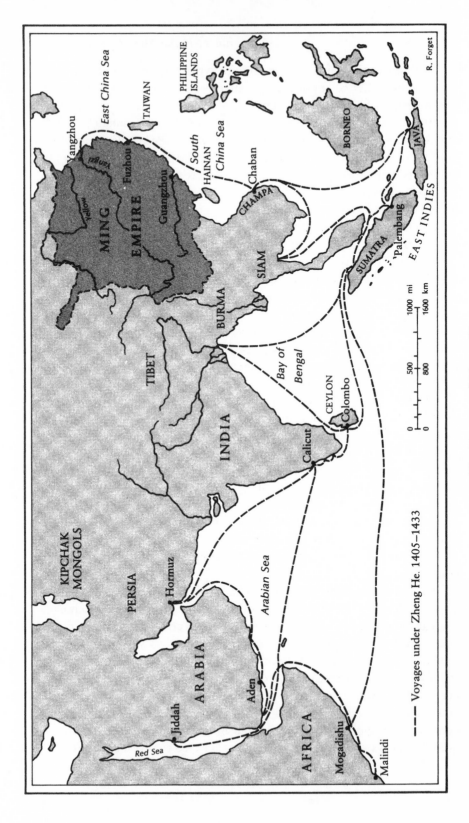

18. The Voyages of Zheng He

portation facilities for the public. In this niggardly situation the extensive commandeering of services from the general population was unavoidable.

Overall, says Ray Huang, when certain sectors of China showed a tendency to grow through industry or foreign trade, the Ming government saw no reason to help them but rather opposed such a growth of imbalance which "in turn would threaten the empire's political unity." It was better to keep all the provinces on the same level as the more backward sectors.

Huang concludes that both Song and Yuan were more sophisticated and showed a higher quality of administration than the Ming. "The T'ang, the Sung and the Yuan never imposed such a rigid fiscal structure as did the Ming" nor did their top government officers assume so little operational responsibility. "The Ming system represents a significant break in Chinese fiscal history. From this time onwards the main aim of governmental finance was to maintain the political status quo and it ceased to exhibit any dynamic qualities." In keeping with this dictum was the spectacular Ming withdrawal from the maritime world.

China Turns Inward

Southern Song and Yuan had seen a great advance in Chinese shipbuilding, nautical technology, and maritime trade to Japan and Southeast and South Asia. By 1400 the countries in sea trade with Ming China had been known for hundreds of years, while Chinese merchant shipping had been exporting silk, porcelain, and copper coins. Concurrently with his five military expeditions north against the Mongols, the Yongle Emperor ordered the Grand Eunuch Zheng He to mount naval expeditions on the routes of trade to the south of China. Zheng He was a Muslim originally surnamed Ma, whose father had made the pilgrimage to Mecca. He led a can-do group of eunuchs whom the emperor commissioned to perform special tasks.

Zheng He's seven voyages between 1405 and 1433 were no small affairs (see Map 18). The shipyards near Nanjing from 1403 to 1419 alone built 2,000 vessels, including almost a hundred big "treasure ships" 370 to 440 feet in length and 150 to 180 feet abeam. J. V. G. Mills (1970) estimates they must have displaced about 3,000 tons apiece. With four to nine masts up to 90 feet high, a dozen water-tight compartments, and stern-post rudders, they could have as many as 50 cabins and carry 450 to 500 men. The fleet of the first voyage of 1405—

1407 set out with an estimated 317 vessels, of which 62 were treasure ships. (The Spanish Armada of 1588 would total 132 vessels.) Zheng He was accompanied by a staff of 70 eunuchs, 180 medical personnel, 5 astrologers, and 300 military officers, who commanded a force of 26,800 men. The first three voyages visited India and many ports en route. The fourth went beyond India to Hormuz, and the last three visited ports on the east coast of Africa, as far south as Malindi (near Mombasa), where Song porcelains and copper coins had long preceded them. Detachments of the fleet made special side trips, one of them to Mecca. As one major function Zheng He carried tribute envoys to China and back home again. He conducted some trade but mainly engaged in extensive diplomatic relations with about 30 countries. Though seldom violently aggressive, he did fight some battles.

Three points are worth noting. First, these official expeditions were not voyages of exploration in the Vasco da Gaman or Columbian sense. They followed established routes of Arab and Chinese trade in the seas east of Africa. Second, the Chinese expeditions were diplomatic, not commercial, much less piratical or colonizing ventures. They exchanged gifts, enrolled tributaries, and brought back geographic information and scientific curiosities like giraffes, which were touted as auspicious unicorns. Third and most striking, once these voyages ceased in 1433 they were never followed up. Instead, the records of them were destroyed by the vice-president of the War Ministry about 1479 and Chinese overseas commerce was severely restricted until 1567. In the great age of sail that was just dawning around the globe, Ming China was potentially far in the lead but refused to go on. It took the Europeans almost another half century even to get started. After 1433 it would be another 37 years before Portuguese explorers on the west coast of Africa got as far south as the Gold Coast, and 59 years before Columbus set sail with three small vessels totaling 450 tons.

Edward Dreyer describes how the great Chinese voyages were stopped by Confucian-trained scholar-officials who opposed trade and foreign contact on principle. Ray Huang stresses the regime's fiscal crisis that made funds really unavailable for these very costly ventures. For example, the Ming intervention in North Vietnam in 1407 had been repulsed by 1428 at considerable cost to the Chinese court, which had to recognize Vietnam as an independent tributary state in 1431. The officials at Beijing were also jealous of the eunuch power that the Yongle Emperor was using in military and security channels to counter the growing hold of the classical examination graduates upon the Ming government.

By mid-century Beijing also faced a revival of Mongol power and border raids. In 1449 a sycophantic chief eunuch took the emperor out to chastise the Mongols. Instead, the Mongols captured him. When the Mongols approached Beijing to trade him in a deal, a new emperor was quickly installed. Ming policy became transfixed by the Mongol menace. Arthur Waldron (1990) has traced the interminable policy discussions among officials who generally feared to attack the Mongols yet refused to let them trade with China so as to reduce their raiding. After 1474 and during the sixteenth century the building of brick-and-stone-faced long walls with their many hundreds of watchtowers created today's Great Wall (see Map 17). It proved to be a futile military gesture but vividly expressed China's siege mentality.

The decline of Ming naval power, once shipbuilding was restricted to small-size vessels, opened the door to a growth of piracy on the South China coast, ostensibly by Japanese but in fact mainly by Chinese. Instead of counterattacking, the Ming forced a costly Chinese withdrawal from the seacoast, vainly aimed at starving out the pirates. This defensive posture included restricting foreign trade by demanding that it all be in the guise of tributary trade. Sarasin Viraphol (1977) describes how the import of Siamese rice by Sino-Siamese merchants had to be conducted as if it were connected with tribute missions. The tribute system reached its high point under the Ming as a form of defense connoting not power but weakness.

In short, anticommercialism and xenophobia won out, and China retired from the world scene. The military declined and bureaucrats ran the show except when the big eunuch establishment, handling surveillance and investigation for the emperor, produced from time to time, under weak rulers, eunuch dictatorships that terrorized the scholars. The contradiction between Ming China's superior capacity for maritime expansion and conservative Neo-Confucian throttling of it suggests that Ming China almost purposely missed the boat of modern technological and economic development.

This disparaging judgment comes out of the context of the late twentieth century, when technology and growth have created innumerable disorders in all aspects of life all over the world without disclosing as yet the principles of order that may postpone the destruction of human civilization. In time the self-contained growth of Ming China with its comparative peace and well-being may be admired by historians, who may see a sort of success where today we see failure.

Factional Politics

In the domain of literati thinking, the ideas of the statesman-philosopher Wang Yangming (Wang Shouren, 1472–1529) gained many adherents and inspired scholars to follow a new bent in Neo-Confucianism. Wang was a very competent scholar-official and general who suppressed rebellions over a number of years and also devoted himself to building up the local community through the use of the Community Compact *(xiang-yue)*. This institution was one of Confucianism's closest approaches to revivalism. As a philosopher, Wang pursued the idea of Zhu Xi's contemporary, Lu Xiangshan, in developing a less practice-centered and more contemplative approach to moral training and self-cultivation. Wang taught that the world of principle is a unity and lies within as well as outside one. Therefore, one should learn to be guided by intuitive knowledge achieved through careful thought and meditation. This had Buddhist overtones. Wang's famous insistence on the unity of theory and practice really demanded, as Willard J. Peterson (1979) notes, "the unity of *moral* knowledge and *social* action." Wang Yangming's teaching had wide influence in Japan as well as in China.

After the Ming collapse, Qing critics would later decry Wang's influence as too abstract, passive, and individual-centered. This contributed to the view that Ming learning had fostered a righteous morality over practical technology. Neo-Confucian classical training in the schools of both Zhu Xi and Wang Yangming taught Ming officials to assert that ethical conduct was the root of good government, while technology was a matter for craftsmen and inferiors.

This stress on moral principles in turn provided the stuff of factional attacks between rival groups of scholar-officials. Factionalism thus inspired the moral homilies of bureaucrats, who criticized the emperor's errant ways or combatted the sinister eunuch influence. The most notorious of many cases began under the Wanli Emperor's reign of 48 years (1573–1620).

In the first decade of this reign, the senior grand secretary (Zhang Juzheng) with great determination enforced austerity and accumulated funds in the central treasuries. He was not afraid to step on toes and attack sinecures, providing he always had the emperor's approval. He did not aim at reform but at making the regime solvent. However, his methods cut corners and flouted conventions. After he died, his high-handed ways were condemned in retrospect.

The Wanli Emperor then became so disenchanted with the moralistic attacks and counterattacks of officials that he was thoroughly alienated from his imperial role. He finally resorted to vengeful tactics of blocking or ignoring the conduct of administration. For years on end he refused to see his ministers or act upon memorials. He refused to make necessary appointments. The whole top echelon of Ming administration became understaffed. In short, Wanli tried to forget about his imperial responsibility while squirreling away what he could for his private purse. Considering the emperor's required role as the kingpin of the state, this personal rebellion against the bureaucracy was not only bankruptcy but treason.

The malfeasance of Wanli and the corruption of powerful eunuchs helped inspire a new level of factionalism in the Lower Yangzi provinces. They produced more than their proportion both of land tax revenues for the court and of prominent officials. Eventually a reform movement centered in the Donglin ("eastern forest") Academy near Wuxi, where a group of these generally high-minded Confucian scholars exhibited a preoccupation with morality that lent animus to their attacks on officials high and low. The practical problems of government were seldom in their sights, but Confucian principles were extolled as absolutes and their targets in the administration were damned accordingly. It has become difficult to say what group had the better of the argument because it concerned ethical demands and personal vituperation more than the practical problems of administration. In the 1620s the eunuch dictator who came into power after the death of Wanli terrorized the Donglin scholars with great violence, though some of them survived to have the last word against him. The factionalism of the late Ming led to divided counsels and imperial inaction just when the dynasty needed vigorous leadership.

By the early 1600s the Dutch and British East India Companies, added to the Portuguese and Spanish trade already under way, were responding to the activity of Japanese and Chinese merchants and officials in a lively international commerce. Within China, large-scale production of ceramics, silk, and cotton cloth accompanied the spread of trade in salt and cereals, the growth of cities, and of a more affluent merchant class engaged in interregional trade. The flow of silver into China was only one factor in this growth. A number of historians point to late Ming achievements in literature, art, and urban life as harbingers of a dynamic renewal in society and culture as well as in the economy. But commerce and Western contact threatened to upset the political order. The Japanese in the early 1600s in decisive fashion closed their country to Western merchants and missionaries. In China a new dynasty supplanted the Ming but inherited their anxiety about foreign trade and Western contact. China's late Ming renewal seems to have been frustrated.

7

The Qing Success Story

The Manchu Conquest

The Manchu conquest of 1644 showed once again that taking over China might be easier from outside than from inside because the essential mixture of militarism and civil administration, *wu* and *wen*, could be put together outside the Wall more readily than within it. Geography was the key to this opportunity. Manchuria in the sixteenth century had been brought under the Chinese type of intensive agriculture only in the southernmost region below Mukden (modern Shenyang). The Ming had recognized the frontier nature of this region by organizing it in military districts rather than under a civil administration only. By establishing hereditary and registered military units at strategic points, separate from the civil administration of the agricultural area, the Ming sought to maintain both a military buffer against nomadic inroads and a check upon any separatist tendencies of local Chinese officials; for they could not overlook the fact that South Manchuria was a hostage to fortune that could be cut off from North China at the bottleneck of Shanhaiguan, where the Great Wall escarpment comes to the sea (see Map 19).

In their rise to power the Manchus took full advantage of their strategic position on a frontier where they could learn Chinese ways and yet not be entirely subjected to Chinese rule. The founder of the state, Nurgaci (1559–1626), began as a minor chieftain on the eastern border of the agricultural basin of South Manchuria. The people he came to lead were a mixed lot but mainly descendants of the seminomadic Ruzhen tribes who had established their Jin dynasty in North China in the twelfth century. Like Chinggis among the Mongols, Nurgaci brought adjoining tribes under his personal rule and early in the seventeenth century set up his Later Jin dynasty, with its capital at Mukden. His son and successor, the very able Hong Taiji (Manchu name Abahai), subjugated Korea on the east and made alliances with the Mongol tribes on the west in Inner Mongolia. In 1636 he gave the name Manchu to his people and proclaimed the Qing ("Pure") dynasty. Meanwhile, a written Manchu language had been developed and some of the Chinese classics translated into it.

By 1644 the Manchus had made several incursions into North China but had not yet been able to defeat the Ming. The Ming regime in China had grown progressively weaker. Rebellion was already endemic. A Chinese rebel named Li Zicheng had raided widely in Northwest China and even into Sichuan and the Yangzi valley. He had finally secured literate advisers and begun to set up a framework of dynastic government. In 1644 he succeeded in capturing Beijing and had the dynastic succession

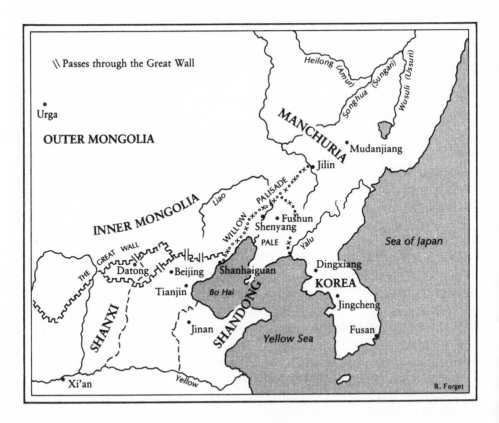

19. Rise of the Manchus

within his grasp. But he proved unable to consolidate institutionally the position that he had won by force.

The Ming military in North and Northeast China had meanwhile become thoroughly disaffected toward the still squabbling literati-officials at the capital, who came mainly from the Lower Yangzi. Through their predominance in the examinations, the landed families of this east-central region were heavily represented in the Beijing government but manifested few warlike capacities. Able Ming commanders were well acquainted with the Manchu striking power, yet as the Ming forces in North China still outnumbered them, some hoped the Manchus could be used within the Wall. This led the Ming general Wu Sangui and several of his colleagues to welcome the Manchus, whom they had been fighting, to come into North China and help suppress the rebels in Beijing. The Manchus, once inside the Wall, proceeded to take over.

Studies of this turbulent period by Frederic Wakeman, Jr. (1985), and Lynn Struve (1984) among others point up the very different concerns animating the Lower Yangzi landed families and the Ming commanders in North China. Between them the Manchus found their opening. In vigorous campaigns they destroyed the rebels in the north and then took over the Lower Yangzi heartland. They made use of Confucian rituals and precedents and showed also a capacity for imperial ruthlessness. For example, the Ming holdouts at Yangzhou on the Grand Canal were massacred in a ten-day orgy that sent a message to all adjoining areas. Ming officials and commanders faced the severe choice between disloyalty and death. When the wife of one Ming official heard in 1621 that the Manchus had captured him, she assumed he would die rather than shift his loyalty and so she led 42 "household retainers and relatives" into suicide. The more practical-minded husband, however, had decided the Mandate had passed, and he had surrendered to serve the Manchus. When in 1677 his grandson, a high Qing official, refused to surrender to the anti-Qing rebels and was killed, his wife led 38 members of his household in suicides that "went on through the night." With such loyalty from Chinese officials (and their wives), the Manchus could govern the empire. Some Ming officials chose death, but some became high administrators for the Manchus and helped smooth the takeover.

Though the Manchus seized Beijing in 1644, their conquest of China remained incomplete for a whole generation. Three of their Chinese collaborators, General Wu Sangui and two others, took over large satrapies in South and Southwest China and entrenched themselves in territorial power. In 1673 these so-called three feudatories rebelled and took over most of the southern provinces. The young Kangxi Emperor, just starting to rule, needed eight years to reestablish Qing control. His rich Lower Yangzi base was of help. So also was the feeling of loyalty to the Qing. Wu Sangui, after all, had been twice disloyal, both to the Ming and to the Qing.

The efficiency of Sino-barbarian rule was quickly proven. Destruction at the end of the Ming was mainly due to Chinese rebellions, particularly the one led by Zhang Xianzhong, which significantly lowered the population of Sichuan. Both Zhang and his competitor Li in the northwest tried in vain to enlist the help of scholars and set up a dynastic-style regime. Both failed. The Manchu success where Chinese rebels had failed was essentially an achievement in the creation of political institutions.

Institutional Adaptation

The Manchus' first problem had been to develop beyond the state of tribal politics. This they did by creating from about 1601 a unified territorial administration over their lands, paralleled by a military organization of all the Manchu fighting men in eight divisions, each with a different flag or banner. The Manchu bannermen had lands assigned to them, but these lands were kept scattered, and the banners did not become territorial units. Mongols and Chinese who came over to the Manchus were taken into the system and organized in their own banner units. The resulting 24 banners were all fighting men personally attached to the emperor. Pamela Crossley (1990) has traced their origin to the Turkic-Mongolian institution of hereditary military servitude. The emperor was not their father in Confucian style but rather their owner in the nomad style. The bannermen enjoyed booty in warfare and stipends of rice and cash in peacetime. They cherished their highly ritualized slavery as "an emblem of their importance to and intimacy with the court." It called forth their loyalty in the highest degree. Witness the fact that about 150,000 invincible bannermen (only 169,000 were even listed on paper at the time) took over Ming China, albeit helped by Chinese collaborators.

Although the banner organization was advertised as multiethnic, Chinese bannermen actually made up three quarters of the total in 1648, while 8 percent were Mongols and only 16 percent Manchus. By 1723 the Manchu component rose to 23 percent, still far from one third of the total. In any case, bannermen (as well as Chinese bondservants) were a great improvement on eunuchs as trustworthy servitors of the emperor and adjuncts of the Inner Court. They formed a talent pool from which individuals could be chosen to function as civil bureaucrats. Nurgaci had appointed his sons to head the banners, but their power was brought under central control in a state council. In this way the originally personal relations between the head of the state and his loyal chieftains and tribesmen were institutionalized.

Finally, the early Manchu rulers, like the Jin and Yuan emperors before them, took over the terminology, forms, and ideas of Confucianism and used them, as they were meant to be used, for the support and maintenance of political authority. They promoted study of the classics and the veneration of ancestors, set up the state cult of Confucius, talked and wrote of the "way of the ruler" (like the Japanese in Manchukuo three centuries later), extolled the Confucian virtues, and accepted the idea that the ruler rules by virtue of his moral goodness.

More than a decade before the Manchus' entrance into China, they had created in Mukden a miniature civil administration in imitation of Beijing. The Six Ministries and other elements typical of Ming government were formally established and staffed by a bureaucracy in which Manchus, Mongols, and Chinese were represented. By the time they entered North China and assumed the Mandate of Heaven they were fully prepared to solve their fundamental problem, how to rule in the Chinese way but maintain their identity as Manchus.

Several circumstances aided them. Unlike the Mongols, they had no vast empire to the west to distract them from the all-important problem of China. Having come from the frontier of South Manchuria, rather than from the Mongolian steppe, they did not have to leap the great cultural gap between the steppe and the sown. Because of the unusually long and vigorous sixty-year reigns of two early emperors, three rulers during 133 years provided a strong executive leadership: the Kangxi Emperor (reigned 1662–1722), Yongzheng (1722–1736), and Qianlong (reigned 1736–1796). They were all hard-working and conscientious sovereigns who commonly saw their ministers every day at dawn, studied the classics assiduously, and maintained a vigorous personal rule.

The various devices by which the Manchus sought to preserve their dynastic vitality and identity are an interesting study. By spending summers in Inner Mongolia, the Manchu emperors set a quite un-Confucian example of physical fitness for riding, hunting, and shooting. They closed their homeland to Chinese immigration and maintained North

Manchuria as a hunting land outside the Chinese agricultural economy. To check Chinese immigration from South Manchuria northward, they reinforced a willow palisade several hundred miles long (a big ditch with willows planted along it) to mark the boundary beyond which the Chinese should not expand (see Map 19). They organized Manchuria under a Manchu military government. North of the Chinese pale in the south, Manchuria remained a sparsely populated vacuum down to the late eighteenth century—a tempting prize for Russian and Japanese imperialists later.

The Manchus also sought to preserve themselves by maintaining their racial purity. They banned intermarriage between Chinese and Manchus and fostered differences of custom between the two groups. Manchu women, for example, did not bind their feet (see Chapter 8). Manchus were not supposed to engage in trade or labor. The Manchu clan organization was preserved by their shamanistic religious system.

Manchu military control of China was maintained by the establishment of banner garrisons at strategic points. The only Chinese troops given a recognized existence were provincial forces that were used mainly as a constabulary on the post routes and against bandits but which lacked any training as a striking force.

In order to preserve strong leadership, the early Manchu emperors arranged that the imperial princes should be pensioned and given wealth but not allowed to become territorial lords. They were kept at Beijing out of power. Until 1860 the dynasty avoided government by empresses and by eunuchs, which had resulted so often in previous dynasties in palace intrigue.

In the civil administration of China the Manchus used a system of dual appointments, whereby both Chinese and Manchus were placed in charge of important functions. Jonathan Spence (1990) has shown how at first they relied on Chinese allies from South Manchuria who had been enrolled usually as Chinese bannermen or bondservants, especially dependent upon and loyal to the Manchu rulers. Eventually the formula was to have capable Chinese do the work and loyal Manchus check up on them. At the capital Manchus outnumbered Chinese, but in the provinces Chinese officials far predominated. In order to draw into their service the most able and promising Chinese, the Manchus saw to it that the examination system continued to function with highest prestige and efficiency.

The devices of synarchy (joint administration by two or more parties) were fully used, not only by having Mongol and Chinese banners within the banner system but also by dual administration through joint Chinese and Manchu presidents of the Six Ministries at the capital (hence called Boards by Westerners) and the pairing in the provinces of Manchu and Chinese governors-general and governors. Often a Manchu governor-general was in charge of two provinces that were each under a Chinese governor. These high officials reported jointly to the emperor direct while in each province the central organization sent its routine reports to the Six Boards at the capital. The censors in 15 different circuits as well as at the capital continued to investigate and report on official conduct. Censorial remonstrances might also be presented (not often) directly to the emperor.

As part of their system of control the Manchu rulers tried to preserve the Manchu language and followed the Qidan, Ruzhen, and Mongol examples in creating a Manchu documentation that was generally unavailable to Chinese officials. Most important was the Imperial Household Department, which had its own treasury and was staffed by the emperor's bannermen and bondservants. As a secret echelon of government parallel to the formal ministries at Beijing, it collected enormous revenues from lands, trade monopolies (including the antigeriatric root from the northeast called ginseng), customs taxes (including the Guangzhou trade), the salt gabelle, silk textile manufactories, loans, fines, and tributes. All this helped the dynasty to profit from the growth of trade and industry. While this inner government began as a device to keep the palace eunuchs under control, to obviate their inveterate corruption, in due time it became corrupt itself. Yet in this way the Qing rulers preserved under their own immediate control large resources beyond the reach of the civil administration.

The Qing established control in Inner Asia by first organizing the Mongols in the Ming fashion under separate leagues and with assigned pasturage. This immobilized and divided the Mongols beyond hope of unification under a new Chinggis Khan. The Qing also supported the Yellow Lamaist sect of Tibetan Buddhism, which had spread among the Mongols and oriented them toward Lhasa. These arrangements in Inner Asia were under a special Ministry of Dependencies, Lifan Yuan, while the Board of Rites continued to handle the tribute missions arriving from contiguous areas like Korea and Vietnam and also arriving from foreign countries by sea.

The Manchus attempted no social revolution. They slaughtered those who resisted but confirmed the status of Chinese gentry families if they accepted Qing rule. The most visible evidence of this, required from all male Chinese, was the distinctive Manchu tonsure—keeping their foreheads shaved and braiding their back hair in a queue. The Qing also had perforce to accept the inadequacies of the Ming government: its fiscal weakness due to a tax structure that collected less than five percent of the gross national product, and its anticommercialism—for instance, the inefficient use of pure silver exchanged in a great variety of units of account (taels or ounces). As Inner Asians themselves, the Manchus also shared the Ming lack of interest in maritime trade and relations.

In his reign from 1722 to 1736 the Yongzheng Emperor propped up the administrative system with useful reforms, first in taxation. He found that especially in the fertile Lower Yangzi provinces, well-connected landlords connived with yamen clerks to reduce their own taxes by wily subterfuges and put the tax burden mainly on the farming populace. Madeleine Zelin (1984) has described how Yongzheng's auditors tried without much success to collect taxes from the gentry landowners. In one reform the accumulated small surcharges were substituted by a single surcharge of 15 to 20 percent on the basic rather low land tax. Provinces used the proceeds partly to pay higher official salaries to "nourish honesty." But the networks of personal connections or *guanxi* that helped each individual's career were far too deeply inlaid in the structure of government to be eliminated. Today they are still a problem.

In administration Yongzheng escaped the stifling effect of bureaucratic procedure by developing an "eyes only" type of dispatch (memorial) inaugurated under Kangxi which came directly to the emperor from certain provincial officials and was returned to them with the emperor's red notations—a whistle-blowing device that gave him informants throughout the bureaucracy. In 1729 he also set up a secret Office of Military Finance of selected top officials to handle urgent business. It became the chief agency of the Inner Court, and became known to foreigners as the Grand Council.

The Grand Council when finally developed was an unusually effective center of Inner Court decision-making—first, because of its informality. The number of councillors averaged about seven. They were Manchus, Chinese, and occasionally Mongols serving for indefinite terms while also carrying on their duties in high posts in the Outer

Court, all in complete secrecy. Their 32 secretaries were talented young men with a future.

Second, Beatrice S. Bartlett (1991) has shown how the Grand Council built up its own secret files, including the eyes-alone palace memorials sent directly to the emperor. Much important documentation was in Manchu. Much of the Council's editorial work concerned bannermen (predominantly Chinese) who were specially devoted to the emperor.

The Jesuit Interlude

The Ming-to-Qing dynastic transition in the first half of the 1600s coincided with the arrival of Europeans in East Asia by sea. Missionaries followed the trade routes. China's first contact with Europe was an extraordinarily fruitful interlude because the Jesuit missionaries were learned men capable of dealing with Chinese scholar-officials in intellectual terms. By 1601 the Italian Jesuit Matteo Ricci was permitted to reside in Beijing on an imperial stipend as a Western scholar. His successors were given charge of the office of astronomy that fixed the official calendar. The Jesuits' success in using astronomy, cartography, European clockwork, the technique of mnemonics (memory training), and other exotica to attract Chinese scholars' interest had been accompanied by a clever policy of "accommodation." They accepted early Confucianism as ancient ethics, attacked only Buddhism and Neo-Confucianism, and sanctioned their Christian converts' reverence for their ancestors as a "civil rite" compatible with Christian faith.

The Jesuit order was under attack in Europe on several fronts. Soon the mendicant friars of the Dominican and Franciscan orders, coming to China from the Spanish Philippines and trying to preach to commoners, denounced the Jesuits, who catered mainly to the Chinese elite. The dispute was referred to the Pope, who sent two envoys to explain to the Qing emperor the papal supremacy in matters of religion. Within the palace Jesuits also became involved in Manchu court politics. Result: in 1724 the emperor banned Christianity as heterodox. Jesuits were allowed to remain only in Beijing.

This self-destruction of the Catholic mission to China is a well-known tale, like the original success story of Matteo Ricci so vividly recounted by Jonathan Spence (1984). Beginning with a translation of Euclid's geometry, the Jesuits published in Chinese, in addition to their Christian works, more than a hundred treatises on Western science and technology. The possible influence of these writings in China awaits fuller exploration, but there is no doubt of the importance of the Jesuit cultural outpost and the exchanges of ideas it did (and did not) make possible.

Meanwhile, China's influence on the eighteenth-century European Enlightenment has been pursued along two main lines: first on the level of political thought among the philosophers, and second through the vogue of "chinoiserie" in gardens, pagodas, furniture, ceramics, and other lines. China's impact on Europe through the Jesuits is a large field of study.

Growth of Qing Control in Inner Asia

The Manchu dynasty's vitality in the eighteenth century was manifested in its expansion in Inner Asia, specifically in Mongolia, Tibet, and Chinese Turkestan. This last was a vast region that included the Yili (Ili) grasslands north of the Mountains of Heaven (Tianshan) and south of them the arid desert and oases of Kashgaria.

Since the peripheries of empires must either be taken under control or be lost, the Qing in the 1600s moved to counter the spread of Russian fur traders and explorers across Siberia and into the Amur valley on the north of Manchuria. By developing water transport from south to north the Qing military were able to outnumber and overawe the few Russians at the end of their trans-Siberian supply route. The result, with Beijing Jesuits doing the interpreting and drafting, was the multilingual landmark treaty of Nerchinsk in 1689. Together with a later treaty of 1727, these negotiations set a Sino–Russian boundary, let a Russian ecclesiastical mission function quietly in Beijing, and permitted a rather exiguous Russian caravan trade to reach the capital.

West of Manchuria the Mongol tribes were kept under control by Qing administrative arrangements and by the religious sect of Yellow Hat Lamaism centered under the Dalai Lama in Lhasa. This made Tibet one key to power in Mongolia and brought Qing forces to stay in Lhasa. Like Khubilai Khan in the thirteenth century, the Manchu emperors used religions for political purposes: Russian Orthodox Christianity for Russians in Beijing, Catholic Christians for European contact at the court, and Yellow sect Lamaism in Tibet and Mongolia.

In between on the Far West, however, lay the mountains and deserts of Chinese Turkestan. Here the Qing confronted an unstable frontier on which the Western Mongol tribes became in the sixteenth and early seventeenth centuries a warlike and expansive force, threatening the stability of the Qing overlordship in Mongolia. To meet this danger, Qing bannermen led a series of expeditionary forces over routes familiar to their Han and Tang predecessors and during the 1750s subjugated the Western Mongols in Yili.

Typically for conquerors, the Qing found it imperative to take over the adjacent oases of Kashgaria south of the Tianshan, and here they found still another but more formidable religious community to deal with—Islam. In Kashgaria the populace generally lived by the Islamic calendar, and their religious, educational, and cultural life was dominated by the leaders of the faith. Once Qing rule was established by conquest in the 1750s, order was imposed on the Muslim population by appointing local chieftains as governors (begs). As Muslims, the begs left legal cases to be settled by Islamic law. The Qing rulers at Beijing collected taxes, especially on trade, and tried to keep order. But imperial Confucianism could not digest and could only occasionally co-opt the self-sufficient and all-embracing order of Islam.

In this way the High Qing rounded out its imperial frontiers far beyond the scope reached by the Ming. In short, Inner Asia was now taken over by the rulers at Beijing, part of whose success no doubt lay in the fact that as Manchus they were Inner Asians themselves and flexible in ideology. The Qing hegemony over Inner Asia after 1755 began a new era in the perpetual interplay between agrarian China and the tribes of the steppe. China was the nomads' supply house for grain, silk, and other products they wanted. The Chinese and the Inner Asian tribal peoples formed a geopolitical community. In the end the Chinese nation of the twentieth century would have its own version of a colonial empire to deal with in Inner Asia.

The era from late Ming to 1800 or so showed continued Manchu creativity but within a context of mounting problems. For example, when we note how the final Qing conquest of the Western Mongols in the 1750s consolidated the Qing continental control over Mongolia, Central Asia, and Tibet, we must also note the Western context. The contemporary struggle between the British and French empires during the Seven Years' War of the 1750s secured Canada and India for British sea power and enterprise. Thus, while the Qing gained control of the marginal caravan routes of arid Central Asia, Britain began to conquer the world's seas at a higher level of power altogether.

The Attempted Integration of Polity and Culture

To retain power, which was their primary aim, the Qing rulers faced two tasks—first to preserve the social and political order of imperial Confucianism, and second to retain power as non-Chinese rulers. These aims overlapped but were not identical. As eventually became evident, Manchu rule was trapped by history into opposing in China the sentiment of ethnic nationalism that was obviously becoming a major motivation among states in the rest of the world.

In the first task—Confucian governance—the dynasty's major aim was to integrate its rule with Chinese culture in mutual dependence. The politics was clearcut: dynastic power established by warfare was sanctioned by the need for unity under one ruler, unchallenged. This unity in turn was sanctioned by the need for order, and order depended upon ceremonies and proper behavior, with punitive force held in reserve.

In today's media environment where citizens observe events directly with less need but more supply of symbols, it is not easy to appreciate the importance of ritual and ceremony in an earlier time. One basis of the government of imperial China was the proper performance of ceremonies at all levels of society. The son kowtowed to his father as his father might do toward the emperor and his officials, for the essence of the civil order was to differentiate the hierarchy of relationships. Proper conduct, it was hoped, externalized one's inner values; but even in the absence of inner feelings, one's performance of ritual could provide a common formal bond with others. In this way the appearance of harmony could assure it. As Naquin and Rawski (1987) put it, "*luan* was the disorder that could arise within the state, the community, the household or the individual when ethical norms and correct ritual were not followed. The desire to promote order and prevent *luan* permeated Chinese society from top to bottom."

The emperor was the great promoter of order. Before the public his position was asserted and reinforced by a variety of activities, beginning with his daily solicitude for his mother and his performance of ceremonies for the reverence of his dynastic ancestors. Another strength of Confucian government lay in its constantly seeking the moral approval of the people governed. This was done by its support of books and education in the teachings of Neo-Confucianism; its maintenance of the rituals marking the seasons of the year and the interplay of relations between man and nature; and its daily demonstration of the exemplary conduct of the ruler which gave him, it was hoped, a virtue that commanded obedience. The ruler's activities included several that aimed at the public welfare, such as dike-building for flood control and maintaining the ever-normal granaries for famine relief and grain loans in time of dearth. The ruler also encouraged morality by the bestowal of rewards on aged and virtuous persons, especially chaste widows.

With this wide support of morality went the menace of the criminal law and punishment of malefactors against morality, especially against the dynasty. This application of the law against evildoers or the mere threat of evildoing included the uninhibited investigation of people in their households and personal lives and the use of judicial torture to encourage confessions. The ankle squeezer used in court was stepped up so as to maximize pressure, and it could turn bones into jelly when skillfully applied. When in doubt as to what law had been violated, the magistrate-judges could fall back on the statute against "doing what ought not to be done," whatever it might have been.

By these rewards and punishments it was hoped the common people could be kept in the proper path. The punishment of relatives was a regular part of the punishment of the criminal. The ancient device of group responsibility meant in effect guilt by association.

In the theocratic Chinese state that extolled the emperor as Son of Heaven, heterodoxy was perpetually guarded against. The strategic elite stratum was the local leadership that began with the roughly one million lower gentry or holders of the first-level (*shengyuan* or *jiansheng*) degrees, which did not qualify one for official appointment but conferred a privileged status and opportunity to seek higher degrees. To these were added possibly five million male commoners, more or less, who had achieved some amount of classical education. With their help, the indoctrination of the common people was pursued by the elite as a Neo-Confucian duty.

As an example let us cite the use of the *Sacred Edict (shengyu)* of the Kangxi Emperor issued in 1670 as 16 maxims for the guidance of daily conduct. Each maxim seven characters long, they conveyed, as Victor Mair (in Johnson et al., 1985) says, "the bare bones of Confucian orthodoxy as it pertained to the average citizen." After 1670 appeared commentaries, paraphrases, adaptations, and so on, in a considerable literature. The idea of explicating classical texts in written colloquial versions seems to have begun in the Yuan dynasty. A precedent in the early Ming appeared as the *Six Maxims* of the Hongwu Emperor. The Qing *Sacred Edict was* now used in the Community Compact or village lecture system originally promoted by Zhu Xi, which in the Ming and

Qing continued to combat heterodoxy and give a religious tinge to the support of orthodoxy.

For example, in the poorest back country among minority peoples, magistrates would use vernacular versions and have the text sung as an incantation. The usual community meetings might use ritual, incense, candles, flower vases, and musicians, plus the singing of a cantor along with drums and clappers. The audience would be told when to kneel, bow, and kowtow. The magistrate might also record notes on the meeting, how the villagers responded, their styles of behavior and the amicable settlement of conflicts. In the early eighteenth century efforts were made to have sessions on the *Sacred Edict* twice a month. The text used would be modified to suit the audience, either in simple vernacular or embellished with classical allusions or with memorable jingles for the simple country folk.

After all this the Yongzheng Emperor had issued in 1724 his "amplified instructions" on the *Sacred Edict,* approximately 10,000 characters long. The emperor wanted things to be clear. However, his text could hardly be comprehended by most of his audience, and officials therefore developed vernacular paraphrases. These versions were generally expected to be read aloud to the people even if the Mandarin dialect could not be understood by them. An orator would speak the local dialect. At a reading session the aged, over 80 or 90, would sit behind the gentry and be served tea while the commoners "were ordered to stand and listen." An increasing concern about heterodoxy is evident in the phraseology of the Ming *Six Maxims,* the *Sacred Edict* of 1670, and the amplified instructions of the *Sacred Edict* of 1724. Mair lists ten versions of the explication, which he sees as examples of "the bearers of high culture consciously and wilfully trying to mold popular culture." But it is still too early to say what was achieved.

Another area for imperial leadership was in popular religion, in particular the deification of public figures famous in earlier times. The most prominent example is that of Guan Yu (162–220), who began as a bodyguard of the founder of one of the Three Kingdoms. Prasenjit Duara (1988) notes how Guan Yu became a ubiquitous folk deity, the god of loyalty, of wealth, of literature, protector of temples, patron of actors and secret societies, as well as the god of war. Many social groups thus used him as a mythic symbol. In 1614 the Ming gave him imperial rank as Guandi. In 1725 "the Guandi cult was brought under systematic imperial control." The best endowed of the hundreds of popular Guandi temples in every county was "selected as the official Guandi temple." By

1853 the Qing raised his worship in the official sacrifices to the same level as that of Confucius. He was thoroughly Confucianized as a master of the classical teachings; Guandi became a heroic protector and provider, a warrior loyal above all to constituted authority and the established order. Duara concludes that cults like those of Guandi served to integrate the village with the larger society. Guandi's many symbolic functions at the popular and imperial levels reinforced one another.

Similarly, James L. Watson (in Johnson et al., 1985) has traced how "the promotion of state-approved cults in South China was so successful that by the mid-Ch'ing [Qing] local gods had been effectively superseded by a handful of approved deities." An example was the Empress of Heaven (Tian Hou), also known as Ma Zu, the patron goddess of fisherpeople, sailors, and maritime merchants. She emerged as a minor deity on the coast of Fujian in the tenth century. The cult began with a woman of the Lin family who took thought for the safety of mariners and became known as "Aunt Lin." Gradually she became a goddess incorporated into the state-approved pantheon through established bureaucratic procedures not unlike the validation of saints in the Catholic Church. The emperor took formal note of the goddess's service to the state and conferred honorific titles upon her, beginning in 1156. In 1278 she was commended by no less than Khubilai Khan. By 1409 she was the celestial concubine who protected the people. The Qing emperors, as they sought to control the southern coast, made her more important. Finally in 1737 the emperor made her "Empress of Heaven." In Taiwan there were official and unofficial temples to this goddess, who became the patron of several merchant guilds with interests in Fujian, as well as of pirates who preyed upon the merchants.

When dominant local lineages adopted her as their patron deity, she provided a useful symbol at both the official and the local levels. The local elites who used the goddess were cooperating in a way approved by the state. She had become a symbol of joining the mainstream Chinese culture. The cult incorporated people from widely varied social backgrounds who might have different beliefs about it. Yet by approving what the people accepted, the state strengthened its integration with the culture.

Another form of integration which amounted to integral subordination was ensured by what David Johnson (in Johnson et al., 1985) terms the "structure of dominance"—the fact that few commoners could be independent of their relations with rural landlords if they were tenants or with urban employers if they were apprentices. This sense of dependence upon superior authority was reflected in the cultural activities of the common people. The written records of popular culture included a wide range, from almanacs to the scriptures of religious sects. Local operas or other dramas were organized and enacted at market towns or at the village level or often by lineages. But throughout the popular culture dissident voices were not permitted to be heard and were destroyed if possible.

The integration of polity and culture sustained the Manchus' legitimacy in their second task—to preserve their power as an alien dynasty. Already the dry rot of assimilation was reducing the Manchu garrison troops to penury. Unable to survive on their farm lands, many troopers had lost both land and livelihood, and had even married Chinese women. Meanwhile the Manchu leadership, still in control of the state, had to keep the loyalty of the Chinese gentry-elite. To absorb the energies of Chinese scholars produced by the examination system far in excess of the posts available, the Manchu emperors became great patrons of literature and sponsored enormous projects of criticism and compilation. This was not simply smart opportunism but inhered in the discharge of imperial duty. Certain emperors of Han, Sui, Tang, Song, and Ming had all sponsored official catalogs of their imperial libraries. In 1409 the third Ming ruler sponsored the *Yongle dadian,* an encyclopedia in 10,000 manuscript volumes into which many works were copied. The Kangxi Emperor produced the famous *Kangxi Dictionary* and an enormous encyclopedia in 5,020 chapters. R. Kent Guy (1987) points out that such projects manifested the emperor's responsibility for and control over all writings in parallel with his responsibility for and control over the education and thought of all scholars.

During the decade after 1772, the Qianlong Emperor, who in his reign sponsored some 60 publications, pursued a project to collect and reproduce all major Chinese works in the four categories of the classics, histories, philosophy, and *belles lettres*. The resulting *Complete Library of the Four Treasuries* was derived from the examination of 10,869 works, of which 3,697 were deemed worthy of inclusion. They were too large to print, and only seven copies each in 36,500 chapters *(juan)* were made by hand. The printed catalog alone ran to 4,490 pages. (Pulitzer Prize committees inundated with books today should take heart.) The advocates of the Qing scholarship of evidential research (*kaozheng,* "rectification through investigation") dominated the project.

Guy shows how the critiques of histories and classical commentaries drafted by unofficial scholars of the conservative "Song Learning" or of the more venturesome "Han Learning" of the *kaozheng* movement were edited by the bureaucrats of the compilation commission under the watchful eye of the paternal autocrat. The whole process buttressed his legitimacy, for it showed he was doing his job. Chinese emperors "had very different prerogatives over scholarship and intellectual life than those to which we are accustomed in the West." They were "not only political leaders, they were sages and stewards of the classical canon." This doctrine, one may add, had survived at the center of the Chinese polity ever since the Shang.

Increasingly the Manchu court used this vast book collection mechanism to conduct a literary inquisition. Although Guy believes it had not been the original aim, as Western scholars first assumed, an effort was made to suppress all works that reflected badly on alien rulers. In searching out rare books and complete texts for inclusion in the master library, the compilers were able at the same time to search out all heterodox works that should be banned or destroyed. They paid high prices for rare works and even conducted house-to-house canvasses. The works proscribed included studies of military or frontier affairs, criticism antibarbarian in tone, and above all items that extolled the preceding Chinese dynasty of the Ming. Altogether, some 2,320 works were suppressed. Ostentatious punishments raised the level of terror among the thousands of literati and officials involved. A certain Wang Xihou had printed a dictionary that criticized the *Kangxi Dictionary* and treasonously printed in full the taboo temple names of the Qing emperors. For this Wang was executed and 21 of his family were enslaved. The Jiangxi governor who had supported the publication was also executed.

Truly the price of alien despotism was eternal vigilance. In the sorcery scare of 1768 Philip Kuhn (1990) has demonstrated how the Qianlong Emperor tried to combat the soul-stealing that was popularly believed to be achievable by clipping off part of a man's queue. It was a form of sorcery that menaced the public. Soon, however, the worried emperor saw in queue-clipping a seditious attack on the Qing tonsure as the symbol of loyal subjection to his rule. Qianlong's worried demands for evidence built up a widespread record because prolonged courtroom torture could elicit from impoverished monks and beggars whatever confessions the officials desired. In the end the Grand Council's closer look revealed that the "evidence" tortured out of people had all been fabricated.

This imperial sensitivity to the slightest sign of sedition, even at the very height of Qing magnificence, calls into question how far the Manchus had really succeeded in both avoiding assimilation themselves and fostering Chinese fealty to them. This raises an unresolved question. Right down to 1911 did not the effort to keep the dynasty in control require an unbudging conservatism that held China back?

The same question may be asked of the scholar-official class. W. T. de Bary (1991) in describing "the trouble with Confucianism," vividly reminds us how defenseless were the Confucian scholars vis-à-vis the state power. They had no power base of their own except as they remained loyal to the ruler or joined in factions formed by like-minded colleagues. Seventeenth-century critics after the Ming disaster had no theoretical basis for questioning the imperial autocracy. They resurrected *fengjian* ("feudal") ideas: for example, to strengthen the local magistrate against the corrupt *yamen* underlings and local gentry by dropping the rule of avoidance and letting him stay longer in office in his native place. This would give the magistrate more incentive and opportunity to improve local conditions. But the Qing would not accept the risk of fostering local interests. Except for a sprinkling of conscientious questioners, Qing scholars found their security lay in supporting orthodoxy. Critical views might seem heterodox. Even the most trenchant critics of dynastic government, like Huang Zongxi in the seventeenth century, assumed the necessity of a single exemplary ruler exercising the final power of the state. Lacking much contact with Western books or ideas, the literati as of 1820 remained integrated in the Neo-Confucian establishment.

Overall, details of city life and literati culture show government playing only a minor role in the mid-Qing era of high civilization. Yet within certain regions of the Chinese subcontinent the state's economic activity was sometimes spectacular. At Jingdezhen the imperial porcelain-making industry employed about 100,000 workers. The fires of two to three hundred kilns would glow in the night. In the late 1600s several million pieces of porcelain were sent to Europe every year. Similarly, the imperial silk manufactory at Suzhou by 1685 counted 800 looms and 2,330 workers. Commercialization continued apace as did privatization of business. Eighteenth-century textile factories with hundreds of looms and workers were hailed in Maoist China as "sprouts of capitalism" that would have modernized China's economy if not cut short by Western imperialism. Meanwhile, the merchant class came to the fore. At Beijing before 1800 there were about 23 native-place guilds catering to merchants from other provinces; by 1875 they would total 387. So one might continue with impressive examples of commercial growth.

In their survey of eighteenth-century China as visible in its macro-regions, S. Naquin and E. S. Rawski (1987) begin by noting the good repute of China in the European Enlightenment before the denigration that accompanied closer contact in the nineteenth century. They point out that European observers of the earlier era were generally "dazzled by Chinese sophistication and splendor." The 120 years after Kangxi's consolidation of Qing rule in the 1680s was a "dynamic" time when the Chinese empire expanded to its greatest extent as part of the resumption of a surge of economic growth and social change that had begun in late Ming. European savants of the Enlightenment were rightly impressed with China's grandeur.

If we ask whether such grandeur amounted to eighteenth-century Chinese "prosperity," we fall into the trap of holistic generalization that our study of macroregions aims to avoid. The vitality of new developments in core areas says something about potentialities for the future, not about current conditions countrywide. We know that gross national product, because it averages millionaires and paupers, may statistically show a nation to be well off even when many of its citizens are destitute. It is even harder to generalize meaningfully about premodern times. Naquin and Rawski caution that "it is important to be impatient with national-level generalizations." In the absence of census and trade figures, research on local history in the High Qing gazetteers and local records faces great but onerous opportunities.

Given the overhang of long-established customs and institutions, a hypothesis may be offered concerning the comparison of China and Europe in early modern times: In China, the economic and social developments of the Late Imperial age were less innovations than continuations. Though comparable to Europe in bulk, activity, and sophistication, eighteenth-century China was at the end of a period of high civilization that had begun in the Northern Song eight centuries before, while Europe of the Enlightenment was just embarking on a quite new phase of world history. Or to put it another way, new things in China could arise only within the inherited matrix of imperial autocracy and gentry society that would remain dominant throughout the nineteenth century. This is the focus of our next section.

PART TWO

Late Imperial China
1600–1911

L ATE IMPERIAL CHINA from 1600 to 1911 saw a doubling if not actually a tripling of population and a corresponding growth in production and trade and the institutions that support them. The disorder of the seventeenth-century transition from Ming to Qing dynastic rule was followed by a High Qing period from about 1680 to the early nineteenth century. Only after ca. 1820 did Western contact begin to get out of control. By that time the decline of the Qing dynasty had already begun.

In this dramatic story of material growth and political decay the autocratic state maintained in theory its claim to dominate all aspects of Chinese life, but in fact it played a minor part in the dynamic growth of Chinese economy and society of Late Ming and Qing. In Part Two our main interest therefore shifts from politics to economics, from the state to the society.

The old Victorian stereotype of a China that remained passive and unchanging while the progressive West exploded over the globe is long since out of date. Instead we have to imagine as of 1750 an Asia of big countries—Japan at 28 million was larger than France or Germany, while both China at, say, 200 million and India at perhaps 100 million were much bigger still. Europe was merely a peninsula of the Eurasian land mass, crowded between the Mediterranean and Baltic Seas. The Americas had perhaps 10 million Native Americans, while the European element consisted mainly of settlements up the St. Lawrence River and along the Atlantic and Gulf coasts, in addition to the older Iberian settlements of Mexico and Central and South America. Thus a mere 250 years ago the world population was distributed much differently than to-day.

After about 1750 the Industrial Revolution brought a great in-crease in the use of steam in manufacturing and transport. Its auto-motive, electronic, and other successors have remade the human condition worldwide. But we still lack unanimous agreement on precisely what has been happening. Even the question of just how the Industrial Revolution got started even today is a subject of dis-pute among economic historians. The importance of a dozen or more factors in the process is still being evaluated. These factors in-clude the growth of the market, use of the factory system, inven-tions, science and technology, public education, the security of pri-vate property, the agricultural revolution, foreign trade, population growth, supply of capital and credit, increased supply and produc-tivity of labor, rate of investment, and the like. These factors all stimulated industrialization in Europe. Perhaps the real dynamic lay in their interaction as mutual stimulants.

Our inherited images of early modern China show her deficient in many if not most of those factors. A comparable industrializa-tion did not occur in nineteenth-century China; yet the disparity in technological and material development that so impressed the Vic-torians is now viewed from a new perspective that stresses the vast size and maturity of China's domestic trade and the growing power of her merchant class in the Ming and early Qing, a power only in-directly acknowledged in the official records. Even Adam Smith could perceive that China's home market was as big as that of all the different countries of Europe put together. The extensive inter-provincial trade meant that China was already highly commercial-ized yet largely self-sufficient. Lancashire textiles, for example, failed to sweep the Chinese market simply because China's hand-woven "Nankeen" cotton cloth was a superior and on the whole cheaper product for local purposes; it still supplied most of North China's needs as late as 1930. After the long struggle to "open" the Chinese market, China's chief imports for mass consumption turned out to be a drug, opium, and a fuel, kerosene—a product more of geological conditions than of Western industrial preemi-nence. China's modern economy when it did develop would be to a large extent in Chinese hands.

The reasons why the late Qing achieved so little industrializa-tion despite its enormous material growth were not only economic but also social, political, and cultural. This is not a question that can be settled simply by applying economic concepts. Thus in Part Two, before turning to the Western invasion after 1820, we will note two elements: first, the extent of China's domestic growth and of certain institutional constraints that would limit its capacity to industrialize; and second, the dynamism of the Chinese overseas—Maritime China—and the foreign trade that would contribute to China's entrance into the outside world.

8

The Paradox of Growth
without Development

The Rise in Population

An increase in population has usually been accompanied (indeed facilitated) by an increase in trade. One can hardly occur without the other. In
the Western experience, commerce provided the conditions that allowed
industrialization to get started, which in turn led to growth in science,
technology, industry, transport, communications, social change, and the
like that we group under the broad term of development. In China such
development did not occur, at least not on anything like the scale in the
West. Researchers like Philip Huang (1990) believe that in looking at
China we must give up our common assumptions based on European experience and the reaction to it of European economic theorists like Adam
Smith and Karl Marx. China's economy had its special problems. For
one thing, China was so large that evidence can be found for very diverse
conditions and trends in different areas at the same time.

To begin with, the massive increase of population that in Europe was
at first attributed to industrialization occurred also and during the same
period in China, even though there was no comparable industrialization.
An estimated population of 60 million as of AD 2 in mid-Han had been
matched by roughly the same figure in mid-Tang, suggesting a thousand
years of ups and downs with only a modest overall increase. Then the estimated total rose under the Song to well above 100 million but was reported as considerably less under the Mongols and the early Ming. By
the time of the Qing takeover in the seventeenth century the total seems
to have risen only slowly during a period of 600 years.

The Manchu dynasty in 1651 recorded 10 million families or households, each of which was estimated at six persons. But we know that the

official population estimates of dynasties erred on the short side. This was because tax payments were due from an administrative area partly according to the estimated population total. This created an incentive for short reporting both by the people and by the authorities responsible for tax payments. China before the 1980s never had a genuine census of the modern type, recording precise data as of a given date on age and sex distribution, marital status, migration, and the other minutiae necessary for scientific analysis. The Chinese figures, on the contrary, resulted from registration and estimation for government purposes, to find out the numbers capable of cultivating land, laboring on public works, bearing arms, or paying taxes. Popular cooperation was not to be expected. Whole categories of persons were omitted. Uniform schedules, accurate maps, trained enumerators, all were lacking. The estimates were often products of bureaucratic ritual. Henan province, for example, during much of the nineteenth century reported an increase of 1,000 persons every other year!

One may guess that the Chinese population by 1600 was close to 150 million. The Ming–Qing transition may have seen a decline. From 1741 to the outbreak of the great Taiping rebellion in 1851 the annual figures rose steadily and spectacularly, beginning with 143 million and ending with 432 million. If we accept these totals, we are confronted with a situation in which the Chinese population doubled in the 50 years from 1790 to 1840. If, with greater caution, we assume lower totals in the early eighteenth century and only 400 million by 1850, we still face a startling fact: something like a doubling of the vast Chinese population in the century *before* Western contact, foreign trade, and industrialization could have had much effect.

To explain this sudden increase we cannot point to factors constant in Chinese society but must find conditions or a combination of factors newly effective during this period. Among these is the almost complete internal peace maintained under Manchu rule during the eighteenth century. There was also an increase in foreign trade through Guangzhou and some improvement of transportation within the empire. Control of disease, like the checking of smallpox by variolation, may have been important. But of most critical importance was the food supply.

Confronted with a multitude of unreliable figures, economists have compared the population records with the aggregate data for cultivated land area and grain production in the six centuries since 1368. Assuming that China's population in 1400 was about 80 million, Dwight Perkins (1969) concludes that its growth to 700 million or more in the

1960s was made possible by a steady increase of the grain supply, which evidently grew five or six times between 1400 and 1800 and rose another 50 percent between 1800 and 1965. This increase of food supply was due perhaps half to the increase of cultivated area, particularly by migration and settlement in the central and western provinces, and half to greater productivity—the farmers' success in raising more crops per unit of land.

This technological advance took many forms: one was the continual introduction from the south of earlier-ripening varieties of rice, which made possible double-cropping. New crops such as corn (maize) and sweet potatoes as well as peanuts and tobacco were introduced from the Americas. Corn, for instance, can be grown on the dry soil and marginal hill land of North China, where it is used for food, fuel, and fodder, and provides something like one seventh of the food energy available in the area. The sweet potato, growing in sandy soil and providing more food energy per unit of land than other crops, became the poor man's food in much of the South China rice area.

Productivity in agriculture was also improved by capital investments, first of all in irrigation. From 1400 to 1900 the total of irrigated land seems to have increased almost three times. There was also a gain in farm tools, draft animals, and human fertilizer (night soil), to say nothing of the population growth itself, which increased half again as fast as cultivated land area and so increased the ratio of human hands and of night soil available per unit of land. Thus the rising population was fed by a more intensive agriculture, applying more labor and fertilizer to the land.

In this broader perspective, population growth in China over the last 600 years has averaged only about four tenths of one percent a year, not a rapid rate overall. But the eighteenth- and early nineteenth-century doubling and redoubling of numbers was something like the contemporary European population explosion triggered partly by the spread of the potato. Recently, some have speculated that the contemporary early modern growth in China, Russia, and Europe was due to a global warming of the climate in early modern times, which lengthened the growing season. Possibly this is a major explanation of China's growth, but it still awaits detailed study and cannot be called a probability.

Diminishing Returns of Farm Labor

Despite enormous growth in population and food supply, the Late Imperial era saw a decline of productivity per laborer in agriculture. This decline struck at the very sector that Confucian scholar-officials regarded as the root of the state and were most committed to fostering. Indeed, their studies and manuals of agricultural technology were models for their day. Unfortunately, the authors were not input–output economists. Because farm families were so busy and hard-working, most observers missed the fact of diminishing returns, especially in rice culture.

The technology of rice culture had steadily advanced along with the increase of production. After the fall of Northern Song to the Jin dynasty in 1126, emigration from North China southward increased, and the Yangzi valley and areas to the south grew in population and rice culture simultaneously. Land was converted to paddy by vigorous effort. Robert Hartwell (1982) reports, for example, that between 1170 and 1225 new dikes or polders "resulted in the reclamation of nearly all the arable land from Lake T'ai to the sea and from the mouth of the Yangtze to the coastal districts of northern Chekiang." All along the southeast coast from Zhejiang to Guangzhou new land was formed by diking fields in the coastal lowlands. Meanwhile, the terracing of hills and mountains increased rice acreage all across South China.

The hand-cultivation of rice requires the fine-tuning of many factors: choice of seed and cropping pattern, the ploughing, irrigating, and fertilizing of fields, the transplanting, weeding, harvesting, winnowing, and drying of the crop, and its storage, transportation, and sale. There are many fine points to consider. Increasing skill and unremitting effort can often increase rice yields in comparison with alternative crops or household handicrafts. Yet the almost indefinite growth of rice yields when abundant labor power is available cannot forever obviate the law of diminishing returns.

Today, looking at the terraced fields that mold the landscape in so many parts of China, an observer may be impressed by the beauty of the level contours imposed by man upon nature and awed by the past investment of muscle power they represent. The economic-minded may calculate the productivity per farmer possible in such a scene. Rice was able to supply more calories per unit of land than any other crop, making it the staff of life in China from Song times onward. But it is indeed labor-intensive.

Consider, for example, the extra labor required to add another terrace on top of several already in use: the physical effort in climbing the terraces to prepare the new top field, to bring up seedlings for transplanting, to adjust the flow of irrigation, to carry up and apply fertilizer, to monitor, weed, and finally hand-harvest the crop. Kang Chao (1986) estimates that in China's labor-intensive farming system, labor input into a unit of land may be 10 to 20 times the labor input usual in extensive plow cultivation elsewhere. In effect, the rice farmer was married to hard labor. As time went on, the total rice crop grew along with the population. Dwight Perkins has shown how the cultivated area increased with population growth, though the new increments of land were of course less accessible and efficient. When effort was shifted from rice to other crops or from agriculture, say, to handicraft production, the same limitation would sooner or later begin to operate. The farmer got less and less product for every increase of his effort.

While "population pressure," meaning a surplus of people making land more scarce than labor and labor therefore cheap, has been one of the major generalizations about China, the judgment of "overpopulation" is a technical question for economic historians. There is as yet no consensus on how great it has been in China at what times and places. Major statistics of land and people are still in dispute. Yet one can point to several facts leading to the general conclusion that population pressure has slowed China's economic and industrial growth.

Land hunger, for one thing, has led to a steady encroachment of farmers on China's lakes. Peter Perdue (1987) has found that around the big Dongting Lake in Hunan by the present century some 900 dikes had been built, stretching almost 4,000 miles. Reduction of lake area reduced the catchment basin for flood waters, exacerbating the flood problem. R. Keith Schoppa (1989) has traced how the Xiang Lake near Hangzhou over the course of nine centuries was filled in and disappeared.

Behind this land hunger lay a steady worsening of the man-to-land ratio. In the era of the equal-field land allotments between 485 and the mid-700s, cultivated land per household had been estimated at 80 *mou* (a *mou* or *mu* is roughly one sixth of an acre). By the twelfth century it was around 20 to 30 *mou*, and in 1936 the average for a family farm in China would be estimated at 3.6 *mou*. The precise significance of terms and statistics in the voluminous but various Chinese records bedevils the work of researchers, but there can be no question as to the long-term downward trend in the man/land ratio.

Another noteworthy datum to indicate the plight of Chinese farmers is the fact that the great Chinese inventions in technology such as silk, porcelain, canal locks, the clock escapement, the stern-post rudder, printing, gunpowder, the mold-board iron plow, and all the rest so copiously set forth by Joseph Needham and his coworkers came generally to an end in the Song. Thereafter the abundance of muscle power made labor-saving inventions less needed. Kang Chao notes that the 77 inventions for use in agriculture (like the bucketed water wheel or *noria* for irrigation) listed in a 1313 handbook were not appreciably added to in later such works.

Farm household industries making silk and tea, or later weaving cotton, offer another line of evidence. It seems strange that after the Song cities of Kaifeng and Hangzhou were established, no great cities of over a million emerge in China until the nineteenth century. This seems to be partly because industry, as Chao puts it, was "ruralized," or as Philip Huang says, "familized." That is, handicrafts by farm women produced goods more cheaply than could city factories or silk filatures. Farm women could run their own unobtrusive sweatshops at home to manufacture household supplies and marketable goods for less than a livable wage. It was less a symptom of incipient capitalism than of the Chinese farmer's ingenuity in supplementing his inadequate return from too-small plots of land. Handicraft products could be sold at the local markets that grew up in the Song and after to eke out a bit of extra income. They bespoke the farm family's abject poverty, which obliged the farmer's wife and children to keep at work spinning and weaving to gain only a pittance that would nevertheless help fend off starvation.

Can the recorded growth in China's population and production be reconciled with evidence of "immiseration," a worsening of living standards at least in some areas? Economists are still arguing over this anomaly. To allege "overpopulation" in a China that doubled its population in the Ming and again in the Qing, preparatory to doubling once again after 1949, may seem to fly in the face of the evidence. The issue, however, is not whether the population could feed itself and continue to increase but whether its overall standard of living could be maintained.

Several results flowed from this population pressure in the late nineteenth century: machines competed with cheap manpower in transport and industry and so seemed to threaten popular livelihood. Poverty meant lack of purchasing power and lack of a market for manufactured goods. Lethargy in mechanization and in standardization handicapped China's capacity to compete even as a source of handicraft products—

witness India's supplanting China in tea production and Japan's rise to dominance in silk production.

China's loss on the land in the per capita productivity of her farm labor force was exacerbated by the artificial weakening of her woman power, through the practice of footbinding.

The Subjection of Women

The low status of women in the old China is cited in all accounts of the family system. But merely to state that women married outside their families of birth, did not own property, and were seldom educated does not give the busy reader a graphic picture. This lack can be met in part by focusing on the very distinct custom of footbinding.

When my wife and I lived in Beijing for four years in the early 1930s, three things impressed us as unusual. First, we were non-Chinese but because of earlier imperialist foreign invasion we enjoyed the privileges of the Chinese ruling-class elite. The police did not bother us. Second, manpower was so abundant and cheap that our easiest transportation was by ricksha with an intelligent human horse between the shafts. He could go faster if you asked him. If trotting about and sweating in the cold gave him a bloody cough, he could always find us a successor. Third, all women of middle age or over had bound feet, stumping about awkwardly on their heels as though the front sections of their feet had been amputated. Traveling in the countryside of five North China provinces, we never met a farmer's wife over the age of 30 whose feet were not bound. All three of these undesirable phenomena—foreign special privileges, an excess of manpower, the bound feet of women—were part and parcel of the culture.

In the old China women were first of all the product and the property of their families. Until well into the present century their subjection was demonstrated and reinforced by the custom of footbinding. So general has been Chinese avoidance of the topic of footbinding that modern Chinese publication on it is meager. Westerners studying China naturally imbibe Chinese sensitivities, and few are muckrakers by temperament. Yet footbinding darkened the lives of most Chinese women for several centuries, with social and psychic repercussions that call for historical appraisal. Most obvious was the economic loss through the impairment of farm women's muscle power and capacity for labor.

The first thing to note about footbinding is that the feet did not cease to grow. They were simply made to grow into a deformed shape. Imagine yourself a girl child who—for some six to ten long years, beginning at age 5 to 8 and lasting until 13 or 15, the years of your childhood and getting your growth—has her feet always bound in long strips of binding cloth night and day with no letup in order to deform them into 3-inch-long "golden lilies." To make your feet thinner under the constant pressure, your four minor toes on each foot are pushed down around and under the balls of your feet. If you tried to walk in a normal way, you would be putting your weight on your toe bones under your feet. Fortunately, however, you cannot do this because in the meantime in order to make your feet shorter the binding cloths have compressed them from front to back. Under this constant pressure your arches have gradually been broken and bowed upward so only the back edge of your heels can support your weight. As the arch is gradually broken, the flat of your heels and the balls of your foot (or plantar) are gradually moved from horizontal to perpendicular, facing each other, so that an object like a silver dollar can be inserted in the narrow space between them. The result is that you will never run again and can walk on the base of your heels only with difficulty. Even standing will be uncomfortable. After your feet have stopped growing the pain will be gone, but you will continue to wear your binding cloths partly to give your feet support, and partly because they are unlovely objects, horribly misshapen and ugly to look at. You let no one see them unshod.

This self-inflicted and inexorable pain in your formative years is welcomed in theory as a way to get a good marriage that may help your family with a fine bride price. Marriage brokers stressed the importance of foot size. Your mother went through it all and helps you do the same. She teaches you the art of not blocking circulation lest it produce gangrene and pus, of keeping your bent-under toenails manicured so they will not puncture your skin, of changing the bindings daily to keep the pressure even, of washing to reduce the smell, massaging your legs to reduce the pain, and wearing cute little shoes to advertise your achievement and entice male attention. As you go into marriage hoping to produce a male baby, you find your life confined largely to household duties. If you happen to be a servant standing before your bound-foot mistress, she may let you lean against the wall to reduce the discomfort of standing. In a very literal sense you cannot run away. Among other things, your unused leg muscles have atrophied and your legs become ungainly spindles.

Missionaries in the 1880s estimated from what they had heard that about 10 percent of the girls who underwent footbinding did not survive it. Of course a large proportion of Chinese children suffered mortality in any case. We shall never be able to quantify such an immeasurable question, but there is evidence that girls during the first years of foot-binding had trouble sleeping, to say nothing of moving about. Some placed their feet at night beneath their mother or rested them on a bed-board, in either case to dull the pain by making their feet numb from lack of blood circulation.

Behind footbinding lay a male sexual fetish that has been noted by many but seldom really investigated. Apparently footbinding had begun at court in the tenth century. Howard Levy (1966) reproduces a poem from the early Song statesman-poet Su Shi (Dongpo, 1036–1101):

Anointed with fragrance, she takes lotus steps;
Though often sad, she steps with swift lightness.
She dances like the wind, leaving no physical trace.
Another stealthily but happily tries on the palace style,
But feels such distress when she tries to walk!
Look at them in the palms of your hands, so wondrously small
that they defy description.

The cruelest aspect of footbinding was that the peasant masses among the Chinese imitated the upper class. Among Mongols, Manchus, and most other minorities footbinding was not practiced. The Manchu (Qing) emperors inveighed against it, as did iconoclastic scholars. But among Chinese farm women who had to lead lives of hard work, footbinding became widespread. We lack studies of when and how far this happened. Apparently the custom was maintained in some areas but not in others. But binding was a widespread practice in the nineteenth century, and its effects were still visible in the 1930s.

What was the psychic and social, to say nothing of the economic, cost of footbinding? Village women accepted it like the pains of childbirth and ridiculed anyone with normal feet. Did they believe the male theory that footbinding produced muscles that increased a husband's enjoyment of copulation? In mutilating themselves did they suffer any loss of self-respect, of self-confidence? Did true Confucianists apply to women the dictum that our bodies as given us by our parents are sacred and should not be allowed to suffer mutilation? Whether the great propagator of Neo-Confucianism Zhu Xi backed footbinding is disputed. He did not champion female freedom. In the end could a bound-foot woman feel anything but inferior? a victim of remorseless fate? fearful of breaking convention? The trauma, conscious or unconscious, must have become part of the personality of Chinese women.

Unfortunately, footbinding is not a social practice that can be studied comparatively. Wasp-waisted Victorian women who had the vapors from fashionably constricting their mid-sections are not comparable, any more than African women who gradually elongated their necks by adding brass rings around them. Possibly the practice of clitoridectomy, in certain parts of Africa, performed by women upon women, is in some ways comparable, yet as a social iniquity visited upon hundreds of millions of women, footbinding is in a class by itself, a unique aspect of Chinese culture. Consequently it is not a topic listed in general works of sociology. Strangely, social historians of China, both men and women, have hardly yet acknowledged its existence. It is the least studied aspect of Chinese society. The fascinating complexity of marriage arrangements and the general inequality meted out to women have been brilliantly explored, but not footbinding. Its avoidance perhaps represents the occupational quirk of sinologists, a secondary patriotism or sinophilia that may lead otherwise hard-headed scholars to want to say no evil of the object of their researches.* Nevertheless, a social evil that becomes institutionalized though shameful to recall must still be faced. African slavery in the United States has been healthily confronted by historians from many angles. Footbinding in China should not be swept under the rug. It was a fact with causes and repercussions still to be understood.

Domestic Trade and Commercial Organization

The expansion of China's domestic trade, which accompanied the growth of population, began with agriculture. Raising farm products and producing farm handicrafts for sale gradually swelled the arteries of trade within macroregions and then between regions. Thus the raw cotton of North China could be taken down the Grand Canal to the textile production centers of the Lower Yangzi. The Shanghai area became for a time a leading exporter of cotton yarn to Guangdong. Specialized products like the ceramics of the Jingdezhen kilns in Jiangxi would naturally be sold across regional boundaries in all directions, while the

---

*For an outstanding example of sentimental sinophilia see my statement in *Foreign Affairs*, October 1972, that in a certain context the Maoist revolution was "the best thing" that had happened to the Chinese people in many centuries.

brick tea supply of central China went up the Han River for exchange at the tea-horse markets on the Inner Asian frontier.

William T. Rowe's (1984, 1989) masterly study of Hankou (1760–1890) offers a primary example of this commercialization. In addition to water transport up and down the Yangzi, Hankou was the crossroads of water-borne commerce on the Han River from the northwest and on the Xiang River south through Hunan all the way to Guangzhou. This route might exchange rice for spices from Southeast Asia. Timber, rice, and later opium came down the Yangzi from Sichuan, and salt came up-river from the salt flats on the coast north of Shanghai. The best tea came north from the hills of Fujian province. By the nineteenth century there was a considerable interregional trade within China, while silk and tea exports were going abroad in greater quantities from Guangzhou and later Shanghai and Fuzhou.

This growth of domestic trade was naturally accompanied by a growth in marketing systems. Villagers visited their standard markets, which in turn were tributary to central markets on up the scale. As itinerant merchants moved about within the area, these markets provided an outlet for a farmer's handicraft products like raw silk or woven cloth, in addition to food products.

More commerce led to the growth of market towns *(zhen)* devoted to trade and industry that were not originally created to be administrative centers. Particularly in the Yangzi delta, the new-grown towns saw handicraft workshops begin to use labor on a capitalist basis. The town elite were merchants, while a freely mobile labor force began to appear as a genuine proletariat, often organized into labor gangs managed by boss contractors. More and more farmers shifted their focus from farming to handicrafts, while others went into the growing sector of transportation.

China's extensive water-transport network was already available to accommodate the growth of trade. One index to growth was the increase of shipping by the many varieties of Chinese junk on the Yangzi and its tributaries and along the coast. They carried the sugar of southeast China from ports like Shantou (Swatow) and Xiamen (Amoy) to southern Manchuria and returned with cargoes of soybean cake to use in the south as fertilizer.

Another index to growth was the proliferation beginning in the late eighteenth century of trade guilds and particularly of native-place guilds, that is, associations in various provincial centers to accommodate merchants and others who shared the same place of origin. Rowe traces the rise of the guild organizations that handled specific trade goods like tea or textiles and the native-place guilds like that of the Ningbo merchants at Hankou. These guilds that served traders from a distance in the inter-regional trade provided them not only with the amenities of a meeting place in their guild halls but also might provide warehouse space, living quarters, a shrine to the patron deity of the guild, an opera stage, a school for examination candidates, and a widespread membership.

Guilds were financed by entrance fees and might own real estate and be landlords with large rent payments coming in. They could also raise funds by bond issues. They put out and enforced regulations concerning trades; they were engaged in and might organize boycotts as well as me-diating disputes. As staple trades became well established, the guilds had increasing functions and influence. With public spirit as well as concern for their own interest, they maintained fire-watching towers and fire-fighting teams in the easily inflammable city. In the local harbor they might maintain rescue boats. They would contribute to charities and pay for soup kitchens in time of famine, and for watchmen against disorder. They might keep up a thoroughfare, build bridges, or improve the water supply. They exhibited a Confucian "public-mindedness." In short, the guilds became municipal institutions, capable of organizing militia or boycotts or mediating in trade disputes but without being under the di-rect control of the local magistrates.

Naturally, the growth of trade led to improvements in fiscal technol-ogy. The Ningbo bankers who from the late eighteenth century domi-nated the Shanghai banking world developed an arrangement known as the transfer tael in order to balance their accounts from day to day. The Shanxi remittance banks, built up by family partnerships in towns along the Fen River, the ancient heartland of the Sui and Tang dynasties, devel-oped during the nineteenth century a capacity to transfer funds by letters of credit and orders on their branches elsewhere so as to obviate the cross-country shipment of silver bullion under convoy against bandits. Rowe lists as innovations "bills of exchange, deposit banking, book transfers of funds between depositors, overdraft credit and . . . negotia-ble and transferable credit instruments."

This admirable commercial growth in Late Imperial China unfortu-nately occurred in a context that enmeshed both farmer and merchant in long-established situations that they could not easily change. Late Imperial China's commercialization was not followed by industrializa-tion on the Western model even though researchers have found abun-dant evidence for the kind of proto-industrialization in China that was followed by industrialization in Europe. Thus the rise of commercial towns, of merchant entrepreneurs managing a putting-out system of household handicraft production, and the appearance of an urban wage-labor class or proletariat can all be documented in certain parts of China like the Yangzi delta. Yet these Europe-like phenomena were superficial to certain long-lasting rural facts in China: the farm household had so little land that sideline and handicraft production especially in silk and cotton became an integral part of its subsistence. The farm household was thus commercialized, to be sure, but through a maximum of labor input, far beyond the point of diminishing returns, and a minimum input of capital. Both their agricultural income and their handicraft income were necessary for the farm family's mere subsistence. The result, as Philip C. C. Huang (1990) puts it, was that "in agriculture wage labor-based farms could not compete with familized peasant cultivation. In industry urban workshops could not compete with low cost home producers." The farm economy was tied to involution, that is, growth of product without any increase of productivity per hour of labor. In this involuted situation a market economy in Adam Smith's sense could not operate. The expectations of economists like Smith and Marx, derived from the European experience, were not adequate to explain the hard facts that had accumulated in China.

Although the merchant class was growing in strength and capacity, it remained subject to the arbitrary action of officials seeking contributions for meeting crises like floods or defense, and also seeking to be paid off with gifts from holders of licenses, monopolies, and properties. Industrial investment by merchants continued to take second place to their investment in land and real estate in an attempt to protect themselves by joining the still dominant class of landed degree-holders (gentry). With the onset of urbanization, subordination of merchants to officials slackened, but merchants never broke free of official supervision, if not domination.

Merchant–Official Symbiosis

The merchant was kept in check by the official as an ally whose activities could be used and milked in the interest of either the officials personally or of the state. As Etienne Balazs pointed out, commercial transactions were always subject to the superintendence and taxation of the officials. Government monopolies of staple articles, like salt and iron in ancient times, or like tea, silk, tobacco, salt, and matches more recently, expressed the overriding economic prerogatives of the state. No merchant class had been allowed to rise independently and encroach upon these prerogatives.

This was ensured in practice by the official disregard for rights of private property. This meant that official patronage and support were necessary to protect any big commercial undertaking. The result was a close community of interest between the merchant and the official. Both could profit where neither could succeed alone. Merchants, bankers, brokers, and traders of all sorts were therefore a class attached as subordinates to the bureaucracy. As handlers and manipulators of goods and capital, they assisted the officials in extracting the surplus not only from commerce but also from agriculture.

By Late Imperial times merchants were accorded a status that reflected the importance of wealth in the growing economy. They could move with some ease into the gentry class through purchase of land and examination degrees and through intermarriage. Unlike Europe, China had little organized foreign trade in which a merchant could invest. Indeed, for 200 years the Ming had banned private trade abroad, as we have seen. Though less profitable than commerce, land was more secure and so remained the great object of investment. The merchant class produced landlords more readily than independent commercial capitalists.

China's premodern financial system also inhibited capitalism. Savings that represented accumulated capital were ordinarily invested in moneylending because of the high interest obtainable. Usurious rates were an index of the farmer's high seasonal demand for money, both to pay his taxes and for subsistence until the next harvest. Short-term credits to farmers paid higher interest than long-term industrial loans. As a result there was less incentive for investment of savings in industrial production.

In short, capitalism failed to prosper in China because the merchant was never able to become established outside the control of the landlord gentry and their representatives in the bureaucracy. In feudal Europe the merchant class developed in the towns. Since the landed ruling class were settled in their manors upon the land, the European towns could grow up outside the feudal system instead of being integrated in it. Medieval burghers gained their independence by having a separate habitat in these new towns, and a new political authority to protect them, in the persons of the kings of nation-states. In China these conditions were lacking. The early abolition of feudalism and the dependence of the emperor and his officials upon the local gentry left no political power outside the established order to which the merchant could turn for special protection. The towns usually grew up first as administrative centers. The essential connection of the gentry with officialdom drew them into the towns both as cultural centers and as walled havens against bandits or irate peasants. The gentry family's best security lay not in a sole reliance upon landowning but in a union of landowning with official prerogatives. Family property in itself was no security, but officials who were family members could give it protection. Thus, the gentry class, as an elite stratum over the peasant economy, found their security in land and office, not in trade and industry. Between them, the gentry and officials saw to it that the merchants remained under control and contributed to their coffers instead of setting up a separate economy.

Private enterprise might develop freely in small-scale farming, brokerage, or petty trading within the grip of government taxation, but this was not a capitalist type of private enterprise. From the peasants' more assiduous cultivation of their privately owned land, the bureaucracy would garner a greater surplus by taxation. By the same principle, they also stood ready to collect from the merchant or industrial producer any surplus he might accumulate. Many merchants appear in the records of ancient China but seldom as a class having political power. The growth of commerce was less important to the rulers than continued supervision of the agricultural economy. The Ming and early Qing depended upon land taxes more than trade taxes.

In premodern China, the merchant had an attitude of mind quite different from that of the Western entrepreneur extolled by our classical economists. According to the latter, the economic man can prosper most by producing goods and securing from his increased production whatever profit the market will give him. In old China, however, the economic man would do best by increasing his own share of what had already been produced. The incentive for innovative enterprise, to win a market for new products, had been less than the incentive for monopoly, to control an existing market by paying for an official license to do so. The tradition in China had been not to build a better mousetrap but to get the official mouse monopoly.

A modern-minded entrepreneur in Late Imperial China had also to contend with the bureaucratism of officials in government. To put Chinese bureaucratism in a Western perspective, let us first recall that in 1800 the great Ohio-Mississippi-Missouri River basin of the Middle West was largely uninhabited, save for a few million Native Americans, whereas the great Yangzi River system supported the livelihood of at least 200 million people. China had invented bureaucracy 2,000 years before, whereas the American civil service legislation began mainly in the 1880s, following the Grant administration and just a hundred years before that of Ronald Reagan. Our brief century of experience has barely begun to acquaint us with institutional pitfalls that are an ancient story in China.

The imperial officials were held responsible for all public events within their jurisdiction but not for all public funds. Budgeting and accounting procedures were rudimentary. The bureaucracy lived by what we today would call systematized corruption, which sometimes became extortion. This went along with the system of intricate personal relationships that each official had to maintain with his superiors, colleagues, and subordinates.

"Squeeze" operated through forms of politeness rather than secrecy. Junior officials in the course of their duties gave their superiors customary "gifts." But like all prices in old China, the amount of such a gift resulted from the working out of a personal relationship. The squeeze system was no more cut-and-dried than any other part of the man-to-man bargaining that pervaded Chinese life. The extralegal sums that passed between officials were larger but no different in kind from the small commissions extracted from every money transaction by underpaid household servants.

Nepotism supported the squeeze or "leakage" system by giving an added sanction for personal arrangements contrary to the public interest. Even classic texts extolled duty to family, and particularly filial piety, as superior to any duty to the state. Thus the interest of the imperial administration at the capital, which needed the sustenance of revenue from the provinces, was constantly in conflict with the multifarious private interests of all the officials, each of whom had to provide for his relatives and his further career.

High office commonly meant riches. The favorite minister of the Qianlong Emperor (Heshen), when tried for corruption and other crimes by that emperor's successor in 1799, was found to have an estate worth in our terms of that period more than one billion dollars—probably an all-time record. I would not suggest that Westerners have been backward or less adept in the art of graft. But in China, corruption has remained longer into modern times an accepted bureaucratic institution, unashamed and unafraid. It did not provide a helpful milieu for entrepreneural capitalism.

Limitations of the Law

It is a minor paradox that dynastic China had a well-developed legal system that was, however, of little help in fostering capitalism. By pre-modern standards the Chinese legal codes were monuments of their kind. The great Tang code of the eighth century and its successors in the Song, Yuan, Ming, and Qing periods still invite analysis. Early European observers were well impressed with Chinese justice. It was only after the eighteenth and nineteenth century reforms of law and punishments in the modern West that Chinese law seemed "backward."

Nevertheless, the Chinese concept of law was fundamentally different from legal conceptions in the West. First of all, the law was not regarded as an external and categorical element in society; there was no "higher law" given to mankind through divine revelation. Moses received his golden tablets on a mountain top, but Confucius reasoned from daily life without the aid of any deity. For his rules of propriety, he did not claim any metaphysical sanction. He merely said they came from the moral character of the natural universe itself, from this world, not from another world beyond human ken. It followed that legal rules were but one expression of this morality—models or examples to be followed, or working rules of administration or ritual observance. So the breaking of such rules was a matter of practical expedience rather than of religious principle. Laws were subordinate to morality. Their sanction lay in reason or the common social experience that underlay morals. This system avoided the unhappy dualism that grew up in the West between the letter of the law and the dictates of commonsense morality.

The Chinese imperial code was chiefly penal, a corrective for the untutored. It was also administrative, and prescribed the details of the rites. The code was partly accumulated out of administrative decisions. It was nearly all public law, referring to procedures, marriage, inheritance, and other matters relative to and important in government administration. The law occupied a comparatively small share of the public scene. The people generally avoided litigation in the magistrate's court, where plaintiffs as well as defendants could be interrogated with prescribed forms of torture and everyone would have to pay fees to the yamen underlings. The magistrates hired personal law secretaries to advise them; aside from these there was no legal profession, no private lawyer class to represent clients. Justice was official, weighted on the side of the state and social order. It operated vertically, from the state upon the individual, more than it did horizontally, to resolve conflicts between one individual and another.

Within its limited sphere, the Qing legal system was elaborately organized, and it functioned, once it got into action, with a good deal of exactitude. The five punishments (beating with the light and heavy bamboo, penal servitude, exile, and death) were imposed by a hierarchy of magistrates' courts running from the county magistrate's yamen up through the prefecture and province to the capital and eventually, for death sentences, to the emperor. Cases were reported to and reviewed by superiors. Appeals could be made. Magistrates were under deadlines to apprehend criminals and could be severely disciplined for wrong judgments. The great Qing code listed 436 main statutes and about 1,900 supplementary or substatutes, which provided specific penalties for specific crimes. The magistrate's problem was to find the statute most applicable to a given case. In doing so he might follow precedent or reason by analogy, but the law was not built up by cases, and although thousands of cases were collected and published with private commentaries to help the magistrates, there was rather little development of generalized doctrine and principles. The statutes were sometimes contradictory and their applicability uncertain. In general, the law was neither primary nor pervasive within the state. To appeal to the letter of the law was to disregard true morality or to admit the moral weakness of one's case.

One major aim of this legal system was to preserve the Confucian hierarchy of relationships, the social order. Thus penalties for the same act varied according to the social and especially the kinship status of the actors. Filial disobedience was the most heinous crime. A son who merely struck his parent could be decapitated, while a parent who beat his son to death, if provoked by the son's disobedience, would deserve only 100 blows (by custom "100" was normally 40 blows) of the heavy bamboo and might be let off entirely. A wife's striking her husband deserved 100 blows, whereas a husband's striking his wife was punishable only if she was badly injured and lodged a complaint. A younger man's scolding his paternal uncle was more heavily punished than his scolding the grandson of his great grandfather's brother. Contributing to the death of one's parent was a capital offense even when quite unintended. T. T. Ch'ü (1961) cites a Qing case: "Teng Feng-ta fell while engaged in a fight, his opponent on top of him. The latter picked up a stone and Teng's son fearing that it would be hurled at his father grabbed a knife and made for the attacker. The latter moved and the knife entered Teng's father's belly, killing him. The authorities considered that the son had sought to rescue his father. They presented his case to the emperor and asked that his sentence be reduced from 'dismemberment' to 'immediate beheading.' This was granted." Behind such provisions lay a concern to maintain the ritual order as one support of the social order. Punishment was the necessary ritual retribution when the social order had been violated.

In short, the law was not an independent specialty, like modern law in America, but a tool of administration in general. Within the broad view of the Confucian philosophy in which the ruling class was educated, the law was a means to be used in the ceaseless struggle to sustain a moral order. Many Chinese officials, in Thomas Metzger's (1977) view, "felt themselves to be poised between harmony and chaos . . . Confucians perceived the society around them as corrupted and in tension with ideals almost beyond the possibility of implementation." But this was a moral problem. They could find no refuge in the mere letter of the law.

Nineteenth-century Westerners were most concerned over the Chinese system's lack of due process to protect the individual. An accused person might be arrested arbitrarily and detained indefinitely, was presumed guilty, might be forced to incriminate himself through confession, and had no advice of counsel nor much chance to make a defense. The individual was unprotected against the state.

Since formal law mainly served the interests of the state, private or civil law remained only informally developed in this legal system. Resolution of conflicts among the people was therefore achieved through various customary and nonofficial channels. Conflicts arising from business deals and contracts might be settled within craft or merchant guilds. Disputes between neighbors might be mediated by village elders, neighborhood associations, or gentry members. In particular, the heads of extended family (lineage) or clan organizations, in addition to maintaining the religious rituals of ancestor reverence, supporting schools for clan members' children, and arranging their marriages, would make every effort to keep their members out of court by assuring their tax payments and settling disputes among them. After all, the legal system was part of the government, which remained superficial, far above the level of daily life in the villages. Most conflicts were therefore resolved extralegally by mediation and appeals to old customs and local opinion.

This nondevelopment of Chinese law along lines familiar to the West was plainly related to the nondevelopment of capitalism and an independent business class in old China. There was no idea of the corporation as a legal individual. Big firms were family affairs. Business relations were not cold impersonal matters governed by the general principles of the law and of contract in a world apart from home and family. Business was a segment of the whole web of friendship, kinship obligations, and personal relations that supported Chinese life. In old China due process of law, sanctity of contract, and free private enterprise never became the sacred trinity that they became in the capitalist West.

This chapter has suggested that nineteenth-century China would be slow to industrialize. The reasons would be social and political as well as economic. The Chinese state and society, in other words, had become inured to counterproductive attitudes, goals, and practices that would impede modernization. The Confucian disesteem of profit, the rulers' concern always to maintain control, the law's unconcern for protecting private investment, the officials' custom of utilizing the merchant, diminishing productivity and footbinding on the farm all combined with the scholars' overweening pride and the common people's xenophobia to create inertia. Late Imperial China could not easily respond to the attack of Western commerce and culture.

Nonofficial capitalist enterprise and state fostering of industry failed to take center stage in nineteenth-century China. We are left with the impression that as of 1750 or so the preindustrial societies of China and Europe had much in common; indeed, they probably seemed in appearance to be more like each other than either one was like the Western states that would emerge transformed by the Industrial Revolution in the nineteenth century. Yet we must acknowledge that such a similarity in appearances was superficial. Beneath the surface lay great differences in social structure, culture, and ideas, as the nineteenth century would demonstrate.

9

Frontier Unrest and the
Opening of China

The Weakness of State Leadership

Whether China was opened by British gunboats or opened of its own accord is no longer a great issue for debate. Growth of population and foreign trade were both impelling China toward greater contact with the outside world. This trend precipitated rebellions on both domestic and foreign frontiers. Meanwhile, the one thing essential for the industrialization of late-comers like Japan or Russia was government leadership. Unfortunately, in nineteenth-century China, government grew weaker and more myopic just when its strength and foresight were needed.

By the end of the eighteenth century, population pressure was increasing the vulnerability of the populace to drought, flood, famine, and disease. These in turn presented the creaking machinery of Qing government with problems it could not meet—flood control, famine relief, increased need for taxes, increased difficulty in getting them. The problem is illustrated by Pierre-Etienne Will's (1990) study of famine relief. In the mid-Qing era, officials maintained the ever-normal granary stocks, combatted price increases, appraised famine conditions, shipped grain in from other provinces, and supervised its careful distribution. But in the 1800s after the population had doubled, the official system broke down, and gentry managers more and more had to take on the public task of famine relief. Such weaknesses combined with official demoralization and self-seeking to make government less effective and weaken its prestige. The nineteenth century became a long story of dynastic decline.

Three motifs dominated China's nineteenth-century experience—domestic rebellion, foreign invasion, and the efforts of the ruling elite to control both and preserve their rule (see Table 4). Since attempts at re-

Table 4. Events in China, 1796–1901

Domestic rebellion	Foreign invasion	Official and elite response
White Lotus 1796–1804		
	Turkestan 1826–1835	
	Anglo–Chinese Opium War 1839–1842	Increasing militarization under local elite
Taiping 1851–1864		Suppression of rebellions
Nian 1853–1868	Anglo–French 1856–1860	
Chinese Muslim SW 1855–1873 NW1862–1873		Qing Restoration ca. 1861–1876
		Self-strengthening 1861–1894
	French 1883–1885	
	Sino– Japanese 1894–1895	Reform movement 1895–1898
	Imperialist encroachment 1898	
Boxer Rising 1898–1901	Boxer War 1900	Qing reforms 1901–1911

bellion, invasion, and control became even greater in the twentieth century, this chapter offers only a foretaste of more recent disasters and achievements.

Recent studies have remade our image of imperialism in China. The Hobson–Lenin thesis at the turn of the century stressed the economic ill effects of imported foreign manufactures destroying native handicraft livelihood and of foreign finance capitalism impoverishing native governments. More recent research has led to a less stark economic picture, in which foreign trade, investment, and technology sometimes stimulated native growth and technological progress. Today's historians are more likely to stress the social disruption and psychological demoralization caused by foreign imperialism. In these dimensions the long-term foreign invasion of China proved to be a disaster so comprehensive and appalling that we are still incapable of fully describing it. Innovations like Christian missions, Western education, and foreign investment became two-edged, often seen as forward steps in our long-term foreign view yet also frequently destructive of China's contemporary well-being. At stake was an entire way of life, a civilization on a grander scale than the economics or psychology of imperialism.

On balance I believe "imperialism" has become a catch-all term like "feudalism," too broad to accept or deny overall, more useful in adjectival form to characterize concrete situations. In any case, China's nineteenth-century troubles began at home with rebellion, not invasion.

The increasing weakness of Qing government was graphically demonstrated in its initial inability to suppress a domestic rebellion at the end of the Qianlong reign. Other small risings followed. Manchu skill was evident in calming domestic rebels in Sichuan and Xinjiang, but the same formula when applied to the handling of Western rebels at Guangzhou would prove disastrous. We therefore look first at the problems of domestic rebellion and then at the forces operating to create rebellion in the foreign trade.

The White Lotus Rebellion, 1796–1804

In the countryside, manpower and food supply were the sinews of warfare, which might be mobilized to unseat the reigning dynasty. Consequently, cults such as the White Lotus Society, a religious sect dating from the Mongol period, sometimes had to be secret in self-defense. In mobilizing its adherents, the White Lotus Society appealed to the hopes of poverty-stricken peasants by its multiple promises that the Maitreya Buddha would descend into the world, that the Ming dynasty would be restored, and that disaster, disease, and personal suffering could be obviated in this life and happiness secured in the next. In the late eighteenth century the sect had spread through the border region where the provinces of Hubei, Sichuan, and Shaanxi join, in the region north of the Yangzi gorges and on the upper waters of the Han River. This mountainous area, rather inhospitable to agriculture, was a domestic frontier area only recently opened to settlement under official Qing auspices. Migration of poor settlers, although encouraged officially, had not been accompanied by an equal development of imperial administration over them. The communities of settlers lived on the very margin of subsistence and tended to be a law unto themselves. The leaders of the White Lotus cult soon added to their popular appeal an anti-Manchu racial doctrine.

The rebellion began in 1796 as a protest against the exactions of minor tax collectors. Though the imperial garrisons were able to get each small uprising under control in turn, new outbreaks continued to erupt, too numerous to control. The populace had already organized self-defense corps against the aborigines to the south and had collected arms and food. When these groups rebelled, they could move into easily defensible mountain redoubts before the imperial forces could arrive. The systematic corruption permitted under the now senile Qianlong Emperor handicapped the imperial military. They lacked supplies, morale, and incentive as well as vigorous leadership. Both sides ravaged the populace instead of fighting.

The White Lotus Rebellion was suppressed only after the Jiaqing Emperor assumed real power upon the death of the Qianlong Emperor in 1799 and supported vigorous Manchu commanders. By pursuing the rebels tenaciously, on the one hand, and establishing tighter control of the manpower and food supply of the area, on the other, the Manchu generals eventually put down the rebellion. First of all, the Qing mobilized the villagers to build several hundred walled enclosures in which the local peasantry could be concentrated. These walled villages were then protected from the rebels by newly organized local militia, who could by this time be enrolled more easily because the devastation of the countryside had seriously hindered their farming and sustenance. In this way the populace was brought under imperial control. Meanwhile the militia were trained to join in the campaign of extermination against the rebels. At the same time a policy of conciliation was pursued toward the men the rebels had impressed into their bands, so as to secure their surrender; and other measures were taken to prevent refugees from continuing to join the rebels. By this combination of force, leniency, and administrative arrangements, the imperial commanders gradually starved the rebels of their new recruits and food supplies.

The policy of "strengthening the walls and clearing the countryside" eventually sapped the strength of the rebellion, and it died out about 1804. But the repercussions of the uprising were enormously damaging to the dynasty. It had cost the imperial regime the rough equivalent of five years' revenue (200 million ounces of silver). Worse still, it had destroyed the Manchu banner forces' reputation for invincibility. It was found that the militia troops when properly trained became professional soldiers, warlike and dangerous, and subsequently an effort had to be made to recover their arms from them.

In 1813 the sect of the Eight Trigrams, a sort of White Lotus off-shoot, staged a rising in a North China county and actually sent a group to try to invade the Forbidden City in Beijing. Even though it was soon suppressed, Susan Naquin (1976) concludes that 70,000 people were killed in the process.

While these stirrings of peasant rebellion gave an ominous cast to the early decades of the nineteenth century, an equally dire situation was developing in China's maritime relations. Here again the bearers of bad news were Chinese, not foreigners, but Chinese who had gone abroad in defiance of Ming and early Qing prohibitions. In short, a neglected wing of the Chinese people, which we call Maritime China, was about to become a major force in Chinese history.

Maritime China: Origins of the Overseas Chinese

The contrast between Maritime China and Continental China was almost as great as that between China and Inner Asia. Few classically educated chroniclers, concentrated as they were upon imperial government, ever went to sea. Chinese seafarers did not write memoirs. Because the sea, unlike the steppe, did not harbor rivals for power, it had been given little importance in Chinese history. Yet Chinese life from the start had had a maritime wing more or less equal and opposite to the Inner Asian wing.

Once we approach the sea from China, we meet a fundamental fact of geography known as the monsoon, a seasonal wind that blew north in summer from the equatorial zone and south in winter. The predictability of these monsoon winds was far more reliable than the rainfall on which North China agriculture depended. Consequently, seafaring had developed in Neolithic times long before written history, a fact that accounts for Neolithic type-sites being found in Taiwan. With the monsoon, navigating to and from the island was not difficult, even if punctuated by summer typhoons.

Many thousands of years later the reliability of sea transport facilitated the Qin-Han absorption of the area of Guangzhou and North Vietnam as part of China's first unified empire. Access to the area by land alone, following barge routes on rivers and portage roads connecting them, could never have reached so far with power adequate to take control. Experienced and massive coastal seafaring was essential to this early extension of the empire to southernmost China. The conclusive evidence is the funerary ship model excavated in Guangzhou of the Han period, with a centered stern-post rudder—a key invention of nautical technology that appeared in Europe only a thousand years later. It bespeaks a high degree of early Chinese nautical sophistication.

Given such early Chinese skill in seafaring, it seems strange to find that the first long-distance international traders in the ports of Southeast China were Arabs. After the founding of Islam in Arabia in the seventh century, Muslim seafarers and invaders took off in all directions, as medieval Europe soon became aware.

Those readers who missed the world history lecture on Islam may be reminded that the religion was founded by the prophet Muhammad in 622 AD in Medina. Called Muslims, his followers believed in the One God, Allah, in the teachings of Muhammad's book, the *Koran*, in God's predestination, and in the Day of Resurrection. Their strict regimen of five daily prayers attesting the faith, along with other duties like a pilgrimage to Mecca, Muhammad's birthplace, prepared them to wage a Holy War against the infidel. Combined with Arab trading skill and seafaring, their faith impelled the Arabs on a Diaspora of expansion east and west.

Muslim forces soon conquered Syria, Persia (Iran), Iraq, and Egypt. Despite rebellions and civil wars, they took over North Africa and Spain and invaded southern France until defeated in 732. Meanwhile, on the east, Muslim forces had taken over Afghanistan, the lower Indus valley in northwest India, and the Central Asian trading cities of Bokhara and Samarkand. More important than the kaleidoscopic flux of wars and rulers, Muslim cities from Baghdad to Bokhara became centers of achievement in science and the arts.

By the tenth century, the Muslim states of conquest linked the sea trade of the Mediterranean with that of the Indian Ocean and so made possible a seaborne commerce that brought spices like pepper, nutmeg, and cinnamon all the way from the islands that produced them in the East Indies to their European market at Alexandria. This spice trade, which eventually helped motivate European expansion to the Far East, much earlier and more easily reached China, where spices were equally prized for preserving food in the absence of refrigeration. The extensive Muslim contact with China under the Mongols was both by land across

Central Asia over the Silk Road and by sea at coastal ports. The story is complicated by the fact that within the Muslim world Arabs were joined by Persians and Turks and some Indians in the shifting configuration of Muslim states and their rivalries. Against this complex background we may imagine a plenitude of Chinese trading junks on well-established coastal routes providing a matrix for the long-distance Muslim commerce at China's big Fujian ports like Quanzhou (Arab Zayton).

While Arab traders had come first to China, Chinese merchant junks began by at least the tenth century to trade at ports along the peninsulas of Southeast Asia and the islands of the East Indies. Beginning even before the Tang, references in the dynastic histories to Chinese trade with Southeast Asia grow more and more numerous. By the time of the Zheng He expeditions of the years 1405–1433, Chinese trade goods were finding markets all across southeast and south Asia and even the east coast of Africa (see Map 18). A score or more of petty states recorded in 1589 as sending tribute to the Ming were mainly the ports of call on the two trade routes that went respectively down the coast of Malaysia to the straits of Malacca and through the Philippines and the island kingdom of Sulu to the East Indies. Chinese traders naturally established their agents or other connections at these ports of trade, where Overseas Chinese communities of sojourners began to grow up. By 1818 ports of call on the Malay peninsula like Ligor, Sungora, Patani, Trengganu, Pahang, and Johore were listed in Chinese government records more realistically as "non-tributary trading countries," that is, places frequented by Chinese merchants that paid no tribute to Beijing. This far-flung Chinese trading community was already established when the Portuguese and Spanish invaded East Asia in the sixteenth century.

As Wang Gungwu (1991) reminds us, Chinese sojourners' communities abroad were not under Chinese official control. Growth of the Overseas Chinese settlement was not fostered nor even countenanced by the Chinese imperial government. In China, while the gentry-elite let no merchant subculture grow up comparable to that in Japan and Europe in the sixteenth century, the Chinese abroad in Southeast Asia were under quite different local, official, and social restraints. They were often able to accumulate capital and became risk-taking entrepreneurs with their own style of life. Their family enterprises in the British, Dutch, and French colonial areas (in Burma, Malaysia, the East Indies, and Indo-China) usefully benefited from the rule of European law. In Bangkok and Manila they advanced through marriage ties with local patricians.

Philanthropy and conspicuous consumption were less useful overseas than in China, while economic development was more appreciated by the local rulers.

In a way curiously reminiscent of the local gentry in China, the Overseas Chinese in Southeast Asia found their social level and functions sandwiched between the European rulers and the local villages. Chinese became brokers who helped in tax collections and in maintaining local services like ferries, bridges, and bazaars. They were generally a stabilizing element in colonial communities, too few to seize power, interested in profiting from services rendered as well as from local trade.

The example of the Chinese role at Manila is instructive. When the Spaniards arrived in the Philippines in force in the 1560s and began to build a colony based on Christian teaching and Filipino plantation labor, they found themselves endangered by the breakdown of the Ming ban on sea trade and the upsurge of Japanese maritime adventurers linked with Chinese coastal pirates. The Ming prohibition of Chinese sea trade, a dead letter long since, was lifted in 1567. By the time the Spaniards began to build their capital at Manila, 150 or so Chinese were on hand. By 1600 there were 25,000 living in a special part of Manila set aside for them. (Chinese converts to Christianity were not so confined.) Two Chinese communities thus began to develop—the commercial one of sojourners who managed all the shops and crafts of a Chinese city, and the mixed one of Christian mestizos who would become Filipino leaders partly of Chinese descent.

In general Overseas Chinese created fraternal associations and secret societies for protection of their interests, as well as guilds with their temples to Guandi and the Empress of Heaven for their commercial welfare. Their trade was not dominated by large corporations with a modern capacity to invest and manage overseas transactions. The durable and seaworthy sailing junks that carried the trade were privately owned, and their cargoes were generally the property of individuals or family merchant firms. Many Chinese quickly learned the European commercial technology of the day.

As time went on, these Chinese trading communities overseas became the active outer fringe of a Maritime China that countered the land-based and agrarian-centered style of the Ming and Qing empires. As a minor tradition from early times, this Maritime China had grown up in the ports where the river traffic from inland China met the ships from Chinese enclaves abroad. Leonard Blusse (1986) notes that despite Beijing's ban on overseas trade, during Ming and early Qing about a hundred big Chinese junks traded every year with Southeast Asia. These traders were ready to expand into international commerce as opportunity allowed. Their principal entrepot on the China coast was Xiamen (Amoy), a port in Fujian that, unlike nearby Quanzhou and Fuzhou, had not been the site of an official superintendency of merchant shipping (*shibosi*).

European Trading Companies and the Canton Trade

Sea trade with Europe quickened the growth rate of Maritime China. The East India Companies, inaugurated about 1600 by the British and Dutch, were powerful corporate bodies that accumulated capital from joint stock investors and were empowered by their national kings to monopolize trade and govern territories abroad. These powerful engines of commercial expansion created British India and the Dutch East Indies. The British developed a staple trade with China in exports of tea, silk, and porcelain and imports of silver, woolen textiles, and eventually opium from India. At first they followed the routes and used the pilots of the Chinese junk trade. Chinese and foreigners in international commerce became a trade-centered community that formed the first Sino–Western meeting place of the modern age.

Although Xiamen had been a major focus of the Chinese trade to Southeast Asia and up the China coast, after 1759 Guangzhou (Canton) was made the sole port open for Europeans. The Canton trade, as it has been known in the West, was organized on typical Chinese lines: the government commissioned a group of Chinese merchant families to act as brokers superintending the foreign traders. Responsibility for each Western ship was taken by one Chinese firm, acting as its security merchant. The security merchants formed a guild, called the Cohong (*hong* means trading firm), which answered the commands of the emperor's specially appointed superintendent of maritime customs for the Guangdong region. This official, usually a Manchu from the Imperial Household Department of the Inner Court in Beijing, was known to foreigners as the Hoppo. The Cohong and the Hoppo had the job of taxing the foreigners' imports and especially their exports of teas and silks.

Until 1834, when the British East India Company lost its royal charter to monopolize British staple trade with China, the Company fitted into this special "Canton system." Its supercargoes sent by the East India Company board of directors in London lived in style in the British Factory (business center and residence) on the banks of the river outside the big provincial capital of Guangzhou during the trading season, from October to March. In the off season from April to September they retired downriver to the Portuguese coastal settlement of Macao.

Since the Hoppo was accustomed to squeezing the Hong merchants for special sums to meet imperial needs, these Chinese merchants were often short of capital to purchase the cargoes of teas and silks to lade on the East Indiamen, as contracted with the Company. Thus they tended to go into debt to the British, and when official exactions kept these licensed merchants in debt or even bankrupt, the British complained about this effect of the merchant guild monopoly. This shortage of investment funds for the tea and silk cargoes to England was a continuing problem for the Company.

Another factor in the Sino–foreign trade was the continued importation into China in the sixteenth and seventeenth centuries of silver, especially from Japan and the Americas. Estimates suggest that as much as $10 million worth of silver annually came into China's domestic trade. As in Europe, this inflow led to rising prices, greater monetization, and increased commerce. In the middle decades of the seventeenth century, however, events in Japan, Spain, and China combined in what some have called a "seventeenth-century crisis" to reduce China's silver import. The consequences, including a sudden fall of prices, were disastrous. In this way China was drawn into the international trading world long before the fact was realized.

Late Imperial China's foreign trade played a subordinate but important role both as a source of imported silver and as a market to stimulate production for export. One estimate is that as much as one seventh of the tea that went to market in China was bought by the British East India Company in its high period after 1759, especially after the rival European smugglers of China tea into the British market were undone by the Commutation Act of 1784, which lowered the duties collected in England.

An omen of China's future was provided in 1793 when the British East India Company, which would continue to rule India until 1858, sent a diplomatic mission to China. Its head, Lord George Macartney, took scientists and artists in an entourage of 100 on a 66-gun man-of-war plus two escort vessels loaded with examples of British manufacturing technology that the Qing court promptly labeled "tribute from England." The Industrial Revolution was gaining momentum, but remained quite unknown to the senescent Qianlong Emperor. The British requests for broader trade opportunities under a published tariff, as well as diplomatic representation at Beijing, were an invitation to China to join the modern world then being born. Beijing politely and complacently turned it all down. Twenty-three years later another embassy under Lord Amherst in 1816 was rudely treated and sent away. By this time Britain and British India were already playing key roles in opening China to international trade. Unfortunately, the Qing court was little concerned with Maritime China and had no idea of the outside world it would soon have to deal with. Its concern was to preserve its authority both within China and on its sea and land frontiers. Early in the nineteenth century while trouble was brewing at Guangzhou, rebellion flared up in Inner Asia over control of non-Chinese on the imperial frontier.

Rebellion on the Turkestan Frontier, 1826–1835

From the oasis cities on the ancient Silk Road in Turkestan (Xinjiang) trade crossed the Pamirs especially between Kashgar and the state of Kokand west of the mountains. Early in the nineteenth century a crisis arose on this frontier. The Central Asianist Joseph Fletcher (in *CHOC* 10) has described how saintly families, descended from the Prophet or other early religious leaders, had great popular influence. In fact, one of these lineages had ruled Turkestan for a time before the Manchu conquest of the 1750s. In exile west of the Pamirs in Kokand, they nursed their claims and sometimes led cavalry raids across the mountain passes into Kashgaria.

One scion of this line was Jahangir, who became a problem just after the Daoguang Emperor came to the throne in 1821. Jahangir's holy war against the Qing was triggered by a dynamic conjunction of faith and commerce. In brief, the westward trade of Kashgar was dominated by merchants of Kokand, whose ruler paid tribute to the Qing emperor, the usual practice in order to smooth the path of foreign trade. Kokand had therefore enrolled as a tributary, had kept Jahangir confined, and in turn had been paid a large yearly gift from the Qing as a reward for such admirable loyalty. But, as Kokandian merchants became more influential in the principal market at Kashgar, Kokand asked for special privileges there—lower taxes on its trade and appointment of its own resident to superintend Kokandian traders in Kashgar.

When these demands were refused in 1817, Kokand released the impetuous Jahangir, who eventually achieved a devastating invasion of Chinese Turkestan in 1816. A Qing relief expedition of 22,000 men crossed the arid trail from one oasis to the next and so reconquered Kashgar in 1827. Jahangir was betrayed and sent to Beijing, where Daoguang had him ritually presented at the imperial temple of ancestors before being quartered.

The Qing reestablished its rule over the area, but Kokand's commercial power and military nuisance capacity had been amply demonstrated. In subsequent negotiations Beijing's envoys gradually worked out an administrative settlement which by 1835 provided that (1) Kokand should station a political representative at Kashgar with commercial agents under him at five other cities; (2) these officials should have consular, judicial, and police powers over foreigners in the area (most of whom came from Kokand); and (3) they could levy customs duties on the goods of such foreigners. In addition, the Qing indemnified traders they had dispossessed during the hostilities.

As we shall see in the rest of this chapter, this was the background from which Daoguang would approach the British problem developing at Guangzhou. That Qing policy toward the British in 1834–1842 would be based on Qing experience on the trading frontier of Central Asia in 1826–1835 was perfectly natural. The Turkestan settlement with Kokand in 1835 had been an exercise in barbarian management, which achieved a stable frontier by giving local commercial concessions and paying some money.

Opium and the Struggle for a New Order at Guangzhou, 1834–1842

After 1759 European trade at Guangzhou under the Cohong and the Hoppo was still nominally conducted as though it were a boon granted to tributary states. Opium imports from India to China now precipitated a crisis.

Opium was produced and sold at auction under official British auspices in India and taken to China by private British and Indian traders licensed by the East India Company that (until 1858) still governed India. Opium sales at Guangzhou paid for the teas shipped to London in a thriving India–China–Britain triangular trade. The drain of silver to pay for ever-increasing imports of opium began to alarm Qing administrators: they noticed silver becoming more dear in terms of the copper coins used by the populace to buy their silver for tax payments, and this threatened both the government's revenues and the popular livelihood. The exhaustive research of Man-houng Lin (unpublished), has analyzed the Qing officials' reactions to this monetary crisis. While pinpointing the outflow of silver to pay for opium, they remained generally unaware of China's fiscal involvement in world trade. Many of the variables involved—such as silver imports from Japan, silver production in Latin America, copper cash production in China, debasement, hoarding, world trade depression—were still invisible to them.

In 1834 London ended the East India Company's monopoly of British trade with China, and a British official was sent to superintend British trade there. Two issues thus urgently arose for China: how to stop the opium trade, and how to deal with the British official.

Under the Guangzhou system the East India Company monopolists had played ball with the brokers called Hong merchants, who handled their trade ship-by-ship and collected duty payments for the Hoppo. But after free trade broke out in 1834, the British private traders like Jardine, Matheson & Co., who had been importing the opium, now began also to export the teas and silks in place of the Company. The British official sent to superintend them refused to deal like a trader with the Hong merchants and demanded to deal with the Qing officials on a basis of diplomatic equality. He was flouting the tribute system.

To accept Britain's diplomatic equality would destroy the emperor's superiority to all other rulers, which helped him to maintain his position in China. To tolerate the opium trade any further would not only further upset the silver/copper exchange rate but would also damage his moral prestige. Opium smoking, though less powerfully addictive than modern derivatives, was a social curse that destroyed both individual smokers and their families. Land was wasted for poppy growing, while the high price of the drug as contraband led to violence and corruption between smugglers and officials. The Chinese demand grew up in situations of demoralization not unlike the American inner cities of today. This tremendous social evil was sparked by the lust for profit among the British Indian government, the foreigners who took opium to China, and the corrupt Chinese distributors. To Americans of today this pattern sounds distressingly familiar.

Several years of argument and uncertainty were due to the Qing administrators' doubts that they could destroy the Chinese smugglers or embargo the trade of the British, whose new steam gunboats were the last word in mobile firepower. Some in 1836 advocated legalizing the opium trade since it could not be stopped. The intransigent opposition to appeasement was led by ambitious Chinese officials who used as their meeting place a poetry reading club at Beijing. This faction's opportunist moral righteousness, which has been newly explored by James Polachek (1992), won out in 1839 when the Daoguang Emperor sent an incorrupt Imperial Commissioner, Lin Zexu, to compel the foreign traders to stop bringing opium to China. Lin suppressed the Chinese opium purveyors in Guangzhou, but he had to barricade the foreigners in their factories before they finally surrendered their current stocks of opium. They knew more opium, now higher priced, was en route from India and, moreover, that the British government might recompense them for their losses.

Commissioner Lin's righteous coercion precipitated war, in which British commercial interests were heavily involved. Dr. William Jardine went to London and helped Lord Palmerston work out the war aims and strategy. The Jardine trading firm leased vessels to the British fleet, lent pilots and translators, provided hospitality and intelligence, and cashed the army quartermaster's bills on London. But the British expeditionary force led by new paddle-wheel steamers was sent to Guangzhou and thence up the coast to secure privileges of general commercial and diplomatic intercourse on a Western basis of equality, and not especially to aid the expansion of the opium trade. The latter was expanding rapidly of its own accord and was only one point of friction in the general antagonism between the Chinese and British schemes of international relations.

In half a dozen engagements along the southeast coast, Britain's gunboats won the Opium War of 1839–1842 and secured Qing agreement to the Treaty of Nanjing in August 1842.

Joseph Fletcher has pointed out how the Anglo–Chinese treaty settlements at Nanjing and later all followed the 1835 example with Kokand. The treaty provisions included (1) extraterritoriality (foreign consular jurisdiction over foreign nationals), an upgrading of an old Chinese practice, (2) an indemnity, (3) a moderate tariff and direct foreign contact with the customs collectors, (4) most-favored-nation treatment (an expression of China's "impartial benevolence" to all outsiders), (5) freedom to trade with all comers, no monopoly (long the custom at Kashgar). Moreover, designated places for trade (now to be called treaty ports) were an old Chinese frontier custom, and equal relations without the kowtow's three kneelings and nine prostrations had been common on the Kokand and Russian frontiers far from China proper.

Manchu statesmanship was consistent on the two frontiers, but there were two major differences: First, Britain, the United States, and France were aggressive maritime powers from another world, a world of seaborne commerce and war, ruled by law and treaty rights, and for them the first treaty settlements of 1842–1844 were only the beginning of encroachment. Second, the concessions that the Qing could use to stabilize Kokand-Kashgar relations far off in Central Asia could only damage Qing prestige if used in China proper. The Manchus, when they took power at Beijing, had inherited the tradition of China's central superiority. Anyone who ruled there had to exact tributary obeisance from outsiders as part of the job of being Son of Heaven. So the unequal treaties were a defeat that grew bigger as time passed.

To appease the British, the Qing gave them the barren island of Hong Kong in perpetuity and opened the first five treaty ports. The top Manchu negotiator even visited Hong Kong on a British gunboat! Yet the principles embodied in the Treaty of Nanjing in 1842 were not fully accepted on the Chinese side, and the treaty privileges seemed inadequate from the British side. Consequently, the treaty system was not really established until the British and French had fought a second war against the Qing and secured treaties at Tianjin in 1858. Even then the new order was not acknowledged by the reluctant dynasty until an Anglo-French expedition occupied Beijing itself in 1860. The transition from tribute relations to treaty relations occupied a generation of friction at Guangzhou before 1840, and twenty years of trade, negotiation, and coercion thereafter.

Inauguration of the Treaty Century after 1842

Although China's treaties with Britain (1842–43), with the United States and France (both in 1844), and with all of them and Russia in 1858 were signed as between equal sovereign powers, they were actually quite unequal. China was placed against her will in a weaker position, open to the inroads of Western commerce and its attendant culture. By the twentieth century, after three generations of energetic Western consuls had developed its fine points, the treaty structure was a finely articulated and comprehensive mechanism. It was based first of all on treaty ports, at first five in number and eventually more than eighty (see Map 20).

The major treaty ports had a striking physical and institutional resemblance to one another. Each had a crowded, noisy waterfront (bund) and godowns (warehouses) swarming with coolies (a foreign word for Chinese laborers), who substituted for machinery. All this activity was under the supervision of Chinese compradors (foreign-hired business managers), who managed affairs beneath the overlordship of the foreign

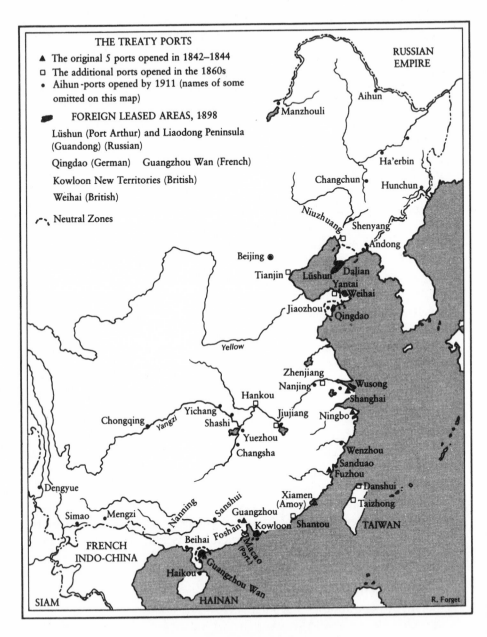

THE TREATY PORTS

▲ The original 5 ports opened in 1842–1844
▢ The additional ports opened in the 1860s
• Aihun -ports opened by 1911 (names of some
  omitted on this map)

⬛ FOREIGN LEASED AREAS, 1898

Lüshun (Port Arthur) and Liaodong Peninsula
(Guandong) (Russian)

Qingdao (German)   Guangzhou Wan (French)

Kowloon New Territories (British)

Weihai (British)

⌒ Neutral Zones

RUSSIAN
EMPIRE

Aihun

Manzhouli

Ha'erbin

Changchun   Hunchun

Niuzhuang   Shenyang

Andong

Beijing

Tianjin   Lüshun   Dalian
                  Yantai
                  Weihai
Jiaozhou
          Qingdao

Yellow

Zhenjiang
Nanjing   Wusong
Hankou   Shanghai
Yichang   Jiujiang   Ningbo
Chongqing   Yangzi   Shashi
                  Yuezhou
          Changsha   Wenzhou
                          Sanduao
                          Fuzhou
Dengyue   Danshui

          Xiamen   Taizhong
          (Amoy)
Simao   Mengzi   Guangzhou
          Nanning   Sanshui   Kowloon   Shantou   TAIWAN
                  Beihai   Foshan   Macao
FRENCH   (Port.)
INDO-CHINA
          Haikou   Guangzhou Wan

SIAM   HAINAN

R. Forget

20. Foreign Encroachments

耕

東皋一犁雨
布榖初催耕
綠野暗春曉
烏犍苦肩頳
我衙勸農字
杖策東郊行
永懷歷山下
往事關聖情

17. Illustrations from an 1808 edition of *Peiwenzhai gengzhitu* show the principal steps in rice cultivation. The first step is the preparation of the seedbed. Here, in South China, the farmer and his water buffalo are ploughing such an area. A long-gowned scholar watches from the dike nearby, and a small boy brings food and drink on his shoulder-pole.

拔秧

新秧初出水渺渺
渺翠毯齊清晨
且拔濯父子爭
提攜既沐青滿
握再櫛根無泥
及時趂芒種散
著畦東西

18. The rice seedlings have sprouted and now stand crowded in the seedbed.
They must be gathered in bundles for transplanting in the paddy fields, where
they will be fertilized with night soil and have room to grow.

插秧

晨雨麥秋潤午風槐
夏凉溪南與溪北笠
歌插新秧抛擲不停
手左右無亂行我教
插秧馬代勞民莫愁

19. Transplanting rice seedlings by hand in orderly rows in the flooded fields is a backbreaking task. The farmers have to stoop and wade backward in water ankle-deep under a hot sun. Millions of farmers in China, Japan, and elsewhere in Asia still grow rice in this way.

灌溉

握苗鄱宋人抱甕慚家荘何
如銜尾鴉倒流渴池塘穏秅
舞翠浪邃除生晨涼斜陽耿
疎柳笑歌間女郎

20. Plentiful water is a requirement for the growth of the rice crop. Here we see two inventions for lifting water from the nearby pond over the dikes and into the paddies. On the left three men leaning their arms on a crossbar press with their feet the treadles which operate a square-pallet chain pump. The square-pallets fill with pond water and lift it on an endless circulating chain. In the foreground the lone worker with his simpler water-moving contraption has protected the dike with a bamboo mat. On hillsides, banked terraces capture the rainfall.

牧刈田鎌手轡穂歡望
刈穫家覓龜折風呼屋
時穫刈倉玗兒色荷山
腰時穫倉日童凌擔月
　時濃永行短歸望
腰永身拾褐望

21. In harvest time the paddies must be dry. The chain pump can be used for draining. The careful planting in rows simplifies the reaping. Men use sickles to cut the long stalks heavy with rice. Boys join in the gathering and binding that follow. Across the pond a woman and child watch the action.

入倉天寒牛在牢
歲暮粟入庚田父
餘樂炙皆臥
賦租胥吏來
樁應却懣催
勾午輸官王
事了索飯
兒叶怒

24. The final step in rice cultivation is storage of the baskets full of winnowed rice. The men are bringing in the heavy baskets and emptying them into a storage room. The side walls can be raised as needed by adding planks. Note the *dou* under the roof. In the distance, men are drinking tea and chatting. A water buffalo nuzzles her calf, and a woman just beyond pats her child.

25. A late Qing edition of the *Qinding shujing tushuo* (1905) depicts craftsmen at work. Carpenters, blacksmiths, bricklayers, and others demonstrate their skills to long-gowned supervisors.

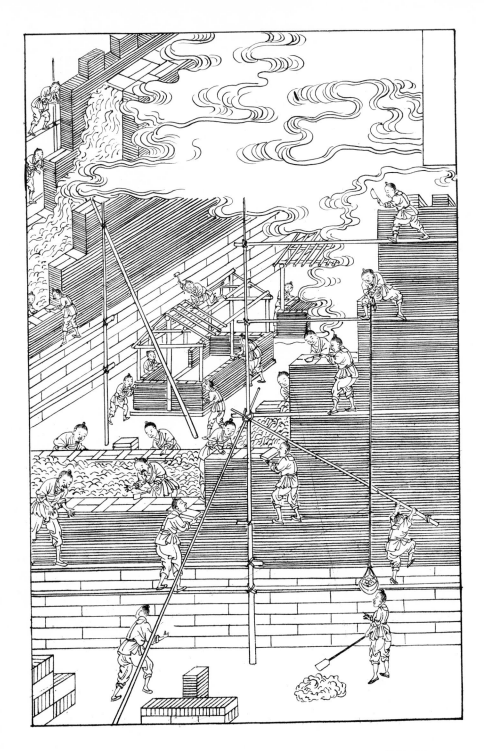

26. A city wall. To be impenetrable by invaders, it is built of two parallel brick walls with earth packed tightly between. Builders on this flimsy scaffolding are raising the walls to forty feet or more.

27. Walling a compound. Unlike the city wall, this wall is built entirely of bricks with a pitched roof of tiles. Two men with trowels are plastering the bricks for elegant effect.

30. A village market. On the busy street, fish, ducks, grain, and other produce are for sale. A shopkeeper at the right is weighing something delicate, probably medicine. Note that none of the shoppers are women.

31. A military workshop. Bows are being strung, arrows tested, swords sharpened, and metal spearheads added to long poles. Soldiers' plumed hats and shields are completed at the back.

32. A hunting scene. The hunters have their horses, dogs, and beaters. A horseman
aims his spear at a speeding fox as a nearby deer escapes. A blundering gunman
misses a rabbit and kills a dog. Birds are the targets of arrows.

taipans (firm managers). Each treaty port centered in a foreign section newly built on the edge of a teeming Chinese city and dominated by the tall white flagstaff of Her Majesty's consulate. Its foreign institutions included the club, the race course, and the church. It was ruled by a proper British consul and his colleagues of other nations and protected by squat gunboats moored off the bund. At Guangzhou, Xiamen, and Fuzhou the foreign community got further protection by being established on an island. At Ningbo, Shanghai, and other places the foreign area was separated from the Chinese city by a river, canal, creek, or other waterway.

These coastal enclaves began as offshoots of Western culture—like cities in European colonies, outposts of empire. Yet from the beginning they had a Chinese component, for alien invaders needed the help of Chinese servants and shopmen just as much as the Chinese upper class did. The treaty ports quickly became Sino–foreign cities where the foreigner played an increasing role in China's urbanization.

Extraterritoriality, under which foreigners and their activities in China remained answerable only to foreign and not to Chinese law, was not a modern invention. In a manner rather like that of the Turks at Constantinople, the Chinese government in medieval times had expected foreign communities in the seaports to govern themselves under their own headmen and by their own laws. This expressed the Chinese imperial preference for minimalist government, getting people to police themselves. This had been true of the early Arab traders in China. The British and Americans at Guangzhou before the Opium War demanded extraterritoriality because they had become accustomed to the protection of their own laws in their relations with the Muslim states of North Africa and the Ottoman Empire and had suffered from Chinese attempts to apply Chinese criminal law to Westerners, without regard for Western rules of evidence or the modern Western abhorrence of torture. Most of all the foreign traders needed the help of their own law of contract.

A further essential of the treaties was the treaty tariff, which by its low rates would have prevented the Chinese from protecting their native industries, in the event that they had recognized the desirability of doing so before the 1890s. In the 1840s Chinese customs collectors were wont to make their own deals with merchants and also lacked authority and means to coerce the foreigners, so that the administration of even the low treaty tariff was not impartial or effective in Chinese hands. Foreign inspectors were therefore appointed as Chinese officials to run the Chinese customhouse at Shanghai in 1854. The Chinese employment of for-

eigners followed ancient precedents and was one of the most constructive features of the treaty system. Under (Sir) Robert Hart as Inspector
General, the Westerners who served as commissioners of Chinese Maritime Customs became leading figures in every port, guardians both of the
equality of competition (by enforcement of the regulations for foreign
trade) and of the modest Chinese revenue of about 5 percent derived
from it. The growth of foreign trade gave Beijing and the coastal provinces important new revenues that could be used for modern needs.

By the most-favored-nation clause (a neat diplomatic device) all foreign powers shared whatever privileges any of them could squeeze out of
China. The treaty system kept on growing as the fortunes of the Qing dynasty deteriorated. The opium trade that had begun as a joint Sino-foreign traffic was taken into the country. After the 1880s China's native
opium production began to supplant the Indian product, importation of
which ceased in 1917. The India-to-China opium trade had continued
for more than a hundred years under British auspices.

The "treaty century" would occupy the years from 1842 until 1943,
when the United States and Britain formally gave up extraterritoriality
as the linchpin of the unequal treaty system. By making the foreigner immune to Chinese legal control, extraterritoriality put the Chinese ruling
class into a situation reminiscent of earlier times, obliged to govern
China under a degree of alien hegemony. The treaty century, measured
chronologically, would last almost as long as the Ruzhen Jin dynasty
(1115–1234) in North China and several years longer than the Mongol
Yuan dynasty (1279–1368). In cultural terms its influence would be
more pervasive than that of the Ruzhen, the Mongols, or the Manchus,
even though China's sovereignty was only impaired and not supplanted
by foreign rule, as happened in the Yuan and Qing periods. This comparison is still to be worked out by historians.

For example, how far was the invasion of Western traders in the
nineteenth century reminiscent of the invasions by Inner Asian tribes
who traded and fought on China's frontier in the fourth to fourteenth
centuries? Or in Linda Cooke Johnson's terms, to what extent was the
Shanghai International Settlement in its beginning stages comparable to
a native-place guild, with its headman (the consul) responsible for its
members and fostering their trade with official permission? The implicit
suggestion is that in China's long experience the nineteenth century
brought less discontinuity than we might think.

The fact remains that 1842–1943 (or 1842–1949) can be seen as a
single period characterized by (1) China's increasing openness to foreign

contact, (2) foreign military invasions running from the peripheral attacks of the British and French to the two invasions by Japan (1894–1895, 1931–1937–1945), (3) Western commercial and religious invasions beginning at Guangzhou as early as the 1830s and steadily increasing at least until the 1930s, and (4) the Chinese comeback first under the Nationalists and second under the Communists.

From the foreign side, the treaty century can be divided into three phases. The first, lasting until the 1870s, was dominated by the British commercial "imperialism of free trade." After setting up the treaty system in the warfare of 1840–1842, 1858, and 1860, Britain supported the weakened Qing regime during its Restoration in the 1860s and later.

The second phase, roughly from the 1870s to 1905, saw the imperialist rivalry in China of the industrializing powers, during which Russia, France, Germany, and Japan as well as Britain all invaded Qing territory. The brief Anglo-Qing co-dominion of the China coast was superseded by the Anglo–Japanese alliance of 1902. The Europeans' imperialist rivalry in Asia and Africa eventuated in their effort to destroy one another in World War I.

Meanwhile, the more constructive third phase of the treaty century in China (to be discussed in Part Three) lasted from the 1900s to the 1930s and 40s.

The treaty century's openness to foreign contact contrasts with the closed posture of the Qing tribute system before 1842. Viewed from outside China, the third (or early twentieth-century) phase of the treaty century was to be the preeminent era of foreign participation in the life of the Chinese people, a high point of cultural interchange in world history before the electronic age. The Chinese patriots' understandable urge is to create and possess their own history, minimizing foreign participation in it. The fact that one cannot leave the Shanghai Municipal Council out of the history of Shanghai nor Jardine, Matheson & Co. out of the history of Hong Kong suggests that we must see the treaty century as an era of international history as well as of Chinese history.

10

Rebellion and Restoration

The Great Taiping Rebellion, 1851–1864

After 1850 the Qing regime was almost overwhelmed by widespread rebellions. The emperor's inability to subdue the British barbarians in
1842, even though the Opium War was fought at only half a dozen
places on the seacoast, had shaken imperial prestige. In 1846–1848,
moreover, flood and famine were widespread among China's expanded
population. It is not surprising that a great uprising finally commenced
in 1850.

It began in the southernmost provinces between the Guangzhou region and its hinterland. This area had been longest connected with the
growing foreign trade and had been last conquered by the Qing. Their
military hold was relatively weak in the very region that had been most
fully subjected to the upsetting effect of foreign trade. The local society,
as analyzed by Frederic Wakeman, Jr. (1966), was dominated by large
land-owning clans, whose militia bands in this area of weak government
often carried on armed feuds between clan villages or groups of villages.
Such local wars were fostered by ethnic fragmentation, due to the fact
that South China had received infusions of migrants from the north,
such as the Hakka people, whose customs set them apart both from the
earlier Han Chinese inhabitants and from the tribal peoples in the hills.
Finally, as population grew and conditions worsened, the foreign opium
trade gave a key opportunity to the antidynastic secret societies, whose
sworn brotherhoods, especially on the trade routes, offered mutual help
and a social subsystem to the alienated and adventurous. In the traditional pattern the natural candidates to lead rebellion would have been

the branches and offshoots of the Triad Society, whose network was already widely dispersed among Chinese overseas and in foreign trade.

The fact that the Taiping movement did not join with these established agencies of revolt springs from the personality of its founder, Hong Xiuquan. The faith Hong preached was his own version of Old Testament Protestant Christianity, and his Heavenly Kingdom of Great Peace (Taiping Tianguo) ruled at Nanjing from 1853 to 1864. But many things doomed it from the start, beginning with its theology. After Hong had failed a fourth time in the Guangzhou examinations of 1843, he exploded in rage at the Manchu domination of China and then read some Christian missionary tracts he had been given. These tracts, which remained Hong's major source of Christian doctrine, had been written by the early Cantonese convert Liang Fa, who saw in the Old Testament a story of a chosen few who with God's help had rebelled against oppression. Liang stressed the righteous wrath of Jehovah, more than the lovingkindness of Jesus, and gave Hong barely a fingerhold on Christian theology. Nevertheless, the tracts seemed to explain the visions he had during an earlier mental illness: God the Father had evidently called him to save mankind, and Jesus was his Elder Brother.

Hong became a militant evangelist for a moral life to serve the one true God. A month with a Baptist missionary with the memorable name of Issachar Jacox Roberts in 1847 gave him examples of how to pray, preach, sing hymns, catechize, confess one's sins, baptize, and otherwise practice fundamentalist Protestantism. With his first two converts Hong created an iconoclastic monotheism potent enough to set up the Taiping theocracy yet too blasphemous to win foreign missionary support, too intent on the one true God to permit cooperation with secret societies like the Triads, and too bizarre and irrational to win over Chinese literati, who were normally essential to setting up a new administration.

The God-Worshipers' Society, as the sect first called itself, got started in a mountain region of Guangxi west of Guangzhou, variously populated by Yao and Zhuang aborigines and Chinese Hakkas like the Hong family, that is, migrants from North China several centuries before, who retained a northern dialect and other ethnic traits, like opposition to footbinding. As a minority in South China, the scattered Hakka communities were uncommonly sturdy and enterprising, as well as experienced in defending themselves against their frequently hostile neighbors.

How Hong became the rebel king of half of China is a story like that of Napoleon Bonaparte or Adolf Hitler, full of drama, the mysteries of chance, and personal and social factors much debated ever since. His converts had the faith that God had ordered them to destroy Manchu rule and set up a new order of brotherhood and sisterhood among God's children. Leadership was taken by six activists who became sworn brothers, among whom Hong was only the first among equals. The chief military leader was an illiterate charcoal burner named Yang, who had the wit to receive God's visitations and speak with His voice in a way that left Hong sincerely speechless. Several of the other leaders were low-level scholars. None was a mere peasant. They got their political–military system from the ancient classic the *Rituals of Zhou*. Their movement was highly motivated, highly organized, and at first austerely puritanical, even segregating men from women.

Taiping Christianity half-borrowed and half-recreated for Chinese purposes a full repertoire of prayers, hymns, and rituals, and preached the brotherhood and sisterhood of all mankind under the fatherhood of the one true and only God. Unlike the political passivity of Daoism and the otherworldliness of Buddhism, the Protestant Old Testament offered trumpet calls to a militant people on the march against their oppressors. The original corps of Hakka true believers were the bravest in battle and the most considerate toward the common people. And no wonder! Hong's teaching created a new Chinese sect organized for war. It used tried and true techniques evolved during 1,800 years of Christian history to inculcate an ardent faith in each individual and ensure his or her performance in its service. Taiping Christianity was a unique East-West amalgam of ideas and practices geared to militant action, the like of which was not seen again until China borrowed and sinified Marxism–Leninism a century later.

Guangxi in 1850 was far from Beijing, lightly garrisoned by Manchu troops, and strongly affected by the influx of opium runners and pirates driven inland along the West River by the British navy's pirate hunting along the coast. The growing disorder inspired the training of local self-defense forces, including both militia and bandits, with little to choose between them since all lived off the people. The small congregation of God-Worshipers, like other groups, armed for self-defense, but secretly and for a larger purpose. By late 1850 some 20,000 true believers answered Hong's call to mobilize, and they battled imperial troops sent to disperse them. On January 11, 1851, his thirty-eighth birthday, Hong proclaimed himself Heavenly King of a new dynasty, the Heavenly Kingdom of Great Peace.

The militant Taiping faith inspired an army of fierce warriors, who in the early years kept to a strict moral discipline, befriended the common people, and by their dedication attracted recruits and terrified opponents. They carried a multitude of flags and banners, partly for identification of units. Instead of shaving their foreheads and wearing the queue that the Qing dynasty required as a badge of loyalty (such a tangible symbol!), the Taipings let their hair grow free and became the "long-haired rebels," even more startling for establishmentarians to behold than student rebels of the Western counterculture a century or so later.

Civil War

The war that raged from 1851 to 1864 was tremendously destructive to life and property (see Map 21). Some 600 walled cities changed hands, often with massacres. While the American Civil War of the early 1860s was the first big contest of the industrial era, when rail and steamship transport and precision-made arms were key factors, the Taiping–imperialist war in China was the last of the premodern kind. Armies moved on their feet and lived off the land. No medical corps attended them. Modern maps and the telegraph were lacking. Artillery was sometimes used in sieges, but the favorite tactic was to tunnel under a wall, plant gunpowder, and blow it up. Navies of junks and sampans fought on the Yangzi and its major lakes to the south, but steamships were a rarity. Muskets were used, but much of the carnage was in hand-to-hand combat with swords, knives, pikes, and staves. This required motivation more than technical training.

An invading army might make up its losses by local recruitment, conscription, or conversion of captives, but a commander could not always count on such troops' standing their ground, much less charging the enemy. Imperial generals brought in Manchu and Mongol hereditary warriors, but the humid South often undid them, and their cavalry was no good in rice fields. The struggle was mainly Chinese against Chinese. Official reports of armies of 20,000 and 30,000 men, sometimes 200,000 and 300,000, make one wonder how they were actually fed and what routes they traveled by, in a land generally without roads. Troop totals were always in round numbers and should probably be scaled down.

In 1851 the Taiping horde erupted northward, captured the Wuhan cities, and early in 1853 descended the Yangzi to take Nanjing and make it their Heavenly Capital. Their strategy was what one might expect of an ambitious committee dominated by an illiterate charcoal burner: ignorant of the outer world, they left Shanghai in imperial hands and failed to develop any foreign relations. Dizzy with success, they sent inadequate forces simultaneously north to conquer Beijing and west to recover central China. Both expeditions failed. Commanders operated pretty much on their own, without reliable intelligence, communications, or coordination, simply coping with situations that arose. Absorbed in religion and warfare, the Taiping leaders were inept in economics, politics, and overall planning.

Lacking trained administrators, they generally failed to take over and govern the countryside as a base area for supplies of men and food. Instead, they campaigned from city to city, living off the proceeds of loot and requisitions, much like the imperial armies. As Philip Kuhn (in CHOC 10), remarks, they remained in effect "besieged in the cities" while the local landed elite remained in place in the countryside. All this resulted from their narrow religiosity, which antagonized, instead of recruiting, the Chinese scholar-gentry class who could have run a government for them.

Meanwhile, a watering down of their original faith and austerity hit the movement. Within Nanjing the leaders soon each had his own army, palace, harem, and supporters. They spent much time elaborating systems of nobility, honors, and ceremonies. Missionaries who called upon the Taiping prime minister in 1860 found him wearing a gold-embroidered crown and clad like his officers in robes of red and yellow silk. Egalitarianism had continued for the rank and file only.

The original leadership had destroyed itself in a bloodbath in 1856 when the Eastern King, Yang, the chief executive and generalissimo, plotted to usurp the position of the Heavenly King, Hong. Hong therefore got the Northern King, Wei, to assassinate Yang and his supporters, only to find that Wei and his supporters, drunk with power, had to be assassinated by the Assistant King, Shi, who then felt so threatened that he took off to the west with much of the army, leaving Hong sitting on a rump of his own incompetent kinfolk.

Both Nationalists and Communists of a later day have tried to salvage from the Taiping movement some positive prototype of anti-Manchu nationalism and social reform. The Taipings were against all the usual evils—gambling, opium, tobacco, idolatry, adultery, prostitution, footbinding; and they gave special scope to women, who supported and sometimes served in the army and ran the palaces in place of eunuchs. But the Taiping calendar and examination system, using tracts and Hong's writings, were no improvement on the old; the ideal communal groupings of twenty-five families with a common treasury never spread over the countryside; the Westernization program of the last prime minister, Hong's cousin, Hong Ren'gan, who had spent some years with missionaries, never got off the ground. Meantime, the ignorance and exclusivity of the Taiping leadership, their lack of an economic program, and failure to build creatively on their military prowess led to the slaughter and destitution of the Chinese populace. Mass rebellion had seldom commended itself in China. Now it gave a bad name to Christianity, too.

The Protestant missionaries resented the infringement on their studious monopoly of God's Word. The more literal-minded were outraged at Hong's claim to be Jesus' younger brother and his injection of the Chinese family system into the Christian Heaven in the person of God's and Jesus' wives. Hong's adaptations may strike us today as undoubtedly the best chance Christianity ever had of actually becoming part of the old Chinese culture. What foreign faith could conquer China without a Chinese prophet? But the few missionaries who ventured to Nanjing, though well received, got the distinct impression that Taiping Christianity did not look to them for basic guidance. Even the Taiping Chinese viewed themselves as central and superior, though generally polite to all "foreign brothers" *(wai xiongdi)*. Their Sixth Commandment, "Thou shalt not kill or injure men," used the traditional Chinese gloss, "The whole world is one family, and all men are brothers." Hong's *Three-Character Classic* for children to memorize recounted God's help to Moses and the Israelites, Jesus' life and death as the Savior, and the ancient Chinese (Shang and Zhou) worship of God (here unwittingly following the Jesuit line). But the rulers of Qin, Han, and Song had gone astray until Hong was received into Heaven in 1837 and commissioned to save the (Chinese) world by driving out the Manchu demons. This was true cultural miscegenation, but few missionaries could stomach it. Meanwhile, Catholic France had opposed Taiping Protestantism on principle as still another outcropping of the evil unleashed by Martin Luther.

The Taiping Heavenly Kingdom went the way of Carthage—only the name survived. The record is biased because the imperialists destroyed most Taiping writings, except for those preserved mainly by foreigners (some were found only in this century in French and British libraries). Leaders of ability emerged in the final years, but too late. A cause for which so many gave their lives must have had much to offer, but only in comparison with the effete old order under the Manchus.

The Qing Restoration of the 1860s

That the Qing managed to survive both domestic and international attacks is due largely to the policy and leadership changes known as the Qing Restoration. By 1861 the Manchu dynasty's mandate seemed truly exhausted. The diehard anti-Western faction in charge of Qing policy had been defeated by the Anglo–French occupation of Beijing in 1860, which secured final acceptance of the unequal treaty system. Meanwhile, a new Taiping commander destroyed the Chinese camp besieging Nanjing, invaded the delta, and in early 1862 would threaten Shanghai. The crisis led to a coup d'etat in Beijing in 1861 that brought into power a new Manchu leadership under the Empress Dowager (Cixi) as regent and headed by two Manchus, Prince Gong and Grand Councillor Wenxiang. They were dedicated to a dual policy: in foreign relations, to accept the treaty system in order to appease the foreign powers; in domestic relations, to put more Chinese in positions of real power in order to defeat the rebels. This more flexible policy began a restoration of Qing power. ("Restoration"—zhongxing—was a traditional term for a dynasty's "revival at midcourse.")

The new commander against the Taipings was a Chinese Confucian scholar from Hunan, Zeng Guofan. Sent home from Beijing to organize militia in 1852, Zeng was appalled by what he saw as the Taiping's blasphemous and violent attack on the whole Confucian order. He was determined to defeat it in the time-honored way, through moral revival. He therefore set himself to build an army for defense. He recruited commanders of similar character, personally loyal to himself, who selected their subordinate officers, who in turn enlisted their soldiers man by man, creating in this way a network of leaders and followers personally beholden to one another and capable of mutual support and devotion in warfare. It was a military application of the reciprocal responsibilities according to status that animated the family system. And it worked. Soldiers were carefully selected from proper families and well paid and trained.

Zeng developed an inland navy on the Yangzi, set up arsenals, and husbanded his resources. As the Taipings' original Hakka soldiers from South China became depleted, Zeng's Hunan Army began to win. Once the Manchus recognized that their best hope lay in trusting Chinese loyal to the old order, Zeng was able to put his chief lieutenants in as provincial governors and so mobilize a concerted war effort. He methodically hemmed the Taipings in from upstream, where the Hubei–Hunan capital of Wuchang had changed hands six times, and from downstream, where Anglo-French forces finally abandoned neutrality and helped defend the Shanghai–Ningbo area.

By accepting the Western treaty system and supporting the conservative Chinese scholar-generals in the provinces, the new leaders at Beijing under the regency of the young Empress Dowager (Cixi) achieved the suppression of the Taipings by 1864 and gave their dynasty a new lease on life. The idealistic picture of this era envisions a genuine conservative effort at a "Restoration" similar to those that had occurred after the founding of the Later Han or after the great mid-Tang rebellion. The pioneer Western historian of the Restoration, Mary Clabaugh Wright (1957), has eloquently described how during the 1860s the components of the traditional Confucian state were energized to function again: a group of high-principled civil officials, chosen by examination in the classics and loyal to the reigning dynasty, sternly suppressed rebellion and tried to minister benevolently to the agrarian economy and the popular welfare. Order was restored in the central provinces, taxes remitted, land reopened to cultivation, schools founded, and men of talent recruited for the civil service, even though more was advocated by the top officials than could be actually achieved at the rice roots. While reviving the traditional order in this fashion, the Restoration leaders also began to Westernize. They set up arsenals to supply modern arms, built steamships, translated Western textbooks in technology and international law, and created a prototype foreign office in the form of a special committee (the Zongli Yamen) under the Grand Council. Soon their new provincial and regional armies with modern arms made peasant uprisings impossible. In these efforts they were aided by the cooperative policy of the Western powers, whose imperialist rivalries did not become intense until the 1870s.

Recent comprehensive appraisals are less upbeat. They note that the Restoration brought into power the ignorant and obscurantist Empress Dowager. Westernization was left largely to the Chinese provincial authorities where Chinese power had become dominant, and this put the Manchu court on the defensive. However, these provincial efforts were uncoordinated and not backed from Beijing. In the end the Qing administration's renewed vitality could not overcome the inertia of the traditional Chinese polity. It could function only on its own terms, which were out of date. The Restoration leaders clung conservatively to the preeminence of agriculture as the basis of state revenue and popular livelihood. They had no conception of economic growth or development in the modern sense but were austerely antiacquisitive; they continued to disparage commerce, including foreign trade, as nonproductive. Rather, they tried to set before the peasantry and bureaucracy the classical ideals of frugality and incorruptibility, so that the product of the land could more readily suffice to maintain the people and the government. To assist agriculture, they tried without much success (as Kwang-Ching Liu has shown (in *CHOC* 10) to reduce land taxes in the lower Yangzi region but did not try to lower rents or limit landlordism. They tried to revive the necessary public works systems for water control but could not control the Yellow River any better than their predecessors.

The Restoration lost vitality after 1870 for many reasons. Its leaders were conscientiously reviving the past instead of facing China's new future creatively. They could not adequately inspire the lower levels of their bureaucracy nor handle the specialized technical and intellectual problems of Westernization. The very strength of their conservative and restorative effort inhibited China's responding to Western contact in a revolutionary way.

Suppression of Other Rebellions

The Restoration's one undoubted success had been in suppressing rebellions. During Taiping control of the lower Yangzi region there arose on their north between the Huai and Yellow rivers another movement of rebel bands called Nian (see Map 21). Based in fortified earth-walled villages on the southern edge of the North China plain, they organized cavalry forces in their own banner system for raiding abroad and controlled their territorial base by taking over the local militia corps. Though lacking the dynastic pretensions of the Taipings, the Nian movement from 1853 to 1868 supplanted the imperial government in a sizable region and harassed it with raids to plunder food supplies from neighboring provinces.

Imperial efforts to root the Nian out of their fortified nests repeatedly failed. Walls were leveled only to rise again. The scholar-generals who had defeated the Taipings tried to deprive the Nian of their popular support in the villages by promising security to the populace, death to the leaders, and pardon to the followers. Meanwhile, other risings flared

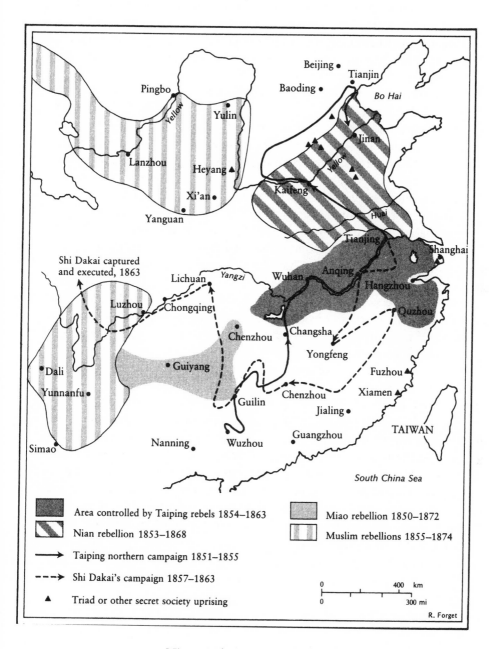

21. Nineteenth-Century Rebellions

up in several parts of North China. They and the Nian were eventually put down by new provincial armies with modern weapons. They cut the rebel cavalry off from their supplies of food and manpower and eventually, with blockade lines and counter-cavalry, destroyed them on the plain.

In the aftermath of these revolts that convulsed Central and North China there were also sanguinary risings of Chinese Muslims in the southwest and northwest during the 1860s and 1870s—bitter struggles that are only now beginning to be studied. All in all, the movement for change in modern China began by following the traditional patterns of peasant-based rebellions and a Restoration that suppressed them. In the process many millions of hapless people were killed. The fighting eventually ran out of steam. Modern estimates are that China's population had been about 410 million in 1850 and, after the Taiping, Nian, Muslim, and other smaller rebellions, amounted to about 350 million in 1873.

Thus, the coercion of China by Western gunboats and even the Anglo–French occupation of Beijing in 1860 were brief, small, and marginal disasters compared with the mid-century rebellions that swept over the major provinces. The Europeans and Americans who secured their special privileges in China's new treaty ports were on the fringe of this great social turmoil, not its creators. For some Chinese at the time they represented a new order and opportunity, but for the majority they were unimportant.

Nevertheless, an informal British–Qing entente took shape in the early 1860s. Britain wanted stability for trade and so, for example, helped Beijing buy a fleet of steam gunboats (the ultimate weapon of the day), although the deal broke up over the question of who would command it. Robert Hart and his Maritime Customs Service, working as Qing officials, spearheaded the British encouragement of modern fiscal administration and facilitation of trade. At the same time, by helping to maintain Qing stability, they played a role in China's domestic politics that patriots later could attack.

11

Early Modernization and the Decline of Qing Power

Self-Strengthening and Its Failure

During the decades following the Qing Restoration of the 1860s, leading personalities, both Manchu and Chinese, tried to adapt Western devices and institutions. This movement, studied by Albert Feuerwerker, Kwang-Ching Liu and others, was posited on the attractive though misleading doctrine of "Chinese learning as the fundamental structure, Western learning for practical use"—as though Western arms, steamships, science, and technology could somehow be utilized to preserve Confucian values. In retrospect we can see that gunboats and steel mills bring their own philosophy with them. But the generation of 1860–1900 clung to the shibboleth that China could leap halfway into modern times, like leaping halfway across a river in flood.

Under the classical and therefore nonforeign slogan of "self-strengthening," Chinese leaders began the adoption of Western arms and machines, only to find themselves sucked into an inexorable process in which one borrowing led to another, from machinery to technology, from science to all learning, from acceptance of new ideas to change of institutions, eventually from constitutional reform to republican revolution. The fallacy of halfway Westernization, in tools but not in values, was in fact apparent to many conservative scholars, who therefore chose the alternative of opposing all things Western.

The leaders in self-strengthening were those who had crushed the Taipings, scholar-officials like Zeng Guofan and his younger coadjutor, Li Hongzhang (1823–1901), who set up an arsenal at Shanghai to make guns and gunboats. As early as 1864 Li explained to Beijing that the foreigners' domination of China was based on the superiority of their weapons, that it was hopeless to try to drive them out, and that Chinese society therefore faced the greatest crisis since its unification under the First Emperor in 221 BC. Li concluded that in order to strengthen herself China must learn to use Western machinery, which implied also the training of Chinese personnel. This simple line of reasoning had been immediately self-evident to the fighting men of Japan after Perry's arrival in 1853. But the movement for Westernization in China was obstructed at every turn by the ignorance and prejudice of the Confucian literati. This lack of responsiveness in China, during the decades when Japan was being rapidly modernized, provides one of the great contrasts of history.

China's difficulties were repeatedly illustrated. To make Western learning available, for example, some eighty Jesuit missionaries during the seventeenth and eighteenth centuries had produced Chinese translations of over 400 Western works, more than half on Christianity and about a third in science. Protestant missionaries of the early nineteenth century published about 800 items, but nearly all as religious tracts or translations of scripture, mainly directed in simple parlance at the common man, not the Chinese literati. At the Shanghai arsenal during the last third of the century, one gifted Englishman (John Fryer) collaborated with Chinese scholars to translate more than a hundred works on science and technology, developing the necessary terminology in Chinese as they went along. But the distribution of all these works was limited, rather few Chinese scholars seem to have read them, and their production depended on the initiative of foreigners or of a few officials concerned with foreign affairs, not under guidance from the throne.

At the capital an interpreters' college had been set up in 1862 as a government institution to prepare young men for diplomatic negotiation. With an American missionary as head and nine foreign professors and with Robert Hart's prompting and Customs support, this new college soon had over 100 Manchu and Chinese students of foreign languages. Yet antiforeign literati objected to the teaching of Western subjects. The erroneous excuse had to be offered that "Western sciences borrowed their roots from ancient Chinese mathematics . . . China invented the method, Westerners adopted it."

The jealousy of a scholar class whose fortunes were tied to Chinese learning was most vigorously illustrated in the case of a Chinese student, Yung Wing, who had been taken to the United States by missionaries in 1847 and graduated from Yale in 1854. When he returned to China after eight years abroad, he had to wait almost a decade before he was

used by Zeng Guofan as an agent to buy machinery and as an interpreter
and translator. Yung Wing's proposal to send Chinese students abroad
was not acted upon until fifteen years after his return. In 1872 he headed
an educational mission that brought some 120 long-gowned Chinese
students to Hartford, Connecticut. Old-style Chinese teachers came with
them to prepare these prospective Westernizers of China for the examinations in the classics, a preparation still essential to their becoming officials. Yung Wing was also given as colleague an obscurantist scholar
whose mission was to see to it that Western contact did not undermine
the students' Confucian morals. In 1881 the whole project was abandoned.

Similar attitudes handicapped early industrialization. Conservatives
feared that mines, railroads, and telegraph lines would upset the harmony between man and nature *(fengshui)* and create all sorts of problems—by disturbing the imperial ancestors, by assembling unruly
crowds of miners, by throwing boatmen and carters out of work, by absorbing government revenues, by creating a dependence on foreign machines and technicians. Even when modernizers could overcome such
fears, they still faced enormous practical difficulties such as the lack of
entrepreneurial skills and capital. Major projects had to be sponsored
by high officials, usually under the formula of "official supervision
and merchant operation." This meant in practice that enterprises were
hamstrung by bureaucratism. Merchant managers remained under the
thumb of their official patrons. Both groups milked the new companies
of their current profits instead of reinvesting them. An ongoing process
of self-sustaining industrial growth through reinvestment was never
achieved.

Thus, China's late-nineteenth-century industrialization proved generally abortive in spite of the early promise of many officially sponsored
projects. For example, the China Merchants' Steam Navigation Company founded by Li in 1872 was subsidized to carry the tribute rice from
the Yangzi delta to feed the capital. Almost every year since 1415 long
flotillas of grain junks had moved these shipments up the Grand Canal.
Now they could go quickly by sea from Shanghai to Tianjin. To provide
coal for the steamer fleet the Kaiping coal mines were opened north of
Tianjin in 1878. To transport this coal, China's first permanent railway
was inaugurated in 1881. Yet by the end of the century these mutually
supporting enterprises had made little progress. The China Merchants'
Company, plundered by its patrons, managers, and employees, lost
ground to British steamship lines. The Kaiping mines, heavily in debt to

foreigners, were taken over by Herbert Hoover and others in 1900. Railroad building was neglected by China and promoted by the imperialist powers in their spheres of influence after 1898.

During the latter part of Li Hongzhang's thirty years of service as governor-general at Tianjin, his chief rival was Zhang Zhidong, who served eighteen years at Wuhan. There he set up an iron foundry that became a steel mill, as well as military academies and technical schools for telegraphy, mining, railways, and industrial arts. Yet Zhang's primary hope was to fit all this technology into the classical Confucian scheme of things.

The modernization of China thus became a game played by a few high officials who realized its necessity and tried to raise funds, find personnel, and set up projects in a generally lethargic if not unfriendly environment. Hope of personal profit and power led them on, but the Empress Dowager's court, unlike the Meiji Emperor's in Japan, gave them no firm or consistent backing. She, on the contrary, let the ideological conservatives stalemate the innovators so that she could hold the balance. Since South China was as usual full of bright spirits looking for new opportunities, especially in the rapidly growing treaty-port cities, the late nineteenth century was a time of much pioneering but little basic change. Westernization was left to the efforts of a few high provincial officials partly because this suited the central–local balance of power—the court could avoid the cost and responsibility—and partly because treaty-port officials in contact with foreigners were the only ones who could see the opportunities and get foreign help.

The payoff from self-strengthening came in the Sino–Japanese War of 1894–1895. Because of her size, the betting was on China, but Li Hongzhang knew differently and tried to forestall the war. China had begun navy building in the 1870s. During the 1880s Li purchased steel cruisers and got instructors and advisors from Britain, but later Krupp outbid Armstrong and two bigger German vessels were added. In the late 1880s, however, funds for the Chinese navy were scandalously diverted by a high-level official conspiracy to build the Empress Dowager's new summer palace instead. By Hart's estimate, the navy "ought to have a balance of 36,000,000 taels [say U.S. $50 million], and lo! it has not a penny." In September 1894 he found "they have no *shells* for the Krupp's, and no *powder* for the Armstrong's." In the war with Japan, only Li Hongzhang's North China army and fleet were involved (not those in Central and South China), and some of the navy's shells were found to be full of sand instead of gunpowder.

When the Japanese intervened in Korea in 1894, ostensibly to quell Korean rebels, they routed Li's North China army, and in one of the first modern naval battles, off the Yalu River, sank or routed his fleet. It was commanded by an old cavalry general who brought his ships out line abreast like a cavalry charge, while the Japanese in two columns circled around them. Today when tourists visit the marble boat which stands in the Summer Palace lake outside Beijing, they should be able to imagine a caption on it: "In memoriam: here lies what might have been the late Qing navy."

From our perspective today, the startling thing is that China's first modern war should have been left on the shoulders of a provincial official as though it were simply a matter of his defending his share of the frontier. The Manchu dynasty has of course been blamed for its non-nationalistic ineptitude, but the trouble was deeper than the dynasty's being non-Chinese; the fault evidently lay in the imperial monarchy itself, the superficiality of its administration, its constitutional inability to be a modern central government.

The Qing dynasty had survived rebellions of the Chinese people, but its foreign relations now got out of hand. Japan's victory over China threw the Far East into a decade of imperialist rivalries. In order to pay off the indemnity, China went into debt to European bondholders. In 1898 Russia, Germany, Britain, Japan, and France all occupied or claimed spheres of influence in China. These consisted usually of a major port as a naval base, a railway through its hinterland, and mines to develop along it. In order to check Japan, China invited Russia into Manchuria—until the Russo–Japanese War of 1905 left Russia confined to the north and Japan triumphant in South Manchuria and Korea.

All in all, China seemed about to perish. Could a new generation with a new teaching come to the rescue? Could the new teaching inspire a national regeneration under a strong ruling power?

The Christian–Confucian Struggle

To most Chinese, Christian missionaries seemed to be the ideological arm of foreign aggression. The conflict, begun in the seventeenth century and resumed in the nineteenth, went on at many levels: political, intellectual, and social.

Politically, Christianity was heterodox. At first it had seemed to be merely another sect of a Buddhist type, with a belief system, a savior, moral guilt, and a way to atone for it—elements that most religions have in common. Since most religious sects in China had long since been proscribed, like the White Lotus, they generally had to be secret organizations. After the spectacular Jesuit contact of the 1600s foundered upon the Rites Controversy that pitted the Pope at Rome against the Emperor of China, Christianity was banned in 1724. The ban was not lifted until 1846 at French insistence. Meanwhile the Chinese Roman Catholic communities had survived, but foreign priests had to work clandestinely.

Protestant missionaries by their calling were reformers at heart, and their efforts at once brought them into conflict with the Confucian establishment, which believed in its own kind of reform. Missionaries and the Chinese gentry-elite were natural rivals. Both were privileged, immune to the magistrate's coercion. Both were teachers of a cosmic doctrine. Rivalry was unavoidable. Paul Cohen quotes as representative an early missionary who saw behind the outward show of the Confucian elite's politeness and refinement "nothing but cunning, ignorance, rudeness, vulgarity, arrogant assumption and inveterate hatred of everything foreign." This view was reciprocated. To the scholar-gentry, missionaries were foreign subversives, whose immoral conduct and teachings were backed by gunboats. Conservative patriots hated and feared these alien intruders, but the conservatives lost out as modern times unfolded, and much of the record thus far available is polemical or else comes mainly from the victorious missionaries and Chinese Christians. The record so ably summarized by Cohen (in *CHOC* 10) shows few Chinese converts to the Christian faith but a pervasive influence from missionary aggressiveness.

The period from 1860 to 1900 saw the gradual spread of mission stations into every province under the treaty right of extraterritoriality, and also under the right of inland residence illegally slipped into one treaty by a devout French interpreter. Building on its old foundations, the Roman Catholic establishment totaled by 1894 some 750 European missionaries, 400 native priests, and over half a million communicants. Protestant missions had begun at Guangzhou, where Robert Morrison was employed by the British East India Company after 1807. The first Americans arrived in 1830. By 1894 the Protestant mission effort supported over 1,300 missionaries, mainly British, American, and Canadian, and maintained some 500 stations—each with a church, residences, street chapels, usually a small school, and possibly a hospital or dispensary—in about 350 different cities and towns. Yet they had made fewer than 60,000 Christian converts among the Chinese. Plainly, China was not destined to become a Christian nation.

After 1860 the increase of contact led to continuing friction between gentry and missionaries. Especially among Hunanese who had resisted the "Christian" Taipings, a militant anti-Christian movement organized ideological defenses and fomented violent action. Typically, gentry would spread rumors of missionary immorality when men and women worshipped together. A lurid pornographic literature, revived from the seventeenth century, described the bestial orgies of priests, nuns, and converts. Gentry had only to post placards stating a time and place for the populace to assemble to touch off a riot. Thousands of incidents occurred and hundreds were reported in diplomatic channels by missionaries demanding redress and official protection of their treaty right to proselytize.

Gunboat blackmail obliged Qing officials to take the foreigners' side and enforce the treaties, further damaging the dynasty's prestige. The Catholics in particular supported their converts in lawsuits. Having little trade, the French championed Catholic missions, whose bishops claimed and sometimes received a sort of official status.

On their part, the Protestant missionaries, organized under a dozen denominations, had an early struggle to master the Chinese language and work out the terminology they needed to convey their message. China had a full vocabulary already in place to designate God, the soul, sin, repentance, and salvation. Missionary translators were up against it: If they used the established term, usually from Buddhism, they could not make Christianity distinctive. But if they used a neologism, they could be less easily understood. This problem became most acute at the central point in Christianity, the term for God. After much altercation, the Catholics ended up with Lord of Heaven, some Protestants with Lord on High, and others with Divine Spirit. One translation into Chinese of the Bible produced a stalemate in which the missionaries could not agree on what to call the basic kingpost of their religion.

In the "Christian occupation of China," as it was unwisely called, Protestant missionaries brought their small schools and rudimentary medicine into the major cities, where examination candidates could occasionally be leafletted. But for the most part the Americans, who had usually come from farms, found that life in the countryside was more congenial and offered a better prospect of competing with Confucianism. The growth of the Protestant Christian church was slow but steady. The number of Chinese converts and practicing Christians rose by 1900 to over 100,000, a mere drop in the Chinese bucket, but the Protestant missionaries were great institution-builders. They set up their compounds with foreign-style houses managed by Chinese servants and soon were developing schools and dispensaries or public-health clinics. The first Chinese they won for Christ were often clients or coworkers, like the cook or the tract distributor, but they also included some gifted and idealistic men who were impressed by foreign ways and were willing to embrace the foreign religion. In the late nineteenth century many Chinese reformers took on Christianity partly because the trinity of industry, Christianity, and democracy seemed to be the secret of Western power and the best way to save China.

The Reform Movement

In Late Imperial China trends in Chinese scholarship took a long time to catch up with the trends in China's foreign relations. During the same years as China's widespread commercial growth, there was a movement in scholarship that Benjamin Elman (1984) calls "from philosophy to philology." The essence was that Confucian scholar-officials' concern to make moral judgments in terms of great principles gave way to more precise technical studies that were less culture-bound, and perhaps better preparation for confronting specific modern problems.

The Lower Yangzi delta where so much of the new interregional trade centered in the late eighteenth century was in the same period the home of a new type of scholarship known as "evidential research" *(kaozhengxue)*. Chinese dismay at the Ming collapse in the early 1600s had pinpointed the cause in Neo-Confucian philosophy, with its subtle admixture of Buddhist-Daoist abstractions. Scholars were "dissatisfied with the empirically unverifiable ideas that had pervaded" Song and Ming interpretations of Confucianism. The stress on moral principles (Song Neo-Confucianism was known as *Lixue,* "the learning of principle") had contributed to the righteous moral denunciations among factions that had hamstrung late Ming administrations. Under the Manchus, some classical scholars therefore turned from philosophy to philology, and also to mathematical astronomy, specifically to the concrete analysis of texts, their authenticity, interpolations, and exact meanings. One result was that from internal evidence forgeries were discovered in venerated classics. They were no longer sacrosanct.

This new look in Qing scholarship was commemorated in 1829 in a collection of 180 works by 75 seventeenth- and eighteenth-century authors, half of whom had held the top degree of *jinshi.* It happened, ironically, that this great achievement of scholarship was due to the editorial leadership of the eminent bibliophile Ruan Yuan, who was also the emperor's top official in charge of Guangdong province and the European trade.

It is true of course that many authors in Ruan Yuan's great collection had come from merchant families. The legendary wealth of the Yangzhou salt merchants, for example, enabled them to finance academies and support talent. With the patronage of high officials, scholars were mobilized to work on big imperial projects of compilation such as the *Ming History* and the Qing geographical gazetteer. There were more than 150 such imperial projects. Out of all this work emerged a sense that evidential research was indeed a profession, separate from office-holding.

Academies and their libraries to foster this research proliferated especially in the Lower Yangzi provinces. Though at first stand-offish, the emperor after 1733 began to sponsor academies that prepared students for the examinations. After 1750, however, officially sponsored but internally somewhat autonomous academies emerged to support study, discussion, and research alone. The "Han learning" of evidential research, basing itself on the New Texts of the Han period, showed the intellectual capacity and vitality of an established community of Qing scholars. They communicated partly by letters written for eventual publication. Their achievements in critical evaluation of the inherited texts led them into epigraphy, phonology, and a beginning of archaeological analysis of bronzes and stone monuments.

By the 1840s the sudden triumph of British seapower led to the drawing together of two lines of Chinese reformist thought—the New Text movement to reappraise the classics and the statecraft movement for the scholar-official elite to become more involved and more effective in administration. The scholar-official Wei Yuan (1794–1857) was a leader in both. In 1826 he had compiled over 2,000 exemplary writings on fiscal and other practical aspects of administration. He proposed carrying Beijing's rice stipend from the Lower Yangzi by sea around Shandong instead of over the toilsome Grand Canal route. He helped reform the salt gabelle, wrote an account of the ten successful Qing military campaigns, and at Guangzhou helped Commissioner Lin by compiling an influential account of the countries overseas—altogether a critical new look at China's problems, none too soon. Wei Yuan brought the outside world that Britain represented onto the horizon of the late Qing reformers.

The continuity between evidential research and modern Chinese scholarship would be evidenced in the 1890s when scholars versed in bronze and stone inscriptions recognized the significance of the "oracle bones" left from the Shang dynasty. This marked the start of modern Chinese archaeology, as noted in Chapter 1, though it did little to help the late Qing meet the Western invasion.

By the 1890s the growth of cities, most of which were treaty ports, had brought great material and social changes. In the coastal and riverine ports, Western-style buildings, street patterns, and city services of gas lighting and water supply, plus steamship transportation and foreign trade, were all connected with (or extensions of) the world outside China. In these ports a modern Chinese economy took shape as a joint product of foreign and Chinese enterprise in commerce, banking, and industry. Simultaneously appeared the modern mass media—Chinese journalists, newspapers, and magazines—and a new intelligentsia of writers and artists not oriented toward careers as government officials. In the modern cities under foreign administration, where Chinese businessmen prospered as bankers and compradors assisting foreign firms, as well as independently, a Chinese public opinion began to find expression.

As Christian converts began to form a decentralized community, missionaries began to put out a Chinese magazine, the *Review of the Times (Wanguo gongbao)*, which reported on the international scene. Weekly from 1875 to 1883 and monthly from 1889 to 1907 this journal spread world news to the Chinese scholar class. Partly because it was so ably written in classical Chinese by the Chinese editors, the journal being first in the field gave the missionaries a direct channel to the scholars and officials who were grappling with the problems of the outside world. In the 1890s the ablest missionaries (like the Welshman Timothy Richard) pursued a program of reaching the scholar class and so had influence on the reform movement.

From China's perspective, Japan's victory of 1895 was not merely a defeat of China by some other civilized power but a real subjection to the powers of darkness represented by the West. Consider that the Westerners had the morals of animals, men and women both holding hands and actually kissing in public. By inventing powerful machines this outside world had overwhelmed the order of man and nature that had created civilization and the good life. Chaos was at hand.

In 1895 several factors had suddenly converged. First was the foreign menace, which had produced four wars and four defeats for China through naval firepower on the coast. New weapons of war, incredibly destructive, were now wielded by these outsiders. To this fact of foreign power was added the second undeniable fact of foreign skill, not only at war-making but in all the practical arts and technology of life. The steam engine on ships and railroads had sped up transportation beyond all compare, and paved roads, gas lighting, water supply, and police systems now characterized port cities such as Shanghai. Third, to those people who felt that technology and the arts were an expression of basic moral and intellectual qualities, it was plain that traditional China was somehow lacking in these capacities that the foreigner demonstrated.

The crisis and humiliation produced by these considerations led to the inescapable conclusion that China must make great changes. Because China's common people did not contribute to the government and most of the elite were too well ensconced in habitual ways to provide intellectual leadership, only scholars could tackle this problem.

The list of desirable reforms had been steadily growing since the Opium War. Several secretaries and advisors of Li Hongzhang had contributed; so had Christian missionaries, Taiping rebels, diplomats who went abroad, and early Chinese journalists in Hong Kong and Shanghai. For such people the Western countries and now Japan offered a cornucopia of new ways that might be adapted to China's needs. On the broadest level, parliaments could create a firmer bond between ruler and people. Government patents or rewards could encourage inventions, repair of roads could help trade, mineralogy could improve mining, agricultural schools could increase production, translations could broaden education—the list was endless.

However, before the reform movement could gain broad support, a philosophical sanction had to be found for China's borrowing from abroad and changing the old ways. This sanction had to be found within Confucianism, for it was still the vital faith of China's ruling class. It called for statesmanship in the service of the Son of Heaven. Only an insider, a latter-day sage, could perform the intellectual task of updating this Confucian tradition. This was Kang Youwei's great contribution. He was a precocious scholar from Guangzhou, imaginative, sublimely self-confident, and expert at finding in China's classical tradition the precedents that would justify its adaptation to the present.

Kang's starting point was the New Text movement, in which Qing scholars had attacked the authenticity of the Ancient Text versions of the classics upon which the Neo-Confucian orthodoxy since the Song period had been based. The whole subject was at a level of complexity like that of the Christian doctrines of the Trinity or of predestination.

No slick summary can do it justice. But for us today the point is that the New Text versions came from the Earlier Han (BC), while the Ancient Text version had become the standard in the Later Han (AD) and had remained so for the Song philosophers who put together the synthesis we call Neo-Confucianism (in Chinese parlance the Song Learning). To repudiate the Ancient Text versions in favor of the New Text versions (which were really older) gave one a chance to escape the Neo-Confucian stranglehold and reinterpret the tradition. The New Text school of thought believed in adapting institutions to the times and so generally favored reform.

As Benjamin Elman (1990) has shown, the New Text reform movement in late Qing was actually a continuation of the late Ming effort of Lower Yangzi scholars (of the Donglin or "Eastern Forest" academy) to extirpate imperial despotism. Instead of an evil eunuch as in the 1620s, the symbol of the autocracy's moral iniquity in the 1790s was the aged Qianlong Emperor's corrupt favorite, Heshen. Beginning in the same Lower Yangzi region as the Donglin (Changzhou prefecture), New Text reformers during the nineteenth century demanded, often in their memorials of remonstrance *(qingyi),* a greater imperial concern for public needs. Kang Youwei, consciously or not, represented a growing gentry interest in government reform.

In 1891 he published his *Study of the Classics Forged during the Xin Period* (AD 9–23). He asserted that "the Classics honored and expounded by the Song scholars are for the most part forged and not those of Confucius." This bombshell was eruditely crafted and very persuasive (though not then nor now generally accepted). Kang also cited New Text classical sources to buttress his theory of the three ages of (1) disorder, (2) approaching peace and small tranquility, and (3) universal peace and great unity. The world was now entering the second age in this progression, which implied a doctrine of progress. Kang Youwei had secured most of his ideas from earlier writers, but he marched to his own drummer. This enabled him to smuggle the ideas of evolution and progress into China's classical tradition at the very moment when these ideas were sweeping the international world.

Indeed, Kang Youwei and his best student, the Cantonese Liang Qichao, were quick to accept the Social Darwinism of the 1890s. They wrote books on the sad fate of hidebound nations like Turkey and India and the success stories of Peter the Great's Russia and Meiji Japan in the struggle for survival of the fittest among nations. In short, these radical reformers at heart were ardent nationalists but still hoped that the Qing monarchy could lead China to salvation. Profiting from the example of Protestant missionaries, they began to use the modern devices of the press and of study societies that sponsored discussion of public problems both in print and in group meetings. Kang even advocated making worship of Confucius into an organized national religion. But his main hope was a traditional one: to gain the ear of the ruler and reform China from the top down. His chance came in 1898, when each imperialist power demanded a sphere of influence and China seemed about to be carved into pieces. Since 1889 the idealistic Emperor Guangxu had been allowed nominally to reign while his aunt, the Empress Dowager, kept watch on him from her newly furbished summer palace. The emperor, now twenty-seven, had been reading books, not a safe activity for a figurehead, and his old imperial tutor, a rival of Li Hongzhang, recommended Kang Youwei to him. As the crisis deepened in 1898 the emperor gave him his confidence.

Between June 11 and September 21, during one hundred days, Guangxu issued some 40 reform decrees aimed at modernizing the Chinese state, its administration, education, laws, economy, technology, military, and police systems. Many of these reforms had been advocated by writers for decades past, only now they were decreed by the emperor. Unfortunately, unlike the first hundred days of Franklin D. Roosevelt, which legislated the New Deal in 1933, the radical reforms of 1898 remained largely on paper while officials waited to see what the Empress Dowager would do. She waited until nearly everyone in the establishment felt threatened by the proposed changes and then staged a military coup d'etat. Kang and Liang escaped to Japan, but she confined Guangxu to the southern island in the palace lake and executed the six radicals she could catch.

Informed mainly by the self-serving writings of Kang and Liang, many have viewed the fiasco of the Hundred Days of 1898 in black and white terms, seeing Kang, Liang, and the emperor as heroes defeated by evil reactionaries. The opening of the Palace Museum Archives in Taibei and the Number One Historical Archives at Beijing has now allowed a revisionist like Luke S. K. Kwong (1984) to reinterpret the events of 1898 and specialists like Benjamin Elman to question some of his questionings. The Beijing politics of 1898 require fuller appraisal.

In any case, the most die-hard Manchu princes, whose palace upbringing had left them ignorant of the world and proud of it, soon became patrons of a peasant secret society, the Boxers. This turning of the Manchu court to active support of a fanatical cult was an obvious act of intellectual bankruptcy.

The Boxer Rising, 1898–1901

In northwest Shandong on the floodplain of the Yellow River, the rather dense population had become so poor that few gentry lived in the villages, and banditry had become a seasonal occupation that inspired intervillage feuds. The Qing government and gentry were losing control. During the 1890s aggressive German missionaries had attracted converts to Catholicism partly by supporting them in lawsuits against non-Christians. After their seizure of Shandong as a sphere of influence in 1898, the Germans' arrogance heightened the anti-Christian sentiment that had long been accumulating as Christian missions spread into the interior while the European powers and Japan repeatedly humbled the Chinese government. Antimissionary riots had led the foreigners to exact such onerous penalties that Qing policy required magistrates to avoid antagonizing the missionaries and their converts. In this situation Shandong peasants defended their interests through secret societies. In southwest Shandong, for example, the Big Sword Society became a force for bandit suppression. In 1898 a disastrous Yellow River flood followed by prolonged drought put the villagers in dire straits. North China became a tinderbox.

Joseph Esherick's (1987) masterly study of the Boxers' origins pinpoints the combining in northwest Shandong of two peasant traditions—the technique of the martial arts or "boxing" (featured in operas and storytelling and visible today in movies of *gongfu* combat) and the practice of spirit possession or shamanism. (We may recall from Chapter 2 that the king of the Shang dynasty had acted as the chief shaman.) The Spirit Boxers, who later took the name Boxers United in Righteousness, put together these two elements. After appropriate rituals, Boxers went into a trance, foamed at the mouth, and arose prepared for combat because they were now invulnerable to swords or bullets. Anyone could be possessed and so for the moment become a leader. No hierarchic organization was necessary. The aim was the simple slogan, "Support the Qing, destroy the foreign." Once ignited in the propitious circumstances of the times, the Boxer movement spread across North China like wildfire. The Manchu princes, and even the Empress Dowager for a time, felt they heard the voice of the common people, the final arbiter of

Chinese politics. They proposed to work with the movement, not against it, and so get rid of foreign imperialism.

In the sequence of events, each side aroused the other. Legation guards in the spring of 1900 went out shooting Boxers to intimidate them. By June 13–14 Boxers broke into Beijing and Tianjin, killing Christians and looting. On June 10, 2,100 foreign troops had started from Tianjin to defend the Beijing legations but got only halfway. On June 17 a foreign fleet attacked the coastal forts outside Tianjin. On June 21 the Empress Dowager and the dominant group at court formally declared war on all the powers. As she said, "China is weak. The only thing we can depend upon is the hearts of the people. If we lose them, how can we maintain our country?" (By country she meant dynasty.)

The Boxer Rising in the long, hot summer of 1900 was one of the best-known events of the nineteenth century because so many diplomats, missionaries, and journalists were besieged by almost incessant rifle fire for eight weeks (June 29–August 14) in the Beijing legation quarter—about 475 foreign civilians, 450 troops of eight nations, and some 3,000 Chinese Christians, also about 150 racing ponies, who provided fresh meat. An international army rescued them, not without bickering, after rumors they had all been killed. The Empress Dowager, with the emperor safely in tow, took off for Xi'an by cart. The allied forces thoroughly looted Beijing. Kaiser Wilhelm II sent a field marshal, who terrorized the surrounding towns, where many thousands of Chinese Christians had been slaughtered; 250 foreigners, mainly missionaries, had been killed across North China. Vengeance was in the air.

But the Chinese provincial governors-general who had led the effort at self-strengthening also coped with this crisis. Li Hongzhang at Guangzhou, Zhang Zhidong at Wuhan, and the others had decided right away in June to ignore Beijing's declaration of war. They declared the whole thing simply a "Boxer Rebellion," and they guaranteed peace in Central and South China if the foreigners would keep their troops and gunboats out. This make-believe worked. The imperialist powers preferred to keep the treaty system intact, together with China's foreign-debt payments. And so the War of 1900, the fifth and largest that the Qing fought with foreign powers in the nineteenth century, was localized in North China.

The Boxer protocol signed in September 1901 by the top Manchu prince and Li Hongzhang with eleven foreign powers was mainly punitive: ten high officials were executed and one hundred others punished;

the examinations were suspended in forty-five cities; the legation quarter in Beijing was enlarged, fortified, and garrisoned, as was the railway, and some twenty-five Qing forts were destroyed. The indemnity was about $333 million, to be paid over forty years at interest rates that would more than double the amount. The only semiconstructive act was to raise the treaty-based import tariff to an actual 5 percent.

Demoralization

The Confucian-based system of government stressed the impeccable conduct of rulers, officials, and leaders in family and community as the sanction for their superior position and privileges. To an unusual degree, China was governed by prestige. Emperors might in fact be knaves or fools, but the imperial institution was sacrosanct. Official pronouncements were aimed at maintaining and improving the image of the power-holders. Losers were stigmatized as lacking in morality, which accounted for their losing out. A man's maintenance of his good name was as important as his life, an idea that applied even more to women. People whose reputations had been blackened could redeem themselves by suicide. In the society as in the government, reputation was all-important. In this context where moral opinion outranked legal considerations, demoralization could be a stark fact of immeasurable significance. Loss of confidence, sense of humiliation, personal or collective loss of face, consciousness of failure in conduct—there were many forms of this disaster in the nineteenth century.

In the most general sense, then, the last century of the Qing stands forth in retrospect as a unified period surcharged with demoralization on many fronts. The century began with the inordinate corruption of the Qianlong Emperor's favorite, Heshen, which besmirched the emperor's reputation. At the same time the failure of the bannermen to quell the White Lotus uprising was a defeat for the dynasty, which had to recruit new troops from the Chinese populace.

If we skip along touching only highlights of moral disaster we must note the rise of the opium trade at Guangzhou and its expansion along the southeast coast. Long since denounced as immoral, opium caused a fiscal crisis when it led to the outflow of silver and upset the silver/copper exchange ratio, to the detriment of peasants who had to pay taxes by purchasing silver with copper coins. China's acceptance of British terms at Nanjing in 1842 could be advertised by the negotiators as skillful deflection of the foreign menace, but the whole empire could see that opium was still arriving in increasing amounts and the problems of Guangzhou were being multiplied at four new ports of trade. While these were peripheral matters of the frontier, they figured at Beijing in the struggle between money-minded appeasement and suppression according to moral principle. Commissioner Lin could not be cashiered without his moral posture being betrayed. The opium trade, legalized by treaty in 1858, was suborning Chinese officialdom, and the court had to go along in a tremendous loss of face. Very shortly came the Taiping Rebellion, which spread so rapidly, once ignited, that one must assume that a lack of imperial repute paved its way from the West River to Nanjing.

Suppression of the rebellion was achieved only after the Qing rulers at Beijing accepted a basic revision of the balance of power between the Manchu dynasty at the capital and loyal Chinese officials in the provinces. Beijing had to put its trust in provincial leaders like Zeng Guofan and Li Hongzhang and their new armies, which were financed by new provincial taxes on trade. It was a fundamental change in the Qing power structure, evidenced, for example, in the fact that Chinese officials thereafter held the top governor-generalships in the metropolitan province around Beijing and in the Lower Yangzi rice basket at Nanjing. The Qing also had to accept a degree of foreign participation in Chinese political life.

To say, as we are justified in doing, that the downward course of Qing fortunes was arrested by the Restoration of the 1860s is nevertheless a confession that the dynasty's days were numbered. The expediency of the Restoration was evident in the Qing acceptance of an informal alliance with the British and French after the humiliating invasion of Beijing and burning of the Summer Palace in 1860. The long process of war and negotiation during the 1850s and 60s between China and the Western powers had been marked by a general Chinese readiness to fight in defense of principle and a general Manchu readiness to appease the invader in the interests of preserving the dynasty. The appeasement achieved by Prince Gong and his backers, including the young Empress Dowager, was a very expedient move and gave the dynasty another generation of existence. Yet its practical implications were to make the Qing in some ways a minor partner in the Anglo–Qing co-dominion of the China coast.

The Imperial Maritime Customs Service built up in the treaty ports by Robert Hart under the wing of the leading Manchu in the Grand Council, Wenxiang, exhibited the double edge of imperialism. During the first half or more of his constructive administration Hart provided the Qing with a modern revenue agency as well as a device for managing bellicose foreigners in their treaty ports. This was on the whole a great boon to the Chinese state, but after 1895 when the loans had to be contracted to pay the indemnities to Japan and after 1901 to the Boxer protocol signers, Customs became an obvious agent of imperialism by levying upon the Chinese state the repayment of indemnities.

Behind this comparative success in Manchu–Chinese cooperation with the treaty powers for the maintenance of order, there was a split between the interests of the Manchu dynasty and the interests of the Chinese people, which could gradually be seen as two separate things. But beneath this was the larger query as to China's capacity to meet the foreign incursion not only in military and economic matters but also on the intellectual plane.

Not only was the performance of the Chinese state inadequate, the basic principles of the Neo-Confucian order were called into question. This was a greater crisis than had faced the late Ming or any earlier dynasty except perhaps the Song. But whereas the Song had shown their cultural superiority even when defeated, the Chinese who became acquainted with Western matters could not conclude that the superiority of Chinese culture was still a fact. The growth of opium addiction throughout the society was a persistent witness to the loss of self-confidence. Jonathan Spence has made a well-informed guess that by 1900 there were about 40 million Chinese consumers of opium, of whom about 15 million were addicts. This meant that for every Chinese converted to Christianity there were some 15 addicted to opium.

Finally, a sense of doom and disaster demoralized the scholar class, the central guardians of the Neo-Confucian faith. The next chapter therefore concentrates on the relations of the dynasty with the gentry-elite.

12

The Republican Revolution
1901–1916

A New Domestic Balance of Power

After its defeat by expeditionary forces of all the major powers in 1900, the Qing dynasty survived until 1912 only because there was no regime in sight to replace it—and because both Chinese and foreigners in China preferred order to disruption. During the decade from 1901 to 1911 the pace of change in the treaty ports on China's coastal and riverine littoral steadily widened the gap between modern-urban China and the countless villages of the interior. This widening gap had begun with the treaty system, which gave reform-minded Chinese their chance to organize and publicize political opinions—something that the Qing regime did not permit. Even so, the early protagonist of rebellion, Sun Yatsen, in 1905 became head of the Revolutionary League at a meeting of Chinese students in Tokyo only with the help of Japanese expansionists. Chinese nationalism was growing but still dormant.

In this buildup of social forces that would emerge in 1911, the key relationship was that between the imperial government and the gentry-elite. In the era from 1850 to 1911 three stages are broadly visible. The first was the success of the gentry-elite in supporting the dynasty against the Taiping and other mid-century rebels. This was done by setting up militia bureaus throughout the countryside, selecting soldiers on the basis of personal loyalty, and financing it all with gentry contributions and the new *likin* tax on trade.

A second stage came in the post-Taiping era of reconstruction, when gentry-elite became active in a revival and growth of Confucian education in academies and became gentry managers of a wide range of urban welfare and other community works. The gentry class changed its composition as landlords moved into cities and merchants were received into gentry status by purchase of degrees and by joining in officially sponsored commercial and industrial projects. Big families had the funds and accounting procedures to join in economic development. Meanwhile, urbanization allowed a large injection of foreign examples, ideas, and connections.

In a third stage beginning in the late 1890s, along with the rise of nationalism came a reformist urban elite, who enlisted under the banner of provincial development, local self-government, and constitutionalism. They started along many lines of modernization, but they found the Manchus too slow, obstructive, and incapable of leading a Chinese nation.

We turn first to the gentry's role in suppressing rural rebellion.

Suppressing Rebellion by Militarization

One consequence of the great Taiping rebellion after 1850 was the militarization of the countryside to maintain order over a swelling and restive rural populace. This raised an institutional problem—how to maintain the dynasty's central control over the military, the *wu*-element in imperial rule. Dynasties had avoided mass conscription of troops ever since the Qin. The Han and later regimes had used prisoners, paupers, mercenaries, or professional, often hereditary, fighting men. Under the Qing, strategic garrisons of bannermen had been supplemented by a dispersed Chinese constabulary, but both had proved inadequate to quell the White Lotus rising. During the early nineteenth century the increase of local disorder led to a proliferation of local militia forces.

Militia were locally supported part-time soldiers, as Philip Kuhn (1970) remarks, "neither purely military nor purely civil" but a bit of both. Their chief feature in late Qing was their management by local gentry. For example, Frederic Wakeman, Jr. (1966), has described how the Guangzhou gentry organized villagers to oppose the British in the 1840s and 50s. Qing officials there were caught in a dilemma: to oppose the popular xenophobia might turn it against the dynasty; to go along with it might provoke British retaliation. Militia as a form of military power in the hands of the people or at least of the local gentry was a two-edged sword. Beijing had backed away from setting up militia *(tuanlian)* under gentry leadership and financing unless they were strictly controlled by the local magistrates in a system of "official supervision and gentry management" *(guandu shenban)*. On this basis hundreds of villages with thousands of militia could be organized over wide areas to respond to official orders transmitted through widespread gentry associations.

Such a mobilization might be assisted by several networks already in place. One was the *baojia* registration of all households with their able-bodied manpower. Another was the strength of lineage networks that connected people through kinship, common property, and ancestor reverence at ancestral halls. Still another was the market community of the villages of a market area. Intermeshed with all these networks—administrative, social, and economic—a militia system had the potential not only to control rural areas but to supplant the government's control over them. Consequently, in the 1850s Beijing had commissioned trusted officials like Zeng Guofan to organize militia in their native areas only as a last recourse in desperate circumstances.

The reliability of a militia network depended upon all its fighting men being locally connected and identified. Secret societies like the Triads, who operated among smugglers along transport routes, and vagrant refugees, who might flood the roads in time of famine, flood, invasion, or other disasters, were incongruous elements that were hard to control. Most dangerous of all were sectarian rebels like the Taipings, who were animated by a specific faith that held them together.

Two things were therefore necessary to check the Taiping rebels' fanaticism. One was a revival of the Confucian ideology of social order expressed in personal relations between commanders and officers and between officers and men. In short, command, to be effective, had to be personal, based on the interpersonal motives of loyalty, respect for authority, and exemplary leadership. Case studies especially from Hunan show how scholar-commanders of the type of Zeng Guofan developed by trial and error the ideas and practices that eventually created the Hunan Army and similar regional forces that defeated the rebellion. From locally based militia, these troops had advanced to the status of full-time warriors (*yong*, "braves").

The other requirement for success was the levy of taxes to finance the war effort. Contributions secured from well-to-do gentry were a primary source once the ideological struggle had been consciously joined. Sale of degree status and even of official posts were other devices of a dynasty *in extremis*. But the main recourse after 1853 was a new tax on trade, collected on goods in transit or in stock, at a very low rate and hence called *likin* (*lijin*, "a tax of one thousandth"). This new tax battened on the recent growth of domestic trade. (Foreign-owned trade goods moved through the interior, subject to a comparable levy of "transit duties" prescribed by treaty.)

The point about *likin* was that it began under local and provincial, not central, control. Susan Mann (1987) has traced how *likin* spread into every province, where elaborate networks of taxing stations were set up on major routes and in cities, all beyond the immediate purview of Beijing. Gradually the central authorities would get a nominal reporting of *likin* receipts and expenditures. By the end of the century *likin* collections would equal the salt taxes in central government revenue accounts. In short, *likin* taxes, like the militia *(tuanlian)* system and the regional armies they supported, were all made agencies of the state in nominal terms, even though they created a new balance between the central and provincial governments that was to shift steadily in favor of the latter.

Thus led and paid for, the regional armies that wiped out the Taipings had been organized by men who not only shared a general outlook and ideology but were also personally related by the bonds that integrated China's ruling class—kinship including marriage, teacher-student relations, same year graduation, and similar relationships. As Kuhn puts it, "the close integration of the Hunan elite" was due to both "the Qing academic system and the network of patronage and loyalty that ran through the bureaucracy." Under the threat of heterodoxy as well as foreign invasion, they had survived as a ruling class loyal to the Confucian order. After the 1860s their unity of thought and action gradually dissipated.

Meanwhile, the regional armies became regular provincial forces, and new naval and military academies began to train officers who had the new prestige of being scholar-soldiers. They became professional officers in the specialties of modern militarism. Their best graduates would lead the warlord generation of 1916–1927 under the Republic.

Elite Activism in the Public Sphere

During the post-rebellion reconstruction of the late Qing decades, the gentry managers who had militarized the countryside had their successors in an urban gentry class who handled activities of value to the community. Many of these matters had been associated with the local elite ever since the Song, but in the rapid rise of cities in the late nineteenth century new responsibilities were taken on. They provided an outlet for the energy of an elite that could not be wholly employed in the bureaucracy. The Qing examinations continued to produce far more degree-holders than the government could absorb into official posts. The Ming–Qing "minimalist form of government," as Mary Rankin (1986) terms it, continued to rely on the gentry to deal with public matters that lay in between the official and the private levels.

In this public *(gong)* sphere, gentry had first of all taken on the management (with official sanction) of irrigation water, including dams and dikes. The old reasoning of K. A. Wittfogel (1957) and others that the need for central control of water resources was responsible for the inevitable rise of an all-powerful Chinese state can now be turned on its head and applied to the rise of power among the local gentry. This critical community resource had to be managed in each case according to local circumstances and could not be imposed from a distance. Along with management responsibilities came a degree of autonomy and power. So quickly are simplistic theories undone!

The urban gentry also made their influence felt in the sphere of education through an increase of academies. Ideally an academy might shelter and sustain a few dozen scholars in a secluded rural spot, where simple living and high thinking might be pursued close to nature. In practice, however, most academies became preparatory schools for examination candidates and were situated in cities. From Song times onward their number steadily accumulated until there were many thousands in the empire—for example, 565 academies had been established between 1506 and 1905 in Guangdong province; almost 500 had been set up between 960 and 1905 in Jiangxi; and Zhejiang had 289 academies during the nineteenth century. Though some were privately founded, most were set up under official sponsorship and continued superintendence. In either case, the land endowment, trust funds, rents, and contributions or subsidies came from officials personally, from gentry and merchants. A spate of academy foundings followed the suppression of the Taipings. Though not funded by the government, they were semiofficial institutions.

Welfare activities traditionally in gentry hands also took on a new urgency. Caring for the ill and for widows and foundlings, maintaining temples, bridges, and ferries, fighting fires, and burying the dead were all customary gentry-aided services. They were now coordinated in many localities under omnicompetent welfare agencies headed by prominent local figures and often backed by native-place guilds. These leaders of the local elite were obeying Confucian moral injunctions and at the same time trying to ensure social stability and community cohesion.

Their motivation harked back to the "feudal" *(fengjian)* ideal of Confucian reformers, who wanted local leaders to bear greater responsibility for local government.

All this elite activism was extra-bureaucratic. In 1878 a famine in North China inspired a mobilization of prominent managers at different urban levels and across provincial boundaries. The managerial elite's capacity to deal with social problems was outpacing that of the Qing bureaucracy. In a variety of forms the gentry had expanded their public functions to meet local community needs, while the Qing bureaucracy grew only informally, by adding on more advisers and deputies. Gentry managers were preferable to the uneducated and corrupt yamen clerks and runners. The bureaucracy's sanction for elite activism, though still nominally required, was becoming less necessary. The public sphere was growing faster than the governmental.

The land-holding gentry who managed the rural militarization that defeated the Taipings and the urban gentry-merchant activists who managed elite education and social welfare in later decades shared certain features. Both remained upper-class, eager to use devices of statecraft to preserve social stability, not by any means ready to lead peasant rebellion to change China's two-level social structure. From the perspective of modern times they were conservatives. Their eventual alienation from the effete Manchu ruling house would be based on the cultural nationalism of Chinese patriots determined to preserve not only their country but also their own social leadership and domination.

The Japanese Influence

Both the late Qing reforms after 1901 and the Revolution of 1911 were nurtured in Japan. In 1890 the poet-diplomat Huang Zunxian published his *Treatise on Japan,* describing to his countrymen the modernization of a country considered by China's elite to be a cultural offshoot of China, where, for example, the philosophy of Wang Yangming (Ō Yōmei) had a wide appeal, especially among the samurai. Japan's unexpected and crushing defeat of China in 1895 made her the country to emulate. Japan's benevolent though arrogant concern for China was expressed in the doctrine that Japan's successful modernization gave her the duty of helping the backward Chinese along the same path. Expansionist secret societies and the Japanese military became thorough investigators of Chinese life and conditions, while scholars studied the common culture *(tongwen, dōbun)* of the two countries. After 1900 Chinese students crowded into Tokyo, about half of them sent by provincial modernizers like Zhang Zhidong.

The Qing reform program of New Policies that he proposed in 1901 followed the Japanese example in many respects: for instance, in the public school system, in the administrative reform of central government, in the promise (made only in 1908) of a constitution and parliament after nine years, and in the emperor's grant to the people of constitutional rights that the emperor could thereafter rescind at will. Both self-government to mobilize the people and police systems to control them were part of the Qing borrowing from Japan. The Qing reforms were in fact aided by Japanese advisers and a generation of Chinese trained in Japan.

Japan's influence on China by example was supplemented after 1905 by Japan's inheritance from the defeated Russians of their leasehold of the Liaodong peninsula in southern Manchuria, together with the South Manchurian Railway. This lodgement of Japanese forces on what was still Qing territory went along with the rapid growth of Japan's "informal empire" in China. Using their privileges under the British-invented unequal treaty system, the Japanese penetrated China's terrain and economy farther than all the Westerners put together. By 1914 Japan was ahead of Britain in direct trade, trading firms, and resident population. By 1930 Japan would have displaced Great Britain as the paramount foreign economic power in China.

Unfortunately, these achievements were cast under a cloud first by Japan's attempt to get ahead of the other imperialists in her 21 Demands of 1915 and finally by her seizure of Manchuria in 1931.

The Qing Reform Effort

With the onset of the twentieth century, the welter of events in China and the wide spectrum of interest groups and actors all take on a modern complexity. This puts a great premium on sorting out the major movements and forces at work. We are dealing here with a decade of reform from 1901 that precipitated the revolution of 1911 and was followed by the setting up of the Chinese Republic and the attempt of the first president, Yuan Shikai, to rule as a new emperor (see Table 5). This sequence of three phases—reforms that stirred things up, a rebellion that led to political confusion, and an effort to reassert central control by dictatorship—seems reminiscent of other great revolutions that led to the rise of a Cromwell, a Bonaparte, or a Stalin.

Table 5. Major turning points, 1901–1916

1901	Proposal of *New Policies* by Zhang Zhidong et al.
1904	New school system decreed
1904–5	Japan's defeat of Russia in Manchuria
1905	Abolition of old examination system
1906	Ancient Six Ministries supplanted by a dozen modern departments of government at Beijing
1908	Constitutional government projected
	October 14 and 15: Death of Emperor Guangxu and Empress Dowager Cixi
1909	Provincial assemblies meet
1910	National Assembly meets
1911	October 10 rebellion at Wuhan cities
1911	January 1: Sun Yatsen provisional president of Chinese Republic at Nanjing
	February: Qing emperor abdicates, Sun resigns, Yuan Shikai provisional president of Chinese Republic at Beijing
1911–13	Struggle between parliament and president
	March: Yuan has Song Jiaoren, parliamentary leader of the new Nationalist Party, assassinated
1913	Yuan dissolves parliament and takes dictatorial powers
1916	Death of Yuan; warlordism ensues

By 1901 the Qing court had got the message that it could become modern only by centralizing power at Beijing. But it was too late to do this. Major governors (including governors-general) had set up bureaus *(ju)* to handle their provinces' foreign relations on such matters as trade, loans, and investments, as well as provincial industry and railways. So many other new developments had outdated the old imperial system that its revival by metamorphosis was a forlorn hope. Nevertheless, the effort was made. The Empress Dowager and her stand-pat Manchu supporters, who had rejected the sweeping blueprints of Guangxu's "Hundred Days of Reform" edicts in 1898, felt obliged by 1901 to embrace reform as unavoidable. But their aim of using it to strengthen the Qing position tarnished the enterprise from the start. Formally the lead was taken by the impeccable loyalist Zhang Zhidong and the remaining member of the Chinese victors over the Taipings, Liu Kunyi. When they put forward in 1901 their New Policies, the most portentous was educational reform.

A hierarchy of modern schools was to be set up in counties, prefectures, and provinces, with a Japanese-style curriculum of old and new subjects. China's many academies would be converted to this use. New school graduates would enter the classical examination system, which would be a bit modernized to accommodate them.

Alas, it was soon found that students would continue to aim mainly at the old examinations as a more prestigious and much cheaper route of advancement, bypassing the difficult modern curriculum and greater cost of the modern schools. There was nothing for it but to abolish the classical examinations entirely in 1905. This great turning point stopped production of the degree-holding elite, the gentry class. The old order was losing its intellectual foundation and therefore its philosophical cohesion, while the student class that replaced it would be buffeted by discordant fragments of Chinese and Western thought. Education began to be the grab-bag that it has since remained, pulling students into technical specialities that in themselves did not constitute a moral order. The Neo-Confucian synthesis was no longer valid, yet nothing to replace it was as yet in sight.

The speed of change now became very unsettling, beginning with the way things looked. Military officers put on Western-style uniforms (and decorations!); high-level ministers and merchants began to wear business suits; radical students began to cut off their queues in defiance of the Manchus. Protestant missionaries assisted in crusades against foot-binding and opium smoking. The training of new armies went on apace on lines already established, and the new press and publications offered broader views of the world as well as of events in China. The spread of literacy and of news helped the emergence of public opinion, more broad and significant than the literati opinion (*qingyi*) of the past. Mass nationalism among the urban population had been aroused as early as the 1880s by the undeclared warfare with France. In the foreign-tinged treaty ports new professions began to be followed—not only those of industrialist, teacher, journalist, engineer, medical doctor, and other scientists but also those of independent writer, artist, and even revolutionary agitator, like Sun Yatsen.

Facing this vortex of change, Beijing pursued systematic policies inspired partly by foreign examples. The aim was to bring the professional activities of the new elite in business, banking, law, education, and agriculture under state regulation and control. This was to be done by setting up professional associations (*fatuan*, "bodies established by law") to form new elite institutions with quasi-administrative functions. The first were chambers of commerce in 1904, which were expected to be four fifths drawn from guilds. They were followed by educational associations (1906), agricultural societies (1907), lawyers' associations (1912), and bankers' associations (1915). In each case the *fatuan* were intended to be subordinate to government and were to be used as mechanisms to control local elites. The most wide-ranging was the program for local self-government, which opened information offices after 1907. The slogans of the day at Beijing focused on rights recovery, constitutionalism, and self-government.

Constitutionalism and Self-Government

Meanwhile, in the dynamic urban environment of the treaty ports, provincial reformers had found many opportunities. This third generation of the late Qing elite were no longer based in the countryside. Landlord bursaries typically collected their rents, dissolving the erstwhile personal bonds between landlord-patron and tenant. Joseph Esherick (1976) sees this generation as neither still a gentry class nor as yet a bourgeoisie. He therefore calls them an "urban reformist elite." They reacted to foreign imperialism by joining in the Rights Recovery movement to combat foreign control of China's industries, especially mines and railways. During the decade from 1901 to 1911 they invested in industrial enterprises with the customary assistance of official connections, monopoly rights, government loans, and tax advantages, all reminiscent of the bureaucratic capitalism of the self-strengthening movement. Whenever their projects' under-capitalization and lack of market demand necessitated the securing of foreign loans, the aim of rights recovery was quite thwarted. Chinese gentry business managers, by aiming at political goals, courted financial disaster.

When Japan's constitutional monarchy defeated Russia's tsarist autocracy in 1905, constitutionalism seemed to have proved its efficacy as a basis for unity between rulers and ruled in a national effort. Even Russia now moved in 1905 toward parliamentary government. Constitutionalism in China, it was hoped, if combined with government reorganization to strengthen the central administrative power, might give the rising provincial interests a meaningful share in the government and so keep them loyal to it. Between 1906 and 1911 Beijing actively pursued this dual program, combining administrative modernization and constitutionalism. Such changes, however, precipitated a struggle for power, both within the central government and between it and the provinces.

In the power struggle at the capital, the Empress Dowager's supporters succeeded in maintaining, or even enlarging, their grip on key posts. This pro-Manchu and therefore anti-Chinese coloration at the capital handicapped Beijing's efforts to create a new and more centralized relationship with the provinces. It ran into anti-Qing sentiment that came not only from the revolutionary students in Tokyo but also from a rising spirit of nationalism within China. This was manifest in 1905 in China's first modern boycott against the United States' discriminatory treatment of Chinese, particularly the total exclusion of laborers. In this boycott, the old tradition of cessation of business by local merchant guilds was expanded nationwide to most of the treaty ports, especially Shanghai and Guangzhou, where students joined merchants in mass meetings and modern press agitation. American trade was damaged for some months, and Beijing hesitated to repress this popular anti-imperialist movement lest it become antidynastic also.

Under the pressure of rising nationalistic sentiment, the court sent two official missions in the first half of 1906 to study constitutionalism abroad. One visited mainly the United States and Germany; the other, Japan, England, and France. Japan's Prince Itō lectured the visitors on the necessity of the emperor's retaining supreme power, not letting it fall into the hands of the people. On their return they recommended following this Japanese view, that a constitution and civil liberties including "public discussion," all granted by the emperor, could actually strengthen his position because he would remain above them all. In September 1906 the Empress Dowager promised a "constitutional polity" after due preparation. Further missions visited Japan and Germany in 1907–1908.

In order to build up a modern central government, the Six Boards in November 1906 were expanded to make eleven ministries (Foreign Affairs, Civil Appointments, Internal Affairs, Finance, Rites, Education, War, Justice, Agriculture-Industry-and-Commerce, Posts-and-Communications, and Dependencies). Parallel with this executive echelon of government it was proposed to retain the old military and censorial structures and add on a purely advisory "popular assembly" to give voice to public opinion. This would be very far indeed from the creation of a legislative branch equal in power to executive and judicial branches. The idea of the separation of powers could not take root in the absence of the supremacy of law.

In August 1908 the Empress Dowager proclaimed a set of constitutional principles to guide a nine-year program to prepare for constitutional self-government. Accordingly, consultative provincial assemblies were to be convened in 1909 and a consultative national assembly in 1910. The electorate for the provincial assemblies of 1909 was carefully limited to those qualified by education (having taught for three years or graduated from middle school, or gained mid-level examination degrees) or by property (worth at least 5,000 Chinese dollars). On this basis about 1,700,000 men were registered to vote, say 0.4 percent of a population of 400 million. Each electoral district was allotted a number of provincial assemblymen according to its number of registered voters. John Fincher (1981) has noted that about nine tenths of those elected were degree-holders of the gentry elite. They were a third generation, counting from the 1850s, and also a final generation. They would have no successors as an identifiable, indoctrinated, and relatively like-minded stratum of society.

Once the provincial assemblies came together in 1909, new patterns of conduct were required. A few members became orators, while most avoided such embarrassing ostentation. The principle of organization was by loyalty to leaders of factions or personal cliques rather than according to legislative programs or principles. The clear definition and support of interests, which would seem selfish, was generally obscured by the utterance of admirable platitudes. Trained lawyers who could draft legislation were hard to find.

Along with constitutionalism, the movement for self-government aimed to mobilize the populace under local elite leadership in support of the reforming imperial state. There were precedents for self-government not only in the ancient *fengjian* idea of local administration by local people but also in modern cities. In Chinese Shanghai outside the foreign-run areas, a Shanghai city council had been set up in 1905. In 1907 a Tianjin county assembly had been established as a model by the reformist official Yuan Shikai. In 1908 Beijing issued regulations to specify the tax levies that could finance subcounty government—mainly excise and land taxes. Local self-government measures at the county level and below were pursued by the local elite, who tried to avoid the onerous taxation and corrupt administration to be expected from sub-officials at that level. Their opening of new schools to educate and mobilize new citizens was combined with the inauguration of police networks for purposes of control. Yuan set the style by having the new police bureaus compile electoral lists for the new local assemblies. As with the national assembly, these local bodies would allow the elite to advise and even participate in reform by setting up public services like electrification and waterworks that would have been customary for gentry in the past. Political power would remain with the officials. The issue of mobilization versus control thus was joined.

The reformist elite wanted separate and honest financing for the reforms. In 1909–1910 self-government regulations were issued for cities, market towns, rural townships, counties, and prefectures, all of which would have assemblies. New commercial and land taxes were levied separate from the old bureaucratic structure. As it turned out, however, the old-style gentry-elite would become fewer and lose their position of leadership in the countryside, and in the end a new official system would supervene.

Insoluble Systemic Problems

The late Qing reformers, too late, made a vigorous effort to increase the dynasty's central power. Two principal means were to build new railways and train the New Army to enhance their control of the state, while the new ministries after 1906 tried to deal with all the specialized aspects of government. But the late Qing official reformers faced impossible tasks, first of all in remaking the structure of state power. The imperial autocracy, undiminished in its claims to absolutism, presided over two bureaucratic structures, one at the capital, the other in the provinces.

At Beijing the Inner Court centered in the Grand Council. Every day its half dozen ministers read incoming memorials and prepared the imperial edicts in reply that energized official action over the land. They used the memorial–edict loop between the high provincial officials and the imperial court directly via the official horse post. The Outer Court of the six ministries, censorate, and other bodies at Beijing handled routine business in correspondence with their subordinate counterparts in the provinces, but on important matters they were also in a memorial–edict loop with the emperor. For this the telegraph was coming into use.

All administration headed up in Beijing. Both reporting memorials and decision-making edicts flowed to and from the emperor, but at two levels, routine and urgent. For routine matters it was a rather centralized unitary system. Provincial offices of personnel, finance, and so on reported to their superior ministries at Beijing. On urgent matters, however, the provincial governors and the capital ministers were on an equal footing under the emperor. There was no way to centralize power so that provincial governors could be put under Beijing ministries.

It was even more impossible to marry the memorial–edict procedure of the imperial law-giver and executive with the attempted legislative efforts of assemblies still labeled "advisory." The incipiently "representative" nature of the assemblies and their voting by majority rule were not held to their credit. No Confucian had ever believed in simply counting heads.

Reform was also checked at every step by Beijing's fiscal weakness. Payment of the Boxer indemnity of 1901 was now taking much of the central government's revenue just at the moment when uncommitted funds were most needed. Here foreign imperialism—the punitive demands of the powers—was plainly holding China back. At the same time, however, the Qing government's capacity to meet the demands of modernization was limited by the revenue system inherited from the Ming. Financial reform was difficult, not only because it threatened so many "rice bowls" (individual incomes) but also because the inherited fiscal system was so superficial and weak to begin with.

In the first place, the actual tax collections over the empire remained largely unknown, unbudgeted, and unaccounted for. Local tax collectors, as well as the provincial regimes above them, had to live on what they collected. What they should report to Beijing was fixed by traditional quotas. At a guess, it was perhaps a third, possibly only a fifth, of the actual collection.

Second, the taxes officially received, more or less according to quota, were not centralized in a "common purse." Instead, they were listed as a congeries of fixed sums due from a multitude of specific sources and allotted to a multitude of specific uses. Sums listed at Beijing were seldom received or disbursed there, for revenues from a province were allotted in bits and pieces to meet needs in it or elsewhere. Of the 18 provinces, 13 regularly forwarded fixed allotments for specific purposes to other provinces. This ad hoc procedure tied the imperial revenues to an infinite number of vested interests, mainly the support of officials and soldiers.

Moreover, even at Beijing there was no single fiscal authority. The imperial revenues around 1905 totaled on the books roughly 102 million taels (say 70 million dollars or 14.5 million pounds sterling), a small sum for so large a country. To make up this total, the Board of Revenue listed its receipts from the land tax and tribute grain still at the traditional figure of about 33 million taels, to which the salt tax added 13 million and other taxes about 7 million. After 1869 the Board had listed the provincial *likin* collections at the nominal figure reported to it (14 million taels in 1905). Meanwhile, the new and growing Maritime Customs revenue, 35 million taels in 1905, was handled separately, and in any case was earmarked for foreign indemnity and loan payments. Thus, the new trade taxes—customs and *likin*—were hardly under Beijing's control, while the traditional land-tax quotas remained inelastic. With authority thus divided, actual revenues unknown, and many expenditures entrenched as vested interests, fiscal reform could come only through an unprecedented assertion of central power, changing the balance on which the Manchu dynasty had so long maintained itself.

Late Qing fiscal development had occurred mainly in the provinces outside or in addition to the established system. When Beijing tried in 1884 to regularize and secure central revenue from the various provincial measures for military financing, the provinces objected to so many details that the effort had to be given up. New provincial agencies like arsenals, factories, steamship lines, and banks were administered by deputed officials *(weiyuan)* or others commissioned for the purpose by provincial officials. Not appointed by Beijing, they did not usually report to Beijing. The ancient Board of Revenue, though reorganized in 1906 as a Ministry of Finance, could not centralize fiscal control. Other ministries continued to receive and expend their traditional revenues and even set up their own banks, like the Bank of Communications (1907).

A novel effort to make a national budget began with nationwide revenue surveys in 1908 and the compilation of budget estimates in 1910, in which central and provincial government revenues and expenditures were differentiated from local. This produced estimates of total revenues (297 million taels) and expenditures (national, including provincial, 338 million taels; local, 37 million taels) which presaged a sizable deficit (78 million taels). Unfortunately, planning and budgeting, collecting statistics, and setting tax rates went on in both the central ministries and the provinces, uncoordinated, with the provinces not subordinate to the ministries and yet expected to supply the revenues.

These inadequacies of the old regime in administration and finance were deeply rooted in Chinese custom, political values, and social structure. It became apparent that the Qing government had been superficial, passive, and indeed parasitic for too long. It could not become modern.

The Revolution of 1911 and Yuan Shikai's Dictatorship

The issue of the Manchu central power's dominating the provinces in the new age of industrial growth and Chinese nationalism came to a head in 1911 over railway-building in Sichuan. Local elite who had invested in promoting railways there were determined not to let central government officials profit from this new venture, to be financed by foreign loans. Qing military efforts at suppression backfired. On October 10 ("double ten"), 1911, a revolt at Wuchang (opposite Hankou) touched off the defection of most provinces, which declared their independence of the Qing regime. The professional agitators of the Revolutionary League, who had made Sun Yatsen their leader in Tokyo in 1905, set up the Chinese Republic on January 1, 1912, at Nanjing, with Sun as provisional president.

There was general agreement that China must have a parliament to represent the provinces, that unity was necessary to forestall foreign intervention, and that the reform-minded Yuan Shikai, Li Hongzhang's successor and chief trainer of China's New Army, was the one man with the capacity to head a government. Through a noteworthy series of compromises, China avoided both prolonged civil war and peasant risings as well as foreign intervention. The Qing emperor abdicated, Dr. Sun resigned, and in March 1912 Yuan became president.

Of the forces active in the 1911 revolution, the strongest in each province was the combination of the military governor with his New Army and the urban reformist elite in the new provincial assembly. These two elements headed each seceding province. In a general way the military governor was the third-generation product of the militarization movement that had defeated the Taipings, while the provincial assembly stemmed from the gentry managers of public projects in the preceding late Qing generation. Constitutionalism had become the slogan of the day, but constitutional monarchy was made impossible by the narrow-minded and self-concerned Manchu princes left in charge by the Empress Dowager after her death in November 1908 (one day after that of the reformist Guangxu Emperor—what a coincidence!). She evidently preferred to be succeeded by a three-year-old baby rather than an adult reformer.

The Chinese Republic began its history with certain attributes of liberalism—an uncontrolled press; elected assemblies representing the local elite in many counties, prefectures, and provinces; and a national parliament organized mainly by the newly created Nationalist Party

(Guomindang). Unfortunately, China's imperial autocracy had not been extirpated, and nothing was found adequate to take its place.

Yuan Shikai, like a dynastic founder, was a military man, later to be called the "father of the warlords." As an experienced Qing official, Yuan was versed in the inherited repertoire of legal, administrative, fiscal, and military arrangements that could manipulate the people from the top down by using regulations as well as arms, rewards, and punishments, playing upon their hopes and fears to secure their compliance. The discordant proposals and political factionalism of 800 parliament members impressed Yuan as adversely as the moralistic rhetoric of his bureaucrats had impressed the Wanli Emperor of the Ming three centuries before. Authority must have a single source, and so Yuan concluded that his only hope of governing China lay in a reassertion of autocracy. He began by eliminating the new revolutionary leader, Song Jiaoren, who had combined Revolutionary League members with smaller groups to form the Nationalist Party. It had won election in 1913 from some 40 million qualified voters, making Song leader of the parliament. In March 1913 Yuan had him assassinated, and then went on to intimidate and abolish the parliament.

The new provincial, prefectural, and county assemblies still threatened to create a pluralistic semirepresentative polity not under central control. By 1914 county assemblies of 20 members drawn from the elite eligible to vote were generally functioning along with the county magistrates, and both coexisted with subcounty assemblies. Yuan abolished all these assemblies in 1914 and followed this by requiring that magistrates appoint a deputy to serve as county self-government manager. In short, the local elite lost their assemblies, and the magistrates regained control. Assemblies continued in demand, however, and in the 1920s would make a comeback, but magistrates still controlled policy and finances by setting up executive boards. As R. Keith Schoppa (1982) would find in studying Zhejiang's political development in the 1920s, the modernizing elite could lead the way in managing public functions in core areas, but the official bureaucracy in league with old-style elite oligarchies would still dominate peripheral areas.

Unfortunately, the centralized polity of the Qing had fragmented. As Ernest Young (1977) demonstrates, Yuan's efforts to modernize were hamstrung by his lack of central government revenues coming in from the provinces. As a result, his reforms (carried over from the late Qing program) often became plans on paper not realized in action. Much talk of an independent judiciary (which would facilitate the abolition of foreign rights of extraterritoriality) led to setting up an active supreme court at Beijing and courts at provincial, prefectural, and county levels, but soon the county-level courts were abolished to save expense and to go back to relying on the magistrate. Prison reform was also pursued. In education Yuan subscribed to four years of universal free schooling plus a second track of special preparatory schools for an elite seeking higher education. Economic development was also on the drawing boards.

Yet all these many programs for modernization were handicapped by a basic assumption that they must be centrally decreed and controlled. The provincial regimes could not be allowed to develop new institutions on their own lest the central government be weakened beyond repair. Yuan's philosophy was not "Trust the people" nor even "Trust the educated men of talent," but "Trust only the central power." Democracy, in short, was not on Yuan's agenda. In 1915 he tried to make himself emperor but died without success in 1916. While provincial and local assemblies had a second vogue in the 1920s, mobilizing popular participation in China's political modernization would soon become the prerogative of a new central power, to be known as party dictatorship. The job could be done from the top down but not from the bottom up.

The young revolutionaries nominally headed by Sun Yatsen, after half a dozen failures to start a conflagration, had no experience in government and little following at the ruling-class level. Their exploits in 1911–1912 later enlivened the heroic founding myth of the Nationalist Party dictatorship. However, the fact that the military governors and provincial assemblies of 1911–1912 had inherited the dominant power of the gentry upper class gave them an aversion to prolonged disorder because it could energize peasant violence. They favored stability. Joseph Esherick (1976) concludes that the imperial autocracy "had not only limited the political freedom and initiatives of the Chinese people, it had also prevented the local elite from excessively oppressing the rest of the population." Having initiated the 1911 revolution that ended the imperial check on their power, the provincial elite now resumed their stance for stability and so "gave pivotal support in 1913," says Esherick, for Yuan's assumption of dictatorial powers. Their instinct was to save China from the chaos that they feared further change would create.

In this way conservatism thwarted any social revolution. Military governors whose power rested on the newly increased armed forces could become no more than regional militarists or warlords. Conservative gentry could not revive the Neo-Confucian faith so as to mobilize the new urban classes in support of a Chinese nationalism. On the contrary, local elites had broken out of the gentry mold, and lineages were preserving their local dominance by all manner of means. Recent research shows in detail how these means included commerce, industries such as silk and salt, warlord power, corporate property, and overall cultural hegemony. Yet these new sprouts of local elite dominance had no new philosophy. It was time for a new leadership to make a fresh beginning with new ideas.

PART THREE

The Republic of China
1912–1949

THIS ERA was sharply bifocal. In a cultural focus it saw an unprecedented influx of foreign goods, ideas, and ways, more comprehensive than at any earlier time. Influences of modernity were piled upon influences from many specific nations. Everything was changing. Yet in another social-political focus were several features characteristic of an interregnum between dynasties. A failed attempt to revive the empire was followed by a decade of warlordism that unsettled the countryside, while foreigners played key economic and administrative roles in the treaty ports. This inspired a nationalist revolution against foreign imperialism, which was accompanied by the crude beginnings of a social revolution to mobilize the farming masses on the land.

Among the great powers, Britain and the United States—the chief sources of Protestant missions—in the Anglo-Saxon fashion preferred reform as more constructive than revolution. Their aid to reform came largely through private nonofficial channels but was both little and late. The USSR, in contrast, supported violent social revolution through aid to both Nationalists and Communists. Meanwhile, Japan's cultural and economic influence on China early in the century gave way to a military aggression that sidetracked China's history from 1931 to 1945. Japan's aggression, merging into World War II, added immeasurably to the Chinese people's desperation.

Partly because the warlord era from 1916 to 1927 was a low point of state power, it was paradoxically a time of considerable achievement along cultural, social, and economic lines. The rela-

tive freedom of this new growth would contrast with the bureaucratic control that would be reimposed upon China after 1927. The
contrast would highlight two themes that continued during China's
era of party dictatorships. One theme was authoritarian statism,
the primacy of state-building, beginning with loyalty to autocratic
central power and putting political unity above all. The other
theme was cultural creativity and social improvement as part of a
process of civil growth. This theme was evident in autonomous developments not under direct control of officialdom in China's adaptation to the modern world. They did not, however, offer much
promise of a unified state power.

13

The Quest for a Chinese Civil Society

The Limits of Chinese Liberalism

Civil society may be defined as the democratic type of society that grew up in Western Europe beginning with the rise of towns independent of the feudal system. It is a pluralist society in which, for example, the church is independent of the state, religion and government are separate, while civil liberties (recently expanded as human rights) are maintained under the supremacy of law. Civil society is a matter of degree, seldom neatly defined. It is part of a country's state-and-society but has a measure of autonomy, freedom within limits. It is not to be found in Islam nor in the modern totalitarian regimes of fascism, Nazism, or communism, nor in the Chinese dynastic empires described in Part One.

However, in Late Imperial China new trends began to move toward the creation of institutions, functions, and individual occupations—a whole sector of society—not under the direct control of the Qing state. This general trend appeared most obviously to foreigners in the treaty ports, but its impulse probably came from within China more than from the outside world, specifically from the expanding activities of the gentry elite in the public *(gong)* sphere of community life. To this tradition of unofficial elite activism were now added after 1911 several modern factors: the growth of the Chinese press, of education, and of business. Civil society was inherent in the expansion of knowledge and of the division of labor, which enabled specialists to claim autonomy within their spheres of special competence. Yet such autonomy always seemed to threaten unity and order in the Chinese state, which its rulers felt depended upon the state's pervasive supervision of the people's lives. This universal social problem of balancing individual autonomy or liberalism against state-imposed unity and order was unusually acute and persistent in China. One evidence was the difficulty of achieving parliamentary government when the supremacy of law was not acknowledged in practice and therefore no division of powers could be accepted between legislature and executive. Parliaments, though convened and often vociferous, functioned less as lawgivers than as symbols of the executive's legitimacy.

Individualism and liberalism in Chinese thinking were strictly limited parts of a larger collectivity. The Chinese individual was subordinate to the group. Chinese laws were less commanding than the claims of morality. The Western concept of civil society had a meaningful counterpart in Chinese thinking, but it had to be defined. For example, individual self-expression and property-holding, the essential features of Victorian liberalism, were to be enjoyed in China only with the blessing of officialdom.

These limitations had been evident in late Qing thought. Although the Neo-Confucian belief system had to accept "foreign matters" (modernization) and the New Learning for their utility at least as part of statecraft, it proved impossible for the last Qing generation to foreswear Confucianism entirely. As we might expect, many tried to find in foreign models a way to reaffirm certain inherited Chinese values.

Japanese reformers facing modernization had proposed to combine "Eastern ethics and Western science." In China, Zhang Zhidong as the top ideology-fixer of his day, put forward his famous formula, "Chinese learning for the substance [the essential principles or *ti*] and Western learning for function [the practical applications or *yong*]." This was slick but inconsistent, because *ti* (substance) and *yong* (function) referred in Chinese philosophy to correlative aspects of any single entity. Thus, Chinese and Western learning each had its own substance and function. The phrase was widely used, nevertheless, since it seemed to give priority to Chinese values and decry Western learning as merely a set of tools.

Confucian-minded Japanese offered one useful concept—that Western-type parliaments could bring harmony between ruler and ruled. But the rationale was different. Western political thought had built up the concept of interests—the personal desires and goals of individuals and groups in their inevitable competition with one another. Interests were seen as motivating political actors in the West, from the king on down to the swineherd. Representative government was a procedure for working out mutual compromises among competing interests. Not so in China. Interests were by definition selfish, and Confucian morality decried selfishness as an antisocial evil. Instead, it extolled the ideal of harmony, which reformers hoped somehow to attain through representative government.

Another liberal concept that was bent out of shape as it moved from West to East was that of individualism. As Benjamin Schwartz (1964) noted long ago, reformers like Yan Fu, who translated the Western liberal classics (Thomas Huxley, Adam Smith, J. S. Mill, and others) at the turn of the century, praised the growth of individualism as a means to support the state, not stand against it. The most influential reformer, Liang Qichao, promoted the notion of each individual's unselfishly developing his capacities, the better to strengthen and enrich the state. Only thus could individuals benefit all their fellow citizens. Liang quoted the Swiss jurist Bluntschli: people are born for the state, not the state for the people. From this statist starting point, which Confucianists had always been taught to begin with, it followed that rights of all sorts were either to be granted by the state or to be withheld by it when in its own interest. All Chinese constitutions have listed many rights but only as programmatic ideals, not necessarily as laws to be enforced.

Behind this Chinese version of "liberalism" lay the prior assumption that the ruler's power was unlimited, still autocratic. His devices of statecraft might expand to include constitutions, parliaments, and citizens' rights (as well as duties), all to improve the state's stability and control. Typically, rights were guaranteed "except as limited by law," that is, by the fiat of the authorities. Chinese constitutions did not become sacred fonts of law, as did the Constitution of the United States, but rather expressed ideals and hopes, more like American party platforms.

This part-way nature of liberalism in China suggests it might best be termed proto- or Sino-liberalism. It had its roots in the *wen* side of Chinese government, where scholar-officials had written proposals in essays and memorials but usually lacked the responsibility or power to put them into practice. The modern Sino-liberal, for example, had a limited freedom of expression because he could not afford to attack local power-holders specifically and in person without danger of violent retaliation from their *wu*-component of government. More serious than this prudential caution was the cast of mind that could not disengage, in Vera Schwarcz's (1986) phrase, from the Neo-Confucian "cult of ritualized subordination . . . the ethic of subservience" implanted in early family training.

Western-type liberalism under law in China was handicapped, finally, by the company it kept, namely, the unequal treaty system. The warlord era in the 1910s and 20s coincided with the high point of foreign influence during the treaty century. Warlord armies despoiling the "interior" outside the ports were potent sanctions for keeping foreign gunboats at hand in the ports. Thus, the stirrings of a Chinese type of civil society in China were modeled in part on Western institutions and yet were protected by the very imperialist presence that had inspired the rise of China's new nationalism.

At bottom we would do well to keep in mind the differing values founded on the difference of historical experience in China and in the West. One need not abandon one's hope for liberal individualism in civil society in order to acknowledge the long-continued efficacy of China's authoritarian collectivism and the modern Chinese intellectuals', excruciating task of having to find some midpoint between them.

The Limits of Christian Reformism

Republican China in the decade after Yuan Shikai consisted of two areas and two regimes—warlord China and treaty-port China. The warlords were military personalities, trained perhaps by Yuan, who controlled regions by commanding troops and keeping them fed. Several had begun as military governors. Their talents were devoted mainly to fighting, or threatening to fight, one another. The treaty-port cities, on the other hand, included most of the centers of urbanization, where most of the modern Chinese banks, industries, universities, and professional classes could be found. It was a joint Chinese and foreign community. The treaty-port part of the Chinese state's power structure provided a degree of stability during the years of warlord disruption. In fact, it set limits to that disruption. Chinese patriots had to confront the paradox that the unequal treaties, while humiliating in principle, were often of material help in fact. For example, in June 1921 Chinese merchants at the treaty port of Yichang, after twice suffering warlord pillaging, asked the foreign ministers in Beijing to set up a foreign concession area in Yichang as a form of protection against the marauding warlord troops.

After the Boxer settlement of 1901, two Chinese and foreign trends had converged: reform-minded Chinese had built up education in the New Learning, while Christian efforts in China more and more stressed the "social gospel," to address the problems of modern city life. The respective Confucian and Christian fundamentalists, who had for years denounced each other but seldom met, were now succeeded by friendly cooperators for the betterment of China. For example, the Chinese Young Men's Christian Association, an offshoot of the international YMCA, found Chinese merchant and upper-class backing for its work among city youths and students with help from its foreign advisers. John Hersey's novel *The Call* offers an inside account of the Y's activity in Sino–foreign cooperation in public education and other projects from 1907 to 1937. The Sino–foreign Christian community enjoyed a brief golden age of about two decades from 1905 to 1925.

This era of Christian cooperation was marked by signal achievements such as the road-building and rural credit work of the China International Famine Relief Commission, the research and training at the Rockefeller-supported Peking Union Medical College, Rockefeller Foundation support of the social sciences as at the Nankai Institute of Economics, growth of Yanjing University and other Christian colleges, including agricultural research at Nanjing University, and the Mass Education Movement under Yan Yangchu (Jimmy Yen).

Three aspects of these institutional accomplishments should be noted: first, they depended more than the Chinese YMCA upon foreign, chiefly American, funding and support. Second, they gave sinophile Americans a sense of satisfactory participation in Chinese life that would later give substance to "the loss of China" feeling in Cold War America. Third, they barely scratched the surface of the Chinese people's problems. Most of these foreign-aided activities were pilot-model treatments, not on a scale capable of transforming China directly.

This superficiality of the Western-inspired or aided projects in China was unavoidable partly because China's educated ruling-class elite, to which the foreigners were attached, was itself such a tiny proportion of the Chinese population. For example, in education, if we accept E. Rawski's (1979) estimate of late Qing male literacy at 30 to 45 percent and female at 2 to 10 percent, we still confront estimates of elementary school enrollment in China running from a million in 1907 to 6.6 million in 1922, while in the same period middle school enrollment rose from 31,000 to 183,000—abysmally small figures for a country teeming with 400 million people.

Liberal efforts at creating a Chinese civil society must therefore be seen as points of growth, like spores growing in a biological laboratory's broth, scattered over a large surface. Given enough time, each group of enterprising reformers—social, scientific, medical, mass educational—

might have expanded their work to reach many of China's people. Yet so massive were the people's problems that in the end only the state could take them on.

The Tardy Rise of a Political Press

The emergence of the independent modern press in China, roughly a century later than in Western Europe and a generation later than in Japan, rounds out our picture of late Qing inertia. The old order had kept a stranglehold on self-expression regarding government policy, which was still the emperor's preserve.

During the millennium since the spread of printed books in the early Song, the ingredients of a modern press had steadily accumulated: official and private libraries, literary connoisseurship and editorial skills, religious texts, great official publication projects, a ceaseless flow of documentation from Beijing to provincial centers, local gazetteers, vernacular literature, private publications—all were on hand. In the early 1890s a dozen Chinese-language newspapers were being published in major port cities. *Shenbao* at Shanghai, started in 1872, had a circulation of 15,000. Their news, partly acquired by telegraph, was mainly commercial. That China's modern press took so long to get into politics was a tribute to the imperial control of thought and print.

Modern Chinese journalism started with treaty-port Chinese like Wang Tao, who had been James Legge's assistant in translating the Confucian classics in the 1860s and spent two years with him in Scotland. In 1874 Wang Tao began in Hong Kong the first newspaper wholly under Chinese auspices, printing both commercial and general news and adding his own reformist editorials. They were informed, as his biographer, Paul Cohen (1974), points out, by Wang's almost unique "field experience" in the West. But in the 1880s Wang still had only a small audience.

Given this brilliant beginning, how could Chinese journalism mark time for 20 years until the crisis of the 1890s inspired the reformist press set up by Liang Qichao and others in Shanghai and provincial centers like Changsha? The reason, in brief, was that the gentry elite were strictly warned not to trespass on the policy-setting prerogative of the imperial regime. Only when specifically permitted could ideas be presented to the throne, and in the 1870s and 80s the strident submissions of literati opinion (*qingyi*) had contributed more moralistic heat than practical light. Only after the Qing dynasty had been defeated in 1900 by *all* the powers, including Japan, did its mandate begin to slip away. Liang Qichao's journals of political opinion published in Japan marked this shift, as the urban reformist elite turned to provincial fields of action.

Once started in the protective environment of the port cities, publication of Chinese newspapers, magazines, and books during the next 20 years increased many times over. Their circulation was aided by the service of the new imperial post office after 1896 as well as by the spread of elementary schooling and literacy. Assuming with Zhang Pengyuan that every copy of a magazine had an average of about 15 readers, Leo Lee and Andrew Nathan (in Johnson et al., 1985) have estimated the total late Qing readership as between 2 and 4 million, say one percent of China's population. The new urban readership and the crises of the 1890s fostered a rapid growth. (By 1893 the urban population was about 23.5 million, say 6 percent of China's population.)

But even as late as the mid-1930s China had only 910 newspapers and about an equal number of magazines. Some papers sold 150,000 copies. Readership of the papers alone totaled between 20 and 30 million. Thus the proportion of the public reached by print was still small compared with other modern nations. Even so, the Shanghai Commercial Press after 1896 became great publishers of textbooks and magazines. Writers of the new literature found that urban readers sought mainly entertainment. The "mandarin duck and butterfly school" of romantic and sentimental fiction, studied by Perry Link (1981), produced some 2,200 novels in the years 1910–1930. Only political discussion was in short supply. This went along with the fact that the higher educational establishment was still minuscule for so large a country.

Modern China's political journalism was generally polemical, aiming to criticize and advocate, not primarily to inform the public as to facts. Lee and Nathan quote Liang Qichao again: "One must intend to use one's words to change the world. Otherwise, why utter them?" Thus the press, despite its small size, became a major tool of politics.

Academic Development

Contrary to the Beijing University (Beida) tradition that China's higher education originated with its forerunner, the Imperial University, inaugurated as one of the 1898 reforms, the recent survey by Wen-hsin Yeh (1990) reminds us that Shanghai was the natural site for the beginning of China's modern education in engineering, technology, and commerce.

Just as St. John's College, opened by the American Episcopal Mission in 1879, became the pioneer Christian college in China, so Nanyang College was founded by the Qing government in 1896. It sent students abroad and later became Jiaotong (Communications) University, a leader in engineering.

The gap between Neo-Confucianism and the New Learning was widened when modern subjects had to be taught with imported English-language textbooks. Chinese vocabularies for technical terms had still to be worked out. College entrance and final examinations were often in English, as was instruction by foreign professors.

When the ancient amalgam of state and society disintegrated in 1912, so did the Neo-Confucian world outlook. In its place flooded in disparate, often conflicting cultural elements in bewildering variety. The generation of the warlord era consequently had to sort things out.

Its problem stands out more starkly if we follow Jon Saari (1990) in his study of the life experience of scholars born in the 1890s, who began with a classical education and yet added onto it in youth an Anglo–American education, including spoken English. This cohort of China's post–gentry-elite had to achieve not one but two liberations—first from the mummified thinking of the old Confucian family system and patriarchal tyranny, second from the polycultural confusion of the New Learning. For the youth who had just finished his elementary classical training, the New Learning brought an explosion that shattered the intellectual environment in which he had just found his place. "Far from being the world, China was now a fragment of the world." The young mind's encounter with the West was often "a crippling experience," full of "confusion and uncertainty." It required "a second liberation perhaps more decisive than the first," a release from confusion by finding "a higher integration or synthesis." To be emancipated from the discredited bonds of Confucianism left one fearfully at sea, in need of a new way to order one's world. A belief in Christianity, or in science, including Darwinism, or a dedication to one of the new professions, or to patriotic revolution—all might help establish one's new self-image. Without intellectual courage, one could hardly survive.

Such was the traumatic breaking in of the first republican generation of intellectuals. Despairing of Japan, they looked to Europe and America for the key to saving China. This task made them pioneers in biculturalism, for the cultural shock of Tokyo was little compared with that of New York, London, Paris, and Berlin.

A government program for training Chinese in America began when the U.S. Congress in 1908 allocated for this purpose roughly half ($12 million) of the American share of the Boxer indemnity. From Qinghua College set up at Beijing as a preparatory school, 1,268 scholars were sent to the United States by 1929. In 1924 the remaining half of the indemnity (which would still have to be paid over by the Chinese government) was allocated to supporting the China Foundation. Guided by a board of ten Chinese and five American trustees, this foundation made private grants for research as well as training. In this era young Chinese scientists trained in the United States formed in 1914 the Science Society. Soon its journal represented the widespread hope of modern scholars that science and the scientific outlook could provide a common approach to China's problems.

Meanwhile, by the 1920s the hundreds of missionary middle schools in China had grown by consolidation into a dozen Christian colleges, usually incorporated in the United States. In the Chinese–American faculties the American members usually enjoyed better housing and were paid by mission boards in America. Protected by extraterritoriality, these American-style institutions like Yanjing University at Beijing during the 1920s and 30s educated children from the new middle class of the port cities.

One influential private and purely Chinese institution was at Tianjin, where Zhang Boling, after 1904, built up Nankai middle school, college, and university with support principally from local Chinese families. Chinese philanthropy also supported Amoy University at Xiamen and two colleges in Shanghai—the Catholic Zhendan (L'Aurore), founded in 1903, and Fudan (1905).

No private institution, however, could outshine Beijing University (Beida) as the focal point of national education. It served to train or retread bureaucrats until two remarkable men came to head it—Yan Fu in 1912 and Cai Yuanpei in 1917. Cai was a Hanlin academician of late Qing vintage who had joined Sun Yatsen's Revolutionary League. He had been the first minister of education in the abortive cabinet under Yuan Shikai and then had studied five years in Germany and France. To foster diversity of thought at Beida he collected talent widely and stood firmly against government interference in education. Cai invited as dean Chen Duxiu, who had absorbed in Paris the spirit of the French Revolution and returned to found in 1915 an influential journal of discussion, *New Youth (La Jeunesse)*. At Beida, Chen led the attack on Confucianism and all its evils in the name of science and democracy.

The New Culture Movement

Japan's aggressive 21 Demands of 1915 tried to set up a sort of Japanese protectorate over China. Though not successful, this incident ended Japan's era of reform leadership in China and heightened China's modern nationalism. Yet at this very time scholars in the New Learning asserted a new role for themselves—to stay out of government service and eschew politics, toward which their forebears had been oriented, in order to scrutinize the old Confucian values and institutions, reject what had held China back, and find in China's past the elements of a new culture.

For this New Culture Movement a first point of attack was the Chinese writing system. In the twentieth century a script and vocabulary largely created about 200 BC were still being used. Any major character had become like an onion, with many layers of meaning accumulated over the ages as it was used for various purposes. For a too simple comparison, suppose the Roman idea expressed as *pater* had come down to us unchanged in written form and today, perhaps combined with other characters, referred to father, patriotism, paternity, patristics, patrimony, patronage, etc., etc. Which meaning to assign to such a character depended on its context, which required knowing the classical texts. This made the classical writing *(wenyan)* not a convenient device ready at hand to help every schoolboy meet life's problems; it was itself one of life's problems. Without long-continued study of it, one was barred from the upper class. The functional literacy for everyday business among ordinary Chinese was far more accessible than the esoteric terms and erudite allusions used by the classical examination graduates.

The first stage in the literary revolution was to use the everyday speech in written form—the step taken in Europe at the time of the Renaissance, when the national vernaculars supplanted Latin. Protestant missionaries had pioneered in this effort, to make the scriptures available to the common man. Among the new scholar class the time was ripe. Leadership was taken by Hu Shi, a student at Cornell and Columbia during World War I, who advocated the use of the *baihua,* or Chinese spoken language, as a written medium for scholarship and all purposes of communication. Many others joined in this revolutionary movement, which denied the superior value of the old literary style. The use of *baihua* spread rapidly; the tyranny of the classics had been broken.

Hu Shi, a student of John Dewey and of pragmatism, also became a leader in the advocacy of scientific methods of thought and criticism.

The value of science in technical studies had long been incontrovertible. Its application, as a way of thought, to Chinese literary criticism and historical scholarship now marked a further step. The new scholarship vigorously attacked the myths and legends of early Chinese history and reassessed the provenance of the classics. It studied Chinese folklore and reappraised the great vernacular novels of Late Imperial times. Its precocity was nurtured by the achievements of evidential scholarship under the Qing.

The creativity of the New Culture Movement is fully visible only in its historical context. The great World War of 1914–1918 disclosed the barbaric potentialities of Europe's arrogant civilization. The empires of Austria–Hungary, of the Russian tsars, and finally Germany all collapsed. Woodrow Wilson proclaimed great principles of self-determination for all peoples and open diplomacy among them. Ideas of several kinds of socialism, of the emancipation of women, and the rights of labor versus capitalists swept around the globe and flooded into Republican China. China's scholar-elite, still a tiny top crust of their ancient society, instinctively took on the task of understanding and evaluating this revolutionary outside world at the same time that it struggled to reevaluate China's inherited culture.

The May Fourth Movement

The incident of May 4, 1919, was provoked by the decision of the peacemakers at Versailles to leave in Japanese hands the former German concessions in Shandong. News of this decision led some 3,000 students from Beida and other Beijing institutions to hold a mass demonstration at the Tiananmen, the gateway to the palace. They burned the house of a pro-Japanese cabinet minister and beat the Chinese minister to Japan. Police attacked the students. They thereupon called a student strike, sent telegrams to students elsewhere, and organized patriotic teams to distribute leaflets and make speeches among the populace. Similar demonstrations were staged in Tianjin, Shanghai, Nanjing, Wuhan, Fuzhou, Guangzhou, and elsewhere. A few students were killed and others were wounded. The prisons were soon full of demonstrators.

The spirit of protest spread when merchants closed their shops in a strike that spread through the major centers in June of 1919. This developed into a boycott of Japanese goods and clashes with Japanese residents. For more than a year student patriots continued to agitate for the destruction of Japan's market in China, with an appreciable effect upon it. Meanwhile, and most significantly, strikes were staged among the recently organized labor unions, which joined in the broadest demonstration of national feeling that China had ever seen.

The startling thing about this movement was that it was led by intellectuals who brought both the new cultural ideas of science and democracy and the new patriotism into a common focus in an anti-imperialist program. More than ever before the student class assumed responsibility for China's fate. They even began through their student organizations to reach the common people.

In mobilizing intellectuals, literature led the way through novels and short stories in the new written vernacular. Most writers were well educated and from the upper class. Leading figures had studied in Japan, but once they returned to China they lived in urban poverty and often under police harassment. Their audience was mainly young students in the cities caught up, like the writers themselves, in a social revolution. They opposed the bonds of the family system and stood for individual self-expression, including sexual freedom. The romantic individualism and self-revelation of some pioneers, telling all in a first-person narrative or diary style, was quite shocking to strict Confucian mores.

The outstanding writer of the 1920s, Lu Xun (1881–1936), came from a Zhejiang gentry family that fell into disgrace. He took the first-level classical examination, studied science at naval and military academies, began medical training in Japan, and finally settled upon literature as a means of social reform. Lu Xun leaped into prominence only in 1918 by publishing in *New Youth* his satire, "The Diary of a Madman," whose protagonist finds between the lines of "benevolence, righteousness, truth, virtue" in his history book two words repeated everywhere: "Eat men." Chinese culture, he wrote, was "a culture of serving one's masters, who are triumphant at the cost of the misery of the multitude."

Student leaders at Beida like Fu Sinian and Luo Jialun in their journal *New Tide (Renaissance)* advocated a Chinese "enlightenment." They denounced the Confucian family bonds as slavery and championed individualistic values. As early as March 1919 the students had set up a lecture society to reach the common people. In this they joined student activists like Zhang Guotao, who were most intent on "saving China."

Thus, some leaders among the tiny minority of intellectuals—professors, students, writers—leaped into the cultural struggle to abolish the out-of-date evils of the old China and establish new values for a new China. As would-be leaders, they faced the crippling fact of China's two-stratum social structure—the ruling elite and the masses. Could their new elite connect with the common people? Or would these new commanders get too far ahead of their troops?

Rise of the Chinese Bourgeoisie

The autonomy of the new academic community was paralleled by a new self-consciousness of functional groups in city life. Recent studies of municipal institutions arising in Shanghai and in Beijing show the mix of new and old, foreign and Chinese, styles of organization.

In Shanghai the nascent bourgeoisie had begun with Chinese merchants in foreign trade. After 1842 the brokers in the trade at Guangzhou, known as Hong merchants, had been succeeded by the compradors ("buyers" in Portuguese), who contracted with foreign merchants to handle the Chinese side of their trade. While the foreigners handled shipping and insurance and invested in imports and exports, the compradors' fortunes came from commissions paid them by their foreign employers, from interest on funds they handled, fees for acting as treasurers and managers of funds, and profits from their own personal investments and businesses. Thus, the compradors of the foreign banks in China had the profitable function of dealing with the Chinese "native" banks that grew up to serve the Chinese merchant community.

Shanghai compradors had come first from Guangzhou in the tea trade and then from Ningbo as well as Jiangsu province. They totaled roughly 250 in 1854, about 700 in 1870, and perhaps 20,000 at the beginning of the twentieth century. Comprador posts were passed down to sons and nephews as hereditary family possessions. Instead of investing in land in the old style, compradors often invested in foreign firms that protected their funds from encroachment by Chinese officials. There is really no way to distinguish (as the Chinese Communist Party liked to do for propaganda purposes) between a "comprador bourgeoisie" and a so-called "national bourgeoisie." They were all one group.

Since agriculture still produced some 65 percent of China's national product, the modern sector of the economy was still marginal. China avoided the role of a semicolony exploited by the foreign powers; it did not become a great source of supplies for the foreigner, nor did it provide a big market for his goods. The only imports with much sale, after opium, were industrial yarns and kerosene. In short, the traditional economic system continued to function so well with its low standard of living that China's modern economy had comparatively little to offer it. The steamship and steam launch, for example, came into the Chinese water network to speed up transport but did not greatly change the system. Chinese merchants soon were using them, whether run by foreigners or by Chinese.

During the late Qing self-strengthening effort, the officials who were leading it had great networks of collaborators, advisers, secretaries, deputies, and partners. This complex had some control over merchants in the "official supervision and merchant management" system, but the officials did not take responsibility for production. Marie-Claire Bergère (1989) comments that the promoters of the early modernization movement depended upon this bureaucratic complex. Power still lay with the bureaucracy. Modernization could be advanced only through personal relations and profit sharing between officials and entrepreneurs. Thus the late Qing had opted not for state capitalism but for the bureaucratic capitalism of officials.

In an imperial edict of 1903 the Qing tried to co-opt the urban elite by upgrading the status of merchants. Between then and 1907 the new Ministry of Trade gave awards to honor investors, technicians, and entrepreneurs. By 1912 there were as many as 794 Chambers of Commerce and 723 education societies along with the local and provincial assemblies. These organizational efforts got out of imperial control when associations developed national programs across provincial boundaries, like that of the Chinese Education Association and the Federation of Provincial Assemblies. Such bodies represented the gentry–merchant elite.

The outbreak in Europe of World War I in August 1914 led to a reduction of foreign shipping and trade in China and a decline of imports, followed shortly by an increased foreign demand for raw materials to be exported. Simultaneously the price of silver on the world market rose spectacularly and so increased the buying power of Chinese currency. The lack of foreign competition gave Chinese entrepreneurs a great opportunity, even though the scarcity of shipping delayed much of the equipment they ordered from Europe. By 1919 the Chinese were benefiting from heavy export demands from Europe and America as well as the rise in the value of silver against gold, which encouraged Chinese imports.

Unlike the self-strengthening movement of the late nineteenth century, this wave of industrialization favored production of consumer goods for immediate consumption and profit. Between 1912 and 1920, says Bergère, Chinese industry achieved an annual growth rate of 13.8 percent. Dozens of cotton mills were established in China, a total of 49 in 1922 alone. Flour mills grew up at Shanghai, and cigarette, paper, and match industries around Guangzhou. In Shanghai between 1912 and 1924 some 200 new workshops for mechanical engineering were set up both to maintain and repair equipment and also to produce knitting machines, looms, and other industrial machinery. By 1920 about half of them were using electric power.

World War I in China also saw the rise of modern-style Chinese banks. These included not only the Bank of China and the Bank of Communications, which had Beijing-government connections. A dozen others were connected with provincial governments handling mainly state funds and loans, but another dozen or so were strictly commercial banks. By 1920 Shanghai also had 71 old-style native banks. Specializing in short-term loans, they handled the funds of opium merchants and the dye trade in chemicals. A stock exchange and a national bank were still lacking.

The population of Shanghai, including the International Settlement and French Concession as well as the surrounding Chinese suburbs and Chinese city, totaled 1.3 million in 1910 and 2.6 million in 1927. Overseas Chinese played a role when in 1919 the big department stores from Hong Kong of the Sincere Company and the Wing On Company (originally of Penang) opened their shops on Nanjing Road. On the Bund arose the big modern buildings of the Hong Kong and Shanghai Banking Corporation and of Jardine, Matheson & Co.

After 1925 the Shanghai Municipal Council of the International Settlement included Chinese councilors; and Chinese administrations grew up in the suburban areas more or less autonomously until their unification in Chinese Greater Shanghai in 1927. The Chinese Ratepayers Association functioned in the International Settlement, and there were many Chambers of Commerce for businessmen. The most prominent was the Shanghai General Chamber of Commerce. The Chinese who developed big textile factories and flour mills formed a new entrepreneurial class linked with but not controlled by landed gentry. This new local elite, especially in Shanghai, stayed clear of government control and secured the appointments of magistrates from among local scholars. Their bureaucrats were recruited on the spot.

In their urge for autonomy, the new entrepreneurs were running parallel with the academics centered in Beijing in the May Fourth Movement of 1919 and later. The industrialists favored the new education, with its teaching of pragmatism and respect for the individual. For example, the New Education Movement led by Jiang Menglin, who followed Cai Yuanpei as head of Beida, was much indebted to the support of the powerful Jiangsu Education Association. Through extended family relations there were many links between the academics and the entrepreneurs in the 1920s. For example, a daughter of Zeng Guofan, the victor over the Taipings, married the director of the Shanghai Arsenal named Nie Qigui. Their sons became directors of cotton mills, and one, Nie Yuntai (C. C. Nieh), became also president of the General Chamber of Commerce.

This new Shanghai bourgeoisie created its own organizations. Publication of the *Bankers' Weekly* in 1917 led to setting up the Shanghai Bankers Association in 1918. This example in Shanghai led to the setting up of bankers' associations in other cities—Hankou, Suzhou, Hangzhou, Beijing, Tianjin, and Harbin. By 1920 they had amalgamated to form the Chinese Bankers Association. A Chinese cotton mill owners' association had also been formed. They studied the world market and switched their allegiance from the traditional aim of monopoly to that of growth. They were international-minded. Some leading bankers had got their higher education in Japan. One of the best known to foreigners, Chen Guangfu (K. P. Chen), had graduated from the Wharton School of Finance at the University of Pennsylvania.

The organization of general partnerships or private companies began to give way to joint stock companies, even though they would still be dominated by family connections. How the family system served as the backbone of the entrepreneurial class was illustrated by the Rong family. About 1896 the founder had opened Chinese banks in Shanghai and Wuxi. In the third generation there were eleven Rong men who served as managers or directors of flour mills and cotton mills. In 1928 the Rong brothers held 54 executive posts in their twelve flour mills and seven cotton mills, constituting more than half of the top management.

The importance of regional and family structures among the new entrepreneurial class indicated that they had not sharply broken away from Chinese society but might instead be called "Confucian modernizers." Bergère questions how far an "entrepreneurial, liberal and cosmopolitan bourgeoisie" could be grafted onto the old mandarin and peasant civilization of China. The one evident fact was that the new type of businessmen had become alienated from the dynasty, and this led them to support the provincial reformist elite in the Revolution of 1911–1912.

In the early 1920s the businessmen agreed with the call of Hu Shi and his Beida colleagues for the Chinese elite to take action, professional

skills to be developed, and good government to succeed in being financially responsible and planning ahead. Hu Shi represented the liberal
Beijing intellectuals, and they found much in common with the Shanghai
business community. For example, the businessmen supported the currently popular concept of provincial federation, reminiscent of the
American states' first form of union (though it proved inadequate). They
all favored provincial autonomy and federalism. Another practical measure was the creation of merchant militia. The contradiction was that
while they sought autonomy and freedom from state control in their
economic functions, they also craved centralized order.

From March 1923 the businessmen through the Chambers of Commerce participated in a national convention at Shanghai that addressed
the problem of political reorganization and unity and the control of
troops and finances. At a high point of their sense of autonomy in June
1923 the Shanghai General Chamber of Commerce declared its independence from Beijing even though it had no territorial or military basis. It
set up a committee of a People's Government, which soon negotiated
with the local warlords to reduce hostilities. Here, however, the Shanghai bourgeoisie, like the Beijing scholars, showed their inability to function in more than the *wen* part of government. The business class were
unable to mount military strength. At Shanghai the Chinese merchants
soon stood opposed to the new and leftist labor movement. In this stance
they had foreign support. In reflecting many years later on his raising
funds at Shanghai for crushing the labor movement, Chen Guangfu
stated the aim had been to topple militarism, the warlords, and support a
modern government. Like Hu Shi, Chen was a Sino-liberal who could
provide leadership in his sector of society but not control the force of the
state. Both these leaders were anti-imperialists and wanted to see China
free of the foreign treaty privileges. They were caught in the dilemma of
craving autonomy but first needing a strong government that might
amount to autocracy.

In the walled capital of Beijing, industry and commerce were secondary to a population of Manchu bannermen and tradesmen serving
mainly the imperial court. After foreign forces occupied the city in 1900,
Japanese initiative led to setting up a police academy that would follow
Japanese and European models to recruit and train uniformed officers,
mainly ex-bannermen, who would be salaried and esteemed as a new
type of civil servant. Yuan Shikai then spread police systems to major
cities. David Strand (1989) notes that "even in dilute form, the Confucianist mentality with its inclination to scold, meddle and mediate, in-

spired effective police work," to say nothing of clientelism and its customary corruption.

The Beijing Chamber of Commerce organized in 1907 was another new agency. Though its membership included only 17 percent of the city's 25,000 commercial establishments, it represented their common interest in such matters as avoiding banknote inflation. Inevitably its leadership was drawn into the politics of the warlord era. Beijing had a hundred or so craft and merchant guilds that had been functioning since time immemorial. The blind storytellers guild, for example, had some 500 members. The old-style Chinese ink makers had about 200 skilled and 300 unskilled workers. When the May Fourth Movement sought to find a "proletarian base for radical politics," it discovered that the guilds made trade unions in the new factories seem less necessary.

Rickshaw travel about town was the new hybrid product of cheap leg muscles and ball-bearing wheels that flourished in East Asia from the 1870s to the 1940s. In the 1920s Beijing had 60,000 rickshaw pullers, and in a riot of 1929 they attacked and damaged 60 of the tramway company's 90 streetcars.

All in all the 1920s in Beijing saw a proliferation of citizens' groups advocating self-government, birth control, and other causes. In the face of warlord battles and devastation in the countryside, leading citizens set up a peace preservation association that imported food, set up soup kitchens to feed up to 80,000 a day, and paid defeated warlord troops to depart quietly. Such activity must have had many precedents in Beijing—in 1644, for instance, when the rebel Li took over the city but was ousted by the Manchus. The 1920s saw a mix of old and new behavior worthy of a civil society, yet final military power could not arise from within it. It had to be imposed from without, as the Nationalist army would do in 1928.

Studies of such cities as Hankou, Shanghai, and Beijing convey an image of self-conscious communities energized from time to time by a moral consensus. This was usually a concern for justice or common welfare (minsheng) that arose among citizens acting through their established groups and institutions. This moral community, needless to say, was inherited from Confucianism and often difficult for outsiders to grasp because it combined popular righteousness with a continued subservience to (military) authority. The semiautonomous elements in a Chinese type of civil society, when they confronted the state power, seemed to have the same vulnerability as Confucian scholar-officials had

had when confronting the emperor. Their moral righteousness could not be the final arbiter.

Origins of the Chinese Communist Party

Whereas Chinese businessmen, like New Culture liberals, aimed to stay outside of politics and government service, some of the activists of May Fourth were drawn into the search for a new state power. Though nurtured in the academic wing of China's nascent civil society, they committed themselves to the age-old effort to create a new government that could bring China unity, social order, wealth, and power. Thus, the May Fourth intellectuals sorted themselves into two groups—academics like Hu Shi and Fu Sinian, who concentrated as scholars on the modern recovery and reappraisal of China's history and culture, and political activists like Chen Duxiu and Zhang Guotao, who joined in forming the Chinese Communist movement.

From the early 1900s Marxism in China was preceded by a widespread interest in anarchism. Until the Soviet revolution brought Leninism to China after 1917, anarchists were the chief socialists on the scene. Chinese students in both Paris and Tokyo were much attracted to Proudhon, Bakunin, and Kropotkin and their denunciation of all authority, beginning with governments, nations, militarism, and the family. Anarchist writers quoted Kropotkin's dictum that the state had become the God of the present day. They eloquently put forward ideas of egalitarianism, especially emancipation of women from family bonds and of the peasantry from exploitation that would become part of the Chinese vocabulary of revolution. Anarchists wanted to rely not on the state but on individual liberation and its bloodless re-creation of the egalitarian community of the far past. Yet Peter Zarrow's (1990) analysis of Chinese anarchist writings gives one a feeling that they indulged in utopian hopes that with one great leap they could somehow jump out of the Confucian straitjacket into complete freedom—a pathetically flawed ideal. No action but assassination ever eventuated. What could really be done?

The New Culture Movement, while attractive to scholars, gave youth little chance to find a new identity as saviors of China by creating a new order of society. In 1919 and afterward student discussion groups, encouraged by Cai Yuanpei at Beida, set an example followed by middle school students and graduates in other centers—Tianjin, Ji'nan, Wuhan,

Changsha, Guangzhou, and especially Shanghai. Most groups founded journals. These activists saw themselves in a new role, not to serve the state but to serve society. Newly aware of the city laboring class, they also wanted to reach the common people. Socialism seemed the great hope; some thought it could bring workers and intellectuals together in time to avert class war. As Arif Dirlik (1989) points out, some Guomindang (Nationalist Party) socialists of this period saw land-holding, not capitalism, as the point to attack.

By 1920 radical study groups were meeting in half a dozen major centers, formed by intellectuals of a self-selected type who knew and encouraged one another. After Professor Li Dazhao formed a specifically Marxist study group at Beida in March 1920, it set a style. Dirlik concludes that Li Dazhao, generally selected by historians as one of the two founders of the Chinese Communist Party, was not really so intent on party-founding. He was an enthusiastic propagator of Marxist theory, but when it came to action he hoped to see the unity of all socialists.

The founding of the CCP seems to have owed most to Chen and to the Comintern. Chen Duxiu's leadership of the New Culture and May Fourth movements had led only to his being jailed for three months in the summer of 1919. He went to Shanghai, dispirited but angry, seeking a vehicle for action. The actual organizing of the CCP nuclei in the fall of 1920 owed much to the Comintern agent Voitinsky. When Voitinsky's successor as Comintern representative, the Dutchman Sneevliet ("Maring"), reached China in 1921, a founding meeting of the CCP could be held at Shanghai in July. Through the propaganda of journals, bookstores, translations, study groups, and labor organizing, Chinese communism quickly established its organizational identity as "an ideology of action." It split with China's anarchists and guild socialists, asserted the primacy of class struggle, and became a secret, exclusive, centralized Bolshevik (that is, Leninist) party seeking power. It left the May Fourth enlightenment far behind. The two "founders," Li Dazhao and Chen Duxiu, did not attend the founding meeting in July 1921, which followed the lead of the Russian Comintern representative. It took another year for the principle of party discipline to be accepted. By that time about half of the original twelve founders had left the movement.

Whether the early CCP members had a real understanding of Marxism–Leninism is open to question. One founder, Mao Zedong, had begun as a disciple of the May Fourth Movement, a gradualist believing in reform. Only after signal frustrations had he concluded that violent revolution was the only feasible course.

Mao had subscribed, like so many others, to the Kropotkin form of anarchism, which stressed mutual aid and concerted efforts. In 1914 at age eighteen he made notes on a Chinese translation by Cai Yuanpei of the German philosopher Friedrich Paulsen's *System der Ethik*. This philosophical popularizer argued that "will is primary to intellect," and ethics are part of nature. The behavior of the universe is ethical and so is that of the individual. Therefore, subjective and objective attitudes are not at loggerheads. This attribution of an ethical posture to development was particularly useful to the Chinese generation that had to reconcile history and value, the Chinese inheritance of ethical teachings with the modern knowledge of the scientific world.

After he returned to Hunan from Beida just before the May Fourth Movement, Mao founded a journal of discussion and put forward the dialectic view that the phase of oppression of the people would be followed by a phase of their transformation, that the humiliation and weakness of China would be followed by China's emergence as a leading nation. This expressed the theme of unity of opposites, which went back a long way in Daoism. Mao's advocacy of "the great union of the popular masses" argued that unified groups in society had long had the upper hand by reason of their standing together, and it was now time for the masses to get the upper hand by doing the same.

While Mao's thinking was cosmopolitan and universal in terms, one of his first activities was in the provincial Hunan self-government movement. It tried to establish a constitution for the province as a reflection of the then-popular idea of federation of independent provinces as the means to bring China into modern government. Self-government must have a popular base and participation, a mobilization of all the people. When his journal was suppressed in late 1919, Mao took another trip to Beijing and Shanghai, where he found kindred spirits. But he was not yet a conspirator or a Marxist, although he organized in 1920 a Russian-affairs study group and a Hunan branch of the Socialist Youth Corps. Even after Mao went to the organizing meeting of the Chinese Communist Party in July 1921 in Shanghai, he was not yet committed to class struggle. In 1923 he organized the Hunan Self-Education College, one object of which was to use the old form of the academy *(shu-yuan)* through which to make available the new content of modern learning. His last activity in Hunan was to work in the labor movement, but he was obliged to flee to Shanghai in April 1923.

These observations on the time it took CCP founders to absorb Marxism–Leninism suggest that the organization of a secret conspiratorial movement for seizing power in China was far easier to achieve in form than was the sophistication of theory needed for guiding it. Countless rebels over thousands of years had formed secret brotherhoods. Sun Yatsen indeed had trouble getting beyond this ancient mode of operation. Records of CCP correspondence between the branches and the center, compiled by Tony Saich (forthcoming), indicate early difficulties in enforcing the discipline of that one-way street called "democratic centralism." The indigenization of communism in China would be a matter both of operating style and of ideas. Bolshevism, stressing party power above all, was only one offshoot of Marxism, which also had its democratic aspirations. Residual anarchist ideas of mutual aid and "labor-learning" (making intellectuals into laborers and vice versa) would remain anti-Bolshevik but of little help for a Chinese type of civil society.

In the 1910s and 20s the experience of New Culture academics and of industrial businessmen alike demonstrated their incapacity to establish state power themselves. Needing a new political order, they would have to wait and see what history might bring them.

14

The Nationalist Revolution
and the Nanjing Government

Sun Yatsen and the United Front

The reunification of warlord-divided China, like many previous re-unifications, required 30 years, from about 1920 to about 1950. Like all such periods, it seemed endlessly confusing because several parallel processes were under way at the same time. In foreign relations there was the Rights Recovery movement of the 1920s to abolish the inequalities of the treaty system. But after 1931 this had to give way to China's patriotic resistance to the Japanese militarists' effort to conquer China, defeated only in 1945. In domestic politics unification was pursued by a united front of two party dictatorships, both inspired by Leninist Russia. The Chinese Communist Party and the Nationalist Party (Guomindang) both cooperated and competed in the 1920s to smash warlordism and roll back imperialism. Breaking apart in 1927, they became deadly rivals despite their nominal cooperation again after 1937 in a second united front against Japan. Meanwhile, a third line of struggle was within the Guomindang itself after it set up the Nationalist Government at Nanjing in an allegedly reunified China in 1928. This intraparty contest was between certain elements of a civil society that were still developing and the military autocracy sanctioned by Japan's invasion.

Each of these three lines of conflict was confusing to observers as well as participants, and altogether they made Republican China an enigma fraught with mystery and misconceptions. Our analysis must start with Sun Yatsen, a patriot whose sincerity permitted him to be startlingly nonideological and opportunistic—just what the circumstances demanded.

Sun was a commoner from the Guangdong delta near Portuguese

Macao. But he grew up partly in Hawaii (winning a school prize for his English!), got a medical education in Hong Kong ("Dr. Sun"), and then in 1896 achieved fame as China's pioneer revolutionary when the Qing legation in London seized him but had to release him. In 1905 the Japanese expansionists helped him pull together the Revolutionary League in Tokyo, and so as a symbolic senior figure he was proclaimed president of the Chinese Republic for a few weeks in 1912 until he gave way to Yuan Shikai.

The ambivalent part-way nature of Sun's Nationalist cause—its limited aims in the reorganizing of Chinese society—emerged quite clearly in the 1920s. The occasion was provided by Sun Yatsen's decision in 1922 to learn from, and his successor, Jiang Jieshi's (Chiang Kaishek's) decision in 1927 to break with, Soviet Russia.

Leninist theory put anti-imperialism on a more than national basis and made it a part of a worldwide movement. Since political thinking in China had always been based on universal principles, and the Chinese empire had traditionally embraced the civilized world, Chinese revolutionists readily sought to base their cause on doctrines of universal validity. Sun Yatsen, while not subscribing to the Communist idea of class struggle, fully recognized the usefulness of Communist methods and accepted Communist collaboration in his Nationalist cause.

The Russian Bolsheviks had organized the Comintern (Communist International) out of scattered groups in various countries. Their first Comintern congress in 1919 encouraged revolution in many parts of Europe. But after 1921, when Lenin turned to his New Economic Policy, though the Comintern still competed with the revived socialist parties of Europe, it was less actively revolutionary, except in China.

Lenin held that Western capitalism was using the backward countries of Asia as a source of profit to bolster the capitalist system. Without imperialist exploitation of Asia, which allowed continued high wages for the workers of the West, capitalism would more rapidly collapse. Nationalist revolutions in Asia, which would deprive the imperialist powers of their profitable markets and sources of raw materials, would therefore constitute a "flank attack" on Western capitalism at its weakest point—that is, in Asian economies, where imperialist domination exploited the working class most ruthlessly.

In China the Soviet Russian government had capitalized upon its own impotence by grandly renouncing the privileges of the tsar's unequal treaties. But it subsequently proved a hard bargainer over the old tsarist rights in Manchuria, and its foreign office continued to deal diplomatically with the Beijing government and warlords in North China while the Comintern worked subversively for revolution.

On his part, Sun Yatsen by 1922, after 30 years of agitation, had reached a low point in his fortunes. He had been proclaimed president of the Chinese Republic in 1912 only to see his country disintegrate into warlordism. His effort to unify China through warlord means had led him into dealings with opportunist militarists at Guangzhou. In June 1922 Sun was outmaneuvered and fled to Shanghai. Just at this moment, when Sun had demonstrated his preeminence as China's Nationalist leader but his incompetence to complete the revolution, he joined forces with the Comintern. In September 1922 he began the reorganization of the Guomindang on Soviet lines.

This marriage of convenience, announced in a joint statement by Dr. Sun and a Soviet representative in January 1923, was a strictly limited arrangement. It stated that Sun did not favor communism for China, since conditions were not appropriate, that the Soviets agreed that China needed unity and independence, and were ready to aid the Chinese Nationalist revolution. As Sun Yatsen wrote to Jiang Jieshi at the time, he had to seek help where he could get it. The Western powers offered no aid. But although Sun now sought and accepted Soviet Russian aid, communism in his mind did not supplant his own Three Principles of the People—Nationalism, People's Rights or Democracy, and People's Livelihood—as the program for the Chinese revolution, even though he found it useful to incorporate in his ideas the Communist emphasis on a mass movement fired by anti-imperialism.

On the basis of this uneasy alliance, Soviet help was soon forthcoming. Having reestablished his government at Guangzhou early in 1923, Sun sent Jiang Jieshi to spend three months in Russia. He returned to head the new Whampoa Military Academy at Guangzhou in 1924. Meanwhile, a Soviet adviser, Michael Borodin, an able organizer who had lived in the United States, became the Guomindang's expert on how to make a revolution. He helped to set up a political institute for the training of propagandists, to teach Guomindang politicians how to secure mass support. On the Soviet model the Guomindang now developed local cells, which in turn elected representatives to a party congress. The first national congress was convened in January 1924 and elected a Soviet-modeled central executive committee as the chief authority in the party. Borodin drafted its new constitution.

In addition to aiding the Nationalist revolution, the ulterior objective of the Comintern was to develop the Chinese Communist Party and get it into a strategic position within the Guomindang (GMD) so as eventually to seize control of it. Members of the Chinese Communist Party were, by agreement with the GMD, admitted to membership in it as individuals, at the same time that the Chinese Communist Party continued its separate existence. This admission of Communists, a "bloc within" strategy, was accepted by the nascent CCP only at the insistence of the Comintern representative. It seemed feasible to Sun Yatsen because the CCP were still so few in number, the two parties were united on the basis of anti-imperialism, and the GMD aimed to lead a broad, national, multiclass movement avoiding class war. Sun also felt that there was little real difference between the People's Livelihood and communism (at least as seen in Lenin's New Economic Policy), that the Chinese Communists were only a group of "youngsters" who hoped to monopolize Russian aid, that Russia would disavow them if necessary to cooperate with the GMD.

On their side, the Chinese Communists were seeking definite class support among urban workers, poor peasants, and students. But they recognized that this class basis was still weak. They therefore sought to go along with and utilize the Nationalist movement without antagonizing the major non-Communist elements within it. It should not be forgotten that the Communist Party in China at this time was still in its infancy. It numbered hardly more than 300 members in 1922, only 1,500 or so by 1925, whereas the GMD in 1923 had some 50,000 members. Tony Saich (forthcoming), surveying the early CCP documents, remarks on the Communists' spurious sense of progress under the "bloc within" strategy. In actual fact, getting CCP members into high GMD posts gave them not power but only influence. When the CCP claimed in May 1926 that it led 1.25 million workers simply because their representatives had attended the CCP-dominated Third Labor Congress, they constructed "no colossus but rather a Buddha" with feet of clay. In the First United Front of the 1920s the CCP failed to establish either urban or rural bases of long-term support.

Thus from the beginning the Guomindang–Communist entente was a precarious thing, held together by the usefulness of each group to the other, by their common enemy, imperialism, and, while he lived, by Sun Yatsen's predominance over the more anti-Communist elements of his Nationalist party.

In 1925 China experienced a great wave of nationwide anti-imperialist sentiment roused by student demonstrations and imperialist gunfire in incidents at Shanghai and Guangzhou (May 30 and June 23,

1925) respectively). These dramatic proofs that the unequal treaties and the foreigners' privileges still persisted gave rise to the nationwide May 30th Movement. It included a prolonged boycott and strike against the British at Hong Kong.

The Accession to Power of Jiang Jieshi (Chiang Kaishek)

After Dr. Sun's untimely death in March 1925, his followers achieved, in 1926–27, the successful Northern Expedition from Guangzhou to the Yangzi valley. The newly trained propagandists of the Nationalist revolution preceded the armies of Jiang Jieshi, who was aided by Russian arms and advisers. By advance propaganda, popular agitation, and the bribery of "silver bullets," the Northern Expedition's six main armies defeated or absorbed some thirty-four warlord forces in South China.

Thus Chinese nationalism in the years from 1925 to 1927 had reached a new height of expression and was focused against Britain as the chief imperialist power. To defend their position, the British on the one hand restored to China their concessions at Hankou and Jiujiang on the Yangzi and on the other hand, with the support of the powers, built up an international force of 40,000 troops to protect Shanghai. In fear of antiforeignism, most of the missionaries, several thousand, evacuated their posts in the interior. In March 1927, when the revolutionary troops reached Nanjing, foreign residents were attacked, six of them killed, and the others evacuated under the protecting shellfire of American and British gunboats.

It was at this point in the spring of 1927 that the latent split between the right and left wings of the revolution finally became complete. For two years the right and left within the movement had generally cooperated, although as early as March 1926 Jiang Jieshi had arrested leftist elements at Guangzhou allegedly to forestall a plot to kidnap him. His three-month view of Russia in 1923 had left him aware of Soviet methods and suspicious of Communist aims. The success of the Northern Expedition finally took the lid off the situation.

In brief, the left wing of the GMD together with the Communists by March 1927 dominated the revolutionary government, which had been moved from Guangzhou to Wuhan. Here were collected, among other leaders, Madame Sun Yatsen and Wang Jingwei, the widow and the chief disciple of the founder, and Borodin, the chief adviser on revolution. Wuhan had been proclaimed the new national capital. This suited Communist strategy because it was a large industrial center. Two members of the CCP had actually been made cabinet ministers. But this government was weak in military strength.

Jiang Jieshi, with the support of the more conservative leaders of the GMD, had aimed at the rich strategic center of the Lower Yangzi. He had come from a merchant-gentry background inland from Ningbo, acquired military training in North China and in Tokyo, and inherited a conventional Sino–Japanese Confucian (not liberal) outlook. In 1927, once the Shanghai–Nanjing region was in his grasp, Jiang was able by military force to forestall the Communists and consolidate his position. In April 1927 at Shanghai foreign troops and warships confronted the Communist-led labor unions, which had seized local control. Under Comintern orders they awaited Jiang as their ally, only to be attacked and decimated by his forces in a bloody betrayal, aided by the Green Gang of the Shanghai underworld.

Jiang set up his capital at Nanjing, and shortly afterward a local general seized power at Wuhan and broke up the left-wing government. Some of its leaders fled to Moscow. The new Nanjing government expelled the Chinese Communists from its ranks and instituted a nationwide terror to suppress the Communist revolutionaries. In this effort it was, for the time being, largely successful. Small contingents of Communist-led troops revolted, and in December 1927 the Communists attempted a coup at Guangzhou. But after this failure to seize power they withdrew to rural mountain areas, especially in Jiangxi province in Central China.

This ignominious failure of the Comintern's laboratory experiment in revolution in China had been affected by a power struggle in Moscow. Trotsky and his followers had criticized the Comintern effort to work through the GMD. They foresaw Jiang Jieshi's betrayal and urged an independent program to develop workers' and peasants' soviets in China under purely Communist leadership. Stalin and his supporters, however, had argued that an independent Communist movement in so backward a country would invite suppression all the sooner. They had looked forward to the time at a later stage of the revolution when, in Stalin's phrase, the Communists could drop their GMD allies as so many "squeezed-out lemons."

Much of the Comintern's ineptitude undoubtedly came from its remoteness from the scene of action. Stalin could hardly succeed in masterminding by the aid of Marxist dialectics the confused stirrings of revolution in a place like Shanghai, where the proletariat were barely getting organized. The Comintern plot in China was also frustrated by the Comintern's own prior act in giving the GMD a centralized Soviet-style party apparatus, which was much harder to subvert than an open Western-style parliamentary party.

Jiang Jieshi's break with the Communists represented an effort to consolidate the gains of the national revolution at a certain level in the revolutionary process, stopping short of class struggle, social revolution, and the remaking of peasant life in the villages. This consolidation in the Nanjing government, combined with military campaigns to check revolt, enabled Jiang and the GMD leaders to achieve a superficial national unity, secure the recognition of the powers, and begin the process of administrative development, which would be a necessary prerequisite to the abolition of the unequal treaties. In the spring of 1928 Jiang led a further northern expedition from the Yangzi to Beijing, which was occupied in June and renamed Beiping ("Northern Peace"). In November the young warlord of Manchuria completed the nominal unification of all China by recognizing the jurisdiction of the Nanjing government. Meantime, the foreign powers one by one made treaties with it and so gave the Nationalist revolution international recognition.

Several conclusions emerge at this point. Although the GMD won power, it was composed of so many disparate elements that it was unable to function as a party dictatorship. Instead, it soon became a Jiang Jieshi dictatorship. In its early history, the driving impulse had been nationalism, first after 1905 against alien Manchu rule, second after 1923 against the imperialism of the treaty powers. The GMD ideology, so necessary to inspire student activists, was nominally Sun Yatsen's Three People's Principles, but these were really a party platform (a set of goals) more than an ideology (a theory of history). The GMD had got no farther than regional warlordism at Guangzhou until in 1923 it allied with the Soviet Union, reorganized itself on Leninist lines, created an indoctrinated Party army, and formed a United Front with the CCP. The four years of Soviet aid and CCP collaboration together with the patriotic Marxist–Leninist animus against the warlords' domestic "feudalism" and the foreign powers' "imperialism" helped the GMD to power.

This tangled story suggests that there has been at bottom only one revolutionary movement in twentieth-century China, that of socialism mainly headed by the CCP. (Perhaps this puts the GMD in a better light, as devoted to state-building and reform rather than to the unending violence of class struggle.) Jiang Jieshi's treacherous slaughter of the CCP at Shanghai in April 1927, though it led to the powers' recognition of his Nanjing government in 1928, tended to dissipate the GMD's revolutionary spirit. Soon it found itself on the defensive against both the CCP and Japan.

The Nature of the Nanjing Government

The Nationalist Government set up at Nanjing in 1928 seemed the most promising since 1912. Many of its officials were patriots educated abroad and competent at the functions of a modern nation-state. Amenities of modern life soon filled the city scene—movies, automobiles, the theatre, arts and crafts, books and magazines, as well as teachers at universities. Chinese institutions included the dozen research institutes of Academia Sinica, the Nationalist Government's Ministry of Public Health, its National Agricultural Research Bureau, the many-sided work of the Maritime Customs Service, the Bank of China's and other research bureaus, and a multitude of similar agencies. This growth carried on the efforts to build up a civil society noted in Chapter 13.

The Nationalist Government's potentialities, what it might have done for the Chinese people, would soon be all but destroyed by Japanese militarism, which seized Manchuria in 1931, encroached on Shanghai in 1932 and then on the Beijing–Tianjin area, and attacked China full scale from 1937 to 1945. In the 1930s and 40s Japan's industrial technology and chauvinist spirit set back the cause of civilization in China, just as similar capacities of the Germans were doing in Europe. The inherent weaknesses of the GMD dictatorship at Nanjing grew worse under the pressures of preparing for war and then having to fight.

A first weakness was the loss of revolutionary aim. In accordance with Sun Yatsen's theory of the three stages of the revolution (military unification, political tutelage, and constitutional democracy), 1929 was proclaimed to be the beginning of the period of political tutelage under the Guomindang dictatorship.

Ever since the First Party Congress had met in January 1924 and adopted a Soviet-style organization, the Central Executive Committee (CEC) had become the chief repository of political authority. High officials of the government were chosen by the CEC and usually from it. Constitutional government was postponed. Party ministries, such as the Ministries of Information, Social Affairs, Overseas Affairs, or Party Organization, functioned as part of the central administration and yet were in form under the Guomindang, not the government. Party and government thus became indistinguishable.

But in this way the Guomindang became a wing of the bureaucracy and lost its revolutionary mission. The earlier party supervision of local administration, its political work in the army, its special criminal courts to try counterrevolutionaries, all were reduced or abandoned. So also were the mass organizations of workers, peasants, youth, merchants, and women. These mass movements had mobilized popular support for the Northern Expedition, but the Nanjing power-holders now looked askance at processions, demonstrations, and mass meetings. They discouraged student movements, looking back upon all these activities of the mid-twenties as useful tools to beat the warlords but no longer of value, now that power was theirs to organize for purposes of control. With this attitude the Guomindang suffered an actual drop in numbers. By late 1929 its membership totaled barely 550,000, of whom 280,000 were military. Members in Shanghai were mainly officials or policemen.

Far from being bourgeois-oriented, the GMD destroyed the semi-autonomy of the Shanghai businessmen. Using gangster methods of abduction and assassination, it intimidated merchants into contributing large funds for the military. By setting up structures parallel to the chambers of commerce while regrouping the guilds and changing personnel, it forced the General Chamber of Commerce to close down and cowed the merchant elite. The new Bureau of Social Affairs now supervised professional organizations, settled conflicts, collected statistics, pursued philanthropic works, maintained hygiene and security arrangements, and organized town planning. Officialdom took over from the merchant class.

The GMD also took over the management of boycotts, which became government-organized and financed against Japanese trade. Boycotts became controlled-spontaneous mass movements that could be turned against leading merchants in terrorist fashion. The Municipality of Greater Shanghai asserted, says Bergère, "what amounted to overseeing rights over the Settlement's officials." The Green Gang of 20,000 or possibly even 100,000 members became GMD agents ready to track down trade union leaders and Communists just as they continued to terrorize wealthy merchants who refused to contribute funds to the government. The Shanghai concession areas no longer provided much refuge for Chinese nationals.

The Shanghai bankers, like those of Beijing and Tianjin, were now making fortunes by giving public loans to the government. Between 1927 and 1931 they underwrote most internal loans, which totaled something like a billion dollars. The government bonds were sold below nominal value and gave the banks an actual interest payment of 20 percent or more.

Improvements under the Nanjing government included the abolition of *likin* in 1931 and recovery of tariff autonomy. A modern mint was established and the tael abolished in March 1933. The National Economic Council was set up to handle foreign-aid funds. Finally the banking coup of 1935 set up the four major banks as a central bank and the national currency as a managed currency subject to inflation. The government gained control over two thirds of the banking sector, taxed business more and more heavily, levied consolidated taxes on production, and raised customs duties.

In general it seemed that the "triumphant bureaucratic apparatus was about to stifle the spirit of enterprise once again," as E. Balazs remarked. High-ranking officials sought personal profits while the government used modern business to strengthen its own authority, not to strengthen the economy by investment in productive enterprise. Having foresworn the land tax and left it to the provincial governments, the Nanjing regime lived parasitically on trade taxes, handicapping the industrial sector it should have tried by all means to encourage. Both productive investment at home and capital loans from abroad were discouraged by these antidevelopment policies. One hypothesis is that the Nanjing decade probably saw continued stagnation in the agrarian economy, with no appreciable increase of per capita productivity. This was accompanied, moreover, by a stultifying growth of "bureaucratic capitalism," that is, domination of industry and finance by officials and political cliques who feathered their private nests by manipulating government monopolies, finances, development schemes, and agencies. As a result, Nanjing was unable to achieve a healthy and solvent fiscal regime, much less a breakthrough into a genuine process of self-sustaining reinvestment and industrialization. Savings were channeled into current government use or private speculation, while the nation's capital resources were not mobilized, even for military purposes.

Modifying this negative view stands the insistence of economic historians like William C. Kirby (1984) that despite its wartime shortcomings the Nationalist regime did achieve a degree of state-building. This was evidenced particularly in the military industries under the National Resources Commission. In either case, most researchers agree that the Nanjing government existed not to represent the interests of a bourgeoisie but rather to perpetuate its own power, much in the manner of dynastic regimes.

If the Nationalist Government was not "bourgeois," was it not at least "feudal"? In other words, representing the landlord interest? The answer is mixed. Since Nanjing left the land tax to be collected by the provinces, the provincial regimes, strapped for revenue, generally left the landlords in place. Central government army officers in particular might become large landowners. Nanjing was against mobilizing peasants, but it was for centralization, not dispersal, of power. "Feudal" lacks precise meaning; it is more useful to see the Nanjing government as having had a dual character—comparatively modern in urban centers and foreign contact, reactionary in its old-style competition with provincial warlords. On its foreign side it could continue the effort to modernize at least the trappings of government, while on its domestic warlord side it continued to suppress social change. Foreigners were more aware of its promise, assuming in Anglo–American fashion that the only way forward in China would be through gradual reform.

Systemic Weaknesses

The Nanjing government's claim to foreign approbation lay first of all in its modernity. The big ministries of foreign affairs, finance, economic affairs, education, justice, communications, war, and navy built imposing office buildings in Nanjing under the wing of the executive branch (*yuan*) of the government. Meanwhile, in addition to the legislative and judicial branches, there were established the control, that is, censorial, and auditing branch, and the examination branch for the civil service. Into these new ministries were recruited educated talent very conscious of China's ignominious place in the world. They began to apply modern science to China's ancient problems. There was at first a new atmosphere of hope in the air.

But this ran into a second weakness—the Nanjing government's limited capacity vis-à-vis the sheer mass of China's 400 million people. GMD China in its equipment and modern plant was a small show. In industrial production it was smaller than Belgium, in air and sea power negligible, in the gadgets and equipment of American life not as big as a Middle Western state. Yet this small and relatively insignificant modern state wanted to spread out over the protean body of a vigorous people in a vast and ancient land. On the whole the Chinese people were not yet heavily taxed. Thomas Rawski's (1989) finding is that in the early 1930s central, provincial, and local taxes all together amounted to only about 5 to 7 percent of China's total output. Yet Nanjing's modernizers wanted to foster modern agronomy, railroads and bus roads, a national press and communications system, and the modern idea of opportunity for youth and women. As a Westernizing influence, Nanjing found its strongest support in the treaty-port cities, its best revenue in the Maritime Customs duties on foreign trade, and its greatest difficulty in reaching the mass of the peasantry. Indeed, it at first controlled only the Lower Yangzi provinces. It was at all times engaged in a political and often military struggle to dominate provincial warlord regimes.

Finally, the Nationalist Government from the start was plagued by systemic weaknesses that began with its personnel. Before the Northern Expedition of 1926 the GMD at Guangzhou had included both the surviving Revolutionary Alliance members of Sun Yatsen's generation and younger idealist-activists who often had a dual membership in the GMD and the CCP. The Soviet input represented by Borodin had been combined with the rising military leadership of Jiang Jieshi. Within five years, however, the vigorous Dr. Jekyll of Guangzhou had metamorphosed into the sordid Mr. Hyde of Nanjing. What had happened to change the character of the Nationalist movement in so short a time?

One factor of course was the slaughter of Communists and the rejection or suppression of those who survived. The CCP kind of youthful idealism was expunged. A second factor was the enormous influence of new GMD members from the ranks of the old bureaucracy and the warlord regimes. The careful selection of members, like the enforcement of party discipline, had never characterized the GMD. It had remained a congeries of competing factions not under central control, and it had customarily admitted to membership anyone who applied. Some warlords brought in whole armies. Once the GMD was in power in Nanjing, its revolutionary idealism was watered down by the admission of corrupt and time-serving officials and the accumulation of opportunists generally lacking in principle. As Lloyd Eastman (1974) has remarked, as early as 1928 Jiang Jieshi, who felt the responsibility of leadership, said that "Party members no longer strive either for principles or for the masses . . . the revolutionaries have become degenerate, have lost their revolutionary spirit and revolutionary courage." They only struggled for power and profit, no longer willing to sacrifice. By 1932 Jiang was declaring flatly, "The Chinese revolution has failed."

By coming to power, in short, the GMD had changed its nature.

After all, it had won power by using the Shanghai Green Gang underworld against the Communists. At the beginning, many Chinese rallied to the support of Nanjing, but the evils of old-style bureaucratism soon disillusioned them. In addition to its white terror to destroy the CCP, the GMD police attacked, suppressed, and sometimes executed a variety of individuals in other parties and the professions. The press, though it persisted, was heavily censored. Publishers were harassed and some assassinated. Colleges and universities were brought under regulation, required to teach the Three Principles of the People, and constantly scrutinized for unorthodox tendencies. Anyone concerned for the masses was regarded as pro-Communist. This anti-Communist stance had the effect of discouraging if not preventing all sorts of projects for the betterment of the people. Thus the GMD cut itself off from revolutionary endeavor. Suppression and censorship were accompanied by corrupt opportunism and inefficient administration. The old watchword "become an official and get rich" was revived with a vengeance.

This disaster put a heavy burden on Jiang Jieshi, who remained an austere and dedicated would-be unifier of his country. By 1932 he was thoroughly disillusioned with his party as well as with the Western style of democracy, which promised no strength of leadership. He began the organization of a fascist body, popularly known as the Blue Shirts, a carefully selected group of a few thousand zealous army officers, who would secretly devote themselves to building up and serving Jiang Jieshi as their leader in the fashion of Mussolini and Hitler. When a public New Life Movement was staged in 1934 for the inculcation of the old virtues and the improvement of personal conduct, much of it was pushed from behind the scenes by the Blue Shirts. This fascist movement under the Nanjing government would have grown stronger if the fascist dictatorships in Europe had not been cut off from China.

One key to Jiang Jieshi's balancing act on the top of the heap was the fact that he committed himself to no one faction. He claimed to be a devout Methodist and got missionary help for reconstruction. He sometimes supported his GMD organizational apparatus against the Blue Shirts but in general he hamstrung the GMD and left it out of participation in administration, while he balanced the Whampoa clique of his former students against other parts of the army or the Political Science (or Political Study) clique of administrators against the CC (Chen brothers) clique of party organizers. His role was such that there could be no other source of final decision, least of all through a participation by the mass of the people. Like Yuan Shikai twenty years before,

Jiang found that Chinese politics seemed to demand a dictator. While he held various offices at various times, he was obviously the one man at the top, and his political tactics would have been quite intelligible to the Empress Dowager. One of Jiang's model figures was Zeng Guofan, who in suppressing the Taipings had been his predecessor in saving the Chinese people from a destructive revolution.

In brief, Jiang was the inheritor of China's ruling-class tradition: his moral leadership was couched in Confucian terms while the work style of his administration showed the old evils of ineffectiveness. As Jiang said in 1932, "When something arrives at a government office it is *yamenized*—all reform projects are handled lackadaisically, negligently, and inefficiently." One result was that paper plans for rural improvement seldom got off the ground, while economic development was similarly short-changed.

Sun Yatsen's five-power constitution fared poorly under the Nanjing government. The Legislative Yuan (branch) was overshadowed by the Executive Yuan, but the latter was rivaled by party ministries not unlike the Executive Yuan ministries. The Examination Yuan really did not function. Eastman reports that "by 1935 for example only 1585 candidates had successfully completed the Civil Service Examinations." Many did not receive official positions at all. Again, the Control Yuan had inherited some of the functions of the censorate of old, but it was almost entirely ineffectual. From 1931 to 1937 it "was presented with cases of alleged corruption involving 69,500 officials. Of these the Yuan returned indictments on only 1800 persons." Worse still, the Control Yuan had no power of judicial decision; and of the 1,800 officials indicted for corruption, only 268 were actually found guilty by the legal system. Of these, 214 received no punishment, and 41 received light punishment, yet only 13 were actually dismissed from office.

All of the five-Yuan civilian government was equaled by the Military Affairs Commission headed by Jiang Jieshi, which used up most of the Nanjing government revenues and set up a de facto military government of its own. Having naturally got rid of the Russian military advisers, Jiang soon began to substitute Germans and establish his military echelon quite separate from the civilian government. The general staff and what became the Military Affairs Commission with its various ministries were under Jiang as commander-in-chief, while the five branches of the civilian government were under him as president. German military advisers set about training an enormous military establishment, for which they planned to get German industrial assistance. By 1930 a China

Study Commission arrived from Germany for three months, and several cultural institutions were set up to develop closer relations. A Sino–German civil aviation line was started.

Spurred by the Japanese seizure of Manchuria in 1931, Beijing intellectuals among others advocated a national industrial buildup for self-defense. Scientists were mobilized. A German-trained geologist became minister of education. In 1932 began the organization of what later became the National Resources Commission (NRC) under the leadership of the geologist Weng Wenhao, a first-level graduate of the examination system, who got his Ph.D. in geology and physics at Louvain in Belgium. Impeccably honest and highly intelligent, Weng rose in the Nationalist Government to high-level posts in economic development. The NRC was directly under Jiang and the military. Its aim was to create state-run basic industries for steel, electricity, machinery, and military arsenals. Part of the plan was to secure foreign investment, particularly from Germany. By 1933 a German military advisory commission was operating in China, aiming at military–industrial cooperation. Chinese tungsten became important for German industry. The organizer of the modern German army, General Hans von Seeckt, visited China twice and advocated building a new elite army with a new officer corps.

Thus at the time of the Japanese attack in 1937 the Nationalist Government had worked out a promising relationship with Nazi Germany, but a parallel development of Nazi relations with Japan and the Nazi–Soviet pact of August 1939 soon left China dependent on a still minimal amount of American aid instead of German.

15

The Second Coming of the
Chinese Communist Party

Problems of Life on the Land

Among the origins of a revolutionary movement, the popular mentality among illiterate farmers is least easy to perceive, whereas material livelihood can be seen in economic conditions and, with luck, statistics. China's economic growth during the Republican era from 1912 down to Japan's attack in 1937 is still being debated. One optimistic view—based largely on overall statistics of production, trade, and investment—cites impressive figures such as China's great increase in the production and consumption of cotton textiles, which in the mid-1930s used more cotton than Britain and Germany combined. Thomas Rawski has marshalled statistics of growth in banking services, money supply, wage rates, transportation and shipping, consumption, and the like, which all go along with continued population growth. He pictures a society that is steadily industrializing. Yet in so big a country this overall landscape may have included large urban slums and numberless impoverished villages.

About China's rural poverty there have been two schools of thought. One school has stressed the exploitation of the farmer by the ruling class through rents, usury, and other exactions, resulting in a maldistribution of income. This idea of landlord-class exploitation fitted Marxist theory and became with many people an article of faith. The other school, as Ramon Myers (1970) points out, has been more "eclectic"; it has stressed the many reasons for the low productivity of the old farm economy: farms of two acres per family were too small; even these tiny plots were improperly used; peasants had insufficient capital and limited access to new technology; there was little control over nature; primitive transport increased marketing costs. Supporters of this interpretation point to the fact that most Chinese farmers owned their land, some were partly owners and partly tenants, and only about one quarter or one fifth were outright tenants, so that landlord exploitation of tenants was far from the general rule and less of a problem than the general lack of capital and technology compared with the abundant supply of labor. The labor supply was assured by the social imperative to beget children who could care for their parents in old age. This care included the presence of a son to carry on the family line and specifically to offer the ritual sacrifices at the family altar that would prevent the spirits of departed parents from roaming about as homeless ghosts.

Whether one stresses inefficiency of production or maldistribution of the product, it remains apparent that village social structure was all-important at the rice-roots level. Subcounty administration, a comparatively neglected area, has been analyzed by Prasenjit Duara (1988) among others. He begins with the fact that "under the late Qing reforms the village was required to develop a fiscal system to finance modern schools, administrative units, and defense organizations." This unprecedented penetration of the state into the rural society was marked by the levy of new taxes not on individuals or on private property as before but on the village as a new fiscal entity. The result was disastrous for the old rural society.

It had been organized by what Duara calls the "cultural nexus of power." He uses this term to describe the *hierarchies* of lineage kinship, or of markets, or of religions or even water control plus the *networks* of patrons and clients or of relations by marriage, and so on, that formed the "framework within which power and authority were exercised." Village leaders, in other words, had derived their authority from the whole criss-crossing interplay of family relations, commercial transactions, religious observances, voluntary associations, and interpersonal and legal relationships that altogether constituted the cultural nexus of village society.

In the reform era beginning early in the century, the chief stimulus to rural change came from the new tax-gathering effort. Clerks were appointed by the county magistrates to keep registers, and rural agents *(difang, dibao)* were appointed without salary to pursue the task of tax-urging and tax-collecting among half a dozen to twenty villages apiece. Duara calls this a "brokerage" function. He finds generally three levels of tax-gathering activity in this unexplored subcounty area. Though terms varied locally, counties *(xian)* were usually divided into wards (qu) and then into townships (xiang) under which were groups of villages. Usually the rural agent would be an entrepreneur acting like a tax farmer, obliged to make his living as well as his expenses from the sums he collected to meet the tax quota. On the other hand, villages might cooperate and club together to pay fees to a rural agent of their own selection, who would represent their interest and be less predatory. In such a case, the agent might serve the community by organizing for self-defense or for crop-watching or to bail out innocent villagers arrested by yamen runners. This kind of "protective brokerage" might thus perform functions that have heretofore been assumed to be those of the local gentry-elite. To be sure, the gentry society sketched in Chapter 4 above was by no means unchanging. Gentry activity has been best documented at the level of the county magistrate. As the population grew, the lower gentry degree-holders' (shengyuan and jiansheng) participation at the subcounty and village levels may have become attenuated at the same time that the quality of such personnel deteriorated.

State penetration of the village generally worsened the already precarious situation of the villagers. In stable times a moral economy had operated on the basis of personal relations of patron and client, as between landlord-moneylender and tenant-borrower. Reciprocal civilities such as presentation of gifts or invitations to feasts lubricated these interpersonal relations. Each party had a proper role to play.

Hard times, however—either disasters of nature or warfare or pressure of the officials—could shatter these social relations and leave the village community leaderless and at sea. Under the state's new pressure for taxes, well-to-do patrons would withdraw from posts of village leadership, to be supplanted by a "local bully" type of tax-farmer who was on the make and often from outside the village. Similarly, respected peasants began to avoid acting as middlemen to oversee and guarantee contracts under customary law. Meantime, large property owners moved to the city. With political power no longer tied into the cultural nexus, villages became the "hunting grounds of political predators." In short, state-building by the government put tax demands on village leaders that alienated them from their constituencies. As unscrupulous tax-farmers took over the tax collecting, corruption increased. In the Lower Yangzi region the breakdown of the cultural nexus came, as we have noted, with the growth of absentee landlordism and the management of landlord–tenant relations by a bursar incapable of maintaining the personal land-owner–tenant or patron–client relationships of former times.

During the warlord era, local administration deteriorated. The landed ruling class, no longer the top elite of the country, no longer indoctrinated in Confucian ideals of community leadership, became more narrowly self-seeking. Secret societies like the Red Spears in Shandong or the Society of Brothers and Elders (Ge Lao Hui) in Sichuan became tools of the local families of property, helping to protect them against both popular disorder and official exaction. Organized in a network of branches, each with its secretariat, treasury, and directorate capable of mobilizing the clandestine brotherhood, such agencies could help the big family lineages dominate the villages in a rich enclave like the Chengdu plain. For a secret society had its executive arm in the person of professional thugs, as well as its income from the protection of illicit activities—gambling houses, brothels, opium dens, or illegal markets where government taxes were evaded. This darker side was combined with the protection of respectable rank-and-file members in their daily pursuits and with clandestine leadership by some of the wealthiest landlords and officials.

When the Guomindang came to power after 1927, the telephone and telegraph, motor roads and bus routes linking local areas with the cities enabled Nanjing and later Chongqing to convey their orders at once to the smallest hamlet. The regime continued the trend toward bureaucratizing the countryside. In place of the magistrates and gentry of imperial times, Philip Kuhn (in *CHOC* 13) has described how the new administrators from Nanjing tried to spread their reforms, and the police organized their anti-Communist security net. Both came further into the local scene than had been the custom under the empire. Where the emperor had appointed the county magistrate but left him under the provincial authorities, the central government now developed direct contact with him. Magistrates were a chief element among the trainees brought to the capital for indoctrination in Jiang Jieshi's Central Training Corps. Meanwhile, the central government established local administrative organs in charge of military, customs, transportation, or other matters, independent of the regular structure of county government. The Guomindang also set up its local cells under central party control, parallel to the official system. Below the county were new levels of wards, districts and subdistricts, groups of towns and villages, leading down to the groups of households that formed the revived *baojia* system.

The Guomindang theory was that through this hierarchy of subunits the government could train the people during the period of political tutelage to prepare them for local autonomy. In 1939 the Nationalist Government issued a new statute to reorganize local government. Families were to be grouped more flexibly, on community lines, to form *jia* and *bao*. Villages and towns were now to become incorporated legal persons able to operate their own local administrations. Each *bao* should form an assembly and elect two representatives, who would in turn function in a village or town assembly to assist the head of the village or town government, who would himself be elected. On paper the law of 1939 was put into effect in nearly all the counties in Free (that is, GMD) China. Yet in the same period the military and police authorities dominated the scene. There is little record of the election process taking hold.

"Local self-government," despite its happy resonance in the minds of Western advocates of democracy, had its own rather different meaning for the Chinese common people. The term in reality usually designated a managerial agency of the local elite, which they used to secure villagers' taxes to support modern improvements. Roadbuilding, setting up modern schools, and paying for police were improvements desired by the modernizing elite, but paying higher taxes to secure them increased the villagers' burden faster than it benefited them. There were many peasant protests against "reform."

Moreover, local self-government had customarily been based on decision making not by an indiscriminate show of hands (one man, one vote) but by consensus, as had been the practice in village leadership councils. Even in the provincial elections of 1909 by a tightly restricted electorate, the persons elected were asked to choose the assemblymen from among their own number by a process of voting that amounted to securing a consensus. If "democracy" in China's two-strata society should try to function by simple majority rule, it would deny the Neo-Confucian faith that disciplined self-cultivation produces men with superior character and worth. Yet, as personal relationships dissipated, this was what modernity seemed to demand.

Looking back on the Nanjing decade, we can see that, ideally, the new government should have attacked the key problem of agricultural production with programs to improve farm technology. Nanjing early sought technical aid from the League of Nations for public health work. Many fine blueprints were offered in the 1930s and 1940s for China's economic regeneration. Land reclamation, reforestation, water conservancy, hydropower, crop and animal breeding, better tools, improved land use, pest control, crop storage facilities, land redistribution, rent reduction, light and heavy industrialization, rural industry and cooperatives, cheaper farm credit, mass education, public health, transportation, law and order all had their advocates and their obvious rationale. The first and foremost object of all such efforts was to increase the productivity of the farmer. This was the crux of China's problem, but the Nationalist Government was unable to get at it. No comprehensive plan was ever devised, much less given effect.

The Nanjing decade was the time for Western aid to China's vigorous economic growth. But Europe was preoccupied with Nazi Germany, while America was absorbed in the Depression and the New Deal. Guomindang China in these years made halting and spotty progress along many lines, to no particular end. The social anthropologist Fei Xiaotong has described the quagmire of old agricultural conditions and practices as an "economy of scarcity." This long-established low-level manpower economy was perpetuated by the Chinese emphasis upon the virtue of contentment and limitation of wants. This age-old acceptance of the institutionalized penury of peasant life, for want of any alternative, was a means by which the individual could fit himself into his kinship group, sustain his lot in life, and actually achieve a high degree of "social integration" of himself in the community. Indeed, the narrow horizon, low efficiency, poor diet, and chronic diseases of the Chinese peasant, which struck the eye of the modern investigator, were always an integral part of the old society, just as they were part of premodern society in Europe.

Rural Reconstruction

During the Nanjing decade the lack of large-scale government aid for the villages was highlighted by a widespread and growing private interest in "rural reconstruction." In several selected areas the problems of peasant life were studied and methods were developed for the promotion of literacy and improvement of living standards. In some of these efforts, Christian missionaries had led the way. Best known to Westerners was the experiment financed partly by the Rockefeller Foundation at Dingxian in North China under the leadership of the dynamic Christian Yan Yangchu (James Yen). A model county also was developed by the government near Nanjing, and an interesting pioneer effort was made in Shandong by the scholar Liang Shuming, whom Guy Alitto (1979) rightly calls "the last Confucian." Fundamentally, these reform efforts tried to give the peasantry some education for citizenship, some public health service, and scientific improvements in crop and animal breeding.

Most studied has been the Mass Education Movement at Dingxian, led by Yan, which reached the most people and had wide influence. After going to Yale, Yan during World War I was one of some 40 Chinese students who worked under the YMCA with the Chinese labor corps in France, writing their letters home. A natural-born evangelist, Yan took on the literacy problem and put out a newspaper. Back in China, he and others applied the YMCA's publicity and mobilization methods to literacy campaigns. This drew him into the problems of the village—not only literacy but also the modern technologies of public health, agricultural improvement, handicrafts, credit and marketing cooperatives, and the recruitment of village elders, landlords, and even local officials to join in a variety of public events and assist in organizing worthy projects. For example, as People's Schools trained teachers, their graduates formed Alumni Associations.

Yan raised funds in America and England to pay a specialist staff, each of whom had to see what could be done by ideas and organization at little or no expense. The health program, for instance, would recruit a farmer to become the village health worker. After 10 days training, he would set about recording vital statistics, identifying and reporting the most obvious diseases, and using his first-aid box to give out eye ointment, calomel, castor oil, and aspirin. He also vaccinated people and disinfected their surroundings. Yet as Charles Hayford's (1990) study makes plain, the crust of custom was hard to break. Midwives, for instance, were customarily unhygienic, sometimes esteeming the curative potential of cow dung and not willing to be taught differently.

After 1932 Dingxian was part of a national Rural Reconstruction Movement that brought many centers and projects into a common fold not under government control. In 1933 Dingxian took the final step of getting its own nominee appointed local magistrate. The experimental work had devised a great many ways to help meet peasant needs, including rural industries, cooperatives, and honest use of tax money. The local conservatives to whom this seemed too close to communism secured the magistrate's transfer.

The movement for rural reconstruction discovered very soon that the problems of economic livelihood were deeply imbedded in social and political institutions. A higher standard of living was a prerequisite for any democratic processes of a Western type. Improvements in living standards in turn depended upon social change. For example, the scientific reforms attempted at Dingxian needed financial support greater than the peasantry could provide, peasant organizations in support of local improvements required official permission, the improvement of crops raised questions of rent and land tenure, an increase of literacy was likely to make the populace more vocal in the pressing of grievances.

In short, any real change in one aspect of the old order on the land implied fundamental changes in the whole system. The problems of the Chinese countryside were so far-reaching and the pressure for change so great that reforms seemed likely to set off a chain reaction toward revolt.

The local self-government program of the Nationalist regime was frustrated by this same syndrome. It was unable to penetrate the village level except superficially from the top down. Plans and legislation that tried to set up elements of local administration representing the central government turned out usually to be in competition with the provincial interests represented by warlord governors and urban chambers of commerce. The modern reforms and improvements brought to the local scene began with the extension of roads and bus lines supplementing the telephone and telegraph. Programs and even institutions for geological survey, crop statistics, agronomic improvement, and maintenance of local order had to be paid for by the effort to collect greater taxes from the villages. The Chinese peasantry still felt that they benefited little from these modern improvements promoted by the city people and the central government. The whole idea of organizing the village for its own self-improvement was foreign to this officialism, with the result that the cause of social revolution, specifically the broadening of land ownership and the lessening of absentee landlordism, could not be pursued under the Nationalist regime. This failure gave the CCP its opportunity in the 1930s.

The Rise of Mao Zedong

While the Nationalist Government was struggling to build up its military power against Japan, the CCP was struggling to survive in the villages. Although the party had some 60,000 members in 1927, Jiang Jieshi's white terror soon literally decimated it. Many dispersed into anonymity and inaction; the most dedicated took off to hole up in remote fastnesses in the countryside. A dozen or so base areas thus developed, small pockets where Red Army (that is, CCP) troops in small numbers supported rebel political leaders. When Mao joined up with the warlord officer Zhu De on the southern Hunan–Jiangxi border, they inaugurated the major base area but soon moved to the hills of Jiangxi to the northeast, with Ruijin as their capital town. Other base areas were established in the Dabie Mountains northeast of Wuhan or around the marshy Hong Lake in northern Jiangsu at the old mouth of the Yellow River.

Ideology and organization have of course been the winning combination in most revolutions. Mao Zedong's organizational principle was like that of any successful bandit: by force and guile (including a new teaching) to curry favor with the local people. Meanwhile, what ideology came from the Soviet Union through the Comintern took a considerable time to find its adaptation to Chinese conditions. For example, the Marxist–Leninist analysis of history gave the key role to the urban proletariat, the industrial working class, and its urban leaders of the Communist party, but the CCP got nowhere until it substituted the peasantry for the proletariat, in effect standing the theory on its head.

After 1927, when Chen Duxiu was expelled for having presided over the near-demise of the CCP, the leadership in China passed to a succession of young men put forward from Moscow by the Comintern. Their ability to wage a successful revolutionary war was severely handicapped by their having to live as underground fugitives in Shanghai and other urban centers. Their doctrinal activities contributed words on paper but never became a public rallying point for mass movement. They still received directives from Moscow, which they transmitted to the base areas.

For a time, the Moscow influence was strengthened by the return of the famous twenty-eight Bolsheviks who took charge of the CCP in early 1931. Their ideas and aims were highly orthodox, not closely suited to the Chinese scene. They continued to talk about the proletarian revolution and tried to seize cities in the hope of establishing independent provinces. This played into the hands of the GMD, and every attempt was thwarted. There was no "rising tide" of rebellion in China. By 1933 the Central Committee was obliged to get out of Shanghai and move to the central base in Jiangxi, of which Mao Zedong was head. There they outranked him but became immersed like him in peasant life and its problems. From this time on the personality and mind of Mao became a central factor in the CCP revolution.

Mao Zedong excelled his colleagues in achieving a unity of theory and practice, a major motif in Confucian philosophy. We can see how Mao's ideas developed, after 1923, as he worked in the united front under the GMD. For a time he was an alternate member of the GMD Central Committee at Guangzhou. There he became director of the Peasant Movement Training Institute, which provided a five-month education in the subject. From May to October 1926 Mao directly taught the sixth class, which had 320 students from all the provinces of China. The institute program seems to have stressed an analysis of peasant problems plus an analysis of class structure in the countryside. On the basis of Mao's own six months' experience back in Hunan in 1925 when he organized peasant unions, his articles of 1926 describe the in-built exploitation of the peasantry all the way from the working peasant landowner to the landless laborer. Peasants are oppressed, he said, by (1) heavy rents, half or more of the crop, (2) high interest rates, between 36 percent and 84 percent a year, (3) heavy local taxes, (4) exploitation of farm labor, and (5) the landowner's cooperation with the warlords and corrupt officials to exploit the peasantry in every way possible. Behind this whole system lay the cooperation of the imperialists, who sought to maintain order for profitable trade in China.

By this time Mao had thoroughly accepted the Leninist concept of a world movement against capitalist imperialism on the basis of class struggle. But, within this generally accepted framework, Mao argued that the key to success in China's revolution must lie, first, in the careful intellectual analysis of the various classes in the countryside and, second, in using an intensely practical tactic of identifying those classes with whom to work and those classes to work against in any given stage of the revolution. Third, the role of the party worker in the village must be one of a guide and catalyst rather than a know-it-all. He must closely examine the villagers' needs and complaints, hopes and fears; only then could he articulate the peasantry's demands and follow the tactic of uniting with the largest possible number to attack the smallest possible target as a step in the revolutionary process.

Unfortunately, while Mao was thinking these thoughts in 1926 the CCP was absorbed in its united-front tactics. Its members still assumed that by definition the Nationalist Revolution of the 1920s was a bourgeois revolution, a view which history was to prove quite doubtful. In this misguided belief, the CCP followed the advice of the Comintern and continued the united front with the GMD at all costs, toning down its ideas of mobilizing the peasantry on the basis of their misery until such time as imperialism had been expelled from China by a new national government. Giving up the social revolution in the countryside seemed to be an unavoidable part of maintaining a united front with the Nationalists. "Peasant excesses" were deplored by the CCP because the mushrooming of peasant associations in the southern provinces during the Northern Expedition had led to savage repression by the landlord–militarist complex still in power. The CCP had no armed forces of its own, and as a result its peasant movement quickly expired after the GMD–CCP split in mid-1927. Thus the CCP contributed to its own disaster.

In this period Mao had dutifully gone along with the line transmitted from Moscow and had vainly attempted to ride the assumed "high tide" that never rose. He found that the peasantry could be mobilized and even seize cities but could not fight the Nationalist Army. Mao therefore got the message that the CCP could survive and prosper only by developing its own armed forces in a territorial base where men and food supply could be combined for fighting. The "Jiangxi Soviet Republic" became the vehicle for this effort from 1931, with Mao as head.

At this time the CCP sought peasant support by land redistribution, dispossessing big landlords if any and giving hope and opportunity to the poor peasantry in particular. One of the many disputes between Mao and the twenty-eight Bolsheviks was over the treatment of rich peasants. Mao saw them as essential to the local economy and tried to reassure them, but the Moscow-trained dogmatists saw them as a threat to the proletarian nature of the movement. Tony Saich comments that part of Mao's effort was to supplant the patron–client relationships that had fostered social stability (and of course problems) in the villages with a new social order based on close analysis as a preparation for class struggle. This was by no means easy to do.

Jiang Jieshi's campaigns to exterminate the Communist "cancer" in Jiangxi obliged the CCP to develop the principles of guerrilla warfare. The first principle was to draw the enemy in along his supply lines until his advance units could be surrounded and cut off. The second principle was never to attack without superior numbers and assurance of success. Eastern Jiangxi with its rugged hills and narrow valleys was ideal for these tactics. The further Jiang's spearheads advanced, the more vulnerable they became. They were successful only in the fifth campaign in 1934, when their German advisers helped devise a system of blockhouses on the hillsides along the invasion routes so placed that gunfire from one could help defend the next. This string of strongpoints supplied by truck could not be dislodged, and Jiang's armies eventually got the upper hand. This made the third principle of guerrilla warfare, that the peasantry be mobilized to provide intelligence as well as men and food, finally ineffective.

The Long March, 1934–1935

In late 1934 the CCP took off on the Long March (see Map 22), which began with perhaps 100,000 people and wound up a year later with something like four to eight thousand. The point of the Long March was to find a new territorial base on the periphery of Nationalist power, not unlike the way in which the Manchus had been on the periphery of the Ming empire. The CCP needed an area it could control and organize. If Yunnan province had been available it might have served, but the local warlords in the provincial regimes had no desire to be taken over by the CCP. Instead, they were gradually taken over by Jiang Jieshi's pursuing armies in a clever strategy by which the pursuit of the CCP justified bringing central government troops into the outlying provinces.

The Long March has always seemed like a miracle, more documented than Moses leading his Chosen People through the Red Sea. (Six thousand miles in a year averages out at seventeen miles every single day.) How did so many troops and party organizers go so far on foot so fast? The answer of course is that only the leaders and a very small proportion of the troops did go all the way.

We must visualize the terrain. Southwest China is a checkerboard of large and small basins within mountain ranges. The populous plains are watered by streams from the inhospitable mountains. To cross Southwest China the Long March had to get across rivers and through the mountains while avoiding the plains and their few motor roads. Most of the route was therefore up hill and down dale, seldom on the flat. Carrying-poles substituted for wheeled vehicles and two-man litters for railroad berths. On the Long March the Red Army–CCP high command rode much of the way asleep on two-man litters, as the column followed the stone paths over hills and paddy fields. Usually the leaders had been up most of the night handling the army's intelligence, logistic, personnel, and strategic problems to prepare for the next day's march or fighting.

The CCP leaders also preserved themselves by having orderlies, aides, and bodyguards as in conventional armies. Like the Americans against the Japanese, they had their secret intelligence sources. Their radio receiver picked up the simply encoded Nationalist military traffic. They knew more about their enemies than their enemies knew about them.

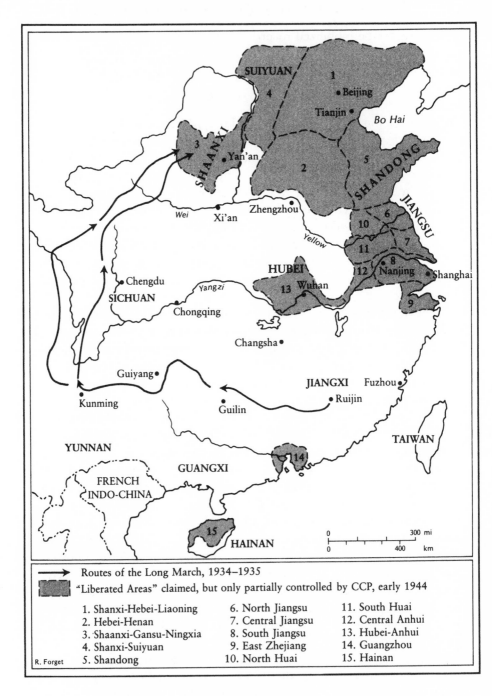

Routes of the Long March, 1934–1935

"Liberated Areas" claimed, but only partially controlled by CCP, early 1944

1. Shanxi-Hebei-Liaoning
2. Hebei-Henan
3. Shaanxi-Gansu-Ningxia
4. Shanxi-Suiyuan
5. Shandong

6. North Jiangsu
7. Central Jiangsu
8. South Jiangsu
9. East Zhejiang
10. North Huai

11. South Huai
12. Central Anhui
13. Hubei-Anhui
14. Guangzhou
15. Hainan

22. The Long March

One major issue as the Long March progressed was where it should go next and who should lead it. Before the march left Jiangxi, Mao had been downgraded by the Soviet-trained faction of the twenty-eight Bolsheviks and their German Communist military adviser sent by the Comintern. The facile Zhou Enlai outranked Mao in the military command. But no one could break Jiang Jieshi's stranglehold. The Comintern ideologists' recourse to positional warfare led only to certain defeat. The flight on the Long March suffered great early losses, especially at river crossings. Mao's unorthodox faith in mobile warfare was finally accepted. On the way west and northwest Mao regained the leadership of the CCP in early 1935 and thereafter never relinquished it. Zhou Enlai, his former superior, became his chief supporter from then on.

Marching speed was so crucial that the original many-mile-long baggage train with its thousands of porters carrying heavy equipment, files, supplies, and also convalescent medical cases, had to be discarded. Military personnel at the start were listed as 86,000. Those arriving a year later in Shaanxi were only a few thousand, even though many new recruits had joined the Red Army along the way. From then on Long March veterans were the aristocracy of the Revolution.

The Long March also helped the new Communist leader to emerge. Mao on the March was already distancing himself from his colleagues. Once he was the One Man at the top, he preferred to dwell in separate quarters away from the rest of the leadership. Like an emperor on the make, from then on he could have no equals or even confidants. He was already caught in the trammels that beset a unifier of China. If we may look both forward and back for a moment, Mao Zedong's rise to power reminds us of the founding of the Han, the Tang, and the Ming. In each case a band of leaders took shape and worked together under one top leader. Once formed, this leadership mobilized the populace in their area to support a military effort and either overthrow tyrants or expel foreigners from the land, in either case, a popular cause. No dynastic founder could do the job alone. So once he was in power he had the problem of dealing with his colleagues in the leadership.

The Role of Zhou Enlai

Another development on the Long March was that Mao found his closest working colleague and future prime minister in Zhou Enlai. An attractive figure of great talent, Zhou instinctively kept a middle position, trying to hold the organization together while at the same time having the good sense never to become a rival for the top post. His forty-eight years on the CCP Politburo set a world record. Zhou thus became one of the great prime ministers of China, devoting himself to the service of the party and its leader, just as earlier prime ministers had served the emperor and the imperial house.

This role was part of Zhou's inheritance. His family came from near Shaoxing in Zhejiang south of Shanghai between Ningbo and Hangzhou, the remarkable center from which so many confidential advisers and secretaries had emerged to serve high officials in the Qing period. Three of Zhou's uncles became provincial graduates under the old examination system, and one became a governor. From the age of ten Zhou went to elementary school in Mukden, Manchuria, and then in 1913 entered the Nankai Middle School at Tianjin, where he came under the influence of that extraordinary liberal educator Dr. Zhang Boling. Zhou absorbed a good deal of education, but he was from the first a student leader. He spent 1917–1919 in Japan, where he became acquainted with socialism. When the May Fourth Movement began, Zhou returned to Nankai, which was now a university, and threw himself into editing a student paper. From then on his life was essentially that of an organizer and propagandist, but he moved rapidly to the left, and his revolutionary stance was confirmed by an experience of several months in jail. In the summer of 1920 he went to France.

Several hundred Chinese students were then in France, in addition to the hundred thousand or so Chinese laborers brought to help the war effort. Most of the students were on a work-and-study program, but many devoted themselves primarily to the great question of the salvation of China. Zhou Enlai immediately rose to the top again as the most impressive, suave, and diplomatic young leader among them. His specialty was not to be the top figure but to bring competing personalities into working agreement. Thus from the very beginning his role was that of a leader who kept the leadership together not by domination but by persuasion. By the time he returned to Guangzhou in 1924 Zhou Enlai was a most accomplished practitioner of united-front revolutionary politics.

In Guangzhou he joined the staff of the new Whampoa Military Academy and became vice director of the political training department—in other words, a leading commissar and at the same time a subordinate and therefore student of young General Jiang. In March 1927 he was in charge in Shanghai when the Communist-led revolt prepared the way for the Nationalist Army, only to be turned upon by Jiang

Jieshi's split. Zhou was a leader again in the uprising at Nanchang in 1927 which became the birthdate of the Red Army. Later he cooperated with the twenty-eight Bolsheviks and supported a succession of party secretaries while avoiding the post himself. In Jiangxi he espoused positional warfare until it brought disaster.

The secret of Zhou's eventual success was that he had the wit to recognize that Moscow's doctrinaire approach to China was futile and that he himself lacked the creative capacity to adjust CCP policy to Chinese conditions. Only because he knew his own limitations was he able, having been Mao's superior, to become his subordinate at the climactic Zunyi Conference early in 1935, when Mao began to take over the CCP leadership in the course of the Long March.

Zhou represented the continuity of a team. With him in France had been Chen Yi and Nie Rongzhen, both of whom would become marshals of the CCP forces. Later at Beijing, Chen would become foreign minister and Nie would take charge of nuclear development. Deng Xiaoping had run the mimeograph machine for Zhou in Paris. The leadership that survived the Long March was indeed closely knit.

Near the end of the Long March, Mao and his Red Army from the Jiangxi base rendezvoused with another part of the Red Army, led by another of the founders of the CCP, Zhang Guotao, who had set up a base in the Dabie Mountains northeast of Wuhan but had moved it westward to north Sichuan in 1933. When they met, Zhang's troops greatly outnumbered Mao's. Although they organized their armies in two major groups, Mao and his colleagues from Jiangxi, as Benjamin Yang (1990) shows in detail, could not accept Zhang's rather vague plans and claim to leadership. Learning suddenly that a small CCP army from the Dabie Mountains had set up a base in northern Shaanxi not far from the Great Wall, Mao and his Jiangxi men decided to make it their goal. Zhang Guotao broke away and later went over to the GMD.

Once arrived in Shaanxi province in the northwest in late 1935, the CCP had little beyond them but desert on the west and the Yellow River on the north and east. Shaanxi had been carved up over the eons by the erosion of the loess plateau. The lack of motor roads made it a defensible area, but it was short of food supply and population, and the Nationalist suppression campaign might have wiped it out had it not been for the Japanese invasion of 1937. In preparation for resistance, the troops of the northeast (Manchuria), stationed at Xi'an to fight the Communists, preferred to fight the Japanese invaders of their homeland. In December of 1936 the northeasterners rebelled and captured Jiang

Jieshi. Before releasing him, they pushed the idea of a Chinese united front instead of Chinese fighting Chinese.

The Second United Front

In 1928 the CCP had reached a low point when its Sixth Congress had to be held in Moscow. While the Comintern directed its destiny for a time thereafter, by 1935 the Russian-trained element was beginning to be superseded by Mao's followers, less because of any conspiracy than because Mao had discovered the key to power in the Chinese countryside. This lay in his feeling for the mentality, needs, and interests of the common people. The "mass line" which he advocated was genuinely concerned to have the revolution guided and supported by the common people. Imported doctrines must be secondary. The people must be carefully listened to, the better to recruit, mobilize, and control them.

A comparable bankruptcy of the Comintern directives had occurred in the white areas under GMD control. Repeated attempts to organize labor unions as an urban proletariat and use strikes to get control of cities never got off the ground. The chief organizer who emerged was another man who knew how to pursue what was possible. Liu Shaoqi headed the Communist effort in the North China cities, where he encouraged the left-wing literary movement, the use of the arts, and the recruitment of students. By dropping Comintern doctrines about proletarian revolution, Liu achieved a parallel indigenization of the CCP methods.

By the time Liu joined Mao at Yan'an in 1937, the second united front had already taken shape. A united front of all Chinese against Japan became the Moscow line in the summer of 1935 in order to combat the rise of fascism in Europe and Japanese aggression in the East. Mao, however, came out for a united front in China against the Japanese but excluding Jiang Jieshi. The key point was that the national revolution to save China from Japan now took precedence over the social revolution on the land, but Mao would not give up the latter to concentrate on the former. Instead, he urged a two-front effort to combat both the Japanese and Jiang Jieshi by developing Soviet bases in a war of resistance. To prove its sincerity, the CCP from Yan'an launched an eastern expedition into Shanxi province in order to get at the Japanese farther east. Just at this time in the spring of 1936 a Comintern directive ordered Mao to join a united front with Jiang. Zhou Enlai went to Shanghai to negotiate the terms.

When the GMD and the CCP finally agreed on a united front alliance in April 1937, Mao began to win out against the remaining twenty-eight Bolsheviks in the CCP. Far from combining with the GMD, Mao planned to carry on the social revolution in Soviet areas as a basis for fighting Japan on the nation's behalf. If this strategy worked, the separate armed forces of the CCP would develop their own bases and popular support while also riding the wave of national resistance to the invader. The basis for Mao's national communism was already at hand.

The force of Chinese nationalism had been mobilized in the early 1920s with the help of Soviet advisers in two competing party dictatorships. However, the senior of these, the GMD, had already become the hope and path of advancement for the urban Sino-liberal professionals who had a Western returned-student or Christian-college background. Thus Nationalist China faced two ways, toward the reformist West in the cities and toward conservatism on the land. Both philosophies might be present in the same family.

Without the devastating Japanese invasion, the Nanjing government might gradually have led the way in China's modernization. As it turned out, however, resisting Japan gave Mao and the CCP their chance to establish a new autocratic power in the countryside, excluding the elements of a nascent urban civil society that were still developing under the Nationalists. In conditions of wartime, the CCP was building a new type of Chinese state geared for class warfare. In the twentieth century, Chinese revolutionaries were thus preparing to assault and reorder a class structure that went back at least 3,000 years.

16

China's War of Resistance
1937–1945

Nationalist Difficulties

Militarist Japan's attempt to conquer China began by seizing Manchuria in 1931 and became a full-fledged invasion from 1937 to 1945 (see Map 23). Japanese historians saw Japan following in the footsteps of the Manchu conquerors of 1644, while Tokyo's modernizers saw Japan shepherding the Chinese people into the modern world. But times had changed. Japan's aggression only strengthened China's new nationalism.

During the eight years of war, a major part of the Chinese people were in Japanese-occupied territory, mainly the coastal cities and railway towns. Another major segment were in the GMD-controlled area, called Free China. The smallest division of China was the CCP area, with its capital at Yan'an. Historians are genetic-minded, looking for origins, and China's future came out of Yan'an. Accordingly, the defeat of the Japanese and then of the Nationalists has been less researched than the rise of the CCP. Success is creative and interesting, failure sad and dull. Who wants it? Moreover, Yan'an being smaller, in size and documentation, is easier to encompass than the vastly variegated experience of Occupied China and Free China. These two areas, though larger than the area under Yan'an, have been less studied.

While the GMD and the CCP were both party dictatorships in form, they were very different political creatures in fact. The GMD had two incarnations, first in the associates of Sun Yatsen in the 1911 revolution, second in the followers of Jiang Jieshi in the Nanjing government after 1927. The GMD's forced removal in 1938 from Nanjing to Wuhan and then beyond the Yangzi gorges to Chongqing cut it off from its roots. Its revenues from the Maritime Customs and the opium trade to Shanghai were knocked out. Its hard-won echelon of modern-trained administrators became refugees. From being the central government of China, the Nationalist regime was now a fugitive in a mountain-ringed redoubt, obliged to work with reactionary provincial militarists and landlords. In West China the Chongqing government tried to keep the local warlords in line and avoid upsetting the social order in the villages.

China's nascent Sino-liberal educational system suffered a grievous destruction of plant and facilities. Missionary colleges kept at work under the Japanese occupation but in purely Chinese universities many students and faculties migrated in 1937–1938 up the Yangzi or to the southwest. The Southwest Associated University at Kunming was set up by Qinghua (Tsing Hua) University and Beijing University from Beijing and Nankai University from Tianjin. Meanwhile, Yanjing University and other Christian institutions, after the Japanese attacked the United States in December 1941, gathered at the site of the West China Union University in Chengdu. Whole industrial plants were dismantled and shipped upriver, where the National Resources Commission had already been developing mines and industries. Intellectuals and government administrators, with great patriotism, put up with displacement from their homes and learned to live primitively in the interior. Unfortunately, although they were the main body of modern China's professional people, their hopes went unrewarded. This was due partly to the ineptitude of their government.

With admirable fortitude but little foresight, the Nationalist regime met its problem by short-term expedients that gave it little strength for the future. The Chongqing government got control of the land tax in grain as the wherewithal to feed its administration. Its industrial developers had arsenals at work to support the war. The spirit of resistance was stimulated by the Japanese bombing of Chongqing, but meanwhile the spirit of the united front deteriorated. Radical intellectuals in Chongqing began to drift northward to Communist Yan'an, except for those who were already "outside cadres" of the CCP assigned to work as ostensible liberals in the GMD area. The secret police of both the party and the government felt more and more compelled to keep the liberals in line as potential subversives. Strong-arm methods against students, publishers, and other seeming enemies steadily widened the split between the intellectuals and the government that hoped to rely upon them for the future.

Jiang Jieshi's regime was as unimaginatively conservative in Chong-

qing as in Nanjing. The peasantry were conscripted and taxed but otherwise left alone. Literacy was not especially promoted, nor did public-
health services reach many villages. The ruling-class stratum of the old
China continued to be quite distinct from the masses in the countryside.
Sichuan province, except for the irrigated rice bowl around the capital at
Chengdu, consisted largely of jagged mountains and swift rivers under
an unpleasantly humid climate, chilly in the winters and oppressive in
the heat of summer. To the ramshackle lack of the amenities of modern
life was added the all-pervasive fact of inflation. Instead of learning to
live off the countryside as the CCP had to do, the GMD lived off the
printing press. Inflation steadily undermined the morale of the upper
class.

The Nationalist Government during World War II displayed all its
earlier weaknesses. Local warlord power-holders in Sichuan, Yunnan,
and Guangxi made Chongqing's extension of local control very difficult.
The governor of Yunnan, where Kunming had become the airbase door-
way to Free China, was able to keep Jiang Jieshi's secret police and
troops largely out of his province until the end of the war in 1945. Nationalist police were unable to suppress the student and faculty movement for a coalition government and against civil war at the Southwest
Associated University in Kunming until the end of 1945.

The Nationalists fared little better in dealing with the farming population. Although inflation at first helped agricultural producers by raising the prices of their crops, this was soon offset by a heavy increase in
taxation—a flagrant proliferation of hundreds of kinds of small taxes or
fees, mainly instituted by the local government heads to finance their administration and private needs. As Lloyd Eastman (1984) recounts,
"There were, for example, a 'contribute-straw-sandals-to-recruits' tax,
a 'comfort-recruits-families' tax, a 'train-antiaircraft-cadres' tax, and a
'provide-fuel-for-garrisoned-troops' tax."

To these burdens were added the Nationalist conscription of men
and grain. Corvée labor was considered at the beck and call of the army,
while the central government also authorized army commanders to live
off the countryside by enforcing grain requisitions. When famine hit the
province of Henan in 1942–1943 it meant starvation either for the
troops or for the people. The requisitions continued unabated, and the
troops were soon being attacked by starving peasants. Famine led to
hoarding supplies for profit and an immense growth of corruption. The
unfortunate result was that the government received little more in the

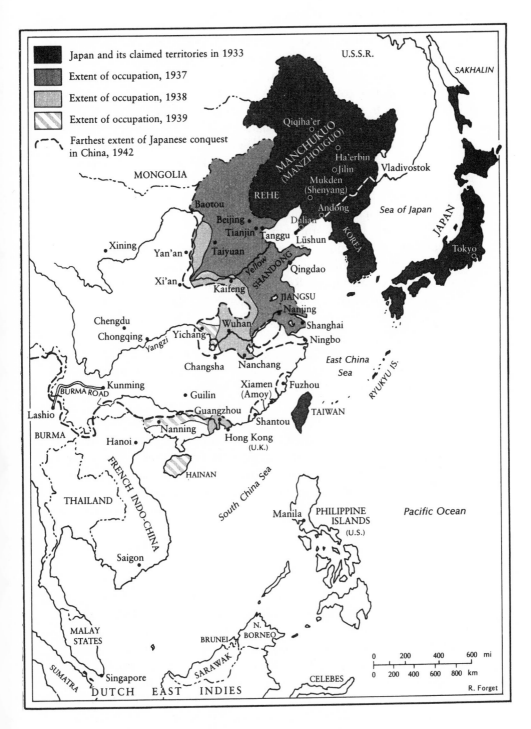

Japan and its claimed territories in 1933

Extent of occupation, 1937

Extent of occupation, 1938

Extent of occupation, 1939

Farthest extent of Japanese conquest in China, 1942

U.S.S.R.

SAKHALIN

Qiqiha'er

MANCHUKUO
(MANZHOUGUO)

Ha'erbin

Jilin

Vladivostok

MONGOLIA

Mukden
(Shenyang)

REHE

Andong

Sea of Japan

JAPAN

Baotou

Dalian

Beijing

Tianjin Tanggu

Lüshun

KOREA

Xining

Yan'an

Taiyuan

Tokyo

Xi'an

Kaifeng

SHANDONG

Yellow

Qingdao

Chengdu

Yichang

JIANGSU

Nanjing

Chongqing

Wuhan

Shanghai

Yangzi

Ningbo

Changsha

Nanchang

East China
Sea

RYUKYU IS.

Kunming

BURMA ROAD

Xiamen
(Amoy)

Fuzhou

Guilin

Lashio

Guangzhou

Shantou

TAIWAN

BURMA

Nanning

Hong Kong
(U.K.)

Hanoi

FRENCH INDO-CHINA

HAINAN

South China Sea

THAILAND

Manila

PHILIPPINE
ISLANDS
(U.S.)

Pacific Ocean

Saigon

MALAY
STATES

N.
BORNEO

BRUNEI

SARAWAK

SUMATRA

Singapore

DUTCH   EAST   INDIES

CELEBES

0   200   400   600 mi

0   200   400   600   800 km

R. Forget

23. The Japanese Invasion of China

way of resources while the petty officials and landlords found out how to profit in the inflation. By the war's end, peasant rebellions were incipient in several provinces of Free China.

Meanwhile, both the Nationalist Government at Chongqing and the CCP at Yan'an fought a two-front war, against Japan and against each other. The war against Japan that had begun outside Beijing on July 7, 1937, led to the announcement in August and September of a united-front agreement between the CCP and the GMD. The CCP agreed to stop its armed revolution to change Chinese society and gave up the forcible confiscation of landlords' land, while its Red Army would be placed under central government command. On its part, the GMD would let the CCP establish liaison offices in several cities, publish its *New China Daily* in Chongqing, and be represented in GMD advisory bodies. From this time on, the form of the united front was maintained. The Red Army was now called the Eighth Route Army, and Zhou Enlai resided in Chongqing to represent it. Having spent 1938 at the transitional capital in Wuhan, he was already the CCP's foreign minister and representative to the world press.

The terms of the united-front agreement remained on paper unchallenged, but in fact developments undid it. Yan'an refused to have Nationalist staff officers in its area. In effect, the Eighth Route Army continued to be an independent force in spite of a small subsidy from the Nationalists. Meanwhile, the CCP in building up its base areas maintained order, encouraged economic production through devices such as mutual-aid teams, and kept on recruiting poor peasant activists, who would eventually get the upper hand over the rich peasants. Party membership grew from some 40,000 claimed in 1937 to an alleged 1,200,000 in 1945, while the armed forces increased from 92,000 in 1937 to perhaps 910,000 in 1945.

Mao's Sinification of Marxism

To control and direct the widespread organization of the CCP movement over the broad stretches of North China required dedicated and disciplined party members, experienced cadres (activists) in the villages, an attempt at self-sufficiency in each base, and the use of radio telegraphy to transmit messages. The principle of centralized control over a decentralized situation was exhibited in the government organization. The Central Committee of the party had its departments at Yan'an dealing with military affairs, organization, united-front work, enemy-occupied areas, labor, women, and the like, a total of twelve categories. Meantime, the territorial organization was divided among half a dozen regional bureaus, such as North China, Northwest China, the Central Plain. Within these regional bureaus were staff sections corresponding to those under the Central Committee at Yan'an. The principle of "integration" *(yiyuanhua)* meant that all directives from the capital at Yan'an to the specialized staff sections of the regional bureaus must go through or at least be fully known to the branch bureau chief, as the local coordinator.

Yan'an in World War II became to a few foreign observers a never-never-land full of sunshine and bonhomie. The revolutionary enthusiasm was infectious, as Edgar Snow and other journalists reported to the world. The homespun democracy apparent among the CCP leaders was a startling contrast to Chongqing. American aid never really got to Yan'an, and the superficiality of contact allowed the cultivation of a mythology that captivated liberals abroad.

The secret of Mao's success at Yan'an was his flexibility at combining short-term and long-term goals. In the short term he espoused in 1940 the New Democracy as a united-front doctrine that would embrace all the Chinese people who would subscribe to CCP leadership. For the long term, he steadily developed the party organization, including its control over intellectuals. The Yan'an rectification movement of 1942–1944 (more fully described below) established the campaign style of mobilization, including individual isolation, terror, struggle, confession, humiliation, and subservience. Party members would come to know it well and, in time, so would the public. It was one of Mao's achievements, with roots both in Leninism–Stalinism and in Imperial Confucianism.

Meantime, the real sinews of power grew up in the CCP mobilization of the peasantry in North China. The Japanese were excellent targets to mobilize against. Invading China along the rail lines, they tried to seal off the areas in between, but their rail-line blockhouses could not control trade and contact across the lines. In general their invasion cultivated the ground for the CCP mobilization. Whether the CCP success in this situation was due to a simple nationalism or to CCP doctrine is essentially a nonquestion because the CCP already represented national communism, not the Comintern, while CCP doctrines grew out of practice in the villages and also enlisted intellectuals in a grand scheme of world salvation.

In the governments of the Border Region and Liberated Areas that the CCP developed in different parts of North China, the first principle was party control based on indoctrination of cadres and enforcement of discipline. The indoctrination had to combine Mao's long-term principles with his tactical flexibility, for the CCP-organized regimes operated at great distances from Yan'an and very much on their own except for unreliable radio communication.

The second principle was to find out what the peasants wanted and give it to them: first of all, local peace and order; second, an army of friendly troops who helped in peasant life, harvesting crops when necessary and fraternizing with the villagers; third, a recruitment of local activists who might very well be found at the upper level of the poor peasantry, people of ability who felt frustrated by circumstance; fourth, a program for economic betterment partly through improved crops but mainly through agricultural cooperation in the form of mutual aid, organized transport, and production of consumer goods in cooperatives.

As these efforts went forward, they became the basis for a third principle: class struggle. This had to be approached in a gingerly fashion because North China landlords were hardly more than rich peasants but might be able to field their own local forces drawn from secret societies and mercenaries. In the early years the GMD also had its forces in parts of North China and so provided an alternative focus of allegiance. The CCP dealt with this by setting up the rather persuasive three thirds system: the Communists would control only one third of the small congresses that sanctioned local government, leaving the other two thirds to the GMD and independents. On this basis, of course, the CCP's superior discipline and dedication let them become leaders on their merits. As their good repute became justified in popular esteem, they could begin to prepare for land reform in addition to economic production programs.

Land reform could be pursued only after three ingredients were present: military control, economic improvement, and recruitment of village activists. In the process itself the trick was to mobilize opinion against landlord despots, such as they were, and—by denouncing or liquidating them—commit the villagers to a revolutionary course. All land-holdings were evaluated and redistributed on a more equal basis according to categories that gave each individual his status as a rich, middle, or poor peasant or landless laborer. If this redistribution could be made to stick, village activists could begin to be indoctrinated in the ethos of the party's leadership. The message was simply that the people could make a better future for themselves if they would organize their efforts in a new unity.

The leadership of this new unity could be found in the CCP. While the individual could achieve nothing alone, he could contribute by sacrificing his individual interests to that of the common cause. The principle of democratic centralism was then extolled as a means whereby all could have their say and make their input, but once a party decision had been made, all would obey it. This would never have gone down in a New England town meeting, but in a North China village, where the alternative was government by landlords and officials from outside the region, it was properly persuasive.

In short, the idea of the "mass line" was here adumbrated: the party must go among the people to discover their grievances and needs, which could then be formulated by the party and explained to the masses as their own best interest. This from-the-masses to-the-masses concept was indeed a sort of democracy suited to Chinese tradition, where the upper-class official had governed best when he had the true interests of the local people at heart and so governed on their behalf.

In this way the war of resistance against Japan provided the sanction for a CCP mobilization of the Chinese masses in the countryside; and this, once achieved, gave a new power to the CCP based not on the cities but on the villages. CCP expansion and base-building across North China and even in the Yangzi region reached a new high point in 1940.

The Japanese had been extending their control by setting up block-houses every one to three miles along the rail lines. They then sent columns out from these strongpoints to invade the villages. But the Japanese, like the Americans in Vietnam or the Russians later in Afghanistan, faced the problem of how to get control of an alien population in the countryside where they lived, partly by the use of puppet troops and partly by their own superior firepower. The Japanese could not be defeated in normal positional warfare but only by the attrition of their resources through guerrilla warfare. To counter this the Japanese spread their network of strongpoints and blockade lines in the effort to starve the guerrillas by cutting off supplies.

In response to this Japanese pressure, the top commander at the CCP military headquarters, Peng Dehuai, prepared a widespread attack known as the Hundred Regiments Offensive that began in August 1940. Japanese rail lines were cut repeatedly all over North China and block-houses destroyed. It was the primary CCP offensive of the entire war, planned by General Peng, possibly without much knowledge of it in Yan'an. After several weeks this offensive was obviously a great victory for the CCP, but then the Japanese retaliated in force and with vengeance. Bringing in more troops, they mounted a "three-all" campaign: "kill all, burn all, loot all." They stopped trying to discriminate between the ordinary peasantry and the Eighth Route Army but simply destroyed everything they could reach. Villages, once destroyed, were garrisoned. The number of blockhouses grew to thousands. The result of this rage and destruction was to break up the CCP position across North China, isolate many sectors, and take over control of most of the county seats that the CCP had acquired. It was a first-rate disaster, and the CCP did not launch another such offensive.

Meanwhile, the Communist expansion in the Yangzi region, particularly through the New Fourth Army, also aroused retaliation from Nationalist forces. Negotiations led to the withdrawal of most of the New Fourth Army from south to north of the Yangzi, but in January 1941 the headquarters unit of several thousand CCP troops was ambushed by the Nationalists and practically destroyed in what was known as the "New Fourth Army incident." While neither party acknowledged the end of the united front, because it was advantageous to both of them in form, it nevertheless had become a fact.

These reverses left Yan'an facing a severe crisis. The GMD and Japanese blockades had cut off nearly all trade, inflation was rising rapidly, and the whole regime had to pull back to survive. While Yan'an had got along with very modest taxation of the peasant grain crop, by 1941 bad weather created shortages and the government began to demand some 10 percent of the grain produced. Confiscations from landlords had dried up. The only way out was to go for self-sufficiency, such as by local production of consumer goods like cotton cloth. Cultivated land and irrigation were greatly increased, the grain yield went up, and livestock were also increased. In short, the economic crisis was met by a great effort to raise production by all possible means.

Parallel with this economic recovery, the early 1940s at Yan'an saw Mao Zedong finally establish his ascendancy over the CCP. Mao's reading of Marxist works had not been extensive until he had some leisure time at Yan'an after 1936. Soon he was giving lectures on dialectical materialism and producing his essays "On Practice" and "On Contradiction." Because he had not yet eliminated the twenty-eight Bolsheviks, his lecturing was designed to show his capacity for intellectual leadership, even though the lectures were rather crude. Nevertheless, Mao showed his originality by his stress on contradictions, which was posited on the "unity of opposites," an idea with a long Chinese history behind it.

His philosophical aim at Yan'an was not merely to establish a nationalistic party concerned for the Chinese nation but also to adapt Marxism to Chinese uses. The political imperative was that the party had to achieve disciplined organization, marked by acceptance of the party line, so that party members could be counted on to operate at a distance in conformity with directives. The GMD had suffered from intense factionalism. The CCP at Yan'an as a smaller organization moved to eradicate it with some success.

Consensus among party activists depended on their being intellectually convinced of the wisdom of the CCP line. The line must invoke theoretical principles to sanction practical action. This was achieved by the gradual creation of the body of ideas popularly known in the West as Maoism but in Chinese more modestly called Mao Zedong Thought. It represented the sinification of Marxism–Leninism, the application of its universal principles to the specific conditions of China. How Mao built it up, piece by piece, is therefore an interesting question worth our pausing to examine.

Mao Zedong Thought

Both Buddhism and Christianity when they came into China had faced a problem of terminology, how to pick Chinese characters that would express the new concepts but keep them distinct from old established Chinese concepts expressed in the same characters. Japanese socialists had pioneered in this effort. Long before Mao, the Chinese adaptation of Marxism had begun at the level of translation of key terms. Marx's "proletariat," the key actor in his cosmic drama, was certainly associated in Western thinking with urban life, specifically early nineteenth-century factory workers in the often unspeakable conditions of Western European industrialization. The translation into Chinese, however, produced the term *wuchan jieji,* meaning "propertyless class," in other words, the very poor who might be either in the city or the countryside, and of course in China were mainly in the countryside. In effect, the European "proletariat" were automatically to be found in China in the poor "peasantry" among the farmers and landless laborers. Granted that Marxist terminology was used by Chinese Marxists in terms consonant with those of Moscow Marxists, there was nevertheless a subtle difference when they spread their doctrine to the Chinese students and common people.

The Chinese term used for "feudal," *fengjian,* had referred in classic

Chinese thinking to the fragmentation of sovereignty in the period of Warring States before the Qin unification in 221 BC. It meant simply decentralized administration, without reference to the land system or the status of the cultivators. However, if feudalism was to be identified in China with landowner exploitation, as Communists wished to do, then feudalism had gone on in China a couple of thousand years. Thus the periods that Marx defined for European history could not be easily applied to China. If all of Chinese history for 2,000 years after 221 BC had been "feudal," the term lost meaning or was humiliating. "Proletariat" and "feudal" were only two of the key terms of Marxism, and they obviously did not fit the Chinese scene without really being bent out of shape.

Quite aside from this terminological problem in sinification, the economic foundation of Chinese life, being mainly in the countryside, gave the Chinese revolution necessarily a rural character more pronounced than that in the Soviet Union. The peasantry had to be the chief revolutionists. The final factor making for sinification was the overriding sentiment of Chinese nationalism based on cultural and historical pride, which meant China could not be the tail of someone else's dog. In effect, the Chinese people could accept only a Chinese Marxism.

In time Chinese historical consciousness would undermine the verisimilitude of Marxism in China. But for Mao's purposes it could be asserted that the domination of the landlord class ("feudalism") was backed by the "imperialist" exploiters from abroad, while the rise of a Chinese merchant class centered in towns produced a capitalist "national bourgeoisie." Only its "comprador" wing sold out to the "imperialist" exploiters, and the situation might be cured by an establishment of central state authority to complete the tasks of the "bourgeois-democratic revolution." Later the revolution would reach the final stage of socialism. In other words, there was enough fit to enable Marxism to get on with the job of revolution by propagating its new world-historical belief system.

Yet sinification was still a two-front enterprise because the CCP had to maintain its credentials as part of international Marxism–Leninism by using orthodox European lingo. Thus, early on the GMD at Guangzhou could not be defined as representing simply a bourgeois class trying to carry through its phase of bourgeois democratic revolution. No, the GMD government, instead of representing the bourgeois capitalist class, had been a multiclass government or "bloc of four classes," in which the proletariat (CCP) could participate. Mao later argued that "the Chinese bourgeoisie and proletariat are new-born and never existed before in Chinese history . . . they are twins born of China's old (feudal) society at once linked to each other and antagonistic to each other." On this basis it was appropriate for the proletariat to lead the bourgeois democratic revolution, a theory which justified the CCP in struggling for power. In China this made sense, whether or not it would in Europe.

For example, in developing his idea of New Democracy in China, Mao began with the Marxist assumption of a bourgeois democratic revolution as the transition from feudalism to capitalism, which would be followed by another revolution as the transition from capitalism to socialism. In Europe the bourgeois democratic revolution was typified by the French Revolution of the 1790s, while the socialist revolution was generally felt to have succeeded only in Russia in 1917. In other words the crowded history of the nineteenth century had represented a bourgeois democratic phase of social development. What was the equivalent in China?

Chinese Marxists could only conclude that the bourgeois democratic revolution had been ushered in by the May Fourth Movement in 1919, which could be characterized by Leninists as an achievement of national capitalism. Since the socialist revolution would be achieved by the CCP at some future time, this application of Marxism–Leninism to China resulted in China's having had 2,000 years of feudalism and only 40 years of capitalism. By European Marxist standards, China was peculiarly out of shape.

The Rectification Campaign of 1942–1944

Now that he was in power, Mao pushed not only to consolidate his position but to unify the party and to ensure discipline. The rectification campaign of 1942–1944 was limited to party members, who had increased in number and lacked the cohesion of the Long March generation. The targets of the campaign were "subjectivism, sectarianism, and party formalism." "Subjectivism" targeted dogmatists who could not combine theory with practice. "Sectarianism" referred to the recent factionalism and the inevitable cleavages between soldiers and civilians, party and nonparty, old and new party members, and so on. "Party formalism" meant the use of jargon instead of practical problem-solving. Other evils were those of creeping bureaucratism and routinization of administration. These could be combatted partly by decentralization—transferring officials down to work in villages closer to practical problems. Also attacked was the individualism of the many intellectuals who had come to Yan'an from the coastal cities.

One principal factor made for friction in the CCP's relationship with intellectuals. Whereas scholars under the imperial order had been oriented toward public service, the writers of the twentieth-century revolution had focused on evils and misdemeanors of government because they had grown up as a class divorced from office-holding. The traditional literati, in short, had now been split into two groups, those in public service and those in public criticism. The modern intellectuals were in the tradition of remonstrance, pointing out the inadequacies of the authorities. Since that great critic of the GMD, Lu Xun, had died in 1936, his name could be safely invoked as that of a paragon.

In Yan'an in the early 1940s the control of literature by the new state authority of the CCP became a central issue. Sino-liberal patriots of all sorts had joined the revolution, and their commitment to attack the imperfections of the GMD naturally led them on to criticize the emerging imperfections of the CCP. Lu Xun's closest followers had continued under the CCP to voice their criticisms. When Mao Zedong gave his two lectures on literature and art at Yan'an early in 1942, he laid down the law that literature should serve the state, in this case the cause of CCP-led revolution. It should therefore be upbeat in the style of socialist realism from the Soviet Union and avoid the kind of revelation of evils and inadequacies that had been a Communist specialty in the GMD period.

The methods whereby Mao's thought-reform movement was carried out at Yan'an in 1942–1944 would become very familiar in CCP history from then on. The individual whose thoughts were to be reformed was first investigated and persuaded to describe himself and his life experience to the point where the group could begin to criticize him. In study-group criticism the individual was at once isolated and subjected to the rebukes or admonishments of everyone else. This shook his self-confidence. As a next step, in public struggle meetings the individual was publicly accused and humiliated before a large and usually jeering audience representing the community. At this point another factor operated, namely, the dependence of the Chinese individual upon group esteem as well as the approval of authority.

As the pressure increased and the individual found no escape from the denigration of his old self, he was led into writing confessions to analyze his evil conduct and his desire to change. Pressure was increased if he was then isolated in jail—subjected to solitary confinement or placed in a cell with others and obliged to wear paper handcuffs, which he could not break without dire consequences. The consequent obliteration of his personality thus prepared him for the final stage of rebirth and reconciliation. When his confession was finally accepted and the party welcomed him back into the fold, he might experience a tremendous elation and willingness to accept the party's guidance. Whether this psychological experience did change personalities is less certain than the fact that it was a highly unpleasant experience to be avoided in the future. One way or the other, the result was conformity to the party line.

Lest we begin to believe in total power and total subjection, we must give due weight to the vigor of Chinese personalities. Those who stood forth as critics were frequently obdurate and essentially uncompromising individuals who felt duty-bound to stick to their principles and criticize evils. The widespread use of thought reform by the CCP thus should not necessarily be taken to mean that Chinese intellectuals were natural slaves. On the contrary, their independence of judgment was hard for the party to overcome.

Mao's sinification of Marxism may fruitfully be compared with the failure of Taiping Christianity. In the 1850s Hong's claim to be the younger brother of Jesus soon made him anathema to the foreign source of his vision, the Western missionaries, whom he did not even deal with in his profound arrogance. In short order he made himself both a Christian heretic and within China a foreign subversive, achieving the worst of both worlds. By contrast, Mao, though eventually anathematized by Moscow, succeeded for some time in cooperating with the Comintern, and when he sinified his Marxism, he masked it in a coating of orthodox terminology. Both Hong and Mao started out with only a rudimentary grasp of the foreign doctrine, and both broke free of the domination of foreigners—Hong of the missionaries, Mao of the Comintern. But of course the differences between them far outweigh such similarities.

In 1943 Mao put forward his doctrine of the "mass line." Like many of Mao's intellectual formulations, this was double-ended and ambiguous so that it could be applied in either of two ways. While it asserted the need of consulting the masses and having a mass participation of some sort in the government, it also reaffirmed the necessity for central control and leadership. At any given time either one could be given the greater emphasis, just as *New Democracy* had provided a theoretical basis for joining with the GMD in a second united front or opposing the GMD as reactionary. Again, one's class status might be defined by reference to one's parents and economic livelihood or it could be defined by one's ideas and aspirations. Similarly, the people were enshrined as the final arbiters and beneficiaries of the revolution, but some persons could be labeled as enemies of the people. This could be done by administrative fiat from above.

It was typical of this line of development that Mao should define contradictions as being some of them antagonistic and some of them non-antagonistic, that is, arguable. Thus some contradictions made you an enemy of the people and some did not, depending on how you were perceived. All in all, it was a very flexible structure of ideas, as though Marx and Engels had been seduced by Yin and Yang. Once Mao had control over it, he was truly in a position of leadership. Unity resulted because those who held out against Mao were vilified, penalized, jailed, or even executed.

American Support of Coalition Government

In 1943 the Soviets successfully defended Stalingrad, the Western Allies won North Africa, the U.S. Navy began to get the upper hand in the Pacific, and American forces had invaded the Solomon Islands on their way to Tokyo. The Japanese had to relax their pressure on the North China Liberated Areas and Border Region. For the Communists the war began to wind down when the long-planned Japanese Ichigo offensive in 1944 rolled down from Henan to the south of the Yangzi, destroying much of the Nationalists' best armies.

In these circumstances CCP expansion was resumed in the period 1943–1945, but its policy was prudent and avoided haste and superficiality. By the time the American Army military observer group, or so-called Dixie Mission, reached Yan'an in mid-1944, the CCP was on an upswing again and preparing for the postwar showdown with the GMD. This resurgent spirit was indicated in the important Seventh Congress of the Chinese Communist Party held in Yan'an from late April to mid-June 1945. It adopted a new constitution, which gave Mao more central power as chairman of the Central Committee and Political Bureau. "The Thought of Mao Zedong" was hailed as the party's guide.

By this time the United States had willy-nilly become an important factor in Chinese politics. To distant outsiders like the Americans, Free China represented an outpost of modern civilization struggling to survive in a sea of antique customs and evil forces. There was no longer anything revolutionary about it, but the Americans found this encouraging and after 1941 adopted Free China as an ally. American ignorance and sentimentality reached the point where President Roosevelt pictured the Nationalist Government moving into the East Asian power vacuum that would be created by the fall of Japan. A clandestine air force recruited from the American military services as mercenaries on leave came to the rescue of Chongqing even before Pearl Harbor. These Flying Tigers, under a retired American airman, Claire Chennault, soon became the 14th Air Force, harassing Japanese communication lines from its base in Kunming. The American China missionary movement got behind United China Relief. American sympathy and largesse had a new lease on life, and General Joseph Stilwell, commander of the China-Burma-India theater of operations, proved that Chinese conscripts, if taken to India and properly fed and trained, could make first-class fighting men.

As Jiang Jieshi had depended in the clinch on the Shanghai underworld, so now he began to depend on the Christian impulses and logistic supply of the Americans. Considering that the Hump airlift in the China-Burma-India Theater was the absolute end of the line in American strategic considerations and supply, this did not put the Nationalists in a strong position. By the time the U.S. Army got an observer mission into Yan'an in 1944, it was too late to use the Washington–Chongqing alliance to prepare the way for a Nationalist victory in the obviously coming civil war.

Nevertheless, the Americans tried. The United States Navy, in its effort to keep up with the Army, sent a mission in 1942 to work with the Chinese secret police and get in on the ground floor of the anti-Communist crusade. But General Stilwell could not get the Nationalist forces trained, supplied, and led to fight the Japanese effectively. The American idea of using Free China as a base for the struggle against Japan absorbed the Americans' attention but at the same time distracted them from the Chinese Revolution. Like the Soviet program in the 1920s, the American aid program to China led into ultimate disaster. For foreigners to work with the Chinese Revolution has never been easy.

The American involvement was flawed by serious anachronism. Every American who had seen warlord China and supported a Christian college had placed hope in the Nanjing government as a representative of American ideals. Unity versus warlordism and China's equality among nations were appealing motifs. The later generation who saw the rising power of the Communists up close were only a small group and had nowhere near the influence in the United States that had been exerted over generations by American missionaries.

These factors produced mixed counsels in the formation of American policy. The foreign service officers and commanders like General Stilwell who were on the spot saw the admirable determination and strength of the Communist movement. In the United States the home-side China constituency, captained by Henry Luce, the China-born publisher of *Time* and *Life,* generally retained their image of an earlier day when the Nanjing government had seemed the last word in Chinese progress.

With the end of the united front in 1941, American observers could see the split widening between the GMD and the CCP party dictatorships. State Department policy, however, was a small drop in the bucket compared with the general American war effort, the logistics of transport over the Hump, the modern training and supply of Chinese troops that Stilwell effected, and his dealing with Jiang Jieshi as a stiff-necked client who felt he was getting the short end of wartime supplies. No Americans in Washington really knew much about the North China Communist area, while they were diplomatically as well as legally compelled to support the Nationalist regime as our ally.

Meanwhile, observers on the spot under the American embassy and military headquarters foresaw a post-World War II civil war in China, which held the danger of Soviet takeover of North China. The extent of Mao's sinification of Marxism or creation of a national communism could not be adequately appreciated by outsiders, who did not know the gruesome details of Mao's relations with Stalin. It therefore became American policy to head off a civil war, and the device thought of was "coalition government." This in effect would be an extension of the united front in its ideal and unrealized form, a combination of the armed forces and representation of both parties in a national assembly. Perceiving this American hope, both of the Chinese parties ostensibly adopted "coalition government" as a postwar aim while privately preparing to fight it out.

The abject unrealism of the American policy was well illustrated by President Roosevelt's special emissary, General Patrick J. Hurley from Oklahoma, a flamboyant and simple-minded American, Reaganesque ahead of his time. His clumsy efforts at heading off the civil war by mediation were followed by Jiang Jieshi's taking him over. Hurley countered the entire embassy staff by plumping for American support of Jiang come what may. By the time it came, of course, Hurley was out of the picture, but his policy was still followed in Washington and led to the Americans' being quite properly put out of China.

After Japan's surrender in August 1945, Jiang and Mao under Hurley's auspices met in Chongqing and in October agreed upon an ideal set of principles that would gladden any liberal in the world. The GMD and CCP regimes would cooperate in a representative assembly, scrambling their armies and meanwhile guaranteeing all civil liberties and good things dear to the hearts of men and women everywhere. This make-believe derived from the recognition that neither side could take a stand against the ideal of peace and cooperation.

The hard facts in the fall of 1945 were far otherwise. As soon as the war with Japan was ended, the Communist forces moved across North China to compel the Japanese to surrender to them. The Nationalists reacted by ordering the Japanese to fight off the Communists and recover from them any territories they had gained. Soon there were numerous Communist–Japanese firefights as the Nationalist Government made use of the ex-imperialist aggressors to fight off the social revolution. Meanwhile, both Nationalist and Communist forces were moving into Manchuria (henceforth called the Northeast) in a competition to take over the area. Typically the Nationalists garrisoned the cities and the Communists mobilized the countryside.

The United States government followed the Nationalist example by moving some 53,000 U.S. Marines into North China to hold Beijing and Tianjin against a possible Soviet incursion, while transporting by air and ship complete Nationalist armies to Manchurian cities and other parts of North China. The United States thus intervened from the beginning on the anti-Communist side. Moreover, as part of the Yalta agreement of February 1945, President Roosevelt had already tried to settle China's fate by arranging with Stalin for a Chinese–Soviet treaty between the Nationalists and the USSR. The terms were that the Soviets would recognize and deal only with the Nationalist Government of China, while the Nationalists in turn acknowledged the Russian recovery of their former imperialist rights in the Northeast along the railways. Stalin promised to withdraw Soviet troops within three months from the Japanese surrender. As it turned out, this would be November 15, 1945, and thus the CCP would have a three-month period in which to infiltrate the Northeast as best they could in competition with the Nationalists, who would be transported by the Americans. Since the Nationalists saw that the CCP even on foot was beating them into the Northeast, they asked the Soviets to stay longer, and Soviet troops did not depart until May 1946, taking with them much of the industrial equipment that could be moved from the new Japanese installations in their puppet state. Having

American backing, Jiang Jieshi fought his way into southern Manchuria against Communist opposition.

Thus the stage was set for the frustration of the mediation effort undertaken by General George C. Marshall on behalf of Washington. As the top commander in World War II, and a devoted but savvy manager, Marshall did what could be done in the direction of coalition government. A Political Consultative Conference convened in Beijing in January 1946, and arrangements were also discussed for the combining of GMD and CCP forces. The center of the civil war, however, had now shifted to the Northeast, which was unfortunately left out of the Chongqing agreements. The United States was buying Jiang Jieshi's acquiescence by a big economic loan, and when Marshall returned to lobby in Congress and secure this part of the bargain, he lost control of the negotiations. By the time he returned, warfare was being quelled in North China by the Executive Headquarters that he had established in Beijing. This headquarters used the device of dispatching American colonels with Communist and Nationalist generals to areas of conflict to stop the fighting. But meanwhile the Northeast was out of control.

Both sides had used the negotiations as a sop to the widespread Chinese peace movement, while preparing to fight it out. In a similar fashion the United States had demanded coalition and reform at Nanjing and Yan'an and yet at the same time had continued to supply the Nationalists. They were all saying one thing while doing another.

33. Sun Yatsen, with his young wife Song Qingling (Soong Ch'ing-ling), en route by ship in late 1924 from Guangzhou to Beijing for talks with warlord leaders on national unification. Sun became ill during the journey, and he died of liver cancer in Beijing on March 12, 1925.

34. Japanese troops met little resistance in their conquest of Manchuria in 1931.

35. *Top:* The Chinese boycott of Japanese goods following the takeover of Manchuria led to fierce fighting in Shanghai in early 1932. Shown here are Japanese troops guarding Chinese prisoners in the city. *Bottom:* Japanese soldiers after a looting expedition.

36. Mao Zedong (right) and Zhang Guotao after the Long March in front of Communist headquarters in the northwest. Zhang was an important figure in the early history of the Communist movement, like Mao attending the first party congress in 1921. He challenged Mao's leadership of the CCP in the course of the Long March and eventually broke with the party. Zhang fled Yan'an in April 1938 and went over to the GMD.

37. Jiang Jieshi (Chiang Kaishek) with two of the most colorful and powerful reformist warlords: the "Christian General" Feng Yuxiang (left) and the "Model Governor"
of Shanxi, Yan Xishan (right). This photograph was taken in 1927–28 after the
Northern Expedition. Unable to accept Jiang's authority, Feng and Yan joined forces
in a bloody war against him in 1929–30. Feng's warlord career ended with Jiang's
victory, but Yan, after a brief retirement, returned to power in Shanxi and remained
there until 1949.

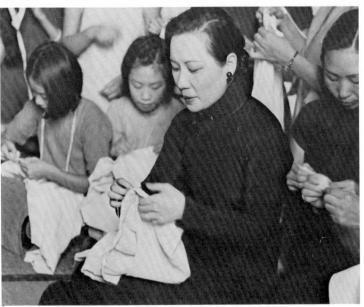

38. *Opposite:* China at war. *Top:* Jiang Jieshi (right) going over war plans with his top generals in Hankou (Wuhan), which became the temporary capital of the Nationalist government after Nanjing's fall to the Japanese in December 1937. *Bottom:* Song Meiling (Soong Meiling), the Wellesley-educated wife of Jiang Jieshi and younger sister of Sun Yatsen's widow, Qingling, helping to sew bandages in a wartime hospital. Madame Jiang's triumphal tour of the United States in 1943 diverted attention from the failing war effort of the GMD in China.

39. *Above:* Youngsters in North China in the 1940s standing watch against attack by agents of Jiang Jieshi. The wall writing above the village entrance says "Mao Zedong is the great liberator of the Chinese people."

40. *Above:* In August 1945, following Japan's surrender, U.S. Ambassador Patrick Hurley (rear right) personally escorted Mao from Yan'an to Chongqing for talks with Jiang.

41. *Opposite, top:* Surface cordiality between Jiang and Mao, here seen toasting each other at a formal banquet in Chongqing in late 1945, failed to mask the profound differences between the two. The Civil War which broke out in the aftermath of the Chongqing talks ended in a decisive Communist victory. The photograph below shows a policeman killing a Communist agent in Shanghai shortly before that city's occupation by the Red Army in 1949.

42. *Top:* Rough justice was meted out to landlords by the Communists in their land reform campaign, largely carried out in North China before 1949 and extended to newly conquered areas of the south in the early 1950s. Estimates of the number killed run to several millions. *Bottom:* Chinese Communist leaders enjoying a lighter moment at a military conference in Guangzhou in January 1960. From right to left: Deng Xiaoping, Mao, Peng Zhen, Luo Ruiqing, Zhou Enlai, He Long, Lin Biao, and Nie Rongzhen. All but Peng were veterans of the Long March. Deng, Peng, Luo, He, and Nie were purged during the Cultural Revolution; Lin died in an alleged coup attempt against Mao in 1971.

43. During the Cultural Revolution Mao became a godlike figure for many Chinese youth. *Top:* Red Guards wave their little red books containing the words of the supreme leader at a September 1966 mass rally in Beijing (one of six, all held in the presence of Mao). *Bottom:* Young members of a production brigade in Jiangsu, hoping to improve the quality of their harvesting, take a break from their work to study a Mao quotation on the importance of being conscientious.

44. *Above:* Zhou Enlai, loyal follower of Mao, long-time premier of the People's Republic, and a member of the Politburo for forty-eight years until his death in January 1976. One of Zhou's last public acts was his call (at the National People's Congress of January 1975) for the Four Modernizations, which became the rallying cry of the reformist 1980s.

45. *Opposite:* The economic reforms of the 1980s encouraged a rampant consumerism that not too many years before would have earned for its practitioners the label of "greedy capitalist-roader," if not worse. *Top:* A couple with a newly purchased washing machine and 20-inch color TV, waiting at the Beijing Railway Station to return to their home in the countryside. *Bottom:* A farmer, from outside Chengdu, driving his ducks to market in the city.

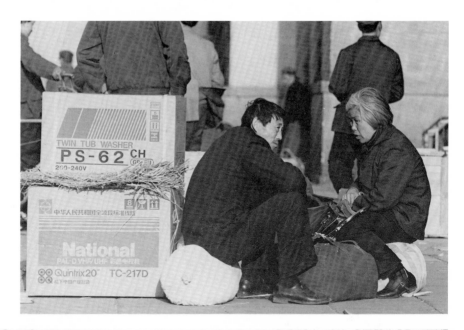

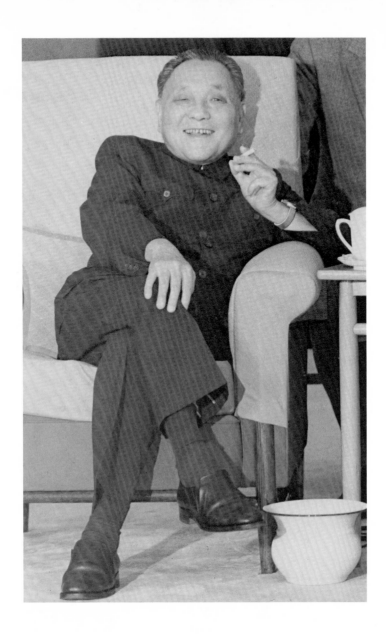

46. *Above:* Deng Xiaoping, a Communist from the earliest days of the movement and one of Zhou Enlai's closest allies, emerged as China's top leader in late 1978, after being twice purged and twice rehabilitated. Deng backed economic reform and China's opening to the outside world; he was less enthusiastic about democratization.

47. *Opposite:* The spring 1989 prodemocracy demonstrations. *Top:* Student activists at Beijing University showing their support of glasnost on the eve of Mikhail Gorbachev's visit to the Chinese capital in May 1989. TV cameras from around the world brought in to cover the visit focused their attention instead on the hunger-striking demonstrators in Tiananmen Square. *Bottom:* A Beijing University student demonstrates in support of journalists protesting the dismissal (in late April) of the editor of the *World Economic Herald* of Shanghai, China's most outspoken newspaper of the late 1980s.

48. Protest and crackdown, spring 1989. *Top:* The huge plaster Goddess of Democracy statue erected by art students in Tiananmen Square as a symbol of the political demands and cosmopolitan spirit of the demonstrators. *Bottom:* A lone unarmed man who blocked the advance of an armored convoy into the center of the capital after the June 4 crackdown.

17

The Civil War and the
Nationalists on Taiwan

Why the Nationalists Failed

When peace broke out in August 1945, the Nationalist armed forces were at least twice the size of the CCP's and moreover had the advantage of American equipment and supplies plus the assistance of the U.S. Navy in transporting troops and the U.S. Marines in the Tianjin–Beijing area. The Nationalists held all of China's major cities and most of its territory. The spirit of the Cold War was emerging in the United States as well as China, and so American backing would obviously continue. In these circumstances, for Jiang Jieshi and the Nationalists to lose the civil war was a remarkable achievement. The reasons they lost were both stupidity on the battlefield and incompetence behind the lines.

In his deployment of forces, Jiang Jieshi continued his out-of-date masterminding of the civil war. He attached great importance to holding provincial capitals once he had seized them. Instead of waging a war from the wealthier Yangzi valley in South China against the Communists in North China, Jiang asserted his unifying power by this symbol of control in capital cities. Since most of them were soon besieged and Jiang had in fact greatly overextended his resources, it is plain that he was moved by anachronistic assumptions as to how to control China. By committing his best American-trained troops directly to the Northeast without consolidating control of the North China area in between, Jiang was asking for military disaster.

The Nationalists' incompetence on the battlefield was matched by their mismanagement behind the lines. It began with the economy. Inflation was skyrocketing as note issue continued to increase. The takeover of China's coastal cities from the Japanese was characterized mainly by a corrupt seizure of assets without much attempt to put them to industrial use. Consumer goods remained inadequate. As industrial production ceased in the Free China area, it was taken up in the recovered cities sufficiently to avoid heavy unemployment. Meanwhile, Nationalists with money made a killing by using their overvalued Nationalist currency to buy up Japanese-occupation currency at its inequitable conversion rate. Starvation and profiteering continued apace in many areas of the countryside, but the return of Nationalist troops to the provinces liberated from the Japanese, if "liberation" could be applied to the situation, only increased the burden of taxation and requisition.

In addition to mishandling the economy, the Nationalist Government mishandled its citizenry and immediately alienated the major components of the Chinese people. It began this process by using the Japanese and their puppet Chinese troops to fight the Communists after the Japanese surrender. This pitting of Chinese forces against Chinese at a time when everyone talked and hoped for peace was highly unpopular. Nationalist treatment of Chinese collaborators, who had functioned under the Japanese and looked forward to liberation, was generally to regard them as enemies not deserving compensation. In a similar fashion the students and faculties in reoccupied China were castigated for their collaboration and subjected to thought reform in Sun Yatsen's Three People's Principles. This put the blame for being under the Japanese on the student class who had survived; it did nothing to mobilize their support. The government continued to tax people while letting the profiteers and self-seeking officials remain untaxed. In effect this represented the worst form of "bureaucratic capitalism," in which officials feathered their nests at the expense of the public.

Another policy failure on the part of the Nationalists was their brushing aside and suppressing the public peace movement, which was widespread and sincere and not, as the Nationalists alleged, simply a Communist conspiracy. The academics wanted a shift from warfare to civilian development and an end of Nationalist reliance on the United States to promote civil war. The government repression with violence against the students successfully alienated them just as the foolish economic policies alienated the urban middle class and industrial capitalists.

In these ways the Nationalist Government lost public support and seemed to be the instigator of the civil war even more than the Communists. It was evident that the Nationalist Government had become so militarized that it could think only of a military solution to the civil war

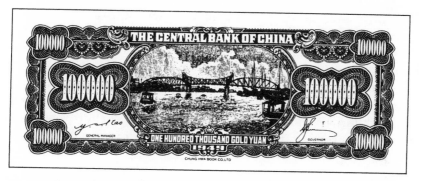

Inflation near the end of World War II. *Top:* The witty cartoonist Ye Qianyu has drawn a ricksha-puller counting the payment from his passenger. Between the knees of the latter is a suitcase for carrying the armfuls of paper money then essential for the requirements of daily life. *Bottom:* To stabilize the currency, the Nationalists in 1948 instituted the gold yuan, valued at four yuan to one American dollar. All the Chinese National Currency (CNC) previously in circulation throughout the population had to be turned over to the government at an exchange value of one gold yuan to *three million* CNC. By 1949 the Central Bank of China was issuing paper money bills of *one hundred thousand* gold yuan for everyday use.

without regard for its functions as a government to serve the public. Liberal Chinese critics of the GMD regime blamed it for allowing the CCP to grow into its position as a more popular regime. Whatever support of the GMD still persisted among the moneyed class was destroyed by the "currency reform" of 1948, when all holdings of specie and foreign currencies were forcibly converted into a new "gold yuan," in terms of which prices would be fixed and the inflation (somehow) would be stopped by decree. But prices soon rose 85,000 times in six months. The moneyed class had been defrauded once again. The GMD had thrown away whatever chance it had of governing China. Thus the Nationalist Government acted out with a vengeance the role attributed in Chinese history to the "bad last ruler" of a dynasty. The modern-trained Sino-liberal leadership in the Free China area did not go over to communism but rather gave up hope in the GMD.

The CCP's consolidation of power after 1946 occurred first of all among the farming populations in the villages of North China. Here the CCP government program shifted back to the land reform that had been generally played down since the united front of 1937. Land reform meant the dispossession and neutralization or destruction of the economic and social influence of landlords and other local magnates, with a corresponding advancement of the activists among the poor peasantry, who under CCP leadership could dominate the villages. With rich peasants thus neutralized or reduced, the Communist leadership could proceed with further reforms. The result of this massive effort was to keep the villages in support of the Communist armies all across North China.

Nationalist Attack and Communist Counterattack

Ironically, the Nationalist forces pursued a war rather similar to what the Japanese had inflicted upon China in their day. By the end of the first year of this three-year struggle the Nationalists held all the major cities and rail lines, and their forces were still far superior in firepower. However, the CCP armies had merely withdrawn, refusing to stand and fight and so avoiding casualties. Thus, in the classic guerrilla strategy, they helped the Nationalists to become overextended. They fought only when they could bring overpowering force to bear on some small GMD unit.

The Nationalists got control of both Yan'an and of the temporary CCP capital at Kalgan (Zhangjiakou). The Communist leadership were refugees, hunted in North Shaanxi by the victorious Nationalist forces. The Nationalists recaptured most of the county seats in the main theaters of North Jiangsu and the Northeast. The destruction of some of their base areas and takeover of the countryside in this fashion was unexpected by the CCP. Their North Jiangsu base area was destroyed, and the common people who had been under their protection were killed or abused by the returning Nationalist landlords.

The battle for the Northeast was commanded for the CCP by General Lin Biao, a master of mobile warfare. After his forces had retreated to northeastern Manchuria beyond the Sungari River, in 1947 Lin staged half a dozen raids across the river to surprise and cut up Nationalist forces. Soon the Nationalist field armies were isolated in their cities.

Research by Steven Levine (1987) explains how the CCP won the Northeast—they mobilized the countryside much as they had in North China. With feverish energy the North China cadres, once infiltrated into the Northeast, carried through many of the procedures of organizing local production, village indoctrination, land reform, thought reform of new cadres, and recruiting of troops and populace to unite in a patriotic war. This was a pervasive achievement, applying their skills of social engineering under forced draft. And it worked. The Chinese of the Northeast, so long frustrated by Japanese occupation, responded to the claims of nationalism and social revolution by supporting the CCP war effort.

The Nationalists as usual assisted this process. Having come from the South, they were distrustful of Manchurian leadership. The area had been under the warlord Zhang Zuolin and his son and then for fifteen years under the Japanese. The Nationalists therefore brought in their own people to head up the regime they were trying to install in the Northeast, while the Communists catered to the local leadership and mobilized it against the intruders from South China. The Nationalist distrust of the local leadership, together with their carpetbagging and exploitative takeover activities, turned sentiment against them. Nationalist arrogance, acquisitiveness, and corruption produced disaster. In effect the Nationalist Army suffered from all the difficulties that had plagued the Japanese: they could not get local intelligence from the pro-Communist populace, they were bogged down by their heavy equipment, and their advancing columns moved too slowly to avoid ambush or piecemeal flank attacks. The Nationalist forces were not trained to fraternize with the populace or to fight at night, nor could they move rapidly.

When the CCP began to counterattack in mid-1947, its forces were soon able not only to dominate Shandong but also to recover the base area between the Yellow River and the Yangzi stretching between the Beijing–Hankou Railway on the west and the Beijing–Nanjing on the east. This gave them a strategic position to menace the whole Yangzi Valley. As the strategic balance shifted, the Communists were more able than ever to capture the Nationalists' American equipment and recruit their surrendered troops into new Communist armies.

On the Nationalist side, Jiang Jieshi refused to evacuate garrisons in major cities while there was still an opportunity to do so. The result was that his best troops, after being besieged and isolated, surrendered with their equipment. By these superior tactics and strategy, the CCP forces not only overwhelmed Nationalist defenders but demoralized them as well. When they finally encircled Beijing in January 1949, the Nationalist commander decided to surrender with all his troops and later had a trusted position in the new regime.

When Mao entered Beijing, his troops were riding in American trucks led by American-made tanks. The American supply of hardware to Jiang Jieshi had been accompanied by professional military advice. But Jiang took the one and not the other. The Americans advised him not to get overextended, but he did so. They advised him to use his planes and tanks and not hoard them as symbols of firepower, but he did not succeed in doing so. They also advised him to let local commanders make tactical decisions, but the Generalissimo persisted in acting like a generalissimo and sending down orders to the division level.

The civil war was fought necessarily in the countryside, where CCP mobilization of the populace gave them both intelligence and logistic superiority. Thus in 1949 in the climactic battle of the Huai–Hai region north of Nanjing, the Nationalist armored corps, which had been held in reserve as a final arbiter of warfare, found itself encircled by tank traps dug by millions of peasants mobilized by party leaders like Deng Xiaoping.

The Americans, after all their investment in troop training and supply of equipment, were disgusted with the outcome. Fortunately, General Marshall had spent a year trying to head off the civil war as a mediator in Chongqing and Nanjing after the Japanese surrender. He knew the score, and when he returned to the United States as Secretary of State in 1947, he succeeded in preventing the Americans from going into a super-Vietnam to quell the Chinese Revolution. American supplies continued, but the marines sent into North China to protect it against the Soviets were withdrawn. The CCP eventually won the war by using surrendered Japanese arms secured through Soviet benevolence in Manchuria and American-supplied arms captured from Jiang's armies as they surrendered. By 1949 nobody could deny that the Chinese Communist Party under Mao Zedong had conquered China fair and square.

Historians' appraisals of the GMD record in China have made use of the extensive criticism put out both by Sino-liberals and by the CCP propagandists, who were making a play for Sino-liberal support and therefore quickly denounced all GMD corruption and infringements of human rights. The fact was that the GMD walked on two legs which unfortunately went in opposite directions, one modernizing and one reactionary. Thus the GMD's evils could be publicized in a partly independent press and by sometimes uncensored foreign journalists while the secret police, not having total power, often succeeded only in adding to their record of dirty work. Although totalitarianism had its activist supporters under Jiang Jieshi, they could not dominate the Chinese scene in the way that CCP totalitarianism, once in power, would be able to do. As a result, the images of the GMD and the CCP as governments of China derive from very different data bases and are not really comparable. The extent of the CCP's executions, for example, were generally unknown to outsiders at the time.

In retrospect Jiang Jieshi is now given credit for solid diplomatic achievements. In the early 1930s he delayed Japan's aggression by negotiating and giving ground while also getting Nazi Germany's aid in building up military forces and industries. In 1937–1939 he secured Soviet military aid against Japan. In the 1940s he got Xinjiang away from Soviet influence, while securing American lend-lease supplies and help in pressuring Moscow, as William Kirby reminds us, "into countenancing China as a 'great power.'" Jiang Jieshi's estimation in history will also rise along with that of the Republic of China on Taiwan.

Taiwan as a Japanese Colony

Among the provinces of China, Taiwan is unique in having been for 50 years (1895–1945) under Japanese rule. Manchuria was only 14 years (1931–1945) under Japan's indirect rule through the puppet state of Manzhouguo (Manchukuo). Moreover, Taiwan was first populated by Malayo-Polynesian aborigines (who totaled 120,000 in 1895). Chinese migrants came mainly after the late sixteenth century, and Manchu rule over the island as a prefecture of Fujian province was not established until 1685. Not until 1885 did Taiwan become a province with a sparse population of 3 million. Although China's self-strengthening movement built up the capital at Taibei, in 1895 Japan—as one of the spoils of victory—took over a subtropical area in which modernization had barely started.

Because Taiwan was Japan's first colony just when she was emerging as a modern power, talented Japanese administrators set out to make the island a model of economic growth. In contrast with European colonial powers in Southeast Asia, the Japanese had a writing system in common with the Taiwan Chinese, as well as Confucian and Buddhist teachings and a common way of life based on rice culture, civil service, and autocratic government. Modern Chinese nationalism, moreover, had not yet developed.

The aborigines had been forced off the broad floodplain on the western side of Taiwan into the spine of the mountains running along the less accessible east coast. Chinese settlers on the western side had developed rice culture under extended lineages dominated by local magnates, among whom rivalry and boundary disputes provoked continual feuds and disorder. Chinese administration had been weak, and the Japanese had to begin in 1895 by suppressing banditry and installing a police force mainly of Taiwanese, recruited and trained for this new work. They became a chief arm of local government—registering all the people and their possessions, supervising the mutual-responsibility system among village households, and enforcing regulations for sanitation and public health while collecting taxes and mediating disputes from day to day.

The variety of landholdings, including topsoil usage, ownership of subsoil, tenants subleasing their rights, and so on, had created an unwieldy complexity in land use and taxation. The Japanese put through a land survey that mapped the terrain, and in 1904 they bought out the noncultivating landlords with public bonds that could be invested in urban enterprises. This created a class of owner-cultivators throughout the countryside and tripled the land tax revenue.

Japan promoted elementary education in Confucianism, science, and Japanese language and fostered farmers' associations as a channel for improving agronomic technology. But they avoided creating an intelligentsia. Middle schools were not started until 1915 and a university only in 1928.

Meanwhile, railroads linked north and south in 1903, and some 6,000 miles of roads eventually knit up the countryside. Japanese-owned sugar mills exporting duty-free cane sugar to Japan became a major industry. Scientific agriculture and peaceful growth produced a skilled citizenry, some of whom agitated to participate in politics but were kept suppressed until Japan's departure in 1945. On balance, Taiwan's modernization under Japan was more substantial than in most provinces of warlord and Nationalist China. Its brick farmhouses with electric appliances were already more advanced than the norm on China's mainland.

Taiwan as the Republic of China

As in the coastal cities of the mainland, the Nationalist occupation of Taiwan after 1945 turned out to be a first-class disaster. Instead of being "liberated," the Taiwan Chinese were treated as enemy collaborators; their goods were seized and the economy despoiled by Nationalist military and politicians seeking personal loot. In February 1947, when unarmed demonstrators protested the corruption of the Nationalist occupation, the military government shot many of them down, sent for mainland reinforcements, and then for several days pursued a pogrom of murdering Taiwanese citizens. A sober estimate is that 8,000 to 10,000 were killed, including much of the potential leadership of the community. This was a triumph for China's backwardness, posited on the assumption of uninhibited autocracy as the primal law of the Chinese political order: policy opponents are disloyal and should be killed. When Jiang Jieshi took refuge on the island in 1949, he found a scene of economic and political collapse. Starting from this low point, the next 40 years saw the unfolding of a remarkable success story in the Republic of China.

Of the several factors in this success, one of the first was the Sino-liberal refugees from the mainland whom Jiang welcomed in his effort to cleanse and revitalize the Nationalist party and government. On Taiwan the Nationalists sought the socialist-minded state control of heavy industry that the National Resources Commission had been pursuing on the mainland. Of 31 Nationalist NRC engineers sent in 1942 to be trained in major American industrial firms, the great majority (21) elected to work for the new state on the mainland. Only seven went to Taiwan. The result is instructive. Of the 21 highly trained engineers on the mainland, none attained ministerial or important executive rank; all suffered political persecution. Of the seven engineers on Taiwan, three headed state-run industries and two became ministers of economic affairs, of whom one later headed all economic planning and development and the other went on to be premier.

Another effort was in education. Professors like Fu Sinian from Beijing and elsewhere helped build up Taiwan National University in Taibei; the research institutes of Academia Sinica resumed their work; and American missionaries set up a major Christian college. When university graduates went for advanced training in the United States, only a few returned at first, but the proportion returning gradually increased.

After the century of American missionary concern for the Chinese people and the traumatic "loss of China" to communism in the 1940s, support for the Republic of China against the People's Republic of China became a major issue in Cold War America. American aid and protection helped Taiwan develop. Though driven from the mainland, the Nationalist Republic of China on Taiwan held the China seat in the United Nations Security Council until 1971, and was recognized by most UN members as being "China." The Korean War (1950–1953), when North Korea invaded South Korea, had led to the U.S. Navy's being assigned to police the Taiwan Strait and prevent a PRC invasion of Taiwan. In 1954 a mutual security treaty between the United States and the Republic of China stabilized the region as part of the American policy of "containment" of the People's Republic. An American aid program continued until 1968 and military aid thereafter.

Building on the Japanese elimination of absentee landlords, the Sino–American Joint Commission on Rural Reconstruction funded by the American Congress in 1948 aided a program to eliminate tenancy altogether. By buying out the remaining landlords with government bonds, the Republic of China created a stable countryside of farmer-owners.

Industry was promoted in the 1950s by transferring to private management the projects that had been confiscated from Japan in 1945. The first aim was to produce consumer goods in light industries as a form of import substitution, but in the 1960s the aim shifted to production for export. Skilled but cheap labor could make consumer electronics. American and Japanese investments were welcomed. The Vietnam War also stimulated the economy. Rural labor flocked to the new cities, yet even so labor was in short supply. This prompted a shift to capital-intensive industries such as steel and petrochemicals, followed in the 1980s by computers, automobiles, and military hardware. By 1988 Taiwan's gross national product totaled about $95 billion, foreign exchange holdings were enormous, and per capita GNP was about $4,800, ten times that of the mainland. This had been accomplished in spite of the Republic of China's being voted out of the UN in 1971 and Washington's recognition of Beijing in 1979. America–Taiwan relations continued like Japan–Taiwan relations as an extra-diplomatic arrangement.

Taiwan's prosperity made political development hard to avoid. The GMD dictatorship claimed still to be the rightful government of all China, though temporarily confined to Taiwan province and some coastal islands of Fujian province. Jiang and his central government, having been displaced from Nanjing, ruled in Taibei superior to the government of Taiwan province at Taizhong. Taiwanese Chinese hatred for the 2 million or so occupying "mainlanders" died away only slowly. But in time Taiwan-born Chinese became a majority both in the party and in the army. Independent Taiwanese politicians were allowed to be elected mayors of major cities. Minor parties, suppressed at first, were finally allowed to compete in elections. After Jiang Jieshi died in 1975, he was succeeded as head of the party and government by his son Jiang Jingguo. Before the son died in 1988 he lifted martial law (in force for 44 years), permitted travel to the mainland, and liberalized domestic politics. His successor was a Japan- and America-trained Taiwanese. A degree of pluralism had been achieved.

Comparisons of Taiwan and the mainland are vitiated by the factor of size. Any PRC province given Taiwan's advantageous concentration of Japanese, American, and other foreign investment, high levels of hygiene, public education and skills, modern infrastructure of transportation, banking, communications, and the like could be equally successful (Guangdong is the likeliest candidate) except for one geographic fact: Taiwan province as an island was protected successively by British, Japanese, and American naval power. It was not invaded after 1947, nor was it taxed to meet the needs of other provinces. Jiang Jieshi remained in charge and stood for development, not revolution. By contrast, the mainland, as we shall see, was kept under central control at all costs, while being revolutionized by mass movements inspired by an activist and demanding ideology. The burden of governing 500 rising to 1,200 million people scattered over a subcontinent is greater than that of governing 20 to 30 million people on a not-very-big island. Those who want to compare Taiwan and the mainland should keep such facts in mind; there is rather little meaningful comparison to make because the facts are so different.

PART FOUR

The People's Republic of China

FROM THE POINT of view of the CCP as distinct from the Chinese people, the first eight years of the People's Republic—from October 1949 to late 1957—were a creative period of reconstruction, growth, and innovation. This promising beginning was followed by two periods of disaster and great disorder among the people: first the Great Leap Forward of 1958–1960, followed by years of economic recovery, 1961–1965; and second the Cultural Revolution of 1966 to Mao Zedong's death in 1976. In this sequence of phases, the first and third saw economic progress under the leadership of able CCP organizers and administrators. The second and fourth periods, however, were dominated by Mao Zedong.

We begin with the CCP consolidation of political control from 1949 to 1953 and then the economic transition to "socialist" (collectivized) agriculture and Soviet-style industrialization from 1954 to 1957. From 1958 the working populace in agriculture would be organized in a system of production that would last for twenty years, until after Mao's death in 1976. So seriously had the violent excesses of Mao Zedong's Cultural Revolution alienated major sectors of Chinese society that the decade from 1966 to 1976 was decried as "ten lost years."

In the 1970s the universities gradually reopened, and an era of consolidation and development under the slogan of the Four Modernizations (in Agriculture, Industry, Science and Technology, and Defense) would begin with Deng Xiaoping's final assumption of power at the end of 1978. The post-Mao era begins a period of economic reforms and opening to the outside world that sparked extraordinary economic growth. In the last two decades of the twentieth century, China's economy grew about 9 percent a year and China was gradually transformed from an agricultural into a modern industrial and service economy on the pattern of its Asian neighbors. The standard of living of the average Chinese quadrupled. At the same time China's move to a market economy and involvement in international trade evoked changes that also transformed its society and culture and weakened the Leninist political structure. Farmers were moving off their farms into towns and cities in search of jobs while workers in state industries were losing their jobs and the accompanying social security benefits as industries were privatized and made more efficient.

The disillusionment caused by Mao's destructive policies plus China's exposure to foreign ideas and cultures undermined the hold of Marxism-Leninism-Mao's Thought and the control of the CCP. Moreover, the move to the market decentralized political power as well as economic power to the local areas and away from the center. The party-state still could repress any threat it perceived to its power, but it was less successful in trying to control the new middle class and burgeoning pluralistic culture. In addition, the weaker center allowed the development of competitive elections in the villages and helped the National People's Congress, China's hitherto rubber-stamp legislature, develop a degree of autonomy. Yet the weakening of the center hindered its ability to collect tax revenues from the local areas and maintain the infrastructure of public education, health care, and irrigation networks, built in the 1950s, that had nurtured China's modernization.

While at the end of the twentieth century China appeared to be on its way to fulfilling the dream of China's reformers since the late nineteenth century to make China "rich and powerful" and recapture its traditional greatness, there was a question whether its leaders would be able to lead China to its destination without basic changes in its political structure.

18

Establishing Control of State and Countryside

Creating the New State, 1949–1953

Control of the people by government rulers and bureaucrats had been the usual basis for peace, order, prosperity, and power in the Chinese state. Under the Chinese Communist Party, efficient control would be by ideological indoctrination and by self-sustaining motivations of fear and hope among the people. Killing need be only enough to keep the motive of terror always in the background.

Just as the Manchus had established their kingdom in southern Manchuria and co-opted Chinese administrators before they took over China in 1644 and later, so the CCP had created a government in North China and the Northeast while in the process of winning the civil war. Under Mao as the now undisputed leader in both theory and strategy, the CCP leadership worked as a team, debating policy issues in the Politburo and adapting central directives to local conditions. Leading field commanders like Peng Dehuai, Lin Biao, Nie Rongzhen, and Chen Yi had all worked with Mao and Zhou Enlai for many years. Party builders like Liu Shaoqi and Deng Xiaoping had been part of the Yan'an organization. It was a tested and close-knit group.

First of all, the People's Liberation Army spread over South and Southwest China as newly liberated areas (see Map 24). Six military administrative regions divided up the country, and military commissions administered them in the initial period until they were abolished in 1954. The CCP generally felt that three years would be required for rehabilitation of the economy and mobilization of the people before they could begin a transformation of society.

Their first decision was to leave the local GMD officials largely in

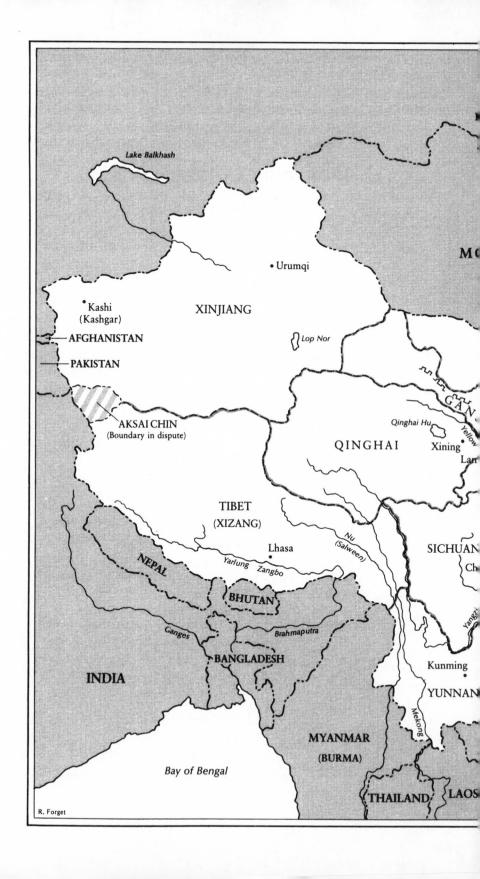

R. Forget

24. The People's Republic of China

place. These retained personnel continued to receive their salaries and perform their functions. After all, they totaled some two million persons, whereas the CCP then had at most three quarters of a million cadres to take over their jobs.

The second move was to bring inflation under control by the concerted use of several devices: (1) by taking over all the banking system, they gained control of all credit; (2) by setting up nationwide trading associations in each major commodity, they gained control of goods; and (3) by paying personnel in market-basket terms, that is, calculating salaries not in money but in basic commodities—so much grain, so much oil, so much cloth, and the like—they reassured the public. By thus making individuals' salaries independent of the inflation and thereby creating a stable basis for commerce, the flow of goods and of money was brought into balance and inflation was reduced to about 15 percent a year. This was literally the salvation of the salaried class.

Rebuilding the railways and reviving steamship lines presented no great logistic problems, but the CCP's plunge into the Korean War after only one year in power seemed at the time like a risky gamble. In October 1950 the Chinese "volunteers" surprised and routed the Americans advancing toward the Yalu River boundary with China. Altogether the PRC sent into Korea more than 2.3 million troops, including about two thirds of its field army, artillery, and airforce and all its tanks. They faced American firepower that by the time of the truce in July 1953 had given them enormous casualties. While some aid came from Moscow, the war was a serious drain of China's resources. On the other hand, it was useful in the reorganization of society. The public campaign to "resist America, aid Korea" provided a wartime sanction, as had the Japanese war and the civil war earlier, in terms of which the populace could be drastically organized.

The initial phase of public sentiment in the cities after 1949 was one of euphoria, based on growing confidence in the CCP. Here was a conquering army of country boys who were strictly self-disciplined, polite, and helpful, at the opposite pole from the looting and raping warlord troops and even the departing Nationalists. Here was a dedicated government that really cleaned things up—not only the drains and streets but also the beggars, prostitutes, and petty criminals, all of whom were rounded up for reconditioning. Here was a new China one could be proud of, one that controlled inflation, abolished foreign privileges, stamped out opium smoking and corruption generally, and brought the citizenry into a multitude of sociable activities to repair public works, spread literacy, control disease, fraternize with the menial class, and study the New Democracy and Mao Zedong Thought. All these activities opened new doors for idealistic and ambitious youth. Only later did they see that the Promised Land was based on systematic control and manipulation. Gradually the CCP organization would penetrate the society, set model roles of conduct, prescribe thought, and suppress individual deviations.

In similar fashion women were liberated from male and family domination, at least in theory. The new marriage law made wives equal to husbands and divorce possible. It sounded like a new day for women. Only later was it seen that women's emancipation had made them full-time salaried workers but mainly in poor-paying jobs. Meanwhile they were still responsible for the home, with little access to contraceptives and subject to male abuse as usual. Having few refrigerators, they still had to queue up endlessly to buy daily necessities.

Long before the CCP could try to transform the economic and social life of the Chinese masses, they faced the problem of creating a new administration that could be relied on to carry out the revolution. Since businessmen as well as GMD officials had been left in place while new CCP cadres had been infiltrated into the government administration, the most urgent task was to weed out and streamline the government apparatus itself. In 1951–52 the Three-Antis Campaign (against corruption, waste, and bureaucratism) was targeted on officials in government, in industry, and in the party. The concurrent Five-Antis Campaign attacked the capitalist class, who at first had been left in place. Under charges of bribery, tax evasion, theft of state assets, cheating in labor or materials, and stealing of state economic intelligence, nearly every employer could be brought to trial. The aim was to get control of the factories and squeeze capital out of the capitalists. Many were eliminated in an atmosphere of terror, and some were left to function as government employees.

Two mechanisms made these movements possible. The first was a new united front, which had been created in 1949 by setting up the Chinese People's Political Consultative Conference as the leading public, though advisory, organ to include both CCP members and non-CCP leaders. The Common Program, which it adopted in 1949, called for gradualism. The government when first set up had a majority of its ministries headed by non-CCP personnel. This represented a mobilization of talent that could be gradually supplanted as competent CCP personnel became available.

The other device was the mass campaign, which made use of the structure of mass organizations. Labor, youth, women, and professional bodies were all enrolled in these organizations. A nationwide administrative structure in each one could reach its membership when a campaign was put on. Thus the early campaigns to eliminate counterrevolutionaries, resist America, and aid Korea, and the Three-Antis and Five-Antis Campaigns, provided an expanding framework for reaching all Chinese who lived in cities. Campaigns not only uncovered and knocked off victims who were of doubtful use or loyalty, they also uncovered activists of ability who could be recruited into the CCP. It had 2.7 million members in 1947 and 6.1 million by 1953.

While this gradual and piecemeal, though sporadic and often terrifying, process of consolidation was going on in the cities and the modern economy, a parallel procedure was the land-reform campaign. This campaign to give all villagers their class status, pull down the landlords, and raise up the landless laborer had been largely carried through in the North China and Northeast areas under Communist control before 1949. But to spread land reform to the larger body of Chinese south of the Yangzi was a daunting task. After military pacification, work teams entered the villages and organized the peasantry to attack and destroy landlords. In this phase, rich peasants might not be attacked but temporarily catered to. But their status shaded off into landlordism above or poor peasant below. The public trials, mass accusations, and executions created an atmosphere of terror. Estimates vary, but apparently some millions of people were killed.

The next step in 1954 was the establishment of a state constitution, which superseded the Common Program and brought the New Democracy phase of China's development to an unexpectedly rapid end. The constitution was based fundamentally on the Soviet constitution established by Stalin in 1936. The net result was to strengthen the Government Administrative Council and its fifty-odd ministries. The administration became the executive arm of the party. Coordination was provided by dual membership. Thus Zhou Enlai was both premier and a Politburo member—number three in the hierarchy, after Mao and Liu. One non-Soviet feature was the establishment of the state chairmanship, held by Mao, an echo of the emperorship of old. The state cult of Mao was already beginning in order to meet the Chinese need for a single authority figure.

In contrast with the Soviet Union, the military and public security forces were kept generally under party control. The armies were under the Military Affairs Commission, headed by Mao, while public security was controlled by the party as well as a ministry. In other words, the secret police were not permitted to become a separate echelon of government or an independent kingdom as they did under Stalin, able to terrorize the rest of the administration as well as the people. Likewise, the military had no separate echelon as had happened under Jiang Jieshi, when the Nationalist Military Affairs Commission had developed ministries that rivaled those of both the party and the government.

Yet the military by its nature formed a separate establishment. Even though many soldiers were party members, the influence of the political commissars who shared command with the officer corps tended to diminish as professionalism increased with time. The army managed its own personnel system *(nomenklatura)* through a MAC department not under detailed supervision by the Party Central Committee. Nor was the MAC's political department closely supervised by the Central Committee's propaganda department. The MAC controlled the several machine-building ministries, its own communications and transport, airfields and ports, factories and research institutes, and in fact its own budget, which was not reviewed by the State Council.

Thus Chinese unity was preserved, as under Jiang Jieshi, by one man's heading the party, government, and army, all three. As Andrew Nathan points out, the only people who would challenge Mao directly would turn out to be his seconds in command of the Military Affairs Commission (Peng Dehuai and Lin Biao). In 1954, however, power remained concentrated in the Standing Committee of the Politburo of the Central Committee of the party.

On the principle of vertical rule, the ministries controlled subordinate agencies at the lower levels of government, while horizontal coordination was supposed to be worked out, if at all, at each territorial level. Meanwhile, a series of People's Congresses on the Soviet model was established at the level of the province and below. Each congress was elected from a single slate of candidates put forward by the congress immediately above. It was responsible more to those above than to those below. This echelon was headed by the National People's Congress, which met from year to year to hear reports and confirm policies. Non-CCP personnel were still prominent in it, but it had no power except as a discussion body. Control was mainly exercised by party committees at all levels of government.

Collectivizing Agriculture

After consolidating the state government, the CCP's next achievement was the collectivization of agriculture. In the Soviet Union in the early 1930s the city cadres had entered the countryside to attack and destroy the rich peasantry *(kulaks)*, who fought back by destroying livestock, fomenting opposition, and generally refusing to go along. The Soviet collectivization had been immensely destructive. In China, however, the CCP had from early on been a rural organization, close to and dependent upon the villages, and it knew how to take gradual steps toward its eventual goal.

The first stage was to get the peasantry into mutual-aid teams, and the second stage was to set up Agricultural Producers' Cooperatives, in which the farmers not only pooled their land and equipment but got a return in proportion to them. This second step kept the rich peasant community from fighting back because its position was not destroyed but at first improved. While this land reform shifted land-holding from the small 2.6 percent of landlord households and left the majority (of cultivating small holders) in place, the situation was not stabilized. Private ownership was simply strengthened by the distribution of landlord land to former tenants and landless laborers. In the early 1950s land could still be bought and sold privately, and so a better-off peasant class could continue. This era after the CCP victory would be looked back upon as a honeymoon period when growth in trade, sideline production, education, small village mutual-aid teams, and cooperatives all seemed promising. Peasants were very loath to give up their private property, however meagre.

But soon came the third stage of cooperativization, which moved from the lower level of Agricultural Producers' Cooperatives to the higher level, which was truly collective and in which all peasants worked for wages regardless of their input of property, tools, animals, and land. Mao's impetuous demand for this further move was debated and resisted by many within the CCP. But during the second stage, when land reform had distributed landlord holdings and some villagers had taken violent communal action in an atmosphere of terror, local activists had been spotted and recruited by the CCP, and their organized zeal gave the third stage of the collectivization campaign momentum. From 1954 to 1956, higher-level collectives spread faster than many expected and became nominally complete. A higher-level Agricultural Producers' Cooperative (APC) was usually part or all of a village. From 1958 to 1978 these units would be called "production teams." They were the bottom layer of a three-tiered structure: production teams forming brigades, and brigades in 1958 forming communes. The PRC had created a rural apparatus such as the Nationalist Government had never even envisaged.

Since under the PRC the state penetrated the populace to the level of the family, which now became part of an APC or (later) production team, this organization of the countryside was far more complete than anything previously attempted in Chinese history. In effect, the farmer no longer owned or rented land or disposed of his own labor or its product. He found himself labeled with a certain class status and obliged to participate in labor, in meetings, and in other collective activities on which his livelihood depended. Survival required sycophancy, lies, betrayals, renunciation of old hopes and loyalties, and other practices of the police state.

What lay behind this official success story of collectivization? After ten years' research in a village (Wugong) about 120 miles south of Beijing, a team headed by Edward Friedman, Paul G. Pickowicz, Mark Selden, and Kay Ann Johnson (1991) finally secured the trust and documentation of major local actors. They record a long, drawn-out, increasingly bitter and in the end devastating struggle to fend off a modern type of serfdom under party control.

The essential happening was the emergence of a new elite from the peasant society in the person of the activists (cadres) of the CCP organization. This new peasant leadership was self-selected, as ambitious and energetic younger people found opportunity to rise in the new power structure. Unlike the democratic egalitarianism and plural opportunities of the American experience, these new power-holders were adept in the creation of *guanxi* (networks or connections), sycophantic ingratiation with superiors, and authoritarian exploitation of inferiors in the traditional Chinese style. Intensely political in every act, these nouveaux cadres instinctively sought status, power, and perquisites that set them apart from the masses and entrenched them as a new local elite. Mouthing ideology, playing up to their patrons, squeezing public funds as the normal spoils of office, they were seldom constrained by a Confucian concern for the populace nor an educated vision of national needs or the public good.

This nominal success in collectivization was hailed as a giant step toward economic benefit in the countryside. In fact, however, it was the final penetration of the state into the farm household, the politicization of peasant life in order to control it.

Collective Agriculture in Practice

During the twenty years from 1958 to 1978 the 75 or 80 percent of the people who constituted rural China would become locked in an umbilical relationship with the new state. As Jean C. Oi (1989) says, though Communist revolutions may remake the power structure, "they do not alter the basic issue of peasant politics: how the harvest shall be divided." This issue became the constant focus of peasant–state relations. How the CCP secured the grain supply to feed the growing cities and help finance industrial expansion is a basic story of the Maoist era.

The structure of agricultural collectivization was capped in 1958 by the establishment of communes. The sheer size of the operation, far bigger than most outsiders can imagine, shows a special Chinese capacity. Once the collectivization structure was completed in 1958, the individual farmer found himself under six levels of administration—at the top was the province, followed by the prefecture, county, commune, brigade, and production team. Under China's 2,000 counties were 70,000 communes. Each commune was generally comparable in size to an old standard market community. Under these 70,000 communes were 750,000 brigades, each of which was roughly the size of a village and had about 220 households, almost 1,000 persons. Beneath the brigades were the 5 million production teams, each of about 33 households or 145 persons (see Table 6).

Over this entire structure the state now established a grain monopoly, procuring and distributing the basic food supply of the whole country. It regulated grain prices and told the farmer what and how much to produce. In historical perspective this was a high point in statecraft—a superb application of the ancient Chinese art of the state's organizing and manipulating the peasantry through the use of local officials.

Villagers obtained their own grain rations by showing their certificates of household registration. These specified where they lived. If they traveled to another region where they did not live, they could not secure rations there. Thus, once the free grain markets were closed, farmers ordinarily could not travel but were fixed upon the land, dependent for food on the production team in which they worked. The paradox was that the revolutionary state, having established its legitimacy by freeing the peasant from landlordism and other constraints, now had him boxed in as never before. The state had become the ultimate landlord, and maintaining legitimacy in that role put statecraft to the test.

Table 6. Rural administrative units and average characteristics, 1974 and 1986

Collectivized agriculture, 1974	Household agriculture, 1986

Commune *(gongshe)* (70,000)
    2,033 hectares
    15 production brigades
    3,346 households
    14,720 persons
    100 production teams
	Township *(xiang/zhen)* (71,521)
	    1,317 hectares"
	    12 villages
	    2,737 households
	    11,886 persons

Brigade *(shengchan dadui)* (750,000)
    133 hectares
    220 households
    980 persons
    7 production teams
	Village *(cun)* (847,894)
	    111 hectares[a]
	    231 households
	    1,002 persons

Team *(shengchan xiaodui)* (5 million)
    33 households
    145 persons
    20 hectares
	<Village Small Group
	    (cun xiaozu)>
	    irregularly organized

Sources: Table reprinted from Jean Oi, *State and Peasant in Contemporary China: The Political Economy of Village Government* (U of California Press, 1989), p. 5.
[a]These figures do not include the 20.63 million hectares of land under cultivation by state farmers.

It met the challenge by performing a very clever two-stage trick. First, it kept the state agricultural tax at a minimum. At first this tax was about 10 percent of the harvest, but gradually it came down to about 4.5 percent. No one could claim the peasant was heavily "taxed." The second step was to establish a level beyond which the harvest was considered a "surplus" and then ask each production team to contribute grain (mainly rice or wheat) from its "surplus" by selling it to the state at the state's low fixed price. What team could give the most to Chairman Mao? The peasant, if sufficiently simple-minded, as few were, could feel himself a benefactor, not a serf!

Specifically, the harvest was divided as follows: First the agricultural tax, the state's share, had to be paid. Second, the "three retained funds" were set aside: for next year's seed, for animal fodder, and for grain rations, the peasant's share, which was distributed to him by the collective owner of the grain, his production team. The peasant ration was partly a basic ration per person and partly work-point grain (usually paid in cash) for labor performed. (The proportion between per capita rations and work-point rations was usually 7 to 3.) Work points were an incentive to do more work. The total ration of grain allocated to each person was set at a subsistence level, but as Jean Oi and others have pointed out, the Chinese definition of subsistence amounted to considerably less grain than the international standard set by relief organizations. "Self-sufficient" rations are internationally defined as 1,700 to 1,900 calories per day while "surplus" begins at 1,900 to 2,100 calories per day. In China these figures were markedly lower, so that "levels considered below subsistence internationally were considered above the surplus level in China."

Having declared the remainder of the harvest "surplus," Mao's China was then prepared to buy a share of the surplus from its producers. The total amount to be so procured by state purchase was set by the higher levels of the six-tier bureaucracy above the production team. Each level received its allotted figure, down to the commune and brigade cadres who oversaw the final acceptance of the commitment among production teams.

In this rather grim process, the key player was the team leader, a local villager who was usually a party member and appointed for a term of years. Given authority over his team, he had to compete with other team leaders in the bargaining and politics that would commit his team to produce and sell part of its "surplus" to the state at the state's below-market price. The team leader was thus the ultimate broker in the grain procurement system, mediating between his team-member inferiors and his brigade-cadre superiors. This function was as old as China's history, a main focus of rural politics and interpersonal village relations. Quite naturally the team leader was involved in patron—client relations with others both above and below his status level. Here was where his connections (guanxi) came into play. Here was where corruption inevitably occurred and often flourished.

The war between farmers and tax gatherers no doubt antedates that between the sexes. It is at least equally subtle and sophisticated. In his two-front operations toward his team and toward his superiors, the team leader could get team cooperation in resisting the state's procurement targets. Falsifying the accounts, even keeping two sets of team books, underreporting, padding expenses, delivering grain after dark to keep it unrecorded, holding back quantities of grain by leaving the fields ungleaned, the better to feed the animals, keeping new fields hidden from the brigade inspectors—a hundred ruses to deceive brigade cadres might be combined with positive efforts to maintain cordial relations with them and even set up some psychological debts through feasts, gifts, and favors. Tales of a team's outwitting the brigade cadres, however, have the pathetic quality of prisoners' legends of successful jail-breaks. They were rare exceptions to the cadres' systematic exploitation of the farmers.

The team leader also had a panoply of methods that he used to get more work out of his team members. But a high level of incentive among the farmers was hard to maintain. After Mao's death in 1976 it would become plain that the state's strategy of putting the farmer in a box the better to squeeze grain out of him had not been very effective. After 1978 when the farmer was given greater opportunity to benefit from his own labor, he produced a great deal more. Until that new day, however, he remained under party–state control.

Beginning Industrialization

The Communist victory in 1949 had stimulated migration from the villages back to the cities. China's urban population grew rapidly from about 57 million in 1949 to almost 100 million in 1957. By 1960 it would be 131 million. Continued migration from rural areas kept city unemployment high until both rural and industrial workers could be brought under institutional control. Industrial labor, China's "proletariat," had been elusive in the Republican era because unskilled workers were recruited from the countryside by labor contractors who cooperated with factory managers in opposing labor unions. In 1949 three fifths of the labor force in manufacturing were still self-employed craftsmen. By 1957 most of them had been absorbed into urban handicraft cooperatives; meanwhile, the labor force had doubled and more than half of it worked in factories.

The Stalinist model of industrialization through emphasis first on heavy industry at the expense of agriculture was ill-suited to the Chinese case because of the great preponderance of the countryside in the economy. Nevertheless, early industrial targets were achieved and the "leap forward" mentality had already appeared in the effort to socialize industry.

State monopoly of industry was helped by the fact that the Nationalists' National Resources Commission (NRC) had already taken control of two thirds of China's industrial investment. In 1949 the NRC's top personnel and their 200,000 employees stayed on the mainland. They wanted to build a state-controlled economy along Soviet lines, and they opposed the American preference for a mixed state-and-private development. NRC engineers led the industrial drive in the People's Republic until the Great Leap Forward of 1958 began to put them out of action—a process completed by the Cultural Revolution after 1966.

Instead of moving over the space of several years to a combination of capitalist and state management of industry, the CCP followed the example of collectivization that they had already established in agriculture. Quickly the collectivization campaign took over industrial management in name, although in practice the capitalist element had to be left to function. The fact was that the CCP cadres across the land knew much more about agriculture than about industry. Their patriotism and personal ambition led them to set high goals for their industrial projects and to report them overfulfilled, without regard for sound and gradual development. Thus the activism of government and party personnel in industry became unrealistic.

After inflation began to come under control, the tax base was broadened and government revenues rose from 6.5 billion yuan in 1950 to 13.3 billion in 1951. The continuing deficit was financed about 40 percent through bond issues. The bonds were not in currency units but in commodity-equivalent units. They could be bank deposits. Where the Nationalist Government revenue had been somewhere around 5 to 7 percent of gross domestic product, the PRC tax share of economic output was estimated at 24 percent in 1952 and 30 percent by 1957.

The process of combining private capitalist industry with state industry made use of discriminatory tax and credit policies, with the result that the private sector, which amounted to more than half in 1949, was reduced to less than a fifth. Local handicrafts, however, remained largely private.

The First Five-Year Plan of the period 1953–1957 was felt to be on the whole a great success. National income grew at an average rate of 8.9 percent. Agricultural output was said to have expanded about 3.8 percent as against a population growth of about 2.4 percent. In other developing countries economic growth averaged about 2.5 percent. India was under 2 percent during the 1950s. The PRC statistics, on paper, were impressive. According to them, the proportion of primary-school children enrolled in school jumped from 25 to 50 percent. In general, it was said that urban wages rose by almost a third and peasant income about a fifth.

The PRC record in industrial investment was almost like that in the Soviet Union during the forced industrialization begun in the USSR in 1928, even though for China per capita national income in 1950 was only about one half to one quarter that of the Soviet Union in 1928. In adopting the Soviet model for rapid industrialization—favoring heavy industry at the expense of agriculture—the CCP was misled by the fact that in the USSR the ratio of population to resources was much more favorable and industrialization was far more advanced before the revolution. About half the PRC's total industrial investment was given to 156 Soviet-aided projects that were large-scale and capital-intensive. Of the 156 Soviet plants, nearly all were in heavy industry and located in inland centers like Wuhan and Baotou in the north so as to get away from dependence on Shanghai and Tianjin on the coast.

The dependence on Soviet aid came at a high price. While the PRC was investing some 25 billion yuan in the First Five-Year Plan, the Soviet contribution was not in the form of grants but only of loans, at the rate of about 60 million yuan a year, all to be repaid. While some 10,000 Soviet specialists came to China and 28,000 Chinese got training in the USSR, these Soviet credits totaled only about 4 percent of China's total investment in industry. To be sure, Soviet technology was more advanced than China's, and on the whole the Soviet relationship proved of crucial value.

All these factors led the planners of the Second Five-Year Plan in 1956 to some very sensible conclusions. They agreed that heavy industry should receive more but that progress in the countryside would be essential to long-term progress in the cities. The planners also felt that large-scale plants would be less effective than smaller-scale ones in the interior. Small local plants, though less advanced in technology, could use labor and materials on the spot, reduce transportation costs, and begin the industrialization of the countryside. Meanwhile, the planners wanted to be less dependent on Soviet aid. A final incentive arose from the fact that collectivization of agriculture had not noticeably increased production of grain and other farm products. It seemed that the growth of the enormous state bureaucracy had reached a point of impeding economic growth, and there was a strong sentiment in favor of less centralization. However, the Second Five-Year Plan discussed in 1956 was never worked out to the point of publication because it was superseded in the spring of 1958 by the Great Leap Forward.

Education and the Intellectuals

How could the revolution succeed if intellectuals were still following the Confucian model of censorial remonstrance and students were still learning classical and liberal stuff in the schools? Mao had not had much of a liberal education, but he knew what he wanted—intellectuals who would support the regime, and education that would reach and remold the peasant masses. Since this was one area where he eventually met defeat, let us pause to look back over China's educational experience.

Under the empire, men of letters had come to be almost universally examination candidates and therefore generally classicists and conservatives. Most of the great achievements of Chinese literature had come within this framework of acceptance of the social order and central authority. No monastic sanctuaries, no clash of sectarian faiths, no division between church and state were allowed, as in Europe, to spawn diversity. Scholarship remained largely in official channels, and the great protagonists of schools of thought like Zhu Xi and Wang Yangming had had official careers.

In modern times two things resulted from this tradition. First, Chinese scholars of the nineteenth century were slow to embrace foreign ideas and begin the process of reform. Second, when the old order did collapse, the spirit of nationalism was so strong that both reformers and counter-revolutionaries among the intellectuals were mainly devoted to "saving China." They were still oriented toward the state.

This orientation had its contradictions, because the role of the scholar-official had always been a dual one—not only to carry out the imperial administration but also to advise the ruler about it and in time of need to remonstrate with him as to policy. The idea that scholars knew what to do and had an obligation to offer their advice became enshrined, for example, in the doctrine of the unity of knowledge and action—that scholarly knowledge should eventuate in action and action should influence knowledge. When scholars of the New Culture Movement after 1912 urged the divorce of scholarship from politics, they were being truly revolutionary. But after 1931, under Japanese attack, even they made their contribution as official advisers and administrators. The great critic of China's decay, Lu Xun, took action to found the League of Left-Wing Writers. His encouragement of criticism and publication had been oriented toward the improvement of the social order and the better exercise of state power, not at all a withdrawal from politics.

Once the Communist Party was in power after 1949, its need for careful thought greatly increased. In theory the transition from revolutionary war to administering a new government required that militant activity shift to the pursuit of revolutionary goals through persuasive means rather than violence. In the second half of the twentieth century, building a modern state would require the intellectual resources not only of engineering and economics but also of the social sciences, history, and literature. This kind of modern learning was now highly valued in the mature societies of postindustrial civilization, whereas Mao and the CCP felt that their most urgent problem in China was to reestablish the strong central power of a unified state and remake its values and social structure according to the new principles of Marxism–Leninism–Mao Zedong Thought. For this purpose they must first establish their control over the thoughts and behavior of the Chinese people. The Communists' tragedy was that they could seldom get beyond the primary imperative of maintaining control.

In the early 1950s the professors of the educational establishment underwent thought reform by the hundreds. Each one was required to expose his former subservience to capitalist imperialism, his profound sense of guilt at having so betrayed the Chinese people, and his gratitude to Chairman Mao for now having led him to a new view. Sons of prominent fathers had to denounce them as reactionaries. Each confession, by the time it was accepted for publication, offered a sometimes ingenious rationale as to why the culprit besmirched with the evils of the old order could no longer be a model for youth to emulate. In this way the professors suffered a disastrous humiliation and neatly destroyed their public image.

Intellectuals in the early 1950s were only one target of thought reform, which grew to major proportions. In nationwide campaigns, certain evils of conduct were targeted in the abstract and then found in individuals who were then victimized in a regular procedure. Each campaign was nationally organized and promoted by activists in each locality, who were often instructed to find a certain quota of victims. Public struggle meetings and humiliation were conducted on a massive scale, with thousands of participants in the audience who were set a warning example of what not to be and do.

The next problem for educational reform was how to produce students devoted to the party line. Since intellectuals were in large part teachers, the whole educational system became an area for revolutionary remaking. Among China's three distinct eras of modern educational policy, the first—the old classical education, lasting until 1905—had trained generalists to be like Oxford and Cambridge graduates—broad-gauge administrators, not technical specialists. In the second era, until the 1940s, the Western liberal arts and sciences were used to produce a modernized elite. The common people were reached only in a preliminary way. In the third era, after 1949, the masses, Mao hoped, could finally become a major focus of educational policy. The expansion of primary school education and of simple public health measures were two of the PRC's major achievements. On the foundation of elementary schools Mao hoped to use the Soviet system to produce ideologically sound technocrats. But the actual system still faced in two directions: to give a modern education and technical skills to the masses, and to train up a broad-gauge elite able to take the place of the old Confucian literati-administrators. But given the PRC's limited resources, how could it achieve both goals simultaneously?

After 1949 the CCP began a vigorous imitation of the Soviet model of education. This model stressed the specialized training of scientific personnel in practical subjects, especially the natural sciences. Accordingly, the CCP dismantled the liberal arts programs inherited from the Christian colleges and national universities. Instead, it created 20 new polytechnic colleges and 26 new engineering institutes. Out of some 200 institutions of higher education, only 13 were designed as comprehensive universities that included both arts and sciences. This reorganization in the early years of the People's Republic had the effect of shifting the majority of students into technical subjects, rather than the liberal arts curriculum, which had previously produced graduates, especially in politics and economics, with political ideas but few skills. The main shift, in other words, had been from a program that produced broad-gauged people for top government jobs to a more practical one that produced technicians; the CCP could through its own channels find administrators. This may be seen as an attempt to cut the linkage between liberal education and public policy.

The Soviet example also led to the regularizing of teaching plans, materials, and textbooks, so that training programs in all specialties were prescribed from the center. A Soviet-type Ministry of Higher Education was set up in November 1952. A large translation program secured Chinese editions of Soviet specialized textbooks, which accounted for a third or more of books published. The teaching of English as a second language gave way to the teaching of Russian. Grading and oral-examination procedures followed Soviet practice. The field of genetics, in particular, was terrorized and stultified by imposition of the unscientific ideas of the Soviet charlatan P. Lysenko.

Inheritances from the Nationalist period and from the CCP Border Region were combined with Soviet influences into an educational system that had many unresolved problems. For example, the highly trained Western-returned students, who were now professors, had to be reconditioned to carry on under communism. Although professors had been prime candidates for thought reform in the 1950s, the fact remained that the teaching staffs on the whole had not adopted communist methods and viewpoints. They were more democratic socialists than totalitarian communists.

Despite their experience of thought reform and many conscious efforts to imbibe the new principles of the revolution, the faculty members were up against the problem of standards in their fields. The CCP aspired to create intellectuals out of workers and peasants without delay, but professors found that the best students still came from families with educational backgrounds and that workers and peasants with only a few years of schooling were simply not capable of university work. The regime could encourage the activity of people's schools *(minban)* at the village level, but it proved impossible to make those schools a pipeline into modern education at higher levels. Because popular education was guided by uneducated party members, it had little chance of achieving the levels of the university.

Most of all the Chinese system of higher education remained quite limited in quantity. A nation of 400 million people had produced annually before 1949 only some 185,000 college graduates; and as the population rapidly increased after that date, the proportion of highly educated personnel did not improve. College graduates comprised somewhere around 1 percent of the population. How could one hope to create a modern country with that proportion of trained personnel? As the 1950s wore on, the goal of a people's school in every village had to be given up. The excess number of middle school graduates competing for college entrance could not be usefully increased lest it create a frustrated class of intellectuals without jobs adequate to their self-esteem.

China still suffered, in short, from the inherited division between the muscle-worker masses and the brain-worker ruling class. Middle school graduates felt it was demeaning not to be in white-collar jobs. In 1956 only about a third of all undergraduate students in universities were of worker-peasant origin. The revolution in education had begun but was far from complete or successful. Combined with the economic inadequacies of the Soviet model of development, this set the stage for a new phase of revolutionary effort to secure the more active support of intellectuals.

Mao began with the premise that the intellectuals' work was essential to the revolution. "We can't get along without them." In early 1956 his position was that just as farmers were amalgamating with industrial workers, so that they were both becoming party members, the same process should apply to the intellectuals. As people doing labor, the farmers, industrial workers, and scholars were all members of the same proletariat. Class struggle was dying away. This was the view of Deng Xiaoping, one of Mao's most loyal followers, who was general secretary of the CCP. Evidence indicates that Mao in early 1956 felt that the intellectuals, while undoubtedly expert, were also Red in their outlook.

At this time the CCP leaders were divided between two views of the intellectuals' value to the party. Some had seen the CCP grow in influence through the united-front strategy that had sought patriotic common ground with nonparty intellectuals, with many of whom they had collaborated and some of whom had eventually joined the party. The intellectuals were relatively few, but they had been essential to the CCP's success in reaching the public through writing and in setting up technical facilities, public services, and administration. CCP leaders like Mao, Zhou, and Deng felt that nonparty intellectual talent should continue to be persuaded to collaborate and their needs should be catered to, whereas hard-line organizers like Liu Shaoqi and the mayor of Beijing, Peng Zhen, were intent on party unity and orthodoxy at all costs.

In intellectual–educational circles this issue was raised in the Hundred Flowers Campaign of 1956–57, so named for the phrase, "Let a hundred flowers bloom together, let the hundred schools of thought contend." As part of a general improvement in their working conditions (more access to foreign publications, more free time and scope for initiative), intellectuals were urged from May 1956 to voice criticisms of the party cadres who had been lording it over them. Mao estimated that among a total of at most 5 million intellectuals—that is, middle school (high school) graduates and above—not more than 3 percent were by this time hostile to Marxism. So the Hundred Flowers criticism of the party's bureaucratic style and methods would be constructive, representing a "nonantagonistic contradiction" among the people, arguable within a context of complete loyalty to the communist system.

China's intellectuals well knew that if you stick your neck out you may lose your head. For a year they said nothing. But then in May 1957 they began to criticize the CCP regime in rapidly escalating terms—its basic premises, working style, doctrines, and practices suddenly came under severe attack. Within five weeks the Hundred Flowers Campaign was closed down.

The Anti-Rightist Campaign, 1957–1958

Once the Hundred Flowers movement in mid-1957 showed the considerable disenchantment of the intellectuals with the CCP regime, Mao then shifted to the principle of class struggle against recalcitrant intellectuals by making them the targets of an Anti-Rightist Campaign from June 1957. A rectification campaign among party members was being mounted at this time because so many CCP bureaucrats had become slack and self-seeking. Some were developing ties with unreliable intellectuals, while the intellectuals were refusing to become Red in their hearts. The two wayward groups could therefore be targeted together.

Chinese emperors had occasionally opened the path for words of criticism *(yanlu),* but they often got more than they expected. In 1957 Mao and his colleagues were appalled and disillusioned by the outburst of criticism, and they quickly retaliated by making intellectuals, as well as some CCP members, targets of the Anti-Rightist Campaign; somewhere between 300,000 and 700,000 skilled people were removed from their jobs and given the devastating title of "rightist," an enemy of the people. The effect was to decapitate the People's Republic, inactivating the very persons in shortest supply. As general secretary of the CCP, Deng Xiaoping took an active part in the Anti-Rightist Campaign.

Up to 1957 two categories of administrators had been leaders in the PRC. One was the patriotic noncommunist liberals who had stayed in China or even come back from abroad to do their bit. The other was the "outside cadres," party members who had been assigned by the CCP before 1949 to make professional careers in Free China. These two categories of people possessed much of the experience, view of the world, and talent needed to set up the new regime. It is not surprising that the outside cadres asked by the CCP to work as ostensible liberal individuals in GMD China should develop a few liberal sentiments of their own. Their ideal of the revolution was to emancipate people, not control them. Such idealists would suffer only after the revolution succeeded. In the tens of thousands of Anti-Rightist cases taken from these two groups of leaders, we see the revolution beginning to devour the revolutionaries.

In the cities, much as in the countryside, by 1957 a new crowd were coming into power, arising from worker or peasant ranks, not well educated, ignorant of the outside world, and suffused with both xenophobia and anti-intellectualism. One way to try to understand this grim story is to see it as a manifestation of struggle between newcomers on the make—"fundamentalists," as Edward Friedman calls them—and the remnants of the modernized ruling elite, whom the newcomers intended to destroy or displace despite the highly skilled service the elite had rendered to the new state. This new group coming into power in the CCP were contemptuous of learning but vengeful and capable of cruel and fanatic destruction now that they had a chance, with only a minimal grasp of China's problems of modernization and how to meet them.

The rise of this new ruling class element revealed the CCP leadership's profound ignorance of modern needs. Both state-building and economic development require trained minds. Casting aside so large a part of China's intellectual elite in favor of "fundamentalists" was stupid and disastrous. In structural terms it destroyed the customary balance between power and learning. For example, in the seventeenth century the Kangxi Emperor had clearly seen how *wu* and *wen* must work together in the governing of China. One may hypothesize that Mao and his colleagues subsequently committed error after error that trained and experienced intellectuals, if used as staff members and collaborators, could have saved them from. The year 1957 was the first of China's "twenty lost years"—lost in the sense that patriotic talent was stultified and not allowed to help the nation's development. The phrase "ten lost years" later used to characterize Mao's Cultural Revolution from 1966 to 1976 was only a continuation of what began in 1957.

Once the intellectuals had been shown by the Hundred Flowers fiasco to be of dubious loyalty, Mao moved to the idea that a new generation of intellectuals should be trained up verily committed to the party because they were of good proletarian-class background. In the contradiction between merit and class status, he saw it necessary to emphasize the latter. He warned the intellectuals that they were simply teachers employed by the proletariat and laboring people to teach their children. They should not venture to have their own ideas separate from those of the party.

In atavistic terms, China's rulers had expected from their followers a degree of unquestioning loyalty of the same priority as filiality toward parents. To say that Mao had lost face by his trust in the Redness of intellectuals hardly begins to describe his motivation. From 1957 on he remained vindictively opposed to them, regarding them with disdain as mere word users and, with some fear, as people he could not control. This reaction led him to many wild statements: that the intellectuals were the most ignorant of the people, that all great intellectual achievements had been made by relatively uneducated youth, that worship of technology was a fetish. In this way he was thrown back upon the source from which he had emerged, namely, the Chinese common people as the fount of wisdom and hope of the future.

19

The Great Leap Forward
1958–1960

Background Factors

In 1958–1960 some 20 to 30 million people lost their lives through malnutrition and famine because of the policies imposed upon them by the Chinese Communist Party. Measured by the statistics showing an increase of mortality, this was one of the greatest of human disasters. Though directly due to Chairman Mao, the Great Leap Forward also expressed the ardor of many millions of rural people. What went wrong?

In the Great Leap Forward (GLF), we can see several factors at work without being able as yet to assign them their ultimate influence. We begin by noting certain residual aspects of the Chinese inheritance—first, that the state authorities had unquestioned control over the populace in the villages. The bifurcation of society into rulers and ruled, the managers and the producers, could now be used by the CCP leaders more intensively than ever before. With the persuasive methods they had developed at Yan'an, once they had set up a Stalinist command economy they could really order the peasantry around.

All central orders, however, had to be applied by local authorities. Part of China's inheritance was that their state of morale, their loyalty to the center, would be a key determinant of the results achieved. CCP activists had now in a general way succeeded to the local leadership position of the lower gentry of imperial times. They could reassert the old practices of officialism, oriented upward toward seeking their superiors' approval rather than downward to serve the people. When morale was high, local authorities might zealously compete to report how well they had carried out the center's orders. In addition to overoptimistic false reporting, they might coerce the populace to get results. When the collectivization of agriculture in 1955–56 had gone much faster than foreseen, it was later disclosed that many Agricultural Producers' Cooperatives had in fact been inaugurated too quickly and were not really able to function as claimed.

Underlying this situation was another inherited factor, the docility of the Chinese peasantry, who were remarkably inured to following the dictates of authority because it represented the peace and order on which their livelihood depended. The vision of the leadership could be imparted to the populace because in the early 1950s the CCP and the Chinese people generally still felt united in the common cause of building up China. The people trusted Chairman Mao. This at once opened the door to utopianism and illusion because the party cadres, drawn increasingly from the upper ranks of the peasantry, were fervently ready to go along, follow the leader, and bring the masses with them. Thus local obedience to the party, plus the personal cult of Mao Zedong, could create mass hysteria, during which people worked around the clock and abandoned established ways.

The impetus for the GLF came from the CCP's shocking recognition in late 1957 that the Stalinist model of industrial growth was not suited to Chinese conditions. China's population in 1950 was four times as big as that of the Soviet Union in the 1920s, while the Chinese standard of living was only half as high. In spite of universal collectivization, farm production had not noticeably increased. From 1952 to 1957 the rural population had increased by about 9 percent while the city population had grown about 30 percent, but the government grain collection had hardly improved at all, and meanwhile China had to begin repaying Soviet loans out of agricultural products. The Soviet model of taxing agriculture to build industry faced a dead end. Moreover, urbanization, having outstripped industrialization, produced urban unemployment, which was added to the underemployment in the populous countryside. The First Five-Year Plan had got results as expected, but to go ahead with more of the same, the Second Five-Year Plan, would invite disaster.

The economist's remedy for this problem, instead of the GLF, would have been to slow down the rate of investment in heavy industry, which at first had reached 48 percent, and direct some of it to light industry, which could produce consumer goods. The availability of consumer goods in turn would provide a material incentive for the peasants' productive activity. By this approach the central government ministries would also play a greater role, and expertise would take precedence over zealotry. The effect would be to carry through an agricultural revolution, which has preceded industrialization in most cases of successful economic development.

This slow approach did not suit Mao Zedong's frame of mind, and he persuaded his colleagues that the countryside could be made over and agricultural production could be increased by a massive organization of rural labor power. The incentive would be the same revolutionary determination that had brought the CCP leadership to success. Economic betterment could be promised, but the material incentives for the individual's work would be reduced, while ideological ardor and self-sacrifice would take their place. This strategy made a very big and uncertain assumption about peasant psychology.

It was just the sort of thing guerrilla warriors could put together. They had learned how to mount campaigns and mobilize the populace to attain specific social objectives, much like capturing positions in warfare—indeed, military terminology was commonly used. The whole apparatus of campaign mechanisms was now to be directed to an economic transformation, the simultaneous development of agriculture and industry. This was a strategy of dualism—or, as Mao said, "Walking on two legs." Mass mobilization would make use of rural labor never before fully employed: first, to use labor intensively to step up irrigation, flood control works and land reclamation; second, to raise agricultural productivity per unit of land by using more hands to plant, weed, and cultivate; and third, to expand small-scale industry locally with materials and equipment at hand in order to produce consumer goods and equipment for agriculture. Meanwhile, the modern industrial economy would produce exports to trade for capital goods from abroad or for investment in further plant construction.

Because economists, like other intellectuals, had suffered downgrading in the Anti-Rightist movement, the enthusiasts for the mass line envisioned the unleashing of productive energies simply through mass mobilization. For this purpose there was a general decentralization of economic management in late 1957. Many enterprises and even monetary controls were decentralized down to the local level. The central statistical bureau was broken up and localized together with functions of economic planning. This was the context in which the overambitious targets of the Great Leap were formulated in each locality, not by economists but by cadres inspired by emulation who were contemptuous of experts but intensely loyal to the cause.

The result in 1958 was a mighty paroxysm of round-the-clock labor. The face of the country was changed with new roads, factories, cities, dikes, dams, lakes, afforestation, and cultivation, for which the 650 million Chinese had been mobilized in nationwide efforts of unparalleled intensity and magnitude. The feat most publicized abroad was the campaign begun in July 1958 to produce steel from small "backyard" iron smelters without special guidance or equipment. Some 30,000 to 50,000 smelting furnaces were reported set up by the end of July, 190,000 in August, 700,000 by the end of September, and a million in October; 100 million people were engaged in this "battle for steel." Unfortunately, the product of all this effort proved largely unusable, though many people had indeed confronted the practical problems of metallurgy. Thus the Great Leap brought small-scale industry into the countryside, applying technology and mobilizing manpower as never before, but the immediate results were chaotic and uneconomic.

The state statistical bureau claimed that in 1958 production of food crops and cotton had nearly doubled in one year, and on this basis the Central Committee set ambitious targets for 1959 to increase again by 50 percent. The leadership became a captive of its own claims.

In late 1958 companies and whole regiments of farmers with their hoes and carrying-baskets marched into the fields in military formation with drums and flags to make war upon recalcitrant nature. It is true that manpower applied to dike-building and irrigation channels, together with the damming up of water and water power and the further reclamation of land, did get results. The Chinese countryside is still dotted with the lakes and water channels constructed by back-breaking labor in 1958–59. One has only to walk through a quarter-mile tunnel built of hand-hewn stone under the surface of a new field (as a means of draining off the water that might otherwise erode the land) to realize what a massive application of muscle power was achieved in the GLF. But all this did not add very much in improved skills, available resources, and capital equipment that could have increased productivity per person.

It was the logic of decentralized mobilization that led to the creation of people's communes, under which the benefits of modernization in health care, education, large-scale production, and the amenities of life were supposed to be distributed equally through their concentration of power and overall planning. Seldom has the willful pursuit of an ideal led to such devastating results.

The Disaster of 1959–1960

Where 1958 had been a good crop year, 1959 had less helpful weather. The farmers marching about to win the revolution on the land had been unable to harvest all the crops, yet the statistics sent in from the provinces and their localities added up to an enormous increase in production, more than a doubling of output. The result was that government requisitions continued high even while production was actually dropping. This led to a first-class manmade famine.

In early 1959 there was a retreat from the GLF program, but the retreat was halted when questions were raised about the GLF's results. In July 1959 the CCP leaders held a climactic meeting at Lushan, a mountain retreat in the Lower Yangzi. One of the top army commanders at Yan'an and in Korea, who was one of the ten marshals of the People's Liberation Army and currently defense minister, Peng Dehuai (who had been with Mao for thirty years, since the very beginning in Hunan), tried to report to Mao the actual deterioration of peasant life, but Mao took it as a personal attack and had Peng thrown out of power.

In retaliation the GLF proponents and Mao as their leader persisted in continuing the GLF program. After the Lushan meeting another Anti-Rightist Campaign was mounted against critics of the GLF strategy. This in turn fired up a renewal of the GLF in 1959, with an exacerbation of the disastrous consequences. The greatest crime of this period was that requisitions of grain from the villages were increased and collected just at a time when the villagers had had trouble getting their harvests in because of the diversion of labor power to public works and also because of poor weather. The net result was to leave the populace in some areas with only half or even one fifth of their usual subsistence grain supply.

The zealotry of the rural GLF managers continued to oppose the technical economic views of the urban central ministries and administrators. This prolongation of the GLF led to another fall in production both in heavy industry and in light-industry consumer goods. The famine of the 1870s in North China, when no rain fell for three years, had been beyond the reach of railways; corpses had dotted the roadsides. In 1959–60 China was better organized, and famine areas full of starved corpses were not seen. But malnutrition due to thin rations made millions more susceptible to disease. The higher-than-usual mortality did not become known until the statistics were worked out. Not until 1960 was it finally realized that many peasants were starving and the whole economy had been thrown into a shambles. China had slid into an economic morass, and Chairman Mao had been shown to have feet of clay. He even had to admit that he knew almost nothing of economics. The GLF had played itself out as a Mao-made catastrophe.

Along with economic disaster had come an ominous political turn. Until this time the top CCP leadership in the Politburo had held discussions every few weeks or months in various parts of the country in order to thrash out their policy decisions. The merit of this system had always been that alternatives were vigorously put forward, but after a decision had been made everybody went along. Now, however, for the first time Mao had transformed the policy argument put forward by Marshal Peng into an illegitimate personal attack on himself. For the moment Mao won the day, but it was a Pyrrhic victory that opened the door to factionalism rather than honest policy discussion. Mao's headstrong denunciation of Peng destroyed the unity of the CCP leadership. Initially nearly everyone had gone along with the GLF strategy, but its failure demonstrated Mao's fallibility and destroyed the solidarity among the leaders.

One of the bones of contention between Mao and Marshal Peng lay also in the latter's desire to make the People's Liberation Army more technically competent, like the Red Army of the USSR. Mao, on the contrary, had been developing the idea of using nuclear bombs as a counterpart to guerrilla warfare, without building up the professional army on Russian lines.

By concentrating solely on Chairman Mao as the leader we would fail to convey the national mood of fervent self-sacrifice and frenetic activity that characterized the Great Leap Forward. Peasants worked around the clock to break their own work records, cadres in charge locally kept on reporting totally unrealistic production figures, and Mao's colleagues such as the economist Chen Yun and Premier Zhou Enlai found no way to stop the fever.

The extent of the disaster was hidden from outside observers by the fact that city populations continued to receive rations from the countryside, and industrial construction continued to expand. But eventually the hard facts could not be avoided. All the marching about with drums and cymbals, carrying flags, and attacking targets, plus the utopian idea of common mess halls for production units and the addition of women to the labor force outside the family farms, was leading the Chinese over a cliff. Several years of saner economic policies in the early 1960s would be necessary to get back to the levels of livelihood of 1957.

Decentralization was one of the several puzzling motifs in the GLF. Local cadres, restive under central orders, welcomed the opportunity to manage the masses in the new projects without interference from the central government. The GLF greatly enhanced the importance of the party as leader of the society. The political result was to give opportunity to the ideologically zealous organizer of mass enthusiasm, the revivalist type rather than the trained expert. The GLF strategy of using mass mobilization to achieve economic development made it difficult for the center to rein in the local activists and get back to an orderly program of central direction, such as economic management requires.

And yet, looming behind the many factors at play in the GLF was the personality and ego of Chairman Mao. He had spent all his life since the 1920s organizing by word and deed a rebellion against the established order. After 1949 he continued to target established groups within Chinese society. Eventually he would break with the Soviet Union as an establishment gone astray. The principal motif of the Maoist style of rebellion was mobilization of the masses and suppression of the intellectuals who formerly had helped to manage them. In this respect Mao was still a rebel against the Confucianism denounced in the May Fourth Movement.

Revival: Seizing Control of Industrial Labor

After the Great Leap Forward, leaders like Liu Shaoqi and Deng Xiaoping secured competent factual reports on communes, industry, science, handicrafts, finance, commerce, literature, and art as bases for practical rehabilitation programs, especially for getting control of the industrial economy. During the GLF, rural migration to the cities had pushed the urban population up to 130 million by 1960. Plant construction and orders for raw materials shot upward out of control. In 1960–1964 retrenchment led to plant closings and a 50 percent drop in employment. This was met by the systematic shipment of many millions of unemployed out of the cities to the countryside, with a net reduction of city population by 14 million. A program of complete household registration, rationing of grain and other daily necessities, and household checks established control over urban residents. Illegal migration was stopped, and urban youths were relocated to rural areas as a regular practice.

As part of this control system, status distinctions developed within city labor. The great bulk of industrial output came from large, capital-intensive state enterprises that became the workplaces *(danwei)* of a skilled and privileged labor force. By the 1980s these permanent workers in state industry would total 27 million and be, in Andrew Walder's (1986) phrase, the only "labor force to participate fully in the welfare state." They had fringe benefits such as housing and subsidized meals, wage supplements, government subsidies, lifetime pensions, and welfare and state insurance arrangements. This well-paid two fifths of the labor force working in some 85,000 enterprises produced three quarters of China's industrial output. Another two fifths of the labor force were a secondary class of workers in urban and rural collective enterprises who produced a third as much output. These smaller and more numerous urban collective enterprises employed craftsmen, women, and youths on less favorable terms than the state enterprises. A still lower category was that of "temporary workers" who performed rather menial muscle-power tasks on contract in construction and transport.

To the privileged worker in a state enterprise, his workplace distributed housing, ration coupons, subsidized food, and staple goods. It also arranged social services, medical care, recreation, and political life. Yet after receiving all these benefits, workers still had to spend more than half of their salaries on food. As a result, the state worker was fully dependent on his workplace, which could discipline him in all the ways a Confucian-minded family used to do. A worker might hope that his son would succeed to his job. Promotion in grade might be due to seniority more readily than to increase of skill. Dissidence or even criticism, on the other hand, might lead to expulsion.

In the early 1960s, in short, no labor movement existed to worry the regime, while in state enterprises the extent of the workers' dependence on their workplaces kept them usually well under control. The essential labor force in heavy industry and other state enterprises in this way was brought into subservience to the state and party as a counterpart to the peasantry's subservience in agriculture.

Meanwhile, economic planners like Chen Yun called for a revival of motivation in agriculture by permitting cultivation of private plots again and selling in local markets, generally fostering the ideal of "individual responsibility." This appeal to material concerns roused Mao to call instead for a renewed ideological effort through class struggle. The lines were being drawn for what became known as the "two-line struggle" between Liu, Deng, and others on the side of expert management and

Mao and his supporters on the side of a romantic, rural-based mobilization as the way to meet China's deepening problems.

Party Rectification and Education

In Mao's two-line struggle with Liu as state chairman and Deng as general secretary of the party, both sides had to agree that the party had suffered badly in its prestige among the people, that corruption had increased, and morale was low. They differed whether to conduct rectification by a new mass movement at the lower levels of the countryside or to keep it within the CCP organization. Mao first tried in 1963 to lead a rectification among the party cadres in the countryside, which he called the Socialist Education Campaign. This would have enabled Mao to create a network of temporary organs in a campaign style, and so the Socialist Education Campaign in 1963 became a battleground between the two approaches. The party organization held back, with the result that in 1964 the CCP mounted another mass campaign, called the Four Cleanups, for class struggle to rectify the village cadres. In practice, the new committee chairmen, secretaries, accountants, warehousemen, and others of the village managerial level had soon begun to lord it over the peasantry from whom they had so recently emerged. They indulged in small peculations, played favorites, did less manual labor, and in general asserted their authority by giving arbitrary orders and making a better life for themselves. The Four Cleanups Campaign therefore targeted cadres whose attitudes (not class origin) had made them exploiters.

To combat these evils the CCP used the device of sending work teams of outside cadres to rectify the conduct of local cadres. The procedure was reminiscent of the original land-reform measures against landlords, local bullies, and small-time despots. Work-team members settled in the village for some weeks, cultivated relations with the poor who had grievances, compiled charges and evidence against the local cadres, and then used endless interrogations, physical exhaustion, and forced confessions as a basis for struggle meetings. These were in the same style as struggle meetings against intellectuals and bureaucrats. They became the chief form of the peasant's participation in political life, manipulated by the CCP on a vast scale. Instead of merely watching an execution in the old style as passive observers, they now became vociferous accusers of victims targeted by the authorities.

Disillusioned by the party officials' reluctance to go along with his approach to rectification through a mass campaign, by 1965 Mao began to look outside the party to find a means for its rectification.

Meanwhile Mao's desire to liberate China's peasants and through education make them knowledgeable citizens—an ideal that Western liberal reformers could readily accept—had also been frustrated. Education had always been a major concern of the people. The GLF had faced a double problem—how to bring education to the common man through new institutions while continuing to train the necessary elite in the established system of middle schools and universities. The new effort now centered on the creation of work–study schools like the "people's schools" *(minban)* used in the Yan'an period. Thousands of middle schools, it was claimed, were established on a work–study basis, while the regular curriculum was reduced from twelve years, as in the American system, to ten years, as in the Soviet. To reach the common man it was also essential to simplify the content of education; textbooks were consequently rewritten. The bottleneck was in personnel adequately trained in special subjects. They were simply unavailable. The makeshift of hailing peasants as "scientists" and bringing them into teaching positions proved to be ineffective. There was no getting around the fact that the work–study schools were inferior to the regular schools.

This palpable fact gave the work–study schools a bad reputation as inferior channels for advancement. Peasant families realized quickly that their children could advance into the upper class only through the regular school system. Rather than have their children enter a work–study program that could lead only to the status of an educated peasant, many peasant families preferred to keep their children at home to work on the farm.

Educators in the regular system, when it was watered down to accommodate relatively untrained worker-peasant students, resorted to a special device in the effort to maintain standards and produce a trained elite. This device, which had been used at Yan'an, was the keypoint school, where the best students, teaching staff, and equipment could be concentrated. Since a national examination system was again functioning, the percentage of graduates who passed it and moved on from senior middle school into universities became the measure of a school's excellence. In the pecking order thus established, the keypoint schools were at the top and the work–study schools at the bottom. Moreover, work–study schools had the largest proportion of worker-peasant children, while the children of political activists or "revolutionary cadres" in the official structure were dominant in the middle schools. However, the winners at the top level in the keypoint schools were likely to be the children of old intellectuals, whose family tradition had given them a head start in education.

Considered as a social program, the educational reforms and innovations of the GLF period directly attacked the old split between upper class and commoner. Mao's dictum, "Never forget class struggle," put the children of intellectuals at a disadvantage. As a consequence, students with a "bad" class background were often penalized or even excluded from the system. Nevertheless, a competition was set up for entrance to college on the basis of examination grades much the same as in earlier times. The result was that by the mid-1960s China's new educational system was bifurcated into two tracks, and the upper track still led into the elite. It had not been possible to change China's class structure through education.

On the contrary, the emergence of elites left a majority out-classed and dissatisfied. When entrance to higher education was restricted in the 1960s for reasons of cost to the state and fear of oversupply of graduates, greater numbers of young people remained unemployed in the cities. In the labor force a similar restiveness arose because of higher wages and more secure jobs afforded skilled workers, while the majority of laborers were plainly expendable. Tensions were growing in major areas of Chinese society as well as within the CCP.

The Sino–Soviet Split

Looking back to 1960, we may now see clearly that the Chinese and the Russians were heading for a split-up. The fact was that American contact with China across the Pacific had been much more extensive and long-lived than the Russian influence from across Siberia and Mongolia. There had been no Russian Orthodox Christian colleges educating Chinese youth. English, not Russian, was the second language of the Chinese upper class. In contrast, the Chinese link with Russia had come through the Communist movement and the few thousands of Chinese that it sent to Moscow. This influence did not begin until the 1920s, and as the Chinese and Russian Communists got to know each other better they did not necessarily become greater friends. The CCP leadership could not forget that Stalin had supported the wrong strategy in the

1920s, and as late as 1945 he had made a treaty with Nationalist China to serve Russian national interests in Manchuria. In short, the Sino–Russian linkup was tenuous and could dissolve as soon as the CCP began to develop its own style of national communism. One solvent would be the fact that, when China again recognized the need for outside aid in economic development, the United States and its allies could supply much more than the Soviet Union.

The Chinese–Russian split developed in the late 1950s in a series of stages. For the fortieth anniversary of the USSR, Chairman Mao made his second trip to Moscow, in the winter of 1957. He said fulsome things about Soviet supremacy in international communism and even went further than the Russians would have liked in claiming prematurely that the Soviet's orbiting of the first satellite, Sputnik, had just shown that "the east wind was prevailing over the west wind" and the days of capitalistic imperialism were numbered. At this time various Sino–Soviet agreements for technical exchange, including assistance in making nuclear bombs, were worked out and China continued to have the help of some 10,000 Soviet experts in its industrial development.

The relationship began to come apart when Nikita Khrushchev became an outspoken critic of the Great Leap Forward. On his two visits to Beijing, in 1958 and 1959, he and Mao did not get along. The Russian leader thought the Chinese leader was a romantic deviationist whose judgment could not be trusted. Khrushchev was incensed at Mao's claim during the GLF that through its commune system China would reach communism sooner than the USSR. Khrushchev was also outraged that in 1958, when Mao was planning to bombard Quemoy Island, garrisoned by Nationalist troops, just outside the port of Xiamen, Mao had told him nothing about it on the grounds that it was a purely domestic matter. This rationalization overlooked the fact that the United States was allied with Taiwan, as was the People's Republic with the USSR, and so this move in a so-called civil war might trigger a superpower—and therefore nuclear—confrontation. Khrushchev was just in the Camp David phase of working out a modus vivendi with President Eisenhower. In the Taiwan Straits crisis in 1958 over possible hostilities between the PRC and the United States, the Soviets refused to back up China and then reneged on the promise to give China an atomic weapon. This falling-out reached the point in mid-1960 where Khrushchev suddenly withdrew all Soviet technicians from China, along with their blueprints. The CCP was soon sending ideological blasts against

Soviet revisionism to the Communist party of the Soviet Union and being paid back in kind. By 1963 this altercation between the two parties was being made public to the world. The falling-out was all the more bitter because as sectarians the CCP and CPSU had once shared a common faith, and now each saw the other as traducing it.

The Great Leap Forward as a Social Movement

The collectivization of agriculture in China had been made possible by years of determined and wholehearted activity on the part of the local cadres who managed the process. These many millions of people, both men and women, were political activists and managers, including both party members and candidates, ambitious to carry through the revolution and at the same time rise in the world with it. They had emerged from the rural masses by their own responsiveness to the opportunities of the revolution. In terms of social structure, they corresponded in a general way to the lower gentry of late imperial and early Republican times—who had been the followers of patrons higher up, managers of bursaries and the affairs of absentee landlords, local officials, heads of gangs and peasant associations, military men, and others in a position to tax, conscript, organize, and tyrannize over the farming population. At the end of the imperial order, this lower gentry had become petty local despots on their own, no longer tied in with the upper gentry, who were then in the cities and towns.

The whole process of land reform under the CCP had been one in which party cadres supplanted the old remnants of the lower gentry. In vitality they represented a new regime, but in structural terms they penetrated much further into village life, backed by the authority of the party. Where the lower gentry had arisen locally with some degree of spontaneity and autonomy, the CCP cadres achieved their dominance by representing higher authority.

Once they had been called into being and had found their way upward in society through the collectivization of agriculture, this new stratum of activists in the countryside needed things to do and were ready to go further. The Great Leap Forward was hard to rein in because once the activists got started reorganizing the villages, they tended to keep on going. "Liberation" in effect had produced a new class who wanted to keep on liberating.

By the late 1950s and early 1960s China was a nation of young people, uprooted from the past and avidly in competition to gain preferment. One may imagine other motives, not necessarily selfish or materialistic. The elimination of the old constraints on peasant life, the spread of literacy and organization, the doctrines of equality and opportunity for all inspired many peasant youth to join a noble cause and sacrifice for it.

In the perspective of Chinese history the GLF also appears as an updated form of the enormous public works built in earlier times. Rebuilding the Great Wall in the Ming, like the constructing of the Chengdu airfields for American B-29 bombers in World War II, was done by labor conscripted from the countryside. Typically a village headman would be ordered to provide so many bodies at the work site over a certain length of time, say ten days. The villagers would bring their food supply and erect mat sheds to sleep in. They worked as a group and after fulfilling their stint would march home again. There were many variations in such labor-service arrangements, but they all added up to tremendous feats of earth-moving in baskets balanced on shoulder-poles and of rock-cutting to provide masonry. The GLF's achievements in building dams, dikes, and irrigation channels was the latest version of an ancient practice that had, for example, erected prehistoric capitals at Anyang and Zhengzhou with walls of earth so well tamped (beaten down within a movable frame) that they are still identifiable today. To command such labor power was the ruler's prerogative. Mao's use of it was quite natural.

Even in the erroneous directions given by minor authorities, such as to cultivate the soil too deep (so salts rose to the surface) or interplant one crop with another (making harvest difficult), we can see a harking back to statecraft theorists of the imperial upper class telling farmers how to farm.

Nor was the reorganization of peasant life under brigades and communes entirely a Maoist invention. The GLF merits comparison, especially in its invasion of the rural scene, with earlier agrarian reforms, such as those of the Northern Wei, Song, and early Ming. We still have much to learn about modern China from her long history.

After some economic recovery in the early 1960s, the next phase of the revolution saw China turn inward again. To be sure, in the 1962 Sino–Indian boundary dispute, after long provocation the People's Liberation Army had scored a quick and spectacular military victory. But as the Sino–Soviet dispute became more vitriolic, Chinese efforts to organize the underdeveloped Third World countries of Africa and Asia against the USSR met frustration. Zhou Enlai's touring Africa got nowhere. Meanwhile, as the United States intervened massively in Vietnam in 1965, it promised not to invade North Vietnam on the ground and so to avoid a Korean-type Sino–American conflict. Frustrated in foreign relations, Mao could feel the times propitious for another great effort to remake the Chinese people.

20

The Cultural Revolution
1966–1976

Underpinnings

Mao's last decade—from 1966 until his death in 1976—saw a domestic political struggle that convulsed China, constantly amazed the outside world, and achieved appalling destruction. It was a fitting finale to China's twenty lost years begun in 1957 with the Anti-Rightist Campaign that dispensed with so many intellectuals. So pervasive was the cataclysm, directly involving something like 100 million people, that its full history is still far from known or written.

Americans trying to understand the Cultural Revolution have to begin by crossing the gap separating the Chinese and American political cultures. Suppose the president in Washington urged high school students all over the United States to put on armbands, accost, upbraid, and harass citizens on the streets and in their homes and finally take over city hall, local business firms, government services, and institutions. The high school students, if they tried it, would be rounded up by nightfall. In the United States the semiautonomous sectors of a civil society—the professions, business, labor, the church, the media, and so on—cannot easily be dragooned.

In looking at the Cultural Revolution (CR) in China, we are therefore obliged to imagine a society that can be run by a Great Leader and a party dictatorship simply because the citizenry are passive in politics and obedient to authority. They have no human rights because they have been taught that the assertion of human rights (such as due process of law) would be selfish and antisocial and therefore ignoble. It would also be severely punished. The problem begins on the ground in the family life of the Chinese village, where the Confucian teaching of social order through dutiful self-subordination has left its mark even today.

One starting point in understanding the CR is to recognize that Mao Zedong had now acquired some of the prerogatives of an emperor. Why he should practically destroy the party he had built up and so endanger the whole revolution is a complex question calling for several lines of analysis.

Initially Mao's aversion to city bureaucratism had expressed his faith that the countryside must be the chief beneficiary of China's revolution. His long rural experience had made him well aware of the impediments to the good life among Chinese peasants. However, the ideal of their "liberation," once Mao was in power, gave way to the obvious need to use them to build up China under CCP leadership and control.

As this effort continued, however, Mao became concerned about the seemingly inevitable buildup of the institutions of the central government and its many levels of officials and cadres who seemed to be taking the place of the local elite of imperial times. He feared a revival of the ruling-class domination of the villagers. Given the modern necessity for expert management, and the irrepressible tendency toward personal privilege and corruption among China's new ruling class, it would be hard to prove him wrong.

A more immediate cause of Mao's concern in the early 1960s was the CCP establishment's widespread and persistent denigration of his record and policies. In a state based upon the ideals of harmony and unity, leaders of factions could not attack one another directly and by name lest they seem to be spoilers and troublemakers. The ancient recourse of Chinese leaders had therefore been to use the penumbra of establishment intellectuals who formed the outer and vocal fringe of their factions. While the Sino-liberal remnants among the intellectuals had generally been purged as rightists, their places as editors, writers, journalists, and organization men of the intelligentsia had been taken by a somewhat younger generation who were inheritors of the intellectuals' tradition. Allied with political leaders, these intraparty intellectuals expressed their attitudes in editorials, essays, commentaries, plays, and other literary productions. In the early 1960s a group of gifted intellectuals representing the CCP establishment used the indirect methods of Aesopian language, allusions, and historical examples to sustain a drumfire of criticism of the errors of the Great Leap Forward and of Mao's mass-mobilization tactics in general. Some went further and questioned Mao's 1942 dictum that all literature should directly serve the revolution. The critical opinion was generated mainly in Beijing, where Peng Zhen was the top man heading the Beijing Party Committee.

Finally, Mao's fear that the popular revolution was going astray in China was increased by the spectacle of the USSR. He resented the heavy-handed ways of Nikita Khrushchev. In the USSR Mao saw "revisionism" at work, that is, a falling away from egalitarian concern for the people and their collective organization and instead the growth of a new ruling class of specially privileged, urban-centered, and technically educated people who were kept in line, like the populace in general, by the powerful secret police. Given the West's general appraisal of the Soviet party dictatorship, Mao's distrust can hardly be faulted. In any case his personal motive was to regain control of the CCP by bringing his own like-minded followers into power.

One result of Mao's attack on Marshal Peng was that he was succeeded as defense minister by Marshal Lin Biao, a brilliant tactician, who now rose to power and pushed the politicization of the army. Lin pulled together the "little red book" of quotations of Chairman Mao as part of his indoctrination program and proved ready to take Mao's side in the developing controversy. Soon he had abolished insignia among army officers and revived the political commissar system, thus downgrading the professional military that Marshal Peng had represented. A campaign was pushed to "learn from the People's Liberation Army (PLA)," as though its military politicization could be a model for the whole society. This broke with the precedent in the CCP that militarism must be kept subordinate.

The Cultural Revolution lasted nominally three years, from early 1966 to April 1969, but many point out that its type of activities really continued for a whole decade to 1976. We begin with Mao himself.

Mao's Aims and Resources

An outsider's understanding of Mao requires a feat of imagination, first to recognize the nature of his supremacy. Mao had two careers, one as rebel leader, one as an updated emperor. He had gained the power of the latter but evidently retained the self-image of the former. Because authority in China came from the top down, as was recognized even in the mass line, once the CCP had taken power its leader became sacrosanct, above all the rest of mankind, not only the object of a cult of veneration but also the acknowledged superior of everyone in the organization. So much of the CCP had been put together by Mao that it could be regarded as his creation, and if he wanted to reform it, that was his privilege. Only if we regard him as a monarch in succession to scores of emperors can we imagine why the leadership of the CCP, trained to be loyal, went along with his piecemeal assault on and destruction of them.

This unique position in people's minds made it possible for Mao, who was also entranced with himself, to regard the emergence of elites as a failure of the revolution, the cure for which must be a revival of egalitarianism, even though this could be attempted only because Mao was so unequal himself. This benevolent despotism was just the opposite of the politics familiar to the Atlantic community, where the chief power-holder is normally the chief object of criticism. In other words, Mao was in such a unique position of acknowledged power that he could do practically anything he wanted to.

But what did Mao think he was doing? Perhaps it can be summed up as an effort to make "democratic centralism" more democratic and less centralist. He saw the new bureaucracy following the ancient pattern of autocratic government from the top down. This would leave the peasant masses where they had always been, at the bottom of society, being exploited by a new elite. To combat this tendency Mao wanted to use the mass-line approach by which the party should elicit and respond to peasant concerns. This new downward-oriented style of government could be aided by decentralization of administration. Local decisions should not all depend on Beijing bureaucrats. The aim of government should be the welfare and indoctrination of the local peasant masses, not merely the old shibboleth of the self-strengthening movement, a "wealthy state and strong army."

This flatly denied one of the basic tenets of the Chinese political tradition, namely that the masses must be governed by a carefully trained and loyal elite of ministers and subordinate officials, of army officers with commanding rank, and of party organizers with special prerogatives. "Revisionism" Mao defined as an abandonment of the goals of the revolution and acceptance of the evils of special status and special accumulation of worldly goods, which could be called a restoration of capitalism.

In promoting and manipulating this social convulsion, Mao staged an instinctive attack on the establishment, even though he had helped set it in place. His rationale centered upon his analysis of class struggle, which he felt still continued under socialism. A struggle against "revisionism" in China was suggested by the example of the Soviet Union, where he felt the ideal of socialist government had been subverted by a corrupt bureaucratism.

Mao also seems to have had in mind the idea that student youth could be mobilized to attack the evils in the establishment and purge China of revisionism. It would be a form of the manipulated mass movement, which his experience told him was the engine of social change. To be sure, by arousing and giving a lead to urban young people, Mao flouted all the principles of party rectification within party ranks. In effect, he declared war on the leaders who had come with him from Yan'an. By manipulating the situation to get the Central Committee's and other directives approved as he wanted, Mao had the party leaders hog-tied by use of their own tradition of disciplined obedience to party commands. This included at certain key points his securing the support of Zhou Enlai, who was performing his usual function of trying to ameliorate the injustices and impracticalities in Mao's attempt to purge his party colleagues. In effect the CCP leadership, intensely loyal to the party, could not foresee what was going to hit them.

To be sure, as the situation got increasingly out of control and into violence, Mao made various efforts to rein it in, but seldom successfully. The Cultural Revolution, like the Hundred Flowers Campaign and the Great Leap Forward, turned out to be something he had not envisioned. Allowing for many variations, the purge rate among party officials was somewhere around 60 percent. It has been estimated that 400,000 people died as a result of maltreatment. In their eventual trial in 1977, the Gang of Four, consisting of Mao's wife Jiang Qing and three of her colleagues in the Central Cultural Revolution Group, were charged with having framed and persecuted more than 700,000 people, of whom some 35,000 were persecuted to death. Many more were physically and mentally crippled, and a great number committed suicide.

Role of the People's Liberation Army

Mao's ability to instigate the Cultural Revolution rested first on the support of the armed forces. There had been a long competition within the People's Liberation Army between military professionalism and ideological politics. Looking way back, we can note how the Red Army of the USSR had worked out the party–army relationship by putting "politics in command," that is, military professionals should be subordinate to political commissars. Gradually, however, military professionalism gained the upper hand in the USSR, along with the growth of the Soviet general staff.

A comparable progression had occurred in China. The Whampoa Military Academy under Jiang Jieshi at Guangzhou had created a party army to spearhead the Northern Expedition, but after the split in 1927 Jiang built up professional forces with no reliance on the masses' help for guerrilla warfare or "people's war." Meanwhile, the CCP in the boondocks had to fall back on the ancient Chinese peasant-bandit techniques—small-unit mobility, deception, and union with the rural populace within a given region. Even in Jiangxi, however, the control group of about a dozen CCP commanders showed a firm belief in professionalism. Several had studied warfare in Moscow, and the rest had absorbed Soviet ideas. The main holdout against them all was Mao Zedong, who believed fervently—then as always—in mobilizing the rural masses in "total war."

In sum, the CCP from the start had had a trained and sophisticated group of central commanders who were intent on the specialization, organization, and discipline of a truly professional army. They held political or military posts as required. During the CCP's rise to power some of them headed field armies, of which there were eventually five. Each of these armies had some local roots, some continuity of command, and certain shared experience, all of which might have led to regionalism and rivalries. But the central leadership (Mao, Zhou, Peng Dehuai, and others) carefully transferred personnel to avoid factionalism. The political leaders, having been commanders themselves, knew how to preserve unity.

By the 1960s, while the PLA was essentially defensive concerning foreign powers, it played a basic role within the country as a support of the political establishment. There were about 38 "main-force" troop units or "armies," which were deployed around the country in eleven military regions. These main-line forces might be contrasted with the regional forces, which were divided among 28 provincial military districts. The regional forces were less well armed and were trained only for local defense work (including, for example, the mobilization of the People's Militia and production-construction corps, who numbered in the tens of millions as part-time soldiers). They were widely dispersed in small commands over the landscape and not trained to be unified field armies. One is reminded of the Late Imperial system under the Qing, in which the Lüying or "Army of the Green Standard" served as a constabulary dispersed in small units to maintain local order while the bannermen formed the striking forces.

Just as military control resided in the emperor, so in the People's Republic the commander-in-chief was the chairman of the CCP, who usually had a concurrent appointment as chairman of the Military Affairs Commission. Under the MAC were three basic command structures to control the military, to command the CCP political apparatus within the military, and to handle administrative and logistic functions. Another echo of the imperial system was the arrangement for troops to grow their own crops and have their own small-scale local industries in order to make them, to some degree, self-supporting, similar to the ancient *tuntian* system of semi-self-sufficient frontier outposts.

Because the party penetrated the army at all levels, many of the military being party members, the regional armies of the PLA in provincial commands took their orders from the local party secretaries and other party authorities. The first party secretary of a province usually served concurrently as the first political commissar of the military district. This political–military web of control handled conscriptions from the millions of applicants each year, the PLA having become a principal channel for upward mobility from the countryside.

Thus the regional PLA interpenetrated local government and public security services and under Lin Biao became both Red and expert. This provided Mao's power base. The armies of the professional main-force troops were at first not involved.

How the Cultural Revolution Unfolded

From late 1965 to the summer of 1966, tensions rose between Mao's group and the CCP establishment. To his support from the repoliticized PLA under Lin Biao Mao added, through his wife Jiang Qing, a group of radical Shanghai intellectuals who later would form his Central Cultural Revolution Group. They formed a rather nondescript team. Lin Biao, though a very able field commander, was a thin and rather quirky, certainly uncharismatic, individual, who was always seen with his cap on (he was bald). No doubt Lin was a gifted infighter and crafty like a fox, but where Mao's being overweight simply added to his magnificence (in the Chinese style, where being thin is not prized), Lin appeared small and unimpressive. Mao's wife, Jiang Qing, though not very successful as a movie actress before she went to Yan'an and captivated the chairman, proved herself a competent politician. She wanted to take over the cultural establishment in order to make radical reforms under the guise of getting back to first principles. She got into power partly by joining Lin Biao as head of his Cultural Department for the PLA. She also teamed up with the radical intellectuals from Shanghai, which became the cultural power base for attack on Beijing.

As a final move in cementing Mao's combination of forces, Luo Ruiqing, a principal officer of the PLA who disagreed with Marshal Lin Biao, was seized late in 1965, accused, interrogated, and dismissed from all his posts in April 1966. The effect was to suppress dissidence in the army. Among the intellectuals, a comparable attack was launched on the vice-mayor of Beijing, Wu Han, for having published at Mao's suggestion a play in which an ancient emperor was rebuked for having wrongfully dismissed an official. Mao was said to be convinced that this was an attack on himself for having dismissed Marshal Peng Dehuai at Lushan in 1959. The top party official in Beijing, Peng Zhen (no relation to the marshal), naturally saw the attack on his vice-mayor as an attack on himself. A Beijing investigation cleared the man of evil intent, but Mao then engineered a Shanghai forum at which Peng Zhen was scathingly denounced, and in April 1966 he was removed from power by the central authorities. This incident showed everyone which way the wind was blowing.

In these preliminary moves Mao knocked off certain officials who were unresponsive to his programs and secured the acquiescence of the party establishment as represented by Zhou Enlai, Liu Shaoqi, and Deng Xiaoping. They were all accustomed to going along with the great man. They did not know that they were being led up a mountain and into a volcano. The Politburo now established a Central Cultural Revolution Group that would report directly to its Standing Committee. It was packed with Mao's supporters. Meanwhile, reorganization of various departments infiltrated Mao's supporters into key positions.

The attack on revisionism and on unnamed members of the party who were "taking the capitalist road" was then heightened during a subphase known as the Fifty Days, from June to August 1966. In this period radical students were mobilized to attack university authorities in wall posters, but Mao stayed in seclusion in central China, leaving his deputy and chief of state, Liu Shaoqi, the urban organizer of the CCP, in charge of Beijing. Always the party builder, Liu could hardly give precedence to mass organizations. He tried to quell the agitation by dispatching work teams to scrutinize the lower levels of the party in major institutions, both universities and factories. Something like 400 teams with about 25 persons each, which would total 10,000 in all, were dispatched to work within the party organization. This thwarted Mao's effort to work through mass organizations.

As the radical and conservative sides became more embittered, Zhou Enlai performed his usual function of trying to bring them together. As late as February 1967 Zhou presided over a meeting between the Central CR Group of radicals on the one hand and an array of conservative military and State Council leaders that included three marshals of the military and five vice premiers on the other. This meeting, later castigated by the radicals as the "February adverse current," represented a recurrent theme of opposition to the worst tendencies in the CR.

In the second phase of the Cultural Revolution, from August 1966 to January 1967, Chairman Mao was a great showman. The dutiful Liu Shaoqi, already doomed for destruction, was orchestrating the antirevisionist movement among the party faithful. In July 1966 the Chinese public was electrified to learn that Mao had come north, pausing on the way to swim across the Yangzi. Since rural Chinese generally could not swim, and few adventurers had ever tried the Yangzi, this was like the news that Queen Elizabeth II had swum the Channel. He was obviously a paragon of athleticism, capable of superhuman feats. (Photos showing his head on top of the water suggest Mao did not use a crawl, sidestroke, backstroke, or breaststroke, but swam instead in his own fashion, standing upright in—not on—the water. He was clocked at an unusually fast speed.)

At Shanghai Mao pulled together in August 1966 the so-called Eleventh Plenum, actually a rump session of the Central Committee packed with his supporters. It demoted Liu Shaoqi from number 2 to number 8 in the CCP hierarchy and promoted General Lin to number 2, which made him Mao's putative successor. The plenum also put forward Mao's general vision of the movement against revisionism, which was intended to achieve a drastic change in the mental outlook of the whole Chinese people. Spiritual regeneration, as he put it, was to take precedence over economic development. The principle of class struggle was to be applied to all intellectuals, bureaucrats, and party members in order to weed out "those in authority taking the capitalist road." As yet nobody knew exactly who these evil people were.

By these maneuvers Mao got nominal legality for stirring up a mass movement against revisionism in the party establishment. This soon took the form of the Red Guard movement.

The Red Guards

Mao's mass movement in the Cultural Revolution consisted primarily of teenage student youth, a very different kettle of fish from the peasant masses who had been activated in the agricultural collectivization of the mid-1950s or in the Great Leap Forward of 1958–1960. The Cultural Revolution at first did not greatly affect the peasantry except in communes near cities. As an essentially urban movement, the CR featured the Red Guards from mid-1966 until they were abolished in mid-1968. These inexperienced youth, trying to "learn revolution by making revolution," were immensely destructive.

The factionalism of the Red Guards, which would lead to open warfare between organized groups in the cities, came from the fact that in the educational system of the 1960s, as we have seen, two types of students vied for top standing and entrance to university from middle school. One group was composed of children from intellectual families, who had a head start in their education at home and were capable of doing high academic work. They gained merit on examinations that could not be denied. The other group was composed of children of the new ruling class of party members, officials, and cadres, whose class background was considered revolutionary and first-rate. They were a rising generation and would have the inside track for official employment. Their level of scholarship, however, was not as high as that of the children of intellectuals, even though the class status of the latter was declared to be very low. This difference in class background would help produce the animus in Red Guard factional fights.

Mao energized the radical students by putting out such slogans as "Bombard the headquarters" and "Learn revolution by making revolution." Youthful support was mobilized in six massive rallies between August 18 and November 26, 1966, at Beijing. To these rallies, which were organized by the PLA and the Cultural Revolution Group, some 10 million youths volunteering as Red Guards from all over China were transported free on the railways and housed in Beijing. They waved aloft the little red book of *Quotations from Chairman Mao* which General Lin had compiled for indoctrinating his troops. Classes were meanwhile suspended and the universities soon closed down.

Whatever may have been Mao's romantic intention, the Red Guards turned to destructive activities that became a brutal reign of terror, breaking into homes of the better-off and the intellectuals and officials, destroying books and manuscripts, humiliating, beating, and even killing the occupants, and claiming all the time to be supporting the revolutionary attack on the "Four Olds"—old ideas, old culture, old customs, old habits. These student youths, boys and girls both, age nine to eighteen, roamed through the streets wearing their red armbands, accosting and dealing their kind of moral justice to people with any touch of foreignism or intellectualism.

By late 1966 Mao's Central Cultural Revolution Group manipulating the situation escalated the depredations of the Red Guards from mere attacks on all persons alleged to have a "bourgeois" taint to a heightened phase of "dragging out" party and government officials for interrogation and punishment. They soon settled on the former chief of state Liu and the secretary-general of the party Deng as the number 1 traitors "following the capitalist road." They and many thousands of others were denounced, detained, and publicly humiliated. By mobilizing a mass attack of urban youth on the central establishment of state and party, Mao and his followers were able to achieve a chaos that they evidently hoped would be a salutary revolution. Confronted with the loosely organized Red Guards in the summer of 1966, the CCP leaders who were under attack fought back by fighting fire with fire and fielding their own Red Guards. The party establishment was strongly structured and not easy to break down, but it was a forlorn hope. Mao had the levers of power and finally emerged as clearly bent on the destruction and rebuilding of the party.

The Seizure of Power

The third phase of the Cultural Revolution began with the movement for "seizure of power" in January of 1967. Seizures were authorized from Beijing and carried out by Red Guards and others all over China's cities. Officials were ousted from their offices, their files examined and often destroyed, and their places taken by young people without previous experience in administration or leadership. Already these young people were breaking into factions, which began to fight one another.

During all this time the People's Liberation Army was kept on the sidelines and so let the destruction go forward. In January 1967, however, Mao directed the army to help the antirevisionist revolution against the conservative counterrevolutionaries. The situation had got out of Mao's control, the PLA remained the only unified force in the society, and it now increasingly had to take power in the local scene. Although thus far only the regional forces, not the main-force units, had been concerned with the CR, they were so intertwined with the CCP local organization that it proved difficult for them to join in the revolutionary committees that were expected to create new provincial governments. The regional forces of the PLA became a weak reed to lean upon. They were supposed to maintain order and protect public services through "military control committees." But, when the regional military garrisons and districts in the provinces were ordered to support the left against the right, they found it impossible to get control over the situation. Only in four provinces did the setting up of revolutionary committees proceed effectively.

One result was an attempt by the Central Cultural Revolution Group to purge the PLA of recalcitrant officers in the provinces. Even so, the Wuhan incident of July 1967 showed how ineffective the regional forces had become as a tool of the Cultural Revolution: an independent division of the Wuhan garrison command helped to kidnap two members of the Cultural Revolution Group of the Central Committee from Beijing. Beijing had to bring in main-force units to control the situation and set up the revolutionary committees.

After Mao ordered the Red Guards to take on the job of dragging out the "capitalist roaders" in the army, the situation soon became violent. China was falling into civil war, in which Red Guard factions battled one another and the regional military joined in and took sides. While the attack on the regional forces' commanders slacked off after September 1967, the spread of factionalism was contagious, and friction developed between regional and main-force units. Beijing dealt with this crisis by ordering the PLA to stop supporting either side and undergo political training. However, by 1968 factional rivalry was becoming evident even within the main-force units. If this developed further, Mao's last card would have been played and he would have lost control of the situation completely.

Under these pressures Mao, in July 1968, finally disbanded the Red Guards, who he said had failed in their mission, and ordered the PLA to carry through the formation of revolutionary committees in all the provinces. The dispersal of the Red Guards led to their being sent down in large numbers to the countryside, casting them from the heights of political importance to the depths. The activists who now took the place

of the Red Guards were called Revolutionary Rebels, and their depredations were equally cruel and fearsome. At the same time, main-force
units were moved about, while the disbandment of the mass organizations relieved the pressure on them to take one side or another. The final
result was that the revolutionary committees were dominated by military men. Most of the party first secretaries were PLA officers. Premier
Zhou was quoted as saying that the 2 million or so of the regional forces
of the PLA had suffered "hundreds of thousands" of casualties.

In the fourth phase of the CR from July 1968 to April 1969, when
Mao attempted to put a new state together, the leadership consisted of
two fifths or more of military men, two fifths of new or old party and official functionaries, with only a slight representation of mass organizations. Military dominance in 1969 was ensured by the low quality of
party and government officials brought into power, who generally could
not compare in ability with their predecessors.

The climax of the Cultural Revolution was reached at the Ninth
Party Congress in April 1969. Lin Biao gave the political report. The
new party constitution, adopted to supplant that of 1956, stressed
Mao's Thought and class struggle. Party membership was limited by
class origin. The new constitution was much briefer than the old and left
party organization obscure, but General Lin Biao as vice chairman to
Chairman Mao was stated to be "Comrade Mao Zedong's close com-
rade-in-arms and successor." Of the 1,500 delegates, two thirds appeared in military uniforms, while in the new Central Committee 45 percent were military (in 1956 it had been 19 percent). On the other hand,
the representation of the masses and mass organizations did not include
many radical student youth. Two thirds of them were from provincial
positions. The great majority were newcomers to the Central Committee, yet their average age was about sixty. The Central Committee was
not only more military but less educated and less prepared to deal with
foreign affairs.

Foreign Affairs

China's foreign relations during the Cultural Revolution suffered from
the same mindless zealotry as did its domestic politics, for the animus of
the time was not only against things old but also against things foreign.
Anti-intellectualism was accompanied by xenophobia. In 1965, when
Zhou Enlai as China's ambassador of good will went on extended tours
in Africa and Asia, the Chinese policy of extending its aid programs,

such as building the Tan-Zam Railway in Africa, became intermixed with revolutionary zeal and espionage. The Chinese attempt to set up a Conference of Third World Countries in Algiers, excluding the Soviet Union, was a fiasco. Meanwhile, the Communist Party of Indonesia staged an attempted coup and was quite thoroughly destroyed by the Indonesian government. Such failures set the stage for China to pull in its horns during the Cultural Revolution.

Nevertheless, the rampaging style of Red Guard attacks damaged the PRC's foreign relations, especially after the Red Guards took over the Foreign Ministry in June 1967. Their squads systematically destroyed records and thoroughly disrupted the continuity of foreign relations. The foreign minister Chen Yi was forced to make self-criticism several times before thousands of jeering students, with Zhou Enlai presiding. What foreign policy could be pursued had to be done through Zhou's office.

As the Red Guard spirit of making revolution on all fronts spread into foreign relations, Chinese embassies abroad became centers of revolutionary proselytism and nondiplomatic incitement of local Communists. From September 1966 to August 1967 this subjective and emotional approach to foreign contact led to the breaking off of relations with several countries, the recall of all but one of the PRC's ambassadors abroad, and a decline in foreign trade. As part of China's domestic disorder, Red Guard mobs invaded the Soviet and British embassies and in fact burned the British Embassy to the ground, as well as the Indonesian Embassy later on. Enormous denunciatory mass meetings were a poor substitute for diplomatic relations.

The Cultural Revolution wound up with a significant shift in the PRC's relations with the United States and the Soviet Union. As the American ground and air war escalated in Vietnam after 1965, both the United States and China took measures to avoid a direct confrontation. As noted earlier, the American crusaders stopped short of fighting China again. They explicitly promised that their planes would try to avoid penetrating Chinese air space. The threat of war with the Americans, who were making war so close to China's borders, was damped down, and Mao concluded he could proceed with his domestic revolution.

The PRC's relations with the Soviet Union went in the opposite direction. The split, begun in 1960 and continued in polemics and exchanges of denunciations between the two parties, steadily intensified the Soviet–Chinese hostility. Incidents began to occur along the 4,000-

mile border, and Soviet forces were built up accordingly. When the Soviet Red Army took over Czechoslovakia in August 1968, the Brezhnev doctrine was soon propounded—that where a Communist regime had been established, it could not be allowed to be subverted. To the Chinese, this sounded rather aggressive. Red Guard attacks in mid-1967 provoked a crisis in Hong Kong, but this tapered off after the PLA took power and curbed the Red Guards in 1968. Revolutionary activity through the Chinese embassies in Burma and Cambodia led to violent incidents and a breaking off of relations. Beijing's revolutionary policy led to a clash with Indian patrols on the Sikkim–Tibet border. This time the Indians were better prepared, and a week's fighting ensued with no outcome. When North Korea went over wholeheartedly to collaboration with the Soviet Union, Chinese–North Korean relations worsened.

The Cultural Revolution's truculence toward the outside world came to a head on March 2, 1969, when the Chinese sent an ambush force onto a disputed island in the Wusuli River, the main tributary of the Amur on China's northeast boundary. The Chinese in their white uniforms overwhelmed the Soviet border patrols. Soviet retaliation was vigorous, not only at that site but in the following year or two at many points along the Sino–Soviet border where incidents erupted, and the Chinese were thus put under pressure. By the end of 1969, as relations with the Soviet Union worsened, they began to improve with the United States.

In the United States the initial impression of the Cultural Revolution had reflected its propaganda. It was seen as Mao's effort to preserve egalitarian populist values and avoid bureaucratism and statism in the course of China's economic development. However, as news of the Red Guard excesses and the maltreatment of intellectuals gradually came out, the movement seemed more like a totalitarian fanaticism under dictatorial leadership. The Nixon–Kissinger policy of seeking normal relations with the PRC had to go slow, even though led by a right-wing Republican.

Decentralization and the Third Front

Though the Cultural Revolution was officially ended in April 1969, many forms of its terrorism continued. During 1970–71 the military security personnel were particularly ruthless in searching for former members of a perhaps fictitious "May 16 Group." Innocent people were tortured into confessing membership and naming others. Several thousand were executed, although it is still uncertain whether any "May 16 Group" ever really existed as charged.

In the 1970s, moreover, the CR spread its coercion into the country-side, where, for example, peasants were required to abandon all sideline occupations such as raising pigs, chickens, and ducks in order to "cut off the tail of capitalism." For many peasants this meant starvation.

Carl Riskin (in Joseph et al., 1991) has analyzed Mao's economic program as seeking a mid-course between the two poles of a market economy and Soviet-type centralization. For one thing, China's sheer size argued against central ministries trying to manage local development all over the country. Mao wanted central control but not central management. He hoped the communes could provide some of the latter. The effort was too involved for us to pursue here in detail. In the end both policy squabbles and practical difficulties produced only, as Riskin says, a "crippled hybrid."

The spectacular politics of the CR at first monopolized foreign attention, but newly published statistics now show that during seven years of the American aggression in Vietnam, from 1964 to 1971, Mao led a massive investment in military–industrial development of the remote inland provinces of China's Northwest and Southwest. Fearful of the designs of both the Soviets and the Americans, he wanted to create self-sufficient bases for defense in mountainous areas difficult of access. In view of the contemporary growth of airpower, this "Third Front" strategy was surely out of date; yet under Mao the CCP blindly poured their scarce resources into it.

At vast expense they built new rail lines through the mountains to link new machine-building and armaments factories, iron mines, steel mills, and hydro-power dams. Typically the new factories were dispersed away from population centers. Barry Naughton (in Joseph et al., 1991) finds that this highly wasteful program put half the nation's capital investment into the Third Front's ten provinces, although in 1965 they had produced only 19 percent of the nation's industrial output. Economically unsound from the start (as the economists cashiered as rightists in 1957–58 could have shown), this gargantuan CR effort was so inadequately planned, so difficult to achieve, and so basically inefficient in its operations that a considerable part of it could never be finished and had to be abandoned. In 1972 some 150 Third Front projects out of 1,600 were suspended, but because they had become vested interests, only 81 could actually be canceled.

Along with this Third Front strategic program went a widespread decentralization of industrial management. Local governments were given autonomy to set up small-scale rural industries outside of central planning. In 1965 there had been under the control of central ministries a total of 10,533 nonmilitary enterprises that produced 47 percent of state-run industrial output. By 1971 these had been reduced to 142 factories that produced only 8 percent of the output.

China's rural industrialization had begun in the Song or earlier when village households used their woman- and child-power to augment farm income by handicrafts to make such products as tea, silk, cotton textiles, bricks, baskets, and the like. In the factory age, small-scale rural industries, as Christine Wong (in Joseph et al., 1991) says, were a "central pillar of Mao's development strategy." By 1979 nearly 800,000 enterprises plus almost 90,000 small hydroelectric stations employed 24 million workers and produced 15 percent of China's industrial output. This included all the farm tools and most small and medium farm machinery, over half the chemical fertilizer, two thirds of the cement, and 45 percent of the coal.

If these achievements had all come from local funding, as propagandists alleged, they would indeed be a model. But recent statistical studies now indicate that state funding was very extensive. "Self-reliance" was a myth. Compared with large-scale plants such as those for fertilizer, the local small-scale plants were inefficient and costly. Many had been started too hastily and grown too big for local supplies. The incentive system was faulty because losses could be charged to the state while profits were retained locally. Cost-accounting procedures were also faulty—for example, new plants could be built in excess of need with funds derived from alleged production "losses." This was acceptable because no one was interested in profitability. Instead of the desired local self-reliance based on local resources and local initiative, the rural industry program "fell prey to a variety of Maoist excesses" (Wong, in Joseph et al., 1991). Too many CCP managers became irresponsible aggrandizers at the expense of the state.

By the early 1970s China thus had three sectors requiring investment—the continuing uncompleted Third Front projects, the provincial and local governments' decentralized and often inefficient small-scale projects, and a new sector of imported foreign technology including whole plants that required port expansion and infrastructure on the east coast. All this economic growth in the CR period was too much for the CCP to handle. By Mao's death in 1976, says Naughton, China's leaders, still divided between the Gang of Four and its opponents, had really

lost control over the economy. At the same time, however, China's economic and population growth had continued unabated. Heavy investment had led industrial growth to average 13.5 percent nationally between 1969 and 1976, while population grew from 725 million in 1965
to about 919 million in 1975. Meanwhile, rural productivity and living
standards had stagnated. The result was that the chief beneficiaries of industrial decentralization seem to have been the new class of CCP cadres
and managers who now constituted a new local elite, not at all what
Mao seems to have wanted.

The Succession Struggle

Under way from 1969 there had been a power struggle to secure the
party's number 2 spot, which would give the holder a presumption of
succession to Chairman Mao in due time. At the formal conclusion of
the Cultural Revolution in 1969, General Lin Biao had brought his military people into increasing prominence in both party and government,
and his own position as number 2 seemed secure.

But from 1969 to 1971, Lin's leading position began to deteriorate.
For one thing, Mao wanted to reduce the role of the military in the political system. Consequently an attack on Lin was orchestrated by Mao,
who had no further use for him, and apparently it was supervised as
usual by Zhou as premier. The attack was pursued on many fronts
through the arcane and Aesopian use of words and symbols that are a
specialty of Chinese politics. For example, when an anti-Lin man was
put in the Central Military Headquarters under Lin, he was ostenta-
tiously accompanied by Premier Zhou and two leading generals of the
old guard. Instead of Mao and Lin appearing side by side in widely dis-
seminated photographs, Lin now appeared in the background. Again, a
one-time aide of Mao, who had developed close relations with Lin, was
accused and in the usual fashion required to give self-criticism. All these
were signs and symbols by which the ultimate power-holder showed
which way the wind was blowing. In short, General Lin had been of
great use, but his usefulness had passed, while Zhou Enlai in the number
3 post continued to work closely with Mao, especially on foreign relations and the rehabilitation of the government.

A final trick of Chairman Mao was to travel around, talk to regional
military commanders, and criticize Lin. As this news was relayed to Lin
by the bamboo telegraph, he realized that his days were numbered, and
he became involved in a conspiratorial effort masterminded by his son,

who was in the central command. The alleged aim was to assassinate Mao and by a military coup take power in his place, as the only alternative to personal disaster. Lin's son made extensive preparations secretly, but someone evidently kept Mao and Zhou informed. In desperation Lin and his wife tried to get away by air, but their plane met destruction on September 13, 1971, far out in Mongolia as it evidently headed for Soviet territory.

In totalitarian fashion this top news of the day was unreported in the official press for more than a year, when a full story was finally released with documents and circumstantial evidence. Exactly what happened to Lin is still a mystery.

After the long buildup of Lin Biao's public image as the leader closest to Mao, his sudden treachery finally bankrupted the people's trust in Mao. The old man had either been a fool to trust him or was a knave now lying about him.

The Cultural Revolution in Retrospect

Statistics used in a short summary do not convey the experience of revolution—neither the heady though transient exhilaration of Red Guards in power nor the bitter suffering of their victims. A "literature of the wounded" soon began to report individuals' disasters—the scholar whose manuscript of an unpublished lifework is burned before his eyes, the husband who tries in vain to save the class status of his children by divorcing his wife, who has been labeled a rightist, the famous novelist who is simply beaten to death, the old school principal who is set to cleaning the latrines.

Since urine and feces (or, in nonliterary parlance, shit) form an essential Chinese fertilizer, it was much easier in China than it would be in the United States to give the upper class some experience of the life of the masses. For intellectuals to clean latrines was not simply a matter of a mop and detergent in a tiled lavatory, even a smelly public one. On the contrary, while cities of a rapidly developing China have both modern and early-modern plumbing, their outskirts as well as the vast countryside have retained the old gravity system. The custom, so admired by ecologists, was to collect the daily accumulation, almost as regular as the action of the tides, for mixture with other organic matter to develop it through composting to fertilize the fields. In fact, one noteworthy sight in any Chinese rural scene is the field latrine, where men and women on opposite sides of the central wall take care to deposit both liquids and solids during the day. The cleaning of latrines was therefore not simply a hygienic task to get rid of unwanted matter but a fundamental supply question, to conserve a resource. When 10 million or so Red Guards, after they got out of hand in 1968, were "sent down to the countryside," they also handled night soil, though they found black pig shit a richer product.

Yet such labor was far less devastating than the public humiliation in "struggle meetings." Targets might be required to stand on a platform, heads bowed respectfully to the masses, while acknowledging and repeating their ideological crimes. Typically they had to "airplane," stretching their arms out behind them like the wings of a jet. In the audience, tears of sympathy might be in a friend's eyes, but from his mouth would come only curses and derisive jeering, especially if the victim after an hour or two fell over from muscular collapse. In the 1920s and 1930s Lu Xun's stories had been especially bitter at the Chinese sadistic laughter over the misery of others. Now Mao's revolution organized it on a massive public scale. Some preferred suicide.

Estimates of the victims of the Cultural Revolution now hover around a million, of whom a considerable number did not survive. To Chinese, so sensitive to peer-group esteem, to be beaten and humiliated in public before a jeering crowd, including colleagues and old friends, was like having one's skin taken off. Generally the victim felt guilty, as anyone may under attack, but especially because they had felt such loyalty and had so venerated Mao and the party. When the charges against them seemed overblown, their experience became meaningless, especially when they so often saw their erstwhile torturers by a sudden shift of line become the tortured. For what cause were they suffering? The systematic cruelty of struggle meetings went along with Chinese audiences' accepting this cruelty and the dictates of higher authority, even when represented only by ignorant teenagers. The CR fed upon this public dependence on, and blind obedience to, authority. There was no idea of morality's being *under* the law.

Andrew Walder (in Joseph et al., 1991) has commented persuasively that observers tend to screen out factors of irrationality that make no sense to them and write them off as "excesses." But as evidence has piled up, the Cultural Revolution is now understood not as a pursuit of abstract ideals but as "an unprecedented wave of state-instigated persecution, torture, gang warfare, and mindless violence." Central to it all was the assumption of conspiracy—"hidden enemies and traitors" among the intellectuals and within the CCP, a theme "borrowed directly" from the Stalinism of show trials and mass liquidations.

This timely image of the CR can be further enlarged if we look back at Imperial Confucianism. In its annals, conspiracy seems to have been a principal mode of operation and a primal source of fear. The founder of the Ming dynasty, for example, extirpated his prime minister's conspiracy of 1380 by executing 40,000 people; the Qing Emperor Qianlong feared conspiracy in the 1760s, and the Qing Restoration began with a conspiracy in 1861. Sun Yatsen indeed pursued conspiracy most of his life. It has been a Chinese specialty in the absence of a "loyal opposition" based on a distinction between the state power and its policies as in the West.

Conspiracy was a continual part of Imperial Confucianism because the ruler's legitimacy was assured only when his proper conduct produced harmony between ruler and ruled. Dissent was disharmonious, and so a dissenter feigned loyalty to protect himself. Sensing this deceit, a ruler easily became suspicious if not actually paranoid. The system had little space for the open expression of opposition because policy was part of the ruler's moral conduct and so of his legitimacy. Opposition must therefore be secret. It might animate a secret society. It implicitly aimed at power. There could be no loyal opposition. In this light, for example, the pro-democracy demonstrators at Tiananmen Square on June 4, 1989, since they wanted changes, seemed to the CCP elders to be their enemies. Those who expect conspiracy can always find it.

Quite aside from Stalinist fears of conspiracy and its home-grown counterpart, Lynn T. White III (1989) pinpoints three administrative practices that contributed to the Cultural Revolution's violence: (1) the pinning of status labels on everyone, which left some families permanently disabled, having been labeled as "rightists" or "bad elements"; (2) the subordination of all people to their work units, whose bosses could control all aspects of their lives; and (3) the threatening of all people in one or another campaign, where targeted victims showed what disaster might befall anyone sooner or later. These were all cheap expedients to control people, but they inspired long-lasting suppressed resentments that surfaced in CR violence.

Many others have offered illuminating analyses of Maoist politics. My own suggestion is that Chinese political history has been left half-finished by the eminently *wen*-minded scholars of Confucian government. Both conspiracy and the violence that usually accompanies it are intrinsically *wu* in nature. The Chinese record often left them in the background, and modern historians have not got very far in working out their story. Political scientists are thus handicapped in adding to their comparative dimension the equally desirable dimension of historical study of China. This new frontier will no doubt soon be well populated.

Aftermath

In the early 1970s, although the Shanghai element headed by the Gang of Four continued to dominate the media of communication and of culture, they had no way, even though backed by Mao, to take over the administration of the government and the economy. The administrative establishment who were intent on economic development gradually coagulated under Zhou Enlai, though Mao remained number 1 in the party. When Zhou, after 1973, became ill with cancer, he moved to make Deng Xiaoping his successor as premier. Though Deng had been targeted for destruction by the Cultural Revolution, he was an experienced old-timer too well connected, especially with the military, and too able and dynamic to be cast aside as Liu Shaoqi had been. Just before the Fourth National People's Congress of January 1975 Deng was made vice chairman of the party and a member of the Standing Committee of the Politburo at the center of power. The National Congress next made him the first vice premier, number 3 in the hierarchy behind Mao and Zhou, and Deng also became chief of the army. The Congress heard Zhou Enlai put forth the call for the Four Modernizations, one of his last public acts.

After Zhou Enlai died in January 1976, the Gang of Four banned any mourning, but on the annual day for the mourning of the dead in April they could not prevent a great crowd of hundreds of thousands from gathering around the Martyrs Memorial in Tiananmen Square to express their veneration of the dead premier. This became the April Fifth (4–5) incident, historically parallel to May Fourth (5–4). Orchestrated by the opposition to the Gang of Four, it represented a pervasive disillusionment at the popular level. The demonstration was suppressed, and in the spirit of the Cultural Revolution Deng Xiaoping was for a second time removed from power.

But the Gang of Four could not suppress the great Tangshan earthquake that in July suddenly killed half a million people east of Beijing and forced its residents to move into the streets. Every peasant believed in the umbilical relationship between man and nature, and therefore between natural disasters and human calamities. After such an overwhelming portent, Mao could only die. He did so on September 9, 1976. He left the succession to his thoroughly unmemorable look-alike, Hua Guofeng, a security chief from Hunan. In October the Gang of Four were arrested and held for trial. In the complex maneuvering for power, Deng Xiaoping won out in late 1978.

Among most Chinese—those in the villages—the final effect of the Cultural Revolution was disillusionment with socialist government and a renewed reliance on the family. Consider these anomalies: Class status, once ascribed in the 1950s, had been inherited by the succeeding generation and now amounted almost to a caste system. Offspring of the 6 percent who had been classified as of the "four bad types" (landlord, rich peasant, counterrevolutionary, and bad element) lived under a permanent cloud. Meanwhile, mobility from city to countryside had continued to be cut off. Peasant life was disesteemed as inferior, uncivilized, and to be avoided. The "sending down" to the villages of some 14 million urban youth had done little to change this image. The collectivized rural economy had signally failed to produce more, and highhanded but ignorant cadres had intervened in it destructively.

In the 1960s the cult of Mao had supplanted the local gods and other figures of the old peasant religion, but by the mid-1970s the violence of the Cultural Revolution and Lin Biao's fall had tarnished Mao's image. Public health successes and the Green Revolution in agriculture (chemical fertilizer, insecticides, better crop strains, and so on) had helped to double the population. Even the great achievements of the revolution in spreading primary school literacy, road transport, and communication by press and radio had partly backfired by revealing how much farther China still had to go. Foreign imperialism was ended but so were foreign stimuli, while the old "feudal" values and corrupt practices remained still embedded in Chinese society.

Future historians may conclude that Mao's role was to try to destroy the age-old bifurcation of China between a small educated ruling stratum and the vast mass of common people. We do not yet know how far he succeeded. The economy was developing, but it was left to his successors to create a new political structure.

21

The Post-Mao Reform Era

Merle Goldman

In the post-Mao era China was transformed from an isolated, poor, rural, and politically turbulent country into a relatively open, stable, urbanizing, and modernizing nation. With an economy expanding on average by over 9 percent a year in the last two decades of the twentieth century and the early years of the twenty-first, China's was the fastest-growing economy in the world. In fact, with per capita incomes more than quadrupling since 1978, China's economy had grown faster than almost any other in history.[1] By the start of the twenty-first century, China had the second-largest economy in the world, behind only the United States in terms of purchasing power parity (PPP).[2] Official government estimates indicate that China had 250 million people living in poverty in 1978; the figure had declined to around 30 million by 2005.[3]

What had happened to cause this transformation? The Chinese Communist Party survivors of the Long March, the party elders, particularly Deng Xiaoping, who returned to power shortly after Mao's death in September 1976, introduced and shaped the reforms that made this extraordinary economic transformation possible. Equally important, they carried them out with a generally literate, healthy population, made possible by the reforms introduced during the early years of the Communist era, which provided education for the younger generation, delivered rudimentary health care, and raised the position of women.

While formally Deng was only the chairman of the Central Military Commission until November 1989, he remained China's paramount leader virtually until his death in February 1997. His authority derived from his status as a member of the original revolutionary generation and from his deep connections with all sectors of the party and the military.

Unlike Mao, who never left China until after 1949 and then only to go to the Soviet Union in the early 1950s, Deng had gone abroad in 1920 at age sixteen as a worker-student in France, where he had a job in a French automobile factory. While there he was recruited into the Communist Party in 1924 by Zhou Enlai, and subsequently spent about nine months in the Soviet Union.

It was not, however, Deng's more worldly experience that led him to reverse three decades of Maoist policies, but the persecution that he, his family, and the other surviving party elders had suffered during the Cultural Revolution that motivated him to move in new directions. Deng and his colleagues officially assumed power at the Third Plenum of the Eleventh Central Committee in December 1978. With the support of the military, they gradually pushed aside Mao's anointed successor, Hua Guofeng, a little-known security official from Hunan province. In 1980, Deng's disciple Hu Yaobang, former head of the Communist Youth League and the youngest Long March survivor, took Hua Guofeng's place as party general secretary. Zhao Ziyang, the reformist party secretary of Guangdong and then of Sichuan province, became prime minister.

Because the Cultural Revolution had decimated the Chinese Communist Party and had caused widespread chaos and destruction, Deng and his colleagues had the support of most of the party's rank and file in their efforts to abandon Maoist policies. Most party members rejected not only Mao's utopian visions of an egalitarian society and unending class struggle, but also the Stalinist model of state control of the economy, collectivization of agriculture, and the emphasis on heavy industry that China had copied from the Soviet Union during its ten-year alliance in the 1950s. By the late 1970s, as in the rest of the Communist world, this model was producing a faltering economy in China.

Although the 1978 Third Plenum marked the formal inauguration of the reform era, the reversal of Mao's policies began soon after Mao's death in 1976. The return to power of purged party leaders gradually shifted the party's emphasis from ideological to pragmatic policies. This shift was expressed in the phrase Mao had negatively attributed to Deng Xiaoping during the Cultural Revolution: "It does not matter whether the cat is white or black, so long as it catches mice." In the late 1970s and early 1980s nationwide ideological campaigns were downgraded in favor of economic development. This change was encapsulated in the slogans "Emancipate the mind," "Seek truth from facts," and "Practice is the sole criterion of truth."

Shortly after the Third Plenum, the reforms were launched that ended the economic stagnation of the late Mao years and triggered China's unprecedented economic growth. Deng believed that the Chinese Communist Party could hold on to its weakened mandate only by improving the standard of living for the majority of the population. These reforms began in the countryside, where 80 percent of the population still lived. Deng was able to win the support of most of the party elders for these rural reforms because during the Cultural Revolution they and/or members of their families had been sent to the countryside, where they experienced the harshness and marginal existence of peasant life. Contrary to party propaganda, they discovered that the peasants' economic livelihood had not improved considerably since 1949. In addition, by the late 1970s China's leaders were also becoming increasingly aware of the economic dynamism of their post-Confucian neighbors in East Asia—South Korea, Hong Kong, Singapore, Taiwan, and Japan— so as China moved away from the Stalinist model, it turned to the East Asian model of development. The Deng leadership sought to restore the party's mandate by emulating the family farms, market economies, consumer goods industries, and involvement in international trade of these countries. This East Asian approach to development also built on long-standing trends in China's own history—periodic land reform, relatively free regional markets, a lively service sector, and local government support of grass-roots enterprises.

Thus, as peasants in the poorer provinces began on their own accord after Mao's death to take their family plots out of the collectives, Deng, unlike Mao, who had stopped such developments in the wake of the Great Leap Forward, allowed this decollectivization to continue and spread to other provinces. When the harvests increased on these family plots, land reform then become official policy. Consequently, in the early 1980s the countryside was the most dynamic sector of China's economy. In contrast to Mao's rigid ideological policies, Deng's economic reforms followed the pragmatic and flexible approach, as purportedly expressed by Deng, of "feeling for the stones as one crosses the river."

Deng's program of reforms, called "socialism with Chinese characteristics," combined the move to a market economy and into the international arena with maintaining the existing Communist party-state. This program resonated with China's late nineteenth-century self-strengthening movement that sought to adopt Western technology and economic methods *(yong)* while still maintaining the traditional Confucian state and values *(ti)*. Likewise, Deng and the party elders in the late 1970s believed they could import Western science, technology, and some economic practices while still maintaining the Communist political system. But just as Western methods had undermined the Chinese state and values at the end of the nineteenth century, so did the market economy undermine the Communist party-state at the end of the twentieth.

China's absorption of Western science, technology, and economic practices as well as its expanding international trade were accompanied by an inflow of Western political ideas and values. By the late 1980s this inflow turned into a tidal wave that poured into China first through books, travel, telephone, films, radio, television, and faxes, and by the mid-1990s through e-mail, the Internet, cell phones, advertising, and popular culture from abroad. In addition, Deng's deliberate downplaying of ideology allowed for more latitude for intellectual, cultural, and individual expression than at any previous time in modern Chinese history, except possibly during the May Fourth period in the early decades of the twentieth century.

The forces unleashed by Deng's opening up and economic reforms challenged not only China's command economy but also the Communist party-state and its official values, which had already been battered by the Cultural Revolution. Although the economic growth and rising incomes generated by the reforms were meant to enhance the party's authority, in practice they weakened it. As land reform took off in the countryside and market reforms moved to the cities by the mid-1980s, the controls of the party-state waned further. The reduced role of the party derived both from the unleashed economic forces and from a conscious decision by the reformers to replace direct government involvement in economic affairs with indirect levers, such as the market and more decentralized decision making.

Deng and his allies deliberately withdrew the party's authority from many other spheres of activity as well. In contrast to the Mao years, when the party held control over virtually all aspects of daily life, now Deng and his fellow reformers, while retaining a tight rein on politics and enforcing the "one-child," policy, loosened the party's grip on personal, social, and cultural life as well as economic activities. The purpose was to repair the damage caused by the imposition of the all-encompassing politicization of everyday life during the Mao era. Even in the political arena the party's relationship to society was gradually transformed by the opening to the outside world, the birth of a nascent civil society, and the introduction of limited grass-roots political reforms, such as elections for village heads and village committees in the countryside and neighborhood committees in the cities, and a limited tenure of two five-year terms for the position of general secretary of the Chinese Communist Party.

Nevertheless, because the market reforms that sparked China's economic dynamism were not accompanied by a regulatory framework or fundamental political reforms of the Communist party-state, they gave rise to rampant corruption, growing social inequalities, regional disparities, and widespread environmental pollution. Furthermore, the influx of Western influences challenged the official ideology and values. Moreover, unlike during the May Fourth period, when foreign influences were confined to Beijing, Shanghai, and the large coastal cities, these influences seeped into the countryside and the hinterland, accelerated by the introduction of the new communications technologies in the mid-1990s.

Although the Communist party-state could and did suppress any perceived political challenges, the leadership's ability to ensure absolute obedience to its commands eroded. The official ideology of Marxism-Leninism and Mao Zedong Thought continued to be invoked, but few still believed in these ideologies and even fewer acted on them. Chinese society became diverse and its culture pluralistic. Growing numbers of Chinese turned to religion, whether evangelical Protestantism, Roman Catholicism, Daoism, or Buddhism. For the first time since 1949, various individuals and groups voiced their own views and pursued their own interests rather than echoing the dictates of the party-state. Even though the party could and did swiftly repress any political challenge to its authority, the changes in the post-Mao period had the potential for a new Chinese revolution.

In comparison to the 1949 revolution, in which it is estimated that from 1 to 2 million landlords lost their lives, the Great Leap Forward and its aftermath, in which more than 30 million peasants died from famine and malnutrition, and the Cultural Revolution, in which half a million people were killed or committed suicide and an estimated 100 million were persecuted, the post-Mao changes were carried out without large-scale violence.[4] With the glaring exceptions of the violent military crackdown on demonstrators in Tiananmen Square on June 4, 1989, in which it is estimated that anywhere from 800 to 1,300 people lost their lives and 10,000 to 30,000 participants were imprisoned,[5] and the continuing persecution of political dissidents and religious groups that tried to practice their beliefs outside party-approved auspices, the post-Mao revolution was conducted without the large-scale repression and episodic turbulence that characterized China's experience in the Mao years.

Forces Unleashed by the Economic Reforms

During the post-Mao era China's predominantly rural and relatively poor economy underwent a massive transition from a command to a market economy and from a predominantly agricultural-based to an increasingly urbanized economy. The changes were transformative, but, unlike in the former Soviet Union, where the reforms were carried out relatively quickly and all at once, China's reforms were carried out gradually and in stages. In further contrast to the experience of the former Soviet Union, particularly Russia, which initially suffered a sudden decline in production, employment, and standard of living, China's agricultural and industrial production increased and the standard of living for the majority of the population improved substantially.

China's greater economic success may be attributed in part to the fact that unlike in Russia, where the Marxist-Leninist system had been in place for almost seventy years, in China it had existed for a mere thirty. Many Chinese still remembered how to function in the pre-1949 market and service economies. Moreover, whereas Russia's economic reforms were imposed from above, several of China's most important reforms, such as land reform, began from below. Although Deng Xiaoping and his colleagues advocated change in the aftermath of the Cultural Revolution, they had no blueprint for economic reform. Consequently they responded to what was already happening at the grass roots. They began by experimenting with various reformist policies that had been briefly tried during the Mao era and were revived spontaneously after Mao's death.

Following the economic disaster of the Great Leap Forward, for example, what was called the "household responsibility system," a return to family farms, appeared in a number of localities. When this led to the dismantling of some communes and a return to market forces and material incentives, Mao brought it to a halt in September 1962. In the aftermath of the Cultural Revolution, however, there was again a return to the household responsibility system, particularly in Anhui province, which was ruled by Deng ally Wan Li, and in Sichuan province, where Zhao Ziyang was party secretary. When productivity in both these provinces increased in the early 1980s, Deng and his reform colleagues made the household responsibility system national policy for the entire country.

Without a leader of Mao's stature to oppose decollectivization, and with a leader of Deng's authority to spearhead it, the communes were dismantled relatively quickly as millions of peasants returned to family farming. This form of land reform, plus a state-mandated increase in the price of grain, provided the material incentives for an agricultural boom in the early years of the Deng era. Although the state still demanded compulsory deliveries of grain and cotton for sale and distribution, it allowed households to pursue profitable sideline activities, such as cultivation of fruits and vegetables and production of livestock and fish, to be sold in relatively free markets, and to engage in local service industries. Between 1980 and 1986, the gross output of rural society more than doubled, while the rural population declined.[6] This increasing wealth of the rural population sparked the growth of a consumer goods industry to absorb the peasants' new discretionary income and a concomitant move away from the Stalinist emphasis on military and heavy industry. With the shift to light industry, China soon began selling relatively inexpensive consumer goods abroad in a pattern similar to that of its East Asian neighbors. These economic changes made it possible for millions of peasants to become small-scale entrepreneurs, involved in services and light industry as well as farming, and provided them with the potential to improve their living standards.

To a certain degree, the subsequent development of township and village enterprises in the 1980s resembles the development of the household responsibility system. Although many of these enterprises were started during the Great Leap Forward, their growth accelerated in the 1980s, and only then did the Deng leadership accept them as national policy. The township and village enterprises began as repair and agricultural tool shops and small light industry factories, but they gradually expanded into larger enterprises, producing consumer goods for international as well as domestic markets. During the Mao period these collective units, mostly in the countryside, represented the unsubsidized part of the public economy that was not guided by the state plan. Therefore, when China began its economic reforms, because this sector was more flexible and did not have the higher labor costs and larger overhead from providing housing, health care, pensions, and education that the state industries did, it was better able to respond to market pressures. In addition, in the post-Mao era the township and village enterprises paid relatively lower taxes, were subject to fewer administrative regulations, and were able to put underutilized labor resources to more productive uses.

A Deng Xiaoping slogan, "To get rich is glorious," sparked the growth of private enterprises (getihu), which initially were family run and small-scale, involved primarily in retail and service trades. When

these private entrepreneurs sought to expand and become more technologically advanced, they usually set themselves up as collective enterprises because they were better able as "collectives" to obtain help from
local governments to secure land, buildings, market opportunities, and
access to resources and loans. Consequently, rural entrepreneurs formed
alliances with local officials to run these collectives.

At the same time that such alliances increased the incomes of nonstate entrepreneurs and workers, they also enriched local officials because ultimate control rested in their hands. As a result, they were inherently corrupt. In some respects these alliances resembled the late Qing
enterprise structure, described as "officials supervise, merchants manage" *(guandu, shangban)*. Although many of these ventures failed, for a
period the nonstate collectives were the most dynamic sector of China's
reform economy. In the 1980s the collectives were growing at a rate of
more than 20 percent per year. As Deng himself noted, this was a development that had not been anticipated.[7] But in the early twenty-first century, the growth of the collectives slackened as the number of individual
and private enterprises was growing at about 37 percent per year.[8]

In October 1984 at the Third Plenum of the Twelfth Central Committee, Deng's disciples Hu Yaobang and Zhao Ziyang officially extended the move to the market from the countryside into the urban areas. Although the planned economy continued to play a role in the major
state-owned enterprises (SOEs), market forces were to guide the urban
economy as they were guiding the rural economy. Shortly after the urban
reforms began, there was a new economic surge. In the second half of the
1980s, the urban economy pushed ahead of the rural economy in terms
of economic growth as the agricultural economy, without new reforms,
began to stagnate, even though the township and village enterprises continued to thrive throughout most of the 1980s.

Other economic reforms introduced in the mid-1980s also resembled
developments in late nineteenth-century China. The establishment of
Special Economic Zones and foreign-joint ventures along China's southeast coast, the Guangdong delta, and the Yangzi River were reminiscent
of the former treaty ports. The major difference, however, was that in the
late twentieth century it was the Chinese government and domestic entrepreneurs rather than foreigners who controlled the zones and the joint
enterprises. To attract foreign investments, the government offered special tax benefits, relaxed regulations, and presented fewer bureaucratic
obstacles than elsewhere in the country; in return, the zones were to
bring in new technologies and promote exports. At first the zones sput-

tered along, but as they continued to be promoted by Deng and his reform colleagues, they took off in the late 1980s when their East Asian
neighbors, particularly Hong Kong and Taiwan, began moving their industries to China to take advantage of lower labor costs. In addition to
the production of labor-intensive, non-durable goods, such as clothing
and shoes, by the 1990s Chinese industry had moved to more sophisticated durable goods, such as electronics, computers, machinery, and
transport.

Another difference from the treaty ports, which had been dominated
by Western nationals, was that in the 1980s almost 70 percent of the foreign investments came from overseas Chinese, especially in Hong Kong,
Taiwan, and Southeast Asia. Many of their ancestors had left China's
coastal areas centuries earlier in search of better lives. They made their
way first to Southeast Asia and then, starting in the mid-nineteenth-cen-
tury, to the Americas, where they prospered as merchants and professionals. Unlike Mao, who had rejected their offers to help China in the
1950s, Deng early on encouraged overseas Chinese in Hong Kong, Thailand, Malaysia, Indonesia, and Singapore to invest in China. By the
1990s, Taiwanese businessmen were increasingly interacting with the
mainland. The capital, entrepreneurial savvy, and management skills of
the overseas Chinese, plus their family contacts and familiarity with Chinese culture, contributed to making China's southeast coast one of the
most dynamic regions in all of Asia. Their enterprises, coupled with the
influx of Western and Japanese firms, accelerated China's move to the
market, involvement in international trade, and rapid economic modernization, thus further reducing economic control by the party-state.

As these foreign enterprises began to spread elsewhere in the country
and domestic collectives and private enterprises continued to grow, more
space was created for nonstate economic activity. The overall balance
between plan and market gradually shifted in favor of the market.[9] This
shift was briefly interrupted after the military crackdown on June 4,
1989, when the conservative party elders and Maoists who returned to
power attempted to reimpose more direct centralized control over the
economy. But after the 1991 collapse of the Soviet Union and Deng's
highly publicized tour in early 1992, called the "southern journey"
(nanxun), aimed at reinvigorating the reforms and staving off a Soviet-
style collapse, the economy began to revive. Deng visited the Special Economic Zone of Shenzhen, between Guangdong and Hong Kong, as well
as Shanghai, to highlight the need to continue the economic reforms
and opening to the outside world. Deng's rejuvenation of the reforms

further dissolved the central planning framework and phased in more unified market prices. By the late 1990s China began moving toward gradual privatization of state industry. Despite continuing discrimination in granting bank loans to private entrepreneurs, the private sector, through the pooling of family resources and other means, was faring much better than the state-owned sector. Growing at an annual rate of 20 percent since the early 1980s, the private sector created more than 60 percent of China's GNP by 2004.[10]

Another major change in the 1990s was the end of the peasants' serf-like ties to their villages that had existed during the Mao period. With greater labor mobility, it is conservatively estimated that by 2003 over 120 million peasants were on the move[11] from the countryside into towns, cities, and particularly to the Special Economic Zones in search of better lives, not just for themselves but for their families back home, to whom they sent remittances. Although people were able to change their jobs in the 1990s, it was still difficult to obtain the permits required to reside permanently in the urban areas. By the early twenty-first century, however, such permits were becoming increasingly less necessary.[12]

Thus the move to a market economy gradually loosened state control over people's personal lives, fostered more autonomous transactions among individuals, and provided much more flexibility, opportunity, and choice in one's economic life. Barry Naughton describes the emergence in the 1990s of the "one household, two systems" model: one family member stays in the state sector in order to get subsidized housing, medical care, pensions, and education benefits, while the spouse enters the market economy.[13]

In addition to bringing about improvements in the standard of living, this arrangement led to increases in household savings that flooded into the banking system, thus funneling funds into the economy for further investment. Rather than embarking on the privatization of state industry at the start of the reforms as the Russians did, China's leaders postponed that process to the late 1990s, in part because the more conservative party elders opposed it on ideological grounds and in part because the leaders knew that privatization would result in the dismissal of millions of redundant workers from state enterprises, possibly provoking widespread unrest. Instead, China's leaders encouraged the expansion of the nonstate sector, foreign-joint ventures, Special Economic Zones, and collective, private, and local enterprises in the expectation that competition would force the state sector to reform itself. As enterprises in the nonstate sector, particularly in the towns, often got their start as subcontractors to state industries, they quickly became more efficient competitors and took business away from the primary contractors. When the competitiveness of the nonstate enterprises accelerated, the state industries were increasingly unable to meet the challenge. Profits of state-sector companies fell from 6 percent of GDP in the early 1980s to less than 1 percent in 1996.[14] This precipitous decline of the state sector in the 1990s also led to the near bankruptcy of China's banks that were ordered to bail out the state industries.

Consequently, at the Fifteenth Party Congress held in September 1997, the party announced the phasing out of most state-owned industries. The state would continue to own key industries—natural resources and strategic sectors such as military industries, chemicals, energy, and grain distribution—but the majority of state industries were to be sold off through a system of shareholding in which factory managers and employees as well as private investors were to be given the opportunity to purchase shares. Although the system was euphemistically called "public ownership," in reality it was privatization. In contrast to Russia, which moved directly from state industry to privatization, causing many disruption and economic hardships, China did not move to privatize until after almost two decades of development of the nonstate sector, which was then able to absorb some of the workers from the SOEs and thus help ease the transition. By late 2002, SOEs accounted for just 15.6 percent of industrial output; even if the output from the state shareholding firms is included, the figure is only 40.8 percent.[15]

Despite this advantage, however, China's reform of state industry had profound implications for Chinese society and government as well as for the economy. In 1996–97 state industries employed about two-thirds of the urban industrial labor force.[16] Although China's nonstate sector had room for some of these workers, it had not expanded sufficiently to absorb the millions of workers who lost their state jobs, in addition to the 120 million who were leaving their villages in search of jobs in the cities, plus the 13 million new workers who came into the marketplace every year. Even before the phasing out of most state-owned industries became official policy in September 1997, workers were already protesting late payment of salaries, furloughs, and layoffs. With the loss of their jobs in state industries, these workers also lost their health care and pension benefits. Such layoffs hit the rust-belt areas of the Northeast (Manchuria) and provinces in the interior, such as Shanxi, Hubei, and Sichuan, especially hard. In 1999 alone, 435 loss-making large and medium state firms, 31,000 small coal mines, and 70 small oil refineries were closed down.[17] By year's end 2002, state-owned and shareholding corporations employed 77 million urban workers, down from 94.7 million at year's end 1998, while private enterprises employed 20 million urban workers, up from 9.7 million at year's end 1998.[18]

Unlike their Russian counterparts, China's state workers did not passively accept their fate. During the 1990s, the number of officially reported protests nearly quadrupled, from 8,700 to 32,000, according to Ministry of Public Security figures.[19] For the most part, these protests were localized and of short duration. The early twenty-first century saw a new phenomenon, however: coordinated workers' protests in a number of different factories, lasting for more than a few days. In the three months from March through May 2002, well-organized joint workers' protests took place in a number of factories in the three Northeast cities of Liaoyang, Daqing, and Fushun, where thousands of laid-off workers protested nonpayment of back wages, loss of pensions and health benefits, insufficient severance pay, and widespread corruption. Some of these protests involved thousands of workers and lasted longer than any previous protests since 1989.[20]

Yet by the end of May 2002 the party was able to defuse the protests. In contrast to its violent handling of the student protests of 1989, the government arrested the main leaders, who were sentenced to long prison terms, but tried to mollify the demonstrators by providing some monetary and health care compensation rather than using force against them. Furthermore, the government arrested some of the officials whom the workers accused of corruption. The sheer number of workers and protests made detention, arrest, or military suppression impractical and would likely only have provoked further unrest. As the process of privatization of state industry accelerated in the early twenty-first century, it was uncertain if such a strategy would continue to mollify increasing numbers of laid-off workers, particularly if there were to be a downturn in the economy. The number of protests continued to grow rapidly. In July 2005 it was reported by Minister of Public Security Zhou Yongkang that 3.76 million people took part in 74,000 protests in 2004.[21]

The decline in state industry had an even greater impact on the Communist party-state. Because the central government received 60 percent of its revenue from state-owned enterprises,[22] this decline meant that the central government lost a substantial share of its revenue. Despite the economy's continuing growth, the central government's revenue base was increasingly depleted. At the same time, because provincial and local governments received less financial support from higher levels than previously, they kept a larger proportion of tax revenues for investment in local projects. Since the moneymaking capacities of the collective and private enterprises benefited both local officials and local entrepreneurs, when directives of the central government diverged from local interests, the officials and entrepreneurs joined together to ignore higher directives. In addition to unchecked corruption, this alliance between local officials and the growing nonstate business community led to increasing economic and political decentralization. It was in the interest of both groups to disregard central government injunctions against product duplication, tax overcharges, corruption, and labor exploitation. As a result, the central government's capacity to wield political authority, let alone economic power, at the local levels was weakened.

Consequently, the development of the nonstate sector not only helped improve the livelihood of the majority of the population but also shifted political and economic power to local officials. Vivienne Shue has described this development as a thinning of power at the center, counterbalanced by a thickening of power at the local levels.[23] Deng and his successors realized that in order to move to the market, it was necessary to decentralize and to reduce the concentration of political and economic power in the central government; but they did not foresee the extent to which such economic and political decentralization would result in a decrease in the flow of taxes to the center, thus diminishing the reach of the party-state's authority and fostering an informal federalism. In the short run, decentralization helps economic development by allowing more tax revenue to stay in the local areas to stimulate growth. But in the long run, as occurred in the late Qing dynasty, it leads to a relative decline of central government revenues and thus decreasing expenditures on education, health, and infrastructure, eventually undermining economic growth, especially in the countryside.

As revenue declined, the government shifted much of the responsibility for investment to the local governments and enterprises. But while they were prepared to invest in economic projects, local governments were less ready to invest in education and health.[24] Central budgetary revenues as a share of gross domestic product (GDP) declined from 35 percent in 1978 to only 12 percent in 1998, though they recovered to 18 percent in 2002. Expenditures show a similar trend. Throughout the 1980s, the central government's expenditures were around 10 percent of GDP, but slipped to 8.4 percent in 1995. In 2002 they recovered to 21 percent.[25] Likewise, with the abolition of the communes which had provided the funds for health care, education, and infrastructure development, particularly public irrigation networks, rural communities could no longer finance their own public activities. Evidence indicates that rural health, education, and public works gradually deteriorated in the 1990s.

Even though the party loosened its authority over people's economic livelihood in the post-Mao era, it increased its authority in the area of birth control. Starting with the Great Leap Forward, Mao had encouraged a large population in the belief that it would make China more powerful. As a result, post-Mao leaders were faced with a population already one-fifth of the world's total and growing at a rate of 15 million a year. In an effort to slow population growth, beginning in the 1980s the party-state imposed draconian birth control policies mandating one child per family. By the mid-1990s, the population growth rate was reduced to about 13 million a year. But the policy provoked much unhappiness, especially in the countryside, where male heirs are desirable in order to continue the family line. Furthermore, because girls marry out of the family, families want a son to take care of the parents in their old age, especially with the loss of social security benefits in the post-Mao era. In addition, the return to the family farm created an incentive to increase family size in order to have more hands to work in the fields. Therefore, during the final years of the twentieth century, peasants in some areas were allowed to have two children if the first child was a girl or if they paid a fine for an extra child. Nevertheless, the strict family planning policy had produced a huge gender gap by the early twenty-first century. Because of ultrasound examinations and selective abortions, and even female infanticide, the government announced in January 2005 that 119 boys were born to every 100 girls, compared with the average world rate of 105 boys to 100 girls. If these trends continue, in a few decades China could have up to 40 million bachelors; the impact of this disparity on society is hard to predict.[26]

Whether the regime can keep the population within the set limit of 1.3 billion other forces may ultimately contribute to a decline in population growth. The movement from agriculture to industry and services had already begun to produce broad structural changes in Chinese society in the 1990s. Because of greater social mobility and migration into the cities and towns,[27] in just two decades the share of China's work force engaged in agriculture plummeted from 71 percent to about 50 percent. It had taken Japan sixty years to attain a similar transformation.[28] As China became increasingly urbanized and household incomes rose substantially, residents spent more money on leisure and consumer goods. By the late 1990s China's economy was less in transition from socialism to capitalism than in transition from a rural society to an urbanized society. If these trends continue, it is likely that the economic, social, and cultural pressures of an urbanized society, rather than the party's birth control policy, will ultimately bring down China's huge population, as has occurred in other urbanized areas of the world.

Whereas the leadership that came to power after the Cultural Revolution was relatively united in the move away from Mao's policies and in introducing rural reforms, differences emerged within the leadership over the speed and direction of the economic reforms. Deng encountered opposition from several of his revolutionary colleagues in the 1980s, particularly Chen Yun, the economic planner, and Deng Liqun, the propagandist of the Mao era. Yet, despite their resistance to the establishment of the Special Economic Zones and to the expansion of the nonstate sector, Deng continued to push ahead with the economic reforms and the opening to the outside world. As he bargained, harangued, and persisted in the face of increasing opposition, he was largely successful in achieving these reforms.

Deng was less consistent, however, in moving ahead with the limited political reforms that he had first encouraged in the aftermath of the Cultural Revolution to ensure that China would never again be convulsed by political disorder.

The Impact of Limited Political Reforms

In the post-Mao era, China is generally contrasted with the former Soviet Union and Eastern Europe as having initiated economic reforms without introducing political reforms. Such a description, however, is not altogether accurate. Shortly after they returned to power in late 1978, Deng Xiaoping and other party leaders introduced several limited political reforms that laid the groundwork for potential political change, though the Communist party-state still remained in charge. In the early years of the Deng era, Deng's reformist disciples Hu Yaobang and Zhao Ziyang, as well as two of the party elders, Peng Zhen and Bo Yibo, moved beyond the economic reforms to implement a series of political reforms to prevent the occurrence of another Cultural Revolution. Initially, the more conservative elders did not oppose these reforms, because they too had suffered in the Cultural Revolution and thus shared similar goals. The political reforms were intended to establish norms, to institutionalize certain procedures, and to rule through collective decision making in order to move away from the unchecked, ad hoc, and dictatorial personal leadership that had caused so much damage during the Mao years.

Even though Deng's overriding concern was with the economy, he, his disciples, and a few of the party elders played pivotal roles in promoting political reforms in the early 1980s. Despite the fact that Deng sought to revive the party's legitimacy through economic means, he blamed the party's loss of authority less on economic factors than on Mao's arbitrary and unlimited concentration of personal political power, which ultimately led to the violence and chaos of the Cultural Revolution. Therefore, despite his own paramount political role, Deng eschewed the highest offices and the personality cult of his predecessor.

Early in the post-Mao era, Deng sought to reestablish the party's authority by reforming the Communist party-state. To that end he and his colleagues called for "socialist democracy" and "socialist legality." The definitions of these terms were vague, however; they clearly did not imply a system of checks and balances, as advocated by some Chinese intellectuals in the mid-1980s. Nor did they mean toleration of public protests. Deng had allowed the Democracy Wall movement of former Red Guards in late 1978 and early 1979, which publicly called for political as well as economic changes, to continue for a number of weeks only because the protesters' demands helped rid the leadership of Mao's appointed successor Hua Guofeng and the remaining Maoist leaders in the leadership. But once that was accomplished and the demonstrators began to criticize the Communist political system for, as one of the Democracy Wall leaders, Wei Jingsheng, publicly stated, turning leaders into dictators, including Deng himself, Deng banned the movement and had Wei and other Democracy Wall leaders imprisoned.[29] Nevertheless, despite Deng's treatment of Wei and the other leaders, shortly thereafter he acknowledged the need to reform the Leninist system's unchecked expansion of political power. As Deng explained in a 1980 speech, the excesses of the Cultural Revolution were the fault not just of the leader but of the party structure that gave the leader so much power: "Even so great a man as Comrade Mao Zedong was influenced to a serious degree by certain unsound systems and institutions, which resulted in grave misfortunes for the party, state and himself."[30]

Thus the Deng leadership early on introduced regulations to limit the concentration of political power in the hands of one or a few individuals. The life tenure of party-state leaders was replaced with fixed terms; the party general secretary and prime minister were to serve a maximum of two five-year terms. In addition, Zhao Ziyang's report to the Thirteenth Party Congress in October 1987 called for the separation of the overlapping functions of party and state; the party was to formulate overall national goals and priorities, and the government was to make and implement policies to carry out the party's goals. Although Deng never questioned the overriding role of the party and its leadership, Zhao's call for the separation of party and state had the potential to diffuse party power and gradually shift some of that power to the government administration. The party's theorists under Hu Yaobang's leadership sought to revise the Marxist-Leninist ideology to make it more appropriate to the reforms, less dogmatic, and more in accord with the Marxist humanism that had inspired the reformers in Eastern Europe.

In addition, the formerly rubber-stamp legislature of the Mao period, the National People's Congress (NPC), asserted a relative degree of independence in the post-Mao era. Unlike during the Mao era, the NPC no longer unanimously approved all legislation sent to it by the party leadership.[31] Deng repeatedly called attention to Article 57 of the Chinese Constitution, which states that the NPC is the "highest organ of the government." During the Deng era, the NPC was headed successively by several powerful party leaders who, for a variety of reasons, sought to increase the NPC's authority: Peng Zhen, former Beijing party chief; Wan Li, former party secretary of Anhui, where the agricultural reforms had begun; and Qiao Shi, formerly responsible for intelligence affairs and a member of the Standing Committee of the Politburo until September 1997. Of course, these NPC chairmen sought to strengthen the NPC's powers in order to enhance their own authority as well, but in the aftermath of the Cultural Revolution they also genuinely believed that it was necessary to increase the power of the legislature in order to limit the power of the party leadership, though they rejected a Western-style system of checks and balances. Toward this end they expanded the NPC's bureaucracy, established a committee system, and put technocrats on the NPC Standing Committee.[32]

While the NPC did not set its own agenda, which was established by the party leadership, at times it did modify, revise, send back, and on certain issues withhold approval of party programs, and it criticized the government for failure to implement its laws. In the 1990s, votes for party policies were no longer automatically unanimous. For example, in the 1992 vote over the controversial issue of the Three Gorges Dam—a massive project to be built on the Yangzi River, which faced opposition because of its potentially destructive impact on the people, environment, and archaeological treasures in the area—one-third of the delegates either were opposed or abstained. In 1995 about one-third of the delegates abstained or voted against one of Jiang Zemin's nominees for vice premier. In 1996, in protest against the leadership's ineffectiveness in stopping the growing lawlessness, 30 percent of the delegates voted against or abstained from supporting the report by China's top prosecutor on law enforcement and corruption.[33] And in 2003 one-tenth of the NPC delegates voted against having Jiang Zemin stay on as chair of the state Central Military Commission after his retirement as general secretary in 2003.[34] Jiang finally stepped down from that post in March 2005. Although the NPC did not reverse policies, it was able to influence and at times force a reconsideration of a number of important issues.[35]

Gradual empowerment of the legislative branches occurred at local levels as well. Beginning in 1980, representatives to the local people's congresses in some areas were chosen by direct vote in multicandidate elections rather than by appointment by higher levels. Although all the candidates had to be vetted by the party, for the first time in the history of the People's Republic some local residents were given an opportunity to choose their own representatives. Although this practice came to a stop in the urban areas after the fall 1980 elections when political dissidents were elected despite the party's disapproval,[36] the practice resumed early in the twenty-first century.

In the rural areas, however, the process of voting for local leaders began in the late 1980s and accelerated in the 1990s. In the effort to rebuild political authority in the countryside, which had begun to erode during the Great Leap Forward famine, had shattered in the Cultural Revolution, and had virtually disappeared with the dismantling of the communes in the post-Mao era, the party, with the prompting of party elders Peng Zhen and Bo Yibo, started to experiment with rural local elections. There was a general recognition that in a period of rapid, potentially destabilizing change, the right to vote could assuage discontent and provide some legitimate leadership in the countryside. The opportunity to elect local leaders was particularly appealing in villages that were lagging economically. Whereas the prosperous province of Guangdong, for example, was one of the last areas to introduce village elections, the slower-developing provinces seized the chance to elect village leaders who promised to improve the livelihood of their constituents.

In 1987 the Organic Law of the Village Committees made official what was already taking place: the right of villagers to choose their own village heads and village committees in multicandidate elections. Even though the candidates had to be approved by officials from the Ministry of Civil Affairs, and the local party committees were in charge of the local elections, these competitive elections resulted in a further devolution of power from the center to the localities. In many cases the elections miscarried, and in most cases the village party secretary won, but sometimes the elections not only allowed villagers to remove abusive, corrupt village leaders from office, but also made the local officials more accountable to the electorate. At the same time, the village leaders who were democratically elected were relatively successful in securing compliance with state policies, such as the unpopular one-child policy and collection of the state's share of grain production, in return for defending the villagers against the illegal, predatory exactions by township and county higher-ups whom the elected officials no longer depended on for their positions.[37]

There is still debate over the number of villages involved in local elections. In the late 1990s estimates ranged from 10 percent, provided by a knowledgeable high party official; to one-third, an estimate given by an NPC official and the International Republican Institute, which helped train villagers in democratic practices; to 31 to 80 percent of China's almost 1 million villages, an estimate provided by the Ministry of Civil Affairs.[38] Whatever the percentage, however, these competitive elections meant that for the first time since China's 1949 revolution, local populations were empowered to make their own decisions and pursue their own interests.

Although the grass-roots multicandidate elections generally did not officially spread beyond the village level, in the late 1990s they were tentatively extended to a small number of townships and urban neighborhood committees. The first township election occurred in Buyun in Sichuan province in December 1998, but this was not because of a change in party policy. Motivated by the removal of the previous township leaders in 1997 on charges of corruption and mismanagement, local officials, with the assistance of Chinese academics, decided to launch a political experiment and organize a multicandidate election for township head, using the secret ballots and transparent vote tabulation methods that were being used in the village elections. Three candidates ran for the position of township magistrate—a schoolteacher, a village head, and a township party vice chairman. Discussing a broad range of local issues, they campaigned actively in the villages that belonged to the township. Ultimately, the party vice chairman was elected by a small margin.[39] But despite the election of a party official and several other township elections that took place in the early twenty-first century, the party leadership did not give its imprimatur to such activities. Unlike the local elections in which the villagers know the people who are running for village head and village committee, elections in townships, which may include up to ten thousand residents, required political organizing, campaigning, and electioneering—methods that could eventually be used to challenge the party's authority. Even though there was greater space for freedom of speech in the post-Mao era, there was still no room for unauthorized political organizing.

Reforms to improve local government in order to reinforce central stability have been a feature of Chinese government since ancient times. Yet, as seen in the last ten years of its rule (1901–1911), when the Qing introduced grass-roots political reforms, including participation through limited suffrage in local self-government, these efforts fueled dissatisfaction with the regime rather than bolstering support for it.[40] A similar fate befell the Guomindang's local political reforms, which were unable to stem the rise of the Communist movement. Local political reforms do not necessarily buttress an authoritarian regime; as seen in China's history, they may hasten its downfall.

In fact, the devolution of political power and efforts at grass-roots reforms at the expense of the weakening central government which dominated the local scene in first half of the twentieth century resonates with the situation in the late twentieth and early twenty-first centuries. In the latter case, however, the devolution was due more to economic than to political factors. Leaders in the economically stronger coastal provinces in post-Mao China have become important figures at the center as well. Even though some were placed on the Politburo when Jiang Zemin, the former party boss and mayor of Shanghai, became the head of the party in the aftermath of the June 4 crackdown on the Tiananmen demonstrators and the dismissal of Zhao Ziyang, they were still likely to identify with local interests.

Another factor diluting the center's power was the inception of a civil society in the People's Republic.[41] In the late 1990s thousands of non-governmental organizations (NGOs) were established. Although they had to be registered with the Ministry of Civil Affairs under the auspices of an official agency and were primarily concerned with educational, social, welfare, gender, and environmental issues rather than political issues, they began to assume some of the duties of the government, such as providing education for children of migrant workers and creating AIDS awareness programs. Nevertheless, even though the growing power of regional leaders and the emergence of NGOs further diluted the center's power, in the early twenty-first century the center still retained ultimate power in its continuing capacity to appoint governors and other important provincial officials[42] and to repress any organized group that it perceived as a threat to its authority.

In 1985–86 a number of intellectuals and technocrats who had been rehabilitated by Hu Yaobang and placed in high government, media, and academic positions called not only for a radical revision of the Marxist-

Leninist ideology but also for a more Western-style political system of checks and balances than in Deng's "socialist democracy." But the senior leaders, particularly the more conservative party elders led by Chen Yun, were not willing to tolerate further political reforms. They worried that existing reforms were already undermining their own power and the power of the party, and they feared the emergence of a Polish Solidarity-like movement or a Czech-style democratic Charter 77 group that could lead to the overthrow of the party. Therefore, they persuaded Deng to redefine "socialist democracy" to mean improvement in the functioning of the bureaucracy rather than the building of institutions to curb political power. When student demonstrations erupted in late 1986 at the University of Science and Technology in Anhui's capital, Hefei, and then spread to the coastal cities and into Tiananmen Square in early January 1987, these party elders prevailed upon Deng to stop the protests, dismiss his disciple Hu Yaobang, who refused to crack down on the demonstrators, and purge several prominent intellectuals whose advocacy of reforming the ideology and institutions, the party elders charged, had provoked the demonstrations. Unlike during the Mao period, however, when such dismissals might lead to ostracism, imprisonment, or worse, Hu Yaobang remained on the Central Committee, even though he lost virtually all his political power, and the purged intellectuals continued to function in their professions, even though they lost their party membership. Despite the crackdown, Deng's treatment of Hu and the intellectual dissidents established a new, more moderate pattern in handling intra-party disputes and intellectual dissent than during the Mao era.

Zhao Ziyang assumed Hu's position as party general secretary in 1987, and Li Peng, an adopted son of Zhou Enlai, took over Zhao's position as prime minister. Li Peng had been trained in Moscow in the 1950s, when China and the former Soviet Union were close allies. Unlike his predecessors who had risen to their positions through revolutionary or party activities, Li Peng came from a background that was representative of the new generation of leaders who dominated the central government in the 1990s. He had risen through the ranks of the technocratic bureaucracy. Although Zhao Ziyang was primarily involved in economic reforms prior to Hu Yaobang's dismissal, when he became general secretary he turned increasingly to political reforms. In addition to calling for the potentially far-reaching reform of separation of party and state, he also promoted the theory of the "primary stage of socialism" which had been formulated by economists associated with Hu Yaobang. The theory maintained that because China was still at an early stage of socialism, it could use capitalist methods to develop its economy. Zhao also introduced a civil service examination system as one way to improve the bureaucracy. Although the examination system represented a return to Chinese tradition, it was an unprecedented political institution in the People's Republic, where appointment generally had been based on political loyalty rather than on merit.

Another reform, approved by the NPC in 1989 and put into effect in October 1990, was the Administrative Litigation Law, which sought to make the bureaucracy function more fairly, particularly at the local levels. This law gave ordinary people the right to bring suit against rapacious, arbitrary officials. As a result, for example, villagers could sue local officials who confiscated their land for industrial and infrastructural development. The number of suits grew from about 13,000 in 1990 to 51,370 in 1995 and an estimated 100,000 in 1997. In 1995 alone it was reported that 70,000 citizens filed suits against government agencies and local officials.[43] With the help of Western legal experts, China also began to formulate property and business laws to deal with disputes between individuals and the state as well as between individuals. The leadership's encouragement of such laws and its numerous rectification campaigns were partly directed at cleaning up the spreading corruption that had accompanied the move to the market.

Neither the laws nor the campaigns, however, were very effective because they were carried out within a system that lacked an independent judiciary and a regulatory framework. Often the officials assigned to clean up the corruption were the very same officials who were engaged in it. As a result, bribery, corruption, and the stripping of assets from the state sector became widespread, further undermining the legitimacy and authority of the party-state. Although some corruption may facilitate the workings of a growing market economy, rampant corruption weakens the entire political structure. In China the general perception is that widespread corruption traditionally has spelled the end of dynasties. It also spelled the end of Guomindang rule in the first half of the twentieth century. Despite the leadership's rhetoric and campaigns against corruption, the party's inability to control it continued to erode the power of the center.

It was the corruption issue, plus a bout of soaring inflation caused in part by efforts at price reform in the late 1980s, that transformed a student-led tribute to Hu Yaobang, who died unexpectedly on April 15, 1989, into massive demonstrations that continued for over six weeks until Deng Xaioping ordered the military crackdown on the demonstrators in Tiananmen Square on June 4. The demonstrations attracted millions of workers and ordinary citizens in Beijing and spread to virtually every city throughout the country. While students and elite intellectuals used Hu's death to demand political reforms, particularly freedom of the press and freedom of association, workers and others used it to demand an end to the corruption, the inflation, and the dissolution of state enterprises that had accompanied the economic reforms. The elders and others in the leadership, however, saw these demonstrations, particularly the one in Tiananmen Square—the symbol of the official seat of government—as a threat both to themselves and to the party-state. In the post-Mao era they had thus far been able to suppress student protests and even intellectual dissent relatively easily with limited campaigns and without the use of violence, the mass mobilizations, and the zealousness that had characterized Mao's campaigns. But because the 1989 demonstrations included such a large proportion of China's urban residents, some in the leadership saw them as a replay of the May Fourth movement, which had led to the fall of the Beijing government in 1919. And as some of the demonstrators became frustrated by the leaders' lack of response to their demands for reform, they began to call for the overthrow of the leadership. The party elders, recalling the Red Guard rampages against them twenty years earlier, feared another Cultural Revolution or an even worse nightmare, a Chinese Solidarity movement.

Consequently, by mid-May Deng had concluded that the demonstrations were a fundamental challenge to the party's power and had to be suppressed with military force. Because Zhao Ziyang refused to go along with the imposition of martial law on May 20, he was charged with splitting the party and dismissed as party general secretary. Until his death in January 2005, he spent the remaining years of his life under a form of house arrest. When the demonstrators remained in Tiananmen Square despite the threat of force, Deng ordered Li Peng to send in troops on June 3–4 and soldiers randomly shot their way into the square. In the aftermath, Jiang Zemin was chosen as party general secretary to replace Zhao Ziyang, because as party secretary of Shanghai Jiang had suppressed demonstrators there with relatively little violence, though reportedly scores of workers had been killed.

While the June 4 military crackdown, the purge of Zhao Ziyang, and the subsequent persecution and imprisonment of the demonstration leaders revealed how little the leadership and the political structure had changed, the demonstrations that had provoked the crackdown revealed how much Chinese society had evolved. The loosening of political controls, opening to the outside world, greater freedom of thought and expression, establishment of NGOs, and priority on improving the standard of living for the majority of the population had led to demands not just from intellectuals but from workers, entrepreneurs, and ordinary urban residents to be treated as citizens rather than as obedient party comrades and passive subjects. Moreover, for the first time in the People's Republic, ordinary citizens and workers joined forces with students to participate in the protests, even though initially the students had not welcomed their participation. Yet June 4 demonstrated that though weakened, the Leninist structure still functioned, and party leaders could suppress any direct challenge they saw as a political threat.

Nevertheless, Deng's death in February 1997 further weakened the party-state. The procedures and norms that Deng and his disciples had attempted to introduce were not sufficiently institutionalized to replace the personal rule that Deng never relinquished. Since Jiang Zemin and his colleagues had already governed the party-state for almost eight years prior to Deng's death, his passing did not leave a vacuum in formal terms. But his death marked the end of a strong leader who was able, through his historic role, military connections, party network, and political savvy, to implement his reforms. Roderick MacFarquhar, in summing up Deng's life, concludes that when the history of China's tortuous road to modernization is written, Deng will be seen as the man who finally found the right path, even if he hesitated to follow it all the way.[44]

Deng left a transformed economic system, a pluralistic society, the beginnings of grass-roots political change, and a National People's Congress that periodically expressed dissent by voting against or abstaining on party directives, but the weakened Communist party-state remained intact. Deng recognized the failings of the political system, but he was reluctant to address them for fear that any change would undermine the power of the party and the leadership. Similarly, in the early years of the twenty-first century, neither the third generation of leaders, led by Jiang Zemin, nor the fourth generation, led by Hu Jintao, whom Deng had designated to succeed Jiang, and who came to power in 2002, showed any inclination to address the issue of political reform.

The Post-Deng Leadership

After November 1989 Jiang assumed all powerful positions in the party and the army, and in 1998 Li Peng was replaced as prime minister by former Shanghai mayor and party secretary Zhu Rongji, who had effectively contained China's inflation in the mid-1990s. Yet none of Deng's successors could ever assume his position as paramount leader. They simply had not played his historic role. Their right to rule came only from Deng's blessing. Whereas Deng had the personal power to get things done, Jiang and his Shanghai colleagues, as well as the fourth generation of party leaders led by General Secretary Hu Jintao and Prime Minister Wen Jiabao, were technocrats. Jiang and his colleagues made their way up the political ladder via state industry and the bureaucracy; Hu Jintao and his colleagues made their way to the pinnacle of power through provincial positions. Even though they paid lip service to Marxism-Leninism, as technocrats they were not ideologically driven. Moreover, as the first cohort of leaders in the People's Republic who had not participated in the revolution, they had less authority to rule than their predecessors, and they were more willing to compromise.[45] After an initial embrace of the neo-Maoists who came to the fore in the aftermath of June 4, Jiang by the mid-1990s was steering a gradual, steady middle course between extremes on both the left and the right.

Unlike Deng, Jiang and his colleagues also lacked deep roots in the military, whose support was still crucial for holding power in China. Jiang tried to build personal ties to the military by granting promotions and by more than doubling the military budget. Because Deng had reduced the size and budget of the military by one-fourth in 1984, units of the People's Liberation Army (PLA) began producing for the market economy to enrich both the military budget and themselves. They refashioned the military factories and established a large number of new enterprises that produced goods for the civilian market at home and abroad. Indeed, in the mid-1990s the PLA was perhaps the largest business conglomerate in China in the post-Mao era. In the late 1990s, however, the military budget was increased so as to create a technologically advanced, well-equipped military power. Concurrently, the military was ordered to cut all its commercial ties. The deaths of a number of military elders and the increasing professionalization of the military reduced the military's political role as well. Yet military leaders were still represented at the highest levels of the Communist party-state, as had been the case throughout the twentieth century, and they remained decisive players in leadership factional struggles. At the start of the twenty-first century, the PLA was still the only organization, with the exception of the party, that had the potential to play a major political role in China.

Despite the silencing of political dissidents after 1989 and the growing nationalistic rhetoric that gradually replaced the waning Marxist-Leninist ideology in the 1990s, Jiang did not slow China's opening to the outside world. Yet China's foreign relations were not without troubles. In the aftermath of June 4, human rights violations were the most emotionally charged issue between China and the United States. Although the threat of American economic sanctions was diluted in 1994 when President Clinton delinked the issue of human rights from China's most-favored-nation status, the United States and other Western nations continued to criticize China for its human rights abuses. Specifically, they condemned the imprisonment of the leaders of the 1989 Tiananmen demonstrations, organizers of independent labor unions, and religious leaders who conducted services under nonofficial auspices, such as Roman Catholics who accepted the authority of the pope and Tibetan monks and nuns who swore allegiance to the Dalai Lama. China's leaders and intellectual spokespersons adamantly rejected criticisms of their human rights practices. Like the leaders of Malaysia, Singapore, and Indonesia, they charged that such criticisms were an imposition of the Western view of human rights on countries with different historical traditions. Jiang extolled "Asian" values as superior to Western values because they were based on collective rights rather than the self-centered individual rights that were responsible for the moral failings of Western societies.

Nevertheless, by the late 1990s there was much less talk of Asian values and more discussion of rights, by both Chinese officials and ordinary citizens. In 1997 China signed the UN Covenant on Economic, Social and Cultural Rights, which was later ratified by the National People's Congress, with the deletion of the right to form labor unions, and in 1998 signed the Covenant on Civil and Political Rights. The signing of these covenants, however, did not limit the party's power or protect the rights of individuals. Nevertheless, the language of rights seeped into the country and spread beyond intellectuals. Laid-off workers, overtaxed peasants, and people whose homes and land were confiscated for development projects without adequate compensation began using this language in their protests.

Despite calling for renewed emphasis on the Communist party-state, the Jiang leadership recognized the impossibility of restoring a centralized controlled economy. Jiang initially tightened political and media controls but not economic controls. In the early years of his leadership he had tried to rein in centrifugal tendencies and preserve the inefficient state-owned enterprises, but at the Fifteenth Party Congress in 1997 he put his own mark on economic policy by launching the major reform of state industry by means of bankruptcies, mergers, selling of shares, foreign-joint ventures, and privatization. Twenty years after China's initial launching of economic reforms, and in the face of mounting social unrest, labor disruptions by laid-off workers, growing inequalities, and criticisms from neo-Maoists, the Jiang leadership made official what had already been taking place informally: the withdrawal of the state from most sectors of the economy and the dissolution of the heavily indebted, overstaffed, and obsolete state-owned industries.

Like Deng, however, Jiang did not embark on a bold program of political reform. Even though Jiang adopted Hu Yaobang's slogan "Emancipate the mind" and talked about political reforms at the Fifteenth Party Congress in 1997, he was slow to carry them out. Indeed, at that Congress he forced the retirement of NPC chairman Qiao Shi, who had actively called for political and legal reforms. In contrast to Jiang, who emphasized strengthening spiritual civilization, a vague term referring to the orthodox ideology and Leninist democratic centralism, Qiao had been the one member of the Politburo's Standing Committee who in the mid-1990s consistently stressed the need to build political and legal institutions and to enforce laws fairly. With Qiao gone, the dichotomy between China's dynamic economy and its obsolete Leninist political structure became even more accentuated. In fact, some of the efforts to separate the party from the government, begun under Zhao Ziyang, were retracted during Jiang's leadership.

Thus, the tragedy of June 4 interrupted the gradual political democratization within the existing framework that had seemed possible earlier in the 1980s. In the aftermath of the military crackdown, the purge of Zhao Ziyang and his supporters, and the suppression of relatively independent organizations of intellectuals who were concerned with political issues, there was a crackdown on independent citizens' associations, professional groups, and trade unions that had been organized during the 1989 demonstrations. The further harsh crackdown on workers seeking to organize their own unions in the mid-1990s and on a coalition of dissident intellectuals, who had participated in the Democracy Wall and the 1989 demonstrations, and disaffected workers attempting to form an opposition political party, the China Democracy Party, in 1998 ensured that there would be no alternative to the party. Although official statistics of the Ministry of Civil Affairs showed that by the end of 1996, 186,666 social organizations were registered nationwide to deal with a wide range of social, professional, gender, environmental, and academic questions, they could expect to survive only as long as they stayed away from political issues.[46] Chinese at the beginning of the twenty-first century could change jobs, travel abroad, complain on talk radio about potholes in the streets, and vote their village leaders out of office, but they still could not publicly criticize the party-state and its leaders. Those who dared to do so were immediately silenced.

There was also a common apprehension among the population that too rapid political change could provoke widespread instability and economic decline, similar to that which had occurred in the former Soviet Union, and thus had the potential of jeopardizing the recent gains in the standard of living. Nevertheless, the gradual introduction in the late 1980s of such institutions as limited grass-roots political reforms in villages and urban neighborhoods and local legal aid offices moved forward. The local equivalents of the NPC continued to assert more autonomy and allowed for more participation by local communities. Established procedures, such as the convening of regular party meetings and the efforts to formulate civil and criminal codes, also continued.

Only a few well-placed intellectuals, however, such as a small number of remaining revolutionary elders, some former participants in the Democracy Wall and the 1989 demonstrations, and a few freelance intellectuals dared publicly express the fear that if political change were too slow, it could also be destabilizing, because China's obsolescent and enfeebled central government could not manage China's new and changing economic and social realities.

A Fluid and Fragmenting Society

The post-Mao move to the market, access to new sources of wealth, devolution of power to local levels, openness to the outside world, and relaxation of controls over daily life caused more far-reaching social changes. Like the economic and political changes, the post-Mao social changes also resonated with the opening up of public space in the late Qing dynasty[47] and the development of an incipient civil society in the early decades of the twentieth century.[48] The reopening of public space marked the end of an increasingly statist trend that had begun during the Republican period (1927–1945), when the Guomindang loosely incorporated various occupational and social groups into the state structure. This process culminated in the 1950s, when the Communist Party imposed virtually complete control over all groups and individuals by organizing them into official party-state federations and associations. During the Mao period, Chinese society was relatively homogeneous, egalitarian, immobile, and vertically organized.

Yet less than ten years after the launching of the economic reforms,

Zhao Ziyang, in his report to the Thirteenth Party Congress in October 1987, officially recognized the emergence of different social groupings across generational, geographic, professional, and economic lines. He urged the establishment of official channels through which these various groups could express their interests in an organized way. In addition to the official occupational and social federations of the Mao period, the party set up intermediate organizations made up of these newly emerging interests. In return for a degree of autonomy within demarcated spheres, such intermediate organizations agreed to accept certain restrictions and obligations.

The party paid particular attention to co-opting the rising economic forces—the self-employed, collectives, small- and large-scale private businesspeople, and revived clans—into organizations in which the party played the dominant role.[49] These organizations not only were to establish some control over their constituent members' activities but also were meant to head off any challenge to the political system from an emerging middle class. In 2001 Jiang Zemin coined the concept of the "Three represents," which was defined as the Communist Party representing the most advanced culture, the most advanced elements, and the broad masses. This idea was used to justify the incorporation of the newly rich entrepreneurs into the Communist Party. Because the new rich either came from officialdom or were dependent on officials for their increasing wealth, they generally supported the political status quo. Although a small number of participants in China's expanding collective and private business community participated in the 1989 demonstrations, after the June 4 crackdown most of them showed seemingly little interest in political reforms and little desire to change their dependent status, primarily because their interests were served by maintaining close relations with party officials.

Even nongovernmental, or "people's" *(minjian)*, associations that were supposedly self-financing had to register and function under some sort of official supervision. Their degree of autonomy was delineated and policed by officials. China's business and professional classes were becoming richer and more numerous, but by the beginning of the twenty-first century they had not yet developed into an independent capitalist or middle class able to assert themselves in their own right. Nevertheless, their organizations and associations opened up spaces in society where they increasingly expressed the interests of their constituencies rather than merely the views of their official sponsors.[50] Professionals and academics, including lawyers, doctors, scientists, engineers, and economists—some of whom established their own private practices and consultancies—set up smaller, more flexible associations. In this respect they resembled the various late nineteenth-century associations that gradually shifted from expressing official Qing views to expressing the views of their associations and in time gained greater political influence.

In some areas, the party's efforts in the 1990s to supervise this emerging intermediary realm were outpaced by informal alliances occurring outside the party's purview. A study of Tianjin reveals that while associations of small-scale merchants remained subservient to officials, associations of large-scale entrepreneurs, as they acquired more wealth and grew less reliant on state resources, increasingly asserted their own interests.[51] Other studies of private entrepreneurs in specific localities, such as Wenzhou along China's thriving southeast coastal area, show that these entrepreneurs were influential in shifting the balance from the public to the private sector. As new economic alliances developed, individuals and groups became bolder in asserting their own interests. While some informal alliances of officials and nonstate entrepreneurs engaged in corruption and clientelism, other alliances promoted more constructive causes, such as improving education and social services, thereby furthering their own interests as well as those of the workers.[52] Although the state was determined to suppress alternative political groups, it was more tolerant of nonpolitical groups and associations. As a result, apolitical associations continued to be established and to proliferate in the 1990s and the early years of the twenty-first century.

Much as in the late Qing dynasty, urban areas became the centers of new markets and trading patterns that helped create public space where new intellectual, cultural, and social interactions took place. Yet similar to what occurred in the late nineteenth century, the public space in the early years of the twenty-first century was unable to develop into a full-fledged civil society involved in political discourse, because periodic government repression, absence of the rule of law, and widespread corruption prevented the establishment of institutions that could protect and sustain an independent civil society. David Strand has pointed out that even though individual and group autonomy cannot survive in a totalitarian society, neither can it thrive without strong institutions and laws to protect it.[53] Unlike in the West, where similar developments led to a clear line between state and society, throughout most of Chinese history and continuing into the twenty-first century, rather than a clear dichotomy between state and society there has been a blend of private, public, and state interactions.

At the same time that post-Mao society became fluid and mobile, it also became "fragmented and fragmenting," to borrow Gordon White's terminology.[54] A manifestation of the social fragmentation caused by the move to the market was the growing gap between the rich and poor and increasing social inequalities. Whereas during the Mao period the workers in state industries were esteemed and well paid, in the post-Mao era the workers' relative status and wages generally declined as state industries increasingly went bankrupt. With salaries frozen, reduced, or simply not paid, their pensions and health care provisions went uncovered, while the salaries of those who worked in nonstate, private, and foreign-joint enterprises increased. The unsettling effects of economic change, plus the loosening of controls, sparked an explosion of collective resistance in the form of industrial strikes, slowdowns, and street demonstrations which accelerated in the late 1990s; in some provinces, such as Sichuan and Hubei, protests turned into large-scale riots.

These economic and social differences were intensified by the accelerating geographic disparities between the coastal areas involved in international trade and private enterprise and the poorer inland provinces dominated by inland trade and SOEs. In 2001, the average income in coastal Shanghai was $1,330; in rural inland Guizhou province it was $165.[55] In the rural sector, widening income disparities likewise occurred between the prospering managers and workers in the collective industries and the farmers who still worked in the fields. There were also mounting economic and social differences between urban and rural areas as the urban rate of growth increased and quickly surpassed rural growth, which had begun to stagnate in the late 1980s. Expenditures on education rose slightly in urban areas, but fell in the rural areas after the dismantling of the communes, which had borne the costs of education and health care during the Mao era. While educational spending at the most advanced end of the educational spectrum, in the universities and research institutes, increased somewhat, it declined at the elementary level, particularly in the countryside, further exacerbating the social disparities between the rural and urban areas.

Similarly, the move to the market widened the gender gap. Since daughters eventually married into their husbands' families, they might be kept home to help with the farming rather than being sent to school. As a result, there was a decline in female literacy in the post-Mao era. In 1990, of the 22 percent of Chinese that made up the illiterate population, 70 percent were female, with a larger percentage of female illiterates in the younger generation: 73 percent of those aged fifteen to twenty-four compared with 68 percent over forty-five years of age.[56] This trend continued to the end of the decade. In 1999 the female illiteracy rate of 15.8 percent contrasted with only 6.9 percent for males.[57]

Because of the growing bankruptcy of SOEs and the state-owned banks that subsidized them, which until the post-Mao era were the major source of the party-state's revenue, and the fact that the center received a progressively smaller share of provincial and local tax revenues, the party-state had fewer resources with which to deal with these intensifying and potentially destabilizing social trends. Nevertheless, the fourth generation of leaders, led by Hu Jintao, committed themselves to closing the disparities between rural and urban areas by reducing taxes on farmers and subsidizing rural education. Whether these measures will work in resolving the income gap remains uncertain.

The disparities between the rural and urban sectors were somewhat mitigated by the easing of restrictions on the movement of people off the farms. Although in the Mao period, peasants were restricted to their home villages through a system of household registration *(hukou)*, decollectivization, the move to the market, and the growth of the nonstate sector and foreign-joint enterprises broke down the immobility of the system. By the mid-1990s China's internal migrants, or "floating population," were on the move everywhere. Nonstate and foreign-joint enterprises attracted young women and adult males from poorer areas to work for low wages, which were nevertheless high relative to their earnings back home. As migrant workers sent a portion of their wages home to their families, they helped lessen the inequalities between the areas. Yet the overall effect of the internal migration was to widen the rural-urban gap still further as farming villages came to be populated primarily by the elderly. The migrant workers, who often were paid late, or sometimes not at all, and worked long hours, often in unsafe conditions, increasingly protested their treatment with demonstrations and walkouts. Back in the countryside, their overtaxed families expressed their anger by protesting, sometimes violently, at the offices of local officials and tax collectors.

In addition, China's migrants increased tensions in the urban communities into which they moved. Transient populations in large cities usually resided with other transients from their own province, county, or village. Most led a marginal existence in makeshift housing. Urban residents, resenting the increased pressure on already burdened urban facilities such as schools, health care services, and space in general, discriminated against and isolated the encroaching migrants. In her study of transient communities, Dorothy Solinger shows that the transients were not well integrated into the urban areas in which they worked.[58] Their rising expectations, as well as their sense of alienation, sometimes resulted in disruptive, criminal acts, threatening stability.

The growing disparities between those at the bottom and those at the top of the economic ladder are seen in a survey of the financial assets per household in Beijing, reported in the *China Daily* in 1997.[59] The survey revealed that the average property value of the richest households was 7.85 times that of the poorest. This percentage has continued to grow. Typical top income earners were managers in private and foreign-joint ventures; families of the unemployed, retired, and transient were at the bottom. These disparities were strikingly visible in China's large cities. While migrant workers lived in shacks alongside construction sites, the newly rich flaunted their wealth with modern condominiums, designer clothes, luxury goods, fancy cars, and trips abroad. In the early twenty-first century it was estimated that 350 million Chinese had cellular phones, the largest number in the world, and a new generation of Chinese yuppies were well equipped with pagers and laptop computers. Rural entrepreneurs built three-story houses in the suburban countryside. Rampant and blatant consumerism was engendering a transformation of values from Maoist utopianism, egalitarianism, and collectivism to post-Mao materialism, self-enrichment, and competitiveness. The exposure to Western culture and living standards, as well as the disillusionment and deprivation caused by the Cultural Revolution, contributed to this growing sense of individual entitlement and rights.

Despite the efforts of Hu Jintao early in the twenty-first century to lessen the inequalities, and despite the continuing economic growth, potentially destabilizing social, economic, and environmental forces unleashed by the economic reforms and rapid development provoked increasing public anger. This anger was expressed in accelerating demonstrations of workers, farmers, pensioners, and ordinary people against widespread corruption, official abuses of power, burdensome local taxes, demolition of housing for development of modern infrastructure, layoffs at failing state-owned enterprises, unpaid health care, pensions, and wages, environmental pollution of the air and water caused by unregulated industrialization, and confiscation of land without adequate compensation. The continuing repression of old and new religious believers and ethnic minorities seeking more autonomy, particularly among the Muslims in China's northwest and Tibetan Buddhists also evoked more frequent, confrontational demonstrations in the early years of the twenty-first century. A pervasive sense of insecurity about the future was widespread, as both ordinary people and the leadership feared chaos *(luan)*, that has haunted the Chinese people since time immemorial.

The reforms thus had a contradictory impact. On the one hand, they made possible upward mobility and improved standards of living, but on the other hand, for those who could not keep up, they fueled a deep sense of dissatisfaction and envy known as "red-eye disease." The accelerating societal changes, with little unemployment insurance and the disappearance of the social welfare network formerly provided by the communes and state industries had a profound psychological impact. Those who suffered the most were women and the elderly in the countryside. Female suicide rates soared. Arthur Kleinman estimates that in 1997, China had the highest per capita rate of female suicide in the world.[60] The official trade unions and the women's federation, as well as the new civil organizations, increasingly tried to address these problems. They provided economic advice and legal education programs to make their constituents aware of ways to deal with their distress other than through protests or suicide. Such services, however, were still in their infancy. The magnitude of the problems and the financial resources needed to deal with them were so great that they could not possibly be handled by the official federations or the nonstate sector on their own. At the same time, the weakening party-state of the post-Mao era was less able to provide help, let alone solutions, for these pressing concerns.

Cultural Pluralism

As the official Marxist-Leninist ideology became bankrupt in the aftermath of the Cultural Revolution and increasingly irrelevant to people's lives, some, especially the youth, turned to nationalism, and others turned to religion. Along with a revival of Buddhism and Daoism, traditional folk religions, and a resurgence of Islam, Christianity rapidly gained new converts in the post-Mao era. Officially there were 200 million religious adherents, but many millions of others worshipped in underground or "house churches," despite the government's harsh repression of any worship outside state auspices. Moreover, a national fever for *qigong* (breathing and other exercises) and other forms of faith healing also developed in the 1990s. One of these *qigong* groups, the Falungong, a Buddhist-Daoist meditation association, grew to a reported 2.1 million followers in the late 1990s until the government harshly suppressed it in the early twenty-first century.[61]

In addition to the emergence of numerous religious beliefs, a variety of ideological views were publicly expressed in the 1990s that further accentuated the growing diversity of Chinese society. Groups of intellectuals inside and outside the official establishment espoused ideas that did not conform to the party's thinking. They used journals, books, public forums, and petitions to argue for economic and political reforms. In the 1980s the most vocal intellectuals were predominantly Marxist humanists and political theorists associated with the intellectual networks of reformist party leaders Hu Yaobang and Zhao Ziyang; in the 1990s and into the twenty-first century, the most vocal intellectuals were unaffiliated with the party leadership. Because of China's move to the market, many of them became independent or freelance intellectuals. Wide-ranging debates, without official direction or ideological constraints, erupted spontaneously on a broad spectrum of topics, ranging from the relevance of the traditional beliefs of Confucianism, Daoism, and legalism to May 4 liberalism, Maoism, and postmodernism.

Even though the People's Republic was never quite as monolithic as depicted in the Maoist period, Chinese society in the post-Mao era became definably pluralistic in its values, religious beliefs, ideological orientation, and ways of living. In addition to these changes, China's embrace in the mid-1990s of the new communications technologies facilitated greater access not only to the outside world and scientific and technological advances, but also to independent discourse and organization of political activities. By June 2005, China had 100 million Internet users, outnumbering by far its 69.6 million Communist Party members,[62] and the figure was predicted to expand to 120 million by the end of the year.[63] Among the Internet users were a small number of "cyber-dissidents," mostly urban, educated youth of the post-1989 generation who used computers and the Internet to criticize party policies and urge political reforms.

Well aware of the political implications of the introduction of the new technologies, which by the early twenty-first century had spread from urban centers along the coast to smaller cities in the interior,[64] the party intensified its efforts to control content it considered "inappropriate" with regulations, censorship, filters, blocked sites, and periodic closure of Internet cafés. A study by Harvard Law School's Berkman Center for the Internet and Society reported in December 2002 that major foreign media outlets were often, though not always, rendered inaccessible to Internet surfers in China.[65] In June 2005 it was ordered that all Chinese Web sites and bloggers be registered with the authorities by the end of the month or face being closed down.[66] Yet, despite these obstacles, some of China's Internet users were able to get around the government blockages because of inconsistent enforcement and through the use of proxy servers in Hong Kong, the United States, and Europe.

Consequently, the Internet provided access to alternate sources of information and created a virtual public space that challenged government propaganda and control of information. It became a new forum where politically dissident views could be expressed and even at times mobilized for political action. An example of the Internet's impact on political issues is revealed in the case of Sun Zhigang, a migrant graphic designer in Guangzhou who was detained and beaten by police on March 17, 2003, for not carrying the proper identity papers. He died three days later while being held in police custody. His case was picked up by the outspoken Guangdong newspaper *Southern Metropolis News (Nanfang dushi bao)*, reprinted across the country, and then posted on China's largest news portal, sina.com, and discussed throughout cyberspace. The official media, including the prime television station CCTV, soon began to focus on the treatment of migrants and police brutality. Although for years advocates of legal reforms had called for the end of arbitrary detention, it was not until widespread outrage was generated on the Internet that the government was pressured to investigate Sun's death. Three months later, in May 2003, the government abolished the system of taking migrants into custody.[67]

The contradictory impact of the reforms on the economy, polity, and society had a similar impact on culture. As China became economically interdependent with the rest of the world in the last two decades of the twentieth century, it initially looked to the West for cultural and intellectual guidance. In the aftermath of the Cultural Revolution and in reaction to their persecution during the Mao era, China's intellectuals and a small number of reformist leaders in the 1980s turned to the Marxist humanist ideas that had been developing in Eastern Europe and then to Western democratic ideas to fill the void. But with the June 4 crackdown, the collapse of the Soviet Union, and the disorder accompanying Russia's move to democracy, there was an intellectual shift away from humanism and liberalism. In the 1990s a small number of older ideologues tried to resuscitate Mao's ideas. A larger contingent, among them a growing number of younger intellectuals, turned to the shared Confucian values and patriarchal structure that they claimed had made possible the economic miracle of East Asia's four little dragons—Taiwan, South Korea, Singapore, and Hong Kong. At the same time, to counter

China's growing intergration with the outside world and its increasing internal regionalism and diversity, the post-Deng leaders and their intellectual spokespersons reemphasized ideological and political unity. At the century's close, they too revived the spirit of nationalism that had also been used to buttress national unity in the early decades of the century.

Even before the inflow of foreign ideas waned, the more conservative elders and remaining Maoists in the mid-1980s put pressure on Deng to stem the swelling Western current. They warned that Western "spiritual pollution," along with the relaxation of internal controls, would lead not just to ideological pluralism but to political pluralism and to an erosion of the party's monopoly over power and ideology. Although Deng in the 1980s, followed by Jiang Zemin in the 1990s, launched a series of campaigns against spiritual pollution in 1983–84, bourgeois liberalization in early 1987, and "all-out Westernization" and peaceful evolution in the early 1990s, these efforts did not silence the expression of dissenting views because they were not backed up with the threat of violence, mass mobilization, and ideological zeal that had characterized the Mao years. Furthermore, China's growing economic and technological international interdependence made it nearly impossible to keep out influences from the West.

As the overwhelming ideological homogeneity of the Mao era gave way to cultural and intellectual pluralism, China's large cities attracted artists, intellectuals, writers, entertainers, foreign visitors, students, and political dissidents. The public and political discourse in the 1980s and the private and popular discourse among an array of diverse groups in the 1990s ranged widely over a variety of subjects. Even though public political debate was suppressed in the aftermath of the June 4 crackdown, the continuing retreat of the state from the cultural realm in terms of financial support and growing tolerance of foreign influences sparked an explosion of artistic experimentation and popular culture in a variety of mediums.[68] So long as the content and style stayed away from politics, the party-state tolerated and at times even encouraged apolitical culture as a diversion from political engagement.

The ideological and political discourse in the post-Mao era until June 4 was relatively free, except during the brief campaigns. In reaction to the Mao era, the dominant themes of the reform leaders and most of the intellectuals in the 1980s were a repudiation of Mao's radicalism and utopianism and interest in Marxist humanism and democratic liberalism. Even though a number of the more conservative elders relentlessly attacked these ideas, they were unable to drown out the prevailing liberal tone of the 1980s. A new school of thought emerged in the late 1980s, called "neo-authoritarianism," formulated by a younger group of intellectuals who were associated with Zhao Ziyang. Attracted to the authoritarian political model of their ethnic and post-Confucian East Asian neighbors, the neo-authoritarians called for several decades of economic reform under a strong centralized leader until a large educated middle class could develop to move the country in the direction of democratization. They engaged in spirited debates with the more liberal-leaning older intellectuals. For the first time in the People's Republic, both sides of a political debate were given relatively equal treatment in prominent intellectual forums, newspapers, and journals. In the aftermath of June 4, however, as a number of Maoist ideologues, led by the conservative elder Deng Liqun, returned to power, both the liberal and neo-authoritarian schools were purged or silenced because of their support for Hu Yaobang and/or Zhao Ziyang.

In the early 1990s there was an attempt to revitalize Mao worship, foment class struggle, and re-indoctrinate the population in Marxism-Leninism. "Mao fever" *(Mao re)* spread to China's major cities with the reappearance of Mao's "little red book" and with Mao medallions ubiquitously hanging from taxicab rearview mirrors. Although the fever was rampantly exploited for self-serving commercial ends, it was also fueled by nostalgia for the supposed order and honest officials of the Mao years in contrast to the disorder and corruption of the post-Mao era.[69] Deng's southern trip to the Shenzhen Special Economic Zones in early 1992 provided him with an opportunity not only to revive the economic reforms but also to attack the "left" as a greater danger than the right. Subsequently, the Mao fever gradually subsided, and beginning in the mid-1990s, a more open political atmosphere emboldened some of the politically engaged intellectuals of the 1980s once again to call publicly for political reform and the release of political prisoners. This political spring, however, was short-lived. By late 1998, public political dissent was once again suppressed.

Despite Deng Xiaoping's attack on the left, neo-Maoists—in a series of public statements and in several theoretical journals under their control—persisted in spreading their Maoist ideological approach, insisting especially on the continuation of the state-controlled economy. This approach found strong support within the bureaucracy, particularly in the planning ministries. In contrast to Deng's nonideological approach, the neo-Maoists continued to stress the struggle between capitalism and socialism. They warned that the decline of state industries would impoverish the workers, leading to the victory of capitalism over socialism. But regardless of the efforts of the neo-Maoists, Jiang Zemin merely paid lip service to reviving ideology. He stressed building "socialists spiritual civilization," but this concept had little to do with socialism. Its major emphasis was on China's revival as a great civilization.

As the post-Deng leadership's reform of state industries in the late 1990s caused the unemployment of workers in SOEs, a new generation of intellectuals, called the "new left," trained primarily in the United States and Europe, denounced China's participation in a global economy called for a revival of the collectivist landholding of the Great Leap Forward and the direct democracy of the Cultural Revolution. At the same time, the liberal intellectuals called for a system of checks and balances as means of controlling the rampant corruption and rent-seeking that had accompanied the economic reforms. Although these various ideological groups contended with one another, most of their ideas also challenged those of the party-state. The Jiang Zemin and Hu Jintao leaderships basically did not interfere with the new left, but they closed down the neo-Maoist journals and off and on throughout the late 1990s and early twenty-first century detained or placed under surveillance liberal intellectuals who called for political reforms.

In contrast, the Jiang Zemin leadership was more tolerant of the revival of Confucianism. Although those espousing Confucianism came from academia rather than from the party and did not refer to Marxism-Leninism in their writings, the leadership found their views more in tune with their own goals. The Confucianists asserted that modernization did not mean Westernization. The seeds of modernization, they argued, could be found in Chinese history and Confucian precepts, with their emphasis on education, moral values, and community. Thus, instead of seeing China's deeply embedded traditional culture as an obstacle to its modernization, as preached by the May Fourth intellectuals, the Maoist ideologues, and party reformers and intellectuals in the 1980s, the Confucianists insisted that Confucianism was conducive to modernization. Citing the dynamic economies of the Confucian-shaped societies of their East Asian neighbors, they asserted that a revived Confucianism could provide the intellectual and cultural underpinnings for China's rapid economic development while helping China avoid the immorality and individualism of Western capitalism. Although the emphasis on Asian values waned in the late 1990s, particularly after the 1997 Asian financial crisis, the revival of Confucianism continued into the twenty-first century among small groups of intellectuals. The government even set up Confucian study centers abroad. The leaders agreed that Confucianism was relevant to the present, but they stressed the Confucian authoritarian values rather than the Confucian obligation of intellectuals to criticize officials who abuse their power or engage in unfair treatment of the population.

Another group of intellectuals advocated a neo-conservative approach in the 1990s. Like the Confucian revival, their views developed in reaction to the pro-Western, anti-traditional discourse of the 1980s, when disillusionment with Maoism initially instilled an unquestioning idealism about Western societies and political life. But as intellectuals learned more about the West and came in closer contact with its realities, their idealism waned. In the 1990s a younger generation of intellectuals who had come of age in the post-Mao era, some of whom were close to the "princeling" children of the party elders, moved to another extreme. Like the neo-authoritarians of the late 1980s, they did not refer to Marxism-Leninism, but neither did they endorse a full-scale move to the market or the development of a middle class that eventually would lead China toward democracy. Rather, like the neo-Maoists, they decried the political decentralization that had accompanied China's move to the market, and called for tighter central controls over the economic regions and cultural life. In addition, they urged that internal migrants be returned to their home villages.

Whereas the neo-Maoists called for a reassertion of the state-owned, centralized economy in ideological terms, the neo-conservatives called for its return in practical terms: that is, a strong central state was necessary to ensure political control and collection of tax revenues. Without a restrengthening of the party-state, they argued, the party would be unable to handle the social instabilities triggered by the economic reforms. Unless the erosion of the party-state were stopped, they warned, the traditional Chinese nightmare of chaos *(luan)* would ensue. The ideas in the popular book *Looking at China through a Third Eye (Disanzhi yanjing kan Zhongguo)*, published in 1994, was representative of this neo-conservative view. The book implicitly criticized Deng's reforms for weakening central control.

With the exception of the liberals, these schools of thought—neo-Maoist, Confucian, new left, and neo-conservative—also increasingly expressed the nationalist sentiments generally embraced by younger intellectuals and urban youth. China's economic achievements had awakened a sense of national pride among the younger generation. In 1993 they spontaneously protested against the rejection of China's bid to host the International Olympics in the year 2000, which they blamed on the United States. They echoed their leaders' charge that the United States was attempting to contain China's rising power. Their indignation was articulated in the book *China Can Say No (Zhongguo keyi shuo bu)* and other books on similar themes that were best-sellers in the mid-1990s. These nationalist sentiments became increasingly vociferous in the early years of the twenty-first century, particularly directed against Japan for not acknowledging the atrocities it committed against China during the Second World War.

Nevertheless, like other developments in post-Mao China, nationalist discourse was diverse and contradictory. Initially its stridency was challenged in articles in the still relatively liberal journal *Reading (Dushu)* and in *The Orient (Dongfang)* until the former came under new left editors in the second half of the 1990s and the later was forced to cease publication in mid-1996. In the late 1990s and again in 2005, the leadership tried to rein in the nationalist fervor lest it turn into xenophobia, which could spin out of control. It tried to ban books with nationalistic themes for fear that they would irreparably damage foreign relations, in particular, with Japan and the United States. In addition, it tried to stop protesters from demanding reparations from Japan or damaging Japanese enterprises in China so as not to frighten off Japanese investors.

Yet, while the leadership pushed the Chinese people in one direction, the youth and intellectuals pushed them in other directions, the new economic realities pulled the Chinese people in a completely different direction. Both the leaders and intellectuals condemned the rampant corruption and commercial crassness that had accompanied China's move to the market. Although they had different reasons—the leadership's concern was the potential for challenges to its authority because of its inability to control the corruption, whereas the intellectuals' concern stemmed from their traditional disdain for "selfish," materialistic behavior and their own increasing impoverishment—both groups berated their countrymen for caring only about making money.

In response, some of the newly rich entrepreneurs tried to redefine "private interests" as part of, rather than in opposition to, the public good.[70] Moreover, ordinary Chinese increasingly defined the public good less in terms of public-spiritedness and more in terms of material well-being and consumerism. Unable to act as citizens, they became absorbed in the pursuit of consumer goods. This pursuit further undermined the party's efforts to impose its ideological views, whatever their content, on the populace. It also undermined the intellectuals' desire to regain their status as value-setters for society. As China's economic reforms shifted the balance of economic power from the state to the nonstate sector, ordinary Chinese also contributed to shifting the balance from officials and intellectuals to consumers and audiences as the shapers of China's cultural life.

At the same time, despite the attempts to revitalize ideology, and the rising nationalism, the inflow of ideas, values, and culture from the West, Taiwan, and Hong Kong could not be stopped. In fact, when Hong Kong was returned to China in 1997 after Great Britain's ninety-nine-year lease expired, under a formula that Deng Xiaoping coined "one country, two systems," Hong Kong's relatively free press had an even more direct impact on China's population. Because of China's persistent and accelerating move to the market, regional decentralization, social diversification, and pluralistic culture, efforts to reassert centralized state control seemed no longer possible, short of another revolution. Equally important, unlike during the Mao period, when China was indifferent to what the rest of the world thought of its actions, China's post-Mao leadership sought political and cultural acceptance as well as economic acceptance by the world community. Because foreigners, including foreign journalists, were engaged in a variety of activities in China and were able to observe events there firsthand, the regime's ability to act ruthlessly to suppress anyone attracted to Western culture was restrained.

Foreign pressure, however, did not restrain China's harsh treatment of political dissidents. Despite the outcry from the outside world, Democracy Wall activist Wei Jingsheng, who had been released from prison in 1993 six months before the conclusion of his fifteen-year sentence as part of China's bid to host the 2000 Olympics, was arrested again in 1994 when he continued to voice dissent publicly. He was sentenced in 1995 to another fourteen years in prison, but was released and exiled to the United States shortly after Jiang Zemin's official visit there in October 1997. In addition, other released political activists, such as Wang Dan, co-leader of the 1989 Tiananmen demonstrations, and Wang Juntao, a founder of a 1980s nongovernmental political think tank, both of whom continued to call for democratic reforms, were exiled to the United States owing in part to the international outcry.

The lively market economy, inflow of foreign ideas, cultural pluralism, intellectual vitality, and social diversity of late twentieth-century China in some ways seemed a replay of the early decades of the century. In both periods, opening to the outside world, new commercial opportunities, growing regionalism, a burgeoning middle class, local elite activism, the lack of an overarching ideology, and the weakening of central control allowed more room for intellectual exploration and individual creativity. In this respect, the Mao era could be regarded as an interregnum between two lively cultural scenes in the twentieth century. Though not yet as brilliant or as original as the urban creativity of the May Fourth period, the innovative literary and artistic works, vibrant popular culture, and intellectual receptivity of the 1980s and 1990s had not been seen since early in the century. Yet, like their May Fourth predecessors, intellectuals in the last two decades of the century discovered that ideological and cultural pluralism, though possibly a precondition, did not necessarily lead to democracy.

After June 4, intellectuals who stayed out of "forbidden areas" of political discourse and politics continued to enjoy relative freedom in their personal, professional, and intellectual lives. Apolitical cultural and intellectual pluralism flourished. While discussion of political issues in the official as well as nonofficial media was constrained, by the late 1990s individuals could privately debate political issues, and journalists had expanding space in which to cover cultural activities, intellectual questions, and international news, especially economic information, at times indirectly touching on political issues. At the same time, the scores of private publishers and thousands of private booksellers that appeared in the 1990s provided further channels for disseminating a variety of views. It thus was no longer possible for the party to sustain even its relatively loose controls over intellectual and cultural life of the 1980s. At the end of the twentieth century, China's population enjoyed more personal, artistic, academic, cultural, professional, economic, and individual freedom than at any time during the Mao period.[71] But those who ventured into the political realm, particularly in organizing political groups and actions, continued to be suppressed. When in 1998 veterans of the Democracy Wall movement and the 1989 Tiananmen demonstrations attempted to establish an opposition political party, the China Democracy Party, they were harshly repressed and their leaders sentenced to long prison terms.

Whereas many of the cultural phenomena in the post-Mao era resembled those during the early decades of the twentieth century, by the beginning of the twenty-first century, China appeared to be moving in a different direction owing to a completely different political and technological context. The May Fourth Movement, in reaction to the chaos stemming from the warlord conflicts, Western imperialism, and China's national weakness, sought to build a more powerful state; the post-Mao era, in reaction to Mao's centralization of state power and politicization of all areas of life, sought to reduce the state's power and its reach. In contrast to the May Fourth intellectuals' efforts to create an atmosphere conducive to establishing a strong state, the post-Mao intellectuals and reformers sought to loosen the state's domination over society and the individual, despite the desire of some "neo-ideologists" to resuscitate the strong central state.

An even more significant difference from the May Fourth era was that in the post-Mao period, access to the outside world was not restricted to elites in Shanghai, Beijing, and other large cities along the coast and riverways. At the dawn of the new century, worldwide information and popular culture were spreading throughout the entire country. Movies, television, radio, and the new communications technologies of cell phones and Internet introduced in the mid-1990s reached virtually every Chinese village. Popular culture, though an alternative to the official party culture, was tolerated not only because its escapism reflected the party's desire for an apolitical public, but also because it expressed the overwhelming desire of the population after June 4 to stay clear of politics. Nevertheless, the spread of international popular culture into virtually the farthermost reaches of China indirectly subverted the party because it promoted values that were alien both to mainstream traditional Chinese culture and to the Marxist-Leninist emphasis on obedience and conformity. At the same time, the party was unable to create a new version of the official ideology that could adopt and incorporate the multiple changes that had taken place in China's society, economy, culture, and values.

The change in the role of the intellectuals, like everything else in the post-Mao era, was contradictory. On the one hand, intellectuals played an important role not because of a strong institutional base or enhanced prestige, but because of the state's weakened authority. Although they were unable to assume their traditional role of political leadership, in the 1980s they helped create an ideological and cultural climate in which students turned to political activism—as evidenced by the spring 1989 demonstrations—which, among other things, called for political reforms. On the other hand, the increasing pluralism and spreading popular culture, particularly in the 1990s, undermined the intellectuals' position as cultural and moral standard-bearers of Chinese society. They no longer played the symbolic role they had held even in the Mao period as supposed leaders of the nation. It was for that very reason that Mao had persecuted them so severely and incessantly.

Although the politically engaged intellectuals were suppressed, as the

economy grew more complex and the nonstate sector expanded, a growing number of intellectuals became less economically dependent on the
state for their livelihood and status. By the end of the century, the position of the intellectuals was changing from a traditionally dependent and
close relationship with the state to one of increasing autonomy. Some
turned to business, others worked as consultants, and still others turned
to popular culture. Regardless of their political views, they became more
and more independent intellectually, if not politically. At century's end
the singular role of intellectuals in Chinese society was thus undergoing
a profound change. As one among a growing number of political, economic, and cultural actors, they helped produce a more pluralistic society, but also a society in which their historic and symbolic leadership role
was less prominent and perhaps even marginalized. Although during the
leaderships of Jiang Zemin and Hu Jintao intellectuals per se no longer
played a pivotal role in the Chinese polity, technocrats, who had been
educated in the Soviet Union during the 1950s, came to the fore not only
in the party, but also in the bureaucracy and institutes that helped shape
public policy. Also, younger and more Western-oriented returnees from
study abroad were filling the ranks of the technocracy in the early
twenty-first century.

Nevertheless, in the aftermath of June 4, new groups of intellectuals
who had been rejected by the establishment because of their past political activities sought to work outside the party-state system to bring
about political reform. At times they were joined by workers and small
entrepreneurs, marking the unprecedented joining together of different
classes to bring about political change in post-1949 China. The 1989
Tiananmen demonstrations and the effort to establish the China Democracy Party were joint class endeavors. Nevertheless, these unprecedented
attempts to bring about political change at the grass-roots level without
the party's permission were harshly suppressed.

By the turn of the century, although the party-state system remained
in place and its corporatist structure still dominated society, because
of the move to the market, the opening to the outside world, and particularly the new communications technologies, the Communist party-
state's command over its many constituencies had been weakened. When
China's post-Mao leaders launched the economic reforms and the opening to the outside world, they certainly could not have realized that the
reforms would give rise to an increasingly independent, pluralist society
that they could not fully control. The energy and fluidity generated by
the reforms produced extraordinary economic growth, but the reforms

also produced a dynamically pluralistic society. The ability of the waning party-state to accommodate China's growing diversity of social interests may well determine whether China undergoes constructive institutional change, stalemate, or chaos in the years ahead.

Thus, the changes in the post-Mao era were just as revolutionary as those of the Mao era. While built on some of the social changes of the Mao era, such as the dramatic increase in literacy, life expectancy close to that in developed countries, and improvement in the position of women, Deng's reforms were carried out with more moderation and responsiveness to the needs of the population. They were also accomplished with relatively little disruption to everyday life and without the chaos and famines that punctuated the first eighty years of the twentieth century in China. With the exception of the military crackdown on the student demonstrators in Tiananmen Square on June 4, 1989, the last two decades of the twentieth century and the early years of the twenty-first century were the longest stretch of domestic and foreign tranquillity in China's modern history.

Notes

1. *China 2020: Development Challenges in the New Century* (Washington, D.C.: World Bank, 1997), p. xiii).

2. PPP is a theoretical exchange rate derived from the parity of purchasing power of one currency in relation to another currency. *World Development Report* (Washington, D.C.: World Bank, 2000).

3. *China: Overcoming Rural Poverty* (Washington, D.C.: World Bank, 2001), p. 1; "Chinese Leaders Stress Poverty Reduction," Xinhua, May 28, 2005.

4. These numbers, from recent scholarship, vary somewhat from those given earlier by Fairbank. Estimates for the number of deaths of landlords come from Frederick C. Teiwes, "The Establishment and Consolidation of the New Regime, 1949–1957," in Roderick MacFarquhar, ed., *The Politics of China: The Eras of Mao and Deng,* 2nd ed. (New York: Cambridge University Press, 1997), p. 36; deaths during the Great Leap Forward from Chen Yizi, former advisor to Zhao Ziyang; estimates of Cultural Revolution deaths in Roderick MacFarquhar, "The Chinese State in Crisis," in MacFarquhar, *The Politics of China,* p. 244; for the numbers of those persecuted in the Cultural Revolution, see Hu Yaobang, interview with Yugoslav journalists, Tanjug, June 21, 1980, translated in *FBIS Daily Report: China,* June 23, 1980, p. L1.

5. Asia Watch, *Punishment Season: Human Rights in China after Martial Law* (New York, March 1990), p. 3.

6. *China Statistical Yearbook, 1990* (Beijing: State Statistical Bureau, 1990), pp. 81, 318.

7. Deng Xiaoping, "We Shall Speed Up Reform" (June 12, 1987), in *Selected Works of Deng Xiaoping (1982–1992)* (Beijing: Foreign Languages Press, 1994), p. 236.

8. *China Statistical Yearbook, 2004* (Beijing: State Statistical Bureau, 2004), p. 513.

9. Barry Naughton, "China's Transition in Economic Perspective," in Merle Goldman and Roderick MacFarquhar, eds., *The Paradox of China's Post-Mao Reforms* (Cambridge, Mass.: Harvard University Press, 1999), p. 34.

10. "Private Firms Outperform State Enterprises Says Official," *South China Morning Post,* December 18, 2004, p. 6.

11. Their number was growing at 13 million per year. Xinhua Domestic Service, October 6, 2002. See also David W. Chen, "China Readies Super ID Card, a Worry to Some," *New York Times,* August 19, 2003, p. 3.

12. As of April 2003 all children born to rural families in Beijing were eligible for urban household registration. Other areas were also loosening controls over the household registration system. In Shenzhen, persons without permanent residency could register with relatives who lived in the city. Xinhua, April 1, 2003.

13. Naughton, "China's Transition in Economic Perspective," pp. 35–36.

14. James Harding, "China's Future Dragons," *Financial Times,* August 14, 1997, p. 17.

15. *China Country Profile, 2004* (London: Economist Intelligence Unit, 2004), p. 47.

16. Harding, "China's Future Dragons," p. 17.

17. According to Sheng Huaren, head of the State Economic and Trade Commission, *China Economic Review* (Financial Times Information), March 12, 2001.

18. *China Country Profile, 2004,* p. 58.

19. Indira A. R. Lakshmanan, "Coping with Broken Promises," *Boston Globe,* November 2, 2002, p. A1.

20. Merle Goldman, From Comrade to Citizen: *The Struggle for Political Rights in Modern China* (Cambridge, Mass.: Harvard University Press, 2005), chap. 8; "Paying the Price: Worker Unrest in Northeast China," *Human Rights Watch* 14, no. 6 (August 2002): 2.

21. Edward Cody, "China Growing More Wary Amid Rash of Protests," *Washington Post,* August 10, 2005, p. A11.

22. "China's Lost Savings," *Asian Wall Street Journal,* March 21–27, 1997, p. 10.

23. Vivienne Shue, *The Reach of the State: Sketches of the Chinese Body Politic* (Stanford: Stanford University Press, 1988).

24. Naughton, "China's Transition in Economic Perspective," p. 38.

25. Ibid., p. 36; *China Country Profile*, 2004, p. 60.

26. Jim Yardley, "Fearing Future China Starts to Give Girls Their Due," *New York Times*, January 31, 2005, p. 3.

27. Naughton, "China's Transition in Economic Perspective," p. 40.

28. *China 2020*, p. 6.

29. Wei Jingsheng, "The Fifth Modernization," in James Seymour, ed., *The Fifth Modernization: China's Human Rights Movement, 1978–1989* (Stanfordville, N.Y.: Human Rights Publishing Group, 1980), pp. 47–69.

30. Deng Xiaoping, "On the Reform of the System of Party and State Leadership" (August 18, 1980); in *Selected Works of Deng Xiaoping (1975–1982)* (Beijing: Foreign Languages Press, 1984), p. 316.

31. Murray Scot Tanner, *The Politics of Lawmaking in Post-Mao China: Institutions, Processes, and Democratic Prospects* (New York: Oxford University Press, 1999).

32. Murray Scot Tanner, "The National People's Congress," in Goldman and MacFarquhar, *The Paradox of China's Post-Mao Reforms*, pp. 114–115.

33. Pei Minxin, "Racing against Time," in William A. Joseph, ed., *China Briefing: The Contradictions of Change* (Armonk, N.Y.: M. E. Sharpe, 1997), p. 39.

34. Elisabeth Rosenthal, "China Leader Steps Down, But Not Out of the Picture," *New York Times*, March 16, 2003, p. 8.

35. The one exception is the reversal of a 1989 law on urban neighborhood committees. NPC assertiveness accompanied passage of the Enterprise Bankruptcy Law (1986), the Central Bank Law (1995), and the Education Law (1995). See Pei Minxin, "Racing against Time," p. 38.

36. Merle Goldman, *Sowing the Seeds of Democracy in China: Political Reform in the Deng Xiaoping Era* (Cambridge, Mass.: Harvard University Press, 1994), p. 79.

37. Kevin J. O'Brien, "Implementing Political Reform in China's Villages," *Australian Journal of Chinese Affairs*, no. 32 (July 1994): 33–59.

38. Li Lianjing, presentation at the Conference on Elections on Both Sides of the Straits, Fairbank Center, Harvard University, May 8, 1997; Xinhua, March 17, 2003, in FBIS-CHI-2003–0317.

39. Li Fan, "Come by the Wind: My Story in Buyun Election," unpublished ms., 2003.

40. Roger R. Thompson, *China's Local Councils in the Age of Constitutional Reform, 1898–1911* (Cambridge, Mass.: Council on East Asian Studies, Harvard University, 1995).

41. Tony Saich, "Negotiating the State: The Development of Social Organizations in China," *China Quarterly*, no. 161 (March 2000): 124–141.

42. Huang Yasheng, *Inflation and Investment Controls in China: The Political Economy of Central-Local Relations during the Reform Era* (New York: Cambridge University Press, 1996).

43. Elisabeth Rosenthal, "Day in Court, and Justice, Sometimes, for the Chinese," *New York Times,* April 27, 1998, p. A1.

44. Roderick MacFarquhar, "Demolition Man," *New York Review of Books,* March 27, 1997, p. 17.

45. Joseph Fewsmith, "Reaction, Resurgence, and Succession: Chinese Politics since Tiananmen," in MacFarquhar, *The Politics of China,* p. 525.

46. Saich, "Negotiating the State," p. 126.

47. Mary Backus Rankin, "Some Observations on a Chinese Public Sphere," *Modern China* 19, no. 2 (April 1993): 158–182.

48. David Strand's study of city politics in Beijing describes the expansion of the public sphere in the 1920s to teahouses, restaurants, and parks, which became places for political discussion. See his *Rickshaw Beijing: City People and Politics in the 1920s* (Berkeley: University of California Press, 1989).

49. Jonathan Unger and Anita Chan, "Corporatism in China: A Developmental State in an East Asian Context," in Barrett L. McCormick and Jonathan Unger, eds., *China after Socialism* (Armonk, N.Y.: M. E. Sharpe, 1996), pp. 95–129.

50. Gordon White, Jude Howell, and Shang Xiaoyuan, *In Search of Civil Society* (Oxford: Clarendon Press, 1996).

51. Christopher Nevitt, "Private Business Associations in China: Evidence of Civil Society or Local State Power," *China Journal,* no. 36 (July 1996): 25–43.

52. Kristen Parris, "The Rise of Private Business Interests," in Goldman and MacFarquhar, *The Paradox of China's Post-Mao Reforms,* pp. 275–282.

53. David Strand, "Conclusion: Historical Perspectives," in Deborah S. Davis et al., eds., *Urban Spaces in Contemporary China: The Potential for Autonomy and Community in Post-Mao China* (New York: Cambridge University Press, 1995), pp. 394–426.

54. White, Howell, and Shang, *In Search of Civil Society,* p. 213.

55. Indira A. Lakshman, "China's Reforms Turn Costly," *Boston Globe,* July 22, 2002, p. A9; *Shehui lanpi shu 2002 nian. Zhongguo shehui xingshi: Fenxi yu yuce* [Blue Book of Chinese Society, 2002: Analysis and Forecast of Chinese Society] (Beijing: Shehui kexue wenxian chubanshe, 2002).

56. Elisabeth Croll, *Changing Identities of Chinese Women* (London: Zed Books, 1995), p. 135.

57. *China Statistical Yearbook, 2000* (Beijing: China Statistics Press, 2000), p. 103.

58. Dorothy J. Solinger, "China's Floating Population: Implications for State and Society," in Goldman and MacFarquhar, *The Paradox of China's Post-Mao Reforms,* p. 238.

59. Xing Zhigang, "Disparity in Assets Widening," *China Daily,* January 8, 1997, p. 3.

60. Arthur Kleinman and Alex Cohen, "Psychiatry's Global Challenge," *Scientific American* (March 1997): 86–89.

61. Bureau of Democracy, Human Rights, and Labor, *International Religious Freedom Report, 2004* (Washington, D.C.: U.S. Department of State, 2004), *www.state.gov/g/drl/rls/irf/2004/35396.htm.*

62. Xinhua, January 20, 2005; Xinhuanet, May 23, 2005, based on statistics of the Organization Department of the Chinese Communist Party; Xinhua, June 29, 2005.

63. Shi Ting, "Search on for 4,000 Web Police for Beijing," *South China Morning Post,* June 17, 2005, p. 9.

64. Guo Liang, *Surveying Internet Usage and Impact in Twelve Chinese Cities* (Beijing: Chinese Academy of Social Sciences, 2003).

65. Sam Allis, "Net Sites Blocked by China Go from Expected to Bizarre," *Boston Globe,* December 5, 2002, p. D2.

66. Robert Marquand, "China Cracks Down on Web and Expats," *Christian Science Monitor,* June 10, 2005, p. 1.

67. Xiao Qiang, "The Great Leap Online That Is Stirring China," *International Herald Tribune,* August 6, 2004, p. 7.

68. Geremie R. Barmé, "CPC and Adcult PRC," paper presented at the Conference on the Non-economic Impact of China's Economic Reforms, Fairbank Center, Harvard University, September 1996; Jianying Zha, "China's Pop Culture in the 1990s," in Joseph, *China Briefing,* pp. 109–150.

69. Geremie Barmé, *Shades of Mao: The Posthumous Cult of the Great Leader* (Armonk, N.Y.: M. E. Sharpe, 1996), pp. 3–73.

70. Parris, "The Rise of Private Business Interests," pp. 271–272.

71. Tony Saich, "Most Chinese Enjoy More Personal Freedom Than Ever Before," *International Herald Tribune,* February 1–2, 1997, p. 6.

Suggested Reading

Barmé, Geremie R. *Shades of Mao: The Posthumous Cult of the Great Leader* (Armonk, NY: M.E. Sharpe, 1996).

Baum, Richard. *Burying Mao: Chinese Politics in the Age of Deng Xiaoping* (Princeton, NJ: Princeton University Press, 1994).

Cheng, Joseph Y. S., ed. *China's Challenges in the Twenty-first Century* (Hong Kong: City University of Hong Kong Press, 2003).

Davis, Michael C., ed. *Human Rights and Chinese Values: Legal, Philosophical, Political Perspectives* (Hong Kong: Oxford University Press, 1995).

Dickson, Bruce. *Red Capitalists in China: The Party, Private Entrepreneurs, and Prospects for Political Change* (New York: Cambridge University Press, 2003).

Fewsmith, Joseph. *China since Tiananmen: The Politics of Transition* (New York: Cambridge University Press, 2001).

Goldman, Merle. *From Comrade to Citizen: The Struggle for Political Rights in Modern China* (Cambridge, MA: Harvard University Press, 2005).

———. *Sowing the Seeds of Democracy in China: Political Reform in the Deng Xiaoping Era* (Cambridge, MA: Harvard University Press, 1994).

Goldman, Merle and Roderick MacFarquhar, eds. *The Paradox of China's Post-Mao Reforms* (Cambridge, MA: Harvard University Press, 1999).

Goldman, Merle and Elizabeth Perry, eds. *The Changing Meanings of Citizenship in Modern China* (Cambridge, MA: Harvard University Press, 2002).

Huang Yasheng. *Selling China: Foreign Direct Investment during the Reform Era* (New York: Cambridge University Press, 2003).

Joseph, William A., ed. *China Briefing: Contradictions of Change 1995–1996* (Armonk, NY: M.E. Sharpe, 1997).

Lieberthal, Kenneth. *Governing China: From Revolution through Reform* (New York: W.W. Norton, 2nd ed., 2004).

MacFarquhar, Roderick, ed. *The Politics of China: The Eras of Mao and Deng* (New York: Cambridge University Press, 2nd ed., 1997).

Naughton, Barry. *Growing Out of the Plan: Chinese Economic Reform, 1978–1993* (New York: Cambridge University Press, 1995).

O'Brien, Kevin. *Reform without Liberalization: China's National People's Congress and the Politics of Institutional Change* (New York: Cambridge University Press, 1990).

Oi, Jean C. *Rural China Takes Off: Institutional Foundations of Rural Reform* (Berkeley: University of California Press, 1999).

Perry, Elizabeth and Mark Selden, eds. *Chinese Society: Change, Conflict, and Resistance* (New York: RoutledgeCurzon, 2nd ed., 2003).

Saich, Tony. *Governance and Politics in China* (New York: Palgrave, 2nd ed., 2004).

Saich, Tony, ed. *The Chinese People's Movement: Perspectives on Spring 1989* (Armonk, NY: M.E. Sharpe, 1990).

Walder, Andrew, ed. *The Waning of the Communist State: Economic Origins of Political Decline in China and Hungary* (Berkeley: University of California Press, 1995).

White, Gordon, Jude Howell, and Shang Xiaoyuan. *In Search of Civil Society* (Oxford: Clarendon Press, 1996).

White, Tyrene, ed. *China Briefing 2000: The Continuing Transformation* (Armonk, NY: M.E. Sharpe, in cooperation with the Asia Society, 2000).

Epilogue: China at the Start
of the Twenty-first Century

The Fourth Generation of Leaders: The Hu Jintao Era

The transition from the third generation of leaders led by Jiang Zemin to the fourth generation of leaders led by Hu Jintao was more orderly than any such transition in China's twentieth-century history. Hu became party general secretary in 2002, president of the People's Republic in 2003, and finally head of the state military commission when Jiang Zemin stepped down in March 2005. A graduate in engineering from Tsinghua University, Hu began his party career in the Communist Youth League. At age thirty-nine he became the youngest member of the party Central Committee in 1982 and at age forty-four the youngest provincial secretary serving in the poor province of Guizhou in 1985. He also served from 1988 to 1992 as party secretary in Tibet, where he put down a Tibetan rebellion in 1989 and became known as a tough administrator. The Politburo that Hu took over in 2002 was split relatively evenly between Jiang's Shanghai associates and party bureaucrats, but by 2005 Hu dominated the party's bureaucracy with his appointments of Communist Youth League associates and younger technocrats to important governmental and provincial positions.

Whereas Jiang Zemin had favored development of the coastal cities and focused on industrial production, particularly for export, Hu and Prime Minister Wen Jiabao, who was trained as a geologist, emphasized the development of the interior and easing the burdens on the farmers. In 2004–5 they attempted to reduce the surging economic disparities between China's rural and urban sectors by dispensing with agricultural taxes[1] and providing rural education and subsidies to farmers. Yet, despite Hu Jintao's earlier association with what has been regarded as the relatively liberal Communist Youth League and Wen Jiabao's prior association with Zhao Ziyang, whom he accompanied on a visit to the Tiananmen demonstrators shortly before June 4, there was little evidence of an interest in political reform during the early years of their rule. In fact, on the NPC's fiftieth anniversary, Hu announced that China would not copy Western political institutions, a course he described as "a blind alley." Rather, he emphasized restrengthening the party's capacity in order to rule more effectively. Consequently, he sought to reinforce the party's monopoly on power, reinvigorate ideological indoctrination, and tighten party discipline to stop the corrosive effects of corruption on party members.

In the later years of Jiang Zemin's leadership, there had been an opening up of public space for political discourse; but shortly after Hu Jintao came to power, there was a crackdown on people who used the Internet to discuss political issues. A number of cyber-dissidents, among them the college student Liu Di, were imprisoned as a warning against discussing issues of political reform on the Internet. Independent intellectuals, such as former literary scholar Liu Xiaobo and writer Yu Jie, who spoke out on controversial political issues, were intermittently detained. The military doctor Jiang Yanyong, who had publicly countered the party's assertion in 2003 that the SARS (severe acute respiratory syndrome) epidemic had been brought under control, was detained and then put under surveillance when in 2004 he called on the party to change its designation of the 1989 Tiananmen demonstrations from a "counterrevolutionary" to a "patriotic" movement.

Ironically, Hu Jintao's tightening of controls over political discourse coincided with the publication of a list of the "Top Fifty Public Intellectuals" in September 2004 in the *Southern People's Weekly (Nanfang renwu zhoukan)*, connected to the Guangzhou Southern media group. With China's move to the market, most of China's media were no longer funded by the state and were forced to be self-financing. One result was that the media became more daring and interesting in order to gain readership and survive financially. The Guangzhou Southern media group was one of the most outspoken. In an accompanying commentary, the *Weekly* praised public intellectuals, pointing out that "this is the time when China is facing the most problems in its unprecedented transformation, and when it most needs public intellectuals to be on the scene and to speak out."[2] Although the list included intellectuals in a variety of professions—writers, artists, film directors, cartoonists, lawyers, environmentalists, and a number of overseas Chinese intellectuals—it was dominated by intellectuals who in the 1990s had called for political reforms, freedom of speech and association, and a system of checks and balances.

In November 2004 an article in the Shanghai Party Committee's more orthodox *Liberation Daily (Jiefang Ribao)* declared that promoting the idea of "public intellectuals" was aimed at "driving a wedge between intellectuals and the party."[3] The article insisted that because China's intellectuals belonged to the working class under the leadership of the party, they therefore could not be independent. Some ten days later the *Liberation Daily* article was reprinted in the party's official newspaper, the *People's Daily,* giving the criticism of public intellectuals the party's official imprimatur.

Although the Hu Jintao leadership was much more concerned than its predecessor with ameliorating the increasing inequalities spawned by China's economic reforms, and particularly with alleviating poverty in the countryside, it suppressed the very people who tried to draw public attention to the growing inequalities and distress in the countryside, other than those they officially designated. This can be seen in its treatment of the January 2004 book *A Survey of Chinese Peasants (Zhongguo nongmin diaocha),* written by Chen Guidi and Wu Chuntao, based on interviews over several years with farmers in the poor province of Anhui. This husband-and-wife team, who were both born in the countryside and spent their early years there, described the developers' seizure of land without providing adequate compensation to rural residents, the imposition of unfair taxes by local officials, and the lack of recourse available to peasants to right these wrongs. The book's vivid depiction of the increasingly impoverished lives of peasants drew attention to exactly what the new generation of leaders had declared it sought to alleviate. Furthermore, the book described official abuses, which the new leadership sought to stop because of fear that it would undermine the party's hold on power. Yet, just one month after its publication, the book was banned. Nevertheless, like other banned books, this book continued to be sold on the black market and by private booksellers on street corners.

Along with the crackdown on cyber-dissidents, a number of well-known independent intellectuals and the critique of "public intellectuals," the Hu Jintao leadership tightened controls over the media. Reports on peasant and worker demonstrations and the growing protests against corruption, abusive officials, and property confiscation were banned. Journalism professor Jiao Guobiao, who had criticized on the Internet the repressive media controls by the Propaganda Department, was no longer allowed to teach at Peking University. Another public intellectual, Wang Yi, a law lecturer at Chengdu University who had called for a system of checks and balances, was also barred from teaching for a period of time, and his writings were not allowed to appear in the state-run media. The journal *Strategy and Management (Zhanlüe yu guanli)*, which had been an outlet for intellectuals of a liberal persuasion, was closed down. Even the editor-in-chief of the *China Youth Daily*, the newspaper affiliated with Hu Jintao's Communist Youth League power base, which had been very aggressive in exposing official corruption, was detained. In 2004 alone, seventeen journalists were arrested for not abiding by the party's dictates and sixty-five media outlets were censored.[4] Several months later, with the explosive growth of Internet use and the development of alternative sources of news, China further tightened restrictions when it blocked off-campus Interent users from the Internet bulletin boards operated by prominent universities.[5]

Nevertheless, despite the renewed crackdown on political dissent, China's move to the market and the outside world and its embrace of the new communications technologies made it increasingly difficult for the party to maintain control over people's views. If a blooger's Web site was blocked, he or she could move to another server or to a Hong Kong or foreign proxy. Moreover, unlike during the Mao period, when millions were harshly persecuted for the acts of a small number, in the post-Mao period persecution for political dissent did not reach far beyond the accused and their immediate associates. Although a number of outspoken intellectuals lost their positions in the establishment and some were imprisoned, others were only briefly detained and then were able to find jobs and outlets for their views in China's expanding market economy and burgeoning civil society. Thus, dissidents voices were not completely silenced as they had been previously. Some intellectuals still tried to function as citizens, either on their own or with others, continuing to express their political views in unofficial publications, on the Internet, and increasingly in organized petitions and protests.

China's Rising

By the beginning of the twenty-first century, China had finally fulfilled the wish of its reformers since the late nineteenth century to make the country "rich and powerful." China's growing economic presence on the world scene represented a revival of its dominant economic power of earlier centuries. Much more than Mao, Deng had made possible the attainment of this century-old dream of transforming China into a great nation. Once again, China was a world power, both economically and strategically. Throughout modern history, however, when great powers have emerged, they have tended to engage in territorial expansion or war, as seen in the case of Germany and Japan during the twentieth century. Perhaps in an effort to reassure the world, the nation's leaders talked confidently of China's "peaceful rise," by which they meant that China would become a global power without causing turmoil in the international community.

When the administration of George W. Bush assumed power in January 2001, however, it considered China, which it referred to as a "strategic competitor," to be its chief foreign policy concern. But after the terrorist attack on the United States on September 11, 2001, China became an ally of the United States in its war on terrorism, which China said it was waging in its northwest province of Xinjiang against Islamic groups, principally the Uighurs, working to set up an independent Islamic state of East Turkestan. The United States then began to refer to China as a "strategic partner." By mid-2005, however, the Bush administration had come to see China's development of its long-range missile capabilities and its military budget that was increasing by more than 10 percent annually as serious threats. Though China's military budget was only a fraction of the Pentagon's annual budget,[6] these threats were regarded not just as dangers to the delicate balance between China and Taiwan, but as overall strategic challenges to the United States' hitherto predominant position in the Pacific.

Furthermore, in contrast to the 1980s, when the United States and China engaged in a tacit alliance against the Soviet Union, with the end of the Cold War in the early 1990s such an alliance was no longer necessary. And by the late 1990s China's relations with Russia gradually warmed as Russia became the main weapons supplier for China's military modernization. China and Russia established military and political ties in a joint effort to counterbalance U.S. global dominance. In October 2004 they settled the last of the old territorial disputes along their 2,700-mile border which had led to violent clashes during the Mao era, and in August 2005 they engaged in joint military exercises. They also sought to cooperate on energy development. Similarly, China settled its disputes along its long border with India, where military confrontations had occurred in the 1960s. China's rise, coupled with India's and Japan's continuing production of technologically advanced goods, thus may signify a gradual shift of world power in the twenty-first century from the West to Asia.

At the same time, a number of previously quiescent conflicts between China and the United States surfaced and further aggravated the Sino-U.S. relationship. Taiwan was the most inflammatory source of conflict. Although the United States acknowledged that Taiwan was part of China, it was unwilling to accept unification through military means and urged a peaceful resolution to the conflict. But as Taiwan became increasingly democratic in the late twentieth century, tensions between China and Taiwan escalated. China held military exercises and conducted missile tests in the Taiwan Straits in an attempt to influence the results of Taiwan's first direct presidential election in March 1996. It could not dissuade voters, however, from electing Lee Teng-hui, their first Taiwan-born and popularly elected president. Nor did China's threats four years later dissuade Taiwan's voters from electing as president Chen Shui-bian of the Democratic Progressive Party, which advocated independence for Taiwan. Even though the economies of China and Taiwan were becoming increasingly interdependent economically, with over 1 million Taiwanese businesspeople living and working in China early in the century,[7] and Taiwan's opposition leader Lien Chan visited China in 2005, marking the first meeting of the Chinese Communist Party and the Guomindang in sixty years, tensions between China and Taiwan remained high.

Although the status of Taiwan was the most volatile issue between China and the United States, there were several other sources of friction as well. The United States continued to be the major critic of China's human rights record, which it periodically criticized at the annual meetings of the UN Commission on Human Rights. In addition, the U.S. State Department repeatedly criticized China in its annual report on the global human rights situation. China rejected all U.S. criticisms as interference in its internal affairs. The United States' negative balance of trade with China, which grew from $44 billion in 1997 to $162 billion by the end of 2004, was another continuing source of friction between the two countries,[8] as was China's disregard of intellectual property rights. When the European Union in 2005 sought to lift the sixteen-year-old arms embargo it had placed on China in the aftermath of June 4, American opposition, along with China's passage of an antisecession law against Taiwan and China's continuing human rights abuses, delayed the lifting of the ban.

In addition, as China entered the twenty-first century and moved into the automobile age, it suffered sporadic power shortages, leading to efforts to gain access to worldwide energy resources that put it in competition with both developed and developing countries. China sought to gain access to energy sources in Africa, Latin America, and Central Asia as well as in the Middle East. In these efforts it was competing not only with the United States and Japan, with which it clashed in the South China Sea over a group of disputed islands that supposedly had deposits of natural gas, but also with India, the other large developing nation, sparking a sharp rise in the global price of energy. In 2004–5, Chinese companies initiated efforts to buy American companies. While the Chinese company Lenovo's buyout of the computer division of IBM aroused relatively little American resistance, the effort of a Chinese state-owned company, China National Offshore Oil Corporation (CNOOC), to buy American Unocal oil corporation sparked concerns and resolutions in the U.S. Congress about the sale of companies to China that threatened America's strategic interests. CNOOC subsequently withdrew its offer. Japan evoked a similar fear when it sought to buy American companies in the 1980s. But whereas Japan was not a military threat to the United States, China is becoming a major military power. Yet, unlike Japan, China is more open to outside economic investment, including American investment, which may act as a restraining force on its strategic ambitions.

China's policy in dealing with the issue of North Korea's nuclear weapons was yet another source of Sino-U.S. friction. China's low-key approach as the major interlocutor with North Korea was not sufficiently tough for the Bush administration. Although the Chinese were no more eager than the Americans to see the development of nuclear weapons on the Korean peninsula, they did not want to push too hard for fear that any kind of radical or destabilizing change might send millions of North Koreans across the border into China's densely populated rust-belt Northeast.

Despite these ongoing tensions between the United States and China, both countries tried to prevent a worsening of relations. Hu Jintao, like Deng and Jiang before him, recognized that China's growing international trade and participation in the world community made it impossible to return to the isolation and belligerence of the Mao years. As China joined international organizations and became part of the global community, including its entry into the World Trade Organization in 2001, it increasingly had to abide by international rules and negotiate with countries with which it had sharp differences. Whether this would reduce China's conflicts with its neighbors and with the United States was still not clear in the early years of the twenty-first century.

An even more worrisome development in China's relations with other countries that became increasingly manifest was an upsurge in the fervent nationalism that filled the ideological vacuum left by the bankruptcy of Marxism-Leninism. This nationalism was expressed most vociferously in the large, widespread demonstrations against Japan in spring 2005. Despite repeated apologies by the leaders of Japan for its actions toward China in World War II, including an apology by Prime Minister Junichiro Koizumi to Hu Jintao at an Asian conference in June 2005, the glossing over of Japan's atrocities during the Second World War in high school textbooks, Koizumi's annual visits to the Yasukuni Shrine which also contained the remains of Second World War Japanese war criminals, and Japan's bid to become a member of the UN Security Council evoked widespread Chinese denunciation and demonstrations by urban youth in Beijing, Shanghai, and other coastal cities in spring 2005.

Although the party had stopped other Chinese demonstrations almost immediately, the leadership allowed the anti-Japanese demonstrations to continue for almost three weeks. Thus, the anti-Japanese message was delivered by the party leadership as well as by China's urban youth, who were the main participants in the demonstrations. But whereas nationalism may unite a nation temporarily against a supposed foreign threat, the anger it engenders may easily be turned on the country's own leadership if it fails to act forcefully against the perceived enemy. Furthermore, the demonstrators' demand that Japan stop glossing over its history may someday be turned against China's own leaders for glossing over the party's turbulent and destructive past. Moreover, the growing nationalism could also become an outlet for expressing anger over increasing economic disparities and rampant official corruption. Thus, although nationalism may temporarily unite disparate sections of the population, it may also lead to a further erosion of party authority.

Disconnection between Socio-economic Changes and China's Political Structure

The party's greatest challenge may come from China's prevailing political system. Despite Marx's dictum that when the substructure—the economic base—changes, the superstructure—the political structure—must also change, China continues to be ruled by the same Communist party-state established at the start of the 1949 revolution. Nevertheless, over the intervening decades of Communist rule, especially in the post-Mao era, there have been dramatic changes. Although China is still an authoritarian state, its market economy and openness to the outside world had loosened the all-encompassing controls of the Mao years, allowing for more intellectual diversity and personal freedom. By 2004, China had developed a growing middle class of some 70 million people who were primarily owners of small and medium-sized private enterprises.[9] One-third of China's private businessmen were party members,[10] and the percentage of party members among large private entrepreneurs was even greater. This rapidly growing sector of society was becoming increasingly wealthy. The question is whether they will be co-opted by the party or in time will attempt to change the party.

Yet despite these transforming economic, and social changes, China's Communist party-state remains in power. Its persistence may be explained by what happened in the former Soviet Union in 1991—the dramatic fall in the standard of living of ordinary Russian citizens, along with the disintegration of the Soviet Union that occurred in the wake of Russian efforts at political reform in the late 1980s. This specter, which haunts both China's population and its leadership, has instilled a widespread belief that fundamental political change will lead to instability and will undermine the gains in livelihood and economic growth enjoyed by most Chinese in the post-Mao period. Yet, without more accommodation of the political structure to the accelerating economic and political decentralization, fragmenting society, cultural pluralism, and sprouting democratization at the grass-roots level, the party-state may ultimately face even greater disorder in the future. In fact, the survival of the party-state may well depend on the success of its political adjustments to these changes.

Even though liberal intellectuals continue to speak out and write about the need for such an adjustments, the party leadership under Hu Jintao has muffled their voices and has yet to acknowledge the necessity for political change because of the fear that it may mark the end of its rule. Instead, the Hu leadership emphasizes economic modernization and redistribution, and reinvigoration of the party. While this approach may be successful in Singapore, a city-state with a population of 4.5 million, it is questionable whether it can be sustained in a diverse nation of 1.3 billion. The experience of China's other post-Confucian neighbors offers a promising alternative. After several decades of economic growth and modernization, guided by an authoritarian political system and supported by a burgeoning middle class, South Korea and Taiwan, starting with gradual political change at the grass-roots, peacefully evolved into democratic polities. Still, China's twentieth-century experience was different from that of its East Asian neighbors in ways that may also influence its future development. It does not have a comparable well-developed educational system or Western-trained bureaucracy, and the decentralization of political power in China has already progressed much further than it has in its still relatively centrally governed neighbors.

In addition, China's post-Mao economic reforms have introduced new problems. Although the shift to the market and the accompanying disintegration of the command economy released suppressed energies and entrepreneurial skills, their success of the economic reforms was accompanied by costs to both China's Communist party-state and various segments of society. Whereas the urban-rural gap of the pre-Communist period had been somewhat mitigated during the Mao era, especially in the areas of health care, education, gender, and income inequalities, the market reforms widened the gap in the 1990s. There is also the potential for great social instability from the by-products of the reforms owing to the accelerating social and economic polarization between the faster-growing coastal areas and the slower-growing interior regions; between the newly rich entrepreneurs and the workers in bankrupt SOEs; between the villages along the coast involved in nonstate enterprises and foreign trade and those still tied to the state in the poorer central and western areas; between the prospering urban dwellers and the disgruntled farmers whose economic growth in the aftermath of the land reform of the early 1980s had leveled off by the end of the decade.

The market reforms also engendered other discontents lying just beneath the surface that were increasingly expressed in workers' demonstrations against loss of jobs, pensions, and health care, farmers' protests against unfair taxes and confiscation of their land for infrastructure projects, migrant laborer riots over unpaid wages and unsafe working conditions, urban homeowners' demands for more compensation for the demolition of their homes to make way for modernization projects, and communities rioting against the contamination of their air and water supplies because of careless, unregulated industrial development. China's environmental problems by the early twenty-first century had become daunting.[11] Fifteen of the world's twenty most polluted cities are in China. Furthermore, in addition to polluted rivers and lakes, there is a rapidly falling water table, extensive desertification, and a steady loss of land due to economic development.[12] These social issues and environmental disasters have sparked a myriad of protests throughout the country.

Another pressing problem facing the leadership as the century began was the estimated 10 million Chinese who would be infected with AIDS by 2010. The leadership of Hu Jintao and Wen Jiabao appeared to recognize the severity of this issue when, in December 2003, Prime Minister Wen Jiabao met with AIDS patients, followed shortly thereafter by a visit from Hu Jintao, and the government doubled its budget for combating AIDS and passed several new AIDS-related policies.[13] Yet the government has generally prevented non-official groups from dealing with AIDS-related problems.

At the same time, the capacity of the party-state to deal with these issues has been weakened. The diffusion of economic decision making to the regions resulted in decreased concentration of political power in Beijing. The efforts of Deng's successors to reestablish strong centralized control and to slow the dynamics of regionalism have been thwarted because China's continued economic growth depends on decentralization and international openness. The regions have become increasingly less responsive to central directives, especially the wealthier provinces along the eastern coast that are involved in international trade. These provinces have closer economic relations with neighboring areas—Guangdong with Hong Kong, Fujian with Taiwan, and Shandong with South Korea—than they have with Beijing, and they are less willing to follow Beijing's directives on such issues as taxes, trade, and social welfare when the directives conflict with their own regional economic interests.

The paradox of the post-Mao era is that an expanding, dynamic economy has undermined the authority of the Communist Party and the political structure that made the economic reforms possible. The reforms have unleashed such compelling forces of change that no leader seeking to reinvigorate the party will be able to manage them without redefining or even changing the Communist party-state. At present there are no procedures or institutionalized structures through which the regions and social groups can interact regularly with the center on policy issues. Nor are there political institutions or an overriding ideology that can bind together China's fragmenting society. Whereas the Confucian bureaucracy held China together through most of its premodern history with a common belief and value system, and indoctrinated party cadres, reinforced by a unified ideology, held the country together during most of the Mao period until Mao created class warfare during the Cultural Revolution by mobilizing groups against one another, there is no such ideology or value system in the post-Mao period to unite China's huge population. In 2005, Hu Jintao launched a nationwide campaign to promote a "harmonious society," stressing the traditional Confucian values of moderation, benevolence, and balance, in an apparent effort to counter the sharpening social tensions caused by the economic reforms. But it appeared to have little impact on the growing protests spreading throughout the country.

In addition, Hu Jintao and his fourth generation of leaders lack the personal history and authority of Deng Xiaoping and his revolutionary colleagues to sustain the already hollowed-out party-state. Nor are there any legitimizing institutions, such as national elections, to grant them authority and power. A factional leadership struggle, an economic downturn, escalating social tensions, or an international crisis could further undermine the authority of the present leaders and even the political system. But who and what can replace them? There are other party leaders to take over, but at present there is no alternative to the Communist Party, which has repeatedly suppressed dissident political voices and any efforts to establish opposition political parties. The military, with representatives at the highest level of the party-state, could wield influence in a factional struggle, but it may be unprepared to govern and too preoccupied with pressuring the government to provide additional funds for military modernization. Short of a systemic collapse, it is also unlikely that a new leadership will emerge from China's dissident community, most of whom are either in prison, in exile, or silenced. Unlike the East European dissidents, Chinese dissidents lack an organization, such as the Solidarity movement in Poland, or a platform of political reform, such as that offered by the Charter 77 group in Czechoslovakia, to challenge the party-state.

Still, the history and experience of other countries, including China's East Asian neighbors, have shown that a growing middle class with rising incomes and educational levels will in time demand a greater voice on political issues. China's emerging middle class is not yet large enough or independent enough of official patronage to exert effective political pressure. Nevertheless, China's post-Confucian neighbors—Japan, South Korea, and Taiwan—demonstrate that there is nothing in China's historical legacy and values that prevents it from moving toward democracy. In fact, the very success of these post-Confucian democracies may reveal that the traditional emphasis on education and desire for civil and humane government could also lead China in a democratic direction.

China's own recent history may also encourage such a process. As we have seen, the impetus for the post-Mao economic reforms and grass-roots political reforms came from pressures from below as well as from Deng Xiaoping and other officials whom Mao had persecuted during the Cultural Revolution. The continuing move to the market and the open-door policies that have led to China's weakening party-state might in time bring about a freer, more democratic society as China's population becomes more prosperous and begins to demand greater rights. China's participation in the global economy means that it will continue to be open and pluralistic. Growing economic integration into the international community will bring increased exposure to the rules, standards, laws, pressures, scrutiny, and regulations of international institutions. Yet the development of appropriate political institutions, such as local elections and the efforts to establish the rule of law, is only at an embryonic stage in China, and could easily be arrested.

Consequently, there is an increasing dichotomy between China's dynamic economic growth and the fragile party-state. Moreover, the unintended consequences of China's reforms—growing geographic disparities, social inequalities, rising expectations, labor unrest, mass protests, and ecological damage—have the potential to lead to massive social upheavals and political instability that could undermine China's extraordinary economic success during the last two decades of the twentieth century. What course China will take in the twenty-first century is still an open question.

Notes

1. "PRC Minister Says 800 Million Farmers to be Exempted from Agricultural Taxes," *Renmin Ribao,* June 29, 2005, trans. *FBIS China,* 20050629. By June 2005 there were twenty-seven generally agriculture tax–free provinces.
2. "Under Fire Again, Intellectuals in China," *The Economist,* December 11, 2004, pp. 40–41.
3. Ibid.
4. Reporters Without Borders, "China: Annual Report 2005," *www.rsf.org/article.php3?id_article=13426&Valider=OK.*
5. Paul Mooney, "China Wages a New War on Academic Dissent," *Chronicle of Higher Education,* June 17, 2005, pp. 29–30.
6. "A New Kind of Challenge," *Newsweek,* May 9, 2005, p. 34.
7. "Why Taiwan Matters," Business Week, May 16, 2005, pp. 76–81.
8. U.S. Census Bureau, Foreign Trade Statistics, *www.census.gov/foreigntrade/balance/c5700.html.*

9. David Barboza, "China, New Land of Shoppers," *New York Times,* May 25, 2005, p. 1.

10. Xinhua, February 10, 2005.

11. In June 2005 the director of the State Environmental Protection Administration (SEPA) announced that China would adopt a series of measures in the coming five years to curb the deteriorating environmental situation. Xinhua, June 29, 2005.

12. Jonathan Watts, "100 Chinese Cities Face Water Crisis, Says Minister," *The Guardian,* June 8, 2005, *www.guardian.co.uk/international/story/ 0,,1501312,00.html.*

13. Jim Yardley, "Chinese City Emerges as Model in AIDS Fight," *New York Times,* June 16, 2005, pp. A1, 13.

Note on Romanization
and Citation

Suggested Reading

Publisher's Note

Illustration Credits

Author Index

General Index

Note on Romanization and Citation

Since the *pinyin* system of romanization introduced some years ago by Beijing seems to have a lock on the future, it is used throughout this book for the transcription of Chinese names and terms. Where an older romanization is likely to be better known to the reader (for example, Chiang Kaishek instead of Jiang Jieshi, or Canton instead of Guangzhou), the familiar form is indicated in parentheses at first use.

Citations in the text are by author and date of publication, except for references to *The Cambridge History of China*, which are identified by *CHOC* and volume number. The Author Index includes authors listed in the Suggested Reading as well as those referred to in the text.

Suggested Reading

The pervasive excitement in Western studies of China is due only in part to the Chinese people's ongoing efforts at revolution and reform. The intensity of our interest arises also from a conjunction of background factors. First, a post–Cold War recognition that scholarship has become a chief hope for global survival. Second, the natural evolution from Area Studies of the 1940s to the use of all the social as well as humanistic sciences to understand history. Third, the growth of a critical mass of linguistically able researchers whose competition enhances their sophistication. Fourth, the increasingly important contributions of Chinese historians in Taiwan, the mainland, and overseas. These and other factors are prompting an unprecedented flow of publication that calls for synthesis.

Aside from basic works of reference, this Suggested Reading list is largely limited to books published after 1970. It omits many items listed in my *United States and China,* 4th ed. revised and enlarged (1983). That volume therefore retains some bibliographic value, particularly concerning American relations with China and the Christian missionary movement, which are less fully dealt with in this volume.

Visible in the literature is a progression of the generations. In the second quarter of the twentieth century the newly trained "sinologists" (mainly historians) still treated China as a single entity, seeking to work out the details of political events, wars, and rebellions as well as seeking overall appraisals of institutional structures. Subsequent generations, more skilled in both language and social science, have aimed to treat China and its history as part of world history within the purview of the social sciences and comparative studies. China is no longer a quaint exception.

This greater maturity in China studies is due partly to the fading out of old parochial distinctions between classical and modern (caricatured as "Confucius say" vs. current events) or between humanities and social sciences (they are now seen to need each other) or between disciplines such as economics and anthropology (which may be mutually dependent). Instead, a China specialist now expects to relate his specialized findings to a larger view of the whole Chinese society within the world scene. This cosmopolitan approach reflects at least two factors. First, the vogue of Marxist–Leninist thinking in connection with the rise of the People's Republic. Second, the worldwide interest in development or, in the broadest terms, modernization. Between them, the communists and the economists have stretched our minds.

One particular trend in China studies received in the 1960s a major stimulus from the work of G. William Skinner, whose influence was noted in the Introduction with reference to marketing systems, macroregions, and urbanization. For example, in order to get below the dynastic histories and official compilations that stress the viewpoint of the imperial institution, Susan Naquin and Evelyn Sakakida Rawski in their *Chinese Society in the Eighteenth Century* (1987) take as a framework Skinner's macroregions, which represent economic-demographic reality more accurately than China's historic provinces.

This approach, by cutting up the Chinese monolith and examining its concrete ingredients, finds great diversity. First of all among the macroregions are the variegated climates and terrains of mountains, plains, rivers, and lakes; then the ethnic or "racial" differences in stature and physical characteristics among the people; then their local dialects (some of them distinct languages); their local products, technologies, and occupations; their domestic architecture, tools, and transport mechanisms; their diverse forms and customs of family life, of folklore, rituals, and religious beliefs. The macroregional approach is a great stimulus to local history, having already produced a number of outstanding studies noted in the following Suggested Reading.

At the beginning of the section entitled "People's Republic of China" one finds reference works listed again. This reflects the original bifurcation between "Chinese History, Ancient to Modern up to 1949," on the one hand, and "Communist China since 1949," as it was called, on the other hand. Michel Oksenberg surveys the special characteristics of research and writing on the PRC in his 48-page essay in *The Cambridge History of China (CHOC)*, vol. 14: "Politics Takes Command: An Essay on the Study of Post-1949 China." We list below only a selection from the writings cited by Oksenberg.

Contents of Suggested Reading

General Works of Reference   478

Bibliographies   478
Geography and Maps   478
Historical Surveys   479
Encyclopedias   480
Dynastic Histories and Other Sources 480
Biographical Dictionaries   480
Philosophy and Religion   481
Technology, Science, and Medicine   482

China before Empire: Prehistory and Early History   483

Archaeological Origins   483
Early History: Zhou Dynasty and Warring States   484

The First Empire: Qin–Han China (221 BC–AD 222)   484

Qin Unification   484
Han Dynasty   485

Sui–Tang China (589–907)   485

Tang Government   485
Tang Society   486

Song China (960–1279)   486

Institutional Studies   486
Society and Economy   486
Zhu Xi and Neo-Confucianism   487

The Role of Inner Asia   487

Sino–Inner Asian Relations   487
The Mongols and the Yuan Dynasty (1279–1368)   488

The Society of Late Imperial China   489

On the Nature of Chinese Society   489
Social Anthropology   490
Late Ming and Qing Social History   490

Ming and Qing Polity   491

The Government of Ming China (1368–1644)   491
Qing Conquest and Governance (1644–1911)   492
Intellectual Trends   493

Early Western Contact   494

The Jesuits and Cultural Controversy   494
Early European Trade   494
The Canton Trading System   495

Domestic Decline and Foreign Invasion   495

General Accounts of the Nineteenth and Twentieth Centuries   495
Relations with the West: The Treaty System   496
Mid-Century Rebellions   498
The Qing Restoration   498
Economic Developments   500
The 1911 Revolution   501

Republican China (1912–1949)   502

General Studies   502
Urban Change   502
Early Politics: Yuan Shikai and Warlord Power   503
Intellectual Revolution: The May 4th Era   503
Guomindang Conquest and Governance (1925–1937)   504
The Early History of the Chinese Communist Party (1921–1936)   505
Economic Conditions in Republican China   506
War with Japan   507
Civil War   508

Republic of China, Taiwan   508

General Works   508
Politics and Government   509
Taiwan's Economic Development   509
Culture and Society   510

People's Republic of China (1949–)   510

Reference Works   510
Periodicals   511
Surveys   511

Sociopolitical Organization and Leadership 511

Mao Zedong 511
Policy and Politics 512
Campaigns 513

Intellectuals and the State 514

Education 514

Great Leap Forward, 1958–1960 515

The Cultural Revolution Period, 1966–1976 515

Red Guards 516
Late Cultural Revolution Period and the Early 1980s 516

The Military 517

The Economy in General 517

Agricultural Development 518
Urbanization and Industry 519
Science and Technology 519

Economic Reform, 1978–1990 520

China's Foreign Affairs 521

Korean War 521
China and the USSR 522
China and the Third World 522
China and the United States 522

Political Reform, 1978–1990 523

Democracy Movement 523
Tiananmen Incident, June 4, 1989 524

Law and Human Rights 524

Domestic Law 524
International Law 525

Social and Public Affairs 525

Medicine and Public Health 525
Environment 525

Demography and Birth Control   526
Women in Society   526
Minorities and Regions   527
Religion   527
Arts and Humanities   528

GENERAL WORKS OF REFERENCE

Bibliographies

G. William Skinner et al., *Modern Chinese Society: An Analytical Bibliography* (Stanford UP, 1973), 3 vols., is highly organized into useful categories; vol. 1 is in Western languages. Charles O. Hucker, *China: A Critical Bibliography* (U of Arizona Press, 1962), contains 2,285 entries by subject to 1961. Continued, after a gap, by Peter Cheng, *China*, World Bibliographical Series, vol. 35 (Clio Press, 1983), an annotated list, categorized by subject, of 1,470 works published 1970–1982. Chun-shu Chang, *Premodern China: A Bibliographical Introduction* (Center for Chinese Studies, U of Michigan, 1971), tells you where to go for what. Note also that *The Cambridge History of China (CHOC)* volumes listed in **Historical Surveys,** below, contain extensive bibliographies more recent than some of the above.

There are now two annual publications for materials published on any East Asian country, and these will contain the most comprehensive listings. The Association for Asian Studies (Ann Arbor) publishes annually the *Bibliography of Asian Studies;* it has also compiled the *Cumulative Bibliography of Asian Studies, 1941–1965,* 8 vols., and *1966–1970,* 6 vols. (G. K. Hall, 1969–70, 1972). In 1990 G. K. Hall began publishing an annual *Bibliographic Guide to East Asian Studies,* the first volume of which surveys 1989 publications.

Geography and Maps

P. J. M. Geelan and D. C. Twitchett, eds., *The Times Atlas of China* (London: Times Books, 1974), contains the best detailed maps of the provinces, some 30 cities, and geoeconomic features like climate and communication. Also recent is the *Atlas of the People's Republic of China* (Beijing: Foreign Languages Press and China Cartographic Publishing House, 1989).

For historical maps consult the new edition of Albert Herrmann, *An Historical Atlas of China,* ed. Norton Ginsburg (Aldine, 1966). Caroline Blunden and Mark Elvin, *Cultural Atlas of China* (Facts on File, 1983), has historical maps, tables, and photographs with a text discussing the development of Chinese culture. Note also Chiao-min Hsieh, *Atlas of China* (McGraw-Hill, 1973), sections on historical, economic, and cultural geography as well as physical geography. T. R. Tregear, *China: A Geographical Survey* (Hodder and Stoughton, 1980), builds on the earlier works of George B. Cressey.

Historical Surveys

The Cambridge History of China, gen. eds. Denis Twitchett and John K. Fairbank (Cambridge UP). Vol. 1: *The Ch'in and Han Empires, 221 BC–AD 220,* ed. Denis Twitchett and Michael Loewe (1986). Vol. 3: *Sui and Tang China, 589–906, Part 1,* ed. Denis Twitchett (1979). Vol. 7: *The Ming Dynasty, 1368–1644, Part 1,* ed. Frederick F. Mote and Denis Twitchett (1988). Vol. 10: *Late Ch'ing, 1800–1911, Part 1,* ed. John K. Fairbank (1978). Vol. 11: *Late Ch'ing, 1800–1911, Part 2,* ed. John K. Fairbank and Kwang-Ching Liu (1980). Vol. 12: *Republican China, 1912–1949, Part 1,* ed. John K. Fairbank (1983). Vol. 13: *Republican China, 1912–1949, Part 2,* ed. John K. Fairbank and Albert Feuerwerker (1986). Vol. 14: *The People's Republic, Part 1: The Emergence of Revolutionary China, 1949–1965,* ed. Roderick MacFarquhar and John K. Fairbank (1987). Vol. 15: *The People's Republic, Part 2: Revolutions within the Chinese Revolution 1966–1982,* ed. Roderick MacFarquhar and John K. Fairbank (1991).

GENERAL WORKS. The best general surveys often come out of teaching experience in major research centers. A comprehensive and sophisticated survey from Paris is Jacques Gernet, *A History of Chinese Civilization* (Cambridge UP, 1982 trans. from *Le Monde Chinois,* Paris, 1972). Paul S. Ropp, ed., *Heritage of China: Contemporary Perspectives on Chinese Civilization* (U of California Press, 1990), is an illuminating symposium volume. From Michigan, Charles O. Hucker, *China's Imperial Past: An Introduction to Chinese History and Culture* (Stanford UP, 1975), is a survey to 1850.

From Harvard, the two volumes by Edwin O. Reischauer and John K. Fairbank, *East Asia: The Great Tradition* (Houghton Mifflin, 1960), and John K. Fairbank, Edwin O. Reischauer, and Albert M. Craig, *East Asia: The Modern Transformation* (Houghton Mifflin, 1965), have been condensed and divided to make *China: Tradition and Transformation* (1978; rev. ed. 1989). Paul A. Cohen and Merle Goldman, eds., *Ideas Across Cultures: Essays on Chinese Thought in Honor of Benjamin I. Schwartz* (Council on East Asian Studies, Harvard U, 1990), contains essays on a wide range of subjects.

From Columbia, Wm. Theodore de Bary, Wing-tsit Chan, and Burton Watson, comps., *Sources of Chinese Tradition* (Columbia UP, 1964), offers 950 pages of carefully selected translations with interpretive comments on the whole sweep of philosophical, religious, and political ideas from Confucius to communism. Patricia Ebrey, *Chinese Civilization and Society: A Sourcebook* (Free Press, 1981), has useful selected translations.

From Oxford, Mark Elvin, *The Pattern of the Chinese Past* (Stanford UP, 1973), pursues socioeconomic themes. From Cambridge, Michael Loewe, *Imperial China: The Historical Background to the Modern Age* (Praeger, 1966), offers interesting analytic notes by a classicist. More recent is Loewe's *The Pride That Was China* (St. Martin's, 1990). Among other surveys, note Ray Huang, *China: A Macro-History* (M. E. Sharpe, 1988), which contains sophisticated highlights. For surveys of modern history see **General Accounts of the Nineteenth and Twentieth Centuries,** below.

Encyclopedias

For compilations by Western scholars see the *Encyclopedia of Asian History,* prepared under auspices of the Asia Society, ed. in chief Ainslie T. Embree, 4 vols. (Scribner's, 1988), with articles by scholars, geared to the nonspecialist; also *The Cambridge Encyclopedia of China,* gen. ed. Brian Hook (Cambridge UP, 1982), on aspects of geography, society, history, and civilization.

Dynastic Histories and Other Sources

W. G. Beasley and E. B. Pulleyblank, *Historians of China and Japan* (Oxford UP, 1961), 2 vols., contains work still of basic value. On the first dynastic history, two works by Burton Watson bring us close to the great pioneer historian Sima Qian: *Records of the Grand Historian of China* (Columbia UP, 1961), 2 vols., a translation of the *Shiji;* and *Ssu-ma Ch'ien: Grand Historian of China* (Columbia UP, 1958). Welcome additions to the corpus of works on the history of the Han dynasty include Burton Watson, *Courtier and Commoner in Ancient China: Selections from the "History of the Former Han" by Pan Ku* (Columbia UP, 1974); and Kan Lao, *The History of the Han Dynasty,* selected trans. (Chinese Linguistics Project, Princeton U, 1984).

Biographical Dictionaries

For biographies in the pre-Han period, see *Selections from the Records of the Historian,* trans. Gladys Yang and Hsien-Yi Yang (Beijing: Foreign Languages Press, 1979). Song dynasty biographies have been compiled in Herbert Franke, ed., *Sung Biographies* (Wiesbaden: Franz Steiner Verlag, 1976), 4 vols., with entries in English, German, and French. On the Ming see L. Carrington Goodrich and Chaoying Fang, eds., *Dictionary of Ming Biography, 1368–1644* (Columbia UP, 1976), 2 vols. Qing biographies are compiled in A. W. Hummel, ed., *Eminent Chinese of the Ch'ing Period, 1644–1912* (U.S. Government Printing Office, 1943, 1944), 2 vols. For twentieth-century personages see entries under **Republican China** and **People's Republic of China.**

Philosophy and Religion

PHILOSOPHY AND THOUGHT. Benjamin I. Schwartz, *The World of Thought in Ancient China* (Harvard UP, 1985), is a widely based distillation reflecting many years of teaching. Also noteworthy is F. W. Mote, *Intellectual Foundations of China,* 2nd ed. (McGraw-Hill, 1989). From a series of conference symposia in the 1950s and 60s on Chinese thought led by Arthur F. Wright, see John K. Fairbank, ed., *Chinese Thought and Institutions* (U of Chicago Press, 1957); other titles are listed in Fairbank, *The United States and China,* 4th ed. (Harvard UP, 1983). The leading general survey is Fung Yu-lan, *A History of Chinese Philosophy,* trans. Derk Bodde (Princeton UP, 1952–53).

CORRELATIVE COSMOLOGY. The main work is John B. Henderson, *The Development and Decline of Chinese Cosmology* (Columbia UP, 1984). Note also Sarah Allan, *The Shape of the Turtle: Myth, Art, and Cosmos in Early China* (SUNY Press, 1991), and Wolfram Eberhard, *A Dictionary of Chinese Symbols: Hidden Symbols in Chinese Life and Thought* (Routledge and Kegan Paul, 1986).

DIVINATION. Richard J. Smith, *Fortune-tellers and Philosophers: Divination in Traditional Chinese Society* (Westview Press, 1991)—a broad survey with extensive sources and bibliography. There is a large literature on this subject.

CONFUCIANISM. Among recent reappraisals of Confucianism, Wm. Theodore de Bary, *The Trouble with Confucianism* (Harvard UP, 1991), is a trenchant critique of the Confucians' moral performance despite the lack of a power base. For introductions see Wei-ming Tu, *Confucian Thought: Selfhood as Creative Transformation* (SUNY Press, 1985); Irene Eber, *Confucianism, the Dynamics of Tradition* (Macmillan, 1986); and Wm. Theodore de Bary, *The Liberal Tradition in China* (Columbia UP, 1983). For studies of Neo-Confucianism, see relevant sections under the Song and Ming periods.

RELIGION IN GENERAL. See Laurence G. Thompson, *Chinese Religion: An Introduction,* 4th ed. (Wadsworth, 1988); Daniel Overmyer, *Religions of China: The World as a Living System* (Harper & Row, 1986); and Christian Jochim, *Chinese Religions: A Cultural Perspective* (Prentice Hall, 1986). For studies of folk sects and modern conditions, see sections under **Republic of China, Taiwan** and **People's Republic of China.**

DAOISM. The most recent version of the core text is Lao Tzu, *Tao Te Ching: The Classic Book of Integrity and the Way,* trans. Victor Mair (Bantam, 1990), based on the Mawangdui manuscripts. A still-fascinating account of Daoism is presented in Holmes Welch, *The Parting of the Way: Lao Tzu and the Taoist Movement* (Beacon Press, 1957); more recent scholarship is reflected in John Lagerwey, *Taoist Ritual in Chinese Society and History* (Collier Macmillan, 1987).

BUDDHISM. Wm. Theodore de Bary, ed., *The Buddhist Tradition in India, China and Japan* (Vintage, 1972), contains selected translations of important texts. On the spread of Buddhism in China the principal monograph is by Eric Zürcher, *The Buddhist Conquest of China: The Spread and Adaptation of Buddhism in Early Medieval China* (Brill, 1959), 2 vols. For a general account, see Kenneth Chen, *Buddhism in China: A Historical Survey* (Princeton UP, 1964). For an interesting brief survey, see Arthur F. Wright, *Buddhism in Chinese History* (Stanford UP, 1959).

Technology, Science, and Medicine

HISTORY OF SCIENCE IN CHINA. For a survey see Nathan Sivin, "Science and Medicine in Imperial China: The State of the Field," *in Journal of Asian Studies,* 47.1 (Feb. 1988): 41–90. Our Western view of China's contribution to world science and technology, traditionally confined to paper, printing, the compass, gunpowder, and similar great inventions, has been revolutionized by the work of Joseph Needham and his several collaborators—Wang Ling, Lu Gwei-djen and others—who are producing a multitomed, seven-volume series, *Science and Civilisation in China* (Cambridge UP, 1954–). Volumes 1 and 2 have been condensed in Colin A. Ronan, *The Shorter Science and Civilisation in China,* vol. 1 (1978). See also Peng Yoke Ho, Li Qi, and Shu An, *Introduction to Science and Civilization in China* (Hong Kong UP, 1985). Selections of Needham's incidental papers and addresses have been published: for example, *Science in Traditional China: A Comparative Perspective* (Harvard UP, 1981); and most recently *Heavenly Clockwork: The Great Astronomical Clocks of Medieval China* (Cambridge UP, 1986).

Note also Shigeru Nakayama and Nathan Sivin, eds., *Chinese Science: Explorations of an Ancient Tradition* (MIT Press, 1973), a symposium including Needham, A. C. Graham, and several Japanese specialists. Useful for social and intellectual context is Derk Bodde, *Chinese Thought, Society, and Science: The Intellectual and Social Background of Science and Technology in Pre-Modern China* (U of Hawaii Press, 1991).

Chinese inventions are surveyed in *Ancient China's Technology and Science,* compiled for the Institute of the History of Natural Sciences, Chinese Academy of Sciences (Beijing: Foreign Languages Press, 1983); and Robert Temple, *The Genius of China: 3,000 Years of Science, Discovery, and Invention* (Simon and Schuster, 1986).

MEDICINE. Recent work is by Paul U. Unschuld, *Medicine in China: A History of Ideas* (U of California Press, 1985); *Medicine in China: A History of Pharmaceutics* (U of California Press, 1986). One basic analysis is Manfred Porkert, *The Theoretical Foundations of Chinese Medicine: Systems of Correspondence* (MIT Press, 1974). See also Lu Gwei-djen and Joseph Needham, *Celestial Lancets: A History and Rationale of Acupuncture and Moxa* (Cambridge UP, 1980). On twentieth-century developments see Nathan Sivin, *Traditional Medicine in Contemporary China* (Center for Chinese Studies, U of Michigan, 1987). On psychology see Arthur Kleinman and T. Y. Lin, eds., *Normal and Abnormal Behavior in Chinese Culture* (Reidel, 1981).

BOOKS AND PRINTING. On the early technical developments see Tsuen-hsuin Tsien, *Science and Civilisation in China,* vol. 5, part 1: *Paper and Printing* (Cambridge UP, 1985). Denis Twitchett has published *Printing and Publishing in Medieval China* (Frederic C. Beil, 1983).

CHINESE LANGUAGE. A fertile field. See John DeFrancis, *The Chinese Language: Fact and Fantasy* (U of Hawaii Press, 1984); S. Robert Ramsey, *The Languages of China* (Princeton UP, 1987); and Jerry Norman, *Chinese* (Cambridge UP, 1988).

MATHEMATICS. Li Yan and Du Shiran, trans. John N. Crossley and Anthony W. C. Lun, *Chinese Mathematics: A Concise History* (Oxford UP, 1987).

MILITARY HISTORY. The field is rather underdeveloped. See Frank A. Kierman, Jr., and John K. Fairbank, eds., *Chinese Ways in Warfare* (Harvard UP, 1974). For a comparative approach that includes China, see William McNeill, *The Pursuit of Power: Technology, Armed Force and Society since AD 1000* (U of Chicago Press, 1982). See also **People's Republic of China,** below.

CHINA BEFORE EMPIRE:
PREHISTORY AND EARLY HISTORY

Archaeological Origins

Thousands of excavations in recent decades have recast the picture of prehistoric times. The most authoritative summary of this archaeological revolution is Kwang-chih Chang, *The Archaeology of Ancient China* (Yale UP, 1963; 4th ed., 1986). Note also K. C. Chang, *Early Chinese Civilization: Anthropological Perspectives* (Harvard UP, 1976), a set of pioneering essays; and K. C. Chang, *Shang Civilization* (Yale UP, 1980). Another major work is the symposium, ed. David N. Keightley, *The Origins of Chinese Civilization* (U of California Press,

1983). See also David N. Keightley, *Sources of Shang History: The Oracle Bone Inscriptions of Bronze Age China* (U of California Press, 1978).

The new evidence is reflected in a thematic survey, Ping-ti Ho, *The Cradle of the East: An Inquiry into the Indigenous Origins of Techniques and Ideas of Neolithic and Early Historic China, 5000–1000 BC* (U of Chicago Press, 1976). The history of the birth of modern Chinese archaeology in the 1920s and 1930s is recorded by a pioneer leader, Li Chi, *Anyang* (U of Washington Press, 1977).

Early History: Zhou Dynasty and Warring States

On the early Zhou, see Cho-yun Hsu and Katheryn Linduff, *Western Chou Civilization* (Yale UP, 1988), which compares the literary and archaeological records. Herrlee G. Creel, *The Origins of Statecraft in China,* vol. 1: *The Western Chou Empire* (U of Chicago Press, 1970), opens a new door to the Legalist administrative tradition. The political institutions of the Warring States period (403–221 BC) have been analyzed by Mark Edward Lewis, *Sanctioned Violence in Early China* (SUNY Press, 1990).

THE CLASSICAL AGE. These are, above all, works of literature. For an introduction see Wm. Theodore de Bary, Ainslie T. Embree, and Amy Vladek Heinrich, eds., *A Guide to Oriental Classics,* 3rd ed. (Columbia UP, 1989); the section on "Classics of the Chinese Tradition" lists complete and partial translations of the *Four Books* with secondary readings and discussion topics. The *Five Classics* are considered with bibliography in another valuable *vademecum* by Jordan D. Paper, *Guide to Chinese Prose* (G. K. Hall, 1973).

On the ancient northern and southern anthologies, see Yeh Shan, *The Bell and the Drum: Shih Ching as Formulaic Poetry in an Oral Tradition,* trans. Wang Ching-hsien (U of California Press, 1974). Recent translations of Warring States philosophers include John Knoblock, *Xunzi: A Translation and Study of the Complete Works, vol. 1, Books 1–6* (Stanford UP, 1988). W. Allyn Rickett has published *Kuan-tzu: A Repository of Early Chinese Thought* (Hong Kong UP, 1965); and recently *Guanzi: Political, Economic, and Philosophical Essays from Early China* (Princeton UP, 1985).

THE FIRST EMPIRE: QIN–HAN CHINA (221 BC–AD 222)

The principal survey work is Denis Twitchett and Michael Loewe, eds., *The Cambridge History of China,* vol. 1: *Qin and Han* (1986).

Qin Unification

On the Qin unification see Derk Bodde in *CHOC* 1 (1986). On Qin legal institutions, see A. F. P. Hulsewe, *Remnants of Ch'in Law: An Annotated Transla-*

tion of the Ch'in Legal and Administrative Rules of the 3rd Century BC. Discovered in Yun-meng Prefecture, Hu-pei Province in 1975 (Brill, 1985).

Han Dynasty

Michele Pirazzoli-t'Serstevens, *The Han Dynasty,* trans. Janet Seligman (Rizzoli, 1982), brilliantly combines text and illustrations, and includes the Mawangdui finds. See also Wang Zhongshu, *Han Civilization,* trans. K. C. Chang (Yale UP, 1982). Note also Hans Bielenstein, *The Bureaucracy of Han Times* (Cambridge UP, 1980). Michael Loewe, *Crisis and Conflict in Han China, 104 BC to AD 9* (Allen and Unwin, 1974), is a political history of cases and crises.

Notable monographs on the Han economy are Ying-shih Yü, *Trade and Expansion in Han China: A Study in the Structure of Sino-Barbarian Economic Relations* (U of California Press, 1967); Cho-yun Hsu, *Han Agriculture: The Formation of Early Chinese Agrarian Economy 206 BC–AD 220* (U of Washington Press, 1980). On law see A. F. P. Hulsewe, *Remnants of Han Law* (Brill, 1955), and more recently A. F. P. Hulsewe, *China in Central Asia: The Early Stage, 125 BC to AD 23* (Brill, 1979).

THOUGHT AND SOCIETY. A product of long-continued scholarship is A. C. Graham, *Disputers of the Tao: Philosophical Argument in Ancient China* (Open Court, 1989). Note also Michael Loewe, *Chinese Ideas of Life and Death: Faith, Myth, and Reason in the Han Period (202 BC–AD 220)* (Allen & Unwin, 1982); and his *Everyday Life in Early Imperial China during the Han Period, 202 BC–AD 220* (Dorset Press, 1988). An exceptional recent work on the Han is Wu Hung, *The Wu Liang Shrine: The Ideology of Early Chinese Pictorial Art* (Stanford UP, 1989).

SUI–TANG CHINA (589–907)

The major recent work is *The Cambridge History of China,* vol. 3: *Sui and T'ang China, 589–906, Part 1,* ed. Denis Twitchett (1979). On the Sui reunification see Arthur F. Wright, *The Sui Dynasty: The Unification of China, AD 581–617* (Knopf, 1978).

Tang Government

On Tang rulership see Howard J. Wechsler, *Mirror to the Son of Heaven: Wei Cheng at the Court of Tang T'ai-tsung* (Yale UP, 1974), introductory to the period. On Tang institutions see Denis C. Twitchett, *Financial Administration under the T'ang Dynasty* (Cambridge UP, 1963; 2nd ed., 1970). Wallace Johnson, ed. and trans., *The T'ang Code, vol. 1: General Principles* (Princeton UP, 1979), makes a basic document available. Recent publications on relations between intellectuals and the state include David McMullen, *State and Scholars in T'ang China* (Cambridge UP, 1988), on the revival of Confucianism; Charles Hartman, *Han Yü and the T'ang Search for Unity* (Princeton UP, 1986).

Tang Society

David Johnson, *The Medieval Chinese Oligarchy* (Westview, 1977), is a basic work on Tang social structure. Note also John C. Perry and Bardwell L. Smith, eds., *Essays on T'ang Society: The Interplay of Social, Political, and Economic Forces* (Brill, 1976). For change over an eight-century span beginning in Tang, see Robert Hartwell, "Demographic, Political, and Social Transformations of China, 750–1550," *Harvard Journal of Asiatic Studies*, 42.2 (Dec. 1982): 365–442.

SONG CHINA (960–1279)

Institutional Studies

LAW, GOVERNMENT, REFORM. On government at the local level, see Brian E. McKnight, *Village and Bureaucracy in Southern Sung China* (U of Chicago Press, 1971). On the changes in the late Northern Song and Southern Song see James T. C. Liu, *Reform in Sung China: Wang An-shih (1021–1086) and His New Policies* (Harvard UP, 1959); and Paul J. Smith, *Taxing Heaven's Storehouse: Horses, Bureaucrats, and the Destruction of the Sichuan Tea Industry, 1074–1224* (Council on East Asian Studies, Harvard U, 1991), which gives basic details on Wang Anshi's tea monopoly and its fate.

SONG EXAMINATION SYSTEM. On the late imperial system's structure and procedures, the basic work is Miyazaki Ichisada, trans. Conrad Schirokauer, *China's Examination Hell: The Civil Service Examinations of Imperial China* (Weatherhill, 1976). On the issue of the system's role in social mobility, see John W. Chaffee, *The Thorny Gates of Learning in Sung China* (Cambridge UP, 1985). Note also Thomas H. C. Lee, *Government Education and Examinations in Sung China* (St. Martin's, 1985); and Winston W. Lo, *An Introduction to the Civil Service of Sung China, with Emphasis on Its Personnel Administration* (U of Hawaii Press, 1987).

Society and Economy

THE RISE OF THE GENTRY. Robert P. Hymes, *Statesmen and Gentlemen: The Elite of Fu-chou, Chiang-hsi, in Northern and Southern Sung* (Cambridge UP, 1986), studies a local community of elite families. Richard L. Davis, *Court and Family in Sung China, 960–1279: Bureaucratic Success and Kinship*

Fortunes for the Shih of Ming-chou (Duke UP, 1986), offers a counterpoint to Hymes. Patricia B. Ebrey, *Family and Property in Sung China: Yüan Tsai's Precepts for Social Life* (Princeton UP, 1984), translates advice from a gentry patriarch. For fuller studies of gentry society see **Late Ming and Qing Social History,** below.

COMMERCIAL DEVELOPMENT. Yoshinobu Shiba, *Commerce and Society in Sung China,* trans. Mark Elvin (Center for Chinese Studies, U of Michigan, 1970), offers a survey of various aspects of the explosion of commerce in the Song. Richard von Glahn, *The Country of Streams and Grottoes: Expansion and Settlement, and the Civilizing of the Sichuan Frontier in Song Times* (Council on East Asian Studies, Harvard U, 1987), looks at a part of the great migrations in the Song. A vivid recreation of Song urban life is Jacques Gernet, *Daily Life in China on the Eve of the Mongol Invasion, 1250–1276,* trans. H. M. Wright (Stanford UP, 1962).

Zhu Xi and Neo-Confucianism

On the intellectual changes during the Tang–Song transition note Peter K. Bol, *"This Culture of Ours": Intellectual Transitions in T'ang and Sung China* (Stanford UP, 1992). James T. C. Liu, *China Turning Inward: Intellectual–Political Changes in the Early Twelfth Century* (Council on East Asian Studies, Harvard U, 1988), is a trenchant survey. Basic texts of Neo-Confucianism are in Chu Hsi, *Learning to Be a Sage: Selections from the Conversation of Master Chu, Arranged Topically,* trans. Daniel K. Gardner (U of California Press, 1990). Recent works on the great synthesizer include: Daniel K. Gardner, *Chu Hsi and the Ta-hsueh: Neo-Confucian Reflection on the Confucian Canon* (Council on East Asian Studies, Harvard U, 1986); Wing-tsit Chan, *Chu Hsi, Life and Thought* (St. Martin's Press, 1987); and Wing-tsit Chan, *Chu Hsi: New Studies* (U of Hawaii Press, 1989), which provide a myriad of interesting details on the philosopher, though still no evidence of his having a sense of humor.

Note also Thomas A. Metzger, *Escape from Predicament: Neo-Confucianism and China's Evolving Political Culture* (Columbia UP, 1977), a major analysis of the Confucian moral experience. See also the studies of Confucianism cited under **Philosophy and Religion,** above, and **Intellectual Trends,** below.

THE ROLE OF INNER ASIA

Sino–Inner Asian Relations

On the origins of Inner Asian peoples the basic work is now Denis Sinor, ed., *The Cambridge History of Early Inner Asia* (Cambridge UP, 1990). Study of Chinese border relations with Manchuria, Mongolia, and Xinjiang (Sinkiang) is pursued in Sechin Jagchid and Van Jay Symons, *Peace, War and Trade along the Great Wall: Nomadic Chinese Interaction through Two Millennia* (Indiana UP, 1989); and Thomas Barfield, *The Perilous Frontier: Nomadic Empires and China* (Basil Blackwell, 1989), a chronological survey.

On Song foreign relations, see Morris Rossabi, *China among Equals: The Middle Kingdom and Its Neighbors* (U of California Press, 1983). For a comparison of Liao, Jin, and Yuan see Herbert Franke's essay in Stuart Schram, ed., *Foundations and Limits of State Power in China* (SOAS, U of London, 1987).

THE LIAO DYNASTY OF THE QIDAN (KHITAN) PEOPLE. For data on the regime of the Qidan Mongols, see K. A. Wittfogel and Chia-sheng Feng, *History of Chinese Society: Liao 907–1125* (American Philosophical Society, 1949). Also see Herbert Franke's chapter in Denis Sinor, ed., *The Cambridge History of Early Inner Asia* (Cambridge UP, 1990).

THE JIN DYNASTY OF THE RUZHEN (JURCHEN) PEOPLE. Notable recent studies on the Jin dynasty in North China include Jing-shen Tao, *The Jurchen in Twelfth-Century China: A Study of Sinicization* (U of Washington Press, 1977); and Hok-lam Chan, *Legitimation in Imperial China: Discussions under the Jurchen Chin Dynasty* (U of Washington Press, 1984).

The Mongols and the Yuan Dynasty (1279–1368)

The most thorough work on the Mongols in history has been done in Europe, beginning in France and Russia. A recent survey is by David Morgan, *The Mongols* (Basil Blackwell, 1986). Among many studies of the founder of the Mongol empire is Leo De Hartog, *Genghis Khan, Conqueror of the World* (I. B. Tauris, 1989). On Chinggis' successor see Thomas T. Allsen, *Mongol Imperialism: The Policies of the Grand Qan Mongke in China, Russia, and the Islamic Lands, 1251–1259* (U of California Press, 1987).

THE YUAN DYNASTY. On the founding of the dynasty see Morris Rossabi, *Khubilai Khan: His Life and Times* (U of California Press, 1988). On Yuan institutions see John D. Langlois, Jr., ed., *China under Mongol Rule* (Princeton UP, 1981); Ch'i-ch'ing Hsiao, *The Military Establishment of the Yüan Dynasty* (Council on East Asian Studies, Harvard U, 1978). On local government see Elizabeth Endicott-West, *Mongolian Rule in China: Local Administration in the Yuan Dynasty* (Council on East Asian Studies, Harvard U, 1989).

On late Yuan political problems see John W. Dardess, *Conquerors and Confucians: Aspects of Political Change in Late Yuan China* (Columbia UP, 1973). On philosophical trends of the period see Hok-lam Chan and Wm. Theodore de Bary, eds., *Yuan Thought: Chinese Thought and Religion under the Mongols* (Columbia UP, 1982).

MARCO POLO ET AL. Polo's best-known European precursors and contemporaries are recorded in Christopher Dawson, *The Mongol Mission: Narratives and Letters of the Franciscan Missionaries in Mongolia and China in the Thirteenth and Fourteenth Centuries* (Sheed and Ward, 1955). For the authoritative English translation of Polo's account, see A. C. Moule and P. Pelliot, *Marco Polo: The Description of the World* (AMS Press, 1976). Of the many popular versions, several are in paperback.

THE SOCIETY OF LATE IMPERIAL CHINA

The late seventeenth through the eighteenth and nineteenth centuries now provide a universe of discourse in themselves, as well as the background to the modern revolution. Surveys of this period include: Susan Naquin and Evelyn Rawski, *Chinese Society in the Eighteenth Century* (Yale UP, 1987); and David Johnson, Andrew Nathan, and Evelyn Rawski, eds., *Popular Culture in Late Imperial China* (U of California Press, 1985). Note also the survey article on approaches to Chinese social history by William Rowe in Olivier Zunz, *Reliving the Past: The Worlds of Social History* (U of North Carolina Press, 1985). For studies on the economy of late imperial China, see **Economic Developments**, below.

On the Nature of Chinese Society

JAPANESE STUDIES. Joshua Fogel's translations and summaries of Japanese studies of China add a much-needed perspective on the China field. On the leading Japanese interpreter, see Joshua Fogel, *Politics and Sinology: The Case of Naitō Konan (1866–1934)* (Council on East Asian Studies, Harvard U, 1984). Recent translations of work by Japanese historians include: Linda Grove and Christian Daniels, eds., *State and Society in China: Japanese Perspectives on Ming–Qing Social and Economic History* (U of Tokyo Press, 1984).

MAX WEBER. A great impetus came from the German sociologist Max Weber, whose pioneer work on China has been largely translated by Hans Gerth as *The Religion of China: Confucianism and Taoism* (Free Press, 1951). The paperback edition (Macmillan, 1964) has an invaluable introduction by C. K. Yang, who puts Weber's work in context and evaluates his contribution.

THE ASIATIC MODE OF PRODUCTION. Another broad impetus through a neo-Marxist approach has come from Karl A. Wittfogel, *Oriental Despotism: A Comparative Study of Total Power* (Yale UP, 1957). See also Timothy Brook, ed., *The Asiatic Mode of Production in China* (M. E. Sharpe, 1989).

AREA SYSTEMS. A vital stimulus, leading toward the study of "local systems," has come from G. William Skinner's three-part article, "Marketing and

Social Structure in Rural China," *Journal of Asian Studies* (1964–65). His framework of macroregions is described and applied in G. William Skinner, ed., *The City in Late Imperial China* (Stanford UP, 1977).

Social Anthropology

Two classic collections in this field are *The Study of Chinese Society: Essays by Maurice Freedman*, intro. by G. William Skinner (Stanford UP, 1979); and Arthur P. Wolf, ed., *Studies in Chinese Society* (Stanford UP, 1978). For work on the family and clan (or lineage), see Maurice Freedman, *Chinese Lineage and Society: Fukien and Kwangtung* (Humanities Press, 1971).

To expand the coverage of Maurice Freedman, see Patricia Ebrey and James L. Watson, *Kinship Organization in Late Imperial China, 1000–1940* (U of California Press, 1986); James L. Watson and Evelyn Rawski, eds., *Death Ritual in Late Imperial and Modern China* (U of California Press, 1988); and Rubie S. Watson and Patricia B. Ebrey, eds., *Marriage and Inequality in Chinese Society* (U of California Press, 1991).

Late Ming and Qing Social History

For historical studies of elites and social structure, Joseph Esherick and Mary Rankin, eds., *Chinese Local Elites and Patterns of Dominance* (U of California Press, 1990), shatters the gentry stereotype to show the great variety of local situations. Also Lloyd Eastman, *Family, Fields, and Ancestors: Constancy and Change in China's Social and Economic History, 1550–1949* (Oxford UP, 1988); and Etienne Balazs, *Chinese Civilization and Bureaucracy: Variations on a Theme*, ed. Arthur Wright, trans. H. M. Wright (Yale UP, 1964), which brings together trenchant essays by a leading European scholar. Among regional studies note Peter Perdue, *Exhausting the Earth: State and Peasant in Hunan, 1500–1850* (Council on East Asian Studies, Harvard U, 1987); and R. Keith Schoppa, *Xiang Lake: Nine Centuries of Chinese Life* (Yale UP, 1989).

SOCIAL AND CULTURAL HISTORY. Recent studies include Ann Waltner, *Getting an Heir: Adoption and the Construction of Kinship in Late Imperial China* (U of Hawaii Press, 1990); Bret Hinsch, *Passions of the Cut Sleeve: The Male Homosexual Tradition in China* (U of California Press, 1990); and Cynthia Brokaw, *The Ledgers of Merit and Demerit: Social Change and Moral Order in Late Imperial China* (Princeton UP, 1991), on social change in the late Ming. A new view of literacy among the Chinese people is suggested by Evelyn S. Rawski, *Education and Popular Literacy in Ch'ing China* (U of Michigan Press, 1979).

THE POSITION OF WOMEN. For recent bibliographic surveys of the field see: Lucie Cheng, Charlotte Furth, and Hon-ming Yip, comps., *Women in*

China: Bibliography of Available English Language Materials (Institute of East Asian Studies, U of California, 1984). The misery and vicissitudes of ordinary life during the Ming are portrayed in Jonathan D. Spence, *The Death of Woman Wang* (Viking, 1978).

Two collections of articles on women are: Richard Guisso and Stanley Johannesen, eds., *Women in China: Current Directions in Historical Scholarship* (Philo Press, 1981); and Margery Wolf and Roxane Witke, eds., *Women in Chinese Society* (Stanford UP, 1975). A survey treatment by Japan's foremost historian of Chinese women is Kazuko Ono, *Chinese Women in a Century of Revolution, 1850–1950,* trans. Joshua Fogel et al. (Stanford UP, 1989). Note also the section **Women in Society,** below. On footbinding the main source so far is Howard S. Levy, *Chinese Footbinding: The History of a Curious Erotic Custom* (Walton Rawls, 1966).

MING AND QING POLITY

The Government of Ming China (1368–1644)

For survey articles by specialists reign by reign see Frederic F. Mote and Denis Twitchett, eds., *The Cambridge History of China,* vol. 7: *Ming China, 1368–1644, Part 1* (Cambridge UP, 1988).

EARLY MING. On the war and politics of the founding of the Ming see Edward Dreyer, *Early Ming China: A Political History, 1355–1435* (Stanford UP, 1982); Edward L. Farmer, *Early Ming Government: The Evolution of Dual Capitals* (East Asian Research Center, Harvard U, 1976), dealing with Nanjing and Beijing; and John Dardess, *Confucianism and Autocracy: Professional Elites and the Founding of the Ming Dynasty* (U of California Press, 1983).

GOVERNMENT INSTITUTIONS. The most concrete study of one of China's primary administrative institutions is by Charles O. Hucker, *The Censorial System of Ming China* (Stanford UP, 1966). Also solid is Ray Huang, *Taxation and Governmental Finance in Sixteenth-Century Ming China* (Cambridge UP, 1974), a basic study. On the notoriously powerful eunuchs, see Mary M. Anderson, *Hidden Power: The Palace Eunuchs of Imperial China* (Prometheus, 1990).

MARITIME CONTACT: ZHENG HE'S VOYAGES. Philip Snow, *The Star Raft: China's Encounter with Africa* (Weidenfeld and Nicolson, 1988), is a lively treatment of Asian–African contacts. J. V. G. Mills, *Ma Huan: Ying-yai shenglan, "The Overall Survey of the Ocean's Shores" (1433)* (Cambridge UP, 1970), translates a primary record of China's overseas trade and the Zheng He expeditions, with a 65-page introduction.

RELATIONS WITH THE MONGOLS: THE GREAT WALL. Arthur Waldron, *The Great Wall of China: From History to Myth* (Cambridge UP, 1990), sums up a basic revision of the whole subject of Ming–Mongol relations. A useful survey is by Morris Rossabi, *China and Inner Asia from 1368 to the Present Day* (Thames & Hudson, 1975).

THE MING–QING TRANSITION. See Jonathan Spence and John Wills, eds., *From Ming to Ch'ing: Conquest, Region, and Continuity in Seventeenth-Century China* (Yale UP, 1979). Chun-shu Chang and Shelley Hsueh-lun Chang, *Crisis and Transformation in Seventeenth-Century China: Society, Culture, and Modernity in Li Yu's World* (U of Michigan Press, 1991), gives a multifaceted portrait of the turbulent seventeenth century. Dynastic decline is dealt with in Ray Huang, *1587, a Year of No Significance: The Ming Dynasty in Decline* (Yale UP, 1981). From this point on, one may best be guided by Jonathan Spence's survey, *The Search for Modern China* (Norton, 1990).

Qing Conquest and Governance (1644–1911)

The major work on the Manchu conquest is Frederic Wakeman, Jr., *The Great Enterprise: The Manchu Reconstruction of Imperial Order in Seventeenth-Century China* (U of California Press, 1985), 2 vols., a very full account from the sources. On the Ming loyalist effort see Lynn Struve, *Southern Ming, 1644–1662* (Yale UP, 1984). Note also Jerry Dennerline, *The Chia-ting Loyalists: Confucian Leadership and Social Change in Seventeenth Century China* (Yale UP, 1981).

EARLY RULERS. There are now several studies of the major rulers, led by a bestseller in the emperor's own words: Jonathan D. Spence, *Emperor of China: Self Portrait of Kang-hsi* (Knopf, 1974).

On Yongzheng see Madeleine Zelin, *The Magistrate's Tael: Rationalizing Fiscal Reform in Eighteenth Century Ch'ing China* (U of California Press, 1984), which deals with his reform efforts.

For studies of Qianlong's reign see Philip A. Kuhn, *Soulstealers: The Chinese Sorcery Scare of 1768* (Harvard UP, 1990), which studies popular, bureaucratic, and especially the emperor's psychology; R. Kent Guy, *The Emperor's Four Treasuries: Scholars and the State in the Late Ch'ien-lung Era* (Council on East Asian Studies, Harvard U, 1987), a new and trenchant look at the great literary inquisition; and Harold L. Kahn, *Monarchy in the Emperor's Eyes: Image and Reality in the Ch'ien-lung Reign* (Harvard UP, 1971), which traces the emperor's education and ritualized daily life.

QING ADMINISTRATION. On the central administration Thomas Metzger, *The Internal Organization of Ch'ing Bureaucracy: Legal, Normative and Communications Aspects* (Harvard UP, 1973), offers new approaches to this whole field. Beatrice S. Bartlett, *Monarchs and Ministers: The Grand Council in Mid-Ch'ing China (1723–1820)* (U of California Press, 1991), is a uniquely insightful study of this powerful policy organ. On the famine relief system see Pierre-Etienne Will, *Bureaucracy and Famine in Eighteenth-Century China,* trans. Elborg Forster (Stanford UP, 1990).

Local administration is analyzed in John R. Watt, *The District Magistrate in Late Imperial China* (Columbia UP, 1972); and Frederic Wakeman, Jr., and Carolyn Grant, eds., *Conflict and Control in Late Imperial China* (U of California Press, 1975).

LAW. Derk Bodde and Clarence Morris, *Law in Imperial China, Exemplified by 190 Ch'ing Dynasty Cases* (Harvard UP, 1967), describes the operation of the imperial legal system and its characteristics, with illustrative cases. T'ung-tsu Ch'ü, *Law and Society in Traditional China* (Mouton, 1961), provides vivid details of the uses of law to regulate the social order. Vivien W. Ng, *Madness in Late Imperial China: From Illness to Deviance* (U of Oklahoma Press, 1990), is based on a very extensive citation of Qing cases. See also the studies under **Law and Human Rights,** below.

QING INNER ASIA. Qing activities concerning Inner Asia are detailed by Joseph Fletcher in John K. Fairbank, ed., *The Cambridge History of China,* vol. 10: *Late Ch'ing, 1800–1911, Part 1* (Cambridge UP, 1978). On the Manchus' control and use of their homeland, see Robert H. G. Lee, *The Manchurian Frontier in Ch'ing History* (Harvard UP, 1970). See also works under **The Role of Inner Asia,** above.

Intellectual Trends

MING NEO-CONFUCIANISM. For analytic treatments of Wang Yang-ming, see Wei-ming Tu, *Neo-Confucian Thought in Action: Wang Yang-ming's Youth (1472–1509)* (U of California Press, 1976); and Julia Ching, *To Acquire Wisdom: The Way of Wang Yang-ming* (Columbia UP, 1976).

Wm. Theodore de Bary has led or inspired several symposia: Wm. Theodore de Bary et al., *Self and Society in Ming Thought* (Columbia UP, 1970); Wm. Theodore de Bary et al., *The Unfolding of Neo-Confucianism* (Columbia UP, 1975); Wm. Theodore de Bary and John W. Chaffee, eds., *Neo-Confucian Education: The Formative Stage* (U of California Press, 1989); and Wm. Theodore de Bary, *The Message of the Mind in Neo-Confucian Thought* (Columbia UP, 1989).

Note also Joanna Handlin, *Action in Late Ming Thought: The Reorientation of Lü K'un and Other Scholar Officials* (U of California Press, 1983); and Willard J. Peterson, *Bitter Gourd: Fang I-chih and the Impetus for Intellectual Change* (Yale UP, 1979).

QING NEO-CONFUCIANISM. A major early Qing thinker is studied in Alison Harley Black, *Man and Nature in the Philosophical Thought of Wang Fuchih* (U of Washington Press, 1989). Benjamin A. Elman, *From Philosophy to Philology: Intellectual and Social Aspects of Change in Late Imperial China* (Council on East Asian Studies, Harvard U, 1984), and his more recent *Classicism, Politics, and Kinship: The Ch'ang-chou School of New Text Confucianism in Late Imperial China* (U of California Press, 1990), lay out and illuminate the growth of schools of criticism, principal leaders, and works.

EARLY WESTERN CONTACT

The Jesuits and Cultural Controversy

Like Marco Polo, the Jesuit pioneers form an entire field in themselves, and it is still full of controversy. The most recent study of Matteo Ricci, including his early life, is by Jonathan Spence, *The Memory Palace of Matteo Ricci* (Viking Penguin, 1984). See also Spence's *The Question of Hu* (Knopf, 1988); and a Jesuit study by John Witek, *Controversial Ideas in China and in Europe: A Biography of Jean-François Foucquet, S.J. (1665–1741)* (Rome: Institutum Historicum, 1982).

Chinese influence on European intellectual disputes is detailed in D. E. Mungello, *Curious Land: Jesuit Accommodation and the Origins of Sinology* (Wiesbaden: Franz Steiner Verlag; U of Hawaii Press, 1989). The Chinese side is probed in depth by Jacques Gernet, *China and the Christian Impact: A Conflict of Cultures,* trans. Janet Lloyd (Cambridge UP, 1985).

Early European Trade

MARITIME CHINA. The Chinese diaspora that preceded and facilitated the early European trade to the Far East (that is, around Africa) has produced few books in Western languages. Sixteen articles of the pioneer in this field are collected in Wang Gungwu, *China and the Chinese Overseas* (Singapore Select Books, 1991). For an example of the potentialities see Leonard Blusse, *Strange Company: Chinese Settlers, Mestizo Women, and the Dutch in VOC Batavia* (Foris Publications, 1986), a conspectus of China's trade to Java using the Dutch archives. New light on the Chinese context of the early European trade comes from Sarasin Viraphol, *Tribute and Profit: Sino–Siamese Trade, 1652–1853* (Council on East Asian Studies, Harvard U, 1977), which details the role of tribute ships, the rice trade, and a great deal more in the growth of China's foreign trade with Siam.

THE PORTUGUESE AND DUTCH. The Portuguese pioneers in China are studied in George B. Souza, *The Survival of Empire: Portuguese Trade and Soci-*

ety in China and the South China Sea, 1630–1754 (Cambridge UP, 1986). The path-breaking work of John E. Wills, Jr., *Pepper, Guns and Parleys: The Dutch East India Company and China, 1622–1681* (Harvard UP, 1974); and *Embassies and Illusions: Dutch and Portuguese Envoys to K'ang-hsi, 1666–1687* (Council on East Asian Studies, Harvard U, 1984), shows the potentialities of the Dutch and Portuguese archives when combined with Chinese records.

RUSSIA. On the early Qing contact with Russia, see Mark Mancall, *Russia and China: Their Diplomatic Relations to 1728* (Harvard UP, 1971); and Eric Widmer, *The Russian Ecclesiastical Mission in Peking during the Eighteenth Century* (East Asian Research Center, Harvard U, 1976).

The Canton Trading System

The major study is by Louis Dermigny, *La Chine et l'occident: le commerce à Canton au XVIIIe siècle, 1719–1833* (Paris: SEVPEN, 1964), 4 vols. See also the recent appraisal and bibliography in the chapter by Frederic Wakeman, Jr., in *The Cambridge History of China,* vol. 10.

DOMESTIC DECLINE AND FOREIGN INVASION

General Accounts of the Nineteenth and Twentieth Centuries

The chief account is by Jonathan Spence, *The Search for Modern China* (Norton, 1990), a summary of major aspects since the late Ming. A survey that is cogent especially in political history and foreign relations is by Immanuel C. Y. Hsu, *The Rise of Modern China,* 4th ed. (Oxford UP, 1990). The period from 1800 to 1911 is dealt with in vols. 10 and 11 of *The Cambridge History of China.*

For a critical overview of American historiography, see Paul A. Cohen, *Discovering History in China: American Historical Writing on the Recent Chinese Past* (Columbia UP, 1984). General accounts include Jean Chesneaux, Marianne Bastid, and Marie-Claire Bergère, *China from the Opium Wars to the 1911 Revolution* (Pantheon, 1976); and Frederic Wakeman, Jr., *The Fall of Imperial China* (Free Press, 1975).

SELECTED PRIMARY SOURCE MATERIALS. S. Y. Teng and J. K. Fairbank, *China's Response to the West: A Documentary Survey, 1839–1923,* 2nd ed. (Harvard UP, 1979), provides translations of works by many of the period's influential figures. Note also Wm. Theodore de Bary et al., eds., *Sources of Chinese Tradition* (Columbia UP, 1964).

Relations with the West: The Treaty System

CHINA'S KNOWLEDGE OF THE WEST. China's first systematic look at the West is skillfully analyzed by Fred W. Drake, *China Charts the World: Hsu Chi-yü and His Geography of 1848* (East Asian Research Center, Harvard U, 1975); and Jane Kate Leonard, *Wei Yuan and China's Rediscovery of the Maritime World* (Council on East Asian Studies, Harvard U, 1984). Note also the writings in Teng and Fairbank, cited in "Selected Primary Source Materials," on p. 457, and the studies cited under "Chinese Intellectuals and the Reform Effort," on p. 461.

THE OPIUM WARS AND NEW-STYLE DIPLOMATIC RELATIONS. A graphic review by Peter Ward Fay, *The Opium War, 1840–1842* (U of North Carolina Press, 1975), opens up new angles of iniquity. James M. Polachek, *The Inner Opium War* (Council on East Asian Studies, Harvard U, 1992), offers new insight on the domestic political context.

For the social forces at work at Canton (Guangzhou) see Frederic Wakeman, Jr., *Strangers at the Gate: Social Disorder in South China, 1839–1861* (U of California Press, 1966). J. Y. Wong, *Yeh Ming-ch'en: Viceroy of Liang Kuang, 1852–8* (Cambridge UP, 1976), gives an inside and revisionist view of a Chinese governor-general at work.

On the setting up of the new system of treaty relations, see John K. Fairbank, *Trade and Diplomacy on the China Coast: The Opening of the Treaty Ports, 1842–1854* (Harvard UP, 1953). On Chinese diplomats, J. D. Frodsham, *The First Chinese Embassy to the West: The Journals of Kuo Sung-t'ao, Liu Hsi-hung, and Chang Te-yi* (Oxford UP, 1970), looks at Chinese diplomatic diaries. On the British consuls in the treaty ports see P. D. Coates, *The China Consuls: British Consular Officers, 1843–1943* (Oxford UP, 1988).

IMPERIALIST EXPANSION AND LATE QING FOREIGN RELATIONS. For a standard Chinese account of nineteenth-century imperialism, see Hu Sheng, *Imperialism and Chinese Politics* (Beijing: Foreign Languages Press, 1981).

On relations with France a recent account is Robert Lee, *France and the Exploitation of China, 1885–1901: A Study in Economic Imperialism* (Oxford UP, 1989). On Germany, John E. Schrecker, *Imperialism and Chinese Nationalism: Germany in Shantung* (Harvard UP, 1971).

On Britain see E. W. Edwards, *British Diplomacy and Finance in China, 1895–1914* (Oxford UP, 1987); and Phillip Darby, *Three Faces of Imperialism: British and American Approaches to Asia and Africa, 1870–1970* (Yale UP, 1987).

On Japan, note Peter Duus, Ramon Myers, and Mark Peattie, eds., *The Japanese Informal Empire in China, 1895–1937* (Princeton UP, 1989).

There is a large corpus of works on Sino–American relations. The best overall account is Michael H. Hunt, *The Making of a Special Relationship: The United States and China to 1914* (Columbia UP, 1983). See John King Fairbank, *The United States and China*, 4th ed. (Harvard UP, 1983), for a more extensive bibliography.

MISSIONARIES. For an overview see Paul A. Cohen's chapter in *The Cambridge History of China*, vol. 10, and John K. Fairbank, ed., *The Missionary Enterprise in China and America* (Harvard UP, 1974). Recent works on the missionary movement include Jane Hunter, *The Gospel of Gentility: American Missionary Women in Turn-of-the-Century China* (Yale UP, 1984); and John Hersey, *The Call* (Knopf, 1985), a historical novel set in the period 1907–1950. There is a huge literature on the missionaries; see John King Fairbank, *The United States and China*, 4th ed. (Harvard UP, 1983), for further reading.

TREATY PORTS. A comprehensive factual overview for 1912–1949 is provided by Albert Feuerwerker in *The Cambridge History of China*, vol. 12. For appraisal of the treaty ports' origins and economic role in general see Rhoads Murphey, *The Outsiders: The Western Experience in India and China* (U of Michigan Press, 1977). One aspect of Shanghai's urbanization under Western, mainly British, influence is studied in Kerrie Macpherson, *A Wilderness of Marshes: The Origins of Public Health in Shanghai, 1843–1893* (Oxford UP, 1987). Sino–foreign contact as seen by Chinese is vividly pictured in Don J. Cohn, ed. and trans., *Vignettes from the Chinese: Lithographs from Shanghai in the Late Nineteenth Century* (Renditions Paperback, 1987).

FOREIGN TRADE. For a survey analysis see Yen-p'ing Hao, *The Commercial Revolution in Nineteenth-Century China: The Rise of Sino–Western Mercantile Capitalism* (U of California Press, 1986). On trade with the United States see Ernest R. May and John K. Fairbank, eds., *America's China Trade in Historical Perspective: The Chinese and American Performance* (Council on East Asian Studies, Harvard U, 1986).

CHINESE MARITIME CUSTOMS. On Robert Hart see Katharine F. Bruner, John K. Fairbank, and Richard J. Smith, eds., *Entering China's Service: Robert Hart's Journals, 1854–1863* (Council on East Asian Studies, Harvard U, 1986); and Richard J. Smith, John K. Fairbank, and Katharine F. Bruner, eds., *Robert Hart and China's Early Modernization: Robert Hart's Journals, 1863–1866* (1991). Hart's role as foreign manager and adviser is glimpsed in John King Fairbank, Katharine Frost Bruner, and Elizabeth MacLeod Matheson, eds., *The I. G. in Peking: Letters of Robert Hart, Chinese Maritime Customs, 1868–1907* (Belknap Press of Harvard UP, 1975), 2 vols.

BANKING. On traditional banking, Andrea Lee McElderry, *Shanghai Old-Style Banks (ch'ien-chuang), 1800–1935* (Center for Chinese Studies, U of Michigan, 1976). On the major British bank, see Frank H. H. King, with Catherine E. King and David S. J. King, *The Hongkong Bank in Late Imperial China, 1864–1902: On an Even Keel* (Cambridge UP, 1987), vol. 1 of a series on the history of the Hong Kong and Shanghai Banking Corporation.

Mid-Century Rebellions

Rebellion and revolution are pursued in several accounts: The social and institutional repercussions of all this disorder are masterfully analyzed in Philip A. Kuhn, *Rebellion and Its Enemies in Late Imperial China: Militarization and Social Structure, 1796–1864* (Harvard UP, 1970). See also Elizabeth J. Perry, *Rebels and Revolutionaries in North China, 1845–1945* (Stanford UP, 1980), an influential study of the connection between environment and rebellion.

For a view of the religious origins of risings, see Daniel L. Overmyer, *Folk Buddhist Religion: Dissenting Sects in Late Traditional China* (Harvard UP, 1976). The fiasco of 1813 is intimately detailed by Susan Naquin, *Millenarian Rebellion in China: The Eight Trigrams Uprising of 1813* (Yale UP, 1976).

TAIPING REBELLION. The most basic study is by Franz Michael in collaboration with Chung-li Chang, *The Taiping Rebellion: History and Documents,* 3 vols. (U of Washington Press, 1966–1971). A detailed and comprehensive account is by a long-time leading specialist, Jen Yuwen, *The Taiping Revolutionary Movement* (Yale UP, 1973).

NIAN AND MUSLIM REBELLIONS. The most recent work is Elizabeth Perry, *Chinese Perspectives on the Nien Rebellion* (M. E. Sharpe, 1981). See also Wen-djang Chu, *The Moslem Rebellion in Northwest China, 1862–1878: A Study of Government Minority Policy* (The Hague: Mouton, 1966).

The Qing Restoration

For an appraisal of the Restoration see the articles by Kwang-Ching Liu in *The Cambridge History of China,* vols. 10 and 11. The major study of Qing policy in the 1860s remains Mary Clabaugh Wright, *The Last Stand of Chinese Conservatism: The T'ung-chih Restoration, 1862–1874* (Stanford UP, 1957).

INSTITUTIONAL CHANGE. For military development under the self-strengthening movement see Bruce Swanson, *Eighth Voyage of the Dragon: A History of China's Quest for Seapower* (Naval Institute Press, 1982); Thomas Kennedy, *The Arms of Kiangnan: Modernization in the Chinese Ordnance Industry, 1860–1895* (Westview, 1978), on arsenals. Provincial and local perspectives are provided in Jonathan K. Ocko, *Bureaucratic Reform in Provincial China: Ting Jih-ch'ang in Restoration Kiangsu, 1867–1870* (Council on East Asian Studies, Harvard U, 1983); and James Cole, *Shaohsing: Competition and Cooperation in Nineteenth-Century China* (U of Arizona Press, 1986).

LATE IMPERIAL POLITICS AND SOCIETY. On the fate of the Manchus as a ruling elite see Pamela Kyle Crossley, *Orphan Warriors: Three Manchu Generations and the End of the Qing World* (Princeton UP, 1990). On the changing nature of Chinese elite participation see Mary Rankin, *Elite Activism and Political Transformation in China, Zhejiang Province, 1865–1911* (Stanford UP, 1986); Min Tu-ki, *National Polity and Local Power: The Transformation of Late Imperial China* (Council on East Asian Studies, Harvard U, 1989), by a leading Korean historian of China; R. Keith Schoppa, *Chinese Elites and Political Change: Zhejiang Province in the Early Twentieth Century* (Harvard UP, 1982); Joseph Esherick and Mary Rankin, eds., *Chinese Local Elites and Patterns of Dominance* (U of California Press, 1990).

CHINESE INTELLECTUALS AND THE REFORM EFFORT. Recent work in this area includes Hao Chang, *Chinese Intellectuals in Crisis: Search for Order and Meaning (1890–1911)* (U of California Press, 1987); and Kwang-Ching Liu, ed., *Orthodoxy in Late Imperial China* (U of California Press, 1990). On one late Qing attempt to profit from Western thought, see Benjamin Schwartz, *In Search of Wealth and Power: Yen Fu and the West* (Belknap Press of Harvard UP, 1964). On the conservative approach to reform, see Daniel H. Bays, *China Enters the Twentieth Century: Chang Chih-tung and the Issues of a New Age, 1895–1909* (U of Michigan Press, 1978).

Leading figures are studied by Paul A. Cohen, *Between Tradition and Modernity: Wang T'ao and Reform in Late Ch'ing China* (Harvard UP, 1974; paperback ed. by Council on East Asian Studies, Harvard U, 1987); and Roger V. DesForges, *Hsi-liang and the Chinese Revolution* (Yale UP, 1973).

On the politics of the Hundred Days reform effort and its aftermath see Luke S. K. Kwong, *A Mosaic of the Hundred Days: Personalities, Politics, and Ideas of 1898* (Council on East Asian Studies, Harvard U, 1984); later reform politics are covered in Stephen MacKinnon, *Power and Politics in Late Imperial China: Yuan Shi-kai in Beijing and Tianjin, 1901–1908* (U of California Press, 1980).

KANG YOUWEI AND LIANG QICHAO. On the radical reform efforts of Kang Youwei see the magistral volume by Kung-ch'uan Hsiao, *A Modern China and a New World: K'ang Yu-wei, Reformer and Utopian, 1858–1927* (U of Washington Press, 1975). On Kang's brilliant disciple see Hao Chang, *Liang Ch'i-ch'ao and Intellectual Transition in China, 1890–1907* (Harvard UP, 1971).

THE BOXER RISING. Most recent is Joseph Esherick, *The Origins of the Boxer Uprising* (U of California Press, 1987). Also, David Buck, *Recent Chinese Studies of the Boxer Movement* (M. E. Sharpe, 1987). There is of course an enormous literature.

Economic Developments

A survey treatment is Ramon Myers, *The Chinese Economy, Past and Present* (Wadsworth, 1980). Major aspects of Sino–Western economic relations are re-searched in Dwight H. Perkins, ed., *China's Modern Economy in Historical Per-spective* (Stanford UP, 1975). Another valuable collection is W. E. Willmott, ed., *Economic Organization in Chinese Society* (Stanford UP, 1972).

RURAL CHINA. This is a major focus of recent work. Among historical studies note Philip C. C. Huang, *The Peasant Economy and Social Change in North China* (Stanford UP, 1985); Huang, *The Peasant Family and Rural Devel-opment in the Yangzi Delta, 1350–1988* (Stanford UP, 1990); David Faure, *The Rural Economy of Pre-Liberation China: Trade Expansion and Peasant Liveli-hood in Jiangsu and Guangdong, 1870–1937* (Oxford UP, 1989); Loren Brandt, *Commercialization and Agricultural Development: Central and Eastern China, 1870–1937* (Cambridge UP, 1989). For a comparison of developments in the sixteenth and eighteenth centuries see Evelyn Sakakida Rawski, *Agricultural Change and the Peasant Economy of South China* (Harvard UP, 1972).

For a lucid theoretically oriented treatment of important areas of scholarly controversy, see Daniel Little, *Understanding Peasant China: Case Studies in the Philosophy of Social Science* (Yale UP, 1989).

DEMOGRAPHY. For an overview see William Lavely, James Lee, and Wang Feng, "Chinese Demography: The State of the Field," *Journal of Asian Studies* 49.4 (Nov. 1990): 807–834. A major historical analysis of the growth of people and food supply is in Dwight H. Perkins, *Agricultural Development in China, 1368–1968* (Aldine, 1969). Most recent is Kang Chao, *Man and Land in Chi-nese History: An Economic Analysis* (Stanford UP, 1986).

INDUSTRIAL ENTERPRISE AND IMPERIALISM. On the "official-control and merchant-operation" system, see Wellington K. K. Chan, *Mer-chants, Mandarins, and Modern Enterprise in Late Ch'ing China* (East Asian Research Center, Harvard U, 1977). On other aspects of the state–merchant re-lationship, see Susan Mann, *Local Merchants and the Chinese Bureaucracy, 1750–1950* (Stanford UP, 1987).

On the silk industry, see Lillian M. Li, *China's Silk Trade: Traditional Industry in the Modern World, 1842–1937* (Council on East Asian Studies, Harvard U, 1981); and Robert Eng, *Economic Imperialism in China: Silk Production and*

Exports, 1861–1932 (Institute of East Asian Studies, U of California, 1986); on the cotton industry, Kang Chao, *The Development of Cotton Textile Production in China* (East Asian Research Center, Harvard U, 1977).

On Western enterprise see Sherman Cochran, *Big Business in China: Sino-Foreign Rivalry in the Cigarette Industry, 1890–1930* (Harvard UP, 1980). The comprador class is researched by Yen-p'ing Hao, *The Comprador in Nineteenth Century China: Bridge between East and West* (Harvard UP, 1970). Most recent is Yuen-sang Leung, *The Shanghai Taotai: Linkage Man in a Changing Society, 1843–1890* (U of Hawaii Press, 1990).

EARLY URBANIZATION. G. William Skinner, ed., *The City in Late Imperial China* (Stanford UP, 1977), maps out broad areas for further research. See as well Mark Elvin and G. William Skinner, eds., *The Chinese City between Two Worlds* (Stanford UP, 1974). Gilbert Rozman, *Urban Networks in Ch'ing China and Tokugawa Japan* (Princeton UP, 1973), uses modern methods of quantification.

On nineteenth-century commercial growth and social community as a major focus of domestic trade, see William T. Rowe, *Hankow: Commerce and Society in a Chinese City, 1796–1889* (Stanford UP, 1984), and *Hankow: Conflict and Community in a Chinese City, 1796–1895* (Stanford UP, 1989).

OVERSEAS CHINESE. Most recent is Lynn Pan, *Sons of the Yellow Emperor: A History of the Chinese Diaspora* (Little, Brown, 1990). On the economic contributions of Chinese abroad see Michael Godley, *The Mandarin-Capitalists from Nanyang: Overseas Chinese Enterprise in the Modernization of China, 1839–1911* (Cambridge UP, 1982); and Sucheng Chan, *This Bittersweet Soil: The Chinese in California Agriculture, 1860–1910* (U of California Press, 1986).

On the role of overseas Chinese in the 1911 Revolution, see Ching Hwang Yen, *The Overseas Chinese and the 1911 Revolution: With Special Reference to Singapore and Malaya* (Oxford UP, 1976); and L. Eve Armentrout Ma, *Revolutionaries, Monarchists, and Chinatowns: Chinese Politics in the Americas and the 1911 Revolution* (U of Hawaii Press, 1990).

The 1911 Revolution

The principal conspectus of the origins of the 1911 Revolution is by Mary Clabaugh Wright, ed., *China in Revolution: The First Phase, 1900–1913* (Yale UP, 1968). More recent is Shinkichi Eto and Harold Schiffrin, eds., *The 1911 Revolution: Interpretive Essays* (U of Tokyo Press, 1984).

Studies of the revolution in specific regions include: Joseph Esherick, *Reform and Revolution in China: The 1911 Revolution in Hunan and Hubei* (U of California Press, 1976); and Edward J. M. Rhoads, *China's Republican Revolution:*

The Case of Kwangtung, 1895–1913 (Harvard UP, 1975). On the political setting see John Fincher, *Chinese Democracy: The Self-Government Movement in Local, Provincial, and National Politics, 1905–1914* (St. Martin's Press, 1981).

THE ROLE OF INTELLECTUALS. Social-intellectual movements are pursued by Michael Gasster, *Chinese Intellectuals and the Revolution of 1911: The Birth of Modern Chinese Radicalism* (U of Washington Press, 1969). On the influence of developments in Russia see Don C. Price, *Russia and the Roots of the Chinese Revolution, 1896–1911* (Harvard UP, 1974), a path-breaking study. Monographs on Sun Yatsen include: Harold Z. Schiffrin, *Sun Yat-sen and the Origins of the Chinese Revolution* (U of California Press, 1968); C. Martin Wilbur, *Sun Yat-sen: Frustrated Patriot* (Columbia UP, 1976).

On other leaders see Young-tsu Wong, *The Search for Modern Nationalism: Zhang Binglin and Revolutionary China, 1869–1936* (Oxford UP, 1989); Mary Backus Rankin, *Early Chinese Revolutionaries: Radical Intellectuals in Shanghai and Chekiang, 1902–1911* (Harvard UP, 1971).

For a pioneer psychological study see Jon Saari, *Legacies of Childhood: Growing up Chinese in a Time of Crisis, 1890–1920* (Council on East Asian Studies, Harvard U, 1990).

REPUBLICAN CHINA (1912–1949)

General Studies

For survey articles by specialists in the field see *The Cambridge History of China*, vols. 12 and 13. O. Edmund Clubb, *Twentieth Century China*, 3rd ed. (Columbia UP, 1978), provides an overview of the period.

On major actors see Howard L. Boorman and Richard C. Howard, eds., *Biographical Dictionary of Republican China* (Columbia UP, 1967), 4 vols., vol. 5, Janet Krompart, *A Personal Name Index* (1979); and Donald Klein and Anne B. Clark, *Biographic Dictionary of Chinese Communism, 1921–1965* (Harvard UP, 1971), 2 vols.

Urban Change

On Shanghai, the major work is by Marie-Claire Bergère, *The Golden Age of the Chinese Bourgeoisie*, trans. Janet Lloyd (Cambridge UP, 1989); see also Joseph Fewsmith, *Party, State, and Local Elites in Republican China: Merchant Organizations and Politics in Shanghai, 1890–1930* (U of Hawaii Press, 1985). David Strand, *Rickshaw Beijing: City People and Politics in the 1920s* (U of California Press, 1989), is an exemplary study of the mixing of old institutions like the guilds and native-place associations with modern elements like the police system and chambers of commerce. Note also the studies on changing elite roles under **The Society of Late Imperial China,** above.

Early Politics: Yuan Shikai and Warlord Power

An outstanding study by Ernest Young, *The Presidency of Yuan Shih-k'ai: Liberalism and Dictatorship in Early Republican China* (U of Michigan Press, 1977), analyzes political developments during the Yuan years. Edward Friedman, *Backward toward Revolution: The Chinese Revolutionary Party* (U of California Press, 1974), looks at the problems of the revolutionaries after 1911. On central government issues in the warlord era proper (1916–1927), see Andrew Nathan, *Peking Politics, 1918–1923: Factionalism and the Failure of Constitutionalism* (U of California Press, 1976). Note also Hsi-sheng Ch'i, *Warlord Politics in China, 1916–1928* (Stanford UP, 1976).

ON WARLORDISM. On regional politics see Diana Lary, *Region and Nation: The Kwangsi Clique in Chinese Politics, 1925–1937* (Cambridge UP, 1974); Robert Kapp, *Szechwan and the Chinese Republic: Provincial Militarism and Central Power, 1911–1938* (Yale UP, 1973); and Donald Sutton, *Provincial Militarism and the Chinese Republic: The Yunnan Army, 1905–1925* (U of Michigan Press, 1980). Recent studies of individual warlords include: Odoric Wou, *Militarism in Modern China: The Career of Wu P'ei-fu, 1916–1939* (Folkestone, Eng.: Dawson and Sons, 1978); and Gavan McCormack, *Chang Tso-lin in Northeast China, 1911–1928: China, Japan, and the Manchurian Idea* (Stanford UP, 1977).

On the relations with foreign powers see Anthony B. Chan, *Arming the Chinese: The Western Armaments Trade in Warlord China* (U of British Columbia Press, 1982).

Intellectual Revolution: The May 4th Era

The major survey remains Chow Tse-tsung, *The May Fourth Movement: Intellectual Revolution in Modern China* (Harvard UP, 1960). On the intellectual life of this period, studies include Jerome Grieder, *Intellectuals and the State in Modern China: A Narrative History* (Free Press, 1981); Jonathan Spence, *The Gate of Heavenly Peace: The Chinese and Their Revolution, 1895–1980* (Viking, 1981); Vera Schwarcz, *The Chinese Enlightenment: Intellectuals and the Legacy of the May Fourth Movement of 1919* (U of California Press, 1986); and Wenhsin Yeh, *The Alienated Academy: Culture and Politics in Republican China, 1919–1937* (Council on East Asian Studies, Harvard U, 1990). Note also Charlotte Furth, ed., *The Limits of Change: Essays on Conservative Alternatives in Republican China* (Harvard UP, 1976); Peter Zarrow, *Anarchism and Chinese*

Political Culture (Columbia UP, 1990); Perry Link, *Mandarin Ducks and Butterflies: Popular Fiction in Early Twentieth-Century Chinese Cities* (U of California Press, 1981).

Analysis of this whole era has been greatly stimulated by the writings of Joseph R. Levenson, *Confucian China and Its Modern Fate,* vol. 1: *The Problem of Intellectual Continuity;* vol. 2: *The Problem of Monarchical Decay;* vol. 3: *The Problem of Historical Significance* (U of California Press, 1958, 1964, 1965). Studies of intellectual leaders include Jerome B. Grieder, *Hu Shih and the Chinese Renaissance: Liberalism in the Chinese Revolution, 1917–1937* (Harvard UP, 1970); Charlotte Furth, *Ting Wen-chiang: Science and China's New Culture* (Harvard UP, 1970); Guy S. Alitto, *The Last Confucian: Liang Shu-ming and the Chinese Dilemma of Modernity* (U of California Press, 1979); and Joey Bonner, *Wang Kuo-wei: An Intellectual Biography* (Harvard UP, 1986).

On the influence of an important Western thinker see James Pusey, *China and Charles Darwin* (Council on East Asian Studies, Harvard U, 1983).

Guomindang Conquest and Governance (1925–1937)

NATIONALIST SENTIMENT AND POLITICS OF THE 1920S. See Richard Rigby, *The May Thirtieth Movement: Events and Themes* (Australian National UP, 1980); Jessie Gregory Lutz, *Chinese Politics and Christian Missions: The Anti-Christian Movements of 1920–1928* (Cross Roads Books, 1988).

THE RISE OF THE GUOMINDANG. Chronicled by C. Martin Wilbur in *The Nationalist Revolution in China, 1923–1928* (Cambridge UP, 1984); and by Donald A. Jordan in *The Northern Expedition: China's National Revolution of 1926–1928* (U of Hawaii Press, 1976). On Soviet relations with the GMD note C. Martin Wilbur and Julie Lien-ying How, *Missionaries of Revolution: Soviet Advisers and Nationalist China, 1920–1927* (Harvard UP, 1989), an important expansion and updating of their work of 1956.

GUOMINDANG RULE: THE NANJING DECADE (1927–1937). Most recent is the volume drawn mainly from *The Cambridge History of China:* Lloyd Eastman, ed., *The Nationalist Era in China, 1927–1949* (Cambridge UP, 1991). The principal studies of the Guomindang in power are by Hung-mao Tien, *Government and Politics in Kuomintang China, 1927–1937* (Stanford UP, 1972), well informed; and Lloyd E. Eastman, *The Abortive Revolution: China under Nationalist Rule, 1927–1937* (Harvard UP, 1974), more iconoclastic.

On the role of foreign aid in the state-building effort see William Kirby, *Germany and Republican China* (Stanford UP, 1984). On relations between state and society in this period note the pioneering study by Prasenjit Duara, *Culture,*

Power, and the State: Rural North China, 1900–1942 (Stanford UP, 1988). For a birds-eye view of the time see Sherman Cochran and Andrew Hsieh, trans. and ed., *One Day in China: May 21, 1936* (Yale UP, 1983), a selection of personal accounts of daily life. Parks M. Coble, *The Shanghai Capitalists and the Nationalist Government, 1927–1937*, 2nd ed. (Council on East Asian Studies, Harvard U, 1986), is an important study of relations between the party and the bourgeoisie. A leader in rural reconstruction is studied in Charles W. Hayford, *To the People: James Yen and Village China* (Columbia UP, 1990).

The Early History of the Chinese Communist Party (1921–1936)

Jacques Guillermaz, *A History of the Chinese Communist Party 1921–1949*, trans. Anne Destenay (Random House, 1972), is a judicious, well-informed, and skeptical account by a long-time French military attaché with firsthand experience.

THE FOUNDING OF THE PARTY. On the party's beginnings see Arif Dirlik, *The Origins of Chinese Communism* (Oxford UP, 1989), on radical Chinese intellectuals; and Michael Y. L. Luk, *The Origins of Chinese Bolshevism: An Ideology in the Making, 1920–1928* (Oxford UP, 1990). On the leading founders of the Communist movement, see Maurice Meisner, *Li Ta-chao and the Origins of Chinese Marxism* (Harvard UP, 1967), a basic study; and Lee Feigon, *Chen Duxiu, Founder of the Chinese Communist Party* (Princeton UP, 1983). Note also Joshua Fogel, *Ai Ssu-ch'i's Contribution to the Development of Chinese Marxism* (Council on East Asian Studies, Harvard U, 1987).

On the role of the Soviet Union see Jane L. Price, *Cadres, Commanders, and Commissars: The Training of the Chinese Communist Leadership, 1920–1945* (Westview, 1976); Dan Jacobs, *Borodin: Stalin's Man in China* (Harvard UP, 1981). Note also Tony Saich, *The Origins of the First United Front in China: The Role of Sneevliet (Alias Maring)* (E. J. Brill, 1991).

THE SOVIET PERIOD, 1928–1934. Warren Kuo, *Analytical History of the Chinese Communist Party* (Taipei: Institute of International Relations, 1966), by a leading researcher in Taiwan, comes up to July 1939. For a history by an early CCP leader, see Chang Kuo-t'ao [Zhang Guotao], *The Rise of the Chinese Communist Party 1921–1927: The Autobiography of Chang Kuo-t'ao*, vol. 1: *1921–1927*; vol. 2: *1928–1938* (U Press of Kansas, 1971–72).

On the early party line, see Arif Dirlik, *Revolution and History: The Origins of Marxist Historiography in China, 1919–1937* (U of California Press, 1978). See also Tony Saich, *The Rise to Power of the Chinese Communist Party: Documents and Analysis, 1920–1949* (forthcoming). On the beginnings in Guangdong, see Roy Hofheinz, Jr., *The Broken Wave: The Chinese Communist Peasant Movement, 1922–1928* (Harvard UP, 1977); and in Jiangxi, see Ilpyong J. Kim,

The Politics of Chinese Communism: Kiangsi under the Soviets (U of California Press, 1973); and William Wei, *Counterrevolution in China: The Nationalists in Jiangxi during the Soviet Period* (U of Michigan Press, 1985).

THE RISE OF MAO. The classic account by Mao himself is in Edgar Snow, *Red Star over China* (Random House, 1938; Bantam, 1978). See also Li Jui, *The Early Revolutionary Activities of Comrade Mao Tse-tung,* trans. Anthony Sariti and ed. James Hsiung (M. E. Sharpe, 1977). On the development of Mao's thought see Stuart Schram, *The Thought of Mao Tse-tung* (Cambridge UP, 1989), which collects his two survey articles from *The Cambridge History of China* and adds a useful introduction.

LOCAL MOVEMENTS. On the early growth of local revolutionary movements see Fernando Galbiati, *Peng Pai and the Hai-Lu-Feng Soviet* (Stanford UP, 1985); Robert Marks, *Rural Revolution in South China: Peasants and the Making of History in Haifeng County, 1570–1930 (U of Wisconsin Press, 1984);* Kamal Sheel, *Peasant Society and Marxist Intellectuals in China: Fang Zhimin and the Origin of a Revolutionary Movement in the Xinjiang Region* (Princeton UP, 1989), in Fujian province; Chong-sik Lee, *Revolutionary Struggle in Manchuria: Chinese Communism and Soviet Interest, 1922–1945* (U of California Press, 1983).

THE LONG MARCH AND THE YAN'AN PERIOD. See Benjamin Yang, *From Revolution to Politics: Chinese Communists on the Long March* (Westview, 1990), a full chronicle that puts Mao, Zhou, and Zhang Guotao in perspective. On developments while the party leadership was at Yan'an see Mark Selden, *The Yenan Way in Revolutionary China* (Harvard UP, 1971). For this period note also relevant works under **War with Japan** and **Civil War,** below.

Economic Conditions in Republican China

Economic development under the Republic is analyzed by Thomas Rawski, *Economic Growth in Prewar China* (U of California Press, 1989); and Albert Feuerwerker, *Economic Trends in the Republic of China, 1912–1949* (Center for Chinese Studies, U of Michigan, 1977), a chapter from *The Cambridge History of China,* vol. 13.

INDUSTRY AND THE LABOR MOVEMENT. The first major study of the labor movement was by Jean Chesneaux, *The Chinese Labor Movement, 1919–1927,* trans. H. M. Wright (Stanford UP, 1968). More recent studies that take issue with his argument include Gail Hershatter, *The Workers of Tianjin, 1900–1949* (Stanford UP, 1986); and Emily Honig, *Sisters and Strangers: Women in the Shanghai Cotton Mills, 1919–1949* (Stanford UP, 1986).

On Communist involvement see S. Bernard Thomas, *Labor and the Chinese Revolution: Class Strategies and Contradictions of Chinese Communism, 1928–1948* (Center for Chinese Studies, U of Michigan, 1983); and Lynda Shaffer, *Mao and the Workers: The Hunan Labor Movement, 1920–1923* (M. E. Sharpe, 1982).

THE RURAL ECONOMY AND RURAL REVOLUTION. For general assessments see Thomas Wiens, *The Microeconomics of Peasant Economy, 1920–1940* (Garland, 1982); and Ramon Myers, *The Chinese Peasant Economy: Agricultural Development in Hopei and Shantung, 1890–1949* (Harvard UP, 1970). Note also Philip C. C. Huang, *The Peasant Economy and Social Change in North China* (Stanford UP, 1985), and *The Peasant Family and Rural Development in the Yangzi Delta, 1350–1988* (Stanford UP, 1990); Prasenjit Duara, *Culture, Power, and the State: Rural North China, 1900–1942* (Stanford UP, 1988).

On the rural revolutionary movement see Kathleen Hartford and Steven M. Goldstein, eds., *Single Sparks: China's Rural Revolutions* (M. E. Sharpe, 1989); Angus McDonald, Jr., *The Urban Origins of Rural Revolution: Elites and the Masses in Hunan Province, 1911–1927* (U of California Press, 1978); and Phil Billingsley, *Bandits in Republican China* (Stanford UP, 1988). For a remarkable on-the-scene account of this period read William Hinton, *Fanshen: A Documentary of Revolution in a Chinese Village* (Monthly Review Press, 1967).

War with Japan

On relations with Japan see Marius Jansen, *Japan and China: From War to Peace, 1894–1972* (Rand McNally, 1975). On the war itself see Lincoln Li, *The Japanese Army in North China, 1937–1941: Problems of Political and Economic Control* (Oxford UP, 1975); James W. Morley, ed., *The China Quagmire: Japan's Expansion on the Asian Continent, 1933–1941, Selected Translations* (Columbia UP, 1983), from a major Japanese work.

On the Guomindang government in wartime see Lloyd Eastman, *Seeds of Destruction: Nationalist China in War and Revolution, 1937–1949* (Stanford UP, 1984); Hsi-sheng Ch'i, *Nationalist China at War: Military Defeats and Political Collapse, 1937–1945* (U of Michigan Press, 1982).

On wartime relations between the CCP and GMD see Kui-kwong Shum, *The Chinese Communists' Road to Power: The Anti-Japanese National United Front, 1935–1945* (Oxford UP, 1988); and Tetsuya Kataoka, *Resistance and Revolution in China: The Communists and the Second United Front* (U of California Press, 1974). Note also Tien-wei Wu, *The Sian Incident: A Pivotal Point in Modem Chinese History* (Center for Chinese Studies, U of Michigan, 1976).

On wartime foreign relations see Christopher Thorne, *Allies of a Kind: The United States, Britain and the War against Japan 1941–1945* (Oxford UP, 1978);

Michael Schaller, *The US Crusade in China, 1938–1945* (Columbia UP, 1979); and John W. Garver, *Chinese–Soviet Relations, 1937–1945: The Diplomacy of Chinese Nationalism* (Oxford UP, 1988).

On the Communist movement in wartime see Yung-fa Chen, *Making Revolution: The Communist Movement in Eastern and Central China, 1937–1945* (U of California Press, 1986); and Peter Schran, *Guerrilla Economy: The Development of the Shensi-Kansu-Ninghsia Border Region, 1937–1945* (SUNY Press, 1976).

Civil War

For an overall account of the period see Suzanne Pepper, *Civil War in China: The Political Struggle, 1945–1949* (U of California Press, 1978). On the Communists during the Civil War see the excellent study by Steven I. Levine, *Anvil of Victory: The Communist Revolution in Manchuria, 1945–1948* (Columbia UP, 1987).

On foreign relations during this period see James Reardon-Anderson, *Yenan and the Great Powers: The Origins of Chinese Communist Foreign Policy, 1944–1946* (Columbia UP, 1980); Yonosuke Nagai and Akira Iriye, eds., *The Origins of the Cold War in Asia* (Columbia UP, 1977), gives the larger context of international relations; Dorothy Borg and Waldo Heinrichs, eds., *Uncertain Years: Chinese–American Relations, 1947–1950* (Columbia UP, 1980).

Note also Gordon Chang, *Friends and Enemies: The United States, China, and the Soviet Union, 1948–1972* (Stanford UP, 1990); Nancy B. Tucker, *Patterns in the Dust: Chinese–American Relations and the Recognition Controversy, 1949–1950* (Columbia UP, 1983).

On the role of foreign journalists and experts note Stephen MacKinnon and Oris Friesen, *China Reporting: An Oral History of American Journalism in the 1930s and 1940s* (U of California Press, 1987).

REPUBLIC OF CHINA, TAIWAN

General Works

For bibliography see J. Bruce Jacobs, Jean Hagger, and Anne Sedgley, comps., *Taiwan: A Comprehensive Bibliography of English-Language Publications* (East Asian Institute, Columbia U, 1984).

EARLY HISTORY. For studies of Taiwan as a province see Johanna Meskill, *A Chinese Pioneer Family: The Lins of Wu-feng, Taiwan, 1729–1895* (Princeton UP, 1979); Ronald Knapp, *China's Island Frontier: Studies in the Historical Geography of Taiwan* (U of Hawaii Press, 1980). On the period of Japanese colonial rule, see Ramon Myers and Mark Peattie, eds., *The Japanese Colonial Empire, 1895–1945* (Princeton UP, 1984).

Among surveys of industrialization, most comprehensive is Samuel P. S. Ho, *Economic Development of Taiwan, 1860–1970* (Yale UP, 1978). For background see E. Patricia Tsurumi, *Japanese Colonial Education in Taiwan, 1895–1945* (Harvard UP, 1977), an able study of the Japanese program and its results. George H. Kerr, *Formosa: Licensed Revolution and the Home Rule Movement, 1895–1945* (U of Hawaii, 1974), concerns Taiwanese reactions to Japanese colonial rule during fifty years.

POST-1949 HISTORY. Among recent surveys note Thomas B. Gold, *State and Society in the Taiwan Miracle* (M. E. Sharpe, 1986); and Hung-mao Tien, *The Great Transition: Political and Social Change in the Republic of China* (Stanford UP, 1989). In Ramon H. Myers, ed., *Two Societies in Opposition: The Republic of China and the People's Republic of China after Forty Years* (Hoover Institution Press, 1991), papers by fifteen specialists compare the two regimes, though without much attention to size.

Politics and Government

On responses to the Guomindang takeover and massacre, note Tse-han Lai, Ramon Myers, and Wou Wei, *A Tragic Beginning: The Taiwan Uprising of February 28, 1947* (Stanford UP, 1990); and George H. Kerr, *Formosa Betrayed* (Houghton Mifflin, 1965).

On political reform note John F. Copper, *A Quiet Revolution: Political Development in the Republic of China* (UP of America, 1988); Harvey Feldman, Michael Y. M. Kau, and Ilpyong Kim, *Taiwan in a Time of Transition* (Paragon, 1988).

Two recent works on Taiwan's foreign policy are Yu San Wang, ed., *Foreign Policy of the Republic of China on Taiwan: An Unorthodox Approach* (Praeger, 1990); and Chiao Chiao Hsieh, *Strategy for Survival: The Foreign Policy and External Relations of the Republic of China on Taiwan, 1949–1979* (Sherwood, 1985). The majority of studies are on relations with the United States or on the reunification issue. Among these note Ramon Myers, ed., *A Unique Relationship: The United States and the Republic of China under the Taiwan Relations Act* (Hoover Institution Press, 1989); Martin Lasater, *Policy in Evolution: The U.S. Role in China's Reunification* (Westview, 1989).

Taiwan's Economic Development

On the issue of values and development see Gilbert Rozman, ed., *The East Asian Region: Confucian Heritage and Its Modern Adaptation* (Princeton UP, 1991).

The different theories about Taiwan's high growth rate are surveyed in Edwin Winckler and Susan Greenhalgh, eds., *Contending Approaches to the Political Economy of Taiwan* (M. E. Sharpe, 1988). Most recent on this subject is Robert

Wade, *Governing the Market: Economic Theory and the Role of Government in East Asian Industrialization* (Princeton UP, 1990), providing strong support for neoclassical theories. The classic optimist argument is John C. H. Fei, Gustav Ranis, and Shirley Kuo, *Growth with Equity: The Taiwan Case* (Oxford UP, 1979). A recent assessment is Kuo-ting Li, *The Evolution of Policy behind Taiwan's Development Success* (Yale UP, 1988).

On the pivotal land reforms see Joseph Yager, *Transforming Agriculture in Taiwan: The Experience of the Joint Commission on Rural Reconstruction* (Cornell UP, 1988).

Culture and Society

RELIGION. There are a number of ethnographic studies of popular religion in Taiwan, among which note David K. Jordan and Daniel L. Overmyer, *The Flying Phoenix: Aspects of Chinese Sectarianism in Taiwan* (Princeton UP, 1986); David K. Jordan, *Gods, Ghosts, and Ancestors: The Folk Religion of a Taiwanese Village* (U of California Press, 1972); and Robert Weller, *Unities and Diversities in Chinese Religion* (U of Washington Press, 1987).

CLASS AND FAMILY. For a survey of approaches see Emily Martin Ahern and Hill Gates, eds., *The Anthropology of Taiwanese Society* (Stanford UP, 1981). For village studies note Stevan Harrell, *Ploughshare Village: Culture and Context in Taiwan* (U of Washington Press, 1982); and Burton Pasternak, *Kinship and Community in Two Chinese Villages* (Stanford UP, 1972). On the family see Myron L. Cohen, *House United, House Divided: The Chinese Family in Taiwan* (Columbia UP, 1976). A recent study is by Hill Gates, *Chinese Working-Class Lives: Getting By in Taiwan* (Cornell UP, 1987).

PEOPLE'S REPUBLIC OF CHINA (1949–)

Reference Works

For surveys by specialists see *The Cambridge History of China*, vol. 14: *The Emergence of Revolutionary China 1949–1965*, and vol. 15: *Revolutions within the Chinese Revolution, 1966–1982* (Cambridge UP, 1987; 1991). Note also the *Bibliography of Asian Studies*, published by the Association for Asian Studies: Cumulative index through 1970, then annual volumes.

BIOGRAPHIES. See Wolfgang Bartke, *Who's Who in the People's Republic of China*, 2 vols., 3rd ed. (K. G. Saur, 1991).

DEMOGRAPHY. Compiled and edited by the Population Census Office of the State Council of the People's Republic of China, Institute of Geography of the Chinese Academy of Sciences, *The Population Atlas of China* (Oxford UP, 1987) gives comprehensive demographic, economic, and social data at the county level.

Periodicals

The leading academic journal for this period is the *China Quarterly* (London: 1960–). *Far Eastern Economic Review,* published in Hong Kong, is a noted weekly. See also the biannual *Australian Journal of Chinese Affairs* (Canberra: 1979–), and the monthly *Asian Survey* (U of California Press, 1971–).

Surveys

HISTORICAL SUMMARIES. Based on long-term observations as a French military attaché, Jacques Guillermaz, *The Chinese Communist Party in Power 1949–1976* (Westview, 1976), emphasizes foreign relations. See also Harold C. Hinton, ed., *The People's Republic of China: A Handbook* (Westview, 1979). Several authors synthesize recent scholarship: Marie-Claire Bergère, Lucien Bianco, and Jürgen Domes, *La Chine au XXe siècle: de 1949 à aujourd'hui* (Paris: Fayard, 1990); Maurice Meisner, *Mao's China and After: A History of the People's Republic* (Free Press, 1986); and Lowell Dittmer, *China's Continuous Revolution: The Post-Liberation Epoch, 1949–1981* (U of California Press, 1987). All analyze the political-ideological situation.

APPRAISALS. Tang Tsou, *The Cultural Revolution and Post-Mao Reforms: A Historical Perspective* (U of Chicago Press, 1986), is a critique of Chinese politics over a twenty-year period. Joyce K. Kallgren, ed., *Building a Nation-State: China after Forty Years* (Institute of East Asian Studies, U of California Press, 1990), offers even more complete coverage. Simon Leys, *Broken Images: Essays on Chinese Culture and Politics* (St. Martin's Press, 1980), is a bitterly disillusioned view by a scholar once devoted to China's high culture.

General accounts by journalists include John Fraser, *The Chinese: Portrait of a People* (Summit, 1980); Fox Butterfield, *China: Alive in the Bitter Sea* (Times Books, 1982), by a *New York Times* correspondent; Jay and Linda Mathews, *One Billion: A China Chronicle* (Random House, 1983), emphasizing social life and customs; John Gittings, *China Changes Face: The Road from Revolution, 1949–89* (Oxford UP, 1989), stressing political history.

SOCIOPOLITICAL ORGANIZATION AND LEADERSHIP

Mao Zedong

Major accounts and appraisals of Mao and his thought are in Stuart R. Schram's chapters in *The Cambridge History of China,* vols. 13 and 15, also published separately as *The Thought of Mao Tse-tung* (Cambridge UP, 1989). See also Benjamin I. Schwartz and Stuart R. Schram, eds. and trans., Mao's *Complete Works before 1949* (M. E. Sharpe, forthcoming). Michael Y. M. Kau and John K. Leung, eds., *The Writings of Mao Zedong, 1949–1976*, vol. 1: *September 1949–December 1955* (M. E. Sharpe, 1986); vol. 2: *January 1956–December 1957* (forthcoming). Roderick MacFarquhar, Timothy Cheek, Eugene Wu, eds., *The Secret Speeches of Chairman Mao: From the Hundred Flowers to the Great Leap Forward* (Council on East Asian Studies, Harvard U, 1989).

ANALYSES. Maurice Meisner, *Marxism, Maoism and Utopianism: Eight Essays* (U of Wisconsin Press, 1982), is a series of critical essays about Karl Marx, Mao, utopias, and communism. Ross Terrill, *Mao: A Biography* (Harper & Row, 1980), covers him very readably. Dick Wilson, ed., *Mao Tse-tung in the Scales of History: A Preliminary Assessment*, organized by the *China Quarterly* (Cambridge UP, 1977), consists of eleven highly qualified contributors dealing with Mao as philosopher, Marxist, political leader, soldier, teacher, economist, patriot, statesman, and Chinese innovator.

PSYCHOLOGICAL ASPECTS OF MAO'S LEADERSHIP. See Lucian W. Pye, *Mao Tse-tung: The Man in the Leader* (Basic Books, 1976). Robert J. Lifton, *Revolutionary Immortality: Mao Tse-tung and the Chinese Cultural Revolution* (Random House, 1968), gives a psychiatrist's different approach.

IDEOLOGY AFTER MAO. Bill Brugger and David Kelly, *Chinese Marxism in the Post-Mao Era* (Stanford UP, 1990), covers communism in politics and government since 1976. William A. Joseph, *The Critique of Ultra-Leftism in China 1958–1981* (Stanford UP, 1984), is an excellent consideration of Mao's ideology and a first study of ideology under Deng Xiaoping. Gilbert Rozman, *The Chinese Debate about Soviet Socialism, 1978–1985* (Princeton UP, 1987), is about communism and opinion about Sino–Soviet relations.

Policy and Politics

Thomas Fingar and Paul Blencoe et al., eds., *China's Quest for Independence: Policy Evolution in the 1970s* (Westview, 1980), discusses policy both internal and foreign from 1949 through the 1970s including the death of Mao. David M. Lampton, ed., *Policy Implementation in Post-Mao China* (U of California Press, 1987), has articles from 1976 to 1983, a number concerning population and environment. John P. Burns and Stanley Rosen, eds., *Policy Conflicts in Post-Mao China: A Documentary Survey, with Analysis* (M. E. Sharpe, 1986), is a textbook of well-chosen primary sources, many from the press, about political events from 1976 to 1985. See also Charles Burton, *Political and Social Change in China since 1978* (Greenwood Press, 1990), which covers politics and government, economic policy, and social conditions since 1976.

THE ROLE OF THE STATE. Stuart R. Schram, ed., *Foundations and Limits of State Power in China* (SOAS and Chinese UP, 1987), draws together European studies of the connections between China's imperial and postimperial periods with specific reference to ritual, religious, and symbolic representations of power. Vivienne Shue, *The Reach of the State: Sketches of the Chinese Body Politic* (Stanford UP, 1988), concerns rural China's integration into Mao's state complex, researching historical precedents and the power of localism.

THE PARTY AND POLITICS. The views of a long-time Jesuit China-watcher can be found in Laszlo Ladany, *The Communist Party of China and Marxism, 1921–1985: A Self Portrait* (Hoover Institution Press, 1988). Hsisheng Ch'i, *The Politics of Disillusionment: The Chinese Communist Party under Deng Xiaoping, 1978–1989* (M. E. Sharpe, 1991), and Hong Yung Lee, *From Revolutionary Cadres to Party Technocrats in Socialist China* (U of California Press, 1991).

OTHER POLITICAL GROUPS. For the Mao period, see Harry Harding, *Organizing China: The Problem of Bureaucracy, 1949–1976* (Stanford UP, 1981), and a pioneering study by Martin King Whyte, *Small Groups and Political Rituals in China* (U of California Press, 1974). Several studies that continue into the post-Mao period emphasize pressure groups. See the discussion in Victor C. Falkenheim, ed., *Citizens and Groups in Contemporary China* (Center for Chinese Studies, U of Michigan, 1987), and in David S. G. Goodman, ed., *Groups and Politics in the People's Republic of China* (M. E. Sharpe, 1984). Also Avery Goldstein, *From Bandwagon to Balance-of-Power Politics: Structural Constraints and Politics in China 1949–1978* (Stanford UP, 1991). Kenneth Lieberthal and Michel Oksenberg, *Policy Making in China: Leaders, Structures, and Processes* (Princeton UP, 1988), presents three case studies on petroleum, the Three Gorges Dam on the Yangzi, and province–center relations.

COMMUNICATION. John Howkins, *Mass Communication in China* (Longman, 1982), covers a range of media.

Campaigns

SURVEYS. Gordon Bennett, *Yundong: Mass Campaigns in Chinese Communist Leadership* (Center for Chinese Studies, U of California, 1976), offers a typology of different kinds of movements. See also Frederick C. Teiwes, *Politics and Purges in China: Rectification and the Decline of Party Norms, 1950–1965* (M. E. Sharpe, 1979).

LAND REFORM AND COLLECTIVIZING AGRICULTURE. Vivienne Shue, *Peasant China in Transition: The Dynamics of Development toward Socialism, 1949–1956* (U of California Press, 1980), suggests that peasants had some freedom to maneuver outside official observation. This thesis is discussed by Jean C. Oi, *State and Peasant in Contemporary China: The Political Economy of Village Government* (U of California Press, 1989), a major contribution to understanding rural China in Maoist and post-Maoist periods. Edward Friedman, Paul Pickowicz, and Mark Selden, with Kay Ann Johnson, *Chinese Village, Socialist State* (Yale UP, 1991), is an inside study of disillusionment during the 1950s and early 1960s, quite devastating.

INTELLECTUALS AND THE STATE

Intellectuals' early trials were covered most completely by Roderick Mac-Farquhar, ed., *The Hundred Flowers Campaign and the Chinese Intellectuals* (Praeger, 1960; Octagon, 1973). Merle Goldman, *Literary Dissent in Communist China* (Harvard UP, 1967; Athenaeum, 1971), is a pioneer work. Carol Lee Hamrin and Timothy Cheek, eds., *China's Establishment Intellectuals* (M. E. Sharpe, 1986); Merle Goldman with Timothy Cheek and Carol Lee Hamrin, *China's Intellectuals and the State: In Search of a New Relationship* (Council on East Asian Studies, Harvard U, 1987), together offer the latest analysis of the subject. Judith Shapiro and Liang Heng, *Cold Winds, Warm Winds: Intellectual Life in China Today* (Wesleyan UP, 1986), is based on travel. Liu Binyan, *A Higher Kind of Loyalty,* trans. Zhu Hong (Random House, 1990), recounts one intellectual's tortuous odyssey through PRC history.

Education

MATERIALS. For general references see Shi Ming Hu and Eli Seifman, eds., *Toward a New World Outlook: A Documentary History of Education in the People's Republic of China 1949–1976* (AMS Press, 1976); it is divided into seven periods, each with commentary and documents. Peter J. Seybolt, *Revolutionary Education in China: Documents and Commentary,* rev. ed. (International Arts & Sciences Press, 1973), thirty-two key documents with comments on all aspects.

POLICY. Many studies reflect the symbiotic relationship between education and the policy needs of the state: Susan L. Shirk, *Competitive Comrades: Career Incentives and Student Strategies in China* (U of California Press, 1982); Jonathan Unger, *Education under Mao: Class and Competition in Canton Schools, 1960–1980* (Columbia UP, 1982); Robert Taylor, *China's Intellectual Dilemma: Politics and University Enrollment, 1949–1978* (U of British Columbia Press, 1981), stressing the conflict between expertise and party promotion.

COMPARISONS. The cognitive psychologist Howard Gardner's *To Open Minds: Chinese Clues to the Dilemma of Contemporary Education* (Basic Books, 1989) concerns U.S. education since 1865, Chinese education since 1976, and the ways of fostering creative thinking in both societies.

EXCHANGES. For the influence of the United States on education see Leo A. Orleans, *Chinese Students in America: Policies, Issues, and Numbers* (National Academy Press, 1988). Joyce K. Kallgren and Denis Fred Simon, eds., *Educational Exchanges: Essays on the Sino–American Experience* (Institute of East Asian Studies, U of California, 1987).

REFORM. Educational reform efforts are detailed in Peter J. Seybolt and Gregory Kuei-ko Chiang, eds. and intro., *Language Reform in China: Documents and Commentary* (M. E. Sharpe, 1978). Suzanne Pepper, *China's Education Reform in the 1980s: Policies, Issues, and Historical Perspectives* (Institute of East Asian Studies, U of California, 1990), is a good discussion of educational changes post-Mao.

GREAT LEAP FORWARD, 1958–1960

See Roderick MacFarquhar, *The Origins of the Cultural Revolution*, vol. 2: *The Great Leap Forward, 1958–1960* (Columbia UP, 1983), a highly skilled textual analysis; David Bachman, *Bureaucracy, Economy, and Leadership in China: The Institutional Origins of the Great Leap Forward* (Cambridge UP, 1991); B. Ashton et al., "Famine in China, 1958–61," *Population and Development Review*, 10.4 (1984), a skilled consideration of the controversial famine.

THE CULTURAL REVOLUTION PERIOD, 1966–1976

Of major importance is the symposium edited by William A. Joseph, Christine P. W. Wong, and David Zweig, *New Perspectives on the Cultural Revolution* (Council on East Asian Studies, Harvard U, 1991).

Several items cover this period in general. Hong Yung Lee, *The Politics of the Chinese Cultural Revolution: A Case Study* (U of California Press, 1978), offers an authoritative political account. Lowell Dittmer, *Liu Shao-ch'i and the Chinese Cultural Revolution: The Politics of Mass Criticism* (U of California Press, 1974), compares Liu's career to Mao's in theory and style. Among accounts by China hands see Edward Rice, *Mao's Way* (U of California Press, 1972), by the then U.S. Consul-General in Hong Kong.

SECRET POLICE. On a different note, Roger Faligot and Rémi Kauffer, trans. from the French by Christine Donougher, *The Chinese Secret Service* (London: Headline, 1989; Morrow, 1990), discusses Kang Sheng (1898–1975) and other intelligence officers and their important role during the Cultural Revolution. It is overfull of names and dates and obviously much based on hearsay, like most secret accounts.

THE CULTURAL REVOLUTION IN RURAL CHINA. Anita Chan, Richard Madsen, and Jonathan Unger, *Chen Village: The Recent History of a Peasant Community in Mao's China* (U of California Press, 1984), is a fine study covering a rural community in the Pearl River delta during the Cultural Revolution. Richard Madsen, *Morality and Power in a Chinese Village* (U of California Press, 1984), is an excellent study of Confucianism and morals in the same village. David Zweig, *Agrarian Radicalism in China, 1968–1981* (Harvard UP, 1989), is an important analysis of the Cultural Revolution in the countryside: elite policy and local implementation.

Red Guards

See Anita Chan, *Children of Mao: Personality Development and Political Activism in the Red Guard Generation* (U of Washington Press, 1985), a fine study of political socialization and activity; William Hinton, *Hundred Day War: The Cultural Revolution at Tsinghua University* (Monthly Review Press, 1972), a gripping account; Nien Cheng, *Life and Death in Shanghai* (Grove, 1986), the best-selling account of the six-and-a-half-year imprisonment of the patrician widow and business associate of a GMD diplomat; B. Michael Frolic, *Mao's People: Sixteen Portraits of Life in Revolutionary China* (Harvard UP, 1980), based on Hong Kong interviews.

Gao Yuan, *Born Red: A Chronicle of the Cultural Revolution* (Stanford UP, 1987), is one of the best accounts by a former Red Guard. Liang Heng and Judith Shapiro, *Son of the Revolution* (Vintage Books, 1984), is an autobiography of a Red Guard who grew up during the Cultural Revolution. Stanley Rosen, *Red Guard Factionalism and the Cultural Revolution in Guangzhou (Canton)* (Westview, 1982), discusses education in China, including the Cultural Revolution, and Guangzhou. Lynn T. White, III, *Policies of Chaos: The Organizational Causes of Violence in China's Cultural Revolution* (Princeton UP, 1989), analyzes the political–social grievances eliciting violence in the Cultural Revolution.

Late Cultural Revolution Period and the Early 1980s

A major German scholar, Jürgen Domes, *The Government and Politics of the People's Republic of China: A Time of Transition* (Westview, 1985), covers 1949–1976. Dealing with the immediate post-Mao time is Roger Garside, *Coming Alive: China after Mao* (McGraw-Hill, 1981). Orville Schell, *In the People's Republic* (Random House, 1977), gives his impressions from travel, factory, and farm.

LATER CAMPAIGNS. For the campaign to send urban youth to the country-side see Thomas P. Bernstein, *Up to the Mountains and Down to the Villages: The Transfer of Youth from Urban to Rural China* (Yale UP, 1977). A major study by Frederick C. Teiwes, *Leadership, Legitimacy, and Conflict in China: From a Charismatic Mao to the Politics of Succession* (M. E. Sharpe, 1984), covers the succession struggles. The Gang of Four are vividly described in the biography by Roxanne Witke, *Comrade Chiang Ch'ing* (Little, Brown, 1977), which is the chief work on the career of Mao's fourth wife. Simon Leys, trans. from French ed. of 1974, *Chinese Shadows* (Viking, 1977), excoriates the anti-intellectual vulgarity of the Jiang Qing (Chiang Ch'ing) era in arts and letters.

THE MILITARY

See Jürgen Domes, *Peng Te-huai: The Man and the Image* (Stanford UP, 1985), an excellent biography of the army commander attacked by Mao in 1959 and later rehabilitated by Deng. For the Mao period see Harvey W. Nelsen, *The Chinese Military System: An Organizational Study of the Chinese People's Liberation Army* (Westview, 1977). Later books emphasize the efforts to revitalize professionalism in the army as against party promotion: Ellis Joffe, *The Chinese Army after Mao* (Harvard UP, 1987); Harlan W. Jencks, *From Muskets to Missiles: Politics and Professionalism in the Chinese Army, 1945–1981* (Westview, 1982); Paul Godwin, ed., *The Chinese Defense Establishment: Continuity and Change in the* 1980s (Westview, 1983). June Teufel Dreyer, ed., *Chinese Defense and Foreign Policy* (Paragon, 1989), discusses China's foreign relations and defense with an excellent analysis of China's role in the global community.

THE ECONOMY IN GENERAL

Alexander Eckstein, *China's Economic Revolution* (Cambridge UP, 1977), is a general survey by a pioneer in the field, strongest on the First Five-Year Plan and the Great Leap Forward. Dwight H. Perkins, *China: Asia's Next Economic Giant* (U of Washington Press, 1986), covers economic conditions since Mao's death. For a neat survey, see Christopher Howe, *China's Economy: A Basic Guide* (Basic Books, 1978). Nicholas R. Lardy, *Economic Growth and Distribution in China* (Cambridge UP, 1978), is an important analysis. See also Chu-yuan Cheng, *China's Economic Development: Growth and Structural Change* (Westview, 1982).

Carl Riskin, *China's Political Economy: The Quest for Development since 1949* (Oxford UP, 1988), emphasizes agriculture, the state, and PRC reforms, with an excellent bibliography. Dorothy J. Solinger, *Chinese Business under Socialism: The Politics of Domestic Commerce 1949–1980* (U of California Press, 1984), is an important book on commerce in a planned socialist economy. Thomas P. Lyons, *Economic Integration and Planning in Maoist China* (Columbia UP, 1987), explains the contradictory tendencies toward both centralization and decentralization.

Agricultural Development

Philip C. C. Huang, "The Paradigmatic Crisis in Chinese Studies," *Modern China*, 17.3 (July 1991), refreshingly objectifies European assumptions applied sometimes unconsciously to Chinese situations. Dwight Perkins and Shahid Yusuf, *Rural Development in China* (Johns Hopkins UP, 1984), a broad review, 1949–c.1982: historical, analytical, and quantitative assessments of Chinese agriculture and related economic issues, mainly intended for development economists. Nicholas R. Lardy, *Agriculture in China's Modern Economic Development* (Cambridge UP, 1983), is an important study of the evolution of the planning system. See also Kenneth R. Walker, *Food Grain Procurement and Consumption in China* (Cambridge UP, 1984). John P. Burns, *Political Participation in Rural China* (U of California Press, 1988), is a pioneering report on the influence of rural population on policy.

VILLAGE CASE STUDIES. See William L. Parish and Martin King Whyte, *Village and Family in Contemporary China* (U of Chicago Press, 1978), a major study; Gordon Bennett et al., *Huadong: The Story of a Chinese People's Commune* (Westview, 1978), a general account of a large suburban commune thirty miles north of Guangzhou; and Anita Chan, Richard Madsen, and Jonathan Unger, *Chen Village: The Recent History of a Peasant Community in Mao's China* (U of California Press, 1984), and Richard Madsen, *Morality and Power in a Chinese Village* (U of California Press, 1984).

DECOLLECTIVIZATION. Sulamith Heins Potter and Jack M. Potter, *China's Peasants: The Anthropology of a Revolution* (Cambridge UP, 1990), covers effects of communism and rural–social conditions. Huang Shu-min, *The Spiral Road: Change in a Chinese Village through the Eyes of a Communist Party Leader* (Westview, 1989), contains interviews with a party secretary on all aspects of the local scene, providing one of the best books about Chinese rural life from land reform to the mid-1980s. The village is situated at Xiamen on the southeast coast. See also Peter Nolan, *The Political Economy of Collective Farms: An Analysis of China's Post-Mao Rural Reforms* (Westview, 1988), a self-criticism of collectivization by a former leftist supporter of the movement; Helen F. Siu, *Agents and Victims in South China: Accomplices in Rural Revolution* (Yale UP, 1989), a historical account of the role of local elites and their changing relation to the state in Huancheng Commune of Xinhui County, Guangdong, 1977–mid-1980s; William L. Parish, ed., *Chinese Rural Development: The Great Transformation* (M. E. Sharpe, 1985), based on field work, 1979–1981, by young interdisciplinary scholars.

RURAL INDUSTRY. See Jon Sigurdson, *Rural Industrialization in China* (Council on East Asian Studies, Harvard U, 1977); Dwight Perkins, ed., *Rural Small-Scale Industry in the People's Republic of China* (U of California Press, 1977), an appraisal by specialists. Also William A. Byrd and Lin Qingsong, eds., *China's Rural Industry: Structure, Development, and Reform* (Oxford UP for the World Bank, 1990), on China's township, village, and private enterprise sectors.

Urbanization and Industry

For the Mao period see John W. Lewis, ed., *The City in Communist China* (Stanford UP, 1971). For post-Mao see Martin King Whyte and William L. Parish, *Urban Life in Contemporary China* (U of Chicago Press, 1984), a major work considering whether China's urban policy can yield a reasonable quality of life; based on interviews and research. See also Christopher Howe, ed., *Shanghai: Revolution and Development in an Asian Metropolis* (Cambridge UP, 1981), on geographical, political, and economic aspects. Ezra F. Vogel, *Canton under Communism: Programs and Politics in a Provincial Capital, 1949–1968,* 2nd ed. (Harvard UP, 1980), a classic study.

MANAGEMENT. See Charles Bettelheim, *Cultural Revolution and Industrial Organization in China: Changes in Management and Division of Labor* (Monthly Review Press, 1974); Stephen Andors, *China's Industrial Revolution: Politics, Planning, and Management, 1949 to the Present* (Pantheon Books, 1977); Peter N. S. Lee, *Industrial Management and Economic Reform in China, 1949–1984* (Oxford UP, 1987), a chronological and theoretical account of the industrial sector.

LABOR AND MANPOWER. Labor productivity in 1957–1975 is analyzed in Thomas G. Rawski, *Economic Growth and Employment in China* (Oxford UP, 1979). Andrew G. Walder, *Communist Neo-Traditionalism: Work and Authority in Chinese Industry* (U of California Press, 1986; paper, 1988), is a superb comparative study of authority, politics, and social structure, noting clientelism in the workplace. On a grimmer note, see Bao Ruo-wang (Jean Pasqualini) and Rudolph Chelminski, *Prisoner of Mao* (Coward, McCann and Geoghegan, 1973), which details the Chinese experience of reform through labor by a Franco-Chinese.

Science and Technology

Richard Baum, ed., *China's Four Modernizations: The New Technological Revolution* (Westview, 1980), has a score of specialist contributors. Richard P. Suttmeier, *Research and Revolution: Science Policy and Societal Change in China*

(D. C. Heath, 1974), uses a historical, organizational, and theoretical approach. Note by the same author, *Science, Technology and China's Drive for Modernization* (Hoover Institution Press, 1980). Tony Saich, *China's Science Policy in the 80s* (Humanities Press International, 1989), traces the development of policy up to 1985, noting that science and technology are the core of the four modernizations promoted to overcome the effect of the Cultural Revolution. Leo A. Orleans, ed., with the assistance of Caroline Davidson, *Science in Contemporary China* (Stanford UP, 1980), is a basic survey describing and appraising the setup in the natural and social sciences as of 1978–79. Denis Fred Simon and Merle Goldman, eds., *Science and Technology in Post-Mao China* (Council on East Asian Studies, Harvard U, 1989), is a historical treatment of organizational changes and requirements.

ECONOMIC REFORM, 1978–1990

Harry Harding, *China's Second Revolution: Reform after Mao* (Brookings Institution, 1987), reports on foreign economic relations as well as economic and political policy. Elizabeth J. Perry and Christine Wong, eds., *The Political Economy of Reform in Post-Mao China* (Council on East Asian Studies, Harvard U, 1985), is a fine analytical study of both agricultural and industrial reform.

INTERNATIONAL ASPECTS AND COMPARISONS. See Robert F. Dernberger, ed., *China's Development Experience in Comparative Perspective* (Harvard UP, 1980); Richard Feinberg et al., eds., *Economic Reform in Three Giants: U.S. Foreign Policy and the USSR, China, and India* (Overseas Development Council, 1990); N. T. Wang, *China's Modernization and Transnational Corporations* (D. C. Heath, 1984), a nonspecialist account of the internal and external constraints on Chinese modernization and the problems of and prospects for reform.

CHINA'S FOREIGN TRADE. See Nicholas R. Lardy, *Foreign Trade and Economic Reform in China, 1978–1990* (Cambridge UP, 1991); Samuel P. S. Ho and Ralph W. Huenemann, *China's Open Door Policy: The Quest for Foreign Technology and Capital: A Study of China's Special Trade* (U of British Columbia Press, 1984), reports on technology transfer, investments, economic policy, and foreign economic relations; Robert Kleinberg, *China's "Opening" to the Outside World: The Experiment with Foreign Capitalism* (Westview, 1990), concerns itself with the Shenzhen Special Economic Zone, foreign investments, economic and commercial policy post-1976.

ENERGY DEVELOPMENT. The energy industry provides a particularly complex problem for modernization. See Vaclav Smil, *Energy in China's Modernization: Advances and Limitations* (M. E. Sharpe, 1988), a review of energy policy, power resources, and the energy industry. Kenneth Lieberthal and Michel Oksenberg, *Policy Making in China: Leaders, Structures, and Processes* (Princeton UP, 1988), is mainly focused on the energy sector.

SPECIAL ECONOMIC ZONES (SEZS). See Yue-man Yeung and Xu-wei Hu, eds., *Chinese Coastal Cities: Catalysts for Modernization* (U of Hawaii Press, 1991), on the post-1978 opening. Ezra F. Vogel, *One Step Ahead in China: Guangdong under Reform* (Harvard UP, 1989), is based on interviews in 30 of 100 counties, which indicated that poor infrastructure was the main problem but was alleviated by the nearness of Hong Kong. See **China's Foreign Affairs** and **Political Reform, 1978–1990**, below.

HONG KONG. On this topic there is a large literature. James L. Watson, *Emigration and the Chinese Lineage: The Mans in Hong Kong and London* (U of California Press, 1975), traces the causes and results of emigration. Wong Siu-lun, *Emigrant Entrepreneurs: Shanghai Industrialists in Hong Kong* (Oxford UP, 1988), considers the distinctive features of Chinese industrial entrepreneurs and how displacement to Hong Kong has helped. See also Peter Wesley-Smith, *Unequal Treaty 1898–1997: China, Great Britain and Hong Kong's New Territories* (Oxford UP, 1980; paperback, 1983); Frank Ching, *Hong Kong and China: For Better or for Worse* (Asia Society and Foreign Policy Association, 1985).

CHINA'S FOREIGN AFFAIRS

See Gerald Segal, ed., *Chinese Politics and Foreign Policy Reform* (Kegan Paul International, 1990), on the interaction between domestic politics and foreign policy up to mid-1989 (post-Tiananmen), noting the influence of the military and of the coastal provinces; A. Doak Barnett, *The Making of Foreign Policy in China: Structure and Process* (Westview, 1985); Harry Harding, ed., *China's Foreign Relations in the 1980s* (Yale UP, 1984); and Samuel S. Kim, ed., *China and the World: New Directions in Chinese Foreign Relations* (Westview, 1989); Michael Yahuda, *China's Foreign Policy: Towards the End of Isolationism* (Macmillan, 1983); John Gittings, *The World and China, 1922–1972* (Harper & Row, 1974), a wide-ranging survey by a correspondent.

Korean War

Bruce Cumings, *The Origins of the Korean War*, vol. 1: *Liberation and the Emergence of Separate Regimes, 1945–1947*; vol. 2: *The Roaring of the Cataract, 1947–1950* (Princeton UP, 1981 and 1990), traces the causes of the Korean War, beginning with the history of Korea and the Allied Occupation, 1945–1948.

China and the USSR

A systematic, historical survey is by O. Edmund Clubb, *China and Russia: The Great Game* (Columbia UP, 1971). See also Herbert J. Ellison, ed., *The Sino-Soviet Conflict: A Global Perspective* (U of Washington Press, 1982); and Gordon H. Chang, *Friends and Enemies: The United States, China, and the Soviet Union, 1948–1972* (Stanford UP, 1990), an innovative, scholarly discussion based on newly available sources concerning American policy toward the Sino-Soviet split, the Taiwan Straits, and China's entry into the Korean War.

China and the Third World

Samuel S. Kim, *The Third World in Chinese World Policy* (Center of International Studies, Princeton U, 1989), discusses foreign relations and economic assistance. See also Lillian Craig Harris and Robert L. Worden, eds., *China and the Third World: Champion or Challenger?* (Auburn House, 1986); Peter Van Ness, *Revolution and Chinese Foreign Policy: Peking's Support for Wars of National Liberation* (U of California Press, 1970).

SOUTHEAST ASIA. See J. A. C. Mackie, ed., *The Chinese in Indonesia: Five Essays* (U of Hawaii Press, in assoc. with the Australian Institute of International Affairs, 1976), on patterns of Chinese political activity and anti-Chinese outbreaks; Robert S. Ross, *The Indochina Tangle: China's Vietnam Policy, 1975–1979* (Columbia UP, 1988), from the fall of Saigon to Beijing's 1979 invasion of Vietnam, noting that the Soviet factor was crucial.

SOUTH ASIA. See Neville Maxwell, *India's China War* (Jonathan Cape, 1970); Alien S. Whiting, *The Chinese Calculus of Deterrence: India and Indochina* (U of Michigan Press, 1975), an important study of the 1962 war and general policy behavior.

AFRICA. See Bruce D. Larkin, *China and Africa, 1949–1970: The Foreign Policy of the People's Republic of China* (U of California Press, 1971), the first historical survey; also Alan Hutchinson, *China's African Revolution* (Westview, 1976).

CHINA'S FOREIGN AID. See Wolfgang Bartke, *The Economic Aid of the P R of China to Developing and Socialist Countries* (K. G. Saur, 1989); and John Franklin Copper, *China's Foreign Aid: An Instrument of Peking's Foreign Policy* (D. C. Heath, 1976), which contains data by regions and countries.

China and the United States

Akira Iriye, *The Cold War in Asia: A Historical Introduction* (Prentice Hall, 1974), appraises Chinese–American relations. James C. Thomson, Jr., Peter W.

Stanley, John Curtis Perry, *Sentimental Imperialists: The American Experience in East Asia* (Harper & Row, 1981), surveys American–East Asian relations. See also Warren I. Cohen, *America's Response to China: A History of Sino–American Relations,* 3rd ed. (Columbia UP, 1990); Roderick MacFarquhar, *Sino–American Relations, 1949–1971* (Praeger, 1972), which contains narrative and analysis with documents showing the evolution of foreign policy.

"LOSS" OF CHINA. Stanley D. Bachrack, *The Committee of One Million: "China Lobby" Politics, 1953–1971* (Columbia UP, 1976), traces the long history of the lobby against admission of Communist China to the UN. Edwin W. Martin, *Divided Counsel: The Anglo–American Response to Communist Victory in China* (UP of Kentucky, 1986), is a well-informed and well-told diplomatic history, 1948–1954. John S. Service, *The Amerasia Papers: Some Problems in the History of US–China Relations* (Center for Chinese Studies, U of California, 1971), is one of the few places where this leading Foreign Service Officer in China states his case. E. J. Kahn, Jr., *The China Hands* (Random House, 1975), puts together the human story of "the loss of China." See also Paul Gordon Lawson, ed., *The China Hands' Legacy: Ethics and Diplomacy* (Westview, 1987).

RAPPROCHEMENT. Robert G. Sutter, *China Watch: Toward Sino–American Reconciliation* (Johns Hopkins UP, 1978), recounts the phases of rapprochement to 1972. William Dudley and Karen Swisher, eds., *China: Opposing Viewpoints* (Greenhaven Press, 1989), concerns human rights, history, and economic conditions since 1976.

POLITICAL REFORM, 1978–1990

For a fairly positive, interpretative assessment of reforms by experienced scholars see A. Doak Barnett and Ralph N. Clough, eds., *Modernizing China: Post-Mao Reform and Development* (Westview, 1986). See also Barrett L. McCormick, *Political Reform in Post-Mao China: Democracy and Bureaucracy in a Leninist State* (U of California Press, 1990); and Carol Lee Hamrin, *China and the Challenge of the Future: Changing Political Patterns* (Westview, 1990), a good political history of the reform movement, including post-1976 economic policy.

Democracy Movement

Andrew J. Nathan, *Chinese Democracy* (Knopf, 1985; paper, U of California Press, 1986), is a fine study of the historical background. Fang Lizhi, *Bringing Down the Great Wall: Writings on Science, Culture and Democracy in China,* ed. and trans. James H. Williams (Knopf, 1991), is an account by the distinguished physicist and leader for reform who, with his wife, took refuge in the U.S. Embassy during Tiananmen. See also Andrew J. Nathan, *China's Crisis: Dilemmas of Reform and Prospects for Democracy* (Columbia UP, 1990). Orville Schell, *Discos and Democracy: China in the Throes of Reform* (Pantheon, 1988), offers a kaleidoscopic view of 1986–87 including portraits of Fang Lizhi, Liu Binyan, and Wang Ruowang, based mainly on talks with intellectuals. See David Bachman and Dali L. Yang, eds. and trans., *Yan Jiaqi and China's Struggle for Democracy* (M. E. Sharpe, 1991), on a leading political scientist and dissident. A penetrating analysis with relevance to China's future political shape is Thomas A. Metzger, "Confucian Thought and the Modern Chinese Quest for Moral Autonomy," in *Renwen ji shehui kexue jikan* (Journal of Social Sciences and Philosophy) (Taibei), 1.1 (Nov. 1988): 297–358.

Tiananmen Incident, June 4, 1989

See Tony Saich, ed., *The Chinese People's Movement: Perspectives on Spring 1989* (M. E. Sharpe, 1990). For documents, see Michel Oksenberg, Lawrence R. Sullivan, and Marc Lambert, eds., *Beijing Spring 1989, Confrontation and Conflict: The Basic Documents* (M. E. Sharpe, 1990). Lee Feigon, author of *China Rising: The Meaning of Tiananmen* (Chicago: Ivan Dee, 1990), spent the spring of 1989 on the People's University campus in Beijing and notes that the protests were launched not by "pro-Western democrats" but by politically well-connected democratic dissidents. Jeffrey N. Wasserstrom and Elizabeth J. Perry, eds., *Popular Protest and Political Culture in Modern China: Learning from 1989* (Westview, 1992), looks at 1989 from a variety of historical and cultural perspectives, with fascinating results. For the official version see Che Muqi, *Beijing Turmoil: More than Meets the Eye* (Beijing: Foreign Languages Press, 1990). George Hicks, ed., *The Broken Mirror: China after Tiananmen* (St. James Press, 1991), offers explanations and predictions by journalists, academics, and diplomats, writing on the first anniversary of June 4.

LAW AND HUMAN RIGHTS

Domestic Law

Anita Chan, Stanley Rosen, and Jonathan Unger, eds., *On Socialist Democracy and the Chinese Legal System: The Li Yizhe Debates* (M. E. Sharpe, 1985), concerns the rule of law, due process, political participation, and the general political-governmental setting. History and criticism of the law in China is provided by Jerome Alan Cohen, R. Randle Edwards, and Fu-mei Chang Chen, eds., *Essays on China's Legal Tradition* (Princeton UP, 1980). Note R. Randle Edwards, Louis Henken, and Andrew J. Nathan, eds., *Human Rights in Contemporary China* (Columbia UP, 1986). See also **Democracy Movement**, above.

International Law

Hungdah Chiu and Jerome Alan Cohen, *People's China and International Law* (Princeton UP, 1974; update forthcoming). See also **Economic Reform, 1978–1990** and **China's Foreign Affairs**, above.

SOCIAL AND PUBLIC AFFAIRS

Problems of contemporary Chinese identity are dealt with in "The Living Tree: The Changing Meaning of Being Chinese Today," *Daedalus,* vol. 120, no. 2, spring 1991, with nine distinguished contributors. Many human variations are noted in Zhang Xinxin and Sang Ye, *Chinese Lives: An Oral History of Contemporary China* (Pantheon, 1987). See also Richard Curt Kraus, *Class Conflict in Chinese Socialism* (Columbia UP, 1981); and James L. Watson, ed., *Class and Social Stratification in Post-Revolution China* (Cambridge UP, 1984).

Medicine and Public Health

Arthur Kleinman, *Social Origins of Distress and Disease: Depression, Neurasthenia, and Pain in Modern China* (Yale UP, 1986), gives a psychiatrist-anthropologist's views. See also Chen Junshi, T. Colin Campbell, et al., eds., *Diet, Life Style and Mortality in China: A Study of the Characteristics of 65 Chinese Counties* (Cornell UP, 1990); Marilyn M. Rosenthal, *Health Care in the People's Republic of China: Moving towards Modernization* (Westview, 1987); and John Z. Bowers, J. William Hess, and Nathan Sivin, eds., *Science and Medicine in Twentieth-Century China: Research and Education* (Center for Chinese Studies, U of Michigan, 1988), deals with a wide range of medical and health-related topics. See also *The Health Sector in China* (World Bank, 1984); *A Barefoot Doctor's Manual* (Philadelphia: Running Press, 1977), dealing with acupuncture, etc.; and C. C. Chen, *Medicine in Rural China: A Personal Account* (U of California Press, 1989).

Environment

See Vaclav Smil, *The Bad Earth: Environmental Degradation in China* (M. E. Sharpe, 1984); the author, a Czech now teaching in Canada, originally praised China's environmental efforts; a visit totally disillusioned him. The book is a polemic but provides much vital information. James E. Nickum, ed. and intro., *Water Management Organization in the People's Republic of China* (M. E. Sharpe, 1982), is an excellent hands-on study about irrigation management. See also S. D. Richardson, *Forests and Forestry in China* (Island Press, 1990). Lester Ross, *Environmental Policy in China* (Indiana UP, 1988), is concerned with the implementation of forestry policy, water conservancy, natural hazards policy, and pollution control using social and environmental sciences and integrating

Chinese political influence. Grainne Ryder, *Damming the Three Gorges: What Dam-Builders Don't Want You to Know* (Toronto: Probe International, 1990), states the arguments against building a huge dam on the Yangzi in hopes of preventing the World Bank funding desired by Li Peng et al. Lyman P. van Slyke, *Yangtze: Nature, History, and the River* (Addison-Wesley, 1988), describes the river as seen in poetry, history, and modern travel accounts.

Demography and Birth Control

The Population Atlas of China (Oxford UP, 1987), ed. Li Chengrui, is an important source of demographic, economic, and social data based on the 1982 census. Leo A. Orleans, *Every Fifth Child: The Population of China* (Stanford UP, 1972), delineates the major issues beginning with the 1953 census. A summary by an eminent demographer is provided by Ansley J. Coale, *Rapid Population Change in China, 1952–1982* (National Academy Press, 1984). See also Judith Banister, *China's Changing Population* (Stanford UP, 1987), a basic study; Elizabeth Croll, Delia Davin, and Penny Kane, eds., *China's One Child Family Policy* (Macmillan, 1985), highly informative; and Burton Pasternak, *Marriage and Fertility in Tianjin, China: Fifty Years of Transition* (East-West Population Institute, East-West Center, 1986), about marriage, human fertility, family, and social customs in Tianjin, a fine case study.

Women in Society

For general treatments see Elizabeth Croll, *The Women's Movement in China: A Selection of Readings, 1949–1973* (London: Anglo-Chinese Educational Institute, 1974). Margery Wolf, *Revolution Postponed: Women in Contemporary China* (Stanford UP, 1985), considers the status, roles, and self-images of Chinese women, noting that patriarchy and socialism co-exist. See also Kay Ann Johnson, *Women, the Family, and Peasant Revolution in China* (U of Chicago Press, 1983); and Arthur P. Wolf and Chieh-shang Huang, *Marriage and Adoption in China* (Stanford UP, 1980).

WOMEN'S RIGHTS. See Marilyn B. Young, ed., *Women in China: Studies in Social Change and Feminism* (Center for Chinese Studies, U of Michigan, 1973). Phyllis Andors, *The Unfinished Liberation of Chinese Women, 1949–1980* (Indiana UP, 1983), indicates that women remain subservient.

BIOGRAPHICAL ACCOUNTS OF WOMEN. Of many biographies, note Vivian Ling Hsu, ed., *Born of the Same Roots: Stories of Modern Chinese Women* (Indiana UP, 1981). Recounted by Yue Daiyun, written by Carolyn Wakeman, *To the Storm: The Odyssey of a Revolutionary Chinese Woman* (U of California Press, 1985), is an amazing account of the personal and political trials of a Beida literature professor. Emily Honig and Gail Hershatter, *Personal Voices: Chinese Women in the 1980s* (Stanford UP, 1988), is about growing up female, a scholarly work based on early 1980s interviews.

Minorities and Regions

On minorities, see Thomas Heberer, *China and Its National Minorities: Autonomy or Assimilation?*, trans. by Michael Vale (M. E. Sharpe, 1989); the author visited minority regions in 1982–1988 but had no interviews, relying on written data; good on history and identification of different minorities and on policy toward regions. June Teufel Dreyer, *China's Forty Millions: Minority Nationalities and National Integration in the People's Republic of China* (Harvard UP, 1976), is a pioneer work on problems and policies.

On regional studies, Dorothy J. Solinger, *Regional Government and Political Integration in Southwest China, 1949–1954: A Case Study* (U of California Press, 1977), remains basic. George V. H. Moseley, III, *The Consolidation of the South China Frontier* (U of California Press, 1973), uses Chinese provincial papers about the 1950–1960 period. See also David S. G. Goodman, *Centre and Province in the People's Republic of China: Sichuan and Guizhou, 1955–1965* (Cambridge UP, 1986); Keith Forster, *Rebellion and Factionalism in a Chinese Province: Zhejiang, 1966–1976* (M. E. Sharpe, 1990), on politics, government, and history, particularly the Cultural Revolution, 1966–1969; Linda Benson and Ingvar Svanberg, eds., *The Kazaks of China: Essays on an Ethnic Minority* (Stockholm: Almquist & Wiksell International, 1988), on Chinese social policy toward the Xinjiang Uighur Autonomous Region; and Dru C. Gladney, *Muslim Chinese: Ethnic Nationalism in the People's Republic* (Council on East Asian Studies, Harvard U, 1991), a monument to field research on the Hui half of twenty million Chinese Muslims.

Religion

Holmes Welch, *Buddhism under Mao* (Harvard UP, 1972), completes a remarkable trilogy on Buddhism in modern China. George Urban, ed. and intro., *The Miracles of Chairman Mao: A Compendium of Devotional Literature, 1966–1970* (Nash Publishing, 1971), deals with faith, abnegation of self, class love, socialist sacrifice, guilt, and confession. G. Thompson Brown, *Christianity in the People's Republic of China*, rev. ed. (John Knox Press, 1986), is a good general book mainly about Protestants. Julian F. Pas, ed., *The Turning of the Tide: Religion in China Today* (Oxford UP, 1989), describes new turnings to various faiths, with historical background about twentieth-century religion in China and Hong Kong.

Arts and Humanities

LITERATURE. See Perry Link, ed., *Stubborn Weeds: Popular and Controversial Chinese Literature after the Cultural Revolution* (Indiana UP, 1983); Hualing Nieh, ed., *Literature of the Hundred Flowers*, 2 vols. (Columbia UP, 1981); Perry Link, Richard Madsen, and Paul G. Pickowicz, eds., *Unofficial China: Popular Culture and Thought in the People's Republic* (Westview, 1989), a significant study based on new data suggesting new ways to study a closed society; Jeanne Tai, comp. and trans., *Spring Bamboo: A Collection of Contemporary Chinese Short Stories* (Random House, 1989), new literary trends by the reform generation; Chen Jo-hsi, *The Execution of Mayor Yin and Other Stories from the Great Proletarian Cultural Revolution* (Indiana UP, 1978), fictionalized examples of experience by a Taiwan-born, U.S.-educated resident of China, 1966–1973, advertised as "dissent" literature; Helen Siu and Zelda Stern, eds., *Mao's Harvest: Voices from China's New Generation* (Oxford UP, 1983), literature of the great disillusionment; Liu Binyan, ed. Perry Link, *People or Monsters? and Other Stories and Reportage from China after Mao* (Indiana UP, 1983), literature including journalistic articles of social commentary.

DRAMA. For theater and opera, see Bonnie S. McDougall, ed., *Popular Chinese Literature and Performing Arts in the People's Republic of China, 1949–1979* (U of California Press, 1984), a fine survey; Rudolf G. Wagner, *The Contemporary Chinese Historical Drama: Four Studies* (U of California Press, 1990), a history and criticism of drama in its political context.

MUSIC. See Richard Curt Kraus, *Pianos and Politics in China: Middle Class Ambitions and the Struggle over Western Music* (Oxford UP, 1989), a highly personal view including biographies of notable Chinese composers and musicians based on written sources and interviews.

ART. Ellen Johnston Laing, *The Winking Owl: Art in the People's Republic of China* (U of California Press, 1988), discusses different approaches to art in the PRC and before. See also Joan Lebold Cohen, *The New Chinese Painting, 1949–1986* (H. N. Abrams, 1987).

FILM. See Paul Clark, *Chinese Cinema: Culture and Politics since 1949* (Cambridge UP, 1987), a useful contribution to the field and to the relationship between the arts and politics through 1983.

Publisher's Note

Professor Fairbank delivered to Harvard University Press on the morning of September 12, 1991, the edited and approved manuscript for *China: A New History*. He suffered a heart attack that afternoon and died two days later, leaving unwritten only this acknowledgments section.

In line with his deep-seated and often-stated conviction that the study of Chinese history must be a collaborative undertaking, drawing on the skills and energies of many individuals, Fairbank sent the typescript of *China: A New History* to more than a dozen colleagues for comment. Among those who offered suggestions for improvement were Marie-Claire Bergère, Peter Bol, Kwang-chih Chang, Lloyd Eastman, Edward Farmer, Herbert Franke, William Kirby, Philip Kuhn, Thomas Metzger, Andrew Nathan, Lucian Pye, John Schrecker, Benjamin Schwartz, James Watson, and especially Paul Cohen, who was in frequent communication with Fairbank during the months preceding his death and agreed to look after the book in the event of his worsening health. The many tasks requiring editorial attention during the production process were performed with gracious expertise by Professor Cohen.

Fairbank's research assistant, Karin Gollin, helped in countless ways in both the development of the text and the compilation of the pre-PRC sections of the Suggested Reading. The PRC portion of the Suggested Reading benefited from the devoted exertions of Martha Henderson Coolidge, who also advised on environmental issues of the post-Mao years. Others who generously shared their bibliographical expertise were William Alford, Paul Cohen, Joan Kaufman, Peter Perdue, Dwight Perkins, Terry Sicular, Nathan Sivin, James Thomson, Rudolf Wagner, David Zweig, and above all Nancy Hearst, librarian at the Fairbank Center for East Asian Research.

As she had done for a number of her husband's previous works, Wilma Fairbank contributed her knowledge and seasoned eye as a historian of Chinese art to the selection and arrangement of the illustrations and wrote many of the accompanying captions. Her aim was to show Chinese people in action, as depicted by Chinese artists through the centuries before photography. Mrs. Fairbank also participated in the selection of the jacket illustration.

For assistance in locating and procuring illustrative material the Press is grateful to Yen-shew Lynn Chao, Timothy Connor, Jing Jun, John Kim, Thomas Lawton, Jeanne Moore, James Watson, Wango Weng, Mark Wilson, and Wu Hung.

Aida Donald, Assistant Director and Editor-in-Chief of Harvard University Press, asked Fairbank to write the book in 1989, mobilized resources to make it possible, and read drafts of the manuscript. Susan Wallace, Senior Editor for Manuscript Development, worked closely with the author during the final stages of manuscript revision and editing. Marianne Perlak, Art Director, designed the book and dust jacket. David Foss, Assistant Production Manager, coordinated typesetting, printing, and binding.

Professor Fairbank's assistant of many years, Joan Hill, took major responsibility for typing the manuscript in several drafts. Olive Holmes compiled the indexes. Under Fairbank's supervision, Robert Forget researched and drew the maps. Maps 1 and 2 are adapted from *The Cambridge History of China,* by permission of Cambridge University Press. Harper & Row generously granted permission to use material from *The Great Chinese Revolution, 1800–1985* (1986).

Illustration Credits

Following page 104:

1. Terracotta army soldier from the First Emperor's buried army. Lintong county, Shaanxi. (Collection housed at site.)
2. Reversed rubbing (white on black) detail from the left shrine of the Wu family, Jiaxiang, Shandong. Restored by Wilma Fairbank. See *Adventures in Retrieval* (Cambridge: Harvard University Press, 1972).
3. Bronze horse, chariot, and occupant from a tomb in Wuwei, Gansu.
4. Side of a stone sarcophagus (detail). Reproduced by permission of the Nelson-Atkins Museum of Art, Kansas City, Missouri (Nelson Fund), 33–8543/2.
5. Guanyin hall and statue, Jixian, Hebei, from Liang Ssu-ch'eng, *A Pictorial History of Chinese Architecture* (1984), reproduced by permission of MIT Press.
6. "Scholars of the Northern Qi Collating Classical Texts" (detail). Denman Waldo Ross Collection 31.123. Courtesy of the Museum of Fine Arts, Boston.
7. Li Tang, "Village Doctor" (detail). Reproduced by permission of the National Palace Museum, Republic of China.
8. Zhang Zeduan, "The Qingming Festival on the River" (detail). Palace Museum, Beijing. Photograph courtesy of Wango H. C. Weng.
9. Li Guanglin, "Guo Ziyi and the Uighurs" (detail). Reproduced by permission of the National Palace Museum, Republic of China.
10. "Palace Ladies Bathing Children." 35.8. Courtesy of the Freer Gallery of Art, Smithsonian Institution, Washington, D.C.
11. Li Song, "The Knickknack Peddler." Reproduced by permission of the National Palace Museum, Republic of China.
12. Portrait of Emperor Ming Taizu. Photograph courtesy of the National Palace Museum, Republic of China.
13. "Tartars on Horseback" (detail). 68.46. Courtesy of the Freer Gallery of Art, Smithsonian Institution, Washington, D.C.
14. "Admonishing in Chains" (detail). 11.235. Courtesy of the Freer Gallery of Art, Smithsonian Institution, Washington, D.C.

15. Zhou Chen, "Beggars and Street Characters" (detail). John L. Severance Fund 64.94. Reproduced by permission of the Cleveland Museum of Art.

16. Yu Zhiting, "Gao Shiqi Whiling Away the Summer." Reproduced by permission of the Nelson-Atkins Museum of Art, Kansas City, Missouri (Bequest of Laurence Sickman), F88–41/17.

Following page 200:

17–24. Illustrations from an 1808 edition of *Peiwenzhai gengzhitu* showing the principal steps in rice cultivation.

25–32. Illustrations from a late Qing edition of the *Qinding shujing tushuo* (1905) depicting craftsmen at work.

Following page 328:

33. Sun Yatsen, with his young wife Song Qingling. Reproduced by permission of Eastfoto.

34. Japanese troops conquering Manchuria in 1931. Reproduced by permission of the Bettmann Archive.

35. *Top:* Japanese troops guarding Chinese prisoners in Shanghai. *Bottom:* Japanese soldiers after a looting expedition. Reproduced by permission of the Bettmann Archive.

36. Mao Zedong and Zhang Guotao after the Long March. Reproduced by permission of the Springer/Bettmann Film Archive.

37. Jiang Jieshi (Chiang Kaishek) with Feng Yuxiang and Yan Xishan. Reproduced by permission of the Hulton-Deutsch Collection of the BBC Hulton Picture Library.

38. *Top:* Jiang Jieshi with his top generals in Hankou (Wuhan). *Bottom:* Song Meiling (Soong Meiling), wife of Jiang Jieshi, helping to sew bandages in a wartime hospital. Reproduced by permission of Robert Capa-Pix/Magnum Photo Library.

39. Youngsters in North China in the 1940s standing watch against attack by agents of Jiang Jieshi. Reproduced by permission of the Bettmann Archive.

40. U.S. Ambassador Patrick Hurley escorting Mao from Yan'an to Chongqing for talks with Jiang. Reproduced by permission of UPI/Bettmann Newsphotos.

41. *Top:* Jiang and Mao toasting each other at a formal banquet in Chongqing in late 1945. *Bottom:* A policeman killing a Communist agent in Shanghai. Reproduced by permission of UPI/Bettmann Newsphotos.

42. *Top:* Rough justice meted out to landlords by the Communists. Reproduced by permission of the Bettmann Archive. *Bottom:* Chinese Communist leaders enjoying a lighter moment. Reproduced by permission of New China Pictures/Magnum Photo Library.

43. *Top:* Red Guards waving their little red books. *Bottom:* Young members

of a production brigade study a Mao quotation. Reproduced by permission of Eastfoto.

44. Zhou Enlai. Reproduced by permission of Marc Riboud/Magnum Photo Library.

45. *Top:* A couple with a newly purchased washing machine and 20-inch color TV. Reproduced by permission of UPI/Bettmann Newsphotos. *Bottom:* A farmer driving his ducks to market in the city. Reproduced by permission of Reuters/Bettmann Newsphotos.

46. Deng Xiaoping. Reproduced by permission of Reuters/Bettmann Newsphotos.

47. *Top:* Student activists at Beijing University showing their support of glasnost. Reproduced by permission of Reuters/Bettmann Newsphotos. *Bottom:* A Beijing University student demonstrating in support of journalists. From *Dedicated to Freedom* (New York: Roxene Corporation, 1989).

48. *Top:* Goddess of Democracy statue. *Bottom:* A lone unarmed man blocking the advance of an armored convoy. Reproduced by permission of Stuart Franklin/Magnum Photo Library.

Page 333:
Inflation near the end of World War II. From Ye Qianyu, *China Today* (Calcutta, 1944).

Author Index

Numbers in bold type indicate year of publication. Numbers in roman type indicate references in the text. Numbers in italic type indicate listings in the Suggested Reading.

Ahern, Emily Martin: **1981**, *510*
Alitto, Guy S.: **1979**, 299, *504*
Allan, Sarah: **1991**, *481*
Allis, Sam: **2002**, *455*
Allsen, Thomas T.: **1987**, *488*
Anderson, Mary M.: **1990**, *491*
Andors, Phyllis: **1983**, *526*
Ashton, B.: **1984**, *515*

Bachman, David: **1991**, *515, 524*
Bachrack, Stanley D.: **1976**, *523*
Balazs, Etienne, 179, 188; **1964**, 45, *490*
Banister, Judith: **1987**, *526*
Bao Ruo-wang (Jean Pasqualini): **1973**, *519*
Barboza, David: **2005**, *470*
Barfield, Thomas J., 110; **1989**, 61–62, *488*
Barmé, Geremie: **1996**, 455n69, *455*
Barnett, A. Doak: **1985**, *521*; **1986**, *523*
Bartke, Wolfgang: **1989**, *522*; **1991**, *510*
Bartlett, Beatrice, S.: **1991**, 151, *493*
Bastid, Marianne: **1976**, *495*
Baum, Richard: **1980**, *519*; **1994**, *455*
Bays, Daniel H.: **1978**, *499*
Beasley, W. G.: **1961**, *480*
Bennett, Gordon: **1976**, *513*; **1978**, *518*
Benson, Linda: **1988**, *527*
Bergère, Marie-Claire, 287; **1976**, *495*; **1989**, 270, 272, *502*; **1990**, *511*

Bernstein, Tomas P.: **1977**, *517*
Bettelheim, Charles: **1974**, *519*
Bianco, Lucien: **1990**, *511*
Bielenstein, Hans: **1980**, *485*
Billingsley, Phil: **1988**, *507*
Black, Alison Harley: **1989**, *494*
Blencoe, Paul: **1980**, *512*
Blunden, Caroline: **1983**, 76, *478*
Blusse, Leonard: **1986**, 194, *494*
Bodde, Derk: **1952–53**, *481*; **1967**, *484, 493*; **1991**, 67, 100, 108, *482*; CHOC 1, 56, *484*
Bol, Peter: **1992**, 94, 96, 109, 117, *487*
Bonner, Joey: **1986**, *504*
Boorman, Howard L.: **1967**, *502*
Borg, Dorothy: **1980**, *508*
Bowers, John Z.: **1988**, *525*
Brandt, Loren: **1989**, *500*
Brokaw, Cynthia: **1991**, *490*
Brook, Timothy: **1989**, *489*
Brown, G. Thompson: **1986**, *527*
Brugger, Bill: **1990**, *512*
Bruner, Katharine F.: **1975**, *497*; **1986**, *497*; **1991**, *497*
Buck, David: **1987**, *500*
Burns, John P.: **1986**, *512*; **1988**, *518*
Burton, Charles: **1990**, *512–513*
Butterfield, Fox: **1982**, *511*
Byrd, William A.: **1990**, *519*

Campbell, T. Colin: **1990**, *525*
Chaffee, John W.: **1985**, 94, *526*; **1989**, *493*

Chan, Anita: 1984, *516, 518;* 1985, *516;* 1985, *524;* 1996, 454n49
Chan, Anthony B.: 1982, *503*
Chan, Hok-lam: 1982, *488;* 1984, 117, *488*
Chan, Sucheng: 1986, *501*
Chan, Wellington, K. K.: 1977, *500*
Chan, Wing-tsit: 1964, *479;* 1987, *487;* 1989, *487*
Chang, Chun-shu: 1971, *478;* 1991, *492*
Chang, Chung-li: 1966–1971, *498*
Chang, Gordon H.: 1990, *508, 522*
Chang, Hao: 1971, *499;* 1987, *499*
Chang, K. C. (Kwang-chih Chang), 31, 34, 44; 1976, *483;* 1980, *485;* 1982, *485;* 1986, 30, *483*
Chang, Kuo-t'ao (Zhang Guotao): 1971–1972, *505*
Chang, Shelley Hsueh-lun: 1991, *492*
Chao, Kang: 172; 1977, *463;* 1986, 171, *500*
Che Muqi: 1990, *524*
Cheek, Timothy: 1986, *514;* 1987, *514;* 1989, *512*
Chelminski, Rudolph: 1973, *519*
Chen, C. C.: 1989, *525*
Chen, David W., 2003, *452*
Chen, Fu-mei Chang: 1980, *524*
Chen Jo-hsi: 1978, *528*
Chen Junshi: 1990, *525*
Chen, Kenneth: 1964, *482*
Chen, Yung-fa: 1986, *508*
Cheng, Chu-yuan: 1982, *517*
Cheng, Joseph Y. S.: 2003, *455*
Cheng, Lucie: 1984, *490–491*
Cheng, Nien: 1986
Cheng, Peter: 1983, *478*
Chesneaux, Jean: 1968, *506;* 1976, *495*
Ch'i, Hsi-sheng: 1976, *503;* 1982, *507;* 1991, *513*
Chiang, Gregory Kuei-ko: 1978, *515*
Ching, Frank: 1985, *521*
Ching, Julia: 1976, *493*
Chiu, Hungdah: 1974, *525*
Chow Tse-tsung: 1960, *503*
Chu, Wen-djang: 1966, *498*
Ch'ü, T'ung-tsu: 1961, 184, *493*
Clark, Anne B.: 1971, *502*
Clark, Paul: 1987, *528*
Clough, Ralph N.: 1986, *523*
Clubb, O. Edmund: 1971, *522;* 1978, *502*
Coale, Ansley J.: 1984, *526*
Coates, P. D.: 1988, *496*

Coble, Parks M.: 1986, *505*
Cochran, Sherman: 1980, *501;* 1983, *505*
Cody, Edward: 2005, *452*
Cohen, A.: 1997, 455n60
Cohen, Jerome Alan: 1974, *525;* 1980, *524*
Cohen, Joan Lebold: 1987, *528*
Cohen, Myron L.: 1976, *510*
Cohen, Paul A., 222; 1974, 262, *499;* 1984, *495;* 1987, *499;* 1990, 51, *479;* CHOC 10, 222, *497*
Cohen, Warren I.: 1990, *523*
Cohn, Don J.: 1987, *497*
Cole, James: 1986, *499*
Copper, John Franklin: 1976, *522;* 1988, *509*
Craig, Albert M.: 1965, *479*
Creel, Herrlee G.: 1970, *484*
Cressey, George B., *479*
Croll, Elizabeth: 1974, *526;* 1985, *526;* 1995, 454n56
Crossley, John N.: 1987, *483*
Crossley, Pamela Kyle: 1990, 146, *499*
Cumings, Bruce: 1981, 1990, *521*

Daniels, Christian: 1984, *489*
Darby, Phillip: 1987, *496*
Dardess, John W.: 1973, *488;* 1983, *491*
Davidson, Caroline: 1980, *520*
Davin, Delia: 1985, *526*
Davis, Michael C.: 1995, *455*
Davis, Richard L.: 1986, *486–487*
Dawson, Christopher: 1955, *489*
de Bary, William Theodore: 1964, *479, 495;* 1970, *493;* 1972, *482;* 1975, *493;* 1982, *488;* 1983, 99, *481;* 1989, *484, 493;* 1991, 63, 160, *481*
de Francis, John: 1984, *483*
de Hartog, Leo: 1989, *488*
Dennerline, Jerry: 1981, *492*
Deng Xiaoping: 1994, 452n7, 453n30
Dermigny, Louis: 1964, *495*
Dernberger, Robert F.: 1980, *520*
Des Forges, Roger V.: 1973, *499*
Destenay, Anne: 1972, *505*
Dickson, Bruce: 2003, *455*
Dirlik, Arif: 1978, *505;* 1989, 276, *505*
Dittmer, Lowell: 1974, *515;* 1987, *511*
Domes, Jürgen: 1985, *516, 517;* 1990, *511*
Donougher, Christine: 1989, *515;* 1990, *515*
Drake, Fred W.: 1975, *496*
Dreyer, Edward, 138; 1982, *491*
Dreyer, June Teufel: 1976, *527;* 1989, *517*

Du Shiran: 1987, *483*

Duara, Prasenjit: 1988, 22, 105, 156, 157, 295, *504–505, 507*

Dudley, William: 1989, *523*

Duus, Peter: 1989, *496*

Eastman, Lloyd: 1974, 290, 292, *504;* 1984, 314, *507;* 1988, *490;* 1991, *504*

Eber, Irene: 1986, *481*

Eberhard, Wolfram: 1986, *481*

Ebrey, Patricia: 1981, *479;* 1984, 107, *487;* 1986, *490;* 1991, *490*

Eckstein, Alexander: 1977, *517*

Edwards, E. W.: 1987, *496*

Edwards, R. Randle: 1980, *524;* 1986, *524*

Ellison, Herbert J.: 1982, *522*

Elman, Benjamin, 229; 1984, 224, *494;* 1990, 228, *494*

Elvin, Mark: 1970, *487;* 1973, 93, *480;* 1974, *501;* 1983, 76, *478*

Embree, Ainsley: 1988, *480;* 1989, *484*

Endicott-West, Elizabeth: 1989, *488*

Eng, Robert: 1986, *500–501*

Esherick, Joseph, 425; 1976, 244, 252, *501;* 1987, 230, *500;* 1990, *490, 499*

Eto, Shinkichi: 1984, *501*

Fairbank, John King: 1953, *496;* 1957, 96, *481;* 1960, 69, *479;* 1965, *479;* 1974, *483, 497;* 1975, *497;* 1979, *495, 496;* 1983, *481, 497;* 1986, *497;* 1991, *497;* CHOC 10–15, *479, 495, 502, 510*

Faligot, Roger: 1989, 1990, *515*

Falkenheim, Victor C.: 1987, *513*

Fang, Chaoying: 1976, *480*

Fang, Lizhi: 1991, *523–524*

Farmer, Edward L., 129; 1976, *491*

Faure, David: 1989, *500*

Fay, Peter Ward: 1975, *496*

Fei, John C. H.: 1979, *510*

Fei Xiaotong, 299

Feigon, Lee: 1983, *505;* 1990, *524*

Feinberg, Richard: 1990, *520*

Feldman, Harvey: 1988, *509*

Feng, Chia-sheng: 1949, 113, *488*

Feuerwerker, Albert, 2, 217; 1977, *506;* CHOC 12, *497;* CHOC 13, *479, 502, 506*

Fewsmith, Joseph: 1985, *502;* 1997, 454n45; 2001, *455*

Fincher, John: 1981, 246, *502*

Fingar, Thomas: 1980, *512*

Fletcher, Joseph, 200; CHOC 10, 197, *493*

Fogel, Joshua: 1984, 126, *489;* 1987, *505;* 1989, *491*

Forster, Keith: 1990, *527*

Franke, Herbert, 123; 1976, *480;* 1987, *488;* 1990, *488*

Fraser, John: 1980, *511*

Freedman, Maurice: 1971, 20, *490;* 1979, *490*

Friedman, Edward, 366; 1974, *503;* 1991, 353, *514*

Friesen, Oris: 1987, *508*

Frodsham, J. D.: 1970, *496*

Frolic, B. Michael: 1980, *516*

Fung Yu-lan: 1952–53, *481*

Furth, Charlotte: 1970, *504;* 1976, *503;* 1984, *490–491*

Galbiati, Fernando: 1985, *506*

Gao Yuan: 1987, *516*

Gardner, Daniel K.: 1986, *587;* 1990, *487*

Gardner, Howard: 1989, *515*

Garside, Roger: 1981, *516*

Garver, John W.: 1988, *508*

Gasster, Michael: 1969, *502*

Gates, Hill: 1981, *510;* 1987, *510*

Geelan, P. J. M.: 1974, *478*

Gernet, Jacques, 46; 1962, *487;* 1972, *479;* 1985, *494*

Gerth, Hans: 1951, *489*

Ginsburg, Norton: 1966, *478*

Gittings, John: 1974, *521;* 1989, *511*

Gladney, Dru C.: 1991, *527*

Godley, Michael: 1982, *501*

Godwin, Paul: 1983, *517*

Gold, Thomas B.: 1986, *509*

Goldman, Merle: 1967, 1971, *514;* 1987, *514;* 1989, *520;* 1990, 51, *479;* 1994, 453n36, *456;* 1999, *456;* 2002, *456;* 2005, *456,* 452n20

Goldstein, Avery: 1991, *513*

Goldstein, Steven M.: 1989, *507*

Goodman, David S. G.: 1984, *513;* 1986, *527*

Goodrich, L. Carrington: 1976, *480*

Graham, A. C.: 1973, *482;* 1989, 62, *485*

Grant, Carolyn: 1975, *493*

Greenhalgh, Susan: 1988, *509*

Grieder, Jerome: 1970, *504;* 1981, *503*

Grove, Linda: 1984, *485*

Guillermaz, Jacques: 1972, *505;* 1976, *511*

Guisso, Richard: 1981, *491*

Guo Liang: 2003, 455
Guy, R. Kent: 1987, 70, 158–159, 492

Hagger, Jean: 1984, 508
Hamrin, Carol Lee: 1986, 514; 1987, 514;
    1990, 523
Handlin, Joanna: 1983, 493
Hao, Yen-p'ing: 1970, 501; 1986, 497
Harding, Harry: 1981, 513; 1984, 521;
    1987, 520
Harding, James: 1997, 452n14,16
Harrell, Stevan: 1982, 510
Harris, Lillian Craig: 1986, 522
Hartford, Kathleen: 1989, 507
Hartman, Charles: 1986, 486
Hartwell, Robert: 1982, 170, 486
Hayford, Charles: 1990, 300, 505
Heberer, Thomas: 1989, 527
Heinrich, Amy Vladek: 1989, 484
Heinrichs, Waldo: 1980, 508
Henderson, John B.: 1984, 64, 481
Henken, Louis: 1986, 524
Herrmann, Albert: 1966, 478
Hersey, John: 1985, 261, 497
Hershatter, Gail: 1986, 506; 1988, 527
Hess, J. William: 1988, 525
Hicks, George: 1991, 524
Hinsch, Bret: 1990, 490
Hinton, Harold C.: 1979, 511
Hinton, William: 1967, 507; 1972, 516
Ho, Peng Yoke: 1985, 482
Ho, Ping-ti, 41, 102; 1976, 484
Ho, Samuel P. S.: 1978, 509; 1984, 520
Hofheinz, Roy, Jr.: 1977, 505
Honig, Emily: 1986, 506; 1988, 527
Hook, Brian: 1982, 480
How, Julie Lien-ying: 1989, 504
Howard, Richard C.: 1967, 502
Howe, Christopher: 1978, 517; 1981, 519
Howell, Jude: 1996, 454n50,54, 456
Howkins, John: 1982, 513
Hsiao, Ch'i-ch'ing: 1978, 122, 488
Hsiao, Kung-ch'uan: 1975, 499
Hsieh, Andrew: 1983, 505
Hsieh, Chiao Chiao: 1985, 509
Hsieh, Chiao-min: 1973, 478
Hsiung, James: 1977, 516
Hsu, Cho-yun: 1980, 485; 1988, 39, 484
Hsu, Immanuel C. Y.: 1990, 495
Hsu, Vivian Ling: 1981, 526
Hu Sheng: 1981, 496
Hu, Shi Ming: 1976, 514

Hu, Xu-wei: 1991, 521
Huang Yasheng: 1996, 453n42, 456
Huang, Chieh-shang: 1980, 526
Huang, Philip C. C., 172, 1985, 500, 507;
    1990, 167, 179, 507; 1991, 518
Huang, Ray: 1974, 132, 133, 134, 137,
    138, 491; 1981, 492; 1988, 480
Huang Shu-min: 1989, 518
Hucker, Charles O., 130; 1962, 478; 1966,
    491; 1975, 109, 479
Huenemann, Ralph W.: 1984, 520
Hulsewe, A. F. P.: 1955, 485; 1979, 485;
    1985, 484–485
Hummel, A. W.: 1943, 1944, 480
Hunt, Michael H.: 1983, 497
Hunter, Jane: 1984, 497
Hutchinson, Alan: 1976, 522
Hymes, Robert P.: 1986, 95, 486

Iriye, Akira: 1974, 522; 1977, 508

Jacobs, Dan: 1981, 505
Jacobs, J. Bruce: 1984, 508
Jagchid, Sechin: 1989, 488
Jansen, Marius: 1975, 507
Jen Yuwen: 1973, 498
Jencks, Harlan W.: 1982, 517
Jochim, Christian: 1986, 481
Joffe, Ellis: 1987, 517
Johannesen, Stanley: 1981, 491
Johnson, David: 1977, 83, 486; 1985, 155,
    157, 263, 489
Johnson, Kay Ann: 1983, 526; 1991, 353,
    514
Johnson, Linda Cooke, 204
Johnson, Wallace: 1979, 485
Jordan, David K.: 1972, 510; 1986, 510
Jordan, Donald A.: 1976, 504
Joseph, William A.: 1984, 512; 1991, 398,
    399, 402, 515

Kahn, E. J., Jr.: 1975, 523
Kahn, Harold L.: 1971, 492
Kallgren, Joyce K.: 1987, 515; 1990, 511
Kane, Penny: 1985, 527
Kapp, Robert: 1973, 503
Kataoka, Tetsuya: 1974, 507
Kau, Michael Y. M.: 1986, 512; 1988, 509
Kauffer, Rémi: 1989, 1990, 515
Keightley, David N., 39; 1978, 484; 1983,
    483–484
Kelly, David: 1990, 512

Kennedy, Thomas: 1978, *498*
Kerr, George H.: 1965, *509*; 1974, *509*
Kierman, Frank A., Jr.: 1974, *483*
Kim, Ilpyong J.: 1973, *505–506*; 1988, *509*
Kim, Samuel S.: 1989, *521, 522*
King, Catherine E.: 1987, *498*
King, David S. J.: 1987, *498*
King, Frank H. H.: 1987, *498*
Kirby, William C., 337; 1984, 288, *504*
Klein, Donald: 1971, *502*
Kleinberg, Robert: 1990, *520*
Kleinman, Arthur: 1981, *483*; 1986, *525*; 1997, *455n60*
Knapp, Ronald: 1980, *508*
Knoblock, John: 1988, *484*
Kraus, Richard Curt: 1981, *525*; 1989, *528*
Krompart, Jane: 1979, *502*
Kuhn, Philip A., 238; 1970, 236, *498*; 1990, 159, *488*; CHOC 13, 297, *479*; CHOC 10, 210, *479*
Kuo, Shirley: 1979, *510*
Kuo, Warren: 1966, *505*
Kwong, Luke S. K.: 1984, 229, *499*

Ladany, Laszlo: 1988, *513*
Lagerwey, John: 1987, *482*
Lai, Tse-han: 1990, *509*
Laing, Ellen Johnston: 1988, *528*
Lakshmarian, Indira A. R.: 2002, *452*
Lambert, Marc: 1990, *524*
Lampton, David M.: 1987, *512*
Langlois, John D., Jr.: 1981, 121, 122, *488*
Lao, Kan: 1984, *480*
Lao, Yan-shuan, 122–123
Lardy, Nicholas R.: 1978, *517*; 1983, *518*; 1991, *506*
Larkin, Bruce D.: 1971, *522*
Lary, Diana: 1974, *503*
Lasater, Martin: 1989, *509*
Lavely, William: 1990, *500*
Lawson, Paul Gordon: 1987, *523*
Lee, Chong-sik: 1983, *506*
Lee, Hong Yung: 1978, *515*; 1991, *513*
Lee, James: 1990, *500*
Lee, Leo, 263
Lee, Peter N. S.: 1987, *519*
Lee, Robert H. G.: 1970, *493*; 1989, *496*
Lee, Thomas H. C.: 1985, *486*
Leonard, Jane Kate: 1984, *496*
Leung, John K.: 1986, *512*

Leung, Yen-sang: 1990, *501*
Levenson, Joseph R.: 1958, 1964, 1965, *504*
Levine, Steven: 1987, 335, *508*
Levy, Howard S.: 1966, 175, *491*
Lewis, John W.: 1971, *519*
Lewis, Mark Edward, 69; 1990, 49, *484*
Leys, Simon: 1977, *523*; 1980, *511*
Li Chengrui: 1987, *526*
Li Chi: 1977, *484*
Li Fan: 2003, *453*
Li Jui: 1977, *506*
Li Lianjing: 1997, *453n38*
Li, Kuo-ting: 1988, *510*
Li, Lillian M.: 1981, *500*
Li, Lincoln: 1975, *507*
Li Qi: 1985, *482*
Li Yan: 1987, *483*
Liang Heng: 1984, *516*; 1986, *514*
Lieberthal, Kenneth: 1988, *513, 521*; 1995, *456*
Lifton, Robert J.: 1968, *512*
Lin, Man-houng, 198
Lin Qingsong: 1990, *519*
Lin, T. Y.: 1981, *483*
Linduff, Katheryn: 1988, 39, *484*
Link, Perry: 1981, 263, *504*; 1983, *528*; 1989, *528*
Little, Daniel: 1989, *500*
Liu Binyan, 419; 1983, *528*; 1990, *514*
Liu, James T. C., 96; 1959, *486*; 1988, 100, *487*
Liu, Kwang-Ching, 217; 1990, 19, 101, *499*; CHOC 10, 214, *479*, CHOC 11, *479, 495, 498*
Lloyd, Janet: 1985, *494*; 1989, *502*
Lo, Winston W.: 1987, *486*
Loewe, Michael: 1966, *480*; 1974, *485*; 1982, *485*; 1988, *485*; 1990, CHOC 1, *479, 484*
Lu Gwei-djen: 1954–, *482*; 1980, *483*
Luk, Michael Y. L.: 1990, *505*
Lun, Anthony W. C.: 1987, *483*
Lutz, Jessie Gregory: 1988, *504*
Lyons, Thomas P.: 1987, *517–518*

Ma, L. Eve Armentrout: 1990, *501*
McCormack, Gavan: 1977, *503*
McCormick, Barrett L.: 1990, *523*
McDonald, Angus, Jr.: 1978, *507*
McDougall, Bonnie S.: 1984, *528*
McElderry, Andrea Lee: 1976, *498*

MacFarquhar, Roderick: 1960, 1973, 514; 1972, 523; 1983, 515; 1989, 512; CHOC 14, 15, 479; 1997, 451n4, 456; 1997, 454n44; 456; 1999, 456

Mackie, J. A. C.: 1976, 522

MacKinnon, Stephen: 1980, 499; 1987, 508

McKnight, Brian E.: 1971, 486

McMullen, David: 1988, 86, 486

McNeill, William: 1982, 483

Macpherson, Kerrie: 1987, 497

Madsen, Richard: 1984, 516, 518; 1989, 528

Mair, Victor, 155, 156; 1990, 481

Mancall, Mark: 1971, 495

Mann, Susan: 1987, 238, 500

Marks, Robert: 1984, 506

Marquand, Robert: 2005, 455

Martin, Edwin W.: 1986, 523

Matheson, Elizabeth MacLeod: 1975, 497

Mathews, Jay: 1983, 511

Mathews, Linda: 1983, 511

Maxwell, Neville: 1970, 522

May, Ernest R.: 1986, 497

Meisner, Maurice: 1967, 505; 1982, 512; 1986, 511

Meskill, Johanna: 1979, 508

Metzger, Thomas A., 51, 1973, 70, 492; 1977, 185, 487; 1988, 524

Michael, Franz: 1966–1971, 498

Mills, J. V. G.: 1970, 137, 491

Min Tu-ki: 1989, 499

Miyazaki Ichisada: 1976, 486

Mooney, Paul: 2005, 469

Morgan, David: 1986, 488

Morley, James M.: 1983, 507

Morris, Clarence: 1967, 493

Moseley, George V. H., III: 1973, 527

Mote, Frederick F.: 1989, 481; CHOC 7, 129, 479, 491

Moule, A. C.: 1976, 489

Mungello, D. E.: 1989, 494

Murphey, Rhoads: 1977, 497

Myers, Ramon H.: 1970, 294, 507; 1980, 500; 1984, 508; 1989, 496, 509; 1990, 509; 1991, 509

Nagai, Yonosuke: 1977, 508

Naitō Konan, 126, 127, 489

Nakayama, Shigeru: 1973, 482

Naquin, Susan: 1976, 191, 498; 1987, 154, 161, 489

Nathan, Andrew, 351; 1976, 503; 1985, 263, 489, 523; 1986, 523, 524; 1990, 524

Naughton, Barry: 1991, 398, 399; 1995, 456; 1999, 452nn9,13,24

Needham, Joseph, 63, 81, 100, 115, 172; 1954–, 3, 482; 1973, 482; 1980, 483; 1981, 482; 1986, 482

Nelsen, Harvey W.: 1977, 517

Nevitt, Christopher: 1996, 454n51

Ng, Vivien W.: 1990, 493

Nickum, James E.: 1982, 525

Nieh, Hualing: 1981, 528

Nolan, Peter: 1988, 518

Norman, Jerry: 1988, 483

O'Brien, Kevin J.: 1990, 456; 1994, 453n37

Ocko, Jonathan, 19; 1983, 498–499

Oi, Jean C.: 1989, 354, 355, 356, 514; 1999, 456

Oksenberg, Michel: 1988, 513, 521; 1990, 524; CHOC 14, 474

Ono, Kazuko: 1989, 491

Orleans, Leo A.: 1972, 526; 1980, 520; 1988, 515

Overmyer, Daniel: 1976, 498; 1986, 481, 510

Pan, Lynn: 1990, 501

Paper, Jordan D.: 1973, 484

Parish, William L.: 1978, 518; 1984, 519; 1985, 518

Parris, Kristen: 1999, 454n52

Pas, Julian F.: 1989, 527

Pasternak, Burton: 1972, 510; 1986, 526

Peattie, Mark: 1984, 508; 1989, 496

Pei Minxin: 1997, 453n33

Pelliot, P.: 1976, 489

Pepper, Suzanne: 1978, 508; 1990, 515

Perdue, Peter: 1987, 171, 490

Perkins, Dwight H., 171; 1969, 168–169, 500; 1975, 500; 1977, 519; 1984, 518; 1986, 517

Perry, Elizabeth J.: 1980, 498; 1981, 498; 1985, 520; 1992, 524; 1999, 456; 2003, 456

Perry, John Curtis: 1976, 486; 1981, 523

Peterson, Willard J.: 1979, 140, 493

Pickowicz, Paul G.: 1989, 528; 1991, 353, 514

Pirazzoli-t'Serstevens, Michele: 1982, 485

Polachek, James M.: 1992, 200, 496

Porkert, Manfred: 1974, 483

Potter, Jack M.: 1990, *518*
Potter, Sulamith Heins: 1990, *518*
Price, Don C.: 1974, *502*
Price, Jane L.: 1976, *505*
Pulleyblank, E. B.: 1961, *480*
Pusey, James: 1983, *504*
Pye, Lucian W.: 1976, *512*

Ramsey, S. Robert: 1987, *483*
Ranis, Gustav: 1979, *510*
Rankin, Mary Backus: 1971, *502*; 1986, 239, *501*; 1990, *490, 499*; 1993, *454n47*
Rawski, Evelyn S.: 1972, *500*; 1979, 261, *490*; 1985, *489*; 1987, 154, 161, *489*; 1988, *490*
Rawski, Thomas, 294; 1979, *519*; 1989, 290, *506*
Reardon-Anderson, James: 1980, *508*
Reischauer, Edwin O.: 1960, 69, *479*
Rhoads, Edward J. M.: 1975, *501–502*
Rice, Edward: 1972, *515*
Richardson, S. D.: 1990, *525*
Rickett, W. Allyn: 1965, *484*; 1985, *484*
Rigby, Richard: 1980, *504*
Riskin, Carl, 398; 1988, *517*
Ronan, Colin A.: 1978, *482*
Ropp, Paul S.: 1990, 2, *479*
Rosen, Stanley: 1982, *516*; 1985, *524*; 1986, *512*
Rosenthal, Elizabeth: 2003, *453*
Rosenthal, Marilyn M.: 1987, *525*
Ross, Lester: 1988, *525*
Ross, Robert S.: 1988, *522*
Rossabi, Morris: 1975, *492*; 1983, 110, *488*; 1988, *488*
Rowe, William T.: 1984, *501*; 1985, *489*; 1989, 177–178, *501*
Rozman, Gilbert: 1973, *501*; 1987, *512*; 1991, *509*
Ryder, Grainne: 1990, *526*

Saari, Jon: 1990, 20, 264, *502*
Saich, Tony, 278, 282, 304; 1989, *520*; 1990, *524*; 1991, *505*; n.s., *505*; 1990, *456*; 1997, *455n71*; 2000, *453n41*, *454n46*; 2004, *456*
Sang Ye: 1987, *525*
Sariti, Anthony: 1977, *506*
Schaller, Michael: 1979, *508*
Schell, Orville: 1977, *516*; 1988, *524*
Schiffrin, Harold Z.: 1968, *502*; 1984, *501*
Schirokauer, Conrad: 1976, *486*

Schoppa, R. Keith: 1982, 251, *499*; 1989, 171, *490*
Schram, Stuart R.: 1987, 45, 123, *488, 513*; 1989, *482, 512*; CHOC 13, 15, *511*; n.d., *512*
Schran, Peter: 1976, *511*
Schrecker, John E.: 1971, *496*
Schwarcz, Vera: 1986, 259, *503*
Schwartz, Benjamin I.: 1964, 259, *499*; 1985, 67, 68, n.d., *512*
Sedgley, Anne: 1984, *508*
Segal, Gerald: 1990, *521*
Seifman, Eli: 1976, *514*
Selden, Mark: 1971, *506*; 1991, 353, *514*; 2003, *456*
Seligman, Janet: 1982, *485*
Service, John S.: 1971, *523*
Seybolt, Peter J.: 1973, *514*; 1978, *515*
Shaffer, Linda: 1982, *507*
Shang Xiaoyuan: 1996, *454nn50,54, 456*
Shapiro, Judith: 1984, *516*; 1986, *514*
Sheel, Kamal: 1989, *506*
Shi Ting: 2005, *455*
Shiba, Yoshinobu: 1970, *487*
Shirk, Susan L.: 1982, *514*
Shu An: 1985, *482*
Shue, Vivienne: 1980, *514*; 1988, *513*; 1988, *452n23*
Shum, Kui-kwong: 1988, *507*
Sigurdson, Jon: 1977, *519*
Simon, Denis Fred: 1987, *515*; 1989, *520*
Sinor, Denis: 1990, *487, 488*
Siu, Helen F.: 1983, *528*; 1989, *518*
Sivin, Nathan, 3; 1973, *482*; 1987, 65, *483*; 1988, *525*
Skinner, G. William, 11, *474*; 1964–1965, 1973, *478*; 1974, *501*; 1977, 106, *490, 501*
Smil, Vaclav: 1979, *490*; 1984, *525*; 1988, *520–521*
Smith, Bardwell L.: 1976, *486*
Smith, Paul J.: 1991, 108, *486*
Smith, Richard J.: 1986, *497*; 1991, *481, 497*
Snow, Edgar: 1983, 1978, *506*
Snow, Philip: 1988, *491*
Solinger, Dorothy J.: 1977, *527*; 1984, *517*; 1999, *454n58*
Souza, George B.: 1986, *494–495*
Spence, Jonathan D., 234; 1974, *492*; 1978, *491*; 1979, *492*; 1981, *503*; 1984, 151, *494*; 1988, *494*; 1990, 148, *492, 495*

Stanley, Peter W.: 1981, 522–523
Stern, Zelda: 1983, 528
Strand, David: 1989, 273, 502; 1989, 454n48; 1995, 454n53
Struve, Lynn: 1984, 145, 492
Sullivan, Lawrence R.: 1990, 524
Sutter, Robert G.: 1978, 523
Suttmeir, Richard P.: 1974, 519–520; 1980, 520
Sutton, Donald: 1980, 503
Svanberg, Ingvar: 1988, 527
Swanson, Bruce: 1982, 498
Swisher, Karen: 1989, 523
Symons, Van Jay: 1989, 488

Tai, Jeanne: 1989, 528
Tao, Jing-shen: 1977, 488
Tanner, Murry Scot: 1999, 453n31
Taylor, Robert: 1981, 514
Teiwes, Frederick C.: 1979, 513; 1984, 517; 1997, 451n4
Temple, Robert: 1986, 482
Teng, S. Y.: 1979, 495–496
Terrill, Ross: 1980, 512
Thomas, S. Bernard: 1983, 507
Thompson, Laurence G.: 1988, 481
Thompson, Roger R.: 1995, 453
Thomson, James C., Jr.: 1981, 522–523
Thorne, Christopher: 1978, 507
Tien, Hung-mao: 1972, 504; 1989, 509
Tregear, R. R.: 1980, 479
Tsien Tsuen-hsuin, 93; 1985, 483
Tsou, Tang: 1986, 511
Tsurumi, E. Patricia: 1977, 509
Tu, Wei-ming: 1976, 493; 1985, 481
Tucker, Nancy B.: 1983, 508
Twitchett, Denis: 1970, 485; 1974, 478; 1983, CHOC 1, 479, 484; CHOC 3, 85, 100, 126, 479, 485; CHOC 7, 479, 491

Unger, Jonathan: 1982, 514; 1984, 516; 1985, 524; 1996, 454n49
Unschuld, Paul U.: 1985, 1986, 483
Urban, George: 1971, 527

Vale, Michael: 1989, 527
Van Ness, Peter: 1970, 494
van Slyke, Lyman P.: 1988, 526
Viraphol, Sarasin: 1977, 139, 494
Vogel, Ezra: 1980, 519; 1989, 521
von Glahn, Richard: 1987, 487

Wade, Robert: 1990, 509–510
Wagner, Rudolf G.: 1990, 528
Wakeman, Carolyn: 1985, 526–527
Wakeman, Frederic, Jr.: 1966, 206, 236, 496; 1975, 493, 495; 1985, 145, 492; CHOC 10, 495
Walder, Andrew: 1986, 375, 519; 1988, 519; 1991, 402; 1995, 456
Waldron, Arthur: 1990, 57, 139, 492
Walker, Kenneth R.: 1984, 518
Waltner, Ann: 1990, 490
Wang Ching-hsien: 1974, 484
Wang Feng: 1990, 500
Wang Gungwu: 1991, 193, 494
Wang Ling: 1954–, 482
Wang, N. T.: 1984, 520
Wang, Yu San: 1990, 509
Wang Zhongshu: 1982, 485
Wasserstrom, Jeffrey N.: 1992, 524
Watson, Burton: 1958, 480; 1961, 480; 1964, 479; 1974, 480; 1984, 525
Watson, James L., 157; 1975, 521; 1986, 490; 1988, 490
Watson, Rubie S.: 1991, 490
Watt, John R.: 1972, 493
Watts, Jonathan: 2005, 470
Weber, Max, 20; 1951, 1964, 489
Wechsler, Howard J.: 1974, 485
Wei Jingsheng: 1980, 453n29
Wei, William: 1985, 506
Wei, Wou: 1990, 509
Welch, Holmes: 1957, 482; 1972, 527
Weller, Robert: 1987, 510
Wesley-Smith, Peter: 1980, 1983, 521
White, Gordon: 1996, 454nn50,54, 456
White, Lynn T., III: 1989, 403, 516
White, Tyrene: 2000, 456
Whiting, Allen S.: 1975, 522
Whyte, Martin King: 1974, 513; 1978, 518; 1984, 519
Widmer, Eric: 1976, 495
Wiens, Thomas: 1982, 507
Wilbur, C. Martin: 1976, 502; 1984, 504; 1989, 504
Will, Pierre-Etienne: 1990, 187, 493
Williams, James H.: 1991, 523
Willmott, W. E.: 1972, 500
Wills, John E., Jr.: 1974, 495; 1979, 492; 1984, 495
Wilson, Dick: 1977, 512
Winckler, Edwin: 1988, 509
Witek, John: 1982, 494

Witke, Roxane: 1975, 491; 1977, 517
Wittfogel, Karl A.: 1949, 113, 488; 1957, 239, 489
Wolf, Arthur P.: 1978, 490; 1980, 526
Wolf, Margery: 1975, 491; 1985, 526
Wong, Christine: 1985, 520; 1991, 399, 515
Wong, J. Y.: 1976, 496
Wong Siu-lun: 1988, 521
Wong, Young-tsu: 1989, 502
Worden, Robert L.: 1986, 522
Wou, Odoric: 1978, 503
Wright, Arthur F., 67, 77, 481; 1959, 75, 482; 1964, 490; 1968, 506; 1978, 485
Wright, H. M.: 1962, 487; 1964, 490
Wright, Mary Clabaugh: 1957, 213, 494; 1968, 501
Wu, Eugene: 1989, 512
Wu Hung: 1989, 485
Wu, Tien-wei: 1976, 507

Xiao Qiang: 2004, 455
Xing Zhigang: 1997, 454n59

Yager, Joseph: 1988, 510

Yahuda, Michael; 1983, 521
Yang, Benjamin: 1990, 309, 506
Yang, C. K.: 1964, 489
Yang, Dali L.: 1991, 524
Yang, Gladys: 1979, 480
Yang, Hsien-yi: 1979, 480
Yardley, Jim: 2005, 453, 470
Yeh Shan: 1974, 484
Yeh, Wen-hsin: 1990, 263, 503
Yen, Ching Hwang: 1976, 501
Yeung, Yue-man: 1991, 521
Yip, Hon-ming: 1984, 490–491
Young, Ernest: 1977, 251, 503
Young, Marilyn B.: 1973, 526
Yü, Ying-shih: 61; 1967, 485
Yusuf, Shahid: 1984, 410, 518

Zarrow, Peter: 1990, 275, 503–504
Zelin, Madeleine: 1984, 150, 492
Zhang Pengyuan, 263
Zhang Xinxin: 1987, 525
Zhu Hong: 1990, 514
Zunz, Olivier: 1985, 489
Zürcher, Eric: 1959, 79, 482
Zweig, David: 1989, 516; 1991, 515

General Index

Aborigines, 207, 337
Academia Sinica, 33, 286, 340
Academies, 67, 81, 100, 104, 122, 220, 225, 235, 238, 239, 243, 272
Administrative Litigation Law, 427
Africa, 92, 138, 193, 203, 381, 395, 396
Agricultural Producers' Cooperatives (APCs), 352–353, 369
Agriculture, 15, 22, 23, 32, 34, 35, 143; primacy of, 67, 129, 170, 176, 214, 269; equal field (*juntian*) system in, 77, 82, 85; productivity in, 169, 170, 411; and CCP, 318, 352–353; collectivized, 343, 352–357, 359, 369, 380, 392, 405, 407; private plots in, 375; Green Revolution in, 405; reform of, 408, 411–412; and economy, 413; and urbanization, 419. *See also* Great Leap Forward; Rice culture Rural area; Trade, domestic
AIDS, 467
Alchemy, 53, 66, 81, 115
Amherst, Lord, 197
Amoy. *See* Xiamen
Analects (*Lunyu*), 98
Anarchism, 275, 276, 277, 278
Ancestor worship, 34, 42, 147, 237
Anhui province, 11, 30
Anti-Communism, 282, 291, 297, 327, 329
Anti-imperialism, 245, 268, 273, 280, 281, 282, 285
Anti-intellectualism, 365, 393, 395, 418
Anti-Rightist Campaign, 365–367, 370, 372, 383
Anyang excavations, 33, 34, 35, 66, 381

Arabs, 82, 92, 122, 124, 138, 192–193, 203
Archaeology, 29–45, 56, 60, 225, 226
Art, 31, 56, 73, 75, 88, 227, 442
Artisans (*gong*), 108, 132
Assemblies, popular, 245–248, 250, 251, 252
Astronomy, 151, 224
Autocracy, 1, 2, 3, 228, 244, 273, 338, 339, 386; family, 18; imperial, 27–28, 96, 111, 127, 160, 161, 163, 247, 251, 252, 256; military, 279
Autonomy, 257, 271, 273, 298, 416

baihua (written vernacular), 266. *See also* Writing system, Chinese
Banditry, 86, 103, 129, 148, 178, 208, 230, 338
Banking, 178, 226, 260, 269, 271, 287–288, 333, 348, 415–416
Bannermen, Manchu, 146–147, 148, 149, 151, 153, 191, 232, 236, 273, 389
baojia (mutual responsibility) system, 97, 130, 132, 237, 297, 298, 338
Beijing, 1, 34, 121, 144, 210, 247, 252, 273, 274; Forbidden City in, 33, 132, 191; Manchu capture of, 145; foreign occupation of, 201, 212, 216, 273; in Boxer rising, 231, 232, 233; renamed Beiping, 285; Political Consultative Conference (1946) in, 330; Mao's entrance into, 336
Beijing University (Beida), 263, 265, 267, 268, 272, 275, 276, 277, 313

Big Sword Society, 230
Birth control, 419–420
Blue Shirts, 291
Bluntschli, Johann, 259
Bo Yibo, 420, 423
Board of Revenue, 248–249
Board of Rites, 149
Bolsheviks, 276, 278, 280; the twenty-eight, 302, 304, 307, 309, 311, 320
Borodin, Michael, 281, 283, 290
Boxer Rising, 230–232, 234, 248, 260, 265
Brezhnev doctrine, 397
British East India Company, 141, 195, 196, 198, 199, 222
Bourgeoisie, Chinese, 269–275, 322
Bronze Age, 23, 35, 37, 41, 44, 49. See also Pottery; Three Dynasties
Buddha, 51, 73, 75; Amitabha (Emituofo or O-mi-to-fo), 74; Maitreya, 189
Buddhism, 47, 56, 72, 73, 74, 76, 78, 79, 140, 321, 439; teachings of, 73–76; Mahayana, 74–75; Chan (Zen), 76; monasteries of, 76, 77, 81, 86, 94; and Christianity, 76, 79, 208, 221, 223; influence of Daoism, 76, 224; and the state, 79, 81; transcendentalism, 98; Yellow Lamaist Sect of, 121, 123, 149, 152
Bureaucracy, 122, 181–182, 240; beginning of, 3, 39, 40, 55, 85; in Tang period, 79, 83; in Song period, 94, 96–97, 104, 108, 126; and ideology, 111, 427; in Jin dynasty, 115; of Ming era, 130, 141; and modernization, 219, 251, 270; in Republican period, 256, 291; in PRC, 356, 359, 386, 427, 443
Bureaucratism, 181, 323, 349, 384, 387, 397
Bush, George W., 461
Buyun, 424

Cadres (CCP activists), 358, 369, 376, 378; recruitment of, 316, 335; as new elite, 353, 384, 400; and tax gathering, 356–357; in Great Leap Forward, 370, 373, 374, 380
Cai Yuanpei, 265, 272, 275, 277
The Call (John Hersey), 261
Canton. See Guangzhou
Capitalism, 180, 181, 183, 185–186, 270, 276, 323, 386, 398, 443–444; Western, and Asia, 188, 280; bureaucratic, 244, 270, 288, 332; and industrial reform, 358

Catholicism, 152, 157, 222, 223, 230, 431. See also Jesuits
CCP. See Chinese Communist Party
Censorate, 78, 130, 149, 247
Central Asia, 1, 23, 29, 38, 48, 61, 77, 78, 121, 124, 153, 193, 198, 201. See also Inner Asia
Central Cultural Revolution Group, 387, 389, 390, 391, 392, 393, 394. See also Cultural Revolution
Centralism, democratic, 278, 319, 386, 432
Chambers of commerce, 244, 270, 271, 273, 274, 287
Chang'an. See Xi'an
Chen Duxiu, 265, 275, 276, 302
Chen Guangfu (K. P. Chen), 272, 273
Chen Guidi, 459
Chen Shui-bian, 462
Chen Yi, 309, 345, 396
Chen Yun, 372, 375, 420, 426
Chennault, Claire, 327
Chiang Kaishek. See Jiang Jieshi
China Can Say No
China Democracy Party, 432, 448, 450
China International Famine Relief Commission, 261
China National Offshore Oil Corporation, 463
Chinese Academy of Sciences
Chinese Communist Party (CCP), 269, 311, 318, 343, 345, 384, 406, 465; and Soviet Union, 255, 302, 350; origins of, 275–278; and class struggle, 276, 280, 285, 364, 365, 395; and GMD, 279, 280–282, 285, 290, 301, 322, 329, 345, 348; and peasants, 302, 303, 311, 316, 350; Central Committee of, 302, 316–317, 326, 351, 371, 387, 391, 395, 407, 413; party congresses of, 310, 326, 351, 391, 395, 416, 421, 431–432; rectification campaigns of, 323–326, 365, 376–378; and intellectuals, 324–325, 359–364; and thought reform, 324–325, 361, 363; struggle meetings of, 324, 376, 402; victory of, 336–337, 357; and military, 350–351, 389; mass campaigns of, 350, 361, 377, 387; "two-line struggle" of, 375–376; succession struggle in, 400–401. See also Guomindang: split with CCP; Mao Zedong; Peasants: mobilization of
Chinese Maritime Customs Service, 195, 203, 216, 218, 233, 234, 249, 286, 290, 312

Chinese People's Political Consultative Conference, Common Program of, 349, 350

Chinggis (Genghis) Khan, 24, 119, 121, 122, 143, 149

Chongqing, 297, 312, 313, 316, 317, 327, 329, 330, 336

Christianity, 47, 121, 194, 207, 211, 218, 234, 321, 410, 439; and Buddhism, 17, 76, 221; banning of, 151, 222. *See also* Buddhism: and Christianity; Confucianism: and Christianity; Taiping rebellion

Civil Society, Chinese, 257–277, 286

Civil War, Chinese, 331–337, 345; of 1851–1864, 209–212; battle for the Northeast in, 329–336; battle of Huai-Hai region in, 336

Cixi, Empress Dowager, 212, 213, 220, 229, 230–231, 233, 242, 292; and constitutionalism, 245, 246, 250

Class struggle, 407, 408, 438, 468

Classic of Changes (*Yijing*), 65, 67

Classic of Documents (or *History; Shujing*), 67

Classic of Poetry (*Shijing*), 38, 67

Clintion, William Jefferson, 431

Cohong, 195, 196, 198. *See also* Guangzhou; Merchants

Cold War, 2, 331, 340

Collective, 412–413, 415, 434

Comintern (Communist International), 276, 280, 281–282, 284–285, 302, 303, 307, 310, 317, 325

Commerce, 59, 60, 160, 176–179, 214, 253, 257, 348. *See also* Trade

Communism, 205, 210, 257, 282, 328, 334, 363, 378; national, 317, 379

Community Compact (*xiangyue*), 79, 99–100, 104, 140, 155. *See also* Confucianism

Compradors, 226, 269, 322

A Comprehensive Mirror for Aid in Government (Sima Guang), 97

Confucianism, 86, 115, 123, 151, 153, 160, 178, 184, 292, 408, 444–445, 467; and loyalty, 19, 68, 69, 124; code of, 51–53; classics of, 53, 67, 79, 98, 100–101, 115, 117, 147, 227, 228, 262, 266–267; and social stability, 53, 384, 468; imperial, 59, 62–63, 67, 72, 147, 153, 154, 403; and Buddhism, 73, 79, 81, 98, 140; and reform, 96–101, 227, 248, 258–259, 264, 265; and militarism, 108–112, 274; and Christianity, 221–224, 260–261, 264; and

CCP, 302, 317, 374, 384. *See also* Neo-Confucianism

Confucius, 47, 51, 52–53, 63, 70, 96, 98, 104, 108, 183; cult of, 147, 157

Constitutionalism, 236, 241, 244–247, 250, 277

Cosmology, 19, 44, 53, 57, 63, 64–66, 117, 118

Cults, 49, 156–157. *See also* Religion

Cultural Revolution, 343, 358, 366, 383–405; underpinnings of, 383–385; Mao's aims and resources in, 385–387; role of PLA in, 387–389; unfolding of, 389–392; Fifty Days in, 390; and higher education, 390, 391, 392; and Deng Xiaoping, 390, 393, 407, 408, 410, 420; and National People's Congress, 422; movement for "seizure of power" in, 393–395; foreign affairs during, 395–397; end of, 397, 400; in retrospect, 401–404; aftermath of, 404–405. *See also* Red Guards

Culturalism, 25, 45, 110, 117

Culture (*wenhua*), 43, 44, 234, 268; influence of Buddhism on Chinese, 73; increasing importance of, in Song era, 126, 127; polity and, 154–161, 256; popular, 158, 442, 449; pluralist, 410, 439–451; and consumerism, 446–447

Currency: copper, 60, 134, 135, 137, 198, 199, 232; paper, 92–93, 124, 134; in Ming era, 133, 134; silver, 134, 135, 141, 150, 178, 196, 198, 199, 232, 270; under Nationalist government, 288; in civil war, 332, 333; reform of 1948, 333, 334

danwei (work units), 375

Daoguang, Emperor, 197, 198, 200

Daoism, 47, 53–54, 75, 81, 98, 123, 208, 277, 439; influence of Buddhism on, 76, 224

darugaci (*daluhuachi*; trouble shooters), 123

Darwinism, Social, 228, 264

de (virtue), 62, 111

Decentralization, 409–410, 418, 425, 445, 447, 449, 465, 466, 467–468

Decollectivization, 408, 411–412, 437

Degree-holders, 95, 103, 105, 106, 110, 117, 239, 243; and land-holding, 102, 104, 179; first-level (*shengyuan* or *jiansheng*), 155, 296; and election of assemblymen, 246. *See also* Examination system

Democratic centralism, 278, 319, 386, 432

Democracy, 1, 224, 252, 265, 268, 291, 344, 432, 442–443, 468–469; Chinese type of, 298, 319
Democracy Wall, 421, 432, 447
Deng Liqun, 420, 443
Deng Xiaoping, 309, 336, 345, 364, 365, 375; reforms of, 343, 374, 406, 408–410, 411, 420–429, 445, 451; and Cultural Revolution, 390, 393, 420; background of, 406–407; and private enterprise, and Special Economic Zone, 413–414; and southern journey, 414, 443; and decentralization, 418–419; opposition to, legacy of, 429; and Westernization, 442; and ideology, 443
Dewey, John, 266
Dissidence, 410, 447, 448, 458, 468. *See also* Protest
Divination, 34, 51, 67
Doctrine of the Mean (Zhongyong), 98
Dong Zhongshu, 67
Dongfeng (The Orient), 446
Donglin ("eastern forest") Academy, 141, 228
Dushu (Reading), 446
Dutch East India Company, 141, 195

East Asia, 408, 414, 441
Economy, 163, 167, 269–270, 373; and geography, 11, 226; farm, 179, 288, 459; in Republican China, 294, 320, 331–332; command, 344, 368, 374; market, 344, 398, 406, 408, 409, 413, 414, 446–447; and Deng Xiaoping, 406–407; state control of, 407; development of, 408; reform of, 408–420, 466–467; planned, 413, 414; and foreign investment, 413–414, 446; and private enterprise, 434; and choice, 415; and decentralization, 418–419; and wages, 436, 437; and income, 436, 438; and East Asia, 441–442; and culture, 444–445. *See also* Trade
Education: Confucian, 52, 62, 70–71, 235, 240, 338; government and, 62, 70–71; Buddhist, 79; growth of, 93–95, 257; reform of, 243; higher, 263, 363, 378; in Taiwan, 338, 339–340; and intellectuals, 359–364; liberal, and public policy, 362; of peasants, 377; and decentralization, 418; and women, 436–437; expenditures on, 436. *See also* Degree-holders; Examination system; Schools

Egalitarianism, 275, 353, 381, 386, 397, 407
Eight Trigrams sect, 191
Eighth Route Army, 316, 320. *See also* Red Army: Chinese
Eisenhower, Dwight, 379
Elites: educated, 20, 95, 103, 378; government and, 52, 82, 83–85, 126, 246, 252, 253, 261, 262; scholar-, 53, 86, 100, 117, 124, 267, 268–269; activism of, 238–240, 257; urban reformist, 244, 247, 250, 263; and revolution, 366, 386; CCP cadres as local, 384, 400. *See also* Degree-holders; Gentry society; Literati
Emperors, 27–28, 46, 126, 132, 232, 403; and cosmology, 57, 65; and bureaucrats, 57, 68–69, 85, 130; ritual observances of, 66, 67, 112; and scholars, 66–71; and education, 70; and reform, 96, 245; and military complex, 110–111; as promoters of order, 154; as patrons of literature, 158; dependence upon local gentry, 180; superiority to other rulers, 199; memorial-edict procedure of, 247–248. *See also* Son of Heaven; *individual emperors*
Empress of Heaven (Tian Hou; Ma Zu), 157, 194
Empresses, 59, 72, 148
Energy, 463
Engels, Friedrich, 326
England, 45, 196, 205, 216, 255, 396; and China, 21, 187, 205, 216, 245, 283. *See also* Opium War; Trade; Treaties
Enlightenment, European, 152, 161
Entrepreneurs, 412–413, 414, 434
Equal-field (*juntian*) system, 171
Erlitou, excavations at, 34–35
Eunuchs, 72, 109, 132, 139, 141, 148, 149, 228; and emperors, 59, 82, 86, 111, 130, 137, 138–139, 140
Europe, 45, 46–47, 93, 124, 138, 180, 186, 323; and China, 3, 11, 14, 106, 151, 152, 161, 163, 180, 264, 270, 299, 360; feudalism in, 102, 180, 322
Examination system, 3, 67, 78, 95, 219, 225, 232, 266, 360, 427; in Tang dynasty, 79, 85; beginning of, 84; in Song dynasty, 93, 94–95, 96, 111; and Qidan, 113; restoration of, 123; in Ming dynasty, 139; in Qing dynasty, 148, 158, 239, 243; Taiping, 211; abolition of, 243; under Nationalists, 292; in PRC, 377, 392.

See also Degree-holders; Intellectuals: children of
Extraterritoriality, 200, 203, 204, 222, 265

Falungong, 439
Family, 48, 103, 272, 268; and lineage, 17–23, 37, 42; status of women in, 18–19, 103; size of, 21; in PRC, 353, 405. *See also* Confucianism; Kinship
Family farm, 411, 419
Famine, 5, 21, 178, 187, 206, 237, 314, 368; and ever-normal granaries, 129, 155, 187; of 1870s, 240, 372. *See also* Great Leap Forward
Fan Zhongyan, 96
Farmers (*nong*), 17–18, 82, 102, 103, 177, 255, 364; and the military, 55, 109, 121; diminishing returns for, 170–173, 431; exploitation of, 294, 303; productivity of, 298–299; and Nationalists, 314; and collectivization, 352–357; and CCP, 381. *See also* Agriculture; Great Leap Forward; Land; Peasants
fatuan (professional associations), 244
fengjian (decentralized or feudal), 39, 160, 240, 246, 321–322
fengshui (harmony between man and nature), 219
Feudalism, 39, 102, 180–181, 321–323
Filial piety, 18, 19, 54, 68, 182, 184, 366
First Emperor (*Shi huangdi*), 55, 56, 57, 70, 78, 218
Five-Antis Campaign, 349, 350
Five Dynasties, 87, 88
Five Phases, 117
Five Relationships, 99
Five-Year Plan: First, 358, 359, 369; Second, 359, 369
Floods, 15, 134, 155, 171, 187, 206, 230, 237
Footbinding, 148, 173–176, 186, 207, 210, 243
Foreign-joint venture, 413–414
Four Books, 98
Four Clean-Ups, 376
Four Modernizations, 343, 404
Four Olds, 393
France, 45, 46, 163, 243, 323; and missionaries, 222, 223; Chinese in, 245, 265, 300, 308, 309. *See also* Treaties
Free China, 312, 314, 326, 327, 332, 334, 365

Fryer, John, 218
Fu Sinian, 268, 275, 339
Fujian province, 35, 157, 177, 193, 195, 337, 341, 467
Fuzhou, 92, 177, 195, 203

Gang of Four, 387, 399, 404, 405
Gentry society, 103, 128, 150, 158, 210; formation of, 101–107, 127; lower, 155, 368, 380; and merchants, 180–181; and missionaries, 222–223; and reform, 228, 243; imperial government and, 234, 235; and rural rebellion, 236–238; urban, 239, 240. *See also* Degree-holders
Geography of China, 4–14, 143, 165
Germany, 163, 245, 267, 286, 292–293, 299, 304, 307, 337
getihu (private enterprise), 412–413
gewu (*ke-wu*; investigation of things), 101
GMD. *See* Guomindang
gong (functions of a public nature), 105, 257
Gong, Prince, 212, 233
Government, 43, 126, 127, 179–180, 240, 298; rise of first central, 37–39, 42, 45; Confucian, 70, 130, 141, 154; parliamentary, 227, 241, 244, 250, 258, 286; and taxation, 417–418; reform of, 420–433, 467–469; tenure in, 421; *vs.* Chinese Communist Party, 421–422; and elections, 423–425; corruption in, 427–428; and pluralism, 442. *See also* Constitutionalism; Decentralization; Party-state
Graeco-Roman world: and China, 47, 51
Grand Canal, 77–78, 86, 89, 115, 124, 133, 145, 176, 219, 225
Grand Council, 150, 151, 159, 213, 247
Great Leap Forward (GLF), 343, 358, 359, 368–382, 387, 392, 410; backyard furnaces in, 371; and decentralization, 371, 374; criticism of, 384; as a social movement, 380–382
Great Learning (*Daxue*), 98
Great Wall of China, 57, 72, 122, 139, 143, 145, 309, 381
Gross domestic product, 418
Guan Yu (Guandi), 156–157, 194
guandu shenban (official supervision and gentry management), 236
Guangdong province, 176, 225, 341, 467
Guangxi province, 207, 208

Guangxu, Emperor, 229, 242, 250
Guangzhou (Canton), 56, 170, 191, 192, 225, 231, 281, 308, 388; trade at, 14, 92, 105, 149, 168, 177, 195–197, 198, 199, 206, 269; opposition to British in, 198–201, 236; foreign community at, 203; Protestant missions at, 222; boycott of American trade at, 245; industries at, 271; Nationalist government at, 281, 290, 322; 1925 incidents at, 282–283. *See also* Invasion, foreign; Trade: opium
guanxi (personal connections), 84, 130, 150, 296, 353, 356
Guanyin (Goddess of Mercy), 74
Guilds: native-place, 160, 177–178, 204, 239; merchant, 185, 194, 195, 244, 245, 274, 287; craft, 274
Guomindang (GMD), 250–251, 252, 276, 283, 297, 311, 341, 425, 427, 433; and Soviet Union, 255, 281, 285, 310; and CCP, 279, 284, 309, 312, 334–337; recognition of,
Guomindang (GMD) *(continued)* by foreign powers, 285; split with CCP, 285, 286, 304, 328; loss of revolutionary mission, 286–287; and Japan, 286, 301, 329, 330; membership of, 287, 311; and Mao Zedong, 302–303, 310; factionalism in, 321; and United States, 327. *See also* Northern Expedition
Guozijian (Directorate of Education), 71

Hakka people, 206, 207, 208, 212
Han Chinese, 23, 25, 115, 117, 206
Han dynasty, 2, 23, 42, 47, 51, 76, 77, 98, 128; consolidation and expansion under, 48, 57–62; Later, 57, 73, 83, 213, 228; scholar-elite of, 62–63; decline of, 72; and class division, 108; and Inner Asia; 110; foreign policy of, 112, 113; Early, 117, 228; army in, 121, 236; seafaring in, 192
Han Learning, 159, 225
Han Wudi (Martial Emperor), 61, 62, 67, 70, 117
Handicrafts, 171, 172, 176, 177, 179, 188, 357, 358
Hangzhou, 78, 92, 171, 172
Hankou, 177, 178, 250, 283, 336
Hart, (Sir) Robert, 204, 216, 218, 220, 233, 234
Heaven (*tian*), 63, 67

Hebei province, 32, 73
Henan province, 32, 33, 35, 168, 314, 326
heqin (peace and kinship), 61
Heshen, 182, 228, 232
Hierarchy, 67–68, 97, 127, 154, 184–185, 295; family, 18–19, 42, 99; government, 20, 123; cosmic, 51; and GMD, 297–298
Hong Kong, 29, 201, 205, 227, 262, 271, 280, 283, 397, 408, 414, 441, 447, 467
Hong Ren'gan, 211
Hong Taiji (Abahai), 144
Hong Xiuquan, 207–211, 325
Hongwu, Emperor (Zhu Yuanzhang), 128–130, 132, 134, 155, 156
Hoover, Herbert, 220
Hoppo, the, 195, 196, 198, 199
Household responsibility system, 411
Hu Jintao, 429, 430, 438, 444, 457–460
Hu Shi, 266, 272–273, 275
Hua Guofeng, 405, 407, 421
Hu Yaobang, 407, 413, 420, 422, 425–426, 427, 432, 440, 443
Huainanzi, 64
Huang Chao, 86
Huang Zongxi, 160
Huang Zunxian, 240
Hubei province, 11, 32, 189, 436
Human rights, 431, 462
Hunan province, 11, 32, 171, 177, 212, 223, 237, 238, 277, 303, 405
Hundred Days of 1898, 229, 242
Hundred Flowers movement, 364, 365, 366, 387
Hundred Regiments Offensive, 319
Hurley, General Patrick J., 328, 329

Imperial Household Department, 149, 195
Imperialism, 119, 121, 160, 188–189, 205, 231, 233–234, 244, 361, 379, 405; cultural, 29; and indemnities, 234, 248, 265; revolution against, 255, 279, 280, 282, 303
India, 51, 53, 72, 163, 173, 228, 327, 358, 463; Chinese expeditions to, 92, 138; British, 153, 195, 196, 197; opium imports from, 198, 200, 204; border with, 461
Individualism, 257–258, 259, 268, 324
Industrial Revolution, 2, 164, 186, 196

Industrialization, 167, 219, 270–271, 288, 370; in Europe, 164, 179, 321; Soviet-style, 343, 357, 369; beginning, in PRC, 357–359; rural, 399, 412–413

Industry, 89, 253, 260; and consumer goods, 270, 320, 332, 340, 369, 370, 372, 412; in Taiwan, 338–339; 340–341; heavy, 359, 369, 372, 375, 407; light, 369, 372, 412; township and village, 412–413; and planned economy, 413; and competition, 415–416; and population, 416–417; and privatization, 415–416; and wages, 436; and tax revenue, 437. *See also* Shanghai: industries in

Infanticide, 2, 18

Inflation, 314, 316, 320, 331, 333, 334, 348, 358, 427, 430

Inner Asia: and China, 3, 23–25, 88, 108, 109, 110, 112–119, 126, 177, 191, 204; armed forces of, 54, 111, 121; Qing control of, 149, 153. *See also* Nomads

Inner Court, 82, 86, 131, 147, 150, 195, 247

Intellectuals: and 20th-century change, 264, 268, 275, 276, 278; and business community, 273; and Nationalist government, 313; and CCP, 317, 324–325, 344, 364, 365, 374, 376, 383, 384; children of, 378, 392; of Shanghai, 389, 390, 404; in Cultural Revolution, 392, 393, 397, 401, 403; and Deng Xiaoping, 425–426; and pluralism, 440, 442, 448, 449; and post-Deng era, 444; and post-Mao era, 445; autonomy of, 450, 458–459. *See also* Education: and intellecutals

Internet, 440–441, 458, 460

Invasion, foreign, 187–189, 205, 226, 309, 312. *See also* Missionaries

Inventions, 88; paper, 3, 56, 93; gun-powder, 3, 81, 89, 115, 172; compass, 3, 81, 93; printing, 3, 88, 93–94, 172; silk, 33, 172; porcelain, 160, 172; patents for, 227

Islam. *See* Muslims

Itō, Prince, 245

Jahangir, 197, 198

Japan, 62, 102, 140, 142, 205, 228, 234, 245, 408, 446; compared with China, 21, 163; attack on China, 33, 255, 279, 286, 309, 311, 312, 334, 360; maritime trade of, 137, 194, 196; seizure of Manchuria, 147, 241, 286, 293, 309, 312; silk pro-

duction in, 173; modernization of, 187, 240, 258; opening of, 218; defeat of China, 226, 230, 240, 263; influence on China, 227, 235, 240–241, 243, 255, 273, 280, 308; 21 Demands of, 241, 266; defeat of Russia, 244; China's war of resistance against, 279, 312–330; occupation of China, 312; attack on United States, 313; Ichigo offensive, 326; surrender of, 329; and CCP, 329, 332; and Taiwan, 338; World War II actions by, 464. *See also* May Fourth Movement; Sino-Japanese War of 1894–1895

Jardine, Dr. William, 200

Jardine, Matheson & Co., 199, 200, 205, 271

Jesuits, 97, 151–152, 218, 222

Jiang Jieshi (Chiang Kaishek), 290, 291–293, 297, 308–309, 310, 313–314; and Soviet Union, 280, 281; accession to power of, 283–286; and GMD, 291, 312; campaigns against CCP, 301, 304, 305, 307, 336, 337; and Mao Zedong, 310, 311; and Americans, 327, 328, 329, 330, 331; diplomatic achievements of, 337; on Taiwan, 339, 341; death of, 341; and military, 351, 388. *See also* Guomindang; Northern Expedition

Jiang Jingguo, 341

Jiang Menglin, 271

Jiang Qing, 387, 389–390

Jiang Yanyong, 458

Jiang Zemin, 422, 423, 425, 428, 429, 430–432, 434, 442, 444, 458

Jiangsu province, 11, 269, 302, 335

Jiangxi province, 159, 176, 307, 309; Communist withdrawal to, 284, 302, 304, 388

jianmin (mean people), 83

Jiao Guobiao, 460

Jiaqing, Emperor, 190

Jin dynasty, 92, 109, 117, 119, 143–144, 170, 204; militarism of, 111–112, 115; and Confucianism, 118, 147; Mongol invasion of, 121, 122, 123, 127. *See also* Ruzhen

jinshi degree, 117, 224

junxian (centralized bureaucratic rule), 56

Kaifeng, 89, 92, 114, 115, 118, 172

Kaiping mines, 219–220

Kalgan (Zhangjiakou), 334

Kang Youwei, 227, 228, 229

Kangxi Dictionary, 158, 159

Kangxi, Emperor, 146, 147, 150, 158, 161, 366; *Sacred Edict (shengyu)* of, 155–156

kaozhengxue (evidential research), 158, 159, 224, 225, 267

Kashgar, 152, 153, 197, 198, 201

Khrushchev, Nikita, 379, 385

Khubilai Khan, 121, 123, 124, 152, 157

Kinship, 20–21, 40, 42, 46, 186, 237, 238, 295, 299; in prehistoric China, 31, 32, 37. *See also* Family

Kokand, 197, 198, 200, 201

Korea, 61, 62, 78, 118, 144, 149, 221, 340, 348, 372, 397, 408, 467, 468

Kropotkin, Pyotr, 275, 277

Labor, 257, 267, 273, 295, 340, 378, 381; agricultural, 15–16, 170–173, 295, 370; corvée, 60, 121, 129, 132, 133, 314; industrial, 374–376

Labor unions, 268, 274, 284, 310, 357

Land, 4–14, 15, 60, 180, 181, 199, 338; erosion of, 11, 17; deforestation of, 11, 17; and loess, 14, 309; and water control, 15; equal division of, 21, 83; shortage of, 21, 105, 171; reallocation of, 77, 82, 304, 318; charitable estates of, 96; conversion of, to rice paddies, 170; purchase of, 102, 352. *See also* Agriculture: equal field system in; Peasants; Taxes: on land

Land reform, 318, 334, 335, 350, 352, 376, 380. *See also* Land: reallocation of

Landlords, 150, 157, 180, 214, 236, 289, 303, 322; exploitation of tenants, 60, 295; absentee, 244, 296, 301, 340, 380; dispossession of, 304, 334; and Nationalist regime, 313, 316; and CCP, 318, 334, 335, 350, 352, 354, 376, 405; in Taiwan, 338, 340. *See also* Taxes: on land

Language: Chinese, 42–43, 44, 101, 223, 264, 321; Sanskrit, 75; Manchu, 144, 149, 151; English, 264, 362, 378; Japanese, 338; Russian, 362, 378

Laozi, 53

Law, 123, 126, 183, 184, 245, 257, 258; as tool of administration, 155, 185; and morality, 183, 184, 258, 402; limitations of, 183–186; lack of due process in Chinese, 185, 186, 383; contract, and international trade, 203; rights and, 259, 383;

and corruption, 427. *See also* Extraterritoriality

League of Left-Wing Writers, 360

League of Nations, 298

Lee Teng-hui, 462

Legalism, 52, 55, 56, 62, 68, 108

Legge, James, 262

Lenin, 280, 303

li ("proper behavior according to status"), 52, 98

Li Dazhao, 276

Li Hongzhang, 217, 218, 219, 220, 221, 227, 229, 231, 233, 250

Li Peng, 426, 428, 429

Li Zicheng, 144, 146

Liang Fa, 207

Liang Qichao, 228, 229, 259, 262, 263

Liang Shuming, 299

Liao dynasty, 111, 113–115, 118, 119, 123, 127

Liberalism, Chinese, 365, 441, 442, 444; limits of, 257–260; Sino-, 337, 339, 384

Lien Chan, 462

Lifan Yuan, 149

lijia system, 132, 135. *See also* Taxes

Lin Biao, 335, 345, 351, 385, 389, 390, 392, 395; as Mao's successor, 391, 395, 400; fall of, 400–401, 405

Lin Zexu, 200, 225, 233

Literacy, 243, 261, 263, 266, 299, 300, 301, 314, 381, 405, 436–437

Literati (*wenren*), 48, 67, 95, 97, 109, 118, 160, 207, 218, 324, 362. *See also* Elites; Gentry society; Scholar-officials

Literature, 262, 268, 324, 360, 384–385. *See also* baihua; Writing system, Chinese

Liu Di, 458

Liu Kunyi, 242

Liu Shaoqi, 310, 345, 350, 364, 374, 375; in Cultural Revolution, 390–391, 393, 404

Liu Xiaobo, 458

Lixue (the learning of principle), 224

Long March, 305–307, 309, 323

Looking at China through a Third Eye (Disanzhi yanjing kan Zhongguo), 445

Lu Xiangshan, 124, 140

Lu Xun, 268, 324, 360, 402

Luce, Henry, 328

Luo Jialun, 268

Luo Ruiqing, 390

Luoyang, 49, 73, 77, 78, 86

Lushan, 372, 390
Lysenko, P., 362

Macao, 196, 280
Macartney, Lord George, 196
Macroregions, 11, 13, 161, 176
Manchuria, 23, 29, 35, 147–148, 177, 221,
  308; in Han dynasty, 61; Sino-nomadic
  government in, 112; Qidan in, 113;
  Ruzhen tribes of, 115; and Ming dynasty,
  143; and Qing dynasty, 152; under Japanese rule, 241, 337; and Russia, 280–
  281, 379; civil war in, 329–330, 335. See
  also Japan: seizure of Manchuria
Manchus, 46, 158, 197, 345; conquest of
  China by, 1, 112, 117, 143–146, 204; institutional adaptation of, 146–151; tonsure of, 150, 159, 209; vs. Chinese, 233,
  234; opposition to, 236, 285
Mandate of Heaven (tianming), 40, 44, 48,
  63, 78, 111, 112, 117, 128, 145, 147
Mao Zedong, 276–277, 301–305, 336, 337,
  345; and class struggle, 2, 277, 303, 311,
  318, 365, 375, 376, 378, 386, 391; and
  peasants, 303, 310, 318, 377, 384; on
  Long March, 307; "mass line" of, 310,
  319, 325, 386; sinification of Marxism,
  316–321, 325, 328; and intellectuals,
  317, 324–325, 360–367, 374; and control of CCP, 320, 389; lectures on literature and art, 324; postwar meeting with
  Jiang Jieshi, 329; death of, 343, 357,
  399, 405; cult of, 350, 369, 385–386,
  405; and role of military, 351, 400; and
  economics, 370, 373, 398; mobilization
  of the masses, 370, 374, 376, 384, 392;
  and Soviet Union, 374, 378–380, 385,
  387; Socialist Education Campaign of,
  376; trips to Moscow, 379; and emergence of elites, 384, 400; on revisionism,
  386–387, 390, 391, 392, 393; and PLA,
  387–389; swim across the Yangzi, 391;
  Third Front strategy of, 398–399; and
  Deng Xiaoping, 407; and household responsibility system, 411; criticism of,
  421–422, 442–443; influence of, 443–
  444. See also Cultural Revolution; Great
  Leap Forward; Mao Zedong Thought;
  Quotations from Chairman Mao
Mao Zedong Thought, 321–323, 326, 349,
  395, 410
Marco Polo, 92, 93, 122

Maritime China, 165, 191–195, 197
Market towns (zhen), 22, 85, 103, 158,
  177, 237, 375
Marshall, General George C., 330, 336
Marx, Karl, 167, 179, 321, 322, 326
Marxism, 275, 277, 278, 284, 294, 321,
  364, 440, 441, 442; Mao's sinification of,
  316–321, 322
Marxism-Leninism, 208, 275, 276, 277,
  280, 285, 302, 322, 323, 361, 410, 411,
  421, 444
Mass Education Movement (Dingxian),
  261, 299, 300
May Fourth Movement, 64, 267–269, 271,
  274, 275, 276, 277, 308, 323, 374, 404,
  410, 428, 444, 448–449
May 30th Movement, 283
Media, mass, 226, 243, 257, 404, 405,
  459–460
Medicine, Chinese, 53, 65, 81
Meiji Emperor, 220
Mencius, 51, 52, 62, 98, 108, 117
Merchants (shang), 97, 141, 142, 160, 164,
  243, 267, 322; itinerant, 22, 177; and
  gentry, 42, 103, 105, 236; status of, 55,
  59, 96, 100, 108, 135, 180, 193, 270,
  435; and officials, 179–182; Hong, 199,
  269; and scholarship, 225; in treaty
  ports, 260; and labor movement, 273;
  and GMD, 287. See also Trade
Metallurgy: iron, 23, 54, 60, 89; bronze,
  23, 37, 41, 49
Middle class, 434, 443, 468
Middle East: and China, 40–41
Migration, 437–438, 445
Military, 45, 110–112, 236, 350–351; Confucian disdain for, 96, 108–109; in Ming
  era, 129, 134, 143, 145; in Qing era,
  145; in PRC, 350–351, 389, 427–428,
  430; budget for, 461
Militia, local (fubing; tuanlian), 82, 121,
  190, 191, 208, 236–237, 238, 273, 388
Mill, John Stuart, 259
minban (people's schools), 363, 377
Mines, 221, 227, 244
Ming dynasty, 99, 110, 122, 127, 128–142,
  403; building during, 34, 57, 381; terrorism in, 129–130; fiscal problems of, 132–
  137, 150; anticommercialism of, 135,
  138, 139, 150; ban on sea trade, 138,
  150, 180, 194; decline of naval power,
  139; tribute system under, 139, 193; fac-

Ming dynasty *(continued)*
  tional politics in, 140–142; collapse of,
  144, 224; revenue system of, 248
Ministries, 78, 130, 270
minsheng (common welfare), 274
Missionaries, 75, 142, 151, 221, 222, 230,
  283; and Chinese language, 75, 223; and
  Taiping rebellion, 207, 210, 211, 223,
  325; Protestant, 218, 222, 223–224, 229,
  243, 255, 266; American, 218, 222, 223,
  327, 340; and Westernization, 218, 227;
  and reform, 223, 243, 255, 299; in Boxer
  Rising, 231. *See also* Catholicism
Modernization, 17, 29, 220, 229, 366, 371;
  slowness of, 186, 236, 248; and
  constitutionalism, 244; and centralization,
  252; and Nationalist government, 289,
  311; in Taiwan, 338–339
Mongolia, 1, 23, 113, 147, 152, 153, 378,
  401; Inner, 144, 147; Outer, 122
Mongols, 73, 109, 111, 113, 118, 119–
  127, 144, 146, 204; conquests of, 92,
  93, 110, 112, 119, 122, 143–144; in
  Ming era, 128, 132, 139; organization of, under Qing, 149, 152, 153;
  Muslims and, 192–193. *See also* Yuan
  dynasty
Monopolies, government, 179–180, 181,
  354
Morrison, Robert, 222
Mukden (Shenyang), 143, 144, 147, 308
Muslims, 92, 121, 124, 137, 153, 192–193,
  203, 216, 257
Mysticism, 53, 74, 75. *See also* Buddhism;
  Daoism

Nan Zhao, 110
Nanchang, uprising at, 309
Nanjing, 34, 76, 250, 336; as Ming capital,
  128, 137; as Heavenly Capital of
  Taipings, 207, 209, 210, 212, 233; as
  Nationalist capital, 279, 283, 284–293,
  297, 312. *See also* Treaty of Nanjing
Nanjing University, 261
Nankai Institute of Economics, 261
Nankai University (Tianjin), 308, 313
National People's Congress (NPC), 422–
  423, 433
Nationalism, 235, 236, 243, 245, 250, 253,
  255, 260, 283, 285, 338, 442–443, 445–
  446, 464; European, 25; ethnic, 154,
  210; cultural, 240; and conservatism,

252, 311; Japanese aggression and, 312;
  and reform, 229, 266, 360
Nationalist Government, 29, 205, 210, 279,
  287, 292, 301, 303; and Soviet Union,
  255, 281, 285, 379; army of, 274, 304,
  308; nature of, 286–289; National Resources Commission (NRC) of, 288, 293,
  313, 339, 357–358; systemic weaknesses
  of, 289–293; difficulties of, 312–316; and
  civil war, 329–337; failure of, 331–334;
  occupation of Taiwan, 339–341
Nationalist Party. *See* Guomindang
Nature, man's relation to, 14–17, 53, 63,
  64, 65, 117, 154, 405. See also *fengshui*
Neo-authoritarianism, 443
Neo-Confucianism, 96–101, 103, 106–107,
  110, 127, 151, 444–445; in Song dynasty,
  67, 93, 95, 118, 124, 125–126, 224, 227,
  228, 234; Buddhist influence on, 81; and
  human rights, 99; in Ming dynasty, 139,
  140, 224, 234; in Qing dynasty, 154,
  155, 160, 234, 243, 258; in Republican
  era, 252–253, 264; and modernization,
  258
Neo-conservatism, 445
Neo-leftism, 444
Neolithic China, 14, 31–33, 35, 37, 38, 44,
  191
New Army, 247, 250
New China Daily, 316
New Culture Movement, 266–267, 275,
  276, 278, 360
New Democracy, 317, 323, 325, 349, 350
New Education Movement, 271–272
New Fourth Army, 320
New Learning, 258, 260, 264, 266
New Life Movement, 291
New Policies, 241, 243. *See also* Qing dy-
  nasty: reforms of
New Text movement, 225, 227–228
New Tide (Renaissance), 268
New Youth (La Jeunesse), 265, 268
Nian rebellion, 214–216
Nie Qigui, 272
Nie Rongzhen, 309, 345
Nie Yuntai (C. C. Nieh), 272
Ningbo, 178, 203, 213, 269, 284
Nomads, 23–24, 57, 61, 72, 73, 77, 117,
  146, 153
Nongovernmental organizations, 425, 434
North China, 29–30, 34, 35, 37, 41, 49,
  61, 78, 86, 87, 329–330; contrast with

South China, 4–14, 20, 76; Yangshao ("painted pottery") culture of, 32; silk production in, 33; Central Plain (*zhongyuan*) of, 44, 54; emigration from, 72, 75, 170; disunion with South China, 72–73; nomad invasions of, 75, 76; industry in, 89; non-Chinese in, 113, 115–119, 121, 145; crops grown in, 169, 176; War of 1900 in, 231; CCP in, 316–320, 328, 329, 331, 345, 350

North Korea, 463

Northern Expedition, 283, 285, 287, 290, 304, 388

Northern Wei dynasty, 73, 84

Nuclear weapons, 373, 379, 463

Nurgaci, 143, 147

Oil, 463

Olympics, 446

Opium War, 200, 203, 206, 227

Oracle bones, 33, 34, 37, 39, 42, 66, 109, 226

ordo (elite guard), 113

Organic Law of the Village Committees, 423–424

Outer Court, 82, 86, 131, 150–151, 247

Overseas Chinese, 165, 191, 193–194, 207, 271, 414

Paleolithic China, 29–31, 32, 33

Palmerston, Lord, 200

Party-state, 410, 420, 437, 465, 467. *See also* Government

Patriarchy, 18, 264

Paulsen, Friedrich, 277

Peasant Movement Training Institute, 303

Peasants, 21, 49, 102, 103, 104, 299; and taxes, 48–49, 60, 132, 232, 314; oppression of, 86, 275, 303; and Nationalist government, 289, 290, 294–295, 314; mobilization of, 304, 305, 310, 317, 318, 319, 335, 336, 373; treatment of rich, 304, 318, 334, 350, 352; and CCP, 316, 354–357, 368, 377, 386; in PRC, 321, 322, 415, 437; docility of, 369, 375; and Cultural Revolution, 392, 398, 405. *See also* Farmers; Land; Villages

Peng Dehuai, 319, 345, 351, 372, 373, 388, 390

Peng Zhen, 364, 385, 390, 422, 423

People's associations, 434–435

People's Liberation Army (PLA), 345, 372, 373, 381, 430; and Cultural Revolution, 385, 387–389, 390, 392, 393, 394, 395

People's Republic of China, 23, 100, 343–446, 464–465; environmentalism in, 15, 17; U.S. recognition of, 340–341; executions in, 350; creation of, 345–351; Military Affairs Commission of, 351, 389; collectivization of agriculture in, 352–357; administrative units of, 354–355; beginning industrialization in, 357–359; education and intellectuals in, 359–364; and Soviet Union, 378, 380; decentralization in, 386, 399–400; and foreign affairs, 395–397; Nixon-Kissinger policy toward, 397

Perry, Matthew C., 218

Piracy, 139, 157, 194, 208

Politics, 127, 266, 360, 420–429; factional, in Ming era, 140–142

Pollution, 466–467

Population, 2, 4–5, 89, 106, 167, 369; and birth control, 2, 274; pressure of, 16, 171, 172, 187; in Han dynasty, 60, 89, 167; in Ming dynasty, 128, 167–168; world, 163–164, 167; in late imperial China, 163, 167–169, 187, 263, 271; growth of urban, 357, 374; in PRC, 400, 415, 417, 419–420, 436–437, 465

Pottery, 32, 34, 35, 37

PRC. *See* People's Republic of China

Press, 262–263, 291. *See also* Chinese Communist Party: and media; Media, mass

Private enterprise, 412–413, 414, 434

Privatization, 415–416

Protest, 416, 417, 421, 426, 427–428, 436, 449, 467. *See also* Dissidence

Qi, state of, 54

Qiang people, 61

Qianlong, Emperor, 147, 159, 182, 189, 190, 196–197, 228, 232, 403

Qiao Shi, 422, 432

Qidan, 110, 111, 113, 115, 123, 149

Qigong, 439

Qin dynasty, 42, 47, 48, 77, 112, 121, 236; unification by, 54–57, 113, 322; burning of books in, 56, 70

Qin Gui, 115

Qing dynasty, 1, 118, 126, 143–161, 258; official documents of, 101; gentry in, 101–107, 161; synarchy in, 149; palace memorials of, 151, 247; control in Inner

Qing dynasty *(continued)*
  Asia, 152–153; literary inquisition of, 159; decline of, 163, 187, 204, 221, 235, 262–263; and international trade, 196–205; scholarship in, 224–225, 227; demoralization of, 232–234; rebellions in, 206–216, 236–238; reforms of, 240, 241–244, 425; Lüying (Army of the Green Standard) in, 389. *See also* Manchus; Restoration, Qing
Qing enterprise structure, 413
Qinghua (Tsing Hua) University, 265, 314
qigong, 439
qingyi (literati opinion), 228, 243, 262
Quanzhou (Zayton), 92, 193, 195
Quotations from Chairman Mao, 385, 392

Railways, 219, 220, 241, 244, 247, 250, 338, 348
Reagan, Ronald, 182, 328
Rebellions: An Lushan, 82–83, 85; mid-Tang, 85, 86, 213; in Qing dynasty, 146, 187, 189, 197, 206; on Turkestan frontier, 197–198; suppression of, 213, 214–216, 236–238; in Free China, 316. *See also* Nian rebellion; Taiping rebellion; White Lotus rebellion
Record of Ceremonies and Proper Conduct (Liji), 67
Records of the Historian (Shiji), 70
Rectification Campaign of 1942–1944, 323–326
Red Army: Chinese, 301, 305, 307, 309, 316; Soviet, 373, 387–388, 397
Red Guards, 392–397, 401, 402, 421, 447
Reform, 248, 289, 295, 360, 361, 381, 425–426; of Confucianism, 96–97, 222; in PRC, 343–344, 408–433, 466. *See also* Deng Xiaoping: reforms of; Land reform
Reform Movement, 224–230
Religion, 17, 31, 70, 156, 221–222, 229, 410, 439. *See also* Buddhism; Christianity; Daoism
Republican era, 241, 250, 255–341
Restoration, Qing, 205, 212–214, 217, 233, 403
Revolution, 275, 310, 311, 323, 370, 401; Sun Yatsen's three stages of, 286; proletariat in, 310, 321–322; bourgeois-democratic, 322–323
Revolution of 1911, 240, 241, 250–253, 272, 312

Revolutionary League, 235, 250, 251, 265, 280, 290. *See also* Sun Yatsen
Ricci, Matteo, 151
Rice culture, 4, 5, 11, 15–16, 23, 169, 170, 338
Richard, Timothy, 226
Rights Recovery movement, 244, 279
Rites Controversy, 222
Rituals, 34, 37, 39, 44, 49, 66, 70, 112, 128, 145, 154. *See also* Religion
Rituals of Zhou, 208
Roberts, Issachar Jacox, 207
Roosevelt, Franklin D., 229, 327, 328, 329
Ruan Yuan, 225
Rural area, 411, 419, 436, 459. *See also* Agriculture
Rural Reconstruction movement, 299–301
Russia, 152, 187, 221, 228, 241, 267, 279, 378, 415, 461. *See also* Soviet Union
Russo-Japanese War (1905), 221
Ruzhen (Jurchen), 92, 110, 111, 115, 117, 118, 122, 123, 143, 149, 204. *See also* Jin dynasty

Scholar-generals, 109, 111, 140, 213, 214, 237, 238
Scholar-officials, 63, 95, 109, 110, 138, 151, 217, 224, 225; and emperor, 70, 160, 274–275, 360; rival groups of, 140, 145; and agriculture, 170; and Sino-liberalism, 259. *See also* Literati
Schools, 94, 227, 243, 246, 261, 265, 313; work-study, 377; keypoint, 377–378. *See also* Education; *minban*
Science, 66, 101, 218, 264, 289, 338; and technology, 3, 151–152, 217, 267; and democracy, 265, 268
Secret societies, 22, 49, 156, 194, 206, 207, 222, 230, 237, 240, 297, 318, 403
Self-criticism, 100, 396, 400
Self-cultivation, 52, 98, 99, 100, 124, 140, 298
Self-government, local, 236, 241, 244–247, 274, 277, 298, 301
Self-strengthening, 217–221, 231, 244, 270, 337, 386
Sericulture, 33
Shaanxi province, 30, 31, 55, 189, 307, 309
Shamanism, 37, 42, 66, 112, 148, 230
Shandong province, 29, 35, 54, 73, 225, 230, 267, 335, 467

Shang dynasty, 33–39, 40, 45, 63, 159, 230; bronzes of, 3, 35, 37, 38, 49; horse-chariot in, 38, 41; conquest by Zhou, 39; writing system of, 42–43; culture of, 112, 117. *See also* Oracle bones; Pottery

Shang Yang (Lord Shang), 55

Shanghai, 227, 245, 246, 265, 269, 271, 272, 281, 308, 414, 425; trade at, 14, 176, 177, 178, 219, 269; International Settlement in, 203, 204, 205, 271; in Taiping rebellion, 210, 212, 213; industries in, 271, 272; 1925 incidents in, 282–283; Green Gang of, 284, 287, 291

Shanxi province, 14, 29, 32, 35, 55, 73, 77, 178, 310

Shenzhen, 414

shi (scholar-gentleman), 83, 93, 106, 109. *See also* Literati

shibosi (official superintendency of merchant shipping), 195

shu (commoners), 83

Sichuan province, 11, 29, 34, 55, 144, 146, 177, 189, 250, 309, 314, 436

Silk Road, 61, 78, 124, 193, 197

Sima Guang, 97

Sima Qian, 69–70

Sima Tan, 70

Singapore, 408, 431, 447, 465

Sino-American Joint Commission on Rural Reconstruction, 340

Sino-British Joint Declaration

Sino-Indian boundary dispute, 381

Sino-Japanese War of 1894–1895, 220–221, 226

Sino-Soviet split, 378–380, 396–397

Six Boards. *See* Six Ministries

Six Dynasties, 73, 76

Six Ministries, 82, 130, 147, 149, 245, 247

Sixteen Kingdoms, 73, 76, 77

Smith, Adam, 164, 167, 179, 259

Sneevliet, Hendrik ("Maring"), 276

Snow, Edgar, 317

Social welfare, 235, 239, 240

Socialism, 267, 276, 322, 323, 363, 408, 443–444

Socialist democracy, 421, 426

Society, 409, 433–439

Son of Heaven, 47, 62, 68, 155, 201, 227. *See also* Emperors

Song dynasty, 85, 88–107, 108–112, 121, 123, 126–127; paintings of, 3, 17; Northern, 86, 88, 98, 114, 119, 161, 170; material growth in, 88–93; examination system during, 93–95, 111; growth of education under, 93–95, 262; creation of Neo-Confucianism in, 96–101; Southern, 98, 109, 110, 115, 121, 122, 137; gentry in, 101–107; and Inner Asia, 108–127; and rise of non-Chinese rule, 112–119; and Mongol conquest, 119–126; population during, 167; handicrafts in, 399. *See also* Neo-Confucianism

Song Jiaoren, 251

Song Learning, 158, 228. *See also* Neo-Confucianism

South China, 20, 40, 72, 169; contrast with North China, 4–14, 76; migration to, 76, 206, 207

South Korea, 466, 467

Southwest Associated University (Kunming), 314, 315

Soviet Union, 280, 281, 310, 324, 350, 352, 362, 379, 461, 465; and United States, 2, 329; support of Chinese revolution, 255, 283, 302; and Nationalists, 329, 336–337; forced industrialization in, 358–359; as model of industrial development, 359, 369, 407; and Cultural Revolution, 396, 397

Special Economic Zones (SEZ), 413–414, 420

Spice Route, 92, 124

Spring and Autumn Annals (*Chunqiu*), 67

Spring-and-Autumn period, 49

Stalin, 241, 284, 328, 329, 350, 351, 368, 378–379, 403

Statecraft, 67, 124, 129, 225, 240, 258, 259, 354, 381

Statism, authoritarian, 256, 259, 397

Stilwell, General Joseph, 327, 328

Su Shi (Dongpo), 175

Sui dynasty, 48, 76, 77, 78, 112, 121

Sui Yangdi, 77, 78

Suicide, 52, 145, 232, 387, 402, 439

Sun Yatsen, 235, 243, 250, 252, 265, 278, 290, 312; and United Front, 279–283; Three People's Principles of, 281, 285, 290, 332; death of, 283; three stages of revolution of, 286; five-power constitution of, 292; and conspiracy, 403. *See also* Revolutionary League

Sun Yatsen, Madame (Song Qingling), 283

Sun Zhigang, 441

Taiping rebellion, 168, 206–209, 223, 227, 233, 236, 237, 238; suppression of, 213, 217, 233, 239, 250, 292, 325; and gentry, 235, 240, 272

Taiwan, 32, 35, 157, 191; as a Japanese colony, 337–339; as the Republic of China, 339–344, 408, 447, 461, 462, 466, 467

Taiwan National University (Taibei), 340

Taixue (imperial academy), 70–71

Tang dynasty, 47, 76, 77, 78, 106, 117, 128; and Inner Asia, 48, 110, 112; Buddhism in, 79; decline of, 81–83, 113; block printing in, 93; foreign policy of, 112; militia system of, 121; law code of, 183

Tang-Song transition, 83–87

Tangshan earthquake, 404–405

Tanguts, 85, 110, 114

Taoism. *See* Daoism

Tariffs, 203, 232, 288

Tax farming, 105, 124, 296

Taxes, 85, 150, 168, 237, 290, 313, 332, 338; on land, 48–49, 60, 85, 92, 129, 132, 133, 135, 141, 150, 181, 214, 246, 247, 249, 288, 289, 338; rural collectors of (*difang, dibao*), 57, 104, 105, 190, 248, 295–296, 298, 356; salt, 92, 149, 238, 249; on trade, 92, 179, 233, 235, 237, 249, 288; in Ming era, 132–133, 135, 181; Single Whip, 135; and customs duties, 149, 195, 249, 288; agricultural, 181, 314, 355, 369; *likin* system of, 235, 237–238, 249, 288; excise, 246; size of revenue from, 248–249, 358; on grain, 249, 320; on business, 288; on villages, 295, 301; and decentralization, 417–418; and industry, 437. *See also* Rebellions

Technocrats, 450, 457

Technology, 3, 140, 220, 359, 367, 371; foreign, 152, 188–189, 217, 227, 359, 399; military, 89, 92, 115; nautical, 93, 137, 192; farm, 298, 338. *See also* Inventions

Ten Kingdoms, 87. *See also* Five Dynasties

Terrorism, 461

Third World, 381, 396

Three-Antis Campaign, 348, 350

Three Bonds, 19, 112

Three Gorges Dam, 422

Three Dynasties, 33–35, 41, 44

Three Feudatories, 146

Three Kingdoms, 73, 156

ti (substance), 258

Tiananmen Massacre, 2

Tiananmen Square, pro-democracy demonstrations in, 403, 410, 426, 427–428, 450; April Fifth incident in, 404; May Fourth demonstrations in, 267

Tianjin, 14, 78, 219, 231, 246, 308, 435. *See also* Treaty of Tianjin

Tibet, 1, 23, 39, 85, 110, 152, 153, 397, 457

tongwen (dōbun; common culture), 240

Totalitarianism, 45, 257, 337, 397, 401

Trade, 39, 85, 127, 193–197, 199, 205; maritime, 14, 16–17, 35, 42, 92, 124, 137, 138, 139; domestic, 89, 141, 164, 176–179, 224, 237–238; silk, 92, 137, 141, 149, 160, 195, 196, 199; foreign, 92, 142, 204, 207, 396, 408, 409, 414, 462; spice, 92, 177, 192; Confucian view of, 129, 135, 138; porcelain, 160, 195; opium, 164, 177, 195, 198–201, 204, 206, 232, 233, 234, 239, 312; kerosene, 164, 269; and population, 167, 176; growth of, in late imperial China, 163, 167–186, 187, 204, 226; tea, 177, 195, 196, 198, 199, 269; salt, 177, 225; cotton textile, 294. *See also* Currency: silver; Merchants; Treaty ports; Tribute system

Trade unions. *See* Labor unions

Treaties, 68, 114, 200, 201, 204, 223; unequal, 61, 201, 204, 212, 213, 241, 260, 279, 280, 285. *See also* Treaty ports; *individual treaties*

Treaty of Kokand, 198, 200

Treaty of Nanjing, 200, 201, 232

Treaty of Nerchinsk, 152

Treaty of Tianjin, 201

Treaty of Versailles, 267

Treaty ports, 200, 201, 203, 216, 220, 244, 245, 255, 260, 290, 414; growth of, 226, 233; foreign commissioners at, 233, 234; change in, 235, 243, 257

Treaty system, 204, 212, 213, 231, 235

Triad Society, 207, 237

Tribute system, 112–113, 139, 149, 199, 201, 205

Trotsky, Leon, 284

tuntian system, 389

Turkestan (Xinjiang), 23, 152–153, 197–198

Tz'u-shi. *See* Cixi, Empress Dowager

Uighur Turks, 110, 122
United Front, 279–283, 285, 303, 304, 317, 320, 334, 349, 364; second, 310–311, 313, 316, 325, 328
United Nations Covenant on Civil and Political Rights, 431
United Nations Covenant on Economic, Social, and Cultural Rights, 431
United States: and China, 1–2, 15, 163, 181–182, 199, 259, 264, 270, 273, 293, 383, 396, 397; Civil War in, 209; Chinese missions to, 245; treatment of Chinese in, 245; attitude to revolution, 255; Constitution of, 259; support of Chinese institutions, 261; Chinese scholars in, 265, 340; and aid to China, 299, 327, 379; Dixie Mission of, 326; support of Chinese coalition government, 326–330; support for Nationalists, 329–331, 332, 336; and Taiwan, 340, 379, 462; and North Vietnam, 382; criticism from, 431, 462; criticism of, 446
Universities, 260, 261, 263–265, 291, 313, 343, 362, 377; and Cultural Revolution, 390, 391, 392. See also *individual universities*
Urbanization, 179, 236, 260, 369, 411, 419–420, 435

Vietnam, 42, 61, 62, 78, 110, 124, 138, 149, 191, 340, 382
Vietnam War, 340, 382, 396, 398
Villages, 17–23, 129, 300, 304, 320, 323–324; cultural nexus of, 295–296; and communism, 317, 318–319, 334, 354; and enterprises, 412; and elections, 423–424
Voitinsky, Grigori, 276
von Seeckt, General Hans, 293

Wan Li, 411, 422
Wang Anshi, 96–97
Wang Dan, 447
Wang Jingwei, 283
Wang Juntao, 447
Wang Tao, 262
Wang Yi, 460
Wang Xihou, 159
Wang Yangming (Wang Shouren; Ō Yōmei), 140, 240, 360
Wanli, Emperor, 140, 141, 251
Warfare, 38, 39, 49, 51, 226–227; guerrilla,

304–305, 307, 319, 334, 370, 388; positional, 307, 309, 319; two-front, 316, 332. See also Rebellions
Warlords, 87, 128, 238, 251, 253, 255, 260, 264, 273, 274, 281; and Nationalist government, 279, 283, 285, 289, 290, 301, 305, 313, 314, 327; and CCP, 279, 305, 348
Warring States period, 40, 49, 51, 52, 54, 57, 67, 69, 113, 322
Wei Jingsheng, 421, 447
Wei Yuan, 225
wen (civil order; culture), 62, 69, 108–112, 129, 143, 259, 273, 366, 403
Wen Jiabao, 430, 457, 458
Weng Wenhao, 293
Wenxiang, 212, 233
wenyan (classical writing), 266
Wenzhou, 435
West China Union University (Chengdu), 313
Westernization, 211, 213, 214, 217, 218, 220, 258, 290, 408–409, 438, 441–442, 445, 447
Whampoa Military Academy, 281, 308, 388
White Lotus rebellion, 189–191, 222, 232, 236
Wilson, Woodrow, 267
Women: subjection of, 18–19, 173–176; position of, in Buddhism, 75, 79; Manchu, 148; farm, 173, 175; in Taiping rebellion, 208, 210–211; reputation of, 232; emancipation of, 267, 275, 349; in labor force, 373; and education, 436–437; and suicide, 439. See also Footbinding
World Trade Organization, 463–464
World War I, 205, 266, 267, 270, 271, 300
World War II, 255, 314, 317, 326, 330, 333, 381, 464
Writing system, Chinese, 56, 101, 266. See also Language: Chinese
wu (military order; force), 62, 69, 108–112, 129, 143, 236, 259, 366, 404
Wu, Empress, 81–82
Wu Chuntao, 459
Wu Han, 390
Wu Sangui, General, 145, 146
Wudi. See Han Wudi
Wuhan, 14, 220, 231, 283, 284, 302, 309, 312, 316, 359

Wuhan incident, 394
wuwei (effortlessness), 54, 75

Xenophobia, 139, 236, 365, 395
Xia dynasty, 33, 35, 37, 38, 41, 42
Xiamen (Amoy), 92, 177, 195, 203, 265, 379
Xi'an (Chang'an), 32, 39, 49, 56, 59, 61, 77, 78, 86, 89, 231, 309
Xianbei, 73
Xinjiang province, 189, 337. *See also* Turkestan
Xiongnu, 61, 70, 73, 110
Xuanzong, Emperor, 82

yahang (wholesale brokers), 105
Yamen clerks, 123, 133, 150, 240
Yan Fu, 259, 265
Yan Yangchu (Y. C. James Yen), 261, 299, 300
Yan'an, 310–326 passim, 334, 345, 368, 372, 377, 387, 390
Yang Guifei, 82
Yangzhou, 78, 105, 145, 225
Yangzi River, 5, 11, 15, 32, 37, 39, 73, 77, 85, 181–182, 209, 283, 336; water transport on, 35, 56, 78, 89, 177; growth in population along, 89; dikes on, 129, 170; inland navy on, 212; migration up, 313; Three Gorges Dam on, 421
Yanjing University, 313
yanlu (path for words of criticism), 365
Ye Qianyu, 333
Yellow (Huang) River, 5, 14, 15, 31–37 passim, 41, 77, 89, 129, 230, 302, 309, 336
yin/yang, 19, 65, 326
yong (function), 258
Yongle, Emperor, 132, 137, 138
Yongle dadian, 158
Yongzheng, Emperor, 147, 150, 156
Young Men's Christian Association, Chinese, 261, 300
Yuan dynasty, 111, 118, 119, 121, 123, 124, 126, 127, 128, 147, 155, 204; expeditions of, 123–124, 137; military system of, 129. *See also* Mongols
Yuan Shikai, 241, 246–247, 250–253, 260, 265, 273, 280, 291
Yu Jie, 458
Yue Fei, General, 115
Yung Wing, 218–219
Yunnan province, 305, 314

Zeng Guofan, 212–213, 217, 219, 233, 237, 272, 292
Zhang Boling, 265, 308
Zhang Guotao, 268, 275, 309
Zhang Juzheng, 140–141
Zhang Xianzhong, 146
Zhang Zhidong, 220, 231, 241, 242, 258
Zhang Zuolin, 335
Zhao Kuangyin, 88
Zhao Ziyang, 407, 411, 413, 420, 421–422, 425, 426, 428, 432, 434, 440, 443, 458
Zhejiang province, 11, 170, 251, 308
Zheng He expeditions, 137–138, 193
Zhengzhou, 33, 34, 381
Zhou (Chou) dynasty, 33, 44, 45, 49, 54, 77, 98, 108; and excavations, 41; philosophers of, 47, 51; Western, 39–40; and class division, 108; and Inner Asia, 112; and Mandate of Heaven, 117
Zhou Enlai, 307–310, 316, 350, 364, 404, 407; and Mao, 307, 345, 400, 401; and Great Leap Forward, 373; tour of Africa, 381–382, 395; in Cultural Revolution, 387, 388, 390, 391, 395, 396; death of, 404
Zhu De, 302
Zhu Rongji, 429
Zhu Xi (Chu Hsi), 98–100, 124, 140, 155, 175, 360
Zhu Yuanzhang. *See* Hongwu, Emperor
Zhuangzi, 54
Zongli Yamen, 213
Zunyi Conference, 309